American BUYERS

Demographics of Shopping

American BUYERS

Demographics of Shopping

New Strategist Publications Inc.

Ithaca, New York

New Strategist Publications, Inc.
P.O. Box 242, Ithaca, New York 14851
800/848-0842; 607/273-0913
www.newstrategist.com

ISBN 978-1-935114-94-9 (paper)
ISBN 978-1-935114-93-2 (hardcover)

Printed in the United States of America

Contents

List of Tables

Chapter 3. Financial Products and Services Buyers, 2008

Chapter 4. Food and Alcoholic Beverages Buyers, 2008

Chapter 5. Buyers of Gifts for People in Other Households, 2008

Chapter 6. Health Care Buyers, 2008

Chapter 7. Housing Buyers: Household Services, Supplies, and Furnishings, 2008

Chapter 10. Transportation Buyers, 2008

Appendix A

Introduction

Welcome to the first edition of *American Buyers: Demographics of Shopping*, a new companion for New Strategist's 15th edition of *Household Spending: Who Spends How Much on What*. This is your exclusive guide to shoppers. The raw spending data presented here are not available on any government web site. They were obtained by special request from the Bureau of Labor Statistics and provide a unique look at household shopping behavior in the United States.

American Buyers provides the data businesses need to manage expectations (how many will walk through the door?) and set prices (how much do buyers typically spend?). Along with *Household Spending*, which reveals the demographic drivers behind household spending patterns, it provides a complete picture of the American consumer in 2008, in the midst of the Great Recession. All spending categories are included in this analysis, from white bread and bananas to cell phone service and prescription drugs.

Consumer spending is the result of a complex mix of wants and needs, hopes and fears. This mix determines the success of individual businesses and the health of our economy. Knowing how many are buying a product or service and how much those buyers spend is the key to inventory management and effective pricing. While most businesses have a feel for what is happening in their own establishment, *American Buyers* lets them see the big picture beyond their walls or web site. It tells them how many buy the products and services they sell and how much those buyers typically spend, all broken down by the demographics that count—age, household income, household type, race and Hispanic origin, region of residence, and education.

American Buyers is based on unpublished data collected by the Bureau of Labor Statistics' Consumer Expenditure Survey, an ongoing, nationwide survey of household spending. In this reference book, New Strategist presents the raw figures showing the percentage of households that buy individual products and services during the average quarter or week. Also presented are calculations done by New Strategist of how much buyers spend on items during the average quarter or week. These data are presented for hundreds of spending categories.

The Bureau of Labor Statistics' Consumer Expenditure Survey is a complete accounting of household expenditures, including everything from big-ticket items such as homes and cars to small purchases like laundry detergent and videogames. The survey does not include expenditures by government, business, or institutions. The lag time between data collection and publication is about two years. The data in this book are from the 2008 Consumer Expenditure Survey, unless otherwise noted.

The Consumer Expenditure Survey uses consumer units as its sampling unit. The Bureau of Labor Statistics defines "consumer unit" as "a single person or group of persons in a sample household related by blood, marriage, adoption or other legal arrangement or who share responsibility for at least two out of three major types of expenses—food, housing, and other expenses." For convenience, consumer units are referred to as households in the text of this book. For more information about the Consumer Expenditure Survey and consumer units, see Appendix B.

Chapters 1 through 10 present buyer statistics by major product and service category (apparel, food, health care, housing, and so on) and include all household expenditures. Within each chapter, buyer statistics are shown by age of householder, household income, household type, race and Hispanic origin of householder, region of residence, and educational attainment of householder. For each of the demographic variables, tables show the percent of households buying during the average quarter or week of 2008 and how much the buyers spent.

How to use the tables in this book

The **QUARTERLY BUYING TABLES** are from the interview portion of the Consumer Expenditure Survey, in which government interviewers ask respondents whether they bought big-ticket or less frequently purchased items over the past three months. Two types of quarterly buying tables are presented here—the percentage of households that bought a particular item and the amount purchasers spent.

• **Percent buying during quarter** These tables show the percentage of households that bought an item during the average quarter of 2008. The percent buying tables give researchers an indication of how commonly items are purchased by demographic characteristic of households. For example, 0.8 percent of households bought new cars during the average quarter of 2008, and 9.9 percent bought airline tickets.

•**Amount buyers spent during quarter** These tables, calculated by New Strategist, show how much households that bought an item during the average quarter spent on the item during the quarter. The 0.8 percent of households that bought new cars during the average quarter of 2008, for example, spent an average of $23,500 on them during the quarter. (Note: The entire cost of an item is included in the purchase amount, whether it is financed or not.) While it is likely that these households purchased only one new car during the quarter, this is not necessarily true for all items in the interview survey. The 9.9 percent of households that bought airline tickets during the average quarter of 2008, for example, spent an average of $868 on tickets. To be sure, many of these purchasers bought more than one airline ticket.

The Top 15, Average Quarter, 2008

(15 products and services bought by the largest percentage of households during an average quarter, 2008)

Groceries (food at home)	99.0%
Electricity	91.6
Gasoline	90.1
Deductions for Social Security	79.8
Meals at restaurants and carry-outs	78.5
Cable and satellite television service	74.1
Residential telephone service	72.4
Property tax	65.3
Health insurance	63.0
Personal care services	61.3
Cellular phone service	59.6
Water and sewerage maintenance	56.9
Computer information services	53.9
Federal income taxes	50.8
Vehicle insurance	50.7

Source: Bureau of Labor Statistics, unpublished data from the 2008 Consumer Expenditure Survey

The Top 15, Average Week, 2008

(15 products and services bought by the largest percentage of households during an average week, 2008)

Groceries (food at home)	82.9%
Gasoline	67.9
Personal taxes (federal, state, and local)	54.7
Lunch at fast-food restaurants, carry-outs	42.3
Dinner at fast-food restaurants, carry-outs	29.9
Dinner at full-service restaurants	27.7
Snacks at fast-food restaurants, carry-outs	24.9
Cleansing, toilet tissue, paper towels, napkins	24.8
Telephone services	22.4
Breakfast at fast-food restaurants, carry-outs	22.1
Lunch at full-service restaurants	21.2
Cosmetics, perfume, and bath products	20.7
Soaps and detergents	20.1
Women's apparel	18.9
Prescription drugs	18.0

Source: Bureau of Labor Statistics, unpublished data from the 2008 Consumer Expenditure Survey

The **WEEKLY BUYING TABLES** come from the diary portion of the Consumer Expenditure Survey, which asks respondents to record their purchases of smaller items for two weeks. Two types of weekly buying tables are presented here, one showing the percentage of households that bought an item during an average week and the other showing the amount buyers spent on the item during the week.

• **Percent buying during week** These tables show the percentage of households that bought an item during the average week of 2008. The percent buying tables give researchers an indication of how commonly items are purchased.

For example, 42 percent of households bought fast-food lunches during the average week of 2008, but only 21 percent bought lunches at full-service restaurants.

• **Amount buyers spent during week** These tables, calculated by New Strategist, show how much the households that bought an item during the average week spent on the item. The 42 percent of households that bought fast-food lunches, for example, spent an average of $17.66 on them. Note that this is not the amount they spent on one fast-food lunch, but how much the household spent on all fast-food lunches during the week. The 21 percent of households that bought full-service lunches during the average week of 2008 spent an average of $26.77 on them.

For more information

The first edition of *American Buyers: Demographics of Shopping* offers businesses and researchers a look at the proportion of households that buy individual products and services and how much the buyers spend. For average household spending figures, indexes, aggregates, market shares, and analyses of the demographic drivers behind household spending patterns, see the companion reference, the 15th edition of Strategist's *Household Spending: Who Spends How Much on What*. To see product-by-product analyses of "best customers," and an examination of how demographic trends are reshaping consumer demand, see the seventh edition of *Best Customers: Demographics of Consumer Demand*. To learn more about these books and to see tables of contents and sample pages, visit New Strategist's web site at http://www.newstrategist.com/. All of New Strategist's reference books are available in print or as downloadable PDF files with links to the Excel version of each table.

For more about the Consumer Expenditure Survey, visit the Bureau of Labor Statistics web site (http://www.bls.gov/cex/) where summary average spending figures are online. The detailed data shown in this book are available from the Bureau of Labor Statistics only by special request.

CHAPTER 1

Apparel Buyers, 2008

Spending on apparel has declined sharply over the years. The average household spent 22 percent less on apparel in 2008 than in 2000, after adjusting for inflation. Nevertheless, clothing needs (and wants) draw millions of people into the marketplace. Women's clothes are most popular, and women's shoes also rank among apparel buyer's top 10 purchases.

Quarterly spending

Nearly three of four households (74 percent) bought apparel products and services during the average quarter of 2008. The purchasers spent an average of $399 on apparel during the quarter. Some 41 percent of households bought women's apparel, making it the most popular apparel category. Households buying women's clothing spent an average of $220 on the item(s) during the quarter. Some 32 percent of households purchased footwear during the quarter, spending $118. Within the footwear category, women's shoes attract the largest percentage of households, with 19 percent buying women's shoes during the average quarter.

Weekly spending

During the average week of 2008, more than one-third of households (35 percent) bought apparel products and services. The purchasers spent $81 on the item(s). Not surprisingly, women's apparel lures the largest percentage of shoppers into the store (or online)—19 percent of households purchased women's apparel during the average week of 2008. Shirts, blouses, and tops are the most popular women's apparel category. Nine percent of households purchased women's tops during the average week of 2008. Those who purchased women's tops spent an average of $27 on the item(s).

Apparel Buyers' Top 10

(apparel categories bought by the largest percentage of households during an average quarter, 2008)

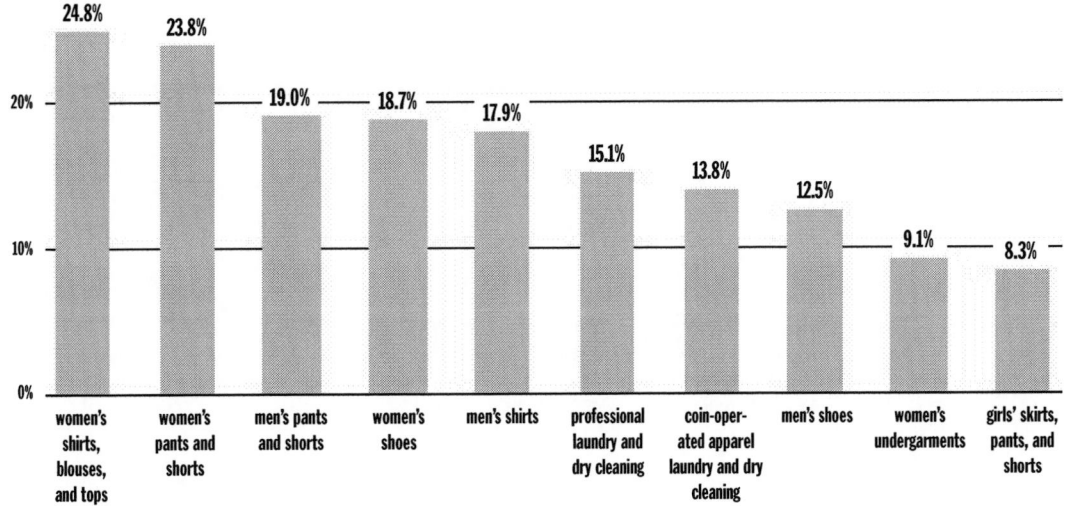

Table 1.1 Percent Buying Apparel by Age, Average Quarter, 2008

(percent of households buying apparel, accessories, and related services during the average quarter, by age of householder, 2008)

	total households	under 25	25 to 34	35 to 44	45 to 54	55 to 64	65 to 74	75+
APPAREL, PERCENT BUYING	**74.3%**	**77.8%**	**81.2%**	**78.8%**	**76.8%**	**73.5%**	**67.1%**	**54.5%**
Men's apparel	**29.6**	**31.5**	**33.7**	**31.6**	**33.4**	**29.8**	**23.5**	**15.4**
Suits	1.3	0.6	1.5	1.4	1.9	1.2	0.9	0.3
Sport coats and tailored jackets	1.1	0.5	1.3	1.2	1.2	1.0	1.0	0.8
Coats and jackets	3.6	4.0	3.7	4.1	3.9	3.9	2.8	1.9
Underwear	5.3	4.1	5.9	6.4	6.1	4.8	4.5	2.6
Hosiery	4.4	3.7	5.5	5.1	5.4	3.8	3.1	2.1
Nightwear	0.9	0.7	0.9	1.3	0.9	0.7	0.6	0.6
Accessories	3.3	3.8	3.8	3.9	3.8	3.0	2.4	1.4
Sweaters and vests	2.5	2.8	2.5	2.7	2.7	2.5	2.4	1.1
Active sportswear	1.5	1.4	1.7	2.1	1.7	1.3	0.9	0.5
Shirts	17.9	22.0	21.0	20.6	20.2	17.1	11.6	6.9
Pants and shorts	19.0	20.6	22.5	20.8	21.9	17.9	14.1	8.7
Uniforms	0.6	0.5	1.1	0.8	0.6	0.5	0.4	0.2
Costumes	0.3	1.0	0.5	0.3	0.3	0.1	0.2	–
Boys' (aged 2 to 15) apparel	**11.3**	**5.1**	**16.2**	**23.0**	**12.1**	**5.2**	**3.4**	**1.7**
Coats and jackets	1.5	0.9	2.1	3.4	1.5	0.8	0.3	0.2
Sweaters	0.7	0.4	1.0	1.5	0.6	0.4	0.2	0.2
Shirts	7.0	3.1	9.7	14.6	7.5	2.9	2.4	0.9
Underwear	2.2	1.2	3.2	5.0	2.0	1.0	0.3	0.0
Nightwear	0.8	0.3	1.3	1.6	0.7	0.6	0.2	0.1
Hosiery	1.4	0.4	2.2	3.1	1.5	0.6	0.2	0.1
Accessories	0.7	0.3	0.8	1.5	0.7	0.4	0.3	0.1
Suits, sport coats, and vests	0.3	0.2	0.3	0.7	0.4	0.2	0.0	0.0
Pants and shorts	8.2	3.6	11.6	17.2	9.1	3.3	2.1	1.0
Uniforms	0.6	0.1	0.9	1.3	0.7	0.1	0.1	0.0
Active sportswear	1.0	0.1	1.3	2.2	1.1	0.4	0.2	0.2
Costumes	0.5	0.1	1.1	1.1	0.3	0.2	0.1	0.1
Women's apparel	**40.8**	**37.2**	**39.9**	**40.8**	**45.7**	**43.9**	**39.9**	**29.6**
Coats and jackets	5.3	4.9	4.8	5.0	6.0	6.5	5.1	3.3
Dresses	7.2	6.8	7.9	7.4	8.8	7.2	5.9	3.2
Sport coats and tailored jackets	1.2	0.8	0.9	1.0	1.6	1.7	1.3	1.0
Sweaters and vests	6.1	5.4	5.6	6.2	7.0	7.2	6.1	4.0
Shirts, blouses, and tops	24.8	23.8	25.1	25.5	28.4	25.8	23.4	15.2
Skirts	3.1	2.3	3.4	3.3	3.6	3.7	2.0	1.6
Pants and shorts	23.8	23.1	23.8	25.9	27.7	24.1	21.4	13.5
Active sportswear	3.2	2.9	3.5	3.9	4.2	2.7	2.6	1.1
Nightwear	4.0	2.6	3.4	4.1	4.1	5.0	4.9	2.8
Undergarments	9.1	7.4	8.4	10.4	10.5	9.2	9.4	5.8
Hosiery	5.7	4.1	5.1	6.0	6.8	6.3	5.3	4.4
Suits	1.6	0.7	1.0	1.6	2.2	1.9	1.7	1.5
Accessories	5.6	5.3	5.5	5.8	6.6	5.5	5.5	3.3
Uniforms	1.0	1.0	1.1	1.2	1.4	1.1	0.6	0.2
Costumes	0.6	1.0	0.9	0.7	0.6	0.4	0.3	0.2
Girls' (aged 2 to 15) apparel	**11.9**	**4.7**	**16.1**	**24.6**	**12.5**	**6.2**	**4.3**	**1.5**
Coats and jackets	1.7	0.6	2.4	3.5	1.5	0.8	0.6	0.3
Dresses and suits	2.2	0.7	3.2	4.1	2.3	1.2	1.1	0.2
Shirts, blouses, and sweaters	7.9	3.4	10.7	16.7	8.2	4.1	2.7	0.9
Skirts, pants, and shorts	8.3	3.3	11.3	18.1	8.8	3.6	2.4	0.8
Active sportswear	1.4	0.4	1.8	3.3	1.1	0.7	0.5	0.0
Underwear and nightwear	3.2	1.1	4.2	7.0	3.4	1.4	0.9	0.2

	total households	under 25	25 to 34	35 to 44	45 to 54	55 to 64	65 to 74	75+
Hosiery	1.6%	0.3%	2.4%	3.5%	1.7%	0.6%	0.6%	0.0%
Accessories	1.1	0.3	1.0	2.6	1.1	0.6	0.3	0.2
Uniforms	0.5	0.2	0.7	1.1	0.7	0.2	0.1	–
Costumes	0.7	0.1	1.2	1.7	0.7	0.3	0.1	–
Children's (under age 2) apparel	**13.1**	**16.5**	**23.4**	**14.3**	**11.2**	**10.9**	**7.7**	**4.1**
Coats, jackets, and snowsuits	1.0	1.7	2.1	0.9	0.9	0.6	0.5	0.3
Outerwear including dresses	7.2	8.9	11.3	7.6	6.6	6.6	4.7	2.4
Underwear	7.1	11.7	16.6	8.4	4.6	3.5	2.4	1.2
Nightwear and loungewear	2.3	2.6	4.2	2.4	1.7	1.9	1.9	0.8
Accessories	3.3	4.0	6.3	3.8	2.7	2.5	1.8	0.9
Footwear	**31.7**	**29.7**	**35.6**	**39.5**	**35.6**	**28.6**	**23.4**	**16.9**
Men's	12.5	14.2	14.7	14.8	14.4	11.0	8.5	5.2
Boys'	6.0	2.3	9.3	13.0	6.3	2.1	1.0	0.3
Women's	18.7	16.9	18.0	19.6	21.5	19.7	17.9	12.8
Girls'	6.2	3.0	9.2	13.4	6.6	2.1	1.4	0.3
Other apparel products and services	**37.3**	**40.4**	**38.7**	**38.5**	**39.1**	**38.6**	**34.6**	**26.8**
Material for making clothes	1.2	0.9	1.1	1.1	1.4	1.4	1.4	0.7
Sewing patterns and notions	1.6	1.4	1.4	1.3	1.6	1.9	2.3	1.2
Watches	3.1	2.0	3.0	3.4	3.7	3.5	3.1	2.0
Jewelry	7.2	6.4	7.0	7.5	8.6	8.5	5.9	3.4
Shoe repair and other shoe services	0.9	0.1	0.7	0.7	1.0	1.2	1.1	0.8
Coin-operated apparel laundry and dry cleaning	13.8	30.5	19.2	13.1	11.0	10.1	10.8	9.7
Apparel alteration, repair, and tailoring services	2.9	2.3	2.9	2.8	3.3	3.4	2.5	2.4
Clothing rental	0.4	0.5	0.5	0.4	0.6	0.2	0.2	–
Watch and jewelry repair	1.8	0.7	0.9	1.7	1.9	2.7	2.5	2.2
Professional laundry, dry cleaning	15.1	4.9	13.3	16.4	18.8	18.1	14.5	10.6
Clothing storage	0.1	–	0.1	0.1	0.2	0.2	0.1	0.0

Note: "–" means sample is too small to make a reliable estimate.
Source: Bureau of Labor Statistics, unpublished data from the 2008 Consumer Expenditure Survey

Table 1.2 Amount Buyers Spent on Apparel by Age, Average Quarter, 2008

(average amount spent by households buying apparel, accessories, and related services during the average quarter, by age of householder, 2008)

	total households	under 25	25 to 34	35 to 44	45 to 54	55 to 64	65 to 74	75+
APPAREL, AMOUNT SPENT	**$399.40**	**$314.51**	**$424.18**	**$457.84**	**$457.42**	**$394.60**	**$312.88**	**$198.84**
Men's apparel	**180.66**	**149.36**	**189.65**	**184.99**	**199.21**	**178.28**	**155.94**	**134.07**
Suits	466.60	347.66	555.65	439.21	441.62	555.63	336.24	352.21
Sport coats and tailored jackets	197.71	82.87	160.80	174.80	280.67	259.86	133.16	101.52
Coats and jackets	114.83	86.85	110.18	116.89	119.24	128.56	104.80	115.36
Underwear	35.86	41.20	34.21	33.44	35.41	34.51	48.66	30.45
Hosiery	20.88	21.24	21.45	17.98	22.56	22.69	19.72	18.05
Nightwear	46.84	29.62	44.72	45.04	60.39	39.53	41.13	52.73
Accessories	51.96	37.90	65.67	47.13	51.70	49.25	42.53	72.45
Sweaters and vests	87.65	62.18	87.40	85.24	94.60	94.92	81.67	89.41
Active sportswear	64.70	65.22	65.91	66.22	70.66	56.34	47.09	61.79
Shirts	81.16	71.12	82.05	75.99	87.74	85.27	77.99	75.07
Pants and shorts	92.63	84.73	93.49	93.07	99.18	88.95	88.46	83.56
Uniforms	149.19	152.40	136.21	133.86	134.17	157.22	343.57	78.95
Costumes	79.03	27.08	96.57	75.00	54.46	171.15	130.43	–
Boys' (aged 2 to 15) apparel	**147.62**	**112.13**	**130.09**	**150.73**	**162.03**	**168.12**	**124.04**	**146.80**
Coats and jackets	75.32	55.28	62.32	69.47	89.33	111.08	96.43	51.67
Sweaters	62.68	71.88	51.46	65.10	63.39	72.62	51.47	75.00
Shirts	69.82	49.26	62.22	67.71	76.64	89.03	65.33	106.18
Underwear	32.52	44.33	31.80	30.89	33.84	34.18	30.47	12.50
Nightwear	41.87	46.32	29.58	36.79	57.77	54.74	59.09	78.13
Hosiery	18.13	13.19	16.67	17.94	18.45	23.77	22.83	10.00
Accessories	43.93	42.86	37.80	32.65	36.64	100.00	63.39	87.50
Suits, sport coats, and vests	75.81	50.00	51.47	74.63	112.84	58.82	25.00	16.67
Pants and shorts	84.63	68.05	77.89	82.80	94.73	93.02	72.90	104.85
Uniforms	135.27	45.00	101.97	152.38	145.00	125.00	131.25	66.67
Active sportswear	44.13	12.50	32.81	53.46	37.96	52.78	42.71	29.17
Costumes	44.61	40.00	50.66	43.40	34.09	46.43	25.00	32.14
Women's apparel	**219.89**	**212.00**	**211.31**	**211.29**	**251.25**	**234.91**	**204.94**	**146.69**
Coats and jackets	115.70	103.27	116.04	102.63	122.93	119.69	132.83	96.70
Dresses	144.90	128.24	150.94	110.89	158.72	159.48	165.24	118.56
Sport coats and tailored jackets	115.65	154.57	70.93	104.37	137.26	114.76	119.27	105.10
Sweaters and vests	94.18	113.37	84.53	85.84	91.61	112.86	91.12	79.87
Shirts, blouses, and tops	86.97	83.65	83.69	79.23	97.22	94.75	82.21	68.66
Skirts	76.46	55.79	56.80	72.45	78.43	93.26	107.25	72.50
Pants and shorts	94.29	98.04	86.36	89.62	103.43	100.77	89.58	78.81
Active sportswear	63.19	47.77	53.33	63.04	68.62	72.22	57.72	75.00
Nightwear	48.30	45.11	43.03	44.47	53.40	51.05	48.72	46.74
Undergarments	55.88	69.47	59.03	51.71	57.10	57.99	52.82	44.93
Hosiery	22.68	20.81	21.26	18.28	26.11	23.93	23.10	23.17
Suits	201.08	128.72	166.00	248.59	208.18	192.14	217.25	147.30
Accessories	$76.75	$55.53	$85.03	$66.60	$91.03	$89.95	$57.16	$44.88
Uniforms	118.51	92.25	114.86	142.68	122.86	101.19	79.46	198.81
Costumes	92.37	49.49	114.66	68.01	110.25	115.34	54.00	86.25
Girls' (aged 2 to 15) apparel	**170.16**	**134.81**	**147.34**	**174.81**	**186.03**	**185.99**	**164.34**	**140.95**
Coats and jackets	65.76	51.36	58.30	58.02	80.92	95.06	65.63	70.69
Dresses and suits	84.49	66.55	61.90	82.73	103.74	117.80	74.07	62.50
Shirts, blouses, and sweaters	77.64	78.12	66.25	78.53	80.61	94.84	84.81	65.29
Skirts, pants, and shorts	88.70	61.97	76.62	89.89	95.76	95.17	114.62	103.57
Active sportswear	43.89	15.00	33.33	47.37	50.71	43.75	50.98	75.00
Underwear and nightwear	44.78	32.14	42.23	41.18	51.55	53.75	48.40	56.25

	total households	under 25	25 to 34	35 to 44	45 to 54	55 to 64	65 to 74	75+
Hosiery	$17.09	$11.54	$17.57	$16.23	$17.25	$21.36	$14.04	$12.50
Accessories	37.73	55.65	42.31	25.67	34.38	72.50	25.78	200.00
Uniforms	131.60	138.16	133.21	124.56	141.07	162.50	86.11	–
Costumes	65.71	30.00	43.75	62.95	101.52	73.15	37.50	–
Children's (under age 2) apparel	**137.48**	**170.25**	**169.00**	**146.99**	**109.65**	**94.81**	**103.02**	**95.11**
Coats, jackets, and snowsuits	70.41	58.76	61.10	56.10	86.05	106.90	79.90	60.16
Outerwear including dresses	81.01	86.36	84.51	82.88	77.01	76.36	75.79	84.81
Underwear	122.94	137.84	137.27	132.18	96.66	79.13	86.05	62.07
Nightwear and loungewear	44.43	37.84	46.93	48.65	37.07	43.62	47.99	37.66
Accessories	56.10	57.48	63.05	53.53	52.15	43.65	54.10	77.84
Footwear	**118.14**	**102.12**	**114.62**	**125.41**	**125.11**	**121.25**	**110.79**	**86.59**
Men's	97.43	100.32	99.51	96.14	99.20	96.99	92.68	88.20
Boys'	67.92	55.48	64.24	68.35	70.08	77.50	73.28	71.00
Women's	91.91	79.09	82.60	89.86	99.09	104.00	90.74	75.69
Girls'	65.83	47.76	57.25	65.89	69.97	92.49	78.13	74.00
Other apparel products and services	**163.68**	**119.26**	**183.24**	**176.60**	**179.76**	**177.77**	**134.82**	**78.67**
Material for making clothes	58.33	43.47	57.30	46.27	71.53	58.09	51.27	66.18
Sewing patterns and notions	28.82	9.93	17.41	24.61	35.28	35.24	35.36	23.73
Watches	171.74	107.25	163.56	270.04	146.65	210.33	80.84	44.62
Jewelry	367.42	327.15	493.35	332.71	348.75	366.90	376.10	212.54
Shoe repair and other shoe services	36.92	39.29	30.43	42.36	29.08	48.33	37.61	27.98
Coin-operated apparel laundry and dry cleaning	76.14	65.00	87.86	93.41	83.30	64.04	56.05	42.95
Apparel alteration, repair, and tailoring services	54.90	43.78	52.87	48.05	67.53	61.27	37.15	49.49
Clothing rental	142.31	88.73	125.93	132.32	126.72	305.43	160.23	–
Watch and jewelry repair	70.36	36.54	52.06	75.86	112.24	60.93	59.14	34.86
Professional laundry, dry cleaning	89.56	60.02	82.68	105.17	96.97	90.79	75.52	54.83
Clothing storage	300.00	–	265.63	243.75	291.25	444.74	186.36	100.00

Note: "–" means sample is too small to make a reliable estimate.
Source: Calculations by New Strategist based on the Bureau of Labor Statistics' 2008 Consumer Expenditure Survey

Table 1.3 Percent Buying Apparel by Age, Average Week, 2008

(percent of households buying apparel, accessories, and related services during the average week, by age of householder, 2008)

	total households	under 25	25 to 34	35 to 44	45 to 54	55 to 64	65 to 74	75+
APPAREL, PERCENT BUYING	**34.6%**	**31.3%**	**39.6%**	**40.8%**	**36.9%**	**32.6%**	**28.8%**	**19.7%**
Men's apparel	**12.2**	**10.2**	**12.1**	**15.6**	**14.2**	**12.2**	**10.2**	**4.8**
Sport coats and tailored jackets	0.1	–	0.0	0.0	–	0.1	0.2	–
Coats and jackets	0.9	0.7	0.9	1.1	0.9	1.0	0.7	0.1
Underwear	2.7	1.9	2.9	4.3	3.0	2.5	1.5	1.0
Hosiery	2.6	2.1	1.8	3.2	3.4	2.8	2.1	1.0
Accessories	3.4	3.6	3.5	3.8	4.0	3.4	2.8	0.9
Sweaters and vests	0.8	1.0	0.9	0.8	0.9	0.7	0.4	0.6
Active sportswear	1.1	1.1	1.3	1.2	1.1	1.2	0.8	0.3
Shirts	5.9	5.7	6.1	8.1	6.7	5.1	4.8	2.0
Pants and shorts	4.0	3.4	3.3	5.3	4.6	4.3	3.3	1.4
Uniforms	0.1	–	0.1	0.1	0.1	–	0.1	–
Boys' (aged 2 to 15) apparel	**3.5**	**2.2**	**5.2**	**7.2**	**3.0**	**1.7**	**1.5**	**0.3**
Shirts	2.2	1.4	3.1	4.5	2.1	1.0	1.3	0.2
Underwear	1.2	0.3	2.0	1.9	1.2	0.7	0.6	–
Nightwear	0.3	0.1	0.4	0.6	0.3	0.2	0.1	0.1
Hosiery	1.1	0.7	1.7	2.3	1.1	0.4	0.4	–
Accessories	0.7	0.5	1.1	1.2	0.6	0.3	0.3	0.1
Suits, sport coats, and vests	0.1	–	0.2	0.1	0.0	–	–	0.1
Women's apparel	**18.9**	**14.9**	**19.6**	**20.6**	**21.5**	**18.8**	**18.7**	**12.0**
Coats and jackets	1.8	1.4	1.3	1.5	2.2	2.4	1.7	1.5
Dresses	2.0	1.5	2.8	1.6	2.7	1.9	1.6	0.7
Sport coats and tailored jackets	0.1	0.1	–	0.1	0.2	0.2	–	–
Sweaters and vests	2.3	1.4	2.9	1.7	3.4	2.1	2.1	1.0
Shirts, blouses, and tops	8.9	8.6	9.1	10.0	10.3	8.9	7.3	5.2
Skirts	0.8	0.7	1.1	0.9	1.2	0.7	0.4	0.2
Pants and shorts	5.8	3.6	6.3	6.3	6.8	5.2	6.2	3.8
Active sportswear	1.7	1.8	1.7	1.7	2.0	1.8	1.4	1.3
Nightwear	2.0	1.8	1.9	2.0	2.7	1.5	2.1	1.5
Undergarments	2.9	1.9	3.1	3.2	3.8	2.8	2.3	2.0
Hosiery	3.8	2.4	2.8	4.4	4.5	3.6	4.2	3.1
Accessories	4.5	3.7	4.1	5.1	5.3	4.7	3.5	3.1
Uniforms	0.2	0.3	0.1	0.4	0.2	0.0	0.2	0.3
Girls' (aged 2 to 15) apparel	**4.9**	**2.1**	**6.6**	**9.6**	**4.8**	**2.7**	**2.5**	**0.6**
Coats and jackets	0.4	–	0.5	0.5	0.5	0.2	0.3	–
Dresses and suits	0.7	0.6	0.8	1.0	1.1	0.5	0.6	–
Shirts, blouses, and sweaters	2.6	0.7	3.7	5.6	2.6	1.2	1.3	0.2
Active sportswear	0.9	0.3	1.0	2.1	1.0	0.5	0.4	0.1
Underwear and nightwear	1.0	0.3	1.5	1.8	1.1	0.6	0.6	0.3
Hosiery	1.2	0.4	1.3	2.9	1.0	0.6	0.3	0.2
Accessories	1.0	0.6	1.6	1.9	0.9	0.3	0.8	0.2
Children's (under age 2) apparel	**5.7**	**9.1**	**12.6**	**7.9**	**3.2**	**2.6**	**2.3**	**1.0**
Outerwear including dresses	1.9	2.6	3.5	2.6	1.4	1.1	0.7	0.3
Underwear	3.9	7.3	9.2	5.5	1.8	1.3	1.4	0.7
Nightwear and loungewear	0.5	0.6	1.0	0.6	0.3	0.4	0.2	0.4
Accessories	1.4	1.2	2.9	2.1	1.1	0.8	0.7	0.4
Footwear	**11.0**	**9.8**	**12.2**	**14.3**	**13.0**	**9.2**	**8.2**	**5.3**
Men's	3.0	2.3	2.9	4.2	3.6	2.8	2.1	1.3
Boys'	1.8	1.4	3.2	3.5	1.6	0.5	0.7	0.1
Women's	6.4	6.4	6.2	7.0	7.6	6.0	5.9	4.0
Girls'	1.8	0.9	2.5	3.3	2.1	0.7	0.7	0.3
Other apparel products and services	**2.6**	**1.5**	**1.7**	**3.1**	**2.9**	**3.1**	**2.9**	**2.6**
Material for making clothes	0.7	0.6	0.4	0.6	1.0	0.9	1.0	0.6
Sewing patterns and notions	1.4	0.7	0.6	1.8	1.5	1.5	1.7	1.4
Watches	0.8	0.4	0.7	0.9	1.0	0.9	0.7	0.8

Note: "–" means sample is too small to make a reliable estimate.
Source: Bureau of Labor Statistics, unpublished data from the 2008 Consumer Expenditure Survey

Table 1.4 Amount Buyers Spent on Apparel by Age, Average Week, 2008

(average amount spent by households buying apparel, accessories, and related services during the average week, by age of householder, 2008)

	total households	under 25	25 to 34	35 to 44	45 to 54	55 to 64	65 to 74	75+
APPAREL, AMOUNT SPENT	$80.93	$68.68	$76.05	$85.33	$93.56	$75.44	$77.55	$62.72
Men's apparel	**49.39**	**46.24**	**43.81**	**53.08**	**47.60**	**50.66**	**57.35**	**42.05**
Sport coats and tailored jackets	140.00	–	66.67	66.67	–	163.64	188.89	–
Coats and jackets	74.12	43.66	67.42	76.32	71.76	93.00	67.61	53.85
Underwear	11.76	6.35	9.76	10.75	11.59	14.80	18.12	14.58
Hosiery	11.37	10.14	9.78	10.56	11.83	12.64	12.62	8.16
Accessories	19.05	15.98	16.71	23.88	22.03	13.99	12.90	26.97
Sweaters and vests	36.84	29.47	25.81	35.06	31.40	29.58	100.00	62.50
Active sportswear	29.25	27.52	32.06	26.50	31.53	28.93	20.00	34.62
Shirts	31.46	28.85	25.45	33.17	32.83	32.15	40.12	19.60
Pants and shorts	39.29	38.69	40.42	38.72	35.13	39.16	49.54	46.10
Uniforms	125.00	–	88.89	269.23	50.00	–	40.00	–
Boys' (aged 2 to 15) apparel	**24.36**	**18.89**	**26.06**	**23.96**	**25.74**	**20.00**	**29.05**	**10.34**
Shirts	20.36	18.98	20.92	21.43	18.05	18.75	23.26	5.88
Underwear	10.43	18.52	8.82	13.54	8.62	6.94	7.02	–
Nightwear	17.24	7.69	17.50	13.79	22.58	13.33	18.18	20.00
Hosiery	10.00	6.15	9.47	10.57	12.15	9.52	11.43	–
Accessories	13.85	10.20	19.63	10.17	16.95	15.38	9.09	14.29
Suits, sport coats, and vests	60.00	–	56.25	62.50	33.33	–	–	–
Women's apparel	**58.55**	**51.58**	**53.90**	**53.24**	**70.96**	**60.19**	**49.20**	**60.62**
Coats and jackets	63.69	37.41	60.90	70.59	68.64	74.58	41.38	53.42
Dresses	70.56	34.64	62.82	55.77	86.19	56.91	124.20	44.78
Sport coats and tailored jackets	44.44	25.00	–	61.54	35.29	31.25	–	–
Sweaters and vests	33.78	27.01	27.72	37.28	32.24	39.05	36.89	44.21
Shirts, blouses, and tops	26.60	24.91	25.88	24.40	29.15	27.75	26.50	25.43
Skirts	27.16	19.72	24.53	24.14	30.25	35.82	17.50	33.33
Pants and shorts	34.20	38.89	32.22	34.88	34.85	34.10	24.80	48.44
Active sportswear	31.21	40.22	29.31	26.95	41.21	23.91	24.48	28.24
Nightwear	24.62	27.62	20.86	20.00	32.48	22.82	17.79	23.97
Undergarments	23.81	21.76	20.26	22.40	26.44	25.54	25.00	22.28
Hosiery	8.53	5.76	7.61	8.39	9.31	9.62	6.41	9.87
Accessories	24.22	19.25	18.25	27.49	25.00	27.10	17.61	30.39
Uniforms	38.10	18.52	85.71	29.73	28.57	66.67	26.32	37.93
Girls' (aged 2 to 15) apparel	**34.50**	**17.29**	**31.00**	**32.22**	**45.85**	**29.59**	**44.08**	**7.94**
Coats and jackets	45.71	–	64.00	26.92	47.06	38.89	56.00	–
Dresses and suits	35.14	23.21	25.00	32.69	50.93	25.00	30.91	–
Shirts, blouses, and sweaters	23.48	15.38	22.68	21.71	29.50	25.64	20.90	8.33
Active sportswear	21.98	6.67	21.88	25.12	19.79	18.37	24.39	–
Underwear and nightwear	16.50	6.25	16.11	16.38	20.72	12.07	20.34	8.00
Hosiery	8.55	5.13	9.02	8.74	7.77	10.94	6.25	6.25
Accessories	15.69	12.70	9.32	17.99	15.38	25.00	29.76	6.25
Children's (under age 2) apparel	**30.05**	**35.57**	**29.71**	**32.02**	**26.96**	**24.61**	**26.75**	**18.95**
Outerwear including dresses	21.62	24.43	23.50	23.19	16.79	20.91	10.81	11.54
Underwear	24.36	25.34	24.59	25.95	24.43	20.93	19.26	16.92
Nightwear and loungewear	19.23	14.29	21.57	17.46	15.15	8.57	78.26	8.33
Accessories	17.48	55.37	15.44	17.45	14.29	12.99	14.71	5.41
Footwear	**54.80**	**49.85**	**54.42**	**54.49**	**61.08**	**50.76**	**51.16**	**48.19**
Men's	65.22	69.60	69.07	61.78	77.18	51.06	66.50	43.18
Boys'	43.41	39.01	45.63	38.81	50.63	41.18	42.47	41.67
Women's	41.85	41.07	36.47	37.29	46.37	46.48	39.70	46.50
Girls'	36.36	13.95	36.51	37.73	40.57	37.88	24.29	17.86
Other apparel products and services	**22.35**	**13.33**	**25.88**	**16.50**	**28.08**	**20.59**	**31.94**	**10.98**
Material for making clothes	19.18	17.86	25.00	15.25	21.00	19.35	23.16	9.52
Sewing patterns and notions	8.09	5.97	6.45	7.30	9.93	10.74	8.14	5.07
Watches	41.98	15.38	43.06	34.09	49.47	33.33	80.00	19.05

Note: "–" means sample is too small to make a reliable estimate.
Source: Calculations by New Strategist based on the Bureau of Labor Statistics' 2008 Consumer Expenditure Survey

Table 1.5 Percent Buying Apparel by Household Income, <u>Average Quarter</u>, 2008

(percent of households buying apparel, accessories, and related services during the average quarter, by before-tax income of household, 2008)

	total households	under $20,000	$20,000–$39,999	$40,000–$49,999	$50,000–$69,999	$70,000–$79,999	$80,000–$99,999	$100,000 or more
APPAREL, PERCENT BUYING	**74.3%**	**63.4%**	**68.7%**	**73.1%**	**76.6%**	**79.4%**	**81.1%**	**87.8%**
Men's apparel	**29.6**	**17.2**	**22.9**	**28.9**	**32.1**	**34.9**	**38.3**	**45.0**
Suits	1.3	0.4	0.6	0.8	1.3	1.1	1.6	3.3
Sport coats and tailored jackets	1.1	0.3	0.7	0.6	1.0	0.9	1.7	2.6
Coats and jackets	3.6	1.8	2.9	3.0	3.8	3.9	5.2	5.8
Underwear	5.3	2.9	4.4	5.3	5.1	6.3	7.1	8.1
Hosiery	4.4	2.4	3.5	4.5	5.1	4.9	6.3	6.4
Nightwear	0.9	0.3	0.5	1.0	0.6	1.2	1.5	1.7
Accessories	3.3	1.9	2.0	2.7	3.5	3.8	4.3	6.2
Sweaters and vests	2.5	1.2	1.6	2.1	2.5	2.0	3.7	4.7
Active sportswear	1.5	0.5	0.9	1.0	1.5	2.1	2.2	3.0
Shirts	17.9	9.6	12.9	17.6	19.0	21.3	23.7	29.1
Pants and shorts	19.0	10.3	13.8	19.5	20.7	22.3	26.2	29.4
Uniforms	0.6	0.3	0.4	0.6	0.9	1.0	1.2	0.7
Costumes	0.3	0.3	0.1	0.3	0.4	0.2	0.4	0.6
Boys' (aged 2 to 15) apparel	**11.3**	**6.0**	**9.0**	**10.9**	**12.8**	**13.7**	**14.8**	**17.0**
Coats and jackets	1.5	0.8	1.0	1.6	2.0	1.8	1.5	2.6
Sweaters	0.7	0.6	0.6	0.8	0.6	0.5	0.9	1.1
Shirts	7.0	3.6	5.3	6.7	8.1	8.1	9.3	10.9
Underwear	2.2	1.4	1.6	2.4	2.4	2.2	3.0	3.0
Nightwear	0.8	0.3	0.5	0.7	0.9	1.0	1.7	1.5
Hosiery	1.4	0.8	1.0	1.5	1.7	1.4	1.7	2.2
Accessories	0.7	0.3	0.5	0.5	0.5	0.6	0.9	1.6
Suits, sport coats, and vests	0.3	0.2	0.3	0.2	0.2	0.4	0.4	0.6
Pants and shorts	8.2	4.0	6.1	7.9	9.9	10.0	11.7	12.4
Uniforms	0.6	0.3	0.4	0.5	0.5	0.4	0.8	1.1
Active sportswear	1.0	0.3	0.5	0.7	0.9	1.4	1.7	2.2
Costumes	0.5	0.2	0.3	0.6	0.5	0.5	0.7	1.0
Women's apparel	**40.8**	**27.1**	**34.3**	**38.9**	**43.5**	**45.3**	**49.8**	**57.9**
Coats and jackets	5.3	3.1	4.3	4.8	4.8	5.3	6.9	8.9
Dresses	7.2	3.7	4.6	6.1	6.8	9.0	9.4	13.5
Sport coats and tailored jackets	1.2	0.6	0.8	0.9	1.0	1.1	0.9	3.1
Sweaters and vests	6.1	3.2	4.7	6.4	6.6	6.2	7.3	10.3
Shirts, blouses, and tops	24.8	15.3	20.0	23.2	27.5	28.9	30.6	36.3
Skirts	3.1	1.6	2.3	2.6	3.0	3.1	4.1	5.7
Pants and shorts	23.8	14.7	18.5	22.5	25.9	27.1	29.6	36.1
Active sportswear	3.2	1.3	2.0	2.8	3.5	3.0	4.9	6.3
Nightwear	4.0	2.3	3.5	3.7	3.7	4.6	5.4	5.9
Undergarments	9.1	6.2	7.7	8.3	9.2	8.6	12.5	13.5
Hosiery	5.7	3.6	4.5	5.7	6.0	5.5	7.2	8.8
Suits	1.6	0.7	1.2	1.2	1.4	1.1	1.5	3.7
Accessories	5.6	3.0	4.2	4.6	5.7	6.0	7.6	9.6
Uniforms	1.0	0.5	0.7	0.9	1.0	1.7	1.1	1.8
Costumes	0.6	0.4	0.4	0.8	0.4	0.6	0.4	1.1
Girls' (aged 2 to 15) apparel	**11.9**	**5.7**	**9.8**	**11.7**	**13.4**	**14.3**	**16.0**	**18.0**
Coats and jackets	1.7	0.7	1.2	1.5	1.9	2.2	2.8	2.5
Dresses and suits	2.2	0.7	1.5	2.8	2.2	2.5	3.3	3.6
Shirts, blouses, and sweaters	7.9	3.8	6.3	7.3	8.4	9.3	11.0	12.8
Skirts, pants, and shorts	8.3	4.0	6.7	7.9	9.1	10.2	12.0	12.5
Active sportswear	1.4	0.3	0.9	1.0	1.8	1.6	2.0	2.6
Underwear and nightwear	3.2	1.2	2.5	2.9	3.6	4.0	4.5	5.1

	total households	under $20,000	$20,000–$39,999	$40,000–$49,999	$50,000–$69,999	$70,000–$79,999	$80,000–$99,999	$100,000 or more
Hosiery	1.6%	0.6%	1.3%	1.6%	1.8%	1.9%	2.3%	2.5%
Accessories	1.1	0.5	0.7	0.7	0.9	1.4	2.2	2.0
Uniforms	0.5	0.4	0.5	0.5	0.5	0.5	0.4	0.9
Costumes	0.7	0.1	0.4	0.5	0.7	0.7	1.5	1.5
Children's (under age 2) apparel	**13.1**	**8.7**	**11.7**	**13.3**	**13.5**	**16.6**	**15.4**	**17.2**
Coats, jackets, and snowsuits	1.0	0.5	1.0	1.1	0.9	1.5	1.0	1.4
Outerwear including dresses	7.2	4.4	6.2	6.8	7.2	10.2	8.2	10.2
Underwear	7.1	5.0	6.3	8.0	7.2	8.5	8.8	8.6
Nightwear and loungewear	2.3	1.5	1.8	2.1	2.2	2.7	2.9	3.7
Accessories	3.3	2.0	3.0	3.2	3.3	3.8	3.8	4.8
Footwear	**31.7**	**21.3**	**27.1**	**30.5**	**34.1**	**36.5**	**37.5**	**44.1**
Men's	12.5	7.3	9.5	12.2	13.0	15.1	15.7	19.4
Boys'	6.0	3.0	4.6	5.8	6.3	8.1	8.1	9.2
Women's	18.7	12.1	15.4	16.3	20.1	20.5	23.1	28.1
Girls'	6.2	3.3	4.9	6.7	6.5	7.4	8.4	9.1
Other apparel products and services	**37.3**	**34.1**	**31.3**	**32.9**	**34.1**	**34.9**	**40.2**	**53.0**
Material for making clothes	1.2	0.7	0.9	1.4	1.5	1.4	1.1	1.8
Sewing patterns and notions	1.6	1.2	1.6	1.3	1.7	2.2	1.8	1.8
Watches	3.1	1.9	2.5	3.5	3.1	2.8	4.3	4.9
Jewelry	7.2	3.8	4.8	6.7	7.9	9.0	9.0	12.1
Shoe repair and other shoe services	0.9	0.4	0.6	0.8	0.8	0.8	0.9	1.8
Coin-operated apparel laundry and dry cleaning	13.8	24.9	16.2	14.0	10.6	8.5	6.9	5.4
Apparel alteration, repair, and tailoring services	2.9	1.3	1.7	2.2	3.0	4.2	3.4	5.9
Clothing rental	0.4	–	0.3	0.2	0.5	0.5	0.5	0.7
Watch and jewelry repair	1.8	0.8	1.4	1.2	2.0	1.9	3.0	3.1
Professional laundry, dry cleaning	15.1	4.9	7.6	11.8	13.1	15.6	20.9	37.2
Clothing storage	0.1	–	0.1	0.0	0.1	0.2	0.2	0.3

Note: "–" means sample is too small to make a reliable estimate.
Source: Bureau of Labor Statistics, unpublished data from the 2008 Consumer Expenditure Survey

Table 1.6 Amount Buyers Spent on Apparel by Household Income, <u>Average Quarter</u>, 2008

(average amount spent by households buying apparel, accessories, and related services during the average quarter, by before-tax income of household, 2008)

APPAREL, AMOUNT SPENT	total households $399.40	under $20,000 $219.30	$20,000–$39,999 $265.15	$40,000–$49,999 $334.29	$50,000–$69,999 $361.88	$70,000–$79,999 $397.18	$80,000–$99,999 $445.51	$100,000 or more $718.38
Men's apparel	**180.66**	**119.45**	**125.55**	**144.77**	**161.37**	**162.55**	**201.19**	**262.10**
Suits	466.60	314.90	271.58	267.99	341.60	240.51	468.91	626.28
Sport coats and tailored jackets	197.71	87.89	127.73	116.95	148.27	146.51	262.50	246.95
Coats and jackets	114.83	89.82	82.26	98.50	108.46	117.69	126.34	145.87
Underwear	35.86	36.70	32.52	35.29	42.00	33.63	33.75	35.69
Hosiery	20.88	18.90	15.99	16.11	21.01	24.34	20.21	26.02
Nightwear	46.84	35.45	45.31	44.39	52.73	41.24	37.41	56.29
Accessories	51.96	45.36	47.57	37.41	54.30	56.58	55.28	55.83
Sweaters and vests	87.65	72.36	81.83	101.30	75.30	72.73	78.30	100.59
Active sportswear	64.70	87.87	42.39	37.24	63.25	56.28	66.48	75.66
Shirts	81.16	62.41	63.53	73.45	73.45	80.31	81.58	104.68
Pants and shorts	92.63	70.99	74.32	81.29	85.57	95.50	100.75	115.59
Uniforms	149.19	142.63	121.46	108.93	195.69	116.84	117.46	184.29
Costumes	79.03	43.84	42.50	20.37	62.50	106.82	147.50	105.45
Boys' (aged 2 to 15) apparel	**147.62**	**135.49**	**125.80**	**136.03**	**137.06**	**147.04**	**132.47**	**184.00**
Coats and jackets	75.32	58.08	66.38	60.74	65.42	96.94	70.27	92.75
Sweaters	62.68	62.96	68.66	54.28	51.29	44.23	46.11	75.45
Shirts	69.82	67.70	58.33	67.96	67.09	72.36	66.49	80.20
Underwear	32.52	25.11	32.46	33.65	32.38	32.59	25.25	38.32
Nightwear	41.87	36.16	51.16	35.77	39.71	36.88	39.85	43.75
Hosiery	18.13	14.07	20.70	14.19	15.23	22.68	17.41	21.23
Accessories	43.93	44.12	48.52	31.86	30.61	23.41	20.43	57.97
Suits, sport coats, and vests	75.81	61.50	76.72	46.59	51.56	67.95	56.40	98.39
Pants and shorts	84.63	84.69	79.40	81.84	79.41	88.82	67.62	98.69
Uniforms	135.27	152.16	136.19	99.50	131.13	142.44	120.78	140.83
Active sportswear	44.13	47.82	38.67	42.54	24.45	36.59	43.67	54.51
Costumes	44.61	24.58	49.21	31.58	35.64	104.35	41.55	45.67
Women's apparel	**219.89**	**152.94**	**160.50**	**190.29**	**191.62**	**213.62**	**220.84**	**329.66**
Coats and jackets	115.70	86.29	95.30	97.37	101.71	118.48	113.05	151.80
Dresses	144.90	100.50	100.20	123.77	134.71	182.31	117.84	187.02
Sport coats and tailored jackets	115.65	117.76	83.28	70.22	124.75	61.59	173.26	134.43
Sweaters and vests	94.18	85.14	72.31	72.17	70.11	98.70	101.95	126.26
Shirts, blouses, and tops	86.97	65.10	71.12	83.29	78.73	83.95	88.23	114.95
Skirts	76.46	50.47	59.94	65.90	53.47	53.18	91.61	105.55
Pants and shorts	94.29	81.01	76.18	81.39	88.90	91.13	93.66	120.64
Active sportswear	63.19	48.15	50.62	46.38	56.47	59.85	63.36	79.55
Nightwear	48.30	52.33	43.90	50.41	45.04	40.08	46.58	54.04
Undergarments	55.88	55.32	49.09	55.15	49.84	50.96	54.32	67.08
Hosiery	22.68	18.91	19.98	22.84	22.93	16.86	19.20	28.88
Suits	201.08	136.98	154.19	137.39	163.73	145.50	162.16	273.93
Accessories	76.75	46.35	57.13	107.65	60.19	68.72	83.32	97.93
Uniforms	118.51	72.41	104.70	108.97	131.19	83.73	86.18	158.42
Costumes	92.37	32.71	131.56	82.10	82.39	109.17	67.61	123.41
Girls' (aged 2 to 15) apparel	**170.16**	**133.43**	**133.70**	**153.49**	**155.80**	**157.30**	**181.37**	**222.30**
Coats and jackets	65.76	55.25	63.40	51.90	54.32	51.50	65.11	89.18
Dresses and suits	84.49	84.47	54.56	71.47	75.11	72.19	70.65	121.96
Shirts, blouses, and sweaters	77.64	71.44	62.17	72.61	76.90	68.62	78.38	94.00
Skirts, pants, and shorts	88.70	64.48	73.30	83.14	89.74	87.92	96.36	105.83
Active sportswear	43.89	44.30	33.11	30.81	40.33	42.28	44.26	53.03
Underwear and nightwear	44.78	35.98	39.71	46.40	37.36	49.43	39.86	54.27

	total households	under $20,000	$20,000–$39,999	$40,000–$49,999	$50,000–$69,999	$70,000–$79,999	$80,000–$99,999	$100,000 or more
Hosiery	$17.09	$42.93	$15.40	$17.04	$15.90	$16.97	$14.80	$16.83
Accessories	37.73	92.67	33.03	16.22	36.92	22.46	29.41	38.38
Uniforms	131.60	81.87	148.43	104.08	112.98	152.78	100.64	172.41
Costumes	65.71	31.71	55.70	145.11	38.26	48.59	47.59	79.14
Children's (under age 2) apparel	**137.48**	**131.49**	**126.16**	**140.08**	**127.28**	**130.26**	**133.94**	**159.03**
Coats, jackets, and snowsuits	70.41	53.26	68.11	77.83	49.73	38.56	71.58	99.26
Outerwear including dresses	81.01	72.46	73.24	77.40	76.49	82.14	84.34	93.59
Underwear	122.94	129.78	119.70	122.15	118.45	112.10	113.67	131.96
Nightwear and loungewear	44.43	34.95	40.36	45.50	37.79	31.60	39.27	59.40
Accessories	56.10	49.47	47.00	60.33	57.69	62.70	50.07	63.16
Footwear	**118.14**	**86.64**	**91.17**	**107.35**	**113.58**	**115.18**	**122.71**	**162.35**
Men's	97.43	84.45	83.49	92.94	98.20	85.31	98.73	115.47
Boys'	67.92	59.22	64.97	62.31	72.75	67.23	59.31	75.87
Women's	91.91	71.92	71.13	83.27	86.67	90.97	87.34	123.98
Girls'	65.83	56.88	57.16	62.97	61.15	68.65	65.10	79.65
Other apparel products and services	**163.68**	**92.10**	**108.76**	**135.16**	**139.99**	**159.29**	**147.14**	**286.61**
Material for making clothes	58.33	36.93	49.71	54.26	47.02	86.59	68.12	72.05
Sewing patterns and notions	28.82	18.35	19.41	33.13	33.04	28.57	36.11	38.71
Watches	171.74	50.72	114.40	79.89	84.79	102.87	69.37	397.34
Jewelry	367.42	288.23	223.17	262.56	285.45	320.57	289.91	577.84
Shoe repair and other shoe services	36.92	25.32	31.75	28.01	31.82	27.33	56.99	42.46
Coin-operated apparel laundry and dry cleaning	76.14	61.30	83.51	86.59	90.83	89.37	93.73	80.14
Apparel alteration, repair, and tailoring services	54.90	30.67	36.36	59.14	46.44	48.40	54.08	72.42
Clothing rental	142.31	–	111.21	134.38	118.37	96.67	108.80	190.28
Watch and jewelry repair	70.36	38.03	46.30	103.93	50.63	37.24	45.47	116.91
Professional laundry, dry cleaning	89.56	50.33	53.82	65.05	64.90	67.38	83.71	120.73
Clothing storage	300.00	–	256.48	500.00	90.00	294.44	222.37	413.46

Note: "–" means sample is too small to make a reliable estimate.
Source: Calculations by New Strategist based on the Bureau of Labor Statistics' 2008 Consumer Expenditure Survey

(percent of households buying apparel, accessories, and related services during the average week, by income of household, 2008)

	total households	under $20,000	$20,000– $39,999	$40,000– $49,999	$50,000– $69,999	$70,000– $79,999	$80,000– $99,999	$100,000 or more
APPAREL, PERCENT BUYING	**34.6%**	**23.0%**	**31.2%**	**30.4%**	**35.5%**	**40.8%**	**42.5%**	**47.7%**
Men's apparel	**12.2**	**6.1**	**9.9**	**9.9**	**14.1**	**12.3**	**17.0**	**19.5**
Sport coats and tailored jackets	0.1	–	0.0	–	0.1	0.2	–	0.1
Coats and jackets	0.9	0.4	0.7	0.9	0.9	0.9	0.8	1.4
Underwear	2.7	1.3	1.8	2.2	3.8	3.4	3.5	4.3
Hosiery	2.6	1.4	2.0	2.6	2.4	2.0	3.5	4.4
Accessories	3.4	1.5	2.4	3.5	3.8	3.9	5.1	5.2
Sweaters and vests	0.8	0.5	0.4	0.5	0.7	1.2	0.7	1.7
Active sportswear	1.1	0.3	0.7	0.6	1.0	1.2	1.8	2.3
Shirts	5.9	2.4	4.7	4.3	7.6	6.2	8.6	9.3
Pants and shorts	4.0	2.1	3.4	2.7	4.6	3.5	5.2	6.5
Uniforms	0.1	–	0.1	–	0.2	0.1	0.1	0.1
Boys' (aged 2 to 15) apparel	**3.5**	**2.2**	**2.9**	**2.6**	**3.5**	**4.8**	**5.2**	**4.9**
Shirts	2.2	1.5	1.8	1.7	2.5	3.4	3.0	2.8
Underwear	1.2	0.8	0.8	0.7	1.0	1.6	1.8	1.9
Nightwear	0.3	0.3	0.2	0.2	0.2	0.5	0.6	0.3
Hosiery	1.1	0.8	0.9	0.7	1.3	1.1	1.5	1.6
Accessories	0.7	0.6	0.6	0.4	0.8	0.3	0.8	0.8
Suits, sport coats, and vests	0.1	–	0.1	–	0.2	0.1	0.1	–
Women's apparel	**18.9**	**12.7**	**17.1**	**15.6**	**18.5**	**21.2**	**23.7**	**27.5**
Coats and jackets	1.8	1.1	1.5	0.8	1.8	2.6	1.9	3.1
Dresses	2.0	1.4	1.5	1.9	1.8	2.3	2.6	3.0
Sport coats and tailored jackets	0.1	0.1	0.1	0.2	0.0	0.1	0.1	0.3
Sweaters and vests	2.3	1.3	1.4	1.5	2.4	3.3	3.1	4.1
Shirts, blouses, and tops	8.9	5.6	8.1	6.7	8.7	10.3	11.6	13.3
Skirts	0.8	0.3	0.6	0.7	1.0	0.9	0.8	1.6
Pants and shorts	5.8	4.4	5.0	3.9	5.9	6.0	8.0	8.2
Active sportswear	1.7	1.1	1.0	1.5	2.2	2.8	2.2	2.6
Nightwear	2.0	1.5	1.4	1.3	2.3	1.6	3.4	2.9
Undergarments	2.9	2.0	2.4	2.3	2.7	3.8	3.7	4.7
Hosiery	3.8	2.7	3.4	4.1	3.1	3.2	4.0	5.9
Accessories	4.5	3.0	4.0	4.2	4.3	5.2	4.0	6.8
Uniforms	0.2	0.4	0.2	0.2	0.4	0.1	0.2	0.2
Girls' (aged 2 to 15) apparel	**4.9**	**3.0**	**3.7**	**4.5**	**4.5**	**6.7**	**6.7**	**7.5**
Coats and jackets	0.4	0.2	0.2	0.3	0.4	0.3	0.5	0.7
Dresses and suits	0.7	0.4	0.4	0.6	1.0	0.7	1.1	1.2
Shirts, blouses, and sweaters	2.6	1.7	1.9	2.6	2.1	3.4	3.3	4.7
Active sportswear	0.9	0.4	0.5	0.6	0.9	1.0	1.9	1.7
Underwear and nightwear	1.0	0.5	1.0	0.8	1.3	1.1	1.4	1.3
Hosiery	1.2	0.7	0.8	1.6	0.8	2.0	1.4	2.0
Accessories	1.0	0.6	0.8	1.0	0.9	1.6	1.4	1.4
Children's (under age 2) apparel	**5.7**	**3.7**	**4.5**	**4.8**	**6.6**	**6.8**	**6.5**	**8.5**
Outerwear including dresses	1.9	1.1	1.4	1.3	1.8	2.3	2.0	3.4
Underwear	3.9	2.5	3.1	3.6	4.7	4.3	4.9	5.3
Nightwear and loungewear	0.5	0.3	0.3	0.5	0.6	0.5	0.4	1.0
Accessories	1.4	0.9	1.2	1.0	1.3	2.2	1.3	2.5
Footwear	**11.0**	**7.5**	**10.0**	**10.0**	**10.9**	**12.1**	**11.8**	**16.3**
Men's	3.0	1.5	2.7	2.5	3.3	4.2	3.4	4.5
Boys'	1.8	1.4	1.8	1.5	1.8	2.0	1.6	2.5
Women's	6.4	4.6	5.6	5.8	6.6	6.2	7.2	9.2
Girls'	1.8	1.2	1.4	1.8	1.4	2.3	2.3	2.7
Other apparel products and services	**2.6**	**1.2**	**2.6**	**2.6**	**2.5**	**2.6**	**3.9**	**3.8**
Material for making clothes	0.7	0.4	0.6	0.9	0.8	0.9	0.8	1.0
Sewing patterns and notions	1.4	0.9	1.5	1.3	0.9	1.3	2.5	1.7
Watches	0.8	0.2	0.8	0.7	1.0	0.5	1.0	1.5

Note: "–" means sample is too small to make a reliable estimate.
Source: Bureau of Labor Statistics, unpublished data from the 2008 Consumer Expenditure Survey

Table 1.8 Amount Buyers Spent on Apparel by Household Income, <u>Average Week</u>, 2008

(average amount spent by households buying apparel, accessories, and related services during the average week, by before-tax income of household, 2008)

	total households	under $20,000	$20,000–$39,999	$40,000–$49,999	$50,000–$69,999	$70,000–$79,999	$80,000–$99,999	$100,000 or more
APPAREL, AMOUNT SPENT	**$80.93**	**$65.47**	**$63.60**	**$61.80**	**$77.35**	**$71.04**	**$90.24**	**$113.00**
Men's apparel	**49.39**	**39.75**	**39.25**	**35.40**	**43.24**	**54.99**	**48.73**	**66.67**
Sport coats and tailored jackets	140.00	–	75.00	–	50.00	318.75	–	142.86
Coats and jackets	74.12	64.60	58.46	58.24	69.23	32.61	48.10	114.79
Underwear	11.76	9.50	10.01	10.86	9.81	13.91	11.02	14.65
Hosiery	11.37	9.36	8.01	7.66	10.83	15.84	12.39	14.19
Accessories	19.05	14.70	13.85	14.77	15.79	14.80	19.53	27.72
Sweaters and vests	36.84	41.05	21.54	22.92	20.27	24.14	39.39	44.51
Active sportswear	29.25	25.28	18.12	24.19	25.26	33.33	33.90	33.33
Shirts	31.46	24.18	24.40	20.75	29.89	31.77	32.48	41.65
Pants and shorts	39.29	34.86	38.70	31.72	31.67	53.62	37.84	45.11
Uniforms	125.00	–	158.33	–	55.56	100.00	671.43	38.46
Boys' (aged 2 to 15) apparel	**24.36**	**20.86**	**22.48**	**20.93**	**27.35**	**24.16**	**22.78**	**27.29**
Shirts	20.36	16.46	22.89	20.24	18.58	21.11	20.07	21.99
Underwear	10.43	9.18	8.12	10.29	9.62	6.92	12.15	12.44
Nightwear	17.24	16.58	14.69	16.67	22.22	25.49	8.93	17.86
Hosiery	10.00	7.69	6.37	8.57	11.20	8.85	12.42	12.74
Accessories	13.85	8.73	12.44	7.14	14.10	6.25	9.33	28.95
Suits, sport coats, and vests	60.00	–	32.68	–	55.56	70.00	66.67	–
Women's apparel	**58.55**	**48.48**	**44.99**	**46.02**	**54.26**	**52.52**	**67.43**	**80.04**
Coats and jackets	63.69	50.41	54.87	46.34	56.74	50.19	87.83	75.00
Dresses	70.56	42.04	61.96	37.57	47.28	58.67	125.78	96.00
Sport coats and tailored jackets	44.44	23.08	33.33	64.71	25.00	33.33	22.22	37.93
Sweaters and vests	33.78	26.46	34.78	29.53	27.97	24.62	30.49	43.83
Shirts, blouses, and tops	26.60	22.73	22.31	23.09	24.45	27.93	28.01	32.96
Skirts	27.16	16.36	21.91	10.61	23.71	35.87	45.68	31.48
Pants and shorts	34.20	29.61	26.93	35.66	33.90	23.92	32.00	46.50
Active sportswear	31.21	26.31	21.41	33.77	30.04	24.73	36.99	37.89
Nightwear	24.62	22.84	20.17	17.56	23.71	17.79	33.93	26.39
Undergarments	23.81	23.50	17.90	21.40	25.28	20.68	21.68	29.18
Hosiery	8.53	6.79	7.34	6.11	8.65	9.69	12.13	9.54
Accessories	24.22	17.88	22.61	22.46	18.89	18.43	18.16	36.22
Uniforms	38.10	75.61	27.29	37.50	38.46	16.67	11.76	30.00
Girls' (aged 2 to 15) apparel	**34.50**	**26.28**	**26.80**	**31.40**	**35.03**	**28.87**	**37.72**	**44.39**
Coats and jackets	45.71	22.51	51.74	28.57	63.16	16.13	30.43	52.94
Dresses and suits	35.14	37.67	27.68	30.36	36.46	24.64	25.00	45.53
Shirts, blouses, and sweaters	23.48	17.46	18.30	21.97	18.93	29.50	31.83	26.65
Active sportswear	21.98	20.83	27.17	20.31	19.77	12.00	22.46	24.71
Underwear and nightwear	16.50	12.97	12.96	14.81	16.54	20.91	15.60	21.60
Hosiery	8.55	9.56	6.67	10.63	9.21	6.50	6.38	8.46
Accessories	15.69	8.22	12.47	15.38	15.05	12.80	22.96	21.90
Children's (under age 2) apparel	**30.05**	**26.05**	**30.91**	**23.19**	**28.66**	**26.62**	**35.97**	**33.22**
Outerwear including dresses	21.62	22.13	19.83	13.53	20.00	18.03	39.30	20.82
Underwear	24.36	20.51	24.25	20.94	22.70	24.88	25.77	28.84
Nightwear and loungewear	19.23	8.04	18.56	12.00	26.56	12.00	16.28	21.21
Accessories	17.48	14.84	25.88	12.24	24.80	11.93	16.54	13.39
Footwear	**54.80**	**53.15**	**47.07**	**46.49**	**56.89**	**47.73**	**62.30**	**62.61**
Men's	65.22	78.99	50.91	58.06	78.29	54.78	61.90	73.13
Boys'	43.41	54.64	46.52	35.53	39.44	47.06	37.74	39.53
Women's	41.85	41.37	35.98	34.77	38.94	29.66	52.35	49.89
Girls'	36.36	27.37	32.83	36.00	25.00	30.34	40.71	48.33
Other apparel products and services	**22.35**	**17.26**	**18.00**	**15.97**	**26.21**	**13.74**	**17.86**	**33.25**
Material for making clothes	19.18	12.28	18.69	13.83	19.51	13.64	20.48	28.00
Sewing patterns and notions	8.09	8.68	6.32	7.14	6.67	10.53	9.39	9.47
Watches	41.98	38.15	36.90	28.99	44.33	20.00	28.16	56.55

Note: "–" means sample is too small to make a reliable estimate.
Source: Calculations by New Strategist based on the Bureau of Labor Statistics' 2008 Consumer Expenditure Survey

Table 1.9 Percent of High-Income Households Buying Apparel, Average Quarter, 2008

(percent of high-income households buying apparel, accessories, and related services during the average quarter, by before-tax income of household, 2008)

	total households	$100,000 or more	$100,000– $119,999	$120,000– $149,999	$150,000 or more
APPAREL, PERCENT BUYING	**74.3%**	**87.8%**	**84.6%**	**87.4%**	**90.7%**
Men's apparel	**29.6**	**45.0**	**41.8**	**44.6**	**47.9**
Suits	1.3	3.3	2.1	2.8	4.7
Sport coats and tailored jackets	1.1	2.6	1.8	2.0	3.7
Coats and jackets	3.6	5.8	4.8	5.3	7.0
Underwear	5.3	8.1	7.0	8.5	8.8
Hosiery	4.4	6.4	6.2	5.6	7.1
Nightwear	0.9	1.7	1.3	1.8	1.9
Accessories	3.3	6.2	4.7	5.5	7.9
Sweaters and vests	2.5	4.7	3.6	5.0	5.4
Active sportswear	1.5	3.0	2.3	2.7	3.8
Shirts	17.9	29.1	26.0	29.0	31.6
Pants and shorts	19.0	29.4	26.9	29.7	31.3
Uniforms	0.6	0.7	0.6	0.4	1.0
Costumes	0.3	0.6	0.4	0.8	0.5
Boys' (aged 2 to 15) apparel	**11.3**	**17.0**	**16.2**	**17.6**	**17.3**
Coats and jackets	1.5	2.6	2.4	2.2	3.1
Sweaters	0.7	1.1	0.9	1.3	1.1
Shirts	7.0	10.9	10.3	11.0	11.3
Underwear	2.2	3.0	3.1	3.2	3.0
Nightwear	0.8	1.5	1.4	1.5	1.6
Hosiery	1.4	2.2	2.7	1.6	2.2
Accessories	0.7	1.6	1.2	1.9	1.8
Suits, sport coats, and vests	0.3	0.6	0.6	0.7	0.6
Pants and shorts	8.2	12.4	11.9	12.7	12.7
Uniforms	0.6	1.1	1.1	0.9	1.2
Active sportswear	1.0	2.2	1.8	1.8	2.6
Costumes	0.5	1.0	1.0	1.0	1.1
Women's apparel	**40.8**	**57.9**	**54.2**	**57.5**	**61.3**
Coats and jackets	5.3	8.9	6.8	8.9	10.7
Dresses	7.2	13.5	10.0	13.5	16.5
Sport coats and tailored jackets	1.2	3.1	1.7	2.6	4.5
Sweaters and vests	6.1	10.3	8.2	9.8	12.3
Shirts, blouses, and tops	24.8	36.3	33.1	34.5	40.1
Skirts	3.1	5.7	4.8	5.3	6.7
Pants and shorts	23.8	36.1	33.5	35.0	39.1
Active sportswear	3.2	6.3	5.7	6.0	6.9
Nightwear	4.0	5.9	5.0	5.3	7.2
Undergarments	9.1	13.5	11.8	13.9	14.6
Hosiery	5.7	8.8	8.3	7.6	10.1
Suits	1.6	3.7	2.8	3.5	4.7
Accessories	5.6	9.6	7.5	10.1	10.9
Uniforms	1.0	1.8	1.7	2.2	1.7
Costumes	0.6	1.1	1.0	0.7	1.5
Girls' (aged 2 to 15) apparel	**11.9**	**18.0**	**16.8**	**18.1**	**18.8**
Coats and jackets	1.7	2.5	2.1	2.5	2.7
Dresses and suits	2.2	3.6	3.3	3.2	4.2
Shirts, blouses, and sweaters	7.9	12.8	11.7	13.2	13.6
Skirts, pants, and shorts	8.3	12.5	12.1	12.8	12.6
Active sportswear	1.4	2.6	2.5	2.1	3.1
Underwear and nightwear	3.2	5.1	4.9	4.8	5.5

	total households	$100,000 or more	$100,000– $119,999	$120,000– $149,999	$150,000 or more
Hosiery	1.6%	2.5%	2.8%	2.2%	2.5%
Accessories	1.1	2.0	2.1	2.1	1.9
Uniforms	0.5	0.9	0.9	0.6	1.0
Costumes	0.7	1.5	1.3	1.7	1.6
Children's (under age 2) apparel	**13.1**	**17.2**	**17.5**	**19.0**	**15.9**
Coats, jackets, and snowsuits	1.0	1.4	1.4	1.2	1.4
Outerwear including dresses	7.2	10.2	11.1	11.1	8.9
Underwear	7.1	8.6	8.9	9.8	7.6
Nightwear and loungewear	2.3	3.7	4.2	4.0	3.0
Accessories	3.3	4.8	4.7	5.4	4.4
Footwear	**31.7**	**44.1**	**39.8**	**45.5**	**46.6**
Men's	12.5	19.4	17.5	20.1	20.6
Boys'	6.0	9.2	8.5	9.6	9.5
Women's	18.7	28.1	23.8	29.7	30.7
Girls'	6.2	9.1	8.3	8.5	10.2
Other apparel products and services	**37.3**	**53.0**	**43.3**	**50.9**	**62.3**
Material for making clothes	1.2	1.8	1.4	2.3	1.7
Sewing patterns and notions	1.6	1.8	1.7	1.6	1.9
Watches	3.1	4.9	3.7	5.3	5.6
Jewelry	7.2	12.1	10.2	12.2	13.7
Shoe repair and other shoe services	0.9	1.8	1.0	1.7	2.5
Coin-operated apparel laundry and dry cleaning	13.8	5.4	6.1	5.0	5.0
Apparel alteration, repair, and tailoring services	2.9	5.9	4.3	5.6	7.4
Clothing rental	0.4	0.7	1.1	0.6	0.5
Watch and jewelry repair	1.8	3.1	2.5	3.7	3.3
Professional laundry, dry cleaning	15.1	37.2	25.9	33.4	48.9
Clothing storage	0.1	0.3	0.4	0.1	0.3

Source: Bureau of Labor Statistics, unpublished data from the 2008 Consumer Expenditure Survey

(average amount spent by high-income households buying apparel, accessories, and related services during the average quarter, by before-tax income of household, 2008)

	total households	$100,000 or more	$100,000–$119,999	$120,000–$149,999	$150,000 or more
APPAREL, AMOUNT SPENT	**$399.40**	**$718.38**	**$506.57**	**$617.31**	**$945.05**
Men's apparel	**180.66**	**262.10**	**204.18**	**230.54**	**323.03**
Suits	466.60	626.28	567.69	457.13	714.61
Sport coats and tailored jackets	197.71	246.95	206.25	180.77	287.74
Coats and jackets	114.83	145.87	123.64	122.78	169.65
Underwear	35.86	35.69	36.11	35.02	35.80
Hosiery	20.88	26.02	20.59	30.98	27.36
Nightwear	46.84	56.29	46.48	64.78	56.48
Accessories	51.96	55.83	37.61	56.82	64.29
Sweaters and vests	87.65	100.59	84.25	95.38	112.99
Active sportswear	64.70	75.66	74.25	86.86	71.10
Shirts	81.16	104.68	92.86	99.37	115.91
Pants and shorts	92.63	115.59	101.71	115.89	125.14
Uniforms	149.19	184.29	87.71	143.92	240.35
Costumes	79.03	105.45	158.33	47.08	129.17
Boys' (aged 2 to 15) apparel	**147.62**	**184.00**	**148.83**	**190.48**	**206.67**
Coats and jackets	75.32	92.75	60.49	127.40	96.63
Sweaters	62.68	75.45	66.48	110.98	53.51
Shirts	69.82	80.20	66.93	88.38	84.76
Underwear	32.52	38.32	30.72	50.71	36.10
Nightwear	41.87	43.75	33.10	38.25	54.81
Hosiery	18.13	21.23	15.37	31.92	21.90
Accessories	43.93	57.97	36.96	50.68	73.62
Suits, sport coats, and vests	75.81	98.39	71.43	112.68	106.05
Pants and shorts	84.63	98.69	83.80	99.45	109.60
Uniforms	135.27	140.83	126.19	161.68	142.62
Active sportswear	44.13	54.51	38.32	41.30	70.08
Costumes	44.61	45.67	54.81	28.47	48.83
Women's apparel	**219.89**	**329.66**	**241.61**	**285.33**	**421.20**
Coats and jackets	115.70	151.80	119.93	107.31	193.01
Dresses	144.90	187.02	134.22	164.70	225.02
Sport coats and tailored jackets	115.65	134.43	79.91	90.59	167.35
Sweaters and vests	94.18	126.26	108.57	87.41	156.44
Shirts, blouses, and tops	86.97	114.95	93.92	103.19	135.92
Skirts	76.46	105.55	78.17	83.95	132.93
Pants and shorts	94.29	120.64	106.55	111.06	136.21
Active sportswear	63.19	79.55	67.26	78.13	88.77
Nightwear	48.30	54.04	42.56	45.49	64.73
Undergarments	55.88	67.08	58.09	67.41	72.79
Hosiery	22.68	28.88	25.15	30.54	30.55
Suits	201.08	273.93	176.59	290.51	313.38
Accessories	76.75	97.93	77.50	82.76	118.74
Uniforms	118.51	158.42	109.79	183.48	175.29
Costumes	92.37	123.41	109.34	185.14	112.16
Girls' (aged 2 to 15) apparel	**170.16**	**222.30**	**206.42**	**197.36**	**249.87**
Coats and jackets	65.76	89.18	74.06	89.33	98.80
Dresses and suits	84.49	121.96	113.69	109.98	133.11
Shirts, blouses, and sweaters	77.64	94.00	80.24	84.22	109.99
Skirts, pants, and shorts	88.70	105.83	100.25	97.43	115.91
Active sportswear	43.89	53.03	39.78	45.79	65.03
Underwear and nightwear	44.78	54.27	55.27	51.30	55.17

	total households	$100,000 or more	$100,000–$119,999	$120,000–$149,999	$150,000 or more
Hosiery	$17.09	$16.83	$15.40	$13.70	$20.04
Accessories	37.73	38.38	37.50	31.01	44.52
Uniforms	131.60	172.41	151.97	172.92	186.89
Costumes	65.71	79.14	122.73	58.18	63.85
Children's (under age 2) apparel	**137.48**	**159.03**	**153.95**	**152.01**	**168.99**
Coats, jackets, and snowsuits	70.41	99.26	70.21	114.74	115.07
Outerwear including dresses	81.01	93.59	83.39	87.28	109.29
Underwear	122.94	131.96	126.95	131.63	136.99
Nightwear and loungewear	44.43	59.40	58.41	48.95	70.15
Accessories	56.10	63.16	63.35	52.80	71.55
Footwear	**118.14**	**162.35**	**142.41**	**144.82**	**187.62**
Men's	97.43	115.47	105.53	101.52	131.42
Boys'	67.92	75.87	69.65	66.68	86.61
Women's	91.91	123.98	112.06	112.47	138.89
Girls'	65.83	79.65	68.54	66.47	94.34
Other apparel products and services	**163.68**	**286.61**	**162.01**	**213.42**	**397.41**
Material for making clothes	58.33	72.05	56.94	50.44	101.45
Sewing patterns and notions	28.82	38.71	34.38	51.42	35.21
Watches	171.74	397.34	112.67	153.38	708.51
Jewelry	367.42	577.84	291.80	423.09	844.94
Shoe repair and other shoe services	36.92	42.46	28.09	37.57	49.20
Coin-operated apparel laundry and dry cleaning	76.14	80.14	66.49	83.00	91.82
Apparel alteration, repair, and tailoring services	54.90	72.42	57.75	70.64	80.46
Clothing rental	142.31	190.28	149.77	156.70	282.21
Watch and jewelry repair	70.36	116.91	65.26	70.96	182.60
Professional laundry, dry cleaning	89.56	120.73	91.22	103.65	141.32
Clothing storage	300.00	413.46	270.95	246.88	592.24

Source: Calculations by New Strategist based on the Bureau of Labor Statistics' 2008 Consumer Expenditure Survey

Table 1.11 Percent of High-Income Households Buying Apparel, Average Week, 2008

(percent of high-income households buying apparel, accessories, and related services during the average week, by before-tax income of household, 2008)

	total households	$100,000 or more	$100,000– $119,999	$120,000– $149,999	$150,000 or more
APPAREL, PERCENT BUYING	**34.6%**	**47.7%**	**47.8%**	**49.8%**	**45.9%**
Men's apparel	**12.2**	**19.5**	**20.2**	**18.8**	**19.2**
Sport coats and tailored jackets	0.1	0.1	0.1	0.3	0.1
Coats and jackets	0.9	1.4	1.3	1.0	1.9
Underwear	2.7	4.3	4.0	5.1	4.0
Hosiery	2.6	4.4	5.4	4.3	3.6
Accessories	3.4	5.2	5.1	4.7	5.8
Sweaters and vests	0.8	1.7	1.6	1.7	1.9
Active sportswear	1.1	2.3	2.1	2.2	2.7
Shirts	5.9	9.3	8.5	9.6	10.0
Pants and shorts	4.0	6.5	6.6	6.3	6.6
Uniforms	0.1	0.1	0.2	0.1	0.1
Boys' (aged 2 to 15) apparel	**3.5**	**4.9**	**5.8**	**4.1**	**4.6**
Shirts	2.2	2.8	3.2	2.2	2.9
Underwear	1.2	1.9	1.7	1.9	2.2
Nightwear	0.3	0.3	0.1	0.6	0.3
Hosiery	1.1	1.6	2.1	1.4	1.2
Accessories	0.7	0.8	1.3	0.3	0.6
Suits, sport coats, and vests	0.1	–	–	–	–
Women's apparel	**18.9**	**27.5**	**27.1**	**27.3**	**27.9**
Coats and jackets	1.8	3.1	2.8	3.1	3.4
Dresses	2.0	3.0	2.7	2.8	3.6
Sport coats and tailored jackets	0.1	0.3	0.1	0.4	0.4
Sweaters and vests	2.3	4.1	3.8	4.2	4.4
Shirts, blouses, and tops	8.9	13.3	13.0	12.8	14.1
Skirts	0.8	1.6	1.0	2.0	2.0
Pants and shorts	5.8	8.2	7.7	8.0	8.8
Active sportswear	1.7	2.6	2.1	2.5	3.1
Nightwear	2.0	2.9	3.1	2.9	2.7
Undergarments	2.9	4.7	4.3	4.8	5.0
Hosiery	3.8	5.9	6.6	6.2	4.9
Accessories	4.5	6.8	7.0	5.8	7.5
Uniforms	0.2	0.2	0.2	0.1	0.2
Girls' (aged 2 to 15) apparel	**4.9**	**7.5**	**8.1**	**8.5**	**6.0**
Coats and jackets	0.4	0.7	0.4	1.2	0.6
Dresses and suits	0.7	1.2	1.2	1.3	1.2
Shirts, blouses, and sweaters	2.6	4.7	5.1	5.5	3.7
Active sportswear	0.9	1.7	2.7	2.1	0.4
Underwear and nightwear	1.0	1.3	1.5	1.6	0.7
Hosiery	1.2	2.0	3.0	2.1	0.9
Accessories	1.0	1.4	1.4	1.3	1.4
Children's (under age 2) apparel	**5.7**	**8.5**	**8.7**	**10.0**	**7.1**
Outerwear including dresses	1.9	3.4	3.3	4.4	2.8
Underwear	3.9	5.3	6.1	5.9	4.1
Nightwear and loungewear	0.5	1.0	1.3	0.9	0.7
Accessories	1.4	2.5	2.1	4.2	1.7
Footwear	**11.0**	**16.3**	**16.3**	**15.3**	**17.2**
Men's	3.0	4.5	4.5	4.7	4.5
Boys'	1.8	2.5	3.4	2.2	1.8
Women's	6.4	9.2	8.4	8.3	10.8
Girls'	1.8	2.7	2.9	3.4	1.9
Other apparel products and services	**2.6**	**3.8**	**4.0**	**4.0**	**3.4**
Material for making clothes	0.7	1.0	1.2	0.9	0.9
Sewing patterns and notions	1.4	1.7	2.0	2.0	1.2
Watches	0.8	1.5	1.2	1.5	1.8

Note: "–" means sample is too small to make a reliable estimate.
Source: Bureau of Labor Statistics, unpublished data from the 2008 Consumer Expenditure Survey

Table 1.12 Amount High-Income Buyers Spent on Apparel, <u>Average Week</u>, 2008

(average amount spent by high-income households buying apparel, accessories, and related services during the average week, by before-tax income of household, 2008)

	total households	$100,000 or more	$100,000– $119,999	$120,000– $149,999	$150,000 or more
APPAREL, AMOUNT SPENT	**$80.93**	**$113.00**	**$90.55**	**$96.45**	**$151.18**
Men's apparel	**49.39**	**66.67**	**42.98**	**55.11**	**101.14**
Sport coats and tailored jackets	140.00	142.86	87.50	207.69	80.00
Coats and jackets	74.12	114.79	67.94	109.18	150.80
Underwear	11.76	14.65	12.25	14.23	17.71
Hosiery	11.37	14.19	11.40	11.48	21.43
Accessories	19.05	27.72	14.03	20.13	45.02
Sweaters and vests	36.84	44.51	52.83	32.76	45.16
Active sportswear	29.25	33.33	32.37	30.88	35.85
Shirts	31.46	41.65	24.59	31.07	64.59
Pants and shorts	39.29	45.11	33.73	37.16	62.65
Uniforms	125.00	38.46	30.00	20.00	77.78
Boys' (aged 2 to 15) apparel	**24.36**	**27.29**	**24.23**	**21.36**	**35.22**
Shirts	20.36	21.99	17.96	17.59	28.62
Underwear	10.43	12.44	10.40	13.90	13.76
Nightwear	17.24	17.86	16.67	13.56	29.63
Hosiery	10.00	12.74	10.53	7.86	21.55
Accessories	13.85	28.95	33.60	16.13	25.81
Suits, sport coats, and vests	60.00	–	–	–	–
Women's apparel	**58.55**	**80.04**	**68.25**	**68.34**	**100.86**
Coats and jackets	63.69	75.00	56.38	70.59	94.33
Dresses	70.56	96.00	147.92	50.36	83.94
Sport coats and tailored jackets	44.44	37.93	30.77	27.03	51.35
Sweaters and vests	33.78	43.83	37.77	36.88	54.50
Shirts, blouses, and tops	26.60	32.96	25.79	38.56	35.91
Skirts	27.16	31.48	23.08	30.46	36.92
Pants and shorts	34.20	46.50	45.11	37.41	54.22
Active sportswear	31.21	37.89	36.92	26.21	45.42
Nightwear	24.62	26.39	20.39	28.52	31.32
Undergarments	23.81	29.18	20.75	25.68	39.44
Hosiery	8.53	9.54	8.62	8.94	11.25
Accessories	24.22	36.22	21.23	28.18	55.36
Uniforms	38.10	30.00	54.17	16.67	15.00
Girls' (aged 2 to 15) apparel	**34.50**	**44.39**	**32.80**	**51.83**	**52.50**
Coats and jackets	45.71	52.94	26.32	57.26	61.82
Dresses and suits	35.14	45.53	17.07	50.39	70.25
Shirts, blouses, and sweaters	23.48	26.65	23.47	32.05	24.93
Active sportswear	21.98	24.71	24.44	28.23	12.20
Underwear and nightwear	16.50	21.60	14.67	19.75	37.84
Hosiery	8.55	8.46	6.35	11.32	10.99
Accessories	15.69	21.90	7.80	12.60	42.25
Children's (under age 2) apparel	**30.05**	**33.22**	**27.86**	**40.36**	**32.02**
Outerwear including dresses	21.62	20.82	17.74	24.66	20.36
Underwear	24.36	28.84	23.93	34.85	29.54
Nightwear and loungewear	19.23	21.21	15.15	27.27	28.77
Accessories	17.48	13.39	9.27	14.96	16.18
Footwear	**54.80**	**62.61**	**52.52**	**56.53**	**76.74**
Men's	65.22	73.13	57.02	53.33	106.00
Boys'	43.41	39.53	34.69	31.25	56.28
Women's	41.85	49.89	45.02	45.77	56.23
Girls'	36.36	48.33	34.13	50.00	68.23
Other apparel products and services	**22.35**	**33.25**	**27.27**	**27.36**	**45.61**
Material for making clothes	19.18	28.00	25.62	36.36	25.29
Sewing patterns and notions	8.09	9.47	8.72	7.00	13.68
Watches	41.98	56.55	51.72	44.52	67.43

Note: "–" means sample is too small to make a reliable estimate.
Source: Calculations by New Strategist based on the Bureau of Labor Statistics' 2008 Consumer Expenditure Survey

Table 1.13 Percent Buying Apparel by Household Type, <u>Average Quarter</u>, 2008

(percent of households buying apparel, accessories, and related services during the average quarter, by type of household, 2008)

	total married couples	married couples, no children	married couples with children				single parent, at least one child <18	single person
			total	oldest child under 6	oldest child 6 to 17	oldest child 18 or older		
APPAREL, PERCENT BUYING	**78.4%**	**73.6%**	**83.2%**	**88.4%**	**84.2%**	**78.2%**	**78.7%**	**66.2%**
Men's apparel	**37.0**	**36.2**	**38.3**	**38.7**	**35.4**	**43.1**	**13.6**	**20.7**
Suits	1.8	1.8	1.8	1.5	1.6	2.3	0.3	0.8
Sport coats and tailored jackets	1.3	1.4	1.4	1.5	1.3	1.4	0.5	0.8
Coats and jackets	4.4	4.6	4.4	3.1	4.1	5.6	2.2	2.6
Underwear	6.5	5.9	7.2	6.3	6.7	8.4	3.1	3.5
Hosiery	5.4	4.4	6.2	5.7	5.8	7.2	3.1	3.2
Nightwear	1.3	1.2	1.4	1.6	1.2	1.6	0.6	0.4
Accessories	4.3	4.2	4.5	4.0	4.7	4.5	1.8	2.4
Sweaters and vests	3.3	3.1	3.5	3.1	3.1	4.3	0.6	1.5
Active sportswear	2.0	1.8	2.4	2.0	2.4	2.5	0.9	0.9
Shirts	22.4	20.1	24.4	24.3	22.7	27.4	8.9	11.8
Pants and shorts	23.8	21.4	26.0	26.3	23.1	30.8	10.2	12.1
Uniforms	0.8	0.5	1.1	0.9	1.0	1.2	0.5	0.4
Costumes	0.3	0.3	0.4	0.2	0.4	0.4	0.1	0.3
Boys' (aged 2 to 15) apparel	**15.9**	**3.8**	**26.5**	**24.0**	**37.1**	**9.9**	**26.6**	**1.8**
Coats and jackets	2.2	0.5	3.6	3.8	5.0	1.2	3.5	0.2
Sweaters	1.0	0.2	1.6	1.7	2.1	0.7	1.9	0.2
Shirts	9.7	2.2	16.2	13.1	23.4	5.7	17.5	1.2
Underwear	2.9	0.3	5.3	4.8	7.5	1.6	6.2	0.3
Nightwear	1.3	0.4	2.1	2.7	2.8	0.6	1.0	0.1
Hosiery	1.9	0.3	3.4	3.0	5.1	0.8	3.9	0.2
Accessories	1.0	0.3	1.6	1.2	2.4	0.5	1.2	0.2
Suits, sport coats, and vests	0.4	0.0	0.7	0.2	0.9	0.6	0.6	0.1
Pants and shorts	11.7	2.2	20.0	15.7	28.5	8.0	20.0	1.1
Uniforms	0.9	0.1	1.5	0.8	2.5	0.3	1.4	0.0
Active sportswear	1.5	0.4	2.6	1.9	4.0	0.5	1.8	0.2
Costumes	0.8	0.1	1.4	1.6	1.9	0.3	1.1	0.1
Women's apparel	**48.9**	**48.8**	**50.1**	**49.6**	**47.8**	**54.4**	**37.0**	**27.4**
Coats and jackets	6.2	6.5	6.1	4.6	5.7	7.5	4.9	3.5
Dresses	8.8	8.1	9.5	8.0	8.5	12.1	6.1	4.2
Sport coats and tailored jackets	1.4	1.5	1.4	1.5	1.0	2.0	0.7	1.0
Sweaters and vests	7.3	7.6	7.2	6.4	6.7	8.7	4.5	4.5
Shirts, blouses, and tops	30.2	28.9	32.0	31.2	30.6	34.8	22.4	15.6
Skirts	3.9	3.4	4.3	3.7	4.0	5.3	2.9	1.9
Pants and shorts	28.9	27.2	31.0	31.4	29.6	33.2	23.7	14.5
Active sportswear	4.0	3.3	4.8	4.3	4.6	5.5	3.3	2.1
Nightwear	4.9	4.9	4.9	4.8	4.4	5.7	3.9	2.4
Undergarments	10.7	10.2	10.9	9.8	10.2	12.7	10.1	6.2
Hosiery	6.9	6.8	6.9	5.6	6.0	9.2	6.3	3.8
Suits	1.8	2.1	1.7	1.0	1.7	2.0	1.5	1.3
Accessories	6.8	6.9	6.7	6.4	6.4	7.5	5.0	3.6
Uniforms	1.3	1.0	1.6	1.1	1.7	1.8	0.9	0.4
Costumes	0.7	0.5	0.9	0.8	0.9	0.8	0.3	0.5
Girls' (aged 2 to 15) apparel	**16.4**	**4.0**	**27.5**	**22.8**	**38.6**	**11.2**	**29.9**	**2.1**
Coats and jackets	2.2	0.4	3.8	3.2	5.4	1.4	5.0	0.3
Dresses and suits	3.0	0.6	5.1	5.4	6.7	2.0	5.4	0.4
Shirts, blouses, and sweaters	11.0	2.4	18.7	15.5	26.1	7.7	20.3	1.3
Skirts, pants, and shorts	11.4	2.2	19.8	15.6	28.1	7.9	22.9	1.0
Active sportswear	2.0	0.5	3.5	2.5	5.3	0.9	3.4	0.1
Underwear and nightwear	4.3	0.8	7.5	6.3	10.6	2.7	8.4	0.5

	total married couples	married couples, no children	married couples with children				single parent, at least one child <18	single person
			total	oldest child under 6	oldest child 6 to 17	oldest child 18 or older		
Hosiery	2.2%	0.3%	3.8%	2.9%	5.5%	1.5%	4.9%	0.2%
Accessories	1.6	0.3	2.7	2.2	3.8	1.1	2.2	0.2
Uniforms	0.7	–	1.3	0.6	2.0	0.4	1.6	0.1
Costumes	1.1	0.0	2.0	1.7	3.0	0.5	1.9	0.0
Children's (under age 2) apparel	**17.1**	**10.4**	**22.3**	**56.0**	**16.9**	**11.4**	**14.3**	**4.7**
Coats, jackets, and snowsuits	1.2	0.9	1.5	5.2	0.8	0.5	1.4	0.3
Outerwear including dresses	9.3	6.8	11.2	27.8	7.9	7.0	7.1	2.6
Underwear	9.6	2.8	14.6	45.3	10.4	3.7	9.5	1.3
Nightwear and loungewear	3.0	2.1	3.9	11.4	2.4	1.9	2.9	0.8
Accessories	4.5	2.7	6.1	16.2	4.6	2.9	3.5	1.1
Footwear	**36.7**	**29.1**	**43.8**	**39.3**	**48.4**	**38.8**	**39.1**	**21.6**
Men's	15.3	13.2	17.4	15.8	16.8	19.1	7.1	8.2
Boys'	8.5	0.9	15.2	11.8	22.1	5.3	14.4	0.7
Women's	22.2	21.5	23.4	20.5	22.8	26.1	17.9	12.7
Girls'	8.5	0.9	15.3	12.8	21.7	5.9	16.8	0.6
Other apparel products and services	**37.6**	**36.9**	**38.8**	**41.0**	**39.0**	**37.1**	**36.8**	**37.7**
Material for making clothes	1.7	1.6	1.9	1.9	1.8	2.0	0.5	0.5
Sewing patterns and notions	2.0	2.0	2.1	2.6	1.8	2.3	1.1	1.0
Watches	3.8	3.8	3.9	3.1	4.0	4.3	2.2	2.2
Jewelry	8.6	8.4	9.2	8.4	9.5	9.2	6.8	5.0
Shoe repair and other shoe services	1.0	1.2	0.9	0.6	0.9	1.1	0.8	0.8
Coin-operated apparel laundry and dry cleaning	6.9	6.1	7.3	11.6	6.9	5.6	20.7	21.9
Apparel alteration, repair, and tailoring services	3.6	3.8	3.6	4.0	3.6	3.2	1.8	2.3
Clothing rental	0.5	0.5	0.5	0.1	0.4	0.9	0.6	0.2
Watch and jewelry repair	2.4	2.9	2.0	1.2	2.1	2.4	0.4	1.3
Professional laundry, dry cleaning	19.1	19.2	19.7	19.4	20.2	19.0	9.7	11.7
Clothing storage	0.2	0.1	0.2	0.1	0.1	0.3	0.0	0.1

Note: "–" means sample is too small to make a reliable estimate.
Source: Bureau of Labor Statistics, unpublished data from the 2008 Consumer Expenditure Survey

Table 1.14 Amount Buyers Spent on Apparel by Household Type, <u>Average Quarter</u>, 2008

(average amount spent by households buying apparel, accessories, and related services during the average quarter, by type of household, 2008)

APPAREL, AMOUNT SPENT	total married couples	married couples, no children	married couples with children				single parent, at least one child <18	single person
			total	oldest child under 6	oldest child 6 to 17	oldest child 18 or older		
	$472.28	**$383.14**	**$539.81**	**$489.54**	**$550.42**	**$553.95**	**$380.97**	**$254.15**
Men's apparel	**183.47**	**167.81**	**194.83**	**169.27**	**184.57**	**222.97**	**187.01**	**174.65**
Suits	474.29	398.19	547.35	643.95	608.70	431.64	320.37	466.56
Sport coats and tailored jackets	216.92	214.13	222.78	246.26	214.68	219.62	124.44	179.22
Coats and jackets	115.19	109.78	118.98	105.67	102.59	143.55	91.29	124.71
Underwear	34.65	35.99	32.41	24.96	32.54	35.64	27.64	40.96
Hosiery	20.95	20.48	21.16	21.83	21.29	20.60	20.54	20.51
Nightwear	46.85	47.86	43.61	26.60	48.32	47.60	45.00	53.21
Accessories	52.63	52.28	52.97	64.48	46.13	59.38	40.14	57.17
Sweaters and vests	87.16	82.13	89.88	66.99	89.14	101.06	98.83	94.33
Active sportswear	62.25	59.20	61.49	49.26	63.87	63.61	75.57	71.88
Shirts	80.85	80.45	80.41	72.55	74.37	93.26	86.58	82.98
Pants and shorts	91.38	87.90	92.41	79.98	84.74	108.64	94.81	96.02
Uniforms	138.58	142.92	140.48	110.34	119.06	184.02	186.96	126.92
Costumes	111.72	140.52	102.86	138.75	132.89	40.38	62.50	43.55
Boys' (aged 2 to 15) apparel	**146.25**	**141.25**	**147.75**	**107.05**	**158.95**	**133.86**	**151.93**	**150.70**
Coats and jackets	75.68	104.90	71.06	60.54	71.79	85.47	72.12	57.89
Sweaters	61.08	78.13	59.34	60.39	58.45	63.24	59.39	75.00
Shirts	69.48	76.56	68.68	43.11	74.18	64.56	65.83	68.35
Underwear	31.38	61.00	29.95	28.21	32.15	16.31	26.96	39.81
Nightwear	39.88	57.14	37.14	41.48	36.59	31.78	51.72	53.85
Hosiery	17.41	22.32	17.26	15.08	18.37	9.38	18.02	33.75
Accessories	42.50	105.83	33.96	28.45	34.35	39.36	35.83	72.22
Suits, sport coats, and vests	68.45	56.25	69.57	28.57	76.39	61.07	107.94	183.33
Pants and shorts	82.78	82.62	83.73	71.62	86.53	80.80	89.08	95.14
Uniforms	135.47	90.00	136.67	105.79	142.14	105.56	145.07	68.75
Active sportswear	43.38	42.07	44.43	26.61	47.11	46.30	53.39	43.33
Costumes	45.67	42.86	48.33	48.02	49.34	33.65	38.29	25.00
Women's apparel	**220.69**	**208.77**	**228.53**	**181.39**	**214.75**	**275.02**	**194.51**	**212.48**
Coats and jackets	110.87	114.85	107.07	104.75	100.70	116.43	104.62	124.86
Dresses	145.43	141.02	147.39	108.23	131.60	182.07	100.24	131.44
Sport coats and tailored jackets	112.68	100.00	121.92	92.29	134.90	123.48	81.94	133.00
Sweaters and vests	91.35	87.42	97.82	64.46	99.36	110.39	66.89	95.18
Shirts, blouses, and tops	87.52	87.92	86.69	75.18	81.85	100.19	77.28	88.24
Skirts	79.61	79.18	81.87	60.28	79.81	93.54	69.37	77.69
Pants and shorts	95.11	93.44	95.45	82.77	91.31	108.95	85.05	93.97
Active sportswear	63.09	67.08	60.08	45.68	56.78	71.57	64.12	61.89
Nightwear	45.88	45.72	45.26	31.88	42.74	55.23	54.36	54.89
Undergarments	52.76	53.62	50.83	51.56	48.99	53.09	50.37	60.17
Hosiery	22.43	22.76	22.13	17.32	18.89	27.48	19.39	23.34
Suits	213.32	193.54	234.39	431.37	218.83	194.95	148.17	211.83
Accessories	73.22	64.70	81.82	56.19	78.30	100.10	58.33	89.69
Uniforms	116.35	100.50	121.76	139.96	123.10	112.64	156.38	119.19
Costumes	108.08	120.56	106.40	42.09	115.49	126.25	218.75	58.65
Girls' (aged 2 to 15) apparel	**173.05**	**131.80**	**175.78**	**121.45**	**186.67**	**176.93**	**176.20**	**156.58**
Coats and jackets	65.57	90.79	62.70	39.66	63.46	89.36	61.97	96.43
Dresses and suits	88.21	77.05	85.19	62.43	91.58	84.24	81.50	88.46
Shirts, blouses, and sweaters	78.56	72.44	77.95	51.81	83.22	78.26	76.93	78.95
Skirts, pants, and shorts	90.01	79.93	89.98	60.98	95.85	88.06	83.48	96.39
Active sportswear	42.33	42.22	42.22	21.18	45.07	48.82	48.47	42.31
Underwear and nightwear	46.19	56.48	45.03	36.63	45.52	53.16	41.50	38.04

	total married couples	married couples, no children	married couples with children				single parent, at least one child <18	single person
			total	oldest child under 6	oldest child 6 to 17	oldest child 18 or older		
Hosiery	$15.86	$16.41	$15.53	$12.67	$16.12	$15.07	$22.01	$18.33
Accessories	34.49	58.82	32.69	33.45	30.62	44.03	38.96	100.00
Uniforms	141.54	–	145.40	168.44	135.51	200.58	97.17	208.33
Costumes	59.58	75.00	61.69	33.63	64.82	86.70	98.78	58.33
Children's (under age 2) apparel	**143.26**	**93.74**	**159.94**	**201.07**	**134.31**	**104.92**	**150.37**	**76.39**
Coats, jackets, and snowsuits	73.76	78.16	64.80	58.64	69.64	89.42	38.69	86.61
Outerwear including dresses	82.17	76.66	82.02	98.04	69.24	69.35	83.10	65.53
Underwear	124.71	57.12	136.39	147.89	128.73	90.21	128.90	55.20
Nightwear and loungewear	45.17	39.08	46.57	48.70	35.61	62.37	54.82	43.90
Accessories	58.04	52.20	59.38	60.71	53.67	70.45	37.28	51.67
Footwear	**123.90**	**112.89**	**129.70**	**97.45**	**132.10**	**143.97**	**111.15**	**106.63**
Men's	93.65	93.47	92.12	78.47	84.87	109.89	94.01	107.44
Boys'	65.15	68.31	65.15	49.60	68.32	62.92	75.99	76.35
Women's	90.19	90.47	90.08	72.84	85.27	105.29	79.74	104.65
Girls'	64.78	58.05	64.70	40.05	69.39	66.78	68.57	65.00
Other apparel products and services	**193.10**	**178.71**	**205.61**	**177.45**	**199.96**	**234.22**	**119.94**	**108.89**
Material for making clothes	62.13	63.66	58.78	61.33	50.14	70.71	38.83	37.98
Sewing patterns and notions	32.97	28.70	38.34	19.85	36.24	53.98	12.39	20.45
Watches	200.98	200.20	218.38	620.39	184.23	101.58	156.05	118.53
Jewelry	365.08	356.32	362.74	197.88	352.98	468.69	161.23	339.97
Shoe repair and other shoe services	40.00	43.70	35.16	22.27	35.96	38.51	22.50	33.55
Coin-operated apparel laundry and dry cleaning	100.61	71.86	114.51	124.46	107.63	116.95	107.30	48.87
Apparel alteration, repair, and tailoring services	58.68	55.97	62.11	33.73	52.35	101.80	41.29	44.33
Clothing rental	156.63	144.71	173.96	84.62	115.97	222.47	91.52	114.29
Watch and jewelry repair	80.71	92.01	63.37	35.89	62.44	73.25	62.20	35.42
Professional laundry, dry cleaning	98.89	83.51	113.73	97.42	118.33	115.31	56.20	71.69
Clothing storage	311.67	540.63	243.06	4.17	255.36	247.06	408.33	156.25

Note: "–" means sample is too small to make a reliable estimate.
Source: Calculations by New Strategist based on the Bureau of Labor Statistics' 2008 Consumer Expenditure Survey

Table 1.15 Percent Buying Apparel by Household Type, <u>Average Week</u>, 2008

(percent of households buying apparel, accessories, and related services during the average week, by type of household, 2008)

APPAREL, PERCENT BUYING	total married couples	married couples, no children	married couples with children				single parent, at least one child <18	single person
			total	oldest child under 6	oldest child 6 to 17	oldest child 18 or older		
	42.3%	32.4%	50.6%	59.6%	49.1%	47.7%	38.6%	21.1%
Men's apparel	**16.5**	**14.0**	**18.8**	**17.9**	**17.8**	**21.1**	**4.7**	**6.8**
Sport coats and tailored jackets	0.1	0.1	0.0	–	0.1	–	–	–
Coats and jackets	1.1	1.0	1.2	1.0	1.1	1.6	0.1	0.6
Underwear	3.6	3.0	4.3	4.0	3.8	5.5	1.8	1.5
Hosiery	3.4	2.6	4.1	3.9	3.4	5.6	1.0	1.3
Accessories	4.7	4.1	5.2	4.7	5.0	5.9	1.1	1.8
Sweaters and vests	0.9	0.7	1.0	0.9	0.8	1.4	0.4	0.5
Active sportswear	1.5	1.2	1.9	2.3	1.7	1.9	0.3	0.4
Shirts	8.0	6.4	9.4	6.8	9.4	11.2	2.2	3.1
Pants and shorts	5.2	4.3	5.8	4.3	5.8	6.8	1.8	2.2
Uniforms	0.1	0.1	0.1	–	0.1	0.3	–	0.1
Boys' (aged 2 to 15) apparel	**4.9**	**1.3**	**8.3**	**7.0**	**11.1**	**4.1**	**8.8**	**0.4**
Shirts	3.0	0.8	5.0	4.0	6.5	2.9	6.3	0.3
Underwear	1.7	0.4	2.8	2.7	3.5	1.7	2.0	0.1
Nightwear	0.4	0.2	0.5	0.9	0.6	–	0.7	0.0
Hosiery	1.6	0.2	2.9	1.6	4.2	1.2	2.3	0.1
Accessories	0.8	0.2	1.4	0.8	2.1	0.5	2.8	0.1
Suits, sport coats, and vests	0.1	0.0	0.1	–	0.2	–	–	–
Women's apparel	**22.8**	**19.3**	**25.4**	**22.8**	**24.5**	**28.8**	**20.2**	**12.1**
Coats and jackets	2.1	2.0	2.2	1.3	1.9	3.1	1.3	1.4
Dresses	2.2	1.6	2.6	2.8	2.1	3.4	2.5	1.4
Sport coats and tailored jackets	0.1	0.2	0.1	–	0.1	0.1	–	0.1
Sweaters and vests	2.7	2.5	2.9	2.6	2.3	3.9	2.9	1.5
Shirts, blouses, and tops	10.7	8.4	12.3	10.4	12.3	13.5	8.9	5.4
Skirts	0.9	0.4	1.3	1.7	0.9	1.6	1.1	0.7
Pants and shorts	7.0	5.7	7.9	7.2	7.9	8.1	7.1	3.6
Active sportswear	2.0	1.9	2.1	1.9	2.0	2.3	1.5	1.4
Nightwear	2.3	2.1	2.3	2.8	1.9	2.7	2.5	1.2
Undergarments	3.8	2.7	4.6	3.5	4.1	6.2	3.4	1.4
Hosiery	4.4	3.9	4.8	3.0	5.2	5.2	4.0	2.5
Accessories	5.3	4.6	5.8	4.4	5.6	7.1	5.0	3.1
Uniforms	0.2	0.3	0.2	0.2	0.2	0.2	0.1	0.1
Girls' (aged 2 to 15) apparel	**6.6**	**1.9**	**10.7**	**10.3**	**14.2**	**4.6**	**10.5**	**1.3**
Coats and jackets	0.5	0.2	0.8	0.3	1.1	0.5	1.1	0.0
Dresses and suits	1.1	0.4	1.6	1.2	2.2	0.7	0.5	0.2
Shirts, blouses, and sweaters	3.7	1.0	6.1	6.0	7.9	3.0	5.6	0.6
Active sportswear	1.4	0.5	2.3	1.4	3.2	1.1	1.9	0.1
Underwear and nightwear	1.4	0.4	2.1	1.9	3.0	0.7	2.6	0.3
Hosiery	1.6	0.3	2.8	2.3	3.8	1.2	2.5	0.3
Accessories	1.3	0.4	2.2	3.1	2.8	0.5	2.0	0.3
Children's (under age 2) apparel	**8.1**	**2.7**	**12.2**	**36.1**	**8.5**	**3.7**	**8.1**	**0.9**
Outerwear including dresses	2.8	1.5	3.5	9.0	2.6	1.4	1.8	0.3
Underwear	5.5	1.2	9.2	28.3	6.3	1.9	5.7	0.5
Nightwear and loungewear	0.7	0.5	0.9	3.4	0.5	0.2	0.3	0.1
Accessories	2.1	0.9	2.9	8.9	1.7	1.2	2.1	0.4
Footwear	**13.5**	**8.6**	**17.6**	**17.1**	**18.0**	**17.3**	**15.3**	**5.9**
Men's	4.0	3.0	4.7	4.3	4.3	5.7	0.9	1.7
Boys'	2.4	0.5	4.2	4.5	5.2	2.1	5.5	0.3
Women's	7.5	5.7	8.9	7.6	8.6	10.4	7.9	3.8
Girls'	2.3	0.4	4.0	3.5	5.4	1.8	5.2	0.3
Other apparel products and services	**3.6**	**3.7**	**3.5**	**2.3**	**3.6**	**4.0**	**1.5**	**1.4**
Material for making clothes	1.0	1.1	0.9	0.9	0.8	1.1	–	0.5
Sewing patterns and notions	1.8	1.9	1.8	1.3	1.5	2.4	0.9	0.9
Watches	1.1	1.1	1.2	0.4	1.5	1.1	0.6	0.3

Note: "–" means sample is too small to make a reliable estimate.
Source: Bureau of Labor Statistics, unpublished data from the 2008 Consumer Expenditure Survey

Table 1.16 Amount Buyers Spent on Apparel by Household Type, Average Week, 2008

(average amount spent by households buying apparel, accessories, and related services during the average week, by type of household, 2008)

	total married couples	married couples, no children	married couples with children				single parent, at least one child <18	single person
			total	oldest child under 6	oldest child 6 to 17	oldest child 18 or older		
APPAREL, AMOUNT SPENT	$84.52	$82.70	$87.50	$65.89	$92.44	$95.60	$73.95	$65.63
Men's apparel	49.36	50.68	50.61	36.01	52.42	55.83	38.98	48.01
Sport coats and tailored jackets	100.00	121.43	100.00	–	80.00	–	–	–
Coats and jackets	80.73	93.00	73.39	64.36	62.28	91.08	33.33	83.33
Underwear	12.57	14.72	11.32	10.08	9.55	14.08	9.24	10.67
Hosiery	11.94	12.02	11.62	12.40	12.02	11.09	9.09	9.92
Accessories	20.04	17.78	22.54	16.95	28.02	17.00	15.89	14.84
Sweaters and vests	37.50	43.28	35.71	21.28	28.00	48.25	26.83	24.53
Active sportswear	29.53	33.62	27.57	26.99	26.79	29.32	19.35	21.43
Shirts	31.62	31.97	32.56	26.67	35.49	30.50	30.59	31.07
Pants and shorts	38.12	40.47	39.04	35.83	40.07	38.74	29.83	42.33
Uniforms	130.00	71.43	175.00	–	50.00	246.15	–	142.86
Boys' (aged 2 to 15) apparel	23.31	17.60	24.15	16.12	26.90	19.61	30.33	24.32
Shirts	19.87	14.47	20.44	13.12	22.19	20.14	26.55	17.86
Underwear	10.00	9.09	10.92	8.15	12.78	6.47	8.33	11.11
Nightwear	16.67	17.39	15.22	17.78	14.55	–	27.69	25.00
Hosiery	10.97	5.88	10.84	7.45	12.03	5.93	10.22	7.69
Accessories	15.19	12.50	15.60	11.25	16.82	10.42	14.75	10.00
Suits, sport coats, and vests	57.14	0.00	61.54	–	58.33	–	–	–
Women's apparel	58.26	60.82	58.36	46.38	55.54	68.70	46.89	56.03
Coats and jackets	61.79	66.83	60.93	26.52	74.35	55.31	46.97	57.35
Dresses	70.45	94.34	63.22	36.33	60.29	79.88	39.37	44.76
Sport coats and tailored jackets	36.36	37.50	28.57	–	33.33	42.86	–	50.00
Sweaters and vests	34.44	41.46	30.53	26.44	24.36	38.87	28.18	38.56
Shirts, blouses, and tops	27.62	28.76	27.99	28.00	25.59	31.78	23.65	22.84
Skirts	26.44	32.50	27.20	23.49	25.53	30.77	11.32	27.94
Pants and shorts	34.00	32.23	36.05	33.38	36.15	37.48	32.21	36.49
Active sportswear	31.98	30.73	34.63	26.74	37.56	34.50	41.50	26.62
Nightwear	22.81	22.49	23.58	13.82	26.06	26.74	14.69	25.83
Undergarments	23.68	19.48	26.25	22.95	23.28	30.82	20.18	25.71
Hosiery	8.33	8.76	8.16	5.74	9.21	7.36	8.21	9.20
Accessories	26.52	31.39	24.70	21.38	23.31	28.01	10.54	20.39
Uniforms	34.78	28.57	42.11	12.50	45.00	50.00	14.29	63.64
Girls' (aged 2 to 15) apparel	36.23	37.11	36.40	24.66	37.21	48.70	33.21	21.09
Coats and jackets	53.19	71.43	46.05	40.00	50.46	35.42	42.98	0.00
Dresses and suits	37.17	35.00	41.51	26.45	42.86	50.00	19.15	35.00
Shirts, blouses, and sweaters	23.50	16.67	24.22	13.67	23.92	38.49	24.82	14.29
Active sportswear	21.43	21.15	21.24	34.03	20.31	16.51	23.81	8.33
Underwear and nightwear	16.30	11.36	16.43	17.65	15.51	23.19	19.22	12.50
Hosiery	8.23	8.00	8.36	7.69	8.18	10.34	9.76	4.00
Accessories	15.04	23.68	14.61	9.39	15.85	21.74	17.50	11.76
Children's (under age 2) apparel	31.55	33.33	30.15	31.07	29.16	28.76	36.31	19.35
Outerwear including dresses	22.18	25.50	20.00	19.42	20.91	19.29	31.69	12.12
Underwear	25.81	22.31	26.45	26.98	24.61	32.81	22.36	17.39
Nightwear and loungewear	21.92	28.00	18.48	16.07	26.09	5.88	35.48	8.33
Accessories	15.79	13.33	14.53	14.80	14.04	13.56	45.33	14.63
Footwear	55.04	61.19	54.65	39.64	61.04	52.14	51.44	52.05
Men's	66.58	84.05	60.47	52.08	66.05	57.02	29.55	64.37
Boys'	39.66	35.56	40.53	24.89	44.32	45.07	60.65	42.31
Women's	40.16	42.51	39.53	37.57	40.77	38.70	30.62	44.74
Girls'	36.32	27.91	39.14	15.47	43.93	43.58	35.25	35.29
Other apparel products and services	22.63	24.25	21.90	26.32	20.06	23.44	16.22	16.31
Material for making clothes	21.43	23.68	20.00	28.09	16.25	20.37	–	15.69
Sewing patterns and notions	8.24	8.56	8.52	7.46	3.90	13.28	4.60	9.20
Watches	41.07	43.40	37.93	62.50	36.49	36.45	34.43	25.93

Note: "–" means sample is too small to make a reliable estimate.
Source: Calculations by New Strategist based on the Bureau of Labor Statistics' 2008 Consumer Expenditure Survey

Table 1.17 Percent Buying Apparel by Race and Hispanic Origin, Average Quarter, 2008

(percent of households buying apparel, accessories, and related services during the average quarter, by race and Hispanic origin of householder, 2008)

	total households	Asian	black	Hispanic	non-Hispanic white and other
APPAREL, PERCENT BUYING	**74.3%**	**76.1%**	**69.7%**	**76.2%**	**74.8%**
Men's apparel	**29.6**	**35.6**	**20.4**	**28.2**	**31.3**
Suits	1.3	1.4	1.9	1.1	1.2
Sport coats and tailored jackets	1.1	1.6	1.0	0.7	1.2
Coats and jackets	3.6	5.9	3.2	2.9	3.8
Underwear	5.3	3.9	5.1	6.0	5.2
Hosiery	4.4	3.7	3.5	4.5	4.6
Nightwear	0.9	0.8	0.5	0.6	1.0
Accessories	3.3	3.5	2.7	3.1	3.5
Sweaters and vests	2.5	4.1	1.6	2.7	2.6
Active sportswear	1.5	1.3	0.7	0.8	1.7
Shirts	17.9	21.3	12.0	17.7	18.8
Pants and shorts	19.0	22.0	13.3	20.4	19.7
Uniforms	0.6	0.7	0.7	0.7	0.6
Costumes	0.3	0.1	0.3	0.2	0.3
Boys' (aged 2 to 15) apparel	**11.3**	**11.2**	**11.5**	**15.1**	**10.8**
Coats and jackets	1.5	1.6	2.3	1.6	1.4
Sweaters	0.7	0.8	0.9	0.9	0.7
Shirts	7.0	6.6	7.3	9.7	6.6
Underwear	2.2	1.7	2.9	2.8	2.0
Nightwear	0.8	0.4	0.6	0.9	0.9
Hosiery	1.4	0.9	1.5	1.6	1.4
Accessories	0.7	0.4	0.8	0.8	0.7
Suits, sport coats, and vests	0.3	0.3	0.6	0.6	0.2
Pants and shorts	8.2	8.3	8.5	11.3	7.7
Uniforms	0.6	0.3	0.8	1.0	0.5
Active sportswear	1.0	1.1	0.5	0.9	1.1
Costumes	0.5	0.2	0.3	0.5	0.6
Women's apparel	**40.8**	**36.5**	**31.9**	**35.8**	**43.0**
Coats and jackets	5.3	6.0	4.6	3.7	5.6
Dresses	7.2	7.9	7.6	7.0	7.1
Sport coats and tailored jackets	1.2	1.7	0.7	0.6	1.4
Sweaters and vests	6.1	6.0	4.0	4.3	6.8
Shirts, blouses, and tops	24.8	19.3	17.3	22.0	26.4
Skirts	3.1	2.9	3.5	3.2	3.0
Pants and shorts	23.8	19.0	17.5	22.4	25.0
Active sportswear	3.2	1.7	1.8	1.8	3.7
Nightwear	4.0	2.5	3.2	2.7	4.3
Undergarments	9.1	6.6	7.7	8.9	9.4
Hosiery	5.7	4.7	6.4	4.2	5.8
Suits	1.6	1.9	2.5	1.1	1.5
Accessories	5.6	5.1	5.4	4.0	5.8
Uniforms	1.0	0.7	1.2	0.7	1.1
Costumes	0.6	1.1	0.2	0.6	0.6
Girls' (aged 2 to 15) apparel	**11.9**	**9.4**	**11.5**	**16.9**	**11.2**
Coats and jackets	1.7	1.7	1.8	1.7	1.6
Dresses and suits	2.2	1.2	2.1	2.9	2.1
Shirts, blouses, and sweaters	7.9	5.7	7.4	11.0	7.5
Skirts, pants, and shorts	8.3	6.1	8.5	12.1	7.7
Active sportswear	1.4	0.9	0.6	1.5	1.5
Underwear and nightwear	3.2	1.7	3.4	3.3	3.1

	total households	Asian	black	Hispanic	non-Hispanic white and other
Hosiery	1.6%	0.9%	1.7%	1.5%	1.6%
Accessories	1.1	0.6	1.0	1.4	1.0
Uniforms	0.5	0.3	0.9	1.2	0.4
Costumes	0.7	0.7	0.4	0.8	0.7
Children's (under age 2) apparel	**13.1**	**11.1**	**14.1**	**17.0**	**12.4**
Coats, jackets, and snowsuits	1.0	0.7	1.2	1.2	0.9
Outerwear including dresses	7.2	6.0	7.3	8.1	7.0
Underwear	7.1	6.0	9.4	11.0	6.1
Nightwear and loungewear	2.3	1.5	2.4	2.3	2.3
Accessories	3.3	2.3	3.8	4.3	3.1
Footwear	**31.7**	**27.9**	**28.8**	**36.0**	**31.5**
Men's	12.5	13.3	10.5	14.2	12.5
Boys'	6.0	5.1	6.5	9.8	5.3
Women's	18.7	14.9	15.9	18.5	19.2
Girls'	6.2	4.3	7.4	9.9	5.4
Other apparel products and services	**37.3**	**42.9**	**39.2**	**39.7**	**36.6**
Material for making clothes	1.2	0.9	0.5	0.6	1.4
Sewing patterns and notions	1.6	1.0	0.7	1.1	1.8
Watches	3.1	3.5	2.4	2.6	3.4
Jewelry	7.2	5.1	4.1	4.3	8.1
Shoe repair and other shoe services	0.9	0.5	0.3	0.9	0.9
Coin-operated apparel laundry and dry cleaning	13.8	24.2	21.8	25.3	10.8
Apparel alteration, repair, and tailoring services	2.9	2.9	2.5	2.1	3.1
Clothing rental	0.4	0.4	0.2	0.3	0.4
Watch and jewelry repair	1.8	1.4	1.0	1.0	2.1
Professional laundry, dry cleaning	15.1	15.7	16.5	10.7	15.6
Clothing storage	0.1	0.0	0.2	–	0.1

Note: "Asian" and "black" include Hispanics and non-Hispanics who identify themselves as being of the respective race alone. "Hispanic" includes people of any race who identify themselves as Hispanic. "Other" includes people who identify themselves as non-Hispanic and as Alaska Native, American Indian, Asian (who are also included in the Asian column), or Native Hawaiian or other Pacific Islander as well as non-Hispanics reporting more than one race. "–" means sample is too small to make a reliable estimate.
Source: Calculations by New Strategist based on the Bureau of Labor Statistics' 2008 Consumer Expenditure Survey

Table 1.18 Amount Buyers Spent on Apparel by Race and Hispanic Origin, <u>Average Quarter</u>, 2008

(average amount spent by households buying apparel, accessories, and related services during the average quarter, by race and Hispanic origin of householder, 2008)

	total households	Asian	black	Hispanic	non-Hispanic white and other
APPAREL, AMOUNT SPENT	**$399.40**	**$445.11**	**$388.53**	**$388.85**	**$402.46**
Men's apparel	**180.66**	**196.67**	**218.43**	**178.79**	**176.97**
Suits	466.60	672.34	343.24	533.04	488.22
Sport coats and tailored jackets	197.71	184.97	172.33	261.81	195.65
Coats and jackets	114.83	125.84	122.41	107.01	114.63
Underwear	35.86	43.97	32.78	36.37	36.20
Hosiery	20.88	18.11	21.13	19.30	21.06
Nightwear	46.84	46.56	43.98	47.27	47.16
Accessories	51.96	69.57	52.35	51.88	51.96
Sweaters and vests	87.65	101.78	74.54	104.81	86.37
Active sportswear	64.70	72.92	73.19	79.67	62.79
Shirts	81.16	92.75	90.06	69.82	81.83
Pants and shorts	92.63	87.64	108.85	87.08	91.74
Uniforms	149.19	125.37	186.19	120.89	148.31
Costumes	79.03	31.25	97.12	53.41	79.55
Boys' (aged 2 to 15) apparel	**147.62**	**148.17**	**162.85**	**146.28**	**145.26**
Coats and jackets	75.32	83.13	70.20	75.00	76.41
Sweaters	62.68	80.95	53.26	48.40	67.69
Shirts	69.82	62.59	73.00	65.15	70.31
Underwear	32.52	65.42	31.01	30.43	33.21
Nightwear	41.87	45.14	31.15	38.66	44.12
Hosiery	18.13	19.68	16.06	21.27	17.88
Accessories	43.93	22.56	37.05	36.56	46.27
Suits, sport coats, and vests	75.81	62.50	92.67	65.00	73.86
Pants and shorts	84.63	91.03	93.53	87.74	82.58
Uniforms	135.27	116.13	121.79	139.66	135.33
Active sportswear	44.13	66.89	29.81	44.66	45.28
Costumes	44.61	48.68	31.67	34.50	46.82
Women's apparel	**219.89**	**230.48**	**229.65**	**198.30**	**221.34**
Coats and jackets	115.70	149.88	121.10	141.71	112.30
Dresses	144.90	159.10	128.19	107.96	153.17
Sport coats and tailored jackets	115.65	95.76	117.31	259.43	105.81
Sweaters and vests	94.18	119.89	70.45	100.94	95.61
Shirts, blouses, and tops	86.97	89.19	76.55	75.65	89.47
Skirts	76.46	89.69	66.57	58.15	81.35
Pants and shorts	94.29	87.74	97.25	88.09	94.88
Active sportswear	63.19	93.13	55.57	56.79	64.13
Nightwear	48.30	60.94	55.42	31.39	49.12
Undergarments	55.88	51.51	60.25	56.40	55.15
Hosiery	22.68	27.93	25.43	20.56	22.42
Suits	201.08	189.87	189.53	181.76	207.14
Accessories	76.75	89.59	113.19	69.12	72.03
Uniforms	118.51	62.50	133.41	132.29	115.33
Costumes	92.37	90.09	162.50	100.00	87.11
Girls' (aged 2 to 15) apparel	**170.16**	**170.04**	**179.51**	**150.69**	**173.06**
Coats and jackets	65.76	71.47	78.11	61.70	64.60
Dresses and suits	84.49	172.46	77.64	82.76	86.22
Shirts, blouses, and sweaters	77.64	85.80	78.39	65.25	80.31
Skirts, pants, and shorts	88.70	88.63	89.18	83.48	89.84
Active sportswear	43.89	66.67	23.31	31.38	47.24
Underwear and nightwear	44.78	31.76	44.40	45.48	44.74

	total households	Asian	black	Hispanic	non-Hispanic white and other
Hosiery	$17.09	$19.17	$24.10	$16.21	$15.88
Accessories	37.73	52.02	35.05	48.16	36.30
Uniforms	131.60	120.83	121.07	136.69	134.72
Costumes	65.71	60.14	206.40	29.82	58.68
Children's (under age 2) apparel	**137.48**	**161.90**	**168.94**	**156.13**	**127.87**
Coats, jackets, and snowsuits	70.41	43.31	56.76	67.02	73.90
Outerwear including dresses	81.01	86.96	100.79	84.65	77.07
Underwear	122.94	165.32	132.20	135.57	117.39
Nightwear and loungewear	44.43	62.16	51.17	49.67	42.47
Accessories	56.10	68.07	59.08	66.36	53.51
Footwear	**118.14**	**121.73**	**130.97**	**122.15**	**115.62**
Men's	97.43	105.95	111.99	100.44	95.08
Boys'	67.92	67.95	80.58	76.10	63.28
Women's	91.91	93.25	96.75	83.95	92.45
Girls'	65.83	61.01	72.41	68.61	63.72
Other apparel products and services	**163.68**	**232.66**	**132.20**	**143.01**	**172.37**
Material for making clothes	58.33	101.06	36.57	51.17	60.25
Sewing patterns and notions	28.82	15.10	25.34	12.39	30.51
Watches	171.74	991.01	98.67	202.35	176.04
Jewelry	367.42	645.50	348.46	226.04	379.98
Shoe repair and other shoe services	36.92	31.02	33.09	41.09	36.70
Coin-operated apparel laundry and dry cleaning	76.14	66.68	82.87	113.19	61.06
Apparel alteration, repair, and tailoring services	54.90	59.35	48.01	41.47	57.39
Clothing rental	142.31	198.65	110.71	163.33	143.02
Watch and jewelry repair	70.36	29.37	49.49	48.54	73.68
Professional laundry, dry cleaning	89.56	73.50	85.94	98.29	89.24
Clothing storage	300.00	362.50	343.75	–	300.00

Note: "Asian" and "black" include Hispanics and non-Hispanics who identify themselves as being of the respective race alone. "Hispanic" includes people of any race who identify themselves as Hispanic. "Other" includes people who identify themselves as non-Hispanic and as Alaska Native, American Indian, Asian (who are also included in the Asian column), or Native Hawaiian or other Pacific Islander as well as non-Hispanics reporting more than one race. "–" means sample is too small to make a reliable estimate.
Source: Calculations by New Strategist based on the Bureau of Labor Statistics' 2008 Consumer Expenditure Survey

(percent of households buying apparel, accessories, and related services during the average week, by race and Hispanic origin of householder, 2008)

	total households	Asian	black	Hispanic	non-Hispanic white and other
APPAREL, PERCENT BUYING	**34.6%**	**35.1%**	**30.5%**	**42.4%**	**34.1%**
Men's apparel	**12.2**	**13.8**	**10.3**	**17.4**	**11.8**
Sport coats and tailored jackets	0.1	–	–	–	0.1
Coats and jackets	0.9	2.3	1.0	1.1	0.8
Underwear	2.7	3.1	3.4	3.4	2.5
Hosiery	2.6	3.1	3.1	3.7	2.3
Accessories	3.4	4.3	2.1	5.2	3.3
Sweaters and vests	0.8	0.9	0.4	1.2	0.8
Active sportswear	1.1	0.6	0.4	1.0	1.2
Shirts	5.9	7.0	5.2	8.5	5.6
Pants and shorts	4.0	3.2	3.9	6.0	3.7
Uniforms	0.1	–	–	0.1	0.1
Boys' (aged 2 to 15) apparel	**3.5**	**2.5**	**4.2**	**4.9**	**3.2**
Shirts	2.2	0.8	3.2	3.3	1.9
Underwear	1.2	–	1.7	1.3	1.1
Nightwear	0.3	0.7	0.2	0.2	0.3
Hosiery	1.1	1.3	1.6	1.7	0.9
Accessories	0.7	0.7	1.0	0.7	0.6
Suits, sport coats, and vests	0.1	–	0.2	0.0	0.0
Women's apparel	**18.9**	**20.1**	**16.5**	**22.3**	**18.9**
Coats and jackets	1.8	1.8	2.5	2.0	1.7
Dresses	2.0	3.2	3.2	2.9	1.7
Sport coats and tailored jackets	0.1	0.4	0.0	0.0	0.1
Sweaters and vests	2.3	2.4	1.3	2.6	2.3
Shirts, blouses, and tops	8.9	8.9	7.2	11.1	8.9
Skirts	0.8	1.1	0.8	1.3	0.7
Pants and shorts	5.8	6.2	5.6	6.8	5.7
Active sportswear	1.7	2.4	0.6	1.8	1.9
Nightwear	2.0	1.6	2.3	2.9	1.9
Undergarments	2.9	2.6	2.1	3.5	3.0
Hosiery	3.8	6.5	3.9	4.0	3.7
Accessories	4.5	5.3	3.6	5.5	4.5
Uniforms	0.2	0.2	0.5	0.4	0.2
Girls' (aged 2 to 15) apparel	**4.9**	**4.2**	**4.6**	**7.0**	**4.6**
Coats and jackets	0.4	0.2	0.7	0.4	0.3
Dresses and suits	0.7	0.7	0.5	1.2	0.7
Shirts, blouses, and sweaters	2.6	1.7	2.8	3.3	2.5
Active sportswear	0.9	0.4	0.4	0.8	1.0
Underwear and nightwear	1.0	0.9	1.0	1.4	1.0
Hosiery	1.2	1.5	1.3	1.2	1.2
Accessories	1.0	0.5	1.0	1.3	1.0
Children's (under age 2) apparel	**5.7**	**2.9**	**5.9**	**9.2**	**5.2**
Outerwear including dresses	1.9	0.2	2.0	3.5	1.6
Underwear	3.9	2.7	3.3	6.0	3.7
Nightwear and loungewear	0.5	0.3	0.7	0.8	0.5
Accessories	1.4	0.4	1.9	2.0	1.3
Footwear	**11.0**	**11.7**	**12.7**	**15.2**	**10.2**
Men's	3.0	3.5	3.3	4.4	2.7
Boys'	1.8	1.3	2.8	2.7	1.6
Women's	6.4	7.3	7.0	7.8	6.1
Girls'	1.8	1.8	2.4	3.1	1.5
Other apparel products and services	**2.6**	**1.8**	**1.7**	**2.9**	**2.8**
Material for making clothes	0.7	0.2	0.3	0.3	0.9
Sewing patterns and notions	1.4	1.3	0.7	1.4	1.5
Watches	0.8	0.5	0.8	1.2	0.8

Note: "Asian" and "black" include Hispanics and non-Hispanics who identify themselves as being of the respective race alone. "Hispanic" includes people of any race who identify themselves as Hispanic. "Other" includes people who identify themselves as non-Hispanic and as Alaska Native, American Indian, Asian (who are also included in the Asian column), or Native Hawaiian or other Pacific Islander as well as non-Hispanics reporting more than one race. Numbers may not add to total because of rounding and missing subcategories. "–" means sample is too small to make a reliable estimate.
Source: Bureau of Labor Statistics, unpublished data from the 2008 Consumer Expenditure Survey

Table 1.20 Amount Buyers Spent on Apparel by Race and Hispanic Origin, <u>Average Week</u>, 2008

(average amount spent by households buying apparel, accessories, and related services during the average week, by race and Hispanic origin of householder, 2008)

APPAREL, AMOUNT SPENT	total households	Asian	black	Hispanic	non-Hispanic white and other
APPAREL, AMOUNT SPENT	**$80.93**	**$87.22**	**$103.58**	**$80.58**	**$77.94**
Men's apparel	**49.39**	**55.18**	**49.42**	**35.71**	**52.42**
Sport coats and tailored jackets	140.00	–	–	–	166.67
Coats and jackets	74.12	76.96	77.88	44.86	79.49
Underwear	11.76	15.02	9.76	7.65	13.04
Hosiery	11.37	13.03	8.74	8.74	12.45
Accessories	19.05	20.14	18.48	17.43	19.58
Sweaters and vests	36.84	22.58	45.24	25.86	38.67
Active sportswear	29.25	46.03	40.48	18.27	29.57
Shirts	31.46	33.33	29.45	22.17	33.87
Pants and shorts	39.29	39.94	36.08	30.28	41.89
Uniforms	125.00	–	–	54.55	150.00
Boys' (aged 2 to 15) apparel	**24.36**	**19.43**	**31.90**	**22.04**	**23.58**
Shirts	20.36	16.05	22.84	21.65	19.47
Underwear	10.43	–	10.71	9.30	10.48
Nightwear	17.24	19.18	13.04	12.50	16.13
Hosiery	10.00	9.85	8.64	8.77	10.64
Accessories	13.85	10.96	11.00	9.23	16.67
Suits, sport coats, and vests	60.00	–	60.87	25.00	33.33
Women's apparel	**58.55**	**70.53**	**72.76**	**60.85**	**56.23**
Coats and jackets	63.69	64.09	117.27	51.76	53.29
Dresses	70.56	48.58	74.92	78.32	67.27
Sport coats and tailored jackets	44.44	88.89	33.33	100.00	45.45
Sweaters and vests	33.78	33.90	36.51	32.70	33.76
Shirts, blouses, and tops	26.60	38.53	25.41	26.33	26.78
Skirts	27.16	33.96	39.74	14.29	28.38
Pants and shorts	34.20	37.18	30.55	32.35	34.98
Active sportswear	31.21	26.36	38.98	25.00	31.75
Nightwear	24.62	19.38	18.94	20.63	26.34
Undergarments	23.81	26.64	14.83	21.10	25.25
Hosiery	8.53	8.59	9.77	7.05	8.65
Accessories	24.22	39.73	22.99	34.79	22.47
Uniforms	38.10	14.29	34.69	48.57	33.33
Girls' (aged 2 to 15) apparel	**34.50**	**25.77**	**39.18**	**31.32**	**34.57**
Coats and jackets	45.71	13.33	65.15	64.86	37.93
Dresses and suits	35.14	37.31	25.00	40.98	34.29
Shirts, blouses, and sweaters	23.48	27.98	26.86	21.10	23.41
Active sportswear	21.98	35.00	26.83	25.00	21.78
Underwear and nightwear	16.50	8.89	15.53	16.91	16.49
Hosiery	8.55	7.33	8.59	10.92	7.76
Accessories	15.69	2.13	10.89	13.64	17.53
Children's (under age 2) apparel	**30.05**	**28.33**	**29.59**	**32.68**	**29.46**
Outerwear including dresses	21.62	11.11	20.40	21.90	21.52
Underwear	24.36	27.41	19.58	27.53	24.32
Nightwear and loungewear	19.23	7.41	18.46	11.84	21.74
Accessories	17.48	11.43	30.81	24.49	13.28
Footwear	**54.80**	**51.32**	**72.53**	**49.93**	**52.45**
Men's	65.22	42.21	87.69	64.60	60.95
Boys'	43.41	41.60	62.55	48.18	36.31
Women's	41.85	47.13	49.50	33.08	42.01
Girls'	36.36	30.39	45.34	27.71	36.91
Other apparel products and services	**22.35**	**23.20**	**20.36**	**17.59**	**23.19**
Material for making clothes	19.18	6.25	18.52	11.76	19.77
Sewing patterns and notions	8.09	13.18	4.23	3.55	8.90
Watches	41.98	46.15	30.95	35.54	43.42

Note: "Asian" and "black" include Hispanics and non-Hispanics who identify themselves as being of the respective race alone. "Hispanic" includes people of any race who identify themselves as Hispanic. "Other" includes people who identify themselves as non-Hispanic and as Alaska Native, American Indian, Asian (who are also included in the Asian column), or Native Hawaiian or other Pacific Islander as well as non-Hispanics reporting more than one race. "–" means sample is too small to make a reliable estimate.
Source: Calculations by New Strategist based on the Bureau of Labor Statistics' 2008 Consumer Expenditure Survey

Table 1.21 Percent Buying Apparel by Region, Average Quarter, 2008

(percent of households buying apparel, accessories, and related services during the average quarter, by region of residence, 2008)

APPAREL, PERCENT BUYING	total households	Northeast	Midwest	South	West
	74.3%	78.1%	75.5%	70.0%	76.9%
Men's apparel	**29.6**	**31.0**	**31.7**	**26.2**	**32.0**
Suits	1.3	1.5	1.2	1.3	1.1
Sport coats and tailored jackets	1.1	1.6	0.8	1.2	0.9
Coats and jackets	3.6	4.3	3.7	2.9	4.1
Underwear	5.3	6.4	5.2	4.8	5.2
Hosiery	4.4	5.3	4.7	3.7	4.6
Nightwear	0.9	1.1	1.0	0.9	0.6
Accessories	3.3	3.6	3.4	2.9	3.7
Sweaters and vests	2.5	3.4	2.3	1.8	2.9
Active sportswear	1.5	1.8	1.7	1.2	1.5
Shirts	17.9	17.6	19.3	16.0	19.7
Pants and shorts	19.0	19.8	19.8	17.4	20.1
Uniforms	0.6	0.6	0.6	0.7	0.6
Costumes	0.3	0.3	0.3	0.3	0.4
Boys' (aged 2 to 15) apparel	**11.3**	**10.6**	**11.5**	**11.2**	**11.9**
Coats and jackets	1.5	1.6	2.0	1.3	1.4
Sweaters	0.7	1.1	0.7	0.5	0.8
Shirts	7.0	6.1	7.1	6.7	8.1
Underwear	2.2	2.2	2.3	2.3	1.9
Nightwear	0.8	0.8	1.0	0.6	1.0
Hosiery	1.4	1.4	1.8	1.2	1.4
Accessories	0.7	1.1	0.7	0.6	0.6
Suits, sport coats, and vests	0.3	0.4	0.2	0.3	0.3
Pants and shorts	8.2	7.8	7.9	8.2	9.0
Uniforms	0.6	0.5	0.3	0.8	0.6
Active sportswear	1.0	1.4	1.1	0.8	0.9
Costumes	0.5	0.7	0.7	0.4	0.4
Women's apparel	**40.8**	**42.7**	**43.7**	**37.9**	**40.9**
Coats and jackets	5.3	7.0	5.7	4.2	5.2
Dresses	7.2	8.4	6.0	7.3	7.1
Sport coats and tailored jackets	1.2	1.5	1.3	0.9	1.5
Sweaters and vests	6.1	8.7	7.0	4.4	6.1
Shirts, blouses, and tops	24.8	24.7	26.8	22.6	26.4
Skirts	3.1	4.1	2.4	2.8	3.5
Pants and shorts	23.8	24.4	25.3	22.5	23.9
Active sportswear	3.2	4.0	3.9	2.5	3.3
Nightwear	4.0	4.4	4.5	3.7	3.5
Undergarments	9.1	10.8	10.4	8.2	8.1
Hosiery	5.7	6.5	6.5	5.2	5.1
Suits	1.6	1.6	1.6	1.9	1.3
Accessories	5.6	7.5	6.1	4.5	5.1
Uniforms	1.0	1.1	1.0	1.2	0.9
Costumes	0.6	0.5	0.5	0.4	1.0
Girls' (aged 2 to 15) apparel	**11.9**	**11.6**	**12.4**	**11.4**	**12.5**
Coats and jackets	1.7	2.1	1.7	1.5	1.6
Dresses and suits	2.2	2.1	1.9	2.2	2.5
Shirts, blouses, and sweaters	7.9	7.6	8.5	7.4	8.6
Skirts, pants, and shorts	8.3	8.3	8.4	8.0	8.7
Active sportswear	1.4	1.6	1.6	1.0	1.6
Underwear and nightwear	3.2	2.5	3.7	3.3	3.1

	total households	Northeast	Midwest	South	West
Hosiery	1.6%	1.2%	2.1%	1.4%	1.6%
Accessories	1.1	1.0	1.4	0.9	1.1
Uniforms	0.5	0.4	0.3	0.7	0.6
Costumes	0.7	0.8	0.7	0.7	0.7
Children's (under age 2) apparel	**13.1**	**10.9**	**13.2**	**13.2**	**14.7**
Coats, jackets, and snowsuits	1.0	1.1	1.1	0.9	1.0
Outerwear including dresses	7.2	5.6	8.0	6.9	8.1
Underwear	7.1	5.8	6.3	7.6	8.0
Nightwear and loungewear	2.3	2.4	2.5	2.2	2.2
Accessories	3.3	3.2	3.1	3.5	3.3
Footwear	**31.7**	**33.3**	**31.4**	**30.1**	**33.3**
Men's	12.5	13.1	13.4	11.2	13.0
Boys'	6.0	5.6	5.4	6.1	6.7
Women's	18.7	20.4	18.9	17.4	19.3
Girls'	6.2	5.7	5.5	6.6	6.6
Other apparel products and services	**37.3**	**45.4**	**35.5**	**32.8**	**39.7**
Material for making clothes	1.2	0.9	1.7	0.8	1.5
Sewing patterns and notions	1.6	1.2	1.7	1.4	2.0
Watches	3.1	3.1	3.6	3.0	2.9
Jewelry	7.2	7.6	8.2	6.0	7.6
Shoe repair and other shoe services	0.9	1.3	0.7	0.6	1.0
Coin-operated apparel laundry and dry cleaning	13.8	20.8	13.2	9.2	16.1
Apparel alteration, repair, and tailoring services	2.9	2.8	3.0	2.9	2.9
Clothing rental	0.4	0.4	0.5	0.3	0.5
Watch and jewelry repair	1.8	2.1	1.9	1.7	1.7
Professional laundry, dry cleaning	15.1	19.4	12.1	15.3	14.5
Clothing storage	0.1	0.2	0.1	0.1	0.1

Source: Bureau of Labor Statistics, unpublished data from the 2008 Consumer Expenditure Survey

Table 1.22 Amount Buyers Spent on Apparel by Region, <u>Average Quarter</u>, 2008

(average amount spent by households buying apparel, accessories, and related services during the average quarter, by region of residence, 2008)

	total households	Northeast	Midwest	South	West
APPAREL, AMOUNT SPENT	**$399.40**	**$449.38**	**$369.68**	**$380.61**	**$415.09**
Men's apparel	**180.66**	**208.39**	**164.40**	**180.25**	**175.48**
Suits	466.60	607.21	371.75	346.46	668.81
Sport coats and tailored jackets	197.71	219.07	227.47	176.29	185.06
Coats and jackets	114.83	143.24	107.77	109.21	103.76
Underwear	35.86	31.86	37.40	35.49	38.93
Hosiery	20.88	23.77	19.31	20.04	20.84
Nightwear	46.84	62.61	44.27	44.12	34.58
Accessories	51.96	57.07	47.55	65.16	35.48
Sweaters and vests	87.65	103.72	85.90	78.87	81.68
Active sportswear	64.70	56.15	62.50	65.04	74.67
Shirts	81.16	84.84	78.12	80.06	82.92
Pants and shorts	92.63	96.08	90.52	95.63	87.66
Uniforms	149.19	208.93	112.89	155.60	131.25
Costumes	79.03	128.70	34.68	37.00	125.00
Boys' (aged 2 to 15) apparel	**147.62**	**171.73**	**138.71**	**142.68**	**146.17**
Coats and jackets	75.32	96.76	63.93	76.92	69.16
Sweaters	62.68	60.23	60.14	54.41	75.33
Shirts	69.82	74.55	69.70	66.88	70.75
Underwear	32.52	28.92	23.33	33.33	44.85
Nightwear	41.87	38.39	44.75	49.60	34.28
Hosiery	18.13	17.02	17.09	17.28	21.53
Accessories	43.93	57.41	16.67	58.19	34.55
Suits, sport coats, and vests	75.81	99.43	104.41	59.68	63.64
Pants and shorts	84.63	97.95	82.95	82.83	79.29
Uniforms	135.27	140.69	97.32	154.75	97.73
Active sportswear	44.13	42.68	58.78	35.00	39.53
Costumes	44.61	37.13	39.62	43.29	66.67
Women's apparel	**219.89**	**252.70**	**202.87**	**206.00**	**231.11**
Coats and jackets	115.70	127.91	113.68	103.29	120.92
Dresses	144.90	175.48	149.54	130.10	135.62
Sport coats and tailored jackets	115.65	112.25	67.12	109.01	168.87
Sweaters and vests	94.18	99.11	84.12	84.89	110.67
Shirts, blouses, and tops	86.97	93.70	85.45	82.42	89.63
Skirts	76.46	79.84	57.04	68.91	96.75
Pants and shorts	94.29	97.72	91.00	91.83	98.89
Active sportswear	63.19	71.12	63.25	58.47	60.08
Nightwear	48.30	49.49	55.04	42.84	47.21
Undergarments	55.88	57.54	47.78	54.72	66.53
Hosiery	22.68	25.73	18.41	24.13	22.56
Suits	201.08	170.52	182.05	218.48	217.80
Accessories	76.75	87.58	62.25	81.12	75.10
Uniforms	118.51	104.44	119.74	146.09	76.63
Costumes	92.37	81.60	46.08	91.46	124.49
Girls' (aged 2 to 15) apparel	**170.16**	**195.61**	**160.86**	**167.15**	**164.82**
Coats and jackets	65.76	76.34	62.13	61.21	65.61
Dresses and suits	84.49	94.23	69.17	88.37	84.68
Shirts, blouses, and sweaters	77.64	88.17	74.70	75.00	76.78
Skirts, pants, and shorts	88.70	105.16	89.71	85.80	78.87
Active sportswear	43.89	56.60	44.35	37.11	39.58
Underwear and nightwear	44.78	51.42	43.56	45.41	40.66

	total households	Northeast	Midwest	South	West
Hosiery	$17.09	$21.17	$15.29	$15.80	$18.21
Accessories	37.73	31.63	21.92	47.04	50.00
Uniforms	131.60	160.90	140.52	117.39	143.44
Costumes	65.71	46.91	57.25	76.45	75.00
Children's (under age 2) apparel	**137.48**	**132.62**	**127.02**	**141.97**	**143.48**
Coats, jackets, and snowsuits	70.41	69.69	71.70	65.29	76.26
Outerwear including dresses	81.01	71.68	75.97	81.18	91.46
Underwear	122.94	111.89	117.18	124.57	131.60
Nightwear and loungewear	44.43	57.33	40.18	43.30	38.71
Accessories	56.10	58.65	52.43	60.10	50.54
Footwear	**118.14**	**127.01**	**107.93**	**116.78**	**122.68**
Men's	97.43	99.37	87.21	104.83	96.41
Boys'	67.92	70.68	56.84	70.79	70.99
Women's	91.91	101.97	83.20	86.22	100.16
Girls'	65.83	79.16	63.89	62.14	63.97
Other apparel products and services	**163.68**	**177.81**	**146.20**	**158.84**	**172.95**
Material for making clothes	58.33	61.70	51.16	48.42	72.56
Sewing patterns and notions	28.82	33.27	35.00	21.01	29.29
Watches	171.74	275.72	113.74	175.17	146.25
Jewelry	367.42	397.59	302.05	371.27	410.16
Shoe repair and other shoe services	36.92	40.04	32.14	38.10	36.30
Coin-operated apparel laundry and dry cleaning	76.14	78.97	64.05	76.56	82.99
Apparel alteration, repair, and tailoring services	54.90	65.60	43.31	51.80	63.96
Clothing rental	142.31	241.67	135.71	89.66	143.48
Watch and jewelry repair	70.36	103.62	50.67	72.27	55.39
Professional laundry, dry cleaning	89.56	95.43	81.73	86.45	95.13
Clothing storage	300.00	276.25	197.50	311.11	416.67

Note: "–" means sample is too small to make a reliable estimate.
Source: Calculations by New Strategist based on the Bureau of Labor Statistics' 2008 Consumer Expenditure Survey

Table 1.23 Percent Buying Apparel by Region, <u>Average Week</u>, 2008

(percent of households buying apparel, accessories, and related services during the average week, by region of residence, 2008)

	total households	Northeast	Midwest	South	West
APPAREL, PERCENT BUYING	**34.6%**	**35.4%**	**33.0%**	**34.4%**	**36.0%**
Men's apparel	**12.2**	**11.1**	**10.9**	**12.3**	**14.5**
Sport coats and tailored jackets	0.1	0.1	0.1	0.0	0.0
Coats and jackets	0.9	0.9	0.7	0.7	1.2
Underwear	2.7	2.5	2.2	2.6	3.6
Hosiery	2.6	2.7	1.9	2.5	3.1
Accessories	3.4	3.1	3.1	3.5	3.5
Sweaters and vests	0.8	0.7	0.8	0.6	1.1
Active sportswear	1.1	1.1	1.3	0.7	1.4
Shirts	5.9	4.9	5.1	6.1	7.2
Pants and shorts	4.0	3.3	3.0	4.3	5.0
Uniforms	0.1	0.1	0.0	0.1	0.1
Boys' (aged 2 to 15) apparel	**3.5**	**3.7**	**3.1**	**3.6**	**3.5**
Shirts	2.2	2.3	1.7	2.4	2.3
Underwear	1.2	1.2	1.0	1.4	0.9
Nightwear	0.3	0.2	0.4	0.3	0.3
Hosiery	1.1	1.1	1.1	1.1	1.0
Accessories	0.7	0.7	0.9	0.6	0.5
Suits, sport coats, and vests	0.1	0.0	0.0	0.1	–
Women's apparel	**18.9**	**20.0**	**17.9**	**18.6**	**19.7**
Coats and jackets	1.8	2.6	1.6	1.5	1.8
Dresses	2.0	2.3	1.1	2.2	2.2
Sport coats and tailored jackets	0.1	0.1	0.2	–	0.1
Sweaters and vests	2.3	2.7	2.4	1.9	2.3
Shirts, blouses, and tops	8.9	8.8	8.0	9.5	9.1
Skirts	0.8	0.9	0.6	0.8	1.0
Pants and shorts	5.8	6.4	5.1	6.0	5.7
Active sportswear	1.7	2.3	1.9	1.1	2.0
Nightwear	2.0	2.3	1.5	2.1	2.0
Undergarments	2.9	2.6	3.3	2.9	2.9
Hosiery	3.8	4.1	3.5	3.3	4.5
Accessories	4.5	5.0	4.3	4.0	4.9
Uniforms	0.2	0.2	0.1	0.4	0.0
Girls' (aged 2 to 15) apparel	**4.9**	**4.4**	**4.8**	**5.1**	**5.0**
Coats and jackets	0.4	0.3	0.5	0.3	0.4
Dresses and suits	0.7	0.6	0.5	1.0	0.7
Shirts, blouses, and sweaters	2.6	2.5	2.9	2.8	2.4
Active sportswear	0.9	0.9	1.1	0.8	0.9
Underwear and nightwear	1.0	1.1	1.0	1.0	1.0
Hosiery	1.2	0.9	1.4	1.0	1.4
Accessories	1.0	1.0	1.1	0.9	1.1
Children's (under age 2) apparel	**5.7**	**5.6**	**6.5**	**5.6**	**5.1**
Outerwear including dresses	1.9	1.7	2.1	1.9	1.7
Underwear	3.9	4.1	4.4	3.8	3.4
Nightwear and loungewear	0.5	0.5	0.8	0.4	0.5
Accessories	1.4	1.3	2.0	1.3	1.3
Footwear	**11.0**	**12.0**	**9.6**	**11.4**	**11.2**
Men's	3.0	3.0	2.3	3.2	3.4
Boys'	1.8	1.7	1.9	2.0	1.6
Women's	6.4	7.5	5.3	6.6	6.2
Girls'	1.8	1.7	1.7	1.7	2.0
Other apparel products and services	**2.6**	**2.1**	**3.4**	**2.4**	**2.7**
Material for making clothes	0.7	0.5	1.0	0.6	0.9
Sewing patterns and notions	1.4	1.1	1.7	1.3	1.3
Watches	0.8	0.9	1.0	0.7	0.8

Note: "–" means sample is too small to make a reliable estimate.
Source: Bureau of Labor Statistics, unpublished data from the 2008 Consumer Expenditure Survey

(average amount spent by households buying apparel, accessories, and related services during the average week, by region of residence, 2008)

	total households	Northeast	Midwest	South	West
APPAREL, AMOUNT SPENT	**$80.93**	**$84.01**	**$77.70**	**$82.02**	**$79.69**
Men's apparel	**49.39**	**52.39**	**42.50**	**48.09**	**54.46**
Sport coats and tailored jackets	140.00	208.33	80.00	33.33	233.33
Coats and jackets	74.12	80.46	70.77	50.00	96.67
Underwear	11.76	14.29	9.55	10.38	12.95
Hosiery	11.37	10.11	10.99	10.28	13.74
Accessories	19.05	16.56	18.53	21.81	16.48
Sweaters and vests	36.84	42.25	29.49	38.18	36.94
Active sportswear	29.25	28.32	26.19	25.35	34.56
Shirts	31.46	31.71	27.15	35.21	29.35
Pants and shorts	39.29	38.18	37.79	39.76	40.48
Uniforms	125.00	385.71	50.00	28.57	107.14
Boys' (aged 2 to 15) apparel	**24.36**	**22.34**	**27.39**	**28.45**	**17.14**
Shirts	20.36	19.91	21.76	23.14	14.78
Underwear	10.43	10.57	15.00	9.63	7.69
Nightwear	17.24	17.65	19.44	16.13	12.90
Hosiery	10.00	8.77	12.61	10.62	9.09
Accessories	13.85	12.68	12.09	21.05	10.87
Suits, sport coats, and vests	60.00	33.33	50.00	60.00	–
Women's apparel	**58.55**	**61.57**	**58.36**	**59.37**	**55.01**
Coats and jackets	63.69	67.19	59.26	74.50	49.44
Dresses	70.56	70.56	119.82	72.60	42.47
Sport coats and tailored jackets	44.44	20.00	50.00	–	35.71
Sweaters and vests	33.78	33.46	33.47	32.12	36.89
Shirts, blouses, and tops	26.60	25.88	28.18	27.14	24.97
Skirts	27.16	25.84	26.56	31.65	21.65
Pants and shorts	34.20	36.68	31.25	34.51	33.63
Active sportswear	31.21	27.35	39.06	30.63	27.72
Nightwear	24.62	20.87	28.10	24.29	25.98
Undergarments	23.81	20.53	26.07	23.02	24.83
Hosiery	8.53	8.05	8.19	8.23	9.44
Accessories	24.22	23.11	20.32	23.00	30.72
Uniforms	38.10	26.32	30.00	41.03	25.00
Girls' (aged 2 to 15) apparel	**34.50**	**44.16**	**35.28**	**32.54**	**29.76**
Coats and jackets	45.71	32.00	40.00	51.85	55.00
Dresses and suits	35.14	60.32	37.50	29.47	28.77
Shirts, blouses, and sweaters	23.48	27.53	23.51	22.66	22.03
Active sportswear	21.98	30.11	19.44	22.62	16.47
Underwear and nightwear	16.50	19.05	17.65	16.50	14.85
Hosiery	8.55	7.61	8.57	8.74	8.70
Accessories	15.69	23.53	12.73	17.39	12.73
Children's (under age 2) apparel	**30.05**	**30.45**	**34.92**	**27.27**	**27.88**
Outerwear including dresses	21.62	17.06	31.71	21.35	13.94
Underwear	24.36	26.39	23.41	22.81	26.74
Nightwear and loungewear	19.23	22.22	13.41	27.50	18.75
Accessories	17.48	17.05	24.62	12.70	15.75
Footwear	**54.80**	**54.99**	**53.03**	**56.73**	**52.77**
Men's	65.22	64.24	63.64	68.89	61.18
Boys'	43.41	49.41	41.49	46.04	34.84
Women's	41.85	43.24	41.86	40.52	42.63
Girls'	36.36	34.12	36.47	40.48	32.34
Other apparel products and services	**22.35**	**27.10**	**18.93**	**23.75**	**21.19**
Material for making clothes	19.18	16.00	18.95	18.03	22.22
Sewing patterns and notions	8.09	8.33	5.36	10.61	8.33
Watches	41.98	48.24	35.58	48.48	32.10

Note: "–" means sample is too small to make a reliable estimate.
Source: Calculations by New Strategist based on the Bureau of Labor Statistics' 2008 Consumer Expenditure Survey

Table 1.25 Percent Buying Apparel by Education, <u>Average Quarter,</u> 2008

(percent of households buying apparel, accessories, and related services during the average quarter, by highest level of education of householder, 2008)

						college graduate		
APPAREL, PERCENT BUYING	total households	less than high school graduate	high school graduate	some college	associate's degree	total	bachelor's degree	master's, professional, doctorate
	74.3%	63.4%	68.7%	75.9%	75.5%	83.1%	81.8%	85.6%
Men's apparel	**29.6**	**20.5**	**26.0**	**30.6**	**29.7**	**36.7**	**36.2**	**37.7**
Suits	1.3	0.6	0.8	1.2	1.3	2.1	1.7	2.9
Sport coats and tailored jackets	1.1	0.5	0.8	0.9	1.2	1.8	1.6	2.2
Coats and jackets	3.6	2.5	2.9	3.2	3.8	4.9	4.9	5.0
Underwear	5.3	4.2	5.1	5.0	5.5	6.1	5.9	6.5
Hosiery	4.4	3.4	4.1	4.5	4.6	5.1	5.1	5.3
Nightwear	0.9	0.4	0.7	0.8	0.8	1.3	1.3	1.4
Accessories	3.3	1.8	2.3	3.5	3.0	5.0	4.6	5.6
Sweaters and vests	2.5	1.3	1.8	2.5	2.3	3.7	3.5	4.0
Active sportswear	1.5	0.5	1.2	1.3	1.9	2.2	2.1	2.5
Shirts	17.9	12.2	14.9	19.1	17.6	22.5	22.4	22.8
Pants and shorts	19.0	14.4	16.7	19.8	18.6	22.8	22.7	23.1
Uniforms	0.6	0.4	0.6	0.5	0.9	0.7	0.8	0.6
Costumes	0.3	0.2	0.2	0.4	0.4	0.4	0.4	0.4
Boys' (aged 2 to 15) apparel	**11.3**	**10.2**	**10.1**	**11.4**	**13.0**	**12.4**	**13.3**	**10.8**
Coats and jackets	1.5	1.5	1.3	1.5	1.9	1.7	1.9	1.3
Sweaters	0.7	0.8	0.6	0.7	0.6	0.8	0.9	0.7
Shirts	7.0	6.7	6.0	7.2	7.8	7.6	8.1	6.7
Underwear	2.2	2.0	1.9	2.4	2.5	2.2	2.5	1.7
Nightwear	0.8	0.5	0.6	0.8	0.8	1.3	1.5	0.7
Hosiery	1.4	1.3	1.4	1.3	1.9	1.4	1.5	1.3
Accessories	0.7	0.6	0.5	0.5	0.8	1.1	1.0	1.1
Suits, sport coats, and vests	0.3	0.3	0.4	0.3	0.4	0.3	0.3	0.3
Pants and shorts	8.2	7.1	7.4	8.2	9.7	9.1	9.8	7.9
Uniforms	0.6	0.3	0.5	0.5	0.6	0.7	0.8	0.7
Active sportswear	1.0	0.4	1.0	0.9	1.2	1.3	1.3	1.3
Costumes	0.5	0.2	0.5	0.5	0.5	0.7	0.7	0.5
Women's apparel	**40.8**	**28.5**	**35.7**	**41.0**	**42.2**	**50.8**	**49.1**	**54.0**
Coats and jackets	5.3	2.9	4.8	5.1	5.3	7.0	6.5	7.9
Dresses	7.2	3.9	5.2	6.9	6.6	10.9	10.4	11.8
Sport coats and tailored jackets	1.2	0.4	0.8	1.1	1.1	2.1	1.9	2.6
Sweaters and vests	6.1	3.1	4.8	5.8	7.1	8.9	8.6	9.4
Shirts, blouses, and tops	24.8	16.7	21.2	25.7	25.1	31.3	30.2	33.2
Skirts	3.1	1.9	2.3	3.0	2.6	4.6	4.1	5.4
Pants and shorts	23.8	15.9	21.0	23.8	24.2	30.1	29.2	31.8
Active sportswear	3.2	1.4	2.3	3.3	4.1	4.7	4.6	5.0
Nightwear	4.0	2.3	4.1	3.9	4.0	4.7	4.6	5.0
Undergarments	9.1	6.7	8.1	9.2	8.6	11.4	11.2	11.9
Hosiery	5.7	4.3	4.9	5.8	5.6	7.1	6.6	8.1
Suits	1.6	0.8	1.0	1.5	1.4	2.7	2.3	3.5
Accessories	5.6	2.9	4.4	5.7	5.4	7.9	7.2	9.2
Uniforms	1.0	0.4	0.9	1.1	1.8	1.2	1.3	1.1
Costumes	0.6	0.1	0.5	0.7	0.6	0.8	0.8	0.9
Girls' (aged 2 to 15) apparel	**11.9**	**9.7**	**11.5**	**11.3**	**13.4**	**13.4**	**13.9**	**12.6**
Coats and jackets	1.7	1.3	1.6	1.6	1.7	1.9	1.8	2.1
Dresses and suits	2.2	1.4	1.8	2.0	2.8	2.9	3.0	2.6
Shirts, blouses, and sweaters	7.9	6.4	7.3	7.4	9.1	9.3	9.8	8.4
Skirts, pants, and shorts	8.3	6.8	8.4	7.8	8.8	9.2	9.8	8.2
Active sportswear	1.4	0.6	1.2	1.4	1.8	1.7	1.8	1.7
Underwear and nightwear	3.2	2.2	3.2	2.9	4.0	3.6	3.8	3.2

	total households	less than high school graduate	high school graduate	some college	associate's degree	college graduate total	bachelor's degree	master's, professional, doctorate
Hosiery	1.6%	1.1%	1.8%	1.4%	1.9%	1.7%	1.9%	1.5%
Accessories	1.1	0.9	0.9	0.8	1.4	1.4	1.4	1.5
Uniforms	0.5	0.5	0.6	0.5	0.4	0.6	0.7	0.5
Costumes	0.7	0.2	0.7	0.6	0.9	1.0	1.0	1.0
Children's (under age 2) apparel	**13.1**	**12.5**	**11.6**	**13.3**	**14.0**	**14.3**	**14.2**	**14.4**
Coats, jackets, and snowsuits	1.0	1.1	0.9	0.9	1.2	1.0	1.1	0.7
Outerwear including dresses	7.2	6.2	6.3	7.5	7.5	8.0	8.3	7.6
Underwear	7.1	8.2	6.0	7.2	7.0	7.3	7.3	7.4
Nightwear and loungewear	2.3	1.6	1.9	2.5	2.1	2.9	2.5	3.7
Accessories	3.3	2.7	2.9	3.5	3.4	3.7	3.6	3.8
Footwear	**31.7**	**25.3**	**28.5**	**32.6**	**32.9**	**36.8**	**36.6**	**37.1**
Men's	12.5	10.2	11.0	13.2	12.9	14.2	14.0	14.4
Boys'	6.0	6.2	5.2	6.1	6.1	6.4	6.7	5.9
Women's	18.7	13.0	16.5	18.4	19.1	23.7	22.8	25.2
Girls'	6.2	5.8	6.0	5.9	6.6	6.7	7.1	6.1
Other apparel products and services	**37.3**	**29.7**	**30.1**	**36.6**	**36.0**	**48.4**	**45.3**	**53.9**
Material for making clothes	1.2	1.2	0.9	1.1	1.2	1.6	1.6	1.5
Sewing patterns and notions	1.6	1.3	1.1	1.7	2.0	1.9	2.0	1.7
Watches	3.1	2.1	2.8	3.2	4.0	3.7	3.5	4.0
Jewelry	7.2	3.0	5.3	7.3	8.2	10.5	10.0	11.4
Shoe repair and other shoe services	0.9	0.3	0.5	0.8	0.7	1.6	1.1	2.3
Coin-operated apparel laundry and dry cleaning	13.8	19.8	13.4	14.9	11.3	11.1	11.3	10.7
Apparel alteration, repair, and tailoring services	2.9	1.2	1.9	2.7	2.4	5.0	4.4	6.0
Clothing rental	0.4	0.0	0.4	0.4	0.4	0.5	0.6	0.3
Watch and jewelry repair	1.8	0.9	1.3	1.8	2.1	2.8	2.6	3.1
Professional laundry, dry cleaning	15.1	4.8	8.8	12.2	13.9	28.5	24.8	35.2
Clothing storage	0.1	–	0.1	0.1	0.2	0.2	0.1	0.2

Note: "–" means sample is too small to make a reliable estimate.
Source: Bureau of Labor Statistics, unpublished data from the 2008 Consumer Expenditure Survey

Table 1.26 Amount Buyers Spent on Apparel by Education, Average Quarter, 2008

(average amount spent by households buying apparel, accessories, and related services during the average quarter, by highest level of education of householder, 2008)

	total households	less than high school graduate	high school graduate	some college	associate's degree	college graduate total	bachelor's degree	master's, professional, doctorate
APPAREL, AMOUNT SPENT	$399.40	$281.03	$320.75	$369.57	$398.94	$522.80	$475.76	$603.46
Men's apparel	**180.66**	**138.64**	**155.00**	**165.20**	**183.99**	**217.35**	**200.72**	**245.99**
Suits	466.60	375.45	408.13	415.17	611.57	492.98	475.00	512.20
Sport coats and tailored jackets	197.71	108.82	255.59	138.44	163.46	219.21	172.12	277.76
Coats and jackets	114.83	93.65	112.80	101.23	114.37	128.50	119.56	144.34
Underwear	35.86	31.41	36.91	33.13	38.11	37.66	35.43	41.40
Hosiery	20.88	20.55	18.54	18.88	22.46	23.49	22.44	25.24
Nightwear	46.84	46.88	44.85	38.41	51.19	50.95	47.85	56.52
Accessories	51.96	30.60	46.71	51.30	46.84	59.48	61.29	56.80
Sweaters and vests	87.65	86.57	74.86	75.91	86.43	99.39	95.80	104.76
Active sportswear	64.70	53.50	51.45	70.45	72.35	67.00	68.90	63.92
Shirts	81.16	66.26	71.93	77.72	74.99	94.29	89.29	103.09
Pants and shorts	92.63	73.96	82.63	88.87	93.14	107.26	103.09	114.64
Uniforms	149.19	102.84	175.81	191.67	106.45	136.79	141.78	127.59
Costumes	79.03	41.67	58.33	92.36	108.33	77.38	76.79	78.57
Boys' (aged 2 to 15) apparel	**147.62**	**142.54**	**140.60**	**138.81**	**144.97**	**161.65**	**154.15**	**178.28**
Coats and jackets	75.32	64.97	73.32	73.10	62.30	87.35	82.31	100.19
Sweaters	62.68	52.11	54.46	77.46	86.51	57.01	48.86	76.07
Shirts	69.82	72.80	68.55	68.07	65.92	71.75	69.74	76.12
Underwear	32.52	30.54	27.03	32.61	38.06	35.02	34.10	37.28
Nightwear	41.87	27.13	56.25	32.69	37.50	44.40	42.53	52.05
Hosiery	18.13	14.50	17.01	18.25	17.30	21.01	21.41	19.92
Accessories	43.93	31.90	65.00	41.51	41.67	40.65	42.07	38.62
Suits, sport coats, and vests	75.81	61.76	75.00	71.00	93.57	84.82	93.10	72.00
Pants and shorts	84.63	88.10	79.48	76.91	83.58	92.66	85.09	109.41
Uniforms	135.27	145.69	118.52	131.02	164.22	137.67	134.54	143.01
Active sportswear	44.13	30.36	45.88	44.83	39.83	46.48	46.12	46.29
Costumes	44.61	37.50	48.58	51.04	32.84	42.80	42.47	43.06
Women's apparel	**219.89**	**147.18**	**179.11**	**214.04**	**206.20**	**272.83**	**252.22**	**306.47**
Coats and jackets	115.70	84.69	95.40	112.60	118.27	135.52	122.46	154.63
Dresses	144.90	107.22	117.17	141.86	119.87	169.63	171.27	166.89
Sport coats and tailored jackets	115.65	131.10	77.13	98.64	83.33	139.02	108.24	180.02
Sweaters and vests	94.18	81.70	72.53	93.49	85.67	108.84	100.99	121.86
Shirts, blouses, and tops	86.97	63.24	74.83	86.78	81.69	102.06	95.65	112.45
Skirts	76.46	59.66	66.27	69.21	55.64	92.01	78.91	109.96
Pants and shorts	94.29	77.74	87.97	92.13	94.44	103.86	96.57	115.87
Active sportswear	63.19	42.86	52.91	51.31	65.37	76.11	73.85	79.68
Nightwear	48.30	42.83	45.06	44.63	47.88	54.43	51.20	59.72
Undergarments	55.88	43.60	48.64	63.07	60.09	58.63	52.76	68.49
Hosiery	22.68	20.36	20.43	21.23	24.24	25.25	24.58	26.15
Suits	201.08	111.51	121.29	189.97	244.16	237.86	249.68	223.36
Accessories	76.75	55.72	61.30	74.87	70.59	90.44	78.06	107.93
Uniforms	118.51	103.66	117.61	117.45	120.28	122.76	122.07	125.44
Costumes	92.37	31.82	110.56	75.35	73.77	104.17	103.27	104.12
Girls' (aged 2 to 15) apparel	**170.16**	**132.50**	**158.46**	**161.47**	**178.74**	**195.68**	**187.82**	**211.17**
Coats and jackets	65.76	64.34	53.40	71.63	59.01	74.34	65.14	87.97
Dresses and suits	84.49	58.27	74.29	82.14	89.29	95.83	87.38	114.29
Shirts, blouses, and sweaters	77.64	67.16	74.39	74.19	75.66	86.34	82.36	94.80
Skirts, pants, and shorts	88.70	68.99	85.55	87.44	91.10	98.54	93.35	109.68
Active sportswear	43.89	32.27	32.61	43.21	42.26	53.30	47.87	63.53
Underwear and nightwear	44.78	42.28	45.51	35.93	56.38	46.20	46.08	46.45

	total households	less than high school graduate	high school graduate	some college	associate's degree	college graduate total	bachelor's degree	master's, professional, doctorate
Hosiery	$17.09	$19.37	$16.81	$16.18	$20.30	$15.84	$16.13	$15.07
Accessories	37.73	36.11	32.58	40.36	53.72	34.86	29.71	42.83
Uniforms	131.60	124.44	110.71	139.67	121.88	152.42	150.00	160.64
Costumes	65.71	38.64	45.90	69.09	100.28	68.93	68.69	69.90
Children's (under age 2) apparel	**137.48**	**151.95**	**129.37**	**138.98**	**119.42**	**141.26**	**139.31**	**144.86**
Coats, jackets, and snowsuits	70.41	77.08	56.12	65.49	77.56	78.35	82.73	66.55
Outerwear including dresses	81.01	81.66	80.01	79.68	69.01	86.05	85.74	86.71
Underwear	122.94	134.79	117.56	124.10	117.63	120.79	113.69	133.50
Nightwear and loungewear	44.43	40.76	41.62	47.66	36.30	46.51	39.82	54.99
Accessories	56.10	53.31	57.82	50.21	48.16	62.40	68.25	52.58
Footwear	**118.14**	**99.26**	**105.22**	**110.95**	**114.87**	**139.21**	**127.67**	**159.68**
Men's	97.43	83.54	90.06	93.88	96.77	110.29	104.81	119.81
Boys'	67.92	74.64	64.21	66.08	63.52	70.12	69.57	71.31
Women's	91.91	64.58	78.94	87.34	90.50	110.42	98.57	129.69
Girls'	65.83	60.59	63.61	62.31	63.74	72.95	68.66	81.71
Other apparel products and services	**163.68**	**122.09**	**128.33**	**146.40**	**173.44**	**203.56**	**175.84**	**245.32**
Material for making clothes	58.33	61.44	53.69	65.93	69.88	51.77	46.02	61.84
Sewing patterns and notions	28.82	25.00	28.21	24.42	36.52	30.26	25.50	40.32
Watches	171.74	112.92	79.86	126.70	134.54	292.69	129.07	552.66
Jewelry	367.42	352.63	295.55	351.79	354.86	412.77	379.98	464.12
Shoe repair and other shoe services	36.92	31.62	26.44	33.88	36.94	41.67	36.61	46.05
Coin-operated apparel laundry and dry cleaning	76.14	94.79	77.93	70.46	72.80	64.40	64.87	63.48
Apparel alteration, repair, and tailoring services	54.90	40.42	42.28	37.55	41.60	70.17	59.26	84.32
Clothing rental	142.31	150.00	113.07	134.52	170.12	165.31	124.15	315.83
Watch and jewelry repair	70.36	21.07	65.08	59.80	63.43	87.64	58.92	129.90
Professional laundry, dry cleaning	89.56	60.81	79.36	75.39	101.57	97.53	92.55	103.82
Clothing storage	300.00	–	333.33	134.62	352.27	375.00	175.00	564.13

Note: "–" means sample is too small to make a reliable estimate.
Source: Calculations by New Strategist based on the Bureau of Labor Statistics' 2008 Consumer Expenditure Survey

Table 1.27 Percent Buying Apparel by Education, Average Week, 2008

(percent of households buying apparel, accessories, and related services during the average week, by highest level of education of householder, 2008)

	total households	less than high school graduate	high school graduate	some college	associate's degree	college graduate total	bachelor's degree	master's, professional, doctorate
APPAREL, PERCENT BUYING	34.6%	30.0%	30.9%	34.4%	38.8%	39.1%	39.5%	38.4%
Men's apparel	**12.2**	**10.4**	**10.7**	**11.6**	**13.1**	**14.7**	**14.8**	**14.6**
Sport coats and tailored jackets	0.1	–	–	0.1	–	0.1	0.0	0.3
Coats and jackets	0.9	0.8	0.5	0.8	0.5	1.3	1.5	1.1
Underwear	2.7	2.0	2.3	2.4	3.1	3.6	3.3	4.0
Hosiery	2.6	2.3	2.3	2.7	2.2	2.9	3.1	2.7
Accessories	3.4	2.6	3.0	3.1	3.7	4.2	4.2	4.1
Sweaters and vests	0.8	0.7	0.3	0.9	0.8	1.1	1.2	0.9
Active sportswear	1.1	0.9	1.0	0.7	1.6	1.4	1.5	1.3
Shirts	5.9	4.4	5.3	5.9	6.3	6.9	7.2	6.5
Pants and shorts	4.0	3.6	3.3	3.9	4.9	4.5	4.3	4.8
Uniforms	0.1	0.1	0.1	0.1	–	0.1	0.1	0.1
Boys' (aged 2 to 15) apparel	**3.5**	**3.7**	**3.1**	**3.4**	**3.7**	**3.8**	**4.1**	**3.3**
Shirts	2.2	2.5	2.0	2.1	2.7	2.2	2.6	1.6
Underwear	1.2	1.0	1.3	1.1	1.0	1.2	1.4	0.9
Nightwear	0.3	0.2	0.5	0.2	0.1	0.3	0.4	0.2
Hosiery	1.1	1.1	1.3	1.0	0.8	1.1	1.0	1.3
Accessories	0.7	0.5	0.6	0.7	1.0	0.6	0.5	0.9
Suits, sport coats, and vests	0.1	–	0.1	0.0	0.1	0.0	0.0	–
Women's apparel	**18.9**	**15.7**	**16.8**	**19.4**	**21.5**	**21.3**	**21.9**	**20.4**
Coats and jackets	1.8	1.2	1.6	1.8	1.9	2.2	2.3	2.0
Dresses	2.0	1.3	1.8	1.7	2.7	2.5	2.3	2.8
Sport coats and tailored jackets	0.1	0.1	–	0.1	0.2	0.2	0.2	0.1
Sweaters and vests	2.3	1.4	1.6	2.1	1.9	3.5	3.8	2.8
Shirts, blouses, and tops	8.9	6.9	8.0	9.3	10.2	10.0	10.3	9.3
Skirts	0.8	0.5	0.5	0.9	1.4	1.0	1.0	1.0
Pants and shorts	5.8	4.8	5.0	6.4	6.2	6.4	6.0	7.0
Active sportswear	1.7	1.3	1.0	1.9	2.0	2.4	2.6	2.1
Nightwear	2.0	2.0	1.8	2.0	1.7	2.2	2.0	2.7
Undergarments	2.9	2.8	2.3	3.4	3.1	3.3	3.2	3.4
Hosiery	3.8	4.1	3.1	4.2	3.7	3.9	3.8	4.1
Accessories	4.5	3.7	3.8	5.1	4.0	5.1	4.8	5.6
Uniforms	0.2	0.1	0.2	0.3	0.2	0.3	0.3	0.2
Girls' (aged 2 to 15) apparel	**4.9**	**4.8**	**3.8**	**5.5**	**6.2**	**5.0**	**5.1**	**5.0**
Coats and jackets	0.4	0.1	0.3	0.5	0.3	0.4	0.4	0.5
Dresses and suits	0.7	0.6	0.7	0.7	0.8	0.8	0.7	1.1
Shirts, blouses, and sweaters	2.6	2.8	2.0	2.6	3.6	2.9	3.0	2.7
Active sportswear	0.9	0.3	0.7	0.9	1.5	1.2	1.2	1.1
Underwear and nightwear	1.0	1.0	0.7	1.2	1.1	1.2	1.3	0.8
Hosiery	1.2	1.1	0.8	1.1	1.5	1.5	1.4	1.7
Accessories	1.0	1.2	0.7	1.2	1.1	1.1	1.0	1.2
Children's (under age 2) apparel	**5.7**	**6.0**	**4.6**	**5.0**	**7.1**	**6.7**	**6.5**	**7.0**
Outerwear including dresses	1.9	2.1	1.4	1.5	2.2	2.4	2.3	2.5
Underwear	3.9	4.0	3.2	3.5	5.2	4.5	4.3	4.7
Nightwear and loungewear	0.5	0.6	0.5	0.3	0.4	0.7	0.8	0.5
Accessories	1.4	1.3	1.3	1.2	1.5	1.7	1.6	2.0
Footwear	**11.0**	**10.7**	**9.6**	**11.4**	**12.2**	**11.8**	**12.7**	**10.2**
Men's	3.0	3.3	2.7	3.1	3.0	3.1	3.2	2.9
Boys'	1.8	2.2	1.7	1.6	2.4	1.8	2.1	1.1
Women's	6.4	5.3	5.5	6.8	6.9	7.2	7.5	6.6
Girls'	1.8	1.9	1.4	1.9	2.3	1.8	2.1	1.2
Other apparel products and services	**2.6**	**2.4**	**2.6**	**2.5**	**2.6**	**2.9**	**2.9**	**3.0**
Material for making clothes	0.7	0.7	0.7	0.7	0.8	0.8	0.7	0.9
Sewing patterns and notions	1.4	1.1	1.3	1.2	1.5	1.6	1.5	1.7
Watches	0.8	0.8	0.8	0.7	0.8	0.9	1.0	0.6

Note: "–" means sample is too small to make a reliable estimate.
Source: Bureau of Labor Statistics, unpublished data from the 2008 Consumer Expenditure Survey

Table 1.28 Amount Buyers Spent on Apparel by Education, <u>Average Week</u>, 2008

(average amount spent by households buying apparel, accessories, and related services during the average week, by highest level of education of householder, 2008)

	total households	less than high school graduate	high school graduate	some college	associate's degree	college graduate total	bachelor's degree	master's, professional, doctorate
APPAREL, AMOUNT SPENT	**$80.93**	**$70.06**	**$69.52**	**$80.09**	**$71.39**	**$96.52**	**$98.05**	**$93.65**
Men's apparel	**49.39**	**35.87**	**38.71**	**51.43**	**44.02**	**61.17**	**64.55**	**54.84**
Sport coats and tailored jackets	140.00	–	–	228.57	–	127.27	266.67	85.19
Coats and jackets	74.12	32.05	68.63	104.94	30.19	78.03	73.29	90.57
Underwear	11.76	9.31	9.40	9.75	11.78	14.61	13.81	16.08
Hosiery	11.37	7.83	9.29	11.81	8.26	14.38	13.07	16.92
Accessories	19.05	15.56	15.67	16.67	11.92	25.06	28.37	19.08
Sweaters and vests	36.84	58.46	28.13	28.74	31.65	38.39	31.45	59.09
Active sportswear	29.25	20.00	29.47	33.82	38.22	25.90	21.38	35.94
Shirts	31.46	22.43	23.26	29.12	31.59	41.62	46.43	31.49
Pants and shorts	39.29	29.95	33.23	41.33	36.66	46.74	51.88	38.46
Uniforms	125.00	66.67	225.00	50.00	–	122.22	127.27	66.67
Boys' (aged 2 to 15) apparel	**24.36**	**19.07**	**29.22**	**22.02**	**31.08**	**22.98**	**23.47**	**21.56**
Shirts	20.36	18.73	20.30	22.12	23.16	19.20	18.77	20.51
Underwear	10.43	7.37	10.08	8.26	8.91	13.93	15.22	10.87
Nightwear	17.24	21.05	17.39	19.05	10.00	12.50	13.89	13.04
Hosiery	10.00	7.41	10.45	7.14	9.76	14.15	15.79	11.90
Accessories	13.85	8.16	14.52	10.77	28.71	12.50	10.42	13.98
Suits, sport coats, and vests	60.00	–	50.00	33.33	50.00	100.00	66.67	–
WOMen's apparel	**58.55**	**47.29**	**48.54**	**60.89**	**48.39**	**71.18**	**69.70**	**74.15**
Coats and jackets	63.69	45.53	56.69	82.51	40.11	66.67	59.03	82.76
Dresses	70.56	129.23	51.43	72.46	52.61	73.90	75.00	71.99
Sport coats and tailored jackets	44.44	20.00	–	50.00	25.00	40.00	50.00	30.77
Sweaters and vests	33.78	24.11	26.22	39.23	34.41	36.23	34.65	40.07
Shirts, blouses, and tops	26.60	20.03	22.91	27.63	22.56	31.96	31.01	33.91
Skirts	27.16	8.51	24.07	33.33	22.63	30.30	25.00	39.42
Pants and shorts	34.20	23.69	30.02	28.95	33.55	45.05	47.19	41.29
Active sportswear	31.21	32.84	34.74	29.26	31.98	30.45	32.56	25.35
Nightwear	24.62	17.65	27.22	27.23	17.24	24.89	28.93	19.62
Undergarments	23.81	17.03	22.91	21.96	25.96	27.52	31.56	20.59
Hosiery	8.53	6.37	8.77	8.89	8.17	9.18	9.38	8.80
Accessories	24.22	18.92	20.31	22.97	19.49	31.23	32.63	28.90
Uniforms	38.10	57.14	23.53	42.86	8.70	44.00	53.85	25.00
Girls' (aged 2 to 15) apparel	**34.50**	**26.03**	**31.75**	**34.98**	**36.06**	**38.84**	**36.56**	**43.64**
Coats and jackets	45.71	25.00	53.33	56.52	21.21	40.48	45.95	36.54
Dresses and suits	35.14	31.25	29.58	43.66	37.18	35.37	27.54	44.86
Shirts, blouses, and sweaters	23.48	19.15	23.98	24.43	31.68	21.65	19.54	25.83
Active sportswear	21.98	16.67	18.31	22.58	21.77	24.17	21.77	30.36
Underwear and nightwear	16.50	14.56	15.07	13.22	20.75	20.00	18.66	23.75
Hosiery	8.55	13.76	7.69	7.96	6.49	8.72	9.49	7.02
Accessories	15.69	13.04	10.81	19.83	10.38	20.00	25.77	11.67
Children's (under age 2) apparel	**30.05**	**37.79**	**28.88**	**23.25**	**24.82**	**33.23**	**34.47**	**30.81**
Outerwear including dresses	21.62	27.49	19.26	15.07	19.07	24.17	27.90	18.18
Underwear	24.36	26.98	21.32	21.97	21.39	28.09	28.01	28.14
Nightwear and loungewear	19.23	45.45	15.38	9.68	15.00	17.14	15.66	21.74
Accessories	17.48	27.20	23.88	12.20	10.81	15.03	16.03	13.30
Footwear	**54.80**	**50.05**	**53.17**	**48.34**	**47.47**	**65.11**	**63.30**	**69.44**
Men's	65.22	59.51	60.67	59.61	54.64	79.03	79.01	78.60
Boys'	43.41	41.47	51.18	38.13	32.20	45.25	45.33	44.25
Women's	41.85	34.33	38.00	37.30	38.01	51.60	50.33	54.01
Girls'	36.36	36.32	38.41	29.10	33.19	41.81	35.10	64.71
Other apparel products and services	**22.35**	**11.62**	**23.94**	**17.39**	**21.71**	**28.28**	**29.72**	**25.84**
Material for making clothes	19.18	10.00	20.00	16.22	12.66	26.58	27.40	26.37
Sewing patterns and notions	8.09	5.56	9.16	7.26	12.75	7.55	5.88	10.06
Watches	41.98	16.87	45.12	31.94	34.18	55.68	54.90	58.06

Note: "–" means sample is too small to make a reliable estimate.
Source: Calculations by New Strategist based on the Bureau of Labor Statistics' 2008 Consumer Expenditure Survey

Entertainment Buyers, 2008

Spending on entertainment has soared over the past few years, despite the Great Recession. The average household spent 22 percent more on entertainment in 2008 than in 2000, after adjusting for inflation. Behind the increase are larger cable bills, new high-definition televisions, and more spending on pets. One-third of households spend on pets during an average quarter, and 21 percent spend during an average week. On a quarterly basis, cable service and video rentals outstrip pets in luring households into the marketplace. On a weekly basis, pets rank number one.

Quarterly spending

During the average quarter of 2008, nearly all—91 percent—of households spent on entertainment. Those who bought devoted an average of $672 to entertainment products and services during the quarter. Seventy-four percent of households spent on cable and satellite television service during the average quarter, making it the most popular entertainment item. Thirty percent bought movie or theater tickets, and 20 percent rented videos. The proportion of households renting videos during the average quarter hovers near 30 percent among householders under age 45, then drops with age to just 4 percent of householders aged 75 or older. One in three households spent on pets during the average quarter, devoting $233 to them. Note that pet food is not among the 10 most popular entertainment items in the chart below only because pet food spending is captured by the weekly (diary) survey rather than the quarterly (interview).

Quarterly spending

During the average week of 2008, a hefty 40 percent of households purchased entertainment products and services. The buyers spent $75 on average. Among entertainment categories examined on a weekly basis, pets attract the largest share of households into the marketplace. More than one in five households bought pet products or services during the average week, spending $40 on them. Eighteen percent of households bought pet food during an average week. Twelve percent of households paid a cable bill during the average week, the purchasers spending $89 on average.

Entertainment Buyers' Top 10

(entertainment categories bought by the largest percentage of households during an average quarter, 2008)

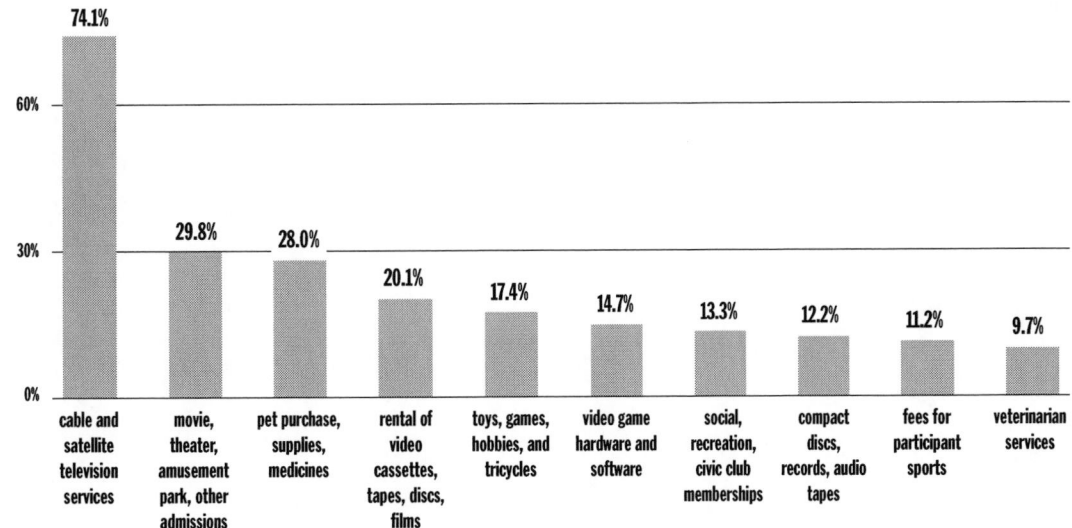

Table 2.1 Percent Buying Entertainment by Age, Average Quarter, 2008

(percent of households buying entertainment during the average quarter, by age of householder, 2008)

	total households	under 25	25 to 34	35 to 44	45 to 54	55 to 64	65 to 74	75+
ENTERTAINMENT, PERCENT BUYING	**91.1%**	**86.8%**	**91.5%**	**92.8%**	**93.2%**	**92.3%**	**90.6%**	**83.3%**
Fees and admissions	**46.5**	**47.9**	**51.2**	**55.1**	**50.4**	**43.9**	**37.6**	**25.1**
Recreation expenses on trips	7.5	4.5	6.6	8.9	9.7	8.6	6.7	2.9
Social, recreation, civic club membership	13.3	8.1	14.2	15.3	14.9	13.8	11.6	8.6
Fees for participant sports	11.2	8.6	11.5	14.9	12.1	9.9	9.9	7.2
Participant sports on trips	3.7	3.0	3.4	4.3	5.2	3.6	3.0	1.0
Movie, theater, amusement park, and other admissions	29.8	37.7	34.4	35.9	32.5	27.4	20.4	12.0
Movie, other admissions on trips	8.2	5.8	8.1	9.4	9.9	9.6	6.9	3.4
Admission to sports events	6.6	9.0	7.6	8.7	8.2	4.9	3.7	1.6
Admission to sports events on trips	8.2	5.8	8.1	9.4	9.9	9.6	6.9	3.4
Fees for recreational lessons	6.2	1.5	5.4	13.0	7.7	3.9	3.2	1.6
Other entertainment services on trips	7.5	4.5	6.6	8.9	9.7	8.6	6.7	2.9
Audio and visual equipment and services	**84.5**	**75.0**	**84.8**	**86.6**	**87.9**	**86.3**	**83.8**	**76.6**
Television sets	4.0	3.8	4.2	4.5	4.7	4.0	3.3	2.5
Cable and satellite television services	74.1	48.1	69.9	75.3	78.8	79.4	78.9	73.5
Satellite radio service	3.1	1.5	3.5	4.2	3.6	3.3	2.3	1.2
Online gaming services	1.0	1.0	1.7	1.5	1.1	0.4	0.3	0.1
VCRs and video disc players	1.9	1.8	2.5	2.1	2.0	2.0	1.1	0.8
Video game hardware and software	14.7	21.3	18.2	18.4	16.1	12.5	7.9	4.2
Video cassettes, tapes, and discs	5.4	7.1	7.8	9.1	5.6	2.8	1.9	0.6
Streamed and downloaded video	0.7	0.9	0.8	1.0	0.8	0.5	0.5	0.1
Repair of TV, radio, and sound equipment	0.5	0.7	0.3	0.7	0.4	0.4	1.0	0.4
Rental of television sets	0.1	0.2	0.1	0.1	0.1	–	0.1	–
Radios	0.7	0.5	0.7	0.6	0.8	0.9	0.9	0.5
Tape recorders and players	0.1	0.1	0.1	0.1	0.2	0.1	0.1	0.1
Personal digital audio players	1.8	2.0	2.2	2.8	2.3	1.1	0.4	0.2
Sound components and component systems	0.7	0.6	0.9	1.0	0.8	0.7	0.2	0.1
Compact discs, records, and audio tapes	12.2	14.4	13.7	13.8	14.2	12.3	8.6	3.8
Streamed and downloaded audio	3.3	4.0	5.2	4.9	3.7	1.9	1.1	0.1
Rental of VCR, radio, and sound equipment	0.1	0.0	0.1	0.1	0.1	0.0	0.0	–
Musical instruments and accessories	1.4	1.6	1.5	2.2	1.6	1.3	0.6	0.1
Rental and repair of musical instruments	0.2	0.1	0.2	0.7	0.2	0.0	0.1	0.1
Rental of video cassettes, tapes, discs, films	20.1	26.9	28.7	26.9	22.5	14.5	8.2	4.3
Rental of computer and video game hardware and software	0.1	–	0.1	0.1	0.1	0.1	0.1	–
Accessories and other sound equipment	1.3	1.6	1.2	1.4	1.5	1.3	1.0	0.7
Satellite dishes	0.3	0.1	0.1	0.3	0.3	0.4	0.5	0.3
Installation of television sets	0.1	0.1	0.1	0.1	0.2	0.2	0.1	0.1
Pets, toys, hobbies, and playground equipment	**43.7**	**29.0**	**47.0**	**52.2**	**49.8**	**44.8**	**37.2**	**23.1**
Pets	33.3	18.3	31.8	38.6	41.9	35.9	28.0	18.6
Pet purchase, supplies, and medicines	28.0	16.2	27.5	33.1	35.4	28.8	22.3	15.3
Pet services	5.7	1.8	4.4	5.6	7.0	8.3	6.3	3.3
Veterinarian services	9.7	3.4	8.8	10.8	12.2	12.0	9.0	4.6
Toys, games, hobbies, and tricycles	17.4	14.8	24.7	24.1	15.6	15.4	12.6	5.9
Stamp and coin collecting	0.9	0.3	0.4	0.7	0.8	1.0	2.2	0.9
Playground equipment	0.4	0.3	0.7	0.7	0.3	0.4	0.2	0.0

	total households	under 25	25 to 34	35 to 44	45 to 54	55 to 64	65 to 74	75+
Other entertainment supplies, equipment, services	**22.5%**	**19.3%**	**26.7%**	**28.2%**	**25.7%**	**20.6%**	**17.5%**	**7.9%**
Unmotored recreational vehicles	0.2	0.1	0.2	0.3	0.1	0.3	0.3	–
Motorized recreational vehicles	0.2	0.2	0.2	0.2	0.2	0.2	0.2	0.2
Rental of recreational vehicles	0.5	0.1	0.5	0.4	0.7	0.5	0.6	0.2
Docking and landing fees	0.4	0.1	0.1	0.5	0.4	0.6	0.4	0.3
Sports, recreation, exercise equipment	10.6	9.6	14.4	15.0	12.3	8.1	5.5	2.1
Athletic gear, game tables, exercise equipment	6.1	6.4	7.8	9.6	7.1	4.2	2.5	1.4
Bicycles	1.4	1.0	2.2	2.1	1.4	1.0	0.4	0.3
Camping equipment	1.0	0.8	1.4	1.2	1.2	0.8	0.6	0.2
Hunting and fishing equipment	2.1	1.3	3.0	2.3	2.6	1.8	1.6	0.2
Winter sports equipment	0.3	0.2	0.4	0.5	0.4	0.2	0.1	0.1
Water sports equipment	0.4	0.1	0.7	0.6	0.5	0.3	0.2	0.1
Other sports equipment	0.9	0.5	1.4	1.3	1.0	0.8	0.6	0.2
Rental and repair of miscellaneous sports equipment	0.3	0.1	0.3	0.5	0.4	0.2	0.1	0.1
Photographic equipment and supplies	14.0	10.6	15.4	17.2	16.2	13.4	12.7	5.5
Film	2.9	1.7	2.3	2.5	3.5	3.4	4.2	2.4
Photo processing	8.9	6.2	9.5	10.4	10.1	9.4	8.8	3.7
Repair and rental of photographic equipment	0.2	0.2	0.1	0.2	0.1	0.2	0.3	0.1
Photographic equipment	2.7	2.4	3.0	3.4	3.4	2.3	2.3	0.7
Photographer fees	2.5	1.9	3.9	4.4	2.6	1.4	0.8	0.3
Live entertainment for catered affairs	0.3	0.3	0.4	0.4	0.4	0.3	0.3	0.1
Rental of party supplies for catered affairs	0.6	0.6	0.8	0.7	0.8	0.5	0.3	0.1

Note: "–" means sample is too small to make a reliable estimate.
Source: Bureau of Labor Statistics, unpublished data from the 2008 Consumer Expenditure Survey

Table 2.2 Amount Buyers Spent on Entertainment by Age, Average Quarter, 2008

(average amount spent by households buying entertainment during the average quarter, by age of householder, 2008)

ENTERTAINMENT, AMOUNT SPENT	total households	under 25	25 to 34	35 to 44	45 to 54	55 to 64	65 to 74	75+
ENTERTAINMENT, AMOUNT SPENT	**$671.81**	**$380.41**	**$644.02**	**$800.23**	**$777.98**	**$719.31**	**$603.68**	**$383.58**
Fees and admissions	**326.61**	**128.43**	**229.96**	**372.14**	**398.49**	**366.06**	**334.40**	**291.75**
Recreation expenses on trips	78.19	56.28	62.05	86.05	78.97	79.71	85.71	87.16
Social, recreation, civic club membership	240.37	119.31	141.42	232.47	277.50	324.38	250.32	248.78
Fees for participant sports	181.17	91.71	140.07	160.50	186.64	233.37	228.88	242.89
Participant sports on trips	186.18	60.75	146.13	210.01	210.71	184.86	149.33	332.84
Movie, theater, amusement park, and other admissions	99.40	58.84	86.36	103.71	109.39	112.54	106.96	104.31
Movie, other admissions on trips	136.07	62.11	114.00	136.15	142.13	153.02	148.98	167.35
Admission to sports events	174.24	83.59	127.27	138.13	211.95	217.06	378.67	153.55
Admission to sports events on trips	45.36	20.68	38.01	45.38	47.38	50.99	49.64	55.76
Fees for recreational lessons	400.32	168.66	307.87	423.75	513.14	301.98	273.91	216.61
Other entertainment services on trips	78.19	56.28	62.05	86.05	78.97	79.71	85.71	87.16
Audio and visual equipment, services	**290.77**	**214.30**	**294.35**	**320.19**	**314.85**	**311.57**	**262.94**	**202.66**
Television sets	1,017.82	714.33	976.90	1,078.56	1,008.35	1,126.13	1,095.77	889.39
Cable and satellite television services	196.78	158.13	198.92	200.09	208.78	206.80	189.68	165.60
Satellite radio service	117.73	94.43	100.00	116.17	140.34	114.26	110.37	119.13
Online gaming services	52.06	74.76	56.02	46.10	50.46	45.14	43.55	40.00
VCRs and video disc players	164.23	85.22	148.02	176.54	183.71	178.79	150.93	168.21
Video game hardware and software	58.23	54.18	58.79	55.75	60.97	63.37	51.74	54.19
Video cassettes, tapes, and discs	213.45	144.15	204.53	235.42	217.75	210.99	227.15	230.36
Streamed and downloaded video	40.58	38.83	41.46	39.74	40.31	43.23	41.67	75.00
Repair of TV, radio, and sound equipment	185.29	152.78	187.10	153.03	165.28	270.63	179.66	234.62
Rental of television sets	221.43	439.71	165.91	206.25	250.00	–	119.23	–
Radios	96.23	82.41	121.23	103.69	80.94	124.42	53.46	89.89
Tape recorders and players	52.78	28.57	35.00	50.00	68.06	28.13	37.50	83.33
Personal digital audio players	192.61	176.72	187.67	191.81	203.82	162.38	307.39	162.50
Sound components and component systems	278.93	146.83	213.89	293.56	293.45	372.18	370.00	143.18
Compact discs, records, and audio tapes	46.57	44.02	47.63	41.67	46.75	48.86	57.60	41.07
Streamed and downloaded audio	41.44	33.27	41.24	44.04	41.02	37.70	56.25	26.92
Rental of VCR, radio, and sound equipment	195.00	12.50	293.18	175.00	115.00	125.00	25.00	–
Musical instruments and accessories	541.73	427.85	346.43	299.77	345.31	1,491.40	1,165.98	85.42
Rental and repair of musical instruments	181.52	71.43	190.00	85.61	515.48	31.25	127.08	137.50
Rental of video cassettes, tapes, discs, films	33.92	31.06	36.39	35.08	34.18	29.82	31.89	28.23
Rental of computer and video game hardware, software	83.33	–	62.50	150.00	55.56	117.86	60.00	–
Accessories and other sound equipment	101.77	89.49	127.46	110.74	103.64	94.29	81.97	53.13
Satellite dishes	132.14	105.56	285.00	141.96	100.00	137.80	152.94	36.72
Installation of television sets	183.93	345.45	141.67	200.00	205.56	188.64	188.89	106.25
Pets, toys, hobbies, and playground equipment	**250.80**	**164.56**	**232.35**	**253.16**	**272.57**	**269.54**	**259.10**	**201.90**
Pets	233.27	154.69	204.45	223.56	255.15	264.43	243.51	183.90
Pet purchase, supplies, and medicines	146.65	122.24	135.42	136.90	159.00	162.66	154.16	115.13
Pet services	160.43	129.37	130.61	143.62	202.95	162.26	135.25	143.07
Veterinarian services	284.95	183.24	249.80	307.24	298.55	290.07	283.24	253.50
Toys, games, hobbies, and tricycles	168.16	128.15	169.60	174.58	171.79	155.35	179.00	188.82
Stamp and coin collecting	137.79	43.94	94.59	59.33	157.44	109.38	201.79	147.09
Playground equipment	316.28	130.77	275.68	460.76	175.00	202.70	509.38	400.00

	total households	under 25	25 to 34	35 to 44	45 to 54	55 to 64	65 to 74	75+
Other entertainment supplies, equipment, services	**$464.72**	**$312.25**	**$423.25**	**$454.30**	**$435.84**	**$550.06**	**$595.45**	**$559.11**
Unmotored recreational vehicles	12,557.89	1,846.88	13,259.72	12,155.83	10,950.00	14,410.34	12,211.21	–
Motorized recreational vehicles	15,326.25	11,595.65	16,756.58	13,702.38	15,367.39	13,700.00	15,987.50	17,398.75
Rental of recreational vehicles	260.94	182.14	225.53	307.05	264.19	275.98	265.52	182.89
Docking and landing fees	461.43	15.00	183.33	167.65	608.55	595.98	575.00	608.65
Sports, recreation, exercise equipment	251.06	168.47	246.25	248.53	266.67	283.66	253.82	189.02
Athletic gear, game tables, exercise equipment	197.92	94.30	187.84	197.94	243.58	212.11	159.82	122.99
Bicycles	261.95	312.98	204.71	273.71	239.15	323.98	208.11	779.00
Camping equipment	199.74	275.00	275.36	230.83	136.23	155.25	142.54	29.69
Hunting and fishing equipment	253.29	275.75	274.08	215.43	228.91	305.39	286.88	31.58
Winter sports equipment	225.86	375.00	152.50	270.00	239.29	169.12	230.00	170.00
Water sports equipment	197.62	40.63	115.15	111.07	350.94	240.52	260.53	133.33
Other sports equipment	177.69	57.07	165.74	119.09	146.84	288.55	418.53	58.33
Rental and repair of miscellaneous sports equipment	268.52	89.29	272.32	256.67	183.78	432.14	604.17	14.29
Photographic equipment and supplies	116.48	114.41	106.33	118.85	133.00	126.68	95.34	57.07
Film	25.43	22.60	27.99	26.00	30.30	23.82	21.10	17.18
Photo processing	38.95	34.46	36.00	42.71	43.83	38.13	31.75	29.62
Repair and rental of photographic equipment	115.63	37.50	103.13	130.56	120.45	170.31	145.54	53.57
Photographic equipment	260.54	222.84	207.46	248.59	246.15	377.53	310.56	180.00
Photographer fees	198.59	214.34	159.09	153.51	289.85	272.63	127.56	152.88
Live entertainment for catered affairs	555.30	189.84	480.63	233.33	858.75	920.83	330.15	162.50
Rental of party supplies for catered affairs	367.98	522.81	258.55	339.77	422.19	432.22	363.00	230.00

Note: "–" means sample is too small to make a reliable estimate.
Source: Calculations by New Strategist based on the Bureau of Labor Statistics' 2008 Consumer Expenditure Survey

Table 2.3 Percent Buying Entertainment by Age, <u>Average Week</u>, 2008

(percent of households buying entertainment during the average week, by age of householder, 2008)

	total households	under 25	25 to 34	35 to 44	45 to 54	55 to 64	65 to 74	75+
ENTERTAINMENT, PERCENT BUYING	**39.6%**	**27.0%**	**38.0%**	**44.0%**	**43.2%**	**42.8%**	**38.4%**	**30.4%**
Fees and admissions	**5.1**	**3.9**	**4.7**	**6.4**	**6.1**	**4.3**	**4.9**	**3.4**
Fees for participant sports	3.9	3.2	3.7	4.0	4.4	3.7	4.2	3.0
Fees for recreational lessons	1.5	0.8	1.1	2.8	1.9	0.8	1.0	0.5
Audio and visual equipment and services	**14.5**	**9.0**	**15.2**	**15.9**	**14.9**	**15.1**	**13.3**	**13.9**
Radios	0.2	0.8	0.0	0.3	0.2	0.1	0.2	–
Cable and satellite television services	11.9	5.5	11.8	11.7	12.0	13.7	12.4	13.5
Tape recorders and players	0.2	–	0.2	0.3	0.2	0.2	0.2	0.1
Miscellaneous sound equipment	0.1	0.1	0.1	0.2	0.1	0.1	–	0.2
Miscellaneous video equipment	0.3	0.3	0.3	0.3	0.3	0.2	0.3	0.1
Sound equipment accessories	0.8	0.7	0.9	1.0	1.1	0.5	0.5	0.2
Video game hardware and software	1.9	1.8	3.4	3.0	2.2	0.9	0.4	–
Pets, toys, hobbies, and playground equipment	**27.0**	**16.4**	**26.2**	**30.0**	**30.4**	**30.5**	**26.1**	**16.7**
Pets	20.9	12.1	18.9	21.2	24.7	25.1	19.9	15.4
Pet food	17.7	9.3	15.2	17.5	21.0	22.1	17.3	14.2
Pet purchase, supplies, and medicines	6.0	3.9	6.6	6.5	6.7	6.3	5.8	2.8
Veterinarian services	1.9	1.3	1.6	1.8	2.3	2.6	2.1	0.8
Toys, games, hobbies, and tricycles	9.6	5.8	12.0	14.0	9.5	8.4	8.5	2.5
Playground equipment	0.1	–	0.1	0.2	0.0	0.1	0.1	–
Other entertainment supplies, equipment, services	**5.6**	**4.1**	**5.7**	**8.7**	**6.7**	**4.2**	**3.8**	**1.7**
Sports, recreation, exercise equipment	4.4	3.3	4.9	6.4	5.2	3.4	2.9	1.5
Athletic gear, game tables, exercise equipment	2.5	1.3	3.0	4.1	3.0	2.0	1.4	0.5
Camping equipment	0.8	0.3	1.0	1.2	0.8	0.5	0.5	0.2
Hunting and fishing equipment	1.3	1.7	1.2	1.6	1.4	1.1	1.2	0.9
Global positioning system devices	0.1	0.2	0.1	0.1	0.1	0.2	0.1	–
Photographic equipment and supplies	0.8	0.4	0.4	1.6	1.1	0.4	0.7	0.2
Other photographic supplies	0.2	0.1	0.1	0.3	0.3	0.2	0.3	0.1
Photographer fees	0.6	0.3	0.4	1.3	0.9	0.2	0.5	0.1
Fireworks	0.1	–	0.1	0.3	0.0	0.2	0.1	–
Souvenirs	0.2	0.2	0.2	0.3	0.3	0.1	0.3	–
Visual goods	0.1	0.2	0.0	0.1	0.1	0.1	0.1	0.0
Pinball, electronic video games	0.1	0.1	0.2	0.3	0.1	0.1	0.1	–

Note: "–" means sample is too small to make a reliable estimate.
Source: Bureau of Labor Statistics, unpublished data from the 2008 Consumer Expenditure Survey

Table 2.4 Amount Buyers Spent on Entertainment by Age, <u>Average Week</u>, 2008

(average amount spent by households buying entertainment during the average week, by age of householder, 2008)

	total households	under 25	25 to 34	35 to 44	45 to 54	55 to 64	65 to 74	75+
ENTERTAINMENT, AMOUNT SPENT	$75.18	$66.48	$81.09	$93.01	$76.60	$70.24	$58.89	$44.19
Fees and admissions	**64.05**	**60.57**	**58.33**	**86.80**	**65.12**	**56.45**	**48.15**	**28.96**
Fees for participant sports	44.94	33.96	61.58	46.53	40.37	47.58	39.57	29.05
Fees for recreational lessons	104.79	157.50	41.96	134.78	112.44	84.15	70.71	23.91
Audio and visual equipment, services	**87.72**	**79.20**	**95.98**	**91.14**	**96.09**	**86.22**	**76.75**	**61.26**
Radios	20.00	18.18	33.33	15.63	27.27	25.00	18.75	–
Cable and satellite television services	89.43	97.99	94.67	98.80	98.75	85.44	78.25	61.26
Tape recorders and players	38.89	–	40.00	14.29	36.84	38.10	70.59	150.00
Miscellaneous sound equipment	18.18	22.22	–	17.65	7.14	–	–	38.10
Miscellaneous video equipment	33.33	10.00	25.00	47.06	13.79	110.00	7.14	15.38
Sound equipment accessories	23.68	39.44	19.54	19.19	27.36	24.00	14.00	20.00
Video game hardware and software	85.94	73.30	91.39	82.55	88.58	91.30	59.52	–
Pets, toys, hobbies, and playground equipment	**40.02**	**40.05**	**42.85**	**54.09**	**35.67**	**36.67**	**32.34**	**21.32**
Pets	40.14	41.72	39.68	58.79	35.60	37.18	33.85	20.92
Pet food	17.74	13.05	15.65	19.83	21.91	15.73	15.60	13.22
Pet purchase, supplies, and medicines	21.31	25.19	19.82	22.46	18.69	28.57	19.01	9.68
Veterinarian services	209.47	211.19	244.23	424.29	127.71	157.14	140.19	130.12
Toys, games, hobbies, and tricycles	24.56	26.56	31.05	26.45	21.26	20.14	19.60	13.47
Playground equipment	50.00	–	22.22	29.41	–	140.00	16.67	–
Other entertainment supplies, equipment, services	**54.59**	**46.44**	**40.56**	**53.44**	**61.50**	**80.33**	**43.16**	**22.29**
Sports, recreation, exercise equipment	52.52	45.51	39.38	46.19	66.47	75.44	40.21	19.59
Athletic gear, game tables, exercise equipment	42.86	32.09	31.86	48.03	44.22	56.35	35.00	16.33
Camping equipment	42.67	39.39	38.83	35.48	53.75	47.83	42.59	42.86
Hunting and fishing equipment	48.09	46.47	39.52	21.25	100.00	45.54	31.93	14.12
Global positioning system devices	227.27	100.00	88.89	230.00	245.45	347.62	100.00	–
Photographic equipment and supplies	79.75	65.00	75.00	94.38	42.48	202.70	51.39	43.75
Other photographic supplies	21.05	75.00	–	16.13	14.29	50.00	7.41	85.71
Photographer fees	96.72	65.63	72.50	113.18	51.16	304.55	77.78	22.22
Fireworks	27.27	–	–	34.48	100.00	6.67	9.09	–
Souvenirs	21.74	56.25	27.27	9.68	26.47	12.50	9.38	–
Visual goods	22.22	5.26	–	11.11	38.46	8.33	16.67	–
Pinball, electronic video games	21.43	9.09	13.64	12.00	20.00	30.00	116.67	–

Note: "–" means sample is too small to make a reliable estimate.
Source: Calculations by New Strategist based on the Bureau of Labor Statistics' 2008 Consumer Expenditure Survey

Table 2.5 Percent Buying Entertainment by Household Income, <u>Average Quarter</u>, 2008

(percent of households buying entertainment during the average quarter, by before-tax income of household, 2008)

	total households	under $20,000	$20,000– $39,999	$40,000– $49,999	$50,000– $69,999	$70,000– $79,999	$80,000– $99,999	$100,000 or more
ENTERTAINMENT, PERCENT BUYING	**91.1%**	**79.2%**	**88.3%**	**93.1%**	**95.6%**	**97.0%**	**97.1%**	**98.6%**
Fees and admissions	**46.5**	**25.2**	**32.5**	**44.9**	**50.5**	**59.3**	**62.2**	**74.6**
Recreation expenses on trips	7.5	2.5	4.0	6.7	7.6	9.8	10.5	16.0
Social, recreation, civic club membership	13.3	4.5	6.9	11.0	13.4	15.8	19.2	28.9
Fees for participant sports	11.2	4.7	7.2	8.1	11.6	15.9	16.4	21.2
Participant sports on trips	3.7	1.2	1.9	3.2	2.8	4.7	5.0	9.0
Movie, theater, amusement park, and other admissions	29.8	16.7	20.0	27.0	32.8	37.6	39.3	49.0
Movie, other admissions on trips	8.2	3.0	4.6	7.2	7.6	10.9	12.1	17.3
Admission to sports events	6.6	3.5	3.5	6.2	6.4	9.1	8.6	12.7
Admission to sports events on trips	8.2	3.0	4.6	7.2	7.6	10.9	12.1	17.3
Fees for recreational lessons	6.2	1.8	2.7	3.9	5.3	7.8	10.3	15.3
Other entertainment services on trips	7.5	2.5	4.0	6.7	7.6	9.8	10.5	16.0
Audio and visual equipment and services	**84.5**	**69.6**	**80.2**	**86.7**	**89.7**	**92.4**	**93.0**	**95.2**
Television sets	4.0	2.5	3.2	3.1	4.2	4.4	6.3	6.1
Cable and satellite television services	74.1	56.8	69.1	74.8	80.0	82.0	84.9	87.8
Satellite radio service	3.1	0.9	2.0	2.6	2.9	5.1	5.1	6.0
Online gaming services	1.0	0.4	0.4	0.8	1.4	1.5	1.9	1.4
VCRs and video disc players	1.9	1.4	1.5	2.1	2.2	2.7	2.0	2.3
Video game hardware and software	14.7	10.0	10.9	13.9	16.2	18.9	18.6	20.8
Video cassettes, tapes, and discs	5.4	2.8	3.4	5.6	5.9	6.6	7.7	9.0
Streamed and downloaded video	0.7	0.3	0.3	0.3	0.8	0.5	1.1	1.6
Repair of TV, radio, and sound equipment	0.5	0.3	0.5	0.4	0.5	0.6	0.7	0.7
Rental of television sets	0.1	0.0	0.1	0.4	0.0	0.0	–	0.0
Radios	0.7	0.7	0.7	0.5	0.7	0.8	0.7	1.0
Tape recorders and players	0.1	0.1	0.0	0.2	0.1	0.1	0.2	0.1
Personal digital audio players	1.8	0.7	1.0	1.5	1.7	3.0	2.3	3.4
Sound components and component systems	0.7	0.4	0.6	0.7	0.7	1.1	1.0	1.0
Compact discs, records, and audio tapes	12.2	6.4	9.8	12.5	12.8	15.1	16.1	18.5
Streamed and downloaded audio	3.3	1.3	1.3	2.6	2.9	3.9	5.0	7.8
Rental of VCR, radio, and sound equipment	0.1	–	0.0	0.1	0.1	–	0.0	0.2
Musical instruments and accessories	1.4	0.7	0.8	1.0	1.5	2.3	2.0	2.5
Rental and repair of musical instruments	0.2	0.1	0.1	0.1	0.4	0.2	0.3	0.5
Rental of video cassettes, tapes, discs, films	20.1	11.0	14.6	21.0	22.7	25.1	27.1	30.1
Rental of computer and video game hardware, software	0.1	0.1	0.1	0.0	0.1	0.2	0.0	0.1
Accessories and other sound equipment	1.3	1.0	1.0	1.0	1.3	1.3	1.8	1.8
Satellite dishes	0.3	0.3	0.3	0.1	0.3	0.3	0.3	0.3
Installation of television sets	0.1	0.1	0.1	0.1	0.2	–	0.2	0.3
Pets, toys, hobbies, and playground equipment	**43.7**	**26.9**	**36.4**	**42.6**	**48.8**	**55.4**	**55.7**	**59.1**
Pets	33.3	19.6	27.4	31.2	37.7	43.8	42.0	46.7
Pet purchase, supplies, and medicines	28.0	17.3	23.8	26.3	31.9	36.8	34.1	37.3
Pet services	5.7	1.8	3.7	5.0	5.4	7.3	8.8	11.6
Veterinarian services	9.7	4.0	6.4	7.9	11.2	12.8	13.8	17.1
Toys, games, hobbies, and tricycles	17.4	9.6	13.6	17.3	19.2	22.2	24.4	25.1
Stamp and coin collecting	0.9	0.5	0.7	0.9	1.3	0.8	1.1	1.0
Playground equipment	0.4	0.2	0.3	0.4	0.4	0.5	0.7	0.8

	total households	under $20,000	$20,000–$39,999	$40,000–$49,999	$50,000–$69,999	$70,000–$79,999	$80,000–$99,999	$100,000 or more
Other entertainment supplies, equipment, services	**22.5%**	**11.2%**	**15.2%**	**23.3%**	**24.7%**	**29.8%**	**31.7%**	**35.9%**
Unmotored recreational vehicles	0.2	0.1	0.2	0.1	0.4	0.3	0.2	0.2
Motorized recreational vehicles	0.2	0.1	0.1	0.2	0.3	0.1	0.4	0.3
Rental of recreational vehicles	0.5	0.2	0.2	0.4	0.2	0.6	0.7	1.3
Docking and landing fees	0.4	0.2	0.2	0.3	0.4	0.3	0.5	0.7
Sports, recreation, exercise equipment	10.6	5.0	6.4	10.2	10.5	14.7	16.5	18.7
Athletic gear, game tables, exercise equipment	6.1	2.7	3.4	5.3	5.6	7.9	10.2	12.0
Bicycles	1.4	0.8	1.0	1.4	1.2	2.0	2.0	2.1
Camping equipment	1.0	0.4	0.5	1.0	1.0	2.0	1.7	1.5
Hunting and fishing equipment	2.1	0.8	1.4	2.6	2.4	3.4	2.8	2.9
Winter sports equipment	0.3	0.1	0.2	0.1	0.2	0.3	0.5	0.7
Water sports equipment	0.4	0.1	0.2	0.6	0.4	0.8	0.8	0.8
Other sports equipment	0.9	0.6	0.5	1.0	0.8	1.3	1.7	1.4
Rental and repair of miscellaneous sports equipment	0.3	0.1	0.2	0.1	0.3	0.2	0.3	0.6
Photographic equipment and supplies	14.0	6.5	9.4	14.8	16.2	18.3	19.7	22.2
Film	2.9	2.0	2.6	3.3	3.4	4.5	3.5	3.2
Photo processing	8.9	3.9	5.9	10.1	10.2	11.8	12.5	14.4
Repair and rental of photographic equipment	0.2	0.1	0.1	0.2	0.3	0.1	0.2	0.1
Photographic equipment	2.7	1.3	1.7	2.4	3.1	3.4	3.8	4.6
Photographer fees	2.5	0.8	1.3	2.9	2.5	3.7	4.3	4.6
Live entertainment for catered affairs	0.3	0.1	0.2	0.2	0.2	0.8	0.4	0.7
Rental of party supplies for catered affairs	0.6	0.1	0.3	0.5	0.6	1.1	0.8	1.2

Note: "–" means sample is too small to make a reliable estimate.
Source: Bureau of Labor Statistics, unpublished data from the 2008 Consumer Expenditure Survey

Table 2.6 Amount Buyers Spent on Entertainment by Household Income, <u>Average Quarter</u>, 2008

(average amount spent by households buying entertainment during the average quarter, by before-tax income of household, 2008)

	total households	under $20,000	$20,000–$39,999	$40,000–$49,999	$50,000–$69,999	$70,000–$79,999	$80,000–$99,999	$100,000 or more
ENTERTAINMENT, AMOUNT SPENT	$671.81	$303.43	$423.84	$457.80	$533.70	$730.88	$904.13	$1,251.53
Fees and admissions	326.61	153.37	176.33	186.31	185.96	269.98	337.10	585.11
Recreation expenses on trips	78.19	70.70	50.55	55.49	58.23	68.40	68.65	102.93
Social, recreation, civic club membership	240.37	181.00	154.95	177.68	129.56	185.41	189.68	348.80
Fees for participant sports	181.17	122.61	149.83	148.20	136.38	155.28	191.61	236.84
Participant sports on trips	186.18	85.66	129.86	112.66	112.10	108.23	175.35	267.60
Movie, theater, amusement park, and other admissions	99.40	54.98	72.13	70.03	77.04	90.83	107.17	144.85
Movie, other admissions on trips	136.07	101.32	104.38	73.03	90.68	102.97	131.23	178.09
Admission to sports events	174.24	75.56	85.62	97.51	132.22	142.99	232.40	256.32
Admission to sports events on trips	45.36	33.78	34.79	24.33	30.20	34.31	43.75	59.36
Fees for recreational lessons	400.32	249.51	215.83	274.67	235.59	327.37	344.85	547.91
Other entertainment services on trips	78.19	70.70	50.55	55.49	58.23	68.40	68.65	102.93
Audio and visual equipment, services	290.77	189.27	224.84	238.58	254.83	315.56	345.45	424.24
Television sets	1,017.82	666.34	709.22	749.02	914.01	1,088.30	1,096.18	1,290.10
Cable and satellite television services	196.78	162.50	179.59	184.62	192.18	204.23	206.30	232.49
Satellite radio service	117.73	126.06	107.70	103.91	111.36	132.75	114.52	116.08
Online gaming services	52.06	99.43	54.69	43.90	65.43	36.66	32.97	53.52
VCRs and video disc players	164.23	105.01	119.23	124.64	129.67	160.43	202.59	268.39
Video game hardware and software	58.23	49.36	52.15	55.42	54.37	59.65	62.43	62.07
Video cassettes, tapes, and discs	213.45	145.34	164.25	174.85	196.40	227.28	181.53	267.28
Streamed and downloaded video	40.58	37.83	22.14	29.17	31.25	38.54	39.22	46.27
Repair of TV, radio, and sound equipment	185.29	116.44	180.42	154.03	125.00	161.64	198.51	195.42
Rental of television sets	221.43	107.85	142.15	87.50	244.32	208.33	–	287.50
Radios	96.23	56.20	67.41	64.22	50.46	175.00	81.99	162.25
Tape recorders and players	52.78	32.24	51.16	37.50	53.57	29.55	47.06	89.29
Personal digital audio players	192.61	179.90	121.65	129.17	197.32	181.27	236.85	217.21
Sound components and component systems	278.93	151.35	174.39	188.21	273.91	401.42	309.31	325.26
Compact discs, records, and audio tapes	46.57	36.32	40.24	39.56	44.85	39.81	54.85	50.56
Streamed and downloaded audio	41.44	30.98	33.35	31.11	35.69	46.85	43.73	46.09
Rental of VCR, radio, and sound equipment	195.00	–	18.17	25.00	54.17	–	66.67	96.67
Musical instruments and accessories	541.73	194.66	431.50	735.16	187.89	348.33	357.82	1,028.87
Rental and repair of musical instruments	181.52	74.23	77.88	156.67	116.67	90.48	186.29	298.50
Rental of video cassettes, tapes, discs, films	33.92	27.35	31.23	32.48	35.85	32.56	34.58	38.09
Rental of computer and video game hardware, software	83.33	7.79	24.56	54.17	31.25	53.33	212.50	91.67
Accessories and other sound equipment	101.77	75.59	78.03	48.64	106.37	82.46	64.97	136.65
Satellite dishes	132.14	69.72	132.67	139.84	75.00	222.79	96.88	246.30
Installation of television sets	183.93	8.90	183.65	218.18	275.00	–	348.33	222.32
Pets, toys, hobbies, and playground equipment	250.80	151.69	190.16	205.43	224.28	248.52	299.83	347.89
Pets	233.27	142.97	174.43	183.18	207.51	220.18	282.13	319.35
Pet purchase, supplies, and medicines	146.65	103.73	118.49	121.30	143.56	142.45	168.46	182.54
Pet services	160.43	106.31	113.67	121.76	131.94	134.08	151.25	214.89
Veterinarian services	284.95	203.00	241.20	243.95	259.28	268.83	345.86	328.66
Toys, games, hobbies, and tricycles	168.16	123.84	144.38	158.78	166.62	171.81	184.04	205.94
Stamp and coin collecting	137.79	71.48	156.74	145.78	107.35	109.33	100.45	171.04
Playground equipment	316.28	171.76	289.16	454.46	232.50	475.00	351.39	412.66

	total households	under $20,000	$20,000– $39,999	$40,000– $49,999	$50,000– $69,999	$70,000– $79,999	$80,000– $99,999	$100,000 or more
Other entertainment supplies, equipment, services	**$464.72**	**$253.42**	**$442.25**	**$470.74**	**$414.98**	**$401.26**	**$567.44**	**$526.21**
Unmotored recreational vehicles	12,557.89	7,958.77	15,725.55	13,925.00	12,818.75	14,382.00	13,459.52	11,740.00
Motorized recreational vehicles	15,326.25	4,586.48	12,503.63	13,127.78	20,085.42	22,650.00	18,835.26	16,280.00
Rental of recreational vehicles	260.94	395.30	219.64	397.12	173.84	377.68	190.85	265.40
Docking and landing fees	461.43	238.80	631.64	401.14	165.83	507.50	428.33	651.45
Sports, recreation, exercise equipment	251.06	149.09	201.20	184.37	225.61	230.19	292.96	324.08
Athletic gear, game tables, exercise equipment	197.92	99.98	114.48	121.62	134.46	188.28	265.75	258.58
Bicycles	261.95	218.08	317.54	362.23	236.33	128.27	217.88	310.14
Camping equipment	199.74	115.12	171.60	134.46	90.00	291.50	236.60	235.17
Hunting and fishing equipment	253.29	184.18	280.33	175.56	332.35	199.05	230.51	325.94
Winter sports equipment	225.86	203.78	145.75	214.06	106.25	71.67	169.44	313.19
Water sports equipment	197.62	88.42	34.01	75.00	90.57	113.16	316.36	259.76
Other sports equipment	177.69	81.04	121.31	109.80	255.30	182.48	143.93	271.43
Rental and repair of miscellaneous sports equipment	268.52	73.79	151.44	160.71	55.56	229.35	264.29	313.67
Photographic equipment and supplies	116.48	71.66	78.19	70.88	80.01	126.15	108.87	181.79
Film	25.43	18.95	22.65	19.94	22.48	32.85	22.65	37.54
Photo processing	38.95	28.20	29.30	27.29	32.96	50.00	39.97	50.51
Repair and rental of photographic equipment	115.63	43.51	118.64	93.75	89.29	177.08	214.29	176.92
Photographic equipment	260.54	189.82	192.61	166.78	196.85	179.55	245.60	369.40
Photographer fees	198.59	90.27	127.00	145.12	102.72	256.54	139.29	318.23
Live entertainment for catered affairs	555.30	34.67	259.35	125.00	203.26	206.02	536.63	1,011.36
Rental of party supplies for catered affairs	367.98	145.83	92.18	130.56	334.57	234.26	307.62	567.31

Note: "–" means sample is too small to make a reliable estimate.
Source: Calculations by New Strategist based on the Bureau of Labor Statistics' 2008 Consumer Expenditure Survey

Table 2.7 Percent Buying Entertainment by Household Income, <u>Average Week</u>, 2008

(percent of households buying entertainment during the average week, by before-tax income of household, 2008)

	total households	under $20,000	$20,000–$39,999	$40,000–$49,999	$50,000–$69,999	$70,000–$79,999	$80,000–$99,999	$100,000 or more
ENTERTAINMENT, PERCENT BUYING	**39.6%**	**26.3%**	**34.8%**	**38.0%**	**43.1%**	**42.2%**	**49.8%**	**52.8%**
Fees and admissions	**5.1**	**2.0**	**2.9**	**4.7**	**5.7**	**6.0**	**7.3**	**9.8**
Fees for participant sports	3.9	1.5	2.5	4.0	4.6	4.6	4.7	6.8
Fees for recreational lessons	1.5	0.5	0.4	1.0	1.2	1.5	3.0	3.6
Audio and visual equipment and services	**14.5**	**10.4**	**13.0**	**14.9**	**15.6**	**14.6**	**18.1**	**18.0**
Radios	0.2	0.0	0.1	0.5	0.2	0.1	0.3	0.3
Cable and satellite television services	11.9	8.9	11.1	13.0	13.0	11.6	13.9	13.8
Tape recorders and players	0.2	–	0.2	–	0.2	0.3	0.3	0.4
Miscellaneous sound equipment	0.1	0.1	0.1	–	0.2	0.2	–	0.2
Miscellaneous video equipment	0.3	0.1	0.1	0.4	0.3	0.4	0.2	0.6
Sound equipment accessories	0.8	0.6	0.4	0.4	0.7	0.6	1.5	1.4
Video game hardware and software	1.9	0.7	1.5	1.2	2.1	2.1	3.2	3.4
Pets, toys, hobbies, and playground equipment	**27.0**	**16.8**	**23.3**	**25.1**	**29.9**	**29.2**	**36.2**	**36.3**
Pets	20.9	12.9	18.2	20.0	23.3	23.6	27.2	27.6
Pet food	17.7	11.3	15.8	17.1	20.7	18.4	22.7	22.2
Pet purchase, supplies, and medicines	6.0	3.3	5.0	5.8	6.6	9.2	7.6	7.8
Veterinarian services	1.9	0.7	1.7	1.3	1.5	2.1	3.0	3.7
Toys, games, hobbies, and tricycles	9.6	6.0	6.9	8.2	10.3	10.3	14.7	14.7
Playground equipment	0.1	0.0	0.1	0.1	0.0	0.1	0.2	0.1
Other entertainment supplies, equipment, services	**5.6**	**2.2**	**3.7**	**3.6**	**5.7**	**6.6**	**8.8**	**10.9**
Sports, recreation, exercise equipment	4.4	1.8	3.1	2.6	5.0	5.1	7.1	7.9
Athletic gear, game tables, exercise equipment	2.5	0.9	1.7	0.6	3.1	2.4	4.2	5.2
Camping equipment	0.8	0.4	0.5	0.9	0.7	0.7	0.9	1.4
Hunting and fishing equipment	1.3	0.6	1.1	1.0	1.5	2.3	1.9	1.8
Global positioning system devices	0.1	–	0.0	0.3	0.0	–	0.2	0.3
Photographic equipment and supplies	0.8	0.4	0.5	0.5	0.5	0.7	1.1	2.0
Other photographic supplies	0.2	0.2	0.2	0.3	0.2	–	0.2	0.3
Photographer fees	0.6	0.2	0.3	0.3	0.3	0.7	0.9	1.8
Fireworks	0.1	–	0.1	–	0.1	0.2	0.3	0.2
Souvenirs	0.2	0.0	0.2	0.4	0.3	0.3	0.3	0.4
Visual goods	0.1	0.0	0.1	0.1	–	0.2	0.1	0.3
Pinball, electronic video games	0.1	–	0.1	0.1	–	0.2	0.3	0.5

Note: "–" means sample is too small to make a reliable estimate.
Source: Bureau of Labor Statistics, unpublished data from the 2008 Consumer Expenditure Survey

Table 2.8 Amount Buyers Spent on Entertainment by Household Income, <u>Average Week</u>, 2008

(average amount spent by households buying entertainment during the average week, by before-tax income of household, 2008)

	total households	under $20,000	$20,000– $39,999	$40,000– $49,999	$50,000– $69,999	$70,000– $79,999	$80,000– $99,999	$100,000 or more
ENTERTAINMENT, AMOUNT SPENT	**$75.18**	**$47.09**	**$56.11**	**$60.54**	**$73.54**	**$86.15**	**$83.22**	**$108.46**
Fees and admissions	**64.05**	**37.41**	**33.52**	**44.73**	**49.74**	**81.34**	**71.47**	**89.26**
Fees for participant sports	44.94	29.21	30.71	32.92	35.14	51.52	54.47	61.63
Fees for recreational lessons	104.79	57.76	43.54	72.82	101.68	166.22	88.93	125.82
Audio and visual equipment, services	**87.72**	**67.36**	**75.90**	**83.49**	**94.29**	**92.72**	**94.75**	**104.78**
Radios	20.00	2.14	17.65	20.00	11.11	22.22	18.75	23.53
Cable and satellite television services	89.43	71.05	80.45	87.79	93.02	103.03	98.99	101.67
Tape recorders and players	38.89	–	27.97	–	62.50	12.00	57.69	33.33
Miscellaneous sound equipment	18.18	29.63	–	–	11.76	5.56	–	19.05
Miscellaneous video equipment	33.33	11.44	17.01	28.21	14.71	65.71	28.57	52.63
Sound equipment accessories	23.68	23.85	12.66	11.36	16.67	13.79	21.38	32.86
Video game hardware and software	85.94	71.63	56.12	64.10	108.25	57.82	87.42	111.11
Pets, toys, hobbies, and playground equipment	**40.02**	**22.26**	**29.84**	**27.81**	**38.40**	**42.46**	**36.31**	**65.55**
Pets	40.14	21.65	29.18	26.22	39.92	44.48	34.72	67.60
Pet food	17.74	12.62	14.12	15.12	17.06	27.21	16.85	23.58
Pet purchase, supplies, and medicines	21.31	16.90	18.54	18.49	23.22	22.77	20.26	25.55
Veterinarian services	209.47	104.00	127.54	121.37	281.46	162.38	136.00	311.48
Toys, games, hobbies, and tricycles	24.56	16.35	23.58	20.90	20.85	17.42	23.59	34.90
Playground equipment	50.00	4.76	17.32	0.00	33.33	112.50	136.84	21.43
Other entertainment supplies, equipment, services	**54.59**	**41.67**	**47.20**	**43.10**	**47.44**	**83.99**	**67.12**	**54.60**
Sports, recreation, exercise equipment	52.52	45.85	47.39	51.55	49.40	60.24	56.88	54.68
Athletic gear, game tables, exercise equipment	42.86	41.07	21.40	33.33	42.48	77.59	39.86	46.24
Camping equipment	42.67	37.99	43.71	44.83	27.40	35.82	34.09	49.65
Hunting and fishing equipment	48.09	20.45	71.32	32.04	58.28	42.04	83.51	17.78
Global positioning system devices	227.27	–	76.88	160.00	200.00	–	200.00	306.90
Photographic equipment and supplies	79.75	47.20	46.39	26.00	34.78	313.89	157.80	63.24
Other photographic supplies	21.05	12.17	12.31	16.00	5.88	–	26.67	46.15
Photographer fees	96.72	44.01	57.16	40.00	51.72	313.89	180.65	66.29
Fireworks	27.27	–	3.84	–	9.09	50.00	37.50	31.58
Souvenirs	21.74	5.12	19.81	12.82	25.93	36.67	8.00	22.86
Visual goods	22.22	4.32	3.55	7.69	–	5.26	0.00	28.00
Pinball, electronic video games	21.43	–	16.49	0.00	–	18.75	12.00	23.40

Note: "–" means sample is too small to make a reliable estimate.
Source: Calculations by New Strategist based on the Bureau of Labor Statistics' 2008 Consumer Expenditure Survey

Table 2.9 Percent of High-Income Households Buying Entertainment, <u>Average Quarter</u>, 2008

(percent of high-income households buying entertainment during the average quarter, by before-tax income of household, 2008)

	total households	$100,000 or more	$100,000–$119,999	$120,000–$149,999	$150,000 or more
ENTERTAINMENT, PERCENT BUYING	**91.1%**	**98.6%**	**97.9%**	**99.2%**	**98.9%**
Fees and admissions	**46.5**	**74.6**	**68.8**	**73.0**	**80.3**
Recreation expenses on trips	7.5	16.0	13.3	15.6	18.4
Social, recreation, civic club membership	13.3	28.9	23.8	27.4	34.0
Fees for participant sports	11.2	21.2	20.0	19.4	23.3
Participant sports on trips	3.7	9.0	7.5	8.0	10.9
Movie, theater, amusement park, and other admissions	29.8	49.0	44.6	49.8	52.1
Movie, other admissions on trips	8.2	17.3	13.9	16.2	20.9
Admission to sports events	6.6	12.7	10.2	12.5	14.9
Admission to sports events on trips	8.2	17.3	13.9	16.2	20.9
Fees for recreational lessons	6.2	15.3	13.3	14.3	17.6
Other entertainment services on trips	7.5	16.0	13.3	15.6	18.4
Audio and visual equipment and services	**84.5**	**95.2**	**94.3**	**96.1**	**95.4**
Television sets	4.0	6.1	5.5	6.6	6.2
Cable and satellite television services	74.1	87.8	87.2	88.4	87.9
Satellite radio service	3.1	6.0	6.3	4.9	6.5
Online gaming services	1.0	1.4	1.7	1.2	1.3
VCRs and video disc players	1.9	2.3	2.2	1.7	2.7
Video game hardware and software	14.7	20.8	20.3	21.5	20.7
Video cassettes, tapes, and discs	5.4	9.0	9.1	9.3	8.8
Streamed and downloaded video	0.7	1.6	1.2	1.3	2.2
Repair of TV, radio, and sound equipment	0.5	0.7	0.8	0.8	0.6
Rental of television sets	0.1	0.0	0.1	–	–
Radios	0.7	1.0	0.5	0.9	1.5
Tape recorders and players	0.1	0.1	0.1	0.0	0.1
Personal digital audio players	1.8	3.4	3.1	3.3	3.7
Sound components and component systems	0.7	1.0	0.5	1.1	1.3
Compact discs, records, and audio tapes	12.2	18.5	16.2	22.0	17.9
Streamed and downloaded audio	3.3	7.8	6.8	6.7	9.3
Rental of VCR, radio, and sound equipment	0.1	0.2	0.2	0.1	0.1
Musical instruments and accessories	1.4	2.5	2.0	2.4	3.0
Rental and repair of musical instruments	0.2	0.5	0.5	0.5	0.5
Rental of video cassettes, tapes, discs, films	20.1	30.1	30.9	29.6	29.7
Rental of computer and video game hardware and software	0.1	0.1	0.1	0.1	0.1
Accessories and other sound equipment	1.3	1.8	1.3	2.7	1.6
Satellite dishes	0.3	0.3	0.1	0.5	0.3
Installation of television sets	0.1	0.3	0.2	0.2	0.4
Pets, toys, hobbies, and playground equipment	**43.7**	**59.1**	**57.3**	**60.1**	**59.9**
Pets	33.3	46.7	45.4	47.2	47.4
Pet purchase, supplies, and medicines	28.0	37.3	37.1	37.7	37.3
Pet services	5.7	11.6	9.0	11.1	14.1
Veterinarian services	9.7	17.1	15.7	16.7	18.5
Toys, games, hobbies, and tricycles	17.4	25.1	23.3	24.7	26.8
Stamp and coin collecting	0.9	1.0	1.3	1.0	0.8
Playground equipment	0.4	0.8	0.3	1.4	0.8

	total households	$100,000 or more	$100,000–$119,999	$120,000–$149,999	$150,000 or more
Other entertainment supplies, equipment, services	**22.5%**	**35.9%**	**34.9%**	**35.7%**	**36.8%**
Unmotored recreational vehicles	0.2	0.2	0.1	0.3	0.1
Motorized recreational vehicles	0.2	0.3	0.2	0.3	0.3
Rental of recreational vehicles	0.5	1.3	1.0	1.5	1.4
Docking and landing fees	0.4	0.7	0.2	0.6	1.1
Sports, recreation, exercise equipment	10.6	18.7	16.7	19.4	19.9
Athletic gear, game tables, exercise equipment	6.1	12.0	10.3	11.9	13.5
Bicycles	1.4	2.1	1.3	2.1	2.6
Camping equipment	1.0	1.5	1.4	1.9	1.2
Hunting and fishing equipment	2.1	2.9	2.8	3.4	2.8
Winter sports equipment	0.3	0.7	0.6	0.9	0.7
Water sports equipment	0.4	0.8	0.5	1.3	0.7
Other sports equipment	0.9	1.4	2.1	1.0	1.1
Rental and repair of miscellaneous sports equipment	0.3	0.6	0.5	0.6	0.8
Photographic equipment and supplies	14.0	22.2	23.5	22.0	21.3
Film	2.9	3.2	3.9	2.8	2.8
Photo processing	8.9	14.4	14.9	14.0	14.2
Repair and rental of photographic equipment	0.2	0.1	0.1	0.2	0.1
Photographic equipment	2.7	4.6	4.6	5.1	4.4
Photographer fees	2.5	4.6	5.1	4.5	4.3
Live entertainment for catered affairs	0.3	0.7	0.6	0.5	0.9
Rental of party supplies for catered affairs	0.6	1.2	1.1	1.0	1.3

Note: "–" means sample is too small to make a reliable estimate.
Source: Bureau of Labor Statistics, unpublished data from the 2008 Consumer Expenditure Survey

Table 2.10 Amount High-Income Buyers Spent on Entertainment, <u>Average Quarter</u>, 2008

(average amount spent by high-income households buying entertainment during the average quarter, by before-tax income of household, 2008)

	total households	$100,000 or more	$100,000– $119,999	$120,000– $149,999	$150,000 or more
ENTERTAINMENT, AMOUNT SPENT	**$671.81**	**$1,251.53**	**$922.86**	**$1,176.52**	**$1,568.34**
Fees and admissions	**326.61**	**585.11**	**410.34**	**460.89**	**782.89**
Recreation expenses on trips	78.19	102.93	69.08	74.34	139.02
Social, recreation, civic club membership	240.37	348.80	248.52	242.83	462.90
Fees for participant sports	181.17	236.84	196.98	212.79	278.05
Participant sports on trips	186.18	267.60	183.96	194.54	350.25
Movie, theater, amusement park, and other admissions	99.40	144.85	112.23	132.91	175.34
Movie, other admissions on trips	136.07	178.09	133.25	154.02	214.93
Admission to sports events	174.24	256.32	165.05	256.45	307.50
Admission to sports events on trips	45.36	59.36	44.42	51.31	71.63
Fees for recreational lessons	400.32	547.91	451.73	409.39	682.55
Other entertainment services on trips	78.19	102.93	69.08	74.34	139.02
Audio and visual equipment and services	**290.77**	**424.24**	**361.81**	**445.71**	**460.47**
Television sets	1,017.82	1,290.10	1,237.64	1,262.48	1,346.11
Cable and satellite television services	196.78	232.49	216.49	223.58	251.47
Satellite radio service	117.73	116.08	108.37	98.82	130.83
Online gaming services	52.06	53.52	46.95	47.65	64.29
VCRs and video disc players	164.23	268.39	259.40	219.91	294.56
Video game hardware and software	58.23	62.07	56.67	62.69	66.00
Video cassettes, tapes, and discs	213.45	267.28	209.72	232.15	340.23
Streamed and downloaded video	40.58	46.27	44.70	44.20	47.95
Repair of TV, radio, and sound equipment	185.29	195.42	154.75	169.33	253.57
Rental of television sets	221.43	287.50	350.00	–	–
Radios	96.23	162.25	100.00	78.49	210.71
Tape recorders and players	52.78	89.29	47.92	125.00	120.83
Personal digital audio players	192.61	217.21	228.56	184.95	227.61
Sound components and component systems	278.93	325.26	423.96	319.68	298.08
Compact discs, records, and audio tapes	46.57	50.56	43.72	44.13	60.88
Streamed and downloaded audio	41.44	46.09	40.36	40.51	52.22
Rental of VCR, radio, and sound equipment	195.00	96.67	41.67	165.91	117.86
Musical instruments and accessories	541.73	1,028.87	221.28	2,517.28	666.37
Rental and repair of musical instruments	181.52	298.50	67.93	111.00	581.60
Rental of video cassettes, tapes, discs, films	33.92	38.09	37.49	37.45	39.00
Rental of computer and video game hardware and software	83.33	91.67	75.00	72.22	120.45
Accessories and other sound equipment	101.77	136.65	128.40	119.03	162.82
Satellite dishes	132.14	246.30	145.00	353.85	132.14
Installation of television sets	183.93	222.32	175.00	162.50	268.42
Pets, toys, hobbies, playground equipment	**250.80**	**347.89**	**297.34**	**317.19**	**407.97**
Pets	233.27	319.35	273.46	281.93	380.06
Pet purchase, supplies, and medicines	146.65	182.54	179.18	171.04	193.01
Pet services	160.43	214.89	143.58	160.49	280.69
Veterinarian services	284.95	328.66	285.62	305.01	373.10
Toys, games, hobbies, and tricycles	168.16	205.94	190.22	210.78	214.22
Stamp and coin collecting	137.79	171.04	69.78	185.35	307.33
Playground equipment	316.28	412.66	442.86	258.52	577.22

	total households	$100,000 or more	$100,000–$119,999	$120,000–$149,999	$150,000 or more
Other entertainment supplies, equipment, services	**$464.72**	**$526.21**	**$315.28**	**$592.69**	**$647.37**
Unmotored recreational vehicles	12,557.89	11,740.00	1,165.63	15,670.00	11,770.00
Motorized recreational vehicles	15,326.25	16,280.00	5,878.26	15,662.50	22,022.06
Rental of recreational vehicles	260.94	265.40	249.74	265.34	273.89
Docking and landing fees	461.43	651.45	1,368.48	243.33	673.89
Sports, recreation, exercise equipment	251.06	324.08	270.84	291.39	381.92
Athletic gear, game tables, exercise equipment	197.92	258.58	210.20	231.51	304.68
Bicycles	261.95	310.14	339.47	184.67	365.34
Camping equipment	199.74	235.17	114.05	275.00	306.50
Hunting and fishing equipment	253.29	325.94	273.14	338.51	360.78
Winter sports equipment	225.86	313.19	324.21	260.00	354.10
Water sports equipment	197.62	259.76	152.45	175.00	430.21
Other sports equipment	177.69	271.43	308.77	204.00	258.26
Rental and repair of miscellaneous sports equipment	268.52	313.67	102.94	306.67	427.56
Photographic equipment and supplies	116.48	181.79	139.92	168.17	229.09
Film	25.43	37.54	42.56	38.36	31.27
Photo processing	38.95	50.51	39.10	54.09	58.00
Repair and rental of photographic equipment	115.63	176.92	210.42	203.75	105.56
Photographic equipment	260.54	369.40	247.57	372.85	471.84
Photographer fees	198.59	318.23	269.17	200.62	447.89
Live entertainment for catered affairs	555.30	1,011.36	1,010.27	1,163.30	966.28
Rental of party supplies for catered affairs	367.98	567.31	546.85	677.48	528.03

Note: "–" means sample is too small to make a reliable estimate.
Source: Calculations by New Strategist based on the Bureau of Labor Statistics' 2008 Consumer Expenditure Survey

Table 2.11 Percent of High-Income Households Buying Entertainment, Average Week, 2008

(percent of high-income households buying entertainment during the average week, by before-tax income of household, 2008)

	total households	$100,000 or more	$100,000– $119,999	$120,000– $149,999	$150,000 or more
ENTERTAINMENT, PERCENT BUYING	**39.6%**	**52.8%**	**49.5%**	**54.0%**	**55.4%**
Fees and admissions	**5.1**	**9.8**	**7.4**	**9.4**	**12.5**
Fees for participant sports	3.9	6.8	5.0	6.8	8.6
Fees for recreational lessons	1.5	3.6	2.7	3.1	5.0
Audio and visual equipment and services	**14.5**	**18.0**	**18.2**	**19.9**	**16.2**
Radios	0.2	0.3	0.5	0.1	0.4
Cable and satellite television services	11.9	13.8	14.2	15.2	12.3
Tape recorders and players	0.2	0.4	0.3	0.5	0.4
Miscellaneous sound equipment	0.1	0.2	0.1	0.1	0.4
Miscellaneous video equipment	0.3	0.6	0.5	0.9	0.4
Sound equipment accessories	0.8	1.4	1.2	1.2	1.8
Video game hardware and software	1.9	3.4	3.7	4.2	2.5
Pets, toys, hobbies, and playground equipment	**27.0**	**36.3**	**33.8**	**36.8**	**38.4**
Pets	20.9	27.6	25.9	26.6	30.0
Pet food	17.7	22.2	20.7	21.3	24.5
Pet purchase, supplies, and medicines	6.0	7.8	8.0	8.3	7.1
Veterinarian services	1.9	3.7	3.2	3.4	4.3
Toys, games, hobbies, and tricycles	9.6	14.7	14.2	15.1	14.9
Playground equipment	0.1	0.1	0.3	–	0.1
Other entertainment supplies, equipment, services	**5.6**	**10.9**	**10.2**	**10.1**	**12.1**
Sports, recreation, exercise equipment	4.4	7.9	7.6	7.1	8.9
Athletic gear, game tables, exercise equipment	2.5	5.2	4.6	3.8	6.9
Camping equipment	0.8	1.4	1.8	1.5	1.0
Hunting and fishing equipment	1.3	1.8	1.7	2.0	1.7
Global positioning system devices	0.1	0.3	0.3	0.2	0.4
Photographic equipment and supplies	0.8	2.0	1.9	2.6	1.8
Other photographic supplies	0.2	0.3	–	0.5	0.4
Photographer fees	0.6	1.8	1.9	2.1	1.4
Fireworks	0.1	0.2	–	0.2	0.4
Souvenirs	0.2	0.4	0.3	0.3	0.4
Visual goods	0.1	0.3	0.4	–	0.3
Pinball, electronic video games	0.1	0.5	0.4	0.5	0.5

Note: "–" means sample is too small to make a reliable estimate.
Source: Bureau of Labor Statistics, unpublished data from the 2008 Consumer Expenditure Survey

Table 2.12 Amount High-Income Buyers Spent on Entertainment, Average Week, 2008

(average amount spent by high-income households buying entertainment during the average week, by before-tax income of household, 2008)

	total households	$100,000 or more	$100,000– $119,999	$120,000– $149,999	$150,000 or more
ENTERTAINMENT, AMOUNT SPENT	**$75.18**	**$108.46**	**$96.10**	**$130.12**	**$103.36**
Fees and admissions	**64.05**	**89.26**	**86.18**	**72.66**	**101.04**
Fees for participant sports	44.94	61.63	54.14	56.78	68.92
Fees for recreational lessons	104.79	125.82	135.29	95.82	134.73
Audio and visual equipment and services	**87.72**	**104.78**	**104.50**	**103.16**	**106.72**
Radios	20.00	23.53	22.92	33.33	25.00
Cable and satellite television services	89.43	101.67	100.21	102.83	102.37
Tape recorders and players	38.89	33.33	38.71	32.65	28.21
Miscellaneous sound equipment	18.18	19.05	7.69	9.09	28.21
Miscellaneous video equipment	33.33	52.63	8.51	60.44	92.50
Sound equipment accessories	23.68	32.86	17.39	36.59	42.46
Video game hardware and software	85.94	111.11	116.71	89.40	131.10
Pets, toys, hobbies, playground equipment	**40.02**	**65.55**	**44.87**	**102.83**	**56.41**
Pets	40.14	67.60	37.53	118.82	58.89
Pet food	17.74	23.58	20.40	23.40	26.42
Pet purchase, supplies, and medicines	21.31	25.55	16.17	22.45	39.33
Veterinarian services	209.47	311.48	130.43	739.40	193.78
Toys, games, hobbies, and tricycles	24.56	34.90	38.06	41.27	26.80
Playground equipment	50.00	21.43	25.00	–	0.00
Other entertainment supplies, equipment, services	**54.59**	**54.60**	**68.36**	**49.31**	**46.12**
Sports, recreation, exercise equipment	52.52	54.68	72.35	40.14	48.09
Athletic gear, game tables, exercise equipment	42.86	46.24	74.84	34.29	31.53
Camping equipment	42.67	49.65	33.71	67.35	59.22
Hunting and fishing equipment	48.09	17.78	16.67	15.92	20.71
Global positioning system devices	227.27	306.90	367.74	140.00	313.51
Photographic equipment and supplies	79.75	63.24	75.81	75.86	36.16
Other photographic supplies	21.05	46.15	–	66.67	22.22
Photographer fees	96.72	66.29	75.81	77.93	39.72
Fireworks	27.27	31.58	–	45.00	26.32
Souvenirs	21.74	22.86	6.67	6.25	45.24
Visual goods	22.22	28.00	11.43	–	51.52
Pinball, electronic video games	21.43	23.40	15.00	14.81	39.58

Note: "–" means sample is too small to make a reliable estimate.
Source: Calculations by New Strategist based on the Bureau of Labor Statistics' 2008 Consumer Expenditure Survey

Table 2.13 Percent Buying Entertainment by Household Type, Average Quarter, 2008

(percent of households buying entertainment during the average quarter, by type of household, 2008)

	total married couples	married couples, no children	married couples with children				single parent, at least one child <18	single person
			total	oldest child under 6	oldest child 6 to 17	oldest child 18 or older		
ENTERTAINMENT, PERCENT BUYING	**94.8%**	**94.2%**	**95.4%**	**94.0%**	**95.8%**	**95.5%**	**89.0%**	**85.1%**
Fees and admissions	**53.5**	**48.6**	**59.5**	**52.7**	**65.3**	**53.8**	**44.4**	**38.3**
Recreation expenses on trips	9.7	9.6	10.3	7.9	11.9	8.8	6.5	5.1
Social, recreation, civic club membership	16.6	16.0	18.1	17.8	19.2	16.2	9.0	10.0
Fees for participant sports	14.1	12.1	16.7	13.3	21.4	10.8	8.1	8.5
Participant sports on trips	4.9	4.8	5.1	4.1	5.9	4.4	3.3	2.4
Movie, theater, amusement park, and other admissions	33.6	28.4	39.3	33.1	43.1	36.6	30.4	24.3
Movie, other admissions on trips	10.4	10.1	11.0	10.0	12.4	9.1	6.6	5.9
Admission to sports events	8.0	6.5	9.6	5.8	11.3	9.0	5.3	5.1
Admission to sports events on trips	10.4	10.1	11.0	10.0	12.4	9.1	6.6	5.9
Fees for recreational lessons	9.1	2.8	15.1	10.5	21.6	6.6	9.2	2.1
Other entertainment services on trips	9.7	9.6	10.3	7.9	11.9	8.8	6.5	5.1
Audio and visual equipment, services	**89.8**	**89.1**	**90.7**	**88.5**	**91.5**	**90.5**	**81.4**	**75.9**
Television sets	4.9	4.6	5.2	3.9	5.6	5.5	3.8	2.6
Cable and satellite television services	81.2	82.5	80.2	74.5	80.6	83.1	67.9	64.0
Satellite radio service	4.2	4.1	4.6	5.8	5.0	3.2	1.6	1.7
Online gaming services	1.2	0.8	1.5	1.6	1.6	1.3	0.9	0.6
VCRs and video disc players	2.1	1.5	2.6	4.3	2.3	2.3	1.5	1.4
Video game hardware and software	16.7	12.4	20.8	24.3	21.9	16.9	14.7	10.4
Video cassettes, tapes, and discs	6.6	2.8	10.1	7.1	13.1	6.6	8.6	2.4
Streamed and downloaded video	0.7	0.5	1.0	0.9	1.0	0.9	0.6	0.6
Repair of TV, radio, and sound equipment	0.7	0.7	0.6	0.8	0.7	0.5	0.3	0.4
Rental of television sets	0.1	0.1	0.1	0.1	0.1	–	0.1	0.0
Radios	0.8	0.9	0.9	0.8	0.9	0.7	0.6	0.7
Tape recorders and players	0.1	0.1	0.1	–	0.1	0.1	0.1	0.1
Personal digital audio players	2.3	1.3	3.1	1.9	4.0	2.5	1.6	0.9
Sound components and component systems	0.8	0.6	0.9	0.8	1.0	0.9	0.7	0.5
Compact discs, records, and audio tapes	13.5	11.8	15.2	12.9	15.5	16.2	12.3	9.3
Streamed and downloaded audio	4.0	2.7	5.3	5.6	6.2	3.6	2.5	2.4
Rental of VCR, radio, and sound equipment	0.1	0.1	0.1	–	0.0	0.2	–	0.0
Musical instruments and accessories	1.7	1.0	2.4	1.4	3.1	1.7	1.6	0.9
Rental and repair of musical instruments	0.4	0.1	0.6	0.3	1.0	0.1	0.2	0.0
Rental of video cassettes, tapes, discs, films	23.6	17.1	30.3	32.0	32.8	25.0	24.4	12.9
Rental of computer and video game hardware, software	0.1	0.1	0.1	–	0.1	0.1	–	0.0
Accessories and other sound equipment	1.4	1.1	1.7	2.2	1.6	1.6	0.5	1.1
Satellite dishes	0.3	0.4	0.3	0.4	0.2	0.3	0.1	0.2
Installation of television sets	0.2	0.2	0.2	0.3	0.2	0.2	0.1	0.1
Pets, toys, hobbies, and playground equipment	**53.1**	**47.1**	**58.9**	**64.3**	**60.3**	**53.3**	**42.2**	**27.8**
Pets	40.6	38.8	42.7	34.2	44.3	45.1	27.1	21.8
Pet purchase, supplies, and medicines	33.5	31.3	35.5	28.3	37.1	37.2	23.5	18.7
Pet services	7.7	8.1	7.6	5.6	8.0	8.1	2.9	3.5
Veterinarian services	12.8	13.3	12.7	9.8	13.1	13.9	6.0	5.4
Toys, games, hobbies, and tricycles	22.9	14.4	30.5	49.0	32.2	16.6	21.3	8.0
Stamp and coin collecting	1.1	1.5	0.8	0.4	0.7	1.4	0.7	0.7
Playground equipment	0.6	0.3	1.0	2.3	0.8	0.5	0.3	0.1

	total married couples	married couples, no children	married couples with children				single parent, at least one child <18	single person
			total	oldest child under 6	oldest child 6 to 17	oldest child 18 or older		
Other entertainment supplies, equipment, services	**29.0%**	**23.7%**	**34.6%**	**39.0%**	**37.7%**	**26.6%**	**22.3%**	**13.5%**
Unmotored recreational vehicles	0.3	0.4	0.3	0.4	0.4	0.1	–	0.0
Motorized recreational vehicles	0.3	0.3	0.3	0.4	0.4	0.3	0.1	0.1
Rental of recreational vehicles	0.6	0.7	0.6	0.6	0.5	0.8	0.3	0.3
Docking and landing fees	0.5	0.6	0.5	0.5	0.5	0.5	0.2	0.1
Sports, recreation, exercise equipment	13.6	9.7	17.8	16.3	22.0	11.3	10.7	6.8
Athletic gear, game tables, exercise equipment	7.8	4.8	10.8	6.7	14.5	6.7	6.9	3.8
Bicycles	1.7	0.8	2.6	3.1	3.1	1.4	1.7	0.9
Camping equipment	1.2	1.0	1.4	1.3	1.7	0.9	1.0	0.6
Hunting and fishing equipment	2.9	2.8	3.3	4.3	3.1	3.0	1.2	1.2
Winter sports equipment	0.4	0.2	0.7	0.7	0.9	0.3	0.1	0.2
Water sports equipment	0.7	0.4	0.9	1.6	0.8	0.5	0.3	0.2
Other sports equipment	1.1	0.8	1.4	1.4	1.7	0.9	1.1	0.6
Rental and repair of miscellaneous sports equipment	0.4	0.3	0.5	0.6	0.6	0.3	0.0	0.2
Photographic equipment and supplies	18.8	15.1	22.6	28.7	23.0	18.5	13.1	7.1
Film	3.8	4.0	3.4	4.3	3.4	3.0	2.8	2.0
Photo processing	12.1	10.4	14.3	19.8	13.6	12.2	6.6	4.5
Repair and rental of photographic equipment	0.2	0.3	0.2	0.1	0.3	0.2	–	0.1
Photographic equipment	3.4	2.7	4.1	4.5	4.0	3.9	2.6	1.6
Photographer fees	3.8	1.2	5.9	8.0	6.7	3.3	3.5	0.3
Live entertainment for catered affairs	0.5	0.5	0.5	0.6	0.5	0.4	0.1	0.2
Rental of party supplies for catered affairs	0.7	0.5	0.9	0.8	1.0	0.8	0.8	0.2

Note: "–" means sample is too small to make a reliable estimate.
Source: Bureau of Labor Statistics, unpublished data from the 2008 Consumer Expenditure Survey

Table 2.14 Amount Buyers Spent on Entertainment by Household Type, <u>Average Quarter</u>, 2008

(average amount spent by households buying entertainment during the average quarter, by type of household, 2008)

	total married couples	married couples, no children	married couples with children				single parent, at least one child <18	single person
			total	oldest child under 6	oldest child 6 to 17	oldest child 18 or older		
ENTERTAINMENT, AMOUNT SPENT	$864.89	$794.37	$956.37	$832.57	$1,079.71	$815.82	$483.33	$407.28
Fees and admissions	403.20	357.05	445.67	314.89	498.58	411.19	245.86	209.24
Recreation expenses on trips	85.50	84.65	86.70	69.38	80.49	110.57	60.72	66.29
Social, recreation, civic club membership	274.85	261.80	295.54	239.81	260.97	402.31	158.01	197.82
Fees for participant sports	196.67	228.58	176.06	112.64	184.96	192.15	147.89	157.94
Participant sports on trips	221.09	215.90	226.36	295.84	221.10	200.74	112.65	102.92
Movie, theater, amusement park, other admissions	110.28	115.72	107.26	89.54	114.50	102.07	82.36	81.66
Movie, other admissions on trips	150.70	145.71	158.01	112.99	158.05	187.04	110.84	96.75
Admission to sports events	209.25	277.75	172.67	126.12	178.42	177.68	72.86	119.35
Admission to sports events on trips	50.22	48.56	52.65	37.66	52.67	62.31	36.95	32.25
Fees for recreational lessons	441.16	250.36	471.11	314.72	498.87	462.41	358.79	201.07
Other entertainment services on trips	85.50	84.65	86.70	69.38	80.49	110.57	60.72	66.29
Audio and visual equipment, services	328.43	306.34	348.67	309.78	362.86	346.63	256.73	215.66
Television sets	1,144.10	1,159.26	1,150.38	1,188.77	1,147.57	1,138.36	819.05	793.58
Cable and satellite television services	207.45	206.18	207.76	199.06	205.19	216.70	187.85	174.09
Satellite radio service	122.58	120.15	124.95	109.47	121.97	149.76	85.58	112.06
Online gaming services	47.41	43.99	50.84	46.79	51.25	53.17	46.63	59.38
VCRs and video disc players	186.54	189.66	193.44	200.47	197.92	179.22	81.86	141.73
Video game hardware and software	58.10	56.95	58.95	56.58	54.06	71.87	48.64	56.10
Video cassettes, tapes, and discs	229.22	246.65	217.57	156.49	234.53	198.71	206.87	156.54
Streamed and downloaded video	39.04	40.22	36.20	32.18	34.41	42.61	43.22	38.33
Repair of TV, radio, and sound equipment	198.85	201.10	189.45	269.21	112.87	295.74	116.67	139.29
Rental of television sets	179.17	158.33	189.29	127.27	230.56	–	371.43	183.33
Radios	116.77	110.92	120.88	119.23	142.20	78.04	57.92	69.20
Tape recorders and players	65.63	56.25	84.38	–	52.27	156.25	82.14	43.75
Personal digital audio players	205.35	187.97	213.54	192.16	208.78	234.56	147.07	192.15
Sound components and component systems	303.80	215.35	310.90	293.21	266.09	410.39	119.59	324.04
Compact discs, records, and audio tapes	44.30	45.95	43.57	35.25	43.62	47.38	38.63	48.51
Streamed and downloaded audio	41.94	34.64	42.61	47.08	41.20	42.98	48.51	33.71
Rental of VCR, radio, and sound equipment	231.25	271.15	104.17	–	62.50	125.00	–	12.50
Musical instruments and accessories	437.35	730.26	316.67	648.73	294.55	223.95	210.00	338.06
Rental and repair of musical instruments	114.58	134.09	112.50	66.67	117.23	117.50	21.88	91.67
Rental of video cassettes, tapes, discs, films	34.78	32.57	35.65	31.10	37.74	34.40	31.53	29.65
Rental of computer and video game hardware, software	107.14	135.71	79.17	–	87.50	62.50	–	50.00
Accessories and other sound equipment	113.83	92.95	120.32	130.41	130.71	92.83	123.58	82.52
Satellite dishes	150.00	121.25	136.11	89.86	229.76	64.17	187.50	67.05
Installation of television sets	186.84	160.29	214.29	285.00	171.59	264.06	25.00	217.86
Pets, toys, hobbies, and playground equipment	276.33	289.32	271.69	249.13	283.24	265.38	181.62	212.35
Pets	250.62	280.47	232.00	211.02	225.82	251.93	164.17	213.97
Pet purchase, supplies, and medicines	159.25	170.75	151.28	137.37	142.19	173.13	109.81	126.10
Pet services	144.65	167.07	131.07	100.63	129.13	146.77	118.38	227.83
Veterinarian services	293.00	315.14	278.38	282.23	282.46	269.97	253.95	283.79
Toys, games, hobbies, and tricycles	180.61	173.38	184.14	161.43	206.48	149.21	147.52	137.67
Stamp and coin collecting	130.23	113.76	166.57	35.63	163.46	189.36	54.79	183.21
Playground equipment	355.08	301.61	346.94	391.63	386.75	86.67	134.68	107.50

	total married couples	married couples, no children	married couples with children				single parent, at least one child <18	single person
			total	oldest child under 6	oldest child 6 to 17	oldest child 18 or older		
Other entertainment supplies, equipment, services	**$560.60**	**$700.13**	**$494.15**	**$467.89**	**$546.77**	**$388.09**	**$157.06**	**$324.81**
Unmotored recreational vehicles	13,279.69	14,888.51	12,570.54	9,198.26	15,132.86	2,835.71	–	27,800.00
Motorized recreational vehicles	16,639.17	17,080.00	16,868.75	18,000.00	18,399.29	10,961.11	1,990.00	14,066.67
Rental of recreational vehicles	294.44	255.63	334.43	440.08	294.23	326.32	165.32	209.85
Docking and landing fees	460.19	520.90	336.70	67.93	309.24	544.27	680.88	681.25
Sports, recreation, exercise equipment	260.12	296.76	241.89	249.98	232.56	266.62	187.00	252.10
Athletic gear, game tables, exercise equipment	211.42	243.59	195.78	195.13	186.19	231.65	162.81	170.14
Bicycles	247.53	391.57	212.16	347.41	163.52	216.31	207.25	389.71
Camping equipment	171.57	161.54	187.50	136.60	230.21	87.92	139.90	197.08
Hunting and fishing equipment	237.41	261.97	214.57	219.67	220.51	201.59	184.62	376.01
Winter sports equipment	236.59	258.33	228.36	48.48	291.48	117.59	146.43	189.71
Water sports equipment	207.69	212.50	212.64	95.50	189.88	505.10	38.89	266.67
Other sports equipment	196.40	281.55	147.99	124.13	155.30	147.94	137.26	87.89
Rental and repair of miscellaneous sports equipment	308.97	397.22	287.75	363.39	277.46	232.03	12.50	118.75
Photographic equipment and supplies	123.57	122.95	125.76	100.03	124.14	152.97	83.55	91.78
Film	26.80	23.76	30.01	37.62	25.88	31.84	19.57	22.21
Photo processing	41.38	37.30	44.56	41.79	46.71	43.07	34.25	29.37
Repair and rental of photographic equipment	120.45	102.00	136.90	295.00	161.00	41.25	–	111.54
Photographic equipment	268.31	324.36	237.25	192.48	260.80	227.81	214.29	241.98
Photographer fees	208.84	375.00	189.11	123.69	155.92	402.85	73.56	214.39
Live entertainment for catered affairs	726.09	780.21	665.69	283.20	610.78	1,105.68	357.14	69.44
Rental of party supplies for catered affairs	409.72	530.56	342.70	326.67	319.95	395.68	154.55	191.67

Note: "–" means sample is too small to make a reliable estimate.
Source: Calculations by New Strategist based on the Bureau of Labor Statistics' 2008 Consumer Expenditure Survey

Table 2.15 Percent Buying Entertainment by Household Type, <u>Average Week</u>, 2008

(percent of households buying entertainment during the average week, by type of household, 2008)

	total married couples	married couples, no children	married couples with children				single parent, at least one child <18	single person
			total	oldest child under 6	oldest child 6 to 17	oldest child 18 or older		
ENTERTAINMENT, PERCENT BUYING	**46.8%**	**44.1%**	**49.2%**	**43.6%**	**51.4%**	**49.0%**	**35.3%**	**29.7%**
Fees and admissions	**6.9**	**5.6**	**8.5**	**4.8**	**10.0**	**8.2**	**3.2**	**3.3**
Fees for participant sports	5.0	4.7	5.6	3.5	5.8	6.5	2.7	2.8
Fees for recreational lessons	2.2	1.1	3.4	1.6	5.0	1.9	0.6	0.6
Audio and visual equipment, services	**16.2**	**15.1**	**17.1**	**16.2**	**17.6**	**16.6**	**14.3**	**12.0**
Radios	0.2	0.2	0.3	0.1	0.4	0.2	0.2	0.1
Cable and satellite television services	13.1	13.5	12.6	13.1	12.5	12.3	9.9	10.7
Tape recorders and players	0.2	0.2	0.3	0.6	0.3	0.1	0.5	0.1
Miscellaneous sound equipment	0.1	0.2	0.1	0.4	0.1	–	0.3	0.0
Miscellaneous video equipment	0.3	0.2	0.4	0.3	0.4	0.3	0.1	0.3
Sound equipment accessories	0.9	0.5	1.2	0.8	1.1	1.7	1.7	0.3
Video game hardware and software	2.4	1.1	3.9	2.5	4.7	3.3	2.5	0.9
Pets, toys, hobbies, and playground equipment	**33.3**	**31.1**	**35.2**	**31.7**	**37.4**	**33.6**	**23.0**	**17.8**
Pets	25.4	26.0	24.7	17.4	25.6	27.7	16.0	14.8
Pet food	21.5	22.6	20.6	14.9	20.8	23.7	13.3	12.5
Pet purchase, supplies, and medicines	6.7	6.8	6.6	3.9	7.6	6.5	5.5	4.8
Veterinarian services	2.4	2.9	2.1	1.5	2.0	2.5	0.8	1.3
Toys, games, hobbies, and tricycles	13.1	7.7	17.7	21.8	20.3	10.5	10.1	4.3
Playground equipment	0.1	0.1	0.1	0.1	0.2	–	0.3	–
Other entertainment supplies, equipment, services	**7.6**	**5.3**	**9.9**	**9.0**	**10.4**	**9.5**	**5.5**	**2.6**
Sports, recreation, exercise equipment	5.9	4.3	7.5	6.5	7.8	7.6	4.0	2.2
Athletic gear, game tables, exercise equipment	3.4	2.3	4.6	3.6	5.2	4.4	2.5	1.2
Camping equipment	1.0	0.6	1.4	1.9	1.5	0.9	1.1	0.2
Hunting and fishing equipment	1.8	1.6	1.8	1.8	1.4	2.7	0.6	0.9
Global positioning system devices	0.2	0.2	0.2	–	0.2	0.3	–	0.0
Photographic equipment and supplies	1.2	0.6	1.7	1.5	2.0	1.2	1.2	0.2
Other photographic supplies	0.3	0.2	0.2	–	0.4	0.1	0.4	0.1
Photographer fees	0.9	0.4	1.4	1.5	1.6	1.1	0.8	0.2
Fireworks	0.2	0.1	0.2	–	0.1	0.4	0.3	–
Souvenirs	0.3	0.2	0.3	0.6	0.3	0.3	0.2	0.1
Visual goods	0.1	0.1	0.2	0.2	0.1	0.3	–	0.1
Pinball, electronic video games	0.2	0.1	0.4	0.8	0.4	0.1	–	0.0

Note: "–" means sample is too small to make a reliable estimate.
Source: Bureau of Labor Statistics, unpublished data from the 2008 Consumer Expenditure Survey

Table 2.16 Amount Buyers Spent on Entertainment by Household Type, <u>Average Week</u>, 2008

(average amount spent by households buying entertainment during the average week, by type of household, 2008)

| | total married couples | married couples, no children | married couples with children | | | | single parent, at least one child <18 | single person |
			total	oldest child under 6	oldest child 6 to 17	oldest child 18 or older		
ENTERTAINMENT, AMOUNT SPENT	**$82.28**	**$83.30**	**$82.95**	**$78.54**	**$88.75**	**$74.67**	**$57.90**	**$63.26**
Fees and admissions	**70.16**	**55.12**	**78.14**	**55.25**	**89.23**	**62.56**	**67.92**	**44.38**
Fees for participant sports	48.39	44.82	51.71	40.00	56.77	47.84	41.73	38.27
Fees for recreational lessons	109.05	89.52	110.53	78.71	114.75	107.98	172.13	64.52
Auido and visual equipment, services	**93.14**	**91.48**	**93.26**	**100.62**	**93.99**	**87.32**	**76.73**	**75.27**
Radios	19.05	20.00	23.33	46.15	20.00	20.83	21.05	20.00
Cable and satellite television services	94.82	90.15	96.82	98.85	98.09	93.19	92.81	73.97
Tape recorders and players	40.91	66.67	28.57	38.18	23.33	25.00	18.75	33.33
Miscellaneous sound equipment	23.08	26.67	23.08	8.11	33.33	–	4.00	–
Miscellaneous video equipment	42.42	62.50	37.84	35.71	47.62	15.15	183.33	14.81
Sound equipment accessories	24.72	30.00	24.79	13.10	28.44	24.10	11.98	30.30
Video game hardware and software	86.07	118.10	80.83	113.25	76.23	76.67	49.39	100.00
Pets, toys, hobbies, and playground equipment	**43.40**	**52.36**	**37.23**	**38.57**	**38.61**	**33.69**	**22.09**	**36.76**
Pets	43.04	56.74	30.73	30.59	30.24	31.61	18.64	39.58
Pet food	18.20	17.67	17.76	14.40	19.07	17.09	12.76	15.12
Pet purchase, supplies, and medicines	22.70	24.78	19.18	14.47	18.25	22.85	13.21	18.07
Veterinarian services	223.36	317.48	129.47	171.71	118.14	130.24	69.51	238.17
Toys, games, hobbies, and tricycles	26.93	19.53	30.93	31.39	32.58	24.40	20.34	15.65
Playground equipment	27.27	11.11	41.67	38.46	36.84	–	7.14	–
Other entertainment supplies, equipment, services	**54.65**	**66.79**	**52.18**	**34.97**	**54.20**	**58.66**	**40.43**	**66.93**
Sports, recreation, exercise equipment	50.42	63.43	46.32	26.39	44.40	60.63	33.58	70.78
Athletic gear, game tables, exercise equipment	42.35	39.30	44.92	16.67	46.21	57.01	37.20	53.23
Camping equipment	41.18	51.61	38.13	35.48	37.84	43.96	27.93	38.89
Hunting and fishing equipment	36.93	61.73	20.65	25.14	17.99	20.90	18.03	93.02
Global positioning system devices	255.56	278.95	247.37	–	152.94	338.24	–	50.00
Photographic equipment and supplies	86.44	104.69	87.27	82.67	101.01	50.43	58.54	54.17
Other photographic supplies	23.08	29.17	13.64	–	13.16	28.57	19.05	28.57
Photographer fees	104.35	152.50	98.60	82.67	121.88	51.85	79.01	64.71
Fireworks	33.33	11.11	40.00	–	33.33	44.44	35.48	–
Souvenirs	21.43	39.13	9.09	12.28	14.29	3.57	23.81	9.09
Visual goods	23.08	–	26.32	6.67	14.29	46.67	–	12.50
Pinball, electronic video games	20.83	–	23.08	12.35	16.67	137.50	–	66.67

Note: "–" means sample is too small to make a reliable estimate.
Source: Calculations by New Strategist based on the Bureau of Labor Statistics' 2008 Consumer Expenditure Survey

Table 2.17 Percent Buying Entertainment by Race and Hispanic Origin, Average Quarter, 2008

(percent of households buying entertainment during the average quarter, by race and Hispanic origin of householder, 2008)

	total households	Asian	black	Hispanic	non-Hispanic white and other
ENTERTAINMENT, PERCENT BUYING	**91.1%**	**85.5%**	**82.4%**	**85.0%**	**93.4%**
Fees and admissions	**46.5**	**49.7**	**26.9**	**33.2**	**51.6**
Recreation expenses on trips	7.5	8.1	3.2	5.0	8.6
Social, recreation, civic club membership	13.3	13.2	5.8	7.1	15.4
Fees for participant sports	11.2	11.3	4.1	5.6	13.2
Participant sports on trips	3.7	3.7	1.2	2.0	4.4
Movie, theater, amusement park, and other admissions	29.8	29.7	18.5	24.2	32.4
Movie, other admissions on trips	8.2	8.6	3.3	4.8	9.5
Admission to sports events	6.6	4.5	3.2	3.6	7.6
Admission to sports events on trips	8.2	8.6	3.3	4.8	9.5
Fees for recreational lessons	6.2	8.5	2.6	3.4	7.2
Other entertainment services on trips	7.5	8.1	3.2	5.0	8.6
Audio and visual equipment and services	**84.5**	**75.9**	**77.0**	**77.3**	**86.8**
Television sets	4.0	3.6	3.3	3.8	4.2
Cable and satellite television services	74.1	62.7	68.4	65.4	76.4
Satellite radio service	3.1	1.8	1.2	3.0	3.5
Online gaming services	1.0	0.6	0.3	0.8	1.1
VCRs and video disc players	1.9	3.0	1.8	1.9	1.9
Video game hardware and software	14.7	10.9	10.3	10.4	16.0
Video cassettes, tapes, and discs	5.4	5.7	3.0	5.0	5.9
Streamed and downloaded video	0.7	0.4	0.4	0.4	0.8
Repair of TV, radio, and sound equipment	0.5	0.5	0.4	0.4	0.6
Rental of television sets	0.1	–	0.0	0.1	0.1
Radios	0.7	0.5	0.5	0.6	0.8
Tape recorders and players	0.1	–	0.0	0.1	0.1
Personal digital audio players	1.8	2.7	1.1	1.8	1.9
Sound components and component systems	0.7	1.1	0.3	0.8	0.7
Compact discs, records, and audio tapes	12.2	8.5	11.3	10.2	12.6
Streamed and downloaded audio	3.3	2.8	1.0	1.9	3.9
Rental of VCR, radio, and sound equipment	0.1	–	–	0.1	0.1
Musical instruments and accessories	1.4	1.1	0.8	0.9	1.6
Rental and repair of musical instruments	0.2	0.2	0.1	0.2	0.3
Rental of video cassettes, tapes, discs, films	20.1	16.1	10.7	15.5	22.3
Rental of computer and video game hardware and software	0.1	0.0	0.0	0.0	0.1
Accessories and other sound equipment	1.3	1.1	0.8	0.8	1.4
Satellite dishes	0.3	0.2	0.2	0.2	0.3
Installation of television sets	0.1	0.3	0.1	0.2	0.1
Pets, toys, hobbies, and playground equipment	**43.7**	**24.7**	**22.7**	**35.6**	**48.3**
Pets	33.3	11.4	12.9	24.6	37.9
Pet purchase, supplies, and medicines	28.0	9.1	11.9	22.2	31.4
Pet services	5.7	1.2	1.3	2.3	6.9
Veterinarian services	9.7	3.0	1.9	4.0	11.8
Toys, games, hobbies, and tricycles	17.4	14.8	12.4	15.2	18.5
Stamp and coin collecting	0.9	1.2	0.2	0.5	1.0
Playground equipment	0.4	0.1	0.2	0.4	0.5

	total households	Asian	black	Hispanic	non-Hispanic white and other
Other entertainment supplies, equipment, services	**22.5%**	**18.5%**	**12.1%**	**15.3%**	**25.3%**
Unmotored recreational vehicles	0.2	–	–	0.0	0.2
Motorized recreational vehicles	0.2	–	0.0	0.1	0.3
Rental of recreational vehicles	0.5	0.8	0.4	0.2	0.5
Docking and landing fees	0.4	–	0.1	0.0	0.4
Sports, recreation, exercise equipment	10.6	9.8	4.8	7.2	12.1
Athletic gear, game tables, exercise equipment	6.1	6.7	3.2	4.4	6.9
Bicycles	1.4	1.1	1.0	1.4	1.4
Camping equipment	1.0	0.8	0.1	0.6	1.2
Hunting and fishing equipment	2.1	0.7	0.3	0.6	2.6
Winter sports equipment	0.3	0.2	0.0	0.1	0.4
Water sports equipment	0.4	0.1	0.1	0.2	0.5
Other sports equipment	0.9	1.0	0.4	0.7	1.0
Rental and repair of miscellaneous sports equipment	0.3	0.1	0.0	0.1	0.3
Photographic equipment and supplies	14.0	9.3	7.9	8.7	15.8
Film	2.9	1.9	2.2	2.0	3.2
Photo processing	8.9	4.8	4.8	4.4	10.3
Repair and rental of photographic equipment	0.2	0.1	0.1	0.1	0.2
Photographic equipment	2.7	3.2	1.1	2.3	3.0
Photographer fees	2.5	1.1	1.3	1.9	2.8
Live entertainment for catered affairs	0.3	0.1	0.2	0.5	0.3
Rental of party supplies for catered affairs	0.6	0.7	0.2	0.9	0.6

Note: "Asian" and "black" include Hispanics and non-Hispanics who identify themselves as being of the respective race alone. "Hispanic" includes people of any race who identify themselves as Hispanic. "Other" includes people who identify themselves as non-Hispanic and as Alaska Native, American Indian, Asian (who are also included in the Asian column), or Native Hawaiian or other Pacific Islander as well as non-Hispanics reporting more than one race. "–" means sample is too small to make a reliable estimate.
Source: Bureau of Labor Statistics, unpublished data from the 2008 Consumer Expenditure Survey

Table 2.18 Amount Buyers Spent on Entertainment by Race and Hispanic Origin, Average Quarter, 2008

(average amount spent by households buying entertainment during the average quarter, by race and Hispanic origin of householder, 2008)

ENTERTAINMENT, AMOUNT SPENT	total households	Asian	black	Hispanic	non-Hispanic white and other
ENTERTAINMENT, AMOUNT SPENT	**$671.81**	**$543.29**	**$380.14**	**$458.91**	**$741.72**
Fees and admissions	**326.61**	**367.69**	**192.65**	**270.34**	**342.97**
Recreation expenses on trips	78.19	86.94	47.21	108.75	77.33
Social, recreation, civic club membership	240.37	181.00	172.66	140.55	251.27
Fees for participant sports	181.17	175.53	139.03	143.72	185.70
Participant sports on trips	186.18	187.33	73.49	220.81	188.56
Movie, theater, amusement park, and other admissions	99.40	91.39	77.94	98.18	101.38
Movie, other admissions on trips	136.07	192.89	93.19	166.96	135.93
Admission to sports events	174.24	221.47	174.31	142.18	176.55
Admission to sports events on trips	45.36	64.29	30.99	55.65	45.31
Fees for recreational lessons	400.32	692.59	311.39	493.31	398.99
Other entertainment services on trips	78.19	86.94	47.21	108.75	77.33
Audio and visual equipment and services	**290.77**	**257.58**	**261.76**	**253.66**	**299.83**
Television sets	1,017.82	1,022.75	862.27	1,020.88	1,035.42
Cable and satellite television services	196.78	173.13	205.49	176.98	198.13
Satellite radio service	117.73	189.44	142.29	117.37	115.90
Online gaming services	52.06	52.50	38.28	40.67	53.35
VCRs and video disc players	164.23	167.03	125.98	109.92	178.04
Video game hardware and software	58.23	42.99	57.69	57.75	58.30
Video cassettes, tapes, and discs	213.45	226.85	213.00	205.20	214.62
Streamed and downloaded video	40.58	72.09	37.82	37.20	41.14
Repair of TV, radio, and sound equipment	185.29	137.50	147.73	188.89	188.18
Rental of television sets	221.43	–	408.33	135.42	266.67
Radios	96.23	68.87	64.62	74.21	102.24
Tape recorders and players	52.78	–	50.00	43.75	55.00
Personal digital audio players	192.61	188.75	182.74	180.87	195.54
Sound components and component systems	278.93	198.58	175.00	232.72	294.59
Compact discs, records, and audio tapes	46.57	49.50	44.36	44.77	47.10
Streamed and downloaded audio	41.44	27.23	44.75	38.48	41.58
Rental of VCR, radio, and sound equipment	195.00	–	–	45.83	208.33
Musical instruments and accessories	541.73	200.66	212.34	158.33	601.76
Rental and repair of musical instruments	181.52	88.54	65.00	63.33	194.44
Rental of video cassettes, tapes, discs, films	33.92	34.56	33.81	35.62	33.73
Rental of computer and video game hardware and software	83.33	587.50	50.00	25.00	89.29
Accessories and other sound equipment	101.77	191.07	98.70	59.81	105.46
Satellite dishes	132.14	53.57	112.50	96.88	141.67
Installation of television sets	183.93	122.00	287.50	96.25	192.86
Pets, toys, hobbies, playground equipment	**250.80**	**190.93**	**163.75**	**168.76**	**266.39**
Pets	233.27	156.56	132.56	155.66	246.31
Pet purchase, supplies, and medicines	146.65	97.70	109.50	119.07	151.82
Pet services	160.43	102.52	85.74	111.35	165.35
Veterinarian services	284.95	259.00	156.22	231.86	291.03
Toys, games, hobbies, and tricycles	168.16	181.71	156.02	136.01	173.49
Stamp and coin collecting	137.79	205.00	108.70	31.86	147.28
Playground equipment	316.28	110.00	194.79	253.47	334.04

	total households	Asian	black	Hispanic	non-Hispanic white and other
Other entertainment supplies, equipment, services	**$464.72**	**$210.43**	**$187.12**	**$287.59**	**$501.59**
Unmotored recreational vehicles	12,557.89	–	–	1,025.00	13,001.04
Motorized recreational vehicles	15,326.25	–	23,158.33	19,166.67	14,913.00
Rental of recreational vehicles	260.94	370.24	132.50	347.06	276.42
Docking and landing fees	461.43	–	1,025.00	112.50	460.23
Sports, recreation, exercise equipment	251.06	186.84	167.01	206.49	260.39
Athletic gear, game tables, exercise equipment	197.92	205.84	181.62	158.58	202.77
Bicycles	261.95	156.98	119.12	226.23	284.64
Camping equipment	199.74	97.59	121.88	316.96	192.52
Hunting and fishing equipment	253.29	55.43	64.81	85.53	262.65
Winter sports equipment	225.86	165.63	100.00	252.08	225.00
Water sports equipment	197.62	206.25	366.67	85.94	198.53
Other sports equipment	177.69	107.03	88.46	240.85	177.88
Rental and repair of miscellaneous sports equipment	268.52	30.56	106.25	300.00	265.44
Photographic equipment and supplies	116.48	178.05	75.25	127.37	118.77
Film	25.43	28.44	18.47	19.92	26.64
Photo processing	38.95	45.29	31.62	39.71	39.44
Repair and rental of photographic equipment	115.63	50.00	209.09	177.08	102.94
Photographic equipment	260.54	406.43	155.48	199.67	273.58
Photographer fees	198.59	84.63	151.91	223.19	198.83
Live entertainment for catered affairs	555.30	150.00	164.29	341.35	629.55
Rental of party supplies for catered affairs	367.98	129.35	150.00	411.76	372.84

Note: "Asian" and "black" include Hispanics and non-Hispanics who identify themselves as being of the respective race alone. "Hispanic" includes people of any race who identify themselves as Hispanic. "Other" includes people who identify themselves as non-Hispanic and as Alaska Native, American Indian, Asian (who are also included in the Asian column), or Native Hawaiian or other Pacific Islander as well as non-Hispanics reporting more than one race. "–" means sample is too small to make a reliable estimate.
Source: Calculations by New Strategist based on the Bureau of Labor Statistics' 2008 Consumer Expenditure Survey

Table 2.19 Percent Buying Entertainment by Race and Hispanic Origin, <u>Average Week</u>, 2008

(percent of households buying entertainment during the average week, by race and Hispanic origin of householder, 2008)

	total households	Asian	black	Hispanic	non-Hispanic white and other
ENTERTAINMENT, PERCENT BUYING	**39.6%**	**29.0%**	**26.9%**	**33.5%**	**42.5%**
Fees and admissions	**5.1**	**4.3**	**1.7**	**2.8**	**6.0**
Fees for participant sports	3.9	1.9	1.3	2.2	4.5
Fees for recreational lessons	1.5	2.5	0.4	0.9	1.7
Audio and visual equipment and services	**14.5**	**14.6**	**13.9**	**14.4**	**14.6**
Radios	0.2	0.1	0.2	0.3	0.2
Cable and satellite television services	11.9	10.9	12.1	11.2	12.0
Tape recorders and players	0.2	0.6	–	0.2	0.2
Miscellaneous sound equipment	0.1	0.1	0.1	0.1	0.1
Miscellaneous video equipment	0.3	0.7	0.3	0.2	0.3
Sound equipment accessories	0.8	0.5	0.6	0.9	0.8
Video game hardware and software	1.9	2.5	2.1	2.3	1.8
Pets, toys, hobbies, and playground equipment	**27.0**	**14.3**	**14.9**	**20.9**	**29.7**
Pets	20.9	8.8	10.6	14.7	23.4
Pet food	17.7	6.6	8.7	12.9	19.8
Pet purchase, supplies, and medicines	6.0	3.2	3.2	3.4	6.8
Veterinarian services	1.9	–	0.6	0.8	2.3
Toys, games, hobbies, and tricycles	9.6	8.0	6.0	8.8	10.3
Playground equipment	0.1	–	–	0.1	0.1
Other entertainment supplies, equipment, services	**5.6**	**3.6**	**3.0**	**4.1**	**6.2**
Sports, recreation, exercise equipment	4.4	2.4	2.5	3.6	4.8
Athletic gear, game tables, exercise equipment	2.5	1.9	1.4	2.1	2.8
Camping equipment	0.8	0.3	0.6	1.1	0.7
Hunting and fishing equipment	1.3	0.8	0.7	0.6	1.5
Global positioning system devices	0.1	0.2	–	–	0.1
Photographic equipment and supplies	0.8	0.8	0.5	0.5	0.9
Other photographic supplies	0.2	0.2	0.1	0.1	0.2
Photographer fees	0.6	0.8	0.4	0.5	0.7
Fireworks	0.1	–	0.1	–	0.1
Souvenirs	0.2	0.3	0.0	0.1	0.3
Visual goods	0.1	0.1	–	0.1	0.1
Pinball, electronic video games	0.1	–	0.0	–	0.2

Note: "Asian" and "black" include Hispanics and non-Hispanics who identify themselves as being of the respective race alone. "Hispanic" includes people of any race who identify themselves as Hispanic. "Other" includes people who identify themselves as non-Hispanic and as Alaska Native, American Indian, Asian (who are also included in the Asian column), or Native Hawaiian or other Pacific Islander as well as non-Hispanics reporting more than one race. "–" means sample is too small to make a reliable estimate.
Source: Bureau of Labor Statistics, unpublished data from the 2008 Consumer Expenditure Survey

Table 2.20 Amount Buyers Spent on Entertainment by Race and Hispanic Origin, <u>Average Week,</u> 2008

(average amount spent by households buying entertainment during the average week, by race and Hispanic origin of householder, 2008)

	total households	Asian	black	Hispanic	non-Hispanic white and other
ENTERTAINMENT, AMOUNT SPENT	**$75.18**	**$180.24**	**$80.39**	**$61.92**	**$76.20**
Fees and admissions	**64.05**	**138.17**	**59.04**	**49.12**	**65.21**
Fees for participant sports	44.94	28.42	36.92	33.95	46.00
Fees for recreational lessons	104.79	211.86	116.28	77.65	105.85
Audio and visual equipment and services	**87.72**	**75.94**	**109.73**	**86.49**	**84.69**
Radios	20.00	15.38	13.04	6.45	22.22
Cable and satellite television services	89.43	76.68	107.30	91.96	86.37
Tape recorders and players	38.89	11.67	–	35.00	40.00
Miscellaneous sound equipment	18.18	7.69	11.11	9.09	18.18
Miscellaneous video equipment	33.33	41.54	7.69	13.64	39.29
Sound equipment accessories	23.68	32.61	10.00	15.73	26.32
Video game hardware and software	85.94	90.61	105.85	81.94	83.70
Pets, toys, hobbies, and playground equipment	**40.02**	**232.73**	**26.91**	**26.65**	**42.38**
Pets	40.14	362.71	22.17	22.90	42.96
Pet food	17.74	19.94	13.92	12.37	18.47
Pet purchase, supplies, and medicines	21.31	40.81	15.77	16.13	22.19
Veterinarian services	209.47	–	105.00	149.38	216.37
Toys, games, hobbies, and tricycles	24.56	17.60	27.53	24.72	24.20
Playground equipment	50.00	–	–	37.50	55.56
Other entertainment supplies, equipment, services	**54.59**	**55.00**	**47.84**	**33.09**	**57.31**
Sports, recreation, exercise equipment	52.52	70.59	45.82	31.94	55.25
Athletic gear, game tables, exercise equipment	42.86	23.40	46.10	35.58	43.84
Camping equipment	42.67	48.39	63.64	25.93	43.24
Hunting and fishing equipment	48.09	54.88	22.06	20.97	50.99
Global positioning system devices	227.27	315.00	–	–	235.71
Photographic equipment and supplies	79.75	27.38	57.78	32.69	84.27
Other photographic supplies	21.05	8.33	88.89	33.33	17.39
Photographer fees	96.72	25.00	50.00	34.78	104.41
Fireworks	27.27	–	20.00	–	30.77
Souvenirs	21.74	21.88	25.00	33.33	21.43
Visual goods	22.22	0.00	–	20.00	18.18
Pinball, electronic video games	21.43	–	25.00	–	23.53

Note: "Asian" and "black" include Hispanics and non-Hispanics who identify themselves as being of the respective race alone. "Hispanic" includes people of any race who identify themselves as Hispanic. "Other" includes people who identify themselves as non-Hispanic and as Alaska Native, American Indian, Asian (who are also included in the Asian column), or Native Hawaiian or other Pacific Islander as well as non-Hispanics reporting more than one race. "–" means sample is too small to make a reliable estimate.
Source: Calculations by New Strategist based on the Bureau of Labor Statistics' 2008 Consumer Expenditure Survey

Table 2.21 Percent Buying Entertainment by Region, <u>Average Quarter</u>, 2008

(percent of households buying entertainment during the average quarter, by region of residence, 2008)

	total consumer units	Northeast	Midwest	South	West
ENTERTAINMENT, PERCENT BUYING	**91.1%**	**92.0%**	**92.1%**	**89.9%**	**91.0%**
Fees and admissions	**46.5**	**46.8**	**49.8**	**40.1**	**53.0**
Recreation expenses on trips	7.5	8.1	7.9	6.3	8.8
Social, recreation, civic club membership	13.3	13.9	13.6	11.0	16.1
Fees for participant sports	11.2	10.1	11.9	9.0	15.0
Participant sports on trips	3.7	3.6	4.0	2.9	4.8
Movie, theater, amusement park, and other admissions	29.8	29.8	32.1	24.7	35.7
Movie, other admissions on trips	8.2	8.3	9.1	6.6	10.0
Admission to sports events	6.6	6.3	9.1	5.6	6.0
Admission to sports events on trips	8.2	8.3	9.1	6.6	10.0
Fees for recreational lessons	6.2	7.2	7.0	4.4	7.5
Other entertainment services on trips	7.5	8.1	7.9	6.3	8.8
Audio and visual equipment and services	**84.5**	**86.7**	**84.8**	**83.8**	**83.5**
Television sets	4.0	4.0	3.9	4.2	4.0
Cable and satellite television services	74.1	79.6	73.0	75.2	69.2
Satellite radio service	3.1	3.9	3.0	2.6	3.5
Online gaming services	1.0	0.9	0.9	0.7	1.5
VCRs and video disc players	1.9	1.9	1.9	1.8	2.1
Video game hardware and software	14.7	12.0	15.6	13.4	18.0
Video cassettes, tapes, and discs	5.4	5.3	6.2	4.9	5.4
Streamed and downloaded video	0.7	1.2	0.4	0.5	0.9
Repair of TV, radio, and sound equipment	0.5	0.5	0.4	0.5	0.6
Rental of television sets	0.1	0.0	0.1	0.1	0.1
Radios	0.7	0.8	1.0	0.6	0.6
Tape recorders and players	0.1	0.1	0.1	0.1	0.2
Personal digital audio players	1.8	1.7	1.9	1.6	1.9
Sound components and component systems	0.7	0.7	0.7	0.6	0.9
Compact discs, records, and audio tapes	12.2	11.7	12.5	11.0	14.0
Streamed and downloaded audio	3.3	3.1	3.3	2.7	4.5
Rental of VCR, radio, and sound equipment	0.1	0.1	0.1	0.0	0.0
Musical instruments and accessories	1.4	1.3	1.7	1.1	1.6
Rental and repair of musical instruments	0.2	0.3	0.3	0.1	0.3
Rental of video cassettes, tapes, discs, films	20.1	16.7	22.9	16.9	25.3
Rental of computer and video game hardware and software	0.1	0.1	0.1	0.0	0.1
Accessories and other sound equipment	1.3	1.1	1.2	1.1	1.7
Satellite dishes	0.3	0.3	0.4	0.2	0.3
Installation of television sets	0.1	0.1	0.1	0.2	0.2
Pets, toys, hobbies, and playground equipment	**43.7**	**41.6**	**45.1**	**43.3**	**44.7**
Pets	33.3	30.9	33.8	34.0	33.8
Pet purchase, supplies, and medicines	28.0	25.9	28.2	29.3	27.3
Pet services	5.7	5.6	6.0	5.0	6.7
Veterinarian services	9.7	10.0	11.0	8.4	10.1
Toys, games, hobbies, and tricycles	17.4	17.5	18.9	16.4	17.5
Stamp and coin collecting	0.9	1.1	1.3	0.5	0.9
Playground equipment	0.4	0.3	0.5	0.5	0.4

	total households	Northeast	Midwest	South	West
Other entertainment supplies, equipment, services	**22.5%**	**21.8%**	**27.0%**	**19.0%**	**24.0%**
Unmotored recreational vehicles	0.2	0.1	0.2	0.1	0.3
Motorized recreational vehicles	0.2	0.2	0.3	0.1	0.2
Rental of recreational vehicles	0.5	0.6	0.5	0.3	0.6
Docking and landing fees	0.4	0.4	0.3	0.4	0.3
Sports, recreation, exercise equipment	10.6	10.2	12.3	8.6	12.6
Athletic gear, game tables, exercise equipment	6.1	6.2	6.8	4.9	7.3
Bicycles	1.4	1.0	1.6	1.1	1.9
Camping equipment	1.0	0.8	0.9	0.7	1.6
Hunting and fishing equipment	2.1	2.1	2.9	1.8	1.6
Winter sports equipment	0.3	0.3	0.4	0.1	0.5
Water sports equipment	0.4	0.3	0.5	0.4	0.5
Other sports equipment	0.9	0.9	1.1	0.7	1.2
Rental and repair of miscellaneous sports equipment	0.3	0.3	0.3	0.1	0.5
Photographic equipment and supplies	14.0	14.3	17.6	12.1	13.2
Film	2.9	3.3	3.5	2.7	2.4
Photo processing	8.9	9.6	11.4	7.5	8.1
Repair and rental of photographic equipment	0.2	0.2	0.1	0.2	0.2
Photographic equipment	2.7	2.7	3.1	2.3	2.9
Photographer fees	2.5	2.6	3.3	2.1	2.2
Live entertainment for catered affairs	0.3	0.3	0.6	0.3	0.3
Rental of party supplies for catered affairs	0.6	0.5	0.7	0.4	0.7

Source: Bureau of Labor Statistics, unpublished data from the 2008 Consumer Expenditure Survey

Table 2.22 Amount Buyers Spent on Entertainment by Region, Average Quarter, 2008

(average amount spent by households buying entertainment during the average quarter, by region of residence, 2008)

	total households	Northeast	Midwest	South	West
ENTERTAINMENT, AMOUNT SPENT	**$671.81**	**$699.06**	**$664.88**	**$601.59**	**$768.76**
Fees and admissions	**326.61**	**376.49**	**293.28**	**295.53**	**360.74**
Recreation expenses on trips	78.19	77.95	68.51	79.07	86.46
Social, recreation, civic club membership	240.37	313.04	222.82	239.16	205.20
Fees for participant sports	181.17	184.69	167.42	182.98	188.84
Participant sports on trips	186.18	172.65	153.65	167.63	240.36
Movie, theater, amusement park, and other admissions	99.40	111.83	89.09	90.00	110.84
Movie, other admissions on trips	136.07	131.25	124.15	145.86	140.16
Admission to sports events	174.24	198.17	149.59	183.99	177.06
Admission to sports events on trips	45.36	43.75	41.38	48.60	46.72
Fees for recreational lessons	400.32	485.29	312.63	357.71	458.40
Other entertainment services on trips	78.19	77.95	68.51	79.07	86.46
Audio and visual equipment and services	**290.77**	**295.00**	**282.20**	**293.64**	**291.49**
Television sets	1,017.82	1,040.82	914.56	1,029.51	1,080.74
Cable and satellite television services	196.78	200.85	187.68	202.01	193.62
Satellite radio service	117.73	95.34	122.35	123.93	126.71
Online gaming services	52.06	37.92	58.91	48.65	56.70
VCRs and video disc players	164.23	187.57	139.29	175.14	154.81
Video game hardware and software	58.23	58.69	56.85	58.92	58.47
Video cassettes, tapes, and discs	213.45	203.85	197.75	232.23	213.05
Streamed and downloaded video	40.58	38.51	43.42	35.56	46.77
Repair of TV, radio, and sound equipment	185.29	253.85	183.75	168.40	161.21
Rental of television sets	221.43	200.00	308.33	200.00	135.00
Radios	96.23	99.67	97.94	93.36	96.25
Tape recorders and players	52.78	35.00	72.22	50.00	48.75
Personal digital audio players	192.61	198.11	185.05	190.29	201.05
Sound components and component systems	278.93	321.07	277.14	299.57	232.30
Compact discs, records, and audio tapes	46.57	49.28	45.12	41.89	52.01
Streamed and downloaded audio	41.44	38.54	32.49	48.21	43.43
Rental of VCR, radio, and sound equipment	195.00	58.33	82.14	108.33	941.67
Musical instruments and accessories	541.73	545.16	862.13	383.18	370.27
Rental and repair of musical instruments	181.52	136.00	379.63	140.38	69.70
Rental of video cassettes, tapes, discs, films	33.92	32.01	31.44	35.27	35.80
Rental of computer and video game hardware and software	83.33	83.33	53.13	58.33	150.00
Accessories and other sound equipment	101.77	85.24	75.00	127.43	101.89
Satellite dishes	132.14	88.46	75.66	187.50	168.27
Installation of television sets	183.93	234.62	208.33	123.33	239.71
Pets, toys, hobbies, playground equipment	**250.80**	**267.39**	**237.90**	**242.57**	**264.25**
Pets	233.27	257.66	217.13	218.42	255.59
Pet purchase, supplies, and medicines	146.65	151.08	136.57	150.60	147.08
Pet services	160.43	153.57	125.76	140.38	221.43
Veterinarian services	284.95	320.16	250.27	275.03	308.28
Toys, games, hobbies, and tricycles	168.16	166.97	163.98	172.02	168.02
Stamp and coin collecting	137.79	149.08	127.54	193.09	94.48
Playground equipment	316.28	285.71	213.68	337.23	458.11

	total households	Northeast	Midwest	South	West
Other entertainment supplies, equipment, services	**$464.72**	**$457.32**	**$443.17**	**$374.83**	**$610.77**
Unmotored recreational vehicles	12,557.89	10,316.07	14,252.63	10,675.00	13,919.53
Motorized recreational vehicles	15,326.25	15,509.21	12,087.10	15,660.42	19,057.61
Rental of recreational vehicles	260.94	256.25	228.00	300.00	266.53
Docking and landing fees	461.43	719.87	708.06	268.92	313.64
Sports, recreation, exercise equipment	251.06	277.62	222.02	241.59	272.80
Athletic gear, game tables, exercise equipment	197.92	258.28	191.18	184.57	176.61
Bicycles	261.95	171.05	231.64	221.43	362.05
Camping equipment	199.74	104.32	137.94	238.54	245.99
Hunting and fishing equipment	253.29	268.63	185.14	266.57	340.43
Winter sports equipment	225.86	166.94	262.84	194.44	239.22
Water sports equipment	197.62	187.12	108.00	316.43	163.94
Other sports equipment	177.69	247.70	133.02	188.24	170.33
Rental and repair of miscellaneous sports equipment	268.52	308.87	299.19	313.64	203.26
Photographic equipment and supplies	116.48	127.42	113.21	103.87	129.99
Film	25.43	27.58	25.28	23.08	27.53
Photo processing	38.95	35.74	40.52	36.44	43.76
Repair and rental of photographic equipment	115.63	210.00	129.17	97.22	78.13
Photographic equipment	260.54	221.39	291.99	240.65	280.92
Photographer fees	198.59	287.74	161.66	165.38	217.32
Live entertainment for catered affairs	555.30	975.00	540.00	418.52	422.22
Rental of party supplies for catered affairs	367.98	458.51	222.89	438.69	409.93

Source: Calculations by New Strategist based on the Bureau of Labor Statistics' 2008 Consumer Expenditure Survey

Table 2.23 Percent Buying Entertainment by Region, Average Week, 2008

(percent of households buying entertainment during the average week, by region of residence, 2008)

	total households	Northeast	Midwest	South	West
ENTERTAINMENT, PERCENT BUYING	**39.6%**	**41.3%**	**39.3%**	**38.8%**	**39.9%**
Fees and admissions	**5.1**	**5.6**	**5.8**	**4.0**	**5.7**
Fees for participant sports	3.9	4.2	4.8	3.2	3.7
Fees for recreational lessons	1.5	1.8	1.2	0.9	2.3
Audio and visual equipment and services	**14.5**	**16.0**	**14.3**	**14.3**	**13.9**
Radios	0.2	0.1	0.2	0.2	0.3
Cable and satellite television services	11.9	14.1	11.6	11.9	10.5
Tape recorders and players	0.2	0.1	0.2	0.2	0.3
Miscellaneous sound equipment	0.1	–	0.1	0.1	0.2
Miscellaneous video equipment	0.3	0.4	0.3	0.2	0.3
Sound equipment accessories	0.8	0.3	1.1	0.6	1.1
Video game hardware and software	1.9	1.6	1.7	2.0	2.2
Pets, toys, hobbies, and playground equipment	**27.0**	**27.4**	**26.1**	**27.3**	**27.0**
Pets	20.9	21.5	20.3	21.0	20.8
Pet food	17.7	18.5	16.9	18.1	17.3
Pet purchase, supplies, and medicines	6.0	6.3	6.2	5.7	6.0
Veterinarian services	1.9	1.8	2.0	1.8	2.1
Toys, games, hobbies, and tricycles	9.6	9.2	9.6	9.7	9.9
Playground equipment	0.1	0.1	0.2	0.1	–
Other entertainment supplies, equipment, services	**5.6**	**5.2**	**5.9**	**5.0**	**6.5**
Sports, recreation, exercise equipment	4.4	4.1	4.6	4.0	4.9
Athletic gear, game tables, exercise equipment	2.5	2.3	2.4	2.5	2.9
Camping equipment	0.8	0.7	0.7	0.7	1.0
Hunting and fishing equipment	1.3	1.3	1.8	1.1	1.3
Global positioning system devices	0.1	0.2	0.1	0.1	0.1
Photographic equipment and supplies	0.8	0.7	0.8	0.7	1.1
Other photographic supplies	0.2	0.2	0.1	0.2	0.4
Photographer fees	0.6	0.5	0.7	0.5	0.7
Fireworks	0.1	0.0	0.2	0.1	0.2
Souvenirs	0.2	0.3	0.3	0.2	0.2
Visual goods	0.1	0.1	0.2	–	0.1
Pinball, electronic video games	0.1	0.2	0.2	0.1	0.1

Note: "–" means sample is too small to make a reliable estimate.
Source: Bureau of Labor Statistics, unpublished data from the 2008 Consumer Expenditure Survey

Table 2.24 Amount Buyers Spent on Entertainment by Region, <u>Average Week</u>, 2008

(average amount spent by households buying entertainment during the average week, by region of residence, 2008)

	total households	Northeast	Midwest	South	West
ENTERTAINMENT, AMOUNT SPENT	**$75.18**	**$79.13**	**$70.07**	**$70.61**	**$84.02**
Fees and admissions	**64.05**	**55.85**	**52.74**	**71.68**	**73.72**
Fees for participant sports	44.94	43.86	35.00	58.82	39.07
Fees for recreational lessons	104.79	73.89	112.90	103.23	121.68
Audio and visual equipment and services	**87.72**	**98.43**	**78.99**	**90.39**	**82.23**
Radios	20.00	15.38	26.32	11.76	25.00
Cable and satellite television services	89.43	95.81	82.82	92.78	83.64
Tape recorders and players	38.89	25.00	26.67	40.00	47.06
Miscellaneous sound equipment	18.18	–	10.00	15.38	27.78
Miscellaneous video equipment	33.33	35.14	15.15	12.50	73.33
Sound equipment accessories	23.68	17.24	30.97	12.07	27.10
Video game hardware and software	85.94	123.75	66.28	80.88	87.21
Pets, toys, hobbies, playground equipment	**40.02**	**39.58**	**35.81**	**33.15**	**55.74**
Pets	40.14	39.62	33.60	31.60	61.07
Pet food	17.74	19.46	16.44	16.77	19.03
Pet purchase, supplies, and medicines	21.31	16.13	23.41	18.02	29.05
Veterinarian services	209.47	220.79	129.50	144.69	367.94
Toys, games, hobbies, and tricycles	24.56	24.70	25.05	24.77	23.51
Playground equipment	50.00	25.00	76.47	16.67	–
Other entertainment supplies, equipment, services	**54.59**	**58.45**	**65.76**	**52.81**	**44.44**
Sports, recreation, exercise equipment	52.52	67.41	57.67	48.13	42.80
Athletic gear, game tables, exercise equipment	42.86	42.79	64.88	41.63	27.30
Camping equipment	42.67	90.91	27.27	29.58	41.00
Hunting and fishing equipment	48.09	53.91	43.09	50.48	46.46
Global positioning system devices	227.27	247.37	127.27	212.50	387.50
Photographic equipment and supplies	79.75	32.84	128.75	89.71	56.19
Other photographic supplies	21.05	18.75	22.22	29.41	17.14
Photographer fees	96.72	39.22	140.28	103.70	74.29
Fireworks	27.27	0.00	35.29	25.00	29.41
Souvenirs	21.74	13.79	15.38	33.33	19.05
Visual goods	22.22	9.09	5.56	–	35.71
Pinball, electronic video games	21.43	11.11	26.32	8.33	57.14

Note: "–" means sample is too small to make a reliable estimate.
Source: Calculations by New Strategist based on the Bureau of Labor Statistics' 2008 Consumer Expenditure Survey

Table 2.25 Percent Buying Entertainment by Education, Average Quarter, 2008

(percent of households buying entertainment during the average quarter, by highest level of education of householder, 2008)

	total households	less than high school graduate	high school graduate	some college	associate's degree	college graduate total	bachelor's degree	master's, professional, doctorate
ENTERTAINMENT, PERCENT BUYING	**91.1%**	**79.7%**	**90.5%**	**92.1%**	**94.3%**	**95.4%**	**94.8%**	**96.5%**
Fees and admissions	**46.5**	**18.2**	**35.4**	**49.6**	**52.8**	**66.0**	**63.6**	**70.4**
Recreation expenses on trips	7.5	2.3	4.7	7.2	8.3	12.7	11.6	14.7
Social, recreation, civic club membership	13.3	2.7	7.2	12.6	15.8	23.7	21.5	27.6
Fees for participant sports	11.2	2.8	8.4	11.4	12.2	17.6	16.7	19.1
Participant sports on trips	3.7	1.0	2.3	3.5	3.4	6.5	6.2	7.1
Movie, theater, amusement park, and other admissions	29.8	11.5	20.7	32.2	32.8	44.2	42.6	47.1
Movie, other admissions on trips	8.2	2.1	5.4	8.1	8.8	13.8	12.1	16.8
Admission to sports events	6.6	2.6	4.6	7.2	7.5	9.6	9.8	9.2
Admission to sports events on trips	8.2	2.1	5.4	8.1	8.8	13.8	12.1	16.8
Fees for recreational lessons	6.2	0.9	3.0	5.5	8.0	11.7	10.9	13.1
Other entertainment services on trips	7.5	2.3	4.7	7.2	8.3	12.7	11.6	14.7
Audio and visual equipment, services	**84.5**	**71.6**	**84.1**	**85.5**	**88.6**	**89.4**	**89.1**	**90.0**
Television sets	4.0	2.9	3.9	4.3	4.9	4.3	4.4	4.2
Cable and satellite television services	74.1	62.9	74.7	72.2	77.3	79.8	79.7	79.8
Satellite radio service	3.1	1.4	2.8	3.1	3.4	4.2	3.9	4.6
Online gaming services	1.0	0.3	0.7	1.2	1.3	1.4	1.5	1.1
VCRs and video disc players	1.9	1.2	1.7	2.0	2.0	2.3	2.0	2.8
Video game hardware and software	14.7	7.6	12.2	17.6	17.6	17.3	17.7	16.6
Video cassettes, tapes, and discs	5.4	2.8	4.8	5.7	6.7	6.6	7.2	5.5
Streamed and downloaded video	0.7	0.2	0.3	0.6	0.7	1.4	1.4	1.3
Repair of TV, radio, and sound equipment	0.5	0.3	0.4	0.5	0.6	0.7	0.7	0.7
Rental of television sets	0.1	0.2	0.1	0.0	0.2	0.0	–	0.0
Radios	0.7	0.6	0.8	0.5	0.7	0.9	0.8	1.2
Tape recorders and players	0.1	0.1	0.0	0.2	0.1	0.1	0.0	0.3
Personal digital audio players	1.8	0.9	1.3	1.6	2.4	2.5	2.6	2.3
Sound components and component systems	0.7	0.5	0.6	0.6	1.0	0.9	0.9	0.8
Compact discs, records, and audio tapes	12.2	7.3	10.7	12.6	13.1	15.3	14.5	16.8
Streamed and downloaded audio	3.3	0.3	1.5	3.3	3.8	6.2	5.9	6.8
Rental of VCR, radio, and sound equipment	0.1	0.0	0.0	0.0	0.2	0.1	0.1	0.1
Musical instruments and accessories	1.4	0.4	0.8	1.4	1.9	2.2	2.2	2.3
Rental and repair of musical instruments	0.2	0.1	0.1	0.2	0.5	0.4	0.3	0.6
Rental of video cassettes, tapes, discs, films	20.1	9.4	15.7	22.8	22.6	26.6	26.9	26.0
Rental of computer and video game hardware, software	0.1	0.1	0.0	0.1	0.0	0.1	0.1	0.0
Accessories and other sound equipment	1.3	0.8	0.9	1.1	1.6	1.9	1.8	2.0
Satellite dishes	0.3	0.4	0.3	0.2	0.4	0.3	0.3	0.2
Installation of television sets	0.1	–	0.2	0.1	0.1	0.2	0.2	0.2
Pets, toys, hobbies, and playground equipment	**43.7**	**29.6**	**40.9**	**44.7**	**50.7**	**50.3**	**49.6**	**51.4**
Pets	33.3	22.1	31.9	33.5	40.0	38.0	37.3	39.1
Pet purchase, supplies, and medicines	28.0	20.0	26.8	28.4	33.8	30.8	30.3	31.9
Pet services	5.7	2.2	5.0	4.9	6.4	8.5	8.1	9.4
Veterinarian services	9.7	4.2	8.0	9.8	11.4	13.3	13.1	13.7
Toys, games, hobbies, and tricycles	17.4	10.8	14.9	18.3	19.0	21.8	21.5	22.3
Stamp and coin collecting	0.9	0.6	0.7	1.0	1.1	0.9	0.9	1.0
Playground equipment	0.4	0.2	0.3	0.5	0.3	0.7	0.6	0.8

	total households	less than high school graduate	high school graduate	some college	associate's degree	college graduate		
						total	bachelor's degree	master's, professional, doctorate
Other entertainment supplies, equipment, services	**22.5%**	**11.0%**	**18.0%**	**23.3%**	**26.6%**	**30.4%**	**29.8%**	**31.5%**
Unmotored recreational vehicles	0.2	0.0	0.2	0.3	0.2	0.2	0.2	0.1
Motorized recreational vehicles	0.2	0.1	0.2	0.1	0.4	0.2	0.3	0.2
Rental of recreational vehicles	0.5	0.1	0.2	0.3	0.6	1.0	0.9	1.2
Docking and landing fees	0.4	0.1	0.3	0.4	0.6	0.4	0.4	0.5
Sports, recreation, exercise equipment	10.6	4.1	7.7	11.0	13.7	15.2	15.6	14.5
Athletic gear, game tables, exercise equipment	6.1	2.1	4.1	6.1	7.9	9.4	9.4	9.5
Bicycles	1.4	0.8	0.9	1.4	1.7	1.9	2.0	1.7
Camping equipment	1.0	0.3	0.7	1.0	1.3	1.5	1.4	1.7
Hunting and fishing equipment	2.1	0.9	1.9	2.5	3.0	2.1	2.4	1.6
Winter sports equipment	0.3	0.0	0.2	0.2	0.3	0.6	0.7	0.5
Water sports equipment	0.4	0.1	0.2	0.5	0.4	0.7	0.7	0.7
Other sports equipment	0.9	0.3	0.6	1.0	1.1	1.4	1.5	1.3
Rental and repair of miscellaneous sports equipment	0.3	0.2	0.2	0.3	0.2	0.5	0.4	0.6
Photographic equipment and supplies	14.0	7.3	11.2	14.4	15.7	19.1	18.7	19.8
Film	2.9	2.6	2.9	2.6	2.8	3.5	3.2	3.9
Photo processing	8.9	4.2	7.2	9.1	9.6	12.6	12.3	13.1
Repair and rental of photographic equipment	0.2	0.1	0.1	0.2	0.2	0.2	0.2	0.2
Photographic equipment	2.7	1.2	2.0	2.9	3.2	3.7	3.6	3.9
Photographer fees	2.5	1.3	1.6	2.6	3.3	3.6	3.8	3.1
Live entertainment for catered affairs	0.3	0.1	0.2	0.5	0.6	0.4	0.3	0.5
Rental of party supplies for catered affairs	0.6	0.2	0.5	0.5	0.7	0.9	0.8	1.0

Note: "–" means sample is too small to make a reliable estimate.
Source: Bureau of Labor Statistics, unpublished data from the 2008 Consumer Expenditure Survey

Table 2.26 Amount Buyers Spent on Entertainment by Education, Average Quarter, 2008

(average amount spent by households buying entertainment during the average quarter, by highest level of education of householder, 2008)

	total households	less than high school graduate	high school graduate	some college	associate's degree	college graduate total	bachelor's degree	master's, professional, doctorate
ENTERTAINMENT, AMOUNT SPENT	**$671.81**	**$338.37**	**$530.61**	**$640.41**	**$745.21**	**$930.04**	**$885.92**	**$1,007.83**
Fees and admissions	**326.61**	**151.43**	**209.67**	**248.53**	**285.75**	**461.12**	**410.76**	**542.71**
Recreation expenses on trips	78.19	55.20	72.60	68.72	75.15	86.80	75.47	102.84
Social, recreation, civic club membership	240.37	163.69	160.76	160.68	203.36	305.99	272.67	352.39
Fees for participant sports	181.17	157.67	166.14	158.00	179.96	201.05	182.57	229.82
Participant sports on trips	186.18	80.75	137.72	137.25	124.18	238.97	186.20	322.38
Movie, theater, amusement park, and other admissions	99.40	67.24	79.66	84.17	84.89	123.56	114.05	138.97
Movie, other admissions on trips	136.07	102.73	118.34	143.13	129.20	142.96	131.56	157.84
Admission to sports events	174.24	97.73	133.30	129.43	122.70	240.48	260.67	202.14
Admission to sports events on trips	45.36	34.24	39.43	47.69	43.04	47.64	43.85	52.61
Fees for recreational lessons	400.32	255.40	256.77	340.05	351.38	470.98	437.37	521.02
Other entertainment services on trips	78.19	55.20	72.60	68.72	75.15	86.80	75.47	102.84
Audio and visual equipment, services	**290.77**	**220.06**	**270.21**	**279.81**	**334.32**	**330.57**	**328.14**	**334.91**
Television sets	1,017.82	725.43	979.80	980.14	992.58	1,181.79	1,177.90	1,190.93
Cable and satellite television services	196.78	175.96	191.05	195.27	202.80	208.99	207.09	212.38
Satellite radio service	117.73	111.63	134.77	111.02	119.53	111.93	115.97	106.20
Online gaming services	52.06	43.27	45.00	64.01	55.62	46.72	50.49	37.26
VCRs and video disc players	164.23	110.68	139.12	147.39	141.08	211.07	225.88	192.74
Video game hardware and software	58.23	59.24	62.09	54.51	57.18	58.82	57.71	60.93
Video cassettes, tapes, and discs	213.45	204.58	211.12	199.96	246.29	215.47	214.97	217.34
Streamed and downloaded video	40.58	31.67	31.03	46.03	33.10	42.59	39.13	48.65
Repair of TV, radio, and sound equipment	185.29	185.48	241.45	127.31	152.92	199.63	229.10	148.57
Rental of television sets	221.43	329.41	143.75	187.50	176.56	350.00	–	333.33
Radios	96.23	85.71	103.29	78.30	64.93	110.11	105.56	118.26
Tape recorders and players	52.78	56.25	112.50	42.19	60.00	56.25	100.00	41.67
Personal digital audio players	192.61	148.91	195.80	209.45	155.79	203.20	193.92	221.47
Sound components and component systems	278.93	240.76	191.27	235.17	352.30	343.39	321.70	391.77
Compact discs, records, and audio tapes	46.57	44.94	47.85	42.06	45.92	49.18	43.08	58.69
Streamed and downloaded audio	41.44	36.76	37.99	50.30	40.31	38.89	41.94	34.14
Rental of VCR, radio, and sound equipment	195.00	25.00	50.00	193.75	364.47	71.43	78.57	53.57
Musical instruments and accessories	541.73	139.77	509.09	357.68	1,493.17	418.58	387.56	470.78
Rental and repair of musical instruments	181.52	30.00	67.86	93.75	131.00	267.31	83.04	438.16
Rental of video cassettes, tapes, discs, films	33.92	35.01	35.12	32.81	35.03	33.50	31.75	36.75
Rental of computer and video game hardware, software	83.33	75.00	87.50	105.00	25.00	90.00	85.71	87.50
Accessories and other sound equipment	101.77	93.09	80.29	90.27	109.53	114.87	105.57	129.21
Satellite dishes	132.14	103.85	58.00	312.50	48.03	149.11	140.63	161.36
Installation of television sets	183.93	–	195.83	175.00	150.00	211.76	246.05	111.67
Pets, toys, hobbies, and playground equipment	**250.80**	**187.29**	**221.39**	**247.08**	**259.12**	**290.53**	**279.15**	**310.28**
Pets	233.27	177.02	190.96	233.86	240.24	278.40	261.82	306.82
Pet purchase, supplies, and medicines	146.65	136.60	135.42	157.83	156.02	147.47	143.55	154.14
Pet services	160.43	98.31	106.83	144.21	141.20	208.24	196.50	225.91
Veterinarian services	284.95	231.88	242.60	270.72	300.11	319.67	294.41	362.42
Toys, games, hobbies, and tricycles	168.16	145.26	186.93	159.90	178.49	165.04	170.75	155.02
Stamp and coin collecting	137.79	39.73	106.60	141.34	88.07	205.05	249.18	132.00
Playground equipment	316.28	206.94	351.79	276.02	132.14	369.12	280.08	492.86

	total households	less than high school graduate	high school graduate	some college	associate's degree	college graduate total	bachelor's degree	master's, professional, doctorate
Other entertainment supplies, equipment, services	**$464.72**	**$266.14**	**$490.41**	**$502.94**	**$466.08**	**$464.83**	**$496.12**	**$412.03**
Unmotored recreational vehicles	12,557.89	6,393.75	13,508.75	13,497.58	9,173.75	12,487.50	11,379.41	15,085.71
Motorized recreational vehicles	15,326.25	10,104.55	14,207.14	16,110.71	11,789.47	18,626.09	21,800.00	10,956.25
Rental of recreational vehicles	260.94	575.00	387.50	195.37	129.51	259.60	251.18	270.16
Docking and landing fees	461.43	67.31	243.33	824.34	534.58	377.50	233.33	578.19
Sports, recreation, exercise equipment	251.06	187.74	215.73	257.97	268.66	266.81	254.77	289.66
Athletic gear, game tables, exercise equipment	197.92	157.42	170.61	168.55	241.29	215.65	223.83	201.15
Bicycles	261.95	227.71	197.85	310.25	140.91	304.50	261.94	397.16
Camping equipment	199.74	69.83	147.01	312.63	263.80	162.33	144.60	189.20
Hunting and fishing equipment	253.29	148.82	247.37	274.41	260.84	256.13	232.64	320.68
Winter sports equipment	225.86	175.00	197.06	231.25	163.97	246.67	277.31	173.56
Water sports equipment	197.62	161.54	117.86	241.15	353.29	172.57	150.00	213.19
Other sports equipment	177.69	149.07	179.69	207.14	163.29	169.68	155.03	201.59
Rental and repair of miscellaneous sports equipment	268.52	229.69	261.76	200.00	226.32	307.07	140.24	520.09
Photographic equipment and supplies	116.48	84.95	90.92	104.26	111.09	144.06	136.10	157.72
Film	25.43	29.05	24.66	24.23	17.82	27.17	24.38	31.30
Photo processing	38.95	46.15	38.29	30.84	40.73	42.11	37.71	49.54
Repair and rental of photographic equipment	115.63	177.08	40.63	130.00	77.94	128.57	140.48	112.50
Photographic equipment	260.54	146.11	229.75	211.60	235.23	330.38	282.89	408.89
Photographer fees	198.59	114.34	128.83	198.75	163.49	250.99	258.40	236.38
Live entertainment for catered affairs	555.30	223.21	538.89	703.13	263.39	592.95	655.30	526.53
Rental of party supplies for catered affairs	367.98	154.55	276.67	426.53	189.86	463.66	461.04	468.38

Note: "–" means sample is too small to make a reliable estimate.
Source: Calculations by New Strategist based on the Bureau of Labor Statistics' 2008 Consumer Expenditure Survey

Table 2.27 Percent Buying Entertainment by Education, Average Week, 2008

(percent of households buying entertainment during the average week, by highest level of education of householder, 2008)

						college graduate		
	total households	less than high school graduate	high school graduate	some college	associate's degree	total	bachelor's degree	master's, professional, doctorate
ENTERTAINMENT, PERCENT BUYING	**39.6%**	**31.7%**	**35.9%**	**41.0%**	**45.3%**	**44.0%**	**43.5%**	**45.1%**
Fees and admissions	**5.1**	**2.1**	**3.7**	**5.1**	**5.3**	**7.7**	**7.3**	**8.4**
Fees for participant sports	3.9	1.7	3.2	4.2	4.2	5.0	5.0	5.1
Fees for recreational lessons	1.5	0.4	0.7	1.1	1.4	3.1	2.6	4.0
Audio and visual equipment and services	**14.5**	**12.4**	**13.8**	**15.4**	**14.1**	**15.5**	**15.1**	**16.3**
Radios	0.2	0.2	0.1	0.4	0.3	0.2	0.2	0.1
Cable and satellite television services	11.9	10.8	11.9	12.6	10.7	12.3	12.1	12.7
Tape recorders and players	0.2	0.1	0.1	0.1	0.2	0.3	0.4	0.2
Miscellaneous sound equipment	0.1	0.0	0.1	0.1	0.1	0.2	0.2	0.3
Miscellaneous video equipment	0.3	0.1	0.1	0.3	0.4	0.4	0.3	0.6
Sound equipment accessories	0.8	0.4	0.4	0.9	0.8	1.2	0.9	1.6
Video game hardware and software	1.9	1.1	1.8	2.0	2.5	2.2	2.3	2.0
Pets, toys, hobbies, and playground equipment	**27.0**	**21.4**	**24.5**	**28.7**	**33.3**	**28.6**	**28.5**	**28.7**
Pets	20.9	16.7	19.4	22.8	25.9	21.1	21.6	20.2
Pet food	17.7	15.5	16.8	18.9	21.7	17.4	17.8	16.7
Pet purchase, supplies, and medicines	6.0	3.2	5.2	7.3	7.4	6.5	6.6	6.2
Veterinarian services	1.9	1.1	1.3	2.3	2.4	2.4	2.6	2.0
Toys, games, hobbies, and tricycles	9.6	6.6	7.6	10.5	11.3	11.6	11.1	12.7
Playground equipment	0.1	0.0	0.1	0.2	–	0.1	0.1	–
Other entertainment supplies, equipment, services	**5.6**	**3.1**	**3.6**	**5.3**	**7.1**	**8.2**	**8.2**	**8.3**
Sports, recreation, exercise equipment	4.4	2.8	3.1	3.8	5.4	6.4	6.7	5.9
Athletic gear, game tables, exercise equipment	2.5	1.3	1.5	2.2	3.3	4.0	4.0	4.1
Camping equipment	0.8	0.6	0.4	0.8	1.0	1.0	1.1	1.0
Hunting and fishing equipment	1.3	0.9	1.3	1.0	1.7	1.7	2.1	1.0
Global positioning system devices	0.1	–	0.1	0.1	0.1	0.2	0.1	0.4
Photographic equipment and supplies	0.8	0.2	0.4	0.8	0.5	1.5	1.4	1.9
Other photographic supplies	0.2	–	0.2	0.2	0.2	0.3	0.2	0.4
Photographer fees	0.6	0.2	0.2	0.6	0.3	1.3	1.1	1.5
Fireworks	0.1	–	0.1	0.1	0.4	0.1	0.1	0.2
Souvenirs	0.2	0.1	0.1	0.4	0.2	0.3	0.3	0.3
Visual goods	0.1	0.0	–	0.2	0.1	0.1	0.2	0.1
Pinball, electronic video games	0.1	–	0.0	0.1	0.5	0.2	0.2	0.2

Note: "–" means sample is too small to make a reliable estimate.
Source: Bureau of Labor Statistics, unpublished data from the 2008 Consumer Expenditure Survey

Table 2.28 Amount Buyers Spent on Entertainment by Education, Average Week, 2008

(average amount spent by households buying entertainment during the average week, by highest level of education of householder, 2008)

	total households	less than high school graduate	high school graduate	some college	associate's degree	college graduate total	bachelor's degree	master's, professional, doctorate
ENTERTAINMENT, AMOUNT SPENT	**$75.18**	**$57.45**	**$61.81**	**$72.36**	**$68.20**	**$95.37**	**$95.33**	**$95.45**
Fees and admissions	**64.05**	**58.54**	**41.29**	**59.77**	**72.45**	**75.33**	**77.34**	**72.28**
Fees for participant sports	44.94	40.23	33.75	47.38	50.71	49.30	50.50	47.16
Fees for recreational lessons	104.79	142.86	72.31	100.94	118.18	107.87	121.48	91.69
Audio and visual equipment, services	**87.72**	**77.82**	**83.94**	**88.75**	**88.62**	**93.43**	**93.58**	**93.21**
Radios	20.00	13.33	16.67	18.42	14.29	29.41	35.00	16.67
Cable and satellite television services	89.43	82.85	84.00	92.69	97.39	92.26	93.12	90.62
Tape recorders and players	38.89	21.43	38.46	30.00	40.91	43.33	51.43	20.00
Miscellaneous sound equipment	18.18	0.00	14.29	14.29	16.67	21.74	20.00	28.57
Miscellaneous video equipment	33.33	25.00	9.09	9.09	15.79	64.29	55.88	71.93
Sound equipment accessories	23.68	13.95	21.62	22.47	15.85	26.72	26.60	26.92
Video game hardware and software	85.94	53.21	77.47	82.83	68.02	109.17	96.02	137.31
Pets, toys, hobbies, and playground equipment	**40.02**	**29.87**	**28.43**	**34.49**	**36.00**	**58.45**	**58.89**	**57.58**
Pets	40.14	28.68	27.43	32.92	36.91	62.44	64.63	58.08
Pet food	17.74	17.75	14.25	16.10	23.70	19.91	19.49	20.71
Pet purchase, supplies, and medicines	21.31	26.71	19.15	21.66	15.60	23.54	20.03	30.61
Veterinarian services	209.47	107.27	146.97	128.19	135.39	347.88	358.98	320.60
Toys, games, hobbies, and tricycles	24.56	24.09	21.10	21.18	21.45	29.98	25.27	37.62
Playground equipment	50.00	0.00	40.00	93.33	–	11.11	14.29	–
Other entertainment supplies, equipment, services	**54.59**	**30.87**	**58.10**	**57.77**	**36.15**	**60.87**	**59.30**	**63.64**
Sports, recreation, exercise equipment	52.52	22.06	47.71	57.59	37.64	61.82	59.40	66.95
Athletic gear, game tables, exercise equipment	42.86	19.40	36.00	61.29	37.54	42.93	45.39	38.42
Camping equipment	42.67	30.65	48.72	28.75	37.50	53.40	42.59	75.79
Hunting and fishing equipment	48.09	18.89	48.03	58.59	14.97	59.76	64.39	42.16
Global positioning system devices	227.27	–	171.43	85.71	125.00	300.00	318.18	288.37
Photographic equipment and supplies	79.75	140.00	155.56	83.95	42.86	61.04	58.82	63.44
Other photographic supplies	21.05	–	13.33	21.74	6.25	30.00	13.04	48.84
Photographer fees	96.72	140.00	261.90	108.62	61.76	66.93	68.14	64.47
Fireworks	27.27	–	33.33	33.33	33.33	25.00	16.67	26.09
Souvenirs	21.74	55.56	12.50	22.50	16.67	20.00	21.88	11.54
Visual goods	22.22	25.00	–	31.25	7.14	7.14	6.25	10.00
Pinball, electronic video games	21.43	–	66.67	9.09	30.61	14.29	13.04	11.11

Note: "–" means sample is too small to make a reliable estimate.
Source: Calculations by New Strategist based on the Bureau of Labor Statistics' 2008 Consumer Expenditure Survey

CHAPTER 3

Financial Products and Services Buyers, 2008

Average household spending on financial products and services increased by 8 percent between 2000 and 2008, after adjusting for inflation. Mixed trends were behind the growth in spending, including less spending on taxes and more spending on charitable contributions. Social Security payroll taxes are the financial item on which the largest percentage of households spent during an average quarter (80 percent). Contributions to churches and other religious organizations rank fourth in the Financial Buyers' Top 10 list.

Quarterly spending

During the average quarter of 2008, 51 percent of households paid federal income tax. Twenty-nine percent of households contributed money to a church or other religious organization, the donors giving an average of $640 during the quarter. Interestingly, "other cash gifts" rank sixth on the Financial Buyers' Top 10 list, as many households give money to their adult children living elsewhere. Gambling losses rank ninth on the list.

Weekly spending

During the average week of 2008, 5 percent of households reported lottery or gambling losses. Among households reporting losses, the average amount lost was $23.

Financial Buyers' Top 10

(financial product and service categories bought by the largest percentage of households during an average quarter, 2008)

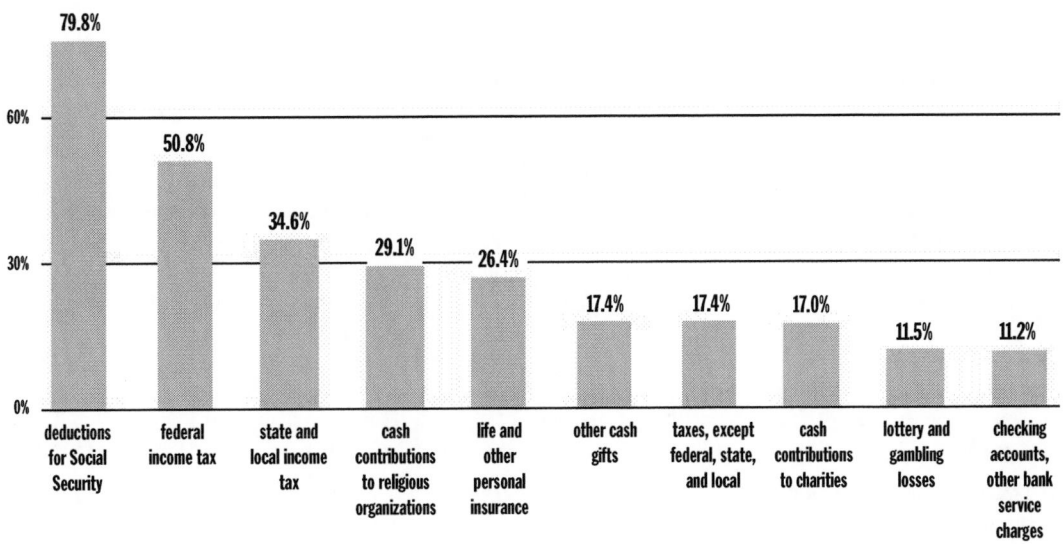

Table 3.1 Percent Buying Financial Products and Services by Age, <u>Average Quarter</u>, 2008

(percent of households buying financial products and services during the average quarter, by age of householder, 2008)

	total households	under 25	25 to 34	35 to 44	45 to 54	55 to 64	65 to 74	75+
FINANCIAL, PERCENT BUYING	**39.6%**	**24.7%**	**35.7%**	**41.0%**	**45.5%**	**46.7%**	**38.0%**	**30.4%**
Lottery and gambling losses	11.5	6.6	8.1	11.1	13.4	14.9	14.6	8.6
Legal fees	2.3	1.4	2.2	2.6	2.6	2.6	1.8	2.1
Funeral expenses	0.9	0.1	0.3	0.5	1.3	1.3	1.2	1.0
Safe deposit box rental	2.2	0.0	0.6	1.0	2.4	3.0	3.9	5.7
Checking accounts, other bank service charges	11.2	11.9	14.2	13.4	13.2	11.1	5.8	2.7
Cemetery lots, vaults, and maintenance fees	0.6	0.1	0.2	0.3	0.3	1.0	1.5	1.0
Accounting fees	5.3	2.1	4.8	5.6	5.8	6.4	5.6	4.8
Finance charges, except mortgage and vehicles	6.2	3.5	7.6	8.0	7.3	6.4	4.0	2.0
Dating services	0.1	–	0.2	0.1	0.1	0.1	0.0	–
Vacation clubs	0.3	0.1	0.2	0.3	0.4	0.4	0.3	0.2
Expenses for other properties	5.1	0.5	1.7	3.5	6.2	8.8	6.8	6.7
Occupational expenses	6.2	1.6	5.8	7.8	9.2	8.3	2.7	0.8
Credit card memberships	0.7	0.3	0.6	0.6	0.7	0.9	0.9	0.4
Shopping club membership fees	3.3	1.2	2.5	3.9	3.8	4.1	4.2	1.9
CASH CONTRIBUTIONS, PERCENT SPENDING	**50.8**	**30.3**	**39.7**	**49.1**	**55.5**	**56.3**	**58.5**	**60.2**
Support for college students	2.9	0.8	0.5	1.7	6.9	3.7	1.9	1.6
Alimony expenditures	0.3	0.1	0.1	0.3	0.3	0.5	0.5	0.1
Child support expenditures	3.0	1.8	4.8	5.5	3.5	1.1	0.3	0.4
Gifts to members of other households of stocks, bonds, and mutual funds	0.2	0.1	0.2	0.1	0.1	0.3	0.6	0.4
Cash contributions to charities and other organizations	17.0	6.7	10.0	13.9	19.2	22.1	22.4	23.2
Cash contributions to church, religious organizations	29.1	13.3	19.5	26.3	30.4	33.0	40.2	41.1
Cash contributions to educational institutions	2.1	0.4	1.4	1.8	2.6	3.0	1.9	2.4
Cash contributions to political organizations	2.4	0.7	1.3	1.8	2.5	3.8	3.7	2.9
Other cash gifts	17.4	12.2	13.0	15.9	19.3	20.5	20.7	19.2
INSURANCE/PENSIONS, PERCENT BUYING	**84.0**	**89.8**	**96.2**	**95.6**	**94.1**	**86.5**	**60.0**	**34.6**
Life and other personal insurance	**27.3**	**5.5**	**19.3**	**30.1**	**34.4**	**35.5**	**29.4**	**19.5**
Life, endowment, annuity, other personal insurance	26.4	5.3	18.6	29.2	33.4	34.8	28.2	18.3
Other nonhealth insurance	2.0	0.5	1.3	2.0	2.5	2.4	2.4	1.9
Pensions and Social Security	**80.1**	**89.8**	**96.1**	**95.4**	**92.9**	**81.8**	**46.5**	**19.6**
Deductions for government retirement	2.7	0.6	2.8	2.9	4.5	3.7	0.9	0.2
Deductions for railroad retirement	0.1	–	0.1	0.2	0.3	0.2	–	–
Deductions for private pensions	11.0	5.5	12.2	14.3	16.6	12.5	2.4	0.5
Nonpayroll deposit to retirement plans	7.9	1.6	8.6	9.0	11.0	9.9	4.6	1.9
Deductions for Social Security	79.8	89.8	96.1	95.4	92.9	81.3	45.7	18.6
PERSONAL TAXES, PERCENT SPENDING	**64.8**	**56.7**	**68.7**	**69.7**	**68.4**	**67.1**	**58.8**	**48.5**
Federal income taxes	**50.8**	**48.8**	**58.9**	**57.9**	**55.7**	**51.6**	**39.6**	**23.6**
Federal income tax deducted	24.5	25.0	31.3	29.4	31.1	24.4	11.2	2.6
Additional federal income tax paid	9.8	2.6	6.1	8.0	10.9	14.5	13.5	10.5
Federal income tax refunds (percent receiving)	35.4	38.2	46.4	42.9	37.6	32.3	22.9	12.9
2008 tax stimulus (percent receiving)	**21.0**	**14.6**	**21.3**	**22.0**	**20.7**	**21.6**	**22.3**	**21.4**
State and local income taxes	**34.6**	**30.5**	**40.1**	**38.4**	**39.4**	**38.5**	**25.7**	**12.4**
State and local income tax deducted	17.2	16.2	21.5	19.5	22.1	19.1	8.3	1.9
Additional state and local income tax paid	7.5	2.9	5.9	6.5	9.2	11.0	8.3	5.1
State and local income tax refunds (percent receiving)	21.8	21.6	27.9	25.8	23.9	21.7	14.7	6.8
Other taxes	**17.4**	**7.0**	**13.8**	**16.0**	**20.2**	**21.4**	**21.4**	**16.3**

Note: "–" means sample is too small to make a reliable estimate.
Source: Bureau of Labor Statistics, unpublished data from the 2008 Consumer Expenditure Survey

Table 3.2 **Amount Buyers Spent on Financial Products and Services by Age, <u>Average Quarter</u>, 2008**

(average amount spent by households buying financial products and services during the average quarter, by age of householder, 2008)

	total households	under 25	25 to 34	35 to 44	45 to 54	55 to 64	65 to 74	75+
FINANCIAL, AMOUNT SPENT	**$500.53**	**$273.73**	**$445.66**	**$484.17**	**$499.75**	**$678.06**	**$423.23**	**$427.85**
Lottery and gambling losses	139.20	71.49	129.50	104.78	128.01	162.30	177.95	179.20
Legal fees	1,543.75	2,129.35	1,492.71	1,275.20	1,172.49	2,363.97	1,549.44	1,279.59
Funeral expenses	1,663.24	3,646.43	1,402.88	2,049.51	1,288.55	1,871.80	1,463.91	2,050.48
Safe deposit box rental	41.82	25.00	31.36	45.00	42.53	44.11	39.51	41.77
Checking accounts, other bank service charges	47.59	56.68	42.88	49.78	47.90	48.17	47.13	34.52
Cemetery lots, vaults, and maintenance fees	868.10	65.63	259.78	754.46	872.50	1,489.18	481.59	699.76
Accounting fees	291.18	149.41	210.17	255.31	327.18	347.32	316.98	305.04
Finance charges, except mortgage and vehicles	722.27	375.00	798.28	762.00	807.94	672.74	510.58	386.57
Dating services	65.00	–	79.69	79.17	77.08	35.00	25.00	–
Vacation clubs	587.10	257.14	501.19	468.94	828.75	569.32	585.16	164.47
Expenses for other properties	842.06	210.65	1,097.40	1,076.85	793.91	1,094.47	466.59	464.80
Occupational expenses	202.92	193.29	218.92	213.59	201.42	201.87	141.61	107.44
Credit card memberships	64.39	36.21	55.26	57.03	85.23	62.77	68.96	41.22
Shopping club membership fees	56.59	44.17	53.73	53.24	58.36	61.53	57.63	53.11
CASH CONTRIBUTIONS, AMOUNT SPENT	**854.42**	**353.06**	**651.81**	**789.33**	**970.04**	**961.04**	**868.52**	**952.08**
Support for college students	907.87	371.65	532.35	759.20	908.66	1,163.46	616.32	1,006.33
Alimony expenditures	3,764.42	421.43	1,378.57	2,025.00	6,117.31	5,006.67	2,581.11	1,903.57
Child support expenditures	1,568.81	1,338.19	1,394.90	1,600.64	1,777.38	1,450.94	943.75	2,138.69
Gifts to members of other households of stocks, bonds, and mutual funds	2,434.09	103.13	1,276.39	335.71	1,027.08	4,729.69	1,346.25	4,007.14
Cash contributions to charities and other organizations	248.28	58.73	175.35	217.26	286.36	258.28	222.09	321.17
Cash contributions to church, religious organizations	640.06	364.86	569.59	579.76	782.54	707.54	650.84	499.63
Cash contributions to educational institutions	555.12	41.67	98.15	745.97	577.30	528.55	215.19	1,078.06
Cash contributions to political organizations	184.81	46.53	109.45	204.17	214.88	245.88	117.30	144.69
Other cash gifts	586.48	211.66	424.23	509.07	430.46	633.76	744.24	1,154.63
INSURANCE AND PENSIONS, AMOUNT SPENT	**1,668.37**	**635.31**	**1,431.64**	**1,872.80**	**2,087.11**	**2,006.32**	**1,089.76**	**724.60**
Life and other personal insurance	**289.92**	**166.56**	**201.15**	**235.86**	**286.64**	**366.10**	**392.18**	**240.11**
Life, endowment, annuity, other personal insurance	286.88	145.10	199.92	235.39	279.41	360.06	396.17	240.87
Other nonhealth insurance	169.70	282.08	117.99	117.29	220.00	190.98	150.53	152.55
Pensions and Social Security	**1,651.12**	**625.29**	**1,393.38**	**1,803.28**	**2,006.60**	**1,962.95**	**1,159.50**	**1,039.24**
Deductions for government retirement	839.43	481.47	559.86	728.67	955.82	1,007.43	887.91	121.88
Deductions for railroad retirement	1,526.79	–	1,369.23	1,576.67	1,571.88	1,321.67	–	–
Deductions for private pensions	1,376.25	734.34	1,068.77	1,470.28	1,393.67	1,690.34	1,113.43	850.48
Nonpayroll deposit to retirement plans	1,670.32	806.72	908.89	1,359.95	1,678.63	2,362.32	2,359.45	3,073.66
Deductions for Social Security	1,271.57	562.81	1,157.45	1,429.97	1,508.13	1,381.89	867.24	763.48
PERSONAL TAXES, AMOUNT SPENT	**690.09**	**96.66**	**388.86**	**683.01**	**1,208.29**	**984.47**	**352.88**	**71.57**
Federal income taxes	**894.74**	**239.31**	**571.43**	**878.57**	**1,337.65**	**1,194.66**	**615.33**	**410.18**
Federal income tax deducted	2,120.94	957.40	1,924.21	2,410.75	2,563.57	2,093.90	1,158.93	1,035.11
Additional federal income tax paid	1,508.11	194.51	762.77	1,736.15	1,545.84	1,984.25	1,393.33	1,095.34
Federal income tax refunds	−604.23	−334.70	−673.92	−790.53	−587.28	−559.04	−325.23	−348.74
2008 tax stimulus	**−932.50**	**−770.52**	**−1,035.25**	**−1,155.66**	**−988.16**	**−882.49**	**−713.87**	**−593.76**
State and local income taxes	**391.90**	**148.77**	**317.61**	**463.65**	**536.61**	**422.56**	**172.76**	**108.70**
State and local income tax deducted	793.11	362.68	719.72	948.66	964.66	734.30	364.43	319.85
Additional state and local income tax paid	377.96	38.79	166.57	482.61	343.66	515.41	363.90	337.77
State and local income tax refunds	−135.41	−66.66	−131.95	−146.32	−140.31	−155.11	−108.89	−149.37
Other taxes	**307.33**	**77.04**	**173.13**	**276.94**	**366.65**	**338.28**	**367.14**	**317.26**

Note: "–" means sample is too small to make a reliable estimate. Negative amounts are money received.
Source: Calculations by New Strategist based on the Bureau of Labor Statistics' 2008 Consumer Expenditure Survey

Table 3.3 Percent Buying Financial Products and Services by Age, <u>Average Week</u>, 2008

(percent of households buying financial products and services during the average week, by age of householder, 2008)

	total households	under 25	25 to 34	35 to 44	45 to 54	55 to 64	65 to 74	75+
Lottery and gambling losses	5.1%	1.8%	3.3%	4.1%	6.1%	7.3%	7.1%	4.8%
Personal taxes	54.7	46.7	62.9	59.4	58.8	53.8	45.8	38.1

Source: Bureau of Labor Statistics, unpublished data from the 2008 Consumer Expenditure Survey

Table 3.4 Amount Buyers Spent on Financial Products and Services by Age, <u>Average Week</u>, 2008

(average amount spent by households buying financial products and services during the average week, by age of householder, 2008)

	total households	under 25	25 to 34	35 to 44	45 to 54	55 to 64	65 to 74	75+
Lottery and gambling losses	$22.96	$21.20	$23.94	$38.11	$14.24	$20.68	$27.50	$18.95
Personal taxes	4,172.14	1,122.52	3,364.04	4,286.86	6,190.53	5,062.13	2,153.34	2,522.61

Source: Calculations by New Strategist based on the Bureau of Labor Statistics' 2008 Consumer Expenditure Survey

Table 3.5 Percent Buying Financial Products and Services by Household Income, <u>Average Quarter</u>, 2008

(percent of households buying financial products and services during the average quarter, by before-tax income of household, 2008)

	total households	under $20,000	$20,000– $39,999	$40,000– $49,999	$50,000– $69,999	$70,000– $79,999	$80,000– $99,999	$100,000 or more
FINANCIAL, PERCENT BUYING	**39.6%**	**24.0%**	**33.2%**	**40.1%**	**44.9%**	**48.1%**	**48.0%**	**54.1%**
Lottery and gambling losses	11.5	7.8	10.6	12.9	13.3	13.0	13.1	13.6
Legal fees	2.3	1.5	2.1	1.9	2.6	2.3	2.7	3.4
Funeral expenses	0.9	0.5	0.8	0.8	0.9	0.7	1.1	1.3
Safe deposit box rental	2.2	1.5	1.8	1.7	2.5	2.5	2.6	3.4
Checking accounts, other bank service charges	11.2	7.1	8.4	11.4	12.8	15.6	13.0	15.8
Cemetery lots, vaults, and maintenance fees	0.6	0.6	0.6	0.7	0.8	0.2	0.5	0.6
Accounting fees	5.3	2.3	4.8	5.8	5.6	4.8	7.4	8.3
Finance charges, except mortgage and vehicles	6.2	3.1	5.4	7.3	7.6	7.2	8.4	7.9
Dating services	0.1	0.0	0.1	0.1	0.1	0.3	0.1	0.1
Vacation clubs	0.3	0.1	0.1	0.3	0.3	0.4	0.4	0.8
Expenses for other properties	5.1	2.4	3.9	4.7	4.9	6.5	6.1	9.2
Occupational expenses	6.2	1.1	2.8	5.7	8.8	9.9	10.3	11.5
Credit card memberships	0.7	0.3	0.4	0.7	0.8	0.8	0.7	1.2
Shopping club membership fees	3.3	1.1	2.3	2.4	3.7	5.3	4.9	6.0
CASH CONTRIBUTIONS, PERCENT SPENDING	**50.8**	**35.6**	**44.8**	**50.0**	**53.7**	**56.7**	**59.2**	**68.2**
Support for college students	2.9	0.7	1.3	2.5	2.7	3.2	4.1	7.1
Alimony expenditures	0.3	0.0	0.2	0.3	0.2	0.3	0.5	0.6
Child support expenditures	3.0	1.4	2.5	3.7	4.0	3.6	3.8	3.4
Gifts to members of other households of stocks, bonds, and mutual funds	0.2	0.2	0.3	0.3	0.1	0.1	0.3	0.3
Cash contributions to charities and other organizations	17.0	8.8	12.4	15.1	17.4	19.6	22.9	29.4
Cash contributions to church, religious organizations	29.1	22.0	26.7	28.4	28.5	30.6	33.3	38.7
Cash contributions to educational institutions	2.1	0.6	1.0	1.5	2.3	2.1	2.3	5.0
Cash contributions to political organizations	2.4	1.0	1.5	1.6	1.9	2.6	2.5	6.0
Other cash gifts	17.4	11.1	15.3	17.2	19.1	20.8	20.6	23.7
INSURANCE/PENSIONS, PERCENT BUYING	**84.0**	**53.7**	**80.8**	**91.8**	**95.4**	**97.1**	**97.9**	**98.8**
Life and other personal insurance	**27.3**	**12.3**	**21.0**	**25.8**	**31.0**	**35.3**	**36.9**	**43.3**
Life, endowment, annuity, other personal insurance	26.4	11.7	20.1	25.0	29.9	34.4	36.3	42.1
Other nonhealth insurance	2.0	0.9	1.5	1.8	2.5	2.3	1.9	3.4
Pensions and Social Security	**80.1**	**45.3**	**74.6**	**89.2**	**93.1**	**96.2**	**97.2**	**98.4**
Deductions for government retirement	2.7	0.2	1.1	2.1	3.1	5.4	5.1	5.7
Deductions for railroad retirement	0.1	–	0.0	0.1	0.2	0.6	0.4	0.2
Deductions for private pensions	11.0	1.0	4.8	9.5	14.1	18.0	18.4	22.7
Nonpayroll deposit to retirement plans	7.9	1.3	2.9	4.9	8.6	10.6	13.7	19.0
Deductions for Social Security	79.8	44.6	74.3	89.1	92.9	96.2	97.1	98.3
PERSONAL TAXES, PERCENT SPENDING	**64.8**	**43.8**	**64.7**	**70.7**	**71.5**	**73.2**	**76.1**	**72.8**
Federal income taxes	**50.8**	**27.9**	**48.0**	**55.3**	**58.5**	**61.4**	**64.9**	**61.9**
Federal income tax deducted	24.5	10.2	20.2	26.9	29.3	34.1	33.7	33.9
Additional federal income tax paid	9.8	3.4	7.2	8.4	11.2	11.2	13.9	17.7
Federal income tax refunds (percent receiving)	35.4	21.0	35.6	40.6	41.0	42.6	43.9	37.9
2008 tax stimulus (percent receiving)	**21.0**	**15.6**	**21.9**	**24.6**	**24.1**	**23.0**	**24.5**	**19.4**
State and local income taxes	**34.6**	**16.4**	**29.6**	**37.6**	**41.0**	**42.1**	**48.5**	**46.1**
State and local income tax deducted	17.2	6.3	12.7	19.1	21.1	23.9	24.3	26.0
Additional state and local income tax paid	7.5	2.4	5.7	7.2	8.4	8.0	11.5	13.1
State and local income tax refunds (percent receiving)	21.8	10.9	19.6	24.6	26.6	27.6	30.4	26.0
Other taxes	**17.4**	**9.9**	**17.0**	**18.7**	**20.1**	**19.7**	**20.3**	**21.4**

Note: "–" means sample is too small to make a reliable estimate.
Source: Bureau of Labor Statistics, unpublished data from the 2008 Consumer Expenditure Survey

Table 3.6 Amount Buyers Spent on Financial Products and Services by Household Income, Average Quarter, 2008

(average amount spent by households buying financial products and services during the average quarter, by before-tax income of household, 2008)

	total households	under $20,000	$20,000–$39,999	$40,000–$49,999	$50,000–$69,999	$70,000–$79,999	$80,000–$99,999	$100,000 or more
FINANCIAL, AMOUNT SPENT	**$500.53**	**$291.69**	**$371.35**	**$412.40**	**$446.74**	**$457.54**	**$504.14**	**$787.45**
Lottery and gambling losses	139.20	102.40	134.27	119.63	162.35	145.23	120.58	166.01
Legal fees	1,543.75	912.97	1,304.33	1,917.16	1,148.64	972.60	1,543.98	2,275.88
Funeral expenses	1,663.24	997.29	1,391.90	1,472.92	1,305.38	1,456.72	1,059.65	2,620.04
Safe deposit box rental	41.82	42.05	38.40	49.11	35.89	36.25	39.03	48.13
Checking accounts, other bank service charges	47.59	39.67	44.67	48.92	51.86	52.09	47.15	49.37
Cemetery lots, vaults, and maintenance fees	868.10	310.27	773.57	369.49	1,185.44	282.61	1,461.54	1,453.64
Accounting fees	291.18	253.73	171.98	188.96	275.45	277.47	265.95	444.07
Finance charges, except mortgage and vehicles	722.27	422.82	579.71	574.45	706.25	875.45	764.43	986.40
Dating services	65.00	30.02	89.75	64.29	89.58	63.28	54.17	55.00
Vacation clubs	587.10	316.31	446.96	267.97	431.73	749.36	533.55	679.82
Expenses for other properties	842.06	640.95	431.93	601.90	676.44	841.38	745.04	1,297.69
Occupational expenses	202.92	139.97	139.40	154.47	162.27	213.08	208.35	262.96
Credit card memberships	64.39	56.68	45.41	54.05	54.28	81.65	76.47	75.21
Shopping club membership fees	56.59	45.69	50.01	57.02	57.01	49.24	56.95	63.52
CASH CONTRIBUTIONS, AMOUNT SPENT	**854.42**	**411.06**	**541.49**	**594.48**	**712.01**	**969.61**	**979.52**	**1,489.43**
Support for college students	907.87	858.84	494.69	634.82	627.66	837.50	1,068.77	1,098.45
Alimony expenditures	3,764.42	2,079.03	1,377.64	2,061.11	2,575.00	6,837.90	4,579.17	4,510.42
Child support expenditures	1,568.81	1,246.70	1,204.00	1,188.81	1,422.37	1,650.97	1,765.56	2,338.57
Gifts to members of other households of stocks, bonds, and mutual funds	2,434.09	935.04	901.58	536.11	373.21	472.73	1,217.74	7,806.25
Cash contributions to charities and other organizations	248.28	142.77	173.59	157.66	167.60	212.55	269.25	391.25
Cash contributions to church, religious organizations	640.06	313.83	398.67	464.95	564.66	811.24	735.36	1,096.13
Cash contributions to educational institutions	555.12	117.62	235.36	172.32	289.76	376.91	383.52	922.54
Cash contributions to political organizations	184.81	107.60	93.82	132.32	110.98	105.04	138.29	272.40
Other cash gifts	586.48	342.44	450.70	402.79	549.36	683.69	606.17	877.64
INSURANCE AND PENSIONS, AMOUNT SPENT	**1,668.37**	**243.24**	**597.66**	**942.32**	**1,362.20**	**1,786.66**	**2,151.83**	**3,996.81**
Life and other personal insurance	**289.92**	**167.31**	**188.88**	**203.74**	**227.90**	**259.47**	**272.11**	**471.45**
Life, endowment, annuity, other personal insurance	286.88	165.42	189.40	198.81	226.34	257.75	270.04	462.79
Other nonhealth insurance	169.70	122.39	114.05	161.03	113.48	122.76	129.06	272.49
Pensions and Social Security	**1,651.12**	**241.98**	**593.28**	**911.21**	**1,319.91**	**1,708.30**	**2,063.82**	**3,804.82**
Deductions for government retirement	839.43	162.28	341.26	475.36	505.34	760.71	868.91	1,204.25
Deductions for railroad retirement	1,526.79	–	332.56	667.50	1,100.00	1,244.55	1,355.63	2,622.37
Deductions for private pensions	1,376.25	180.80	357.12	576.29	709.59	848.12	1,157.88	2,451.82
Nonpayroll deposit to retirement plans	1,670.32	1,680.76	1,355.13	725.46	1,226.63	1,153.15	1,028.23	2,333.43
Deductions for Social Security	1,271.57	190.59	514.82	798.46	1,082.66	1,373.69	1,650.22	2,713.75
PERSONAL TAXES, AMOUNT SPENT	**690.09**	**–199.46**	**–154.31**	**39.56**	**248.21**	**483.14**	**781.17**	**2,972.61**
Federal income taxes	**894.74**	**–82.43**	**25.26**	**263.62**	**467.92**	**696.50**	**982.04**	**2,904.95**
Federal income tax deducted	2,120.94	267.46	701.16	1,056.13	1,445.13	1,739.09	2,288.83	4,799.39
Additional federal income tax paid	1,508.11	1,011.81	470.24	820.73	712.12	988.73	1,224.91	2,938.02
Federal income tax refunds	–604.23	–405.66	–458.93	–510.27	–559.86	–649.32	–692.81	–922.25
2008 tax stimulus	**–932.50**	**–552.43**	**–740.61**	**–919.74**	**–1,035.11**	**–1,127.80**	**–1,175.50**	**–1,235.24**
State and local income taxes	**391.90**	**37.28**	**76.21**	**162.01**	**249.81**	**312.76**	**353.26**	**1,036.39**
State and local income tax deducted	793.11	115.41	260.15	393.05	550.87	665.26	801.97	1,661.09
Additional state and local income tax paid	377.96	325.82	127.44	151.17	217.78	141.06	191.72	784.82
State and local income tax refunds	–135.41	–92.74	–91.03	–102.78	–119.68	–139.58	–149.75	–215.64
Other taxes	**307.33**	**157.81**	**157.74**	**252.43**	**252.85**	**273.90**	**365.96**	**591.42**

Note: "–" means sample is too small to make a reliable estimate. Negative amounts are money received.
Source: Calculations by New Strategist based on the Bureau of Labor Statistics' 2008 Consumer Expenditure Survey

Table 3.7 Percent Buying Financial Products and Services by Household Income, <u>Average Week</u>, 2008

(percent of households buying financial products and services during the average week, by before-tax income of household, 2008)

	total households	under $20,000	$20,000– $39,999	$40,000– $49,999	$50,000– $69,999	$70,000– $79,999	$80,000– $99,999	$100,000 or more
Lottery and gambling losses	5.1%	2.5%	5.1%	5.0%	6.5%	5.1%	6.4%	6.3%
Personal taxes	54.7	29.5	51.6	59.7	61.1	64.2	66.5	69.5

Source: Bureau of Labor Statistics, unpublished data from the 2008 Consumer Expenditure Survey

Table 3.8 Amount Buyers Spent on Financial Products and Services by Household Income, <u>Average Week</u>, 2008

(average amount spent by households buying financial products and services during the average week, by before-tax income of household, 2008)

	total households	under $20,000	$20,000– $39,999	$40,000– $49,999	$50,000– $69,999	$70,000– $79,999	$80,000– $99,999	$100,000 or more
Lottery and gambling losses	$22.96	$10.95	$24.91	$32.60	$35.83	$13.73	$21.54	$15.17
Personal taxes	4,172.14	758.56	172.70	1,648.12	2,441.42	3,767.84	3,717.90	12,774.60

Source: Calculations by New Strategist based on the Bureau of Labor Statistics' 2008 Consumer Expenditure Survey

Table 3.9 Percent of High-Income Households Buying Financial Products and Services, Average Quarter, 2008

(percent of high-income households buying financial products and services during the average quarter, by before-tax income of household, 2008)

	total households	$100,000 or more	$100,000–$119,999	$120,000–$149,999	$150,000 or more
FINANCIAL, PERCENT BUYING	**39.6%**	**54.1%**	**51.9%**	**55.3%**	**55.2%**
Lottery and gambling losses	11.5	13.6	14.1	14.0	12.9
Legal fees	2.3	3.4	3.3	2.6	4.0
Funeral expenses	0.9	1.3	1.0	1.3	1.5
Safe deposit box rental	2.2	3.4	2.6	3.3	4.0
Checking accounts, other bank service charges	11.2	15.8	14.8	15.4	16.7
Cemetery lots, vaults, and maintenance fees	0.6	0.6	0.7	0.5	0.5
Accounting fees	5.3	8.3	6.7	8.1	9.7
Finance charges, except mortgage and vehicles	6.2	7.9	7.4	10.0	7.0
Dating services	0.1	0.1	0.0	–	0.1
Vacation clubs	0.3	0.8	1.1	0.6	0.7
Expenses for other properties	5.1	9.2	8.6	8.6	10.1
Occupational expenses	6.2	11.5	12.7	12.6	9.9
Credit card memberships	0.7	1.2	0.9	1.1	1.5
Shopping club membership fees	3.3	6.0	5.9	5.0	6.8
CASH CONTRIBUTIONS, PERCENT SPENDING	**50.8**	**68.2**	**63.5**	**69.4**	**71.2**
Support for college students	2.9	7.1	4.4	7.4	9.1
Alimony expenditures	0.3	0.6	0.4	0.1	1.1
Child support expenditures	3.0	3.4	3.6	3.2	3.4
Gifts to members of other households of stocks, bonds, mutual funds	0.2	0.3	0.3	0.2	0.3
Cash contributions to charities and other organizations	17.0	29.4	23.4	29.0	34.5
Cash contributions to church, religious organizations	29.1	38.7	37.5	39.5	39.3
Cash contributions to educational institutions	2.1	5.0	2.8	4.9	6.8
Cash contributions to political organizations	2.4	6.0	3.7	5.8	8.0
Other cash gifts	17.4	23.7	22.7	24.1	24.2
INSURANCE AND PENSIONS, PERCENT BUYING	**84.0**	**98.8**	**98.5**	**98.7**	**99.1**
Life and other personal insurance	**27.3**	**43.3**	**39.7**	**44.5**	**45.4**
Life, endowment, annuity, other personal insurance	26.4	42.1	38.7	43.7	43.9
Other nonhealth insurance	2.0	3.4	2.7	3.1	4.1
Pensions and Social Security	**80.1**	**98.4**	**98.1**	**98.0**	**98.9**
Deductions for government retirement	2.7	5.7	6.6	5.9	4.9
Deductions for railroad retirement	0.1	0.2	0.2	0.5	–
Deductions for private pensions	11.0	22.7	22.1	24.0	22.4
Nonpayroll deposit to retirement plans	7.9	19.0	15.4	16.5	23.7
Deductions for Social Security	79.8	98.3	98.1	98.0	98.8
PERSONAL TAXES, PERCENT SPENDING	**64.8**	**72.8**	**75.1**	**73.9**	**70.2**
Federal income taxes	**50.8**	**61.9**	**62.9**	**63.4**	**60.2**
Federal income tax deducted	24.5	33.9	34.6	34.0	33.3
Additional federal income tax paid	9.8	17.7	13.4	16.3	22.2
Federal income tax refunds (percent receiving)	35.4	37.9	42.9	40.2	32.2
2008 tax stimulus (percent receiving)	**21.0**	**19.4**	**24.0**	**20.7**	**14.8**
State and local income taxes	**34.6**	**46.1**	**45.2**	**46.6**	**46.6**
State and local income tax deducted	17.2	26.0	26.2	25.6	26.0
Additional state and local income tax paid	7.5	13.1	9.9	12.6	16.1
State and local income tax refunds (percent receiving)	21.8	26.0	28.0	28.3	23.0
Other taxes	**17.4**	**21.4**	**21.7**	**20.8**	**21.5**

Note: "–" means sample is too small to make a reliable estimate.
Source: Bureau of Labor Statistics, unpublished data from the 2008 Consumer Expenditure Survey

Table 3.10 Amount High-Income Buyers Spent on Financial Products and Services, Average Quarter, 2008

(average amount spent by high-income households buying financial products and services during the average quarter, by before-tax income of household, 2008)

	total households	$100,000 or more	$100,000–$119,999	$120,000–$149,999	$150,000 or more
FINANCIAL, AMOUNT SPENT	**$500.53**	**$787.45**	**$599.73**	**$716.27**	**$979.44**
Lottery and gambling losses	139.20	166.01	159.71	231.52	124.67
Legal fees	1,543.75	2,275.88	1,551.20	1,522.57	3,084.37
Funeral expenses	1,663.24	2,620.04	1,527.50	3,133.93	2,962.67
Safe deposit box rental	41.82	48.13	35.80	40.74	58.75
Checking accounts, other bank service charges	47.59	49.37	42.96	51.98	52.47
Cemetery lots, vaults, and maintenance fees	868.10	1,453.64	824.66	3,086.98	1,114.44
Accounting fees	291.18	444.07	311.94	354.09	568.71
Finance charges, except mortgage and vehicles	722.27	986.40	977.92	927.70	1,049.14
Dating services	65.00	55.00	68.75	–	47.22
Vacation clubs	587.10	679.82	582.52	344.17	992.47
Expenses for other properties	842.06	1,297.69	832.40	1,200.44	1,674.73
Occupational expenses	202.92	262.96	248.40	236.71	300.28
Credit card memberships	64.39	75.21	79.94	63.41	79.08
Shopping club membership fees	56.59	63.52	58.63	63.02	67.22
CASH CONTRIBUTIONS, AMOUNT SPENT	**854.42**	**1,489.43**	**928.34**	**1,099.95**	**2,152.04**
Support for college students	907.87	1,098.45	822.94	953.16	1,285.20
Alimony expenditures	3,764.42	4,510.42	2,512.50	3,331.25	5,144.42
Child support expenditures	1,568.81	2,338.57	1,778.94	1,904.21	3,088.20
Gifts to members of other households of stocks, bonds, and mutual funds	2,434.09	7,806.25	3,975.00	85.53	13,653.03
Cash contributions to charities and other organizations	248.28	391.25	217.36	258.16	561.97
Cash contributions to church, religious organizations	640.06	1,096.13	726.43	953.17	1,480.77
Cash contributions to educational institutions	555.12	922.54	241.91	234.08	1,478.51
Cash contributions to political organizations	184.81	272.40	166.53	157.81	367.96
Other cash gifts	586.48	877.64	590.95	659.04	1,241.92
INSURANCE AND PENSIONS, AMOUNT SPENT	**1,668.37**	**3,996.81**	**2,737.40**	**3,533.16**	**5,330.19**
Life and other personal insurance	**289.92**	**471.45**	**316.77**	**385.83**	**637.95**
Life, endowment, annuity, other personal insurance	286.88	462.79	311.75	375.64	629.35
Other nonhealth insurance	169.70	272.49	192.15	242.71	331.74
Pensions and Social Security	**1,651.12**	**3,804.82**	**2,621.10**	**3,381.93**	**5,045.20**
Deductions for government retirement	839.43	1,204.25	962.84	1,061.05	1,589.23
Deductions for railroad retirement	1,526.79	2,622.37	1,897.50	2,969.68	–
Deductions for private pensions	1,376.25	2,451.82	1,509.87	2,148.61	3,428.87
Nonpayroll deposit to retirement plans	1,670.32	2,333.43	1,236.77	1,856.61	3,141.33
Deductions for Social Security	1,271.57	2,713.75	2,018.64	2,464.04	3,443.81
PERSONAL TAXES, AMOUNT SPENT	**690.09**	**2,972.61**	**1,192.88**	**1,772.45**	**5,370.84**
Federal income taxes	**894.74**	**2,904.95**	**1,361.44**	**1,852.90**	**4,960.39**
Federal income tax deducted	2,120.94	4,799.39	2,917.75	3,534.71	7,257.56
Additional federal income tax paid	1,508.11	2,938.02	1,329.04	1,899.57	4,241.18
Federal income tax refunds	−604.23	−922.25	−773.21	−839.80	−1,153.19
2008 tax stimulus	**−932.50**	**−1,235.24**	**−1,284.79**	**−1,291.30**	**−1,115.56**
State and local income taxes	**391.90**	**1,036.39**	**580.60**	**669.96**	**1,642.81**
State and local income tax deducted	793.11	1,661.09	1,065.65	1,216.66	2,443.96
Additional state and local income tax paid	377.96	784.82	383.67	426.94	1,172.90
State and local income tax refunds	−135.41	−215.64	−195.84	−186.98	−258.80
Other taxes	**307.33**	**591.42**	**396.21**	**435.35**	**852.46**

Note: "–" means sample is too small to make a reliable estimate. Negative amounts are money received.
Source: Calculations by New Strategist based on the Bureau of Labor Statistics' 2008 Consumer Expenditure Survey

Table 3.11 Percent of High-Income Households Buying Financial Products and Services, Average Week, 2008

(percent of high-income households buying financial products and services during the average week, by before-tax income of household, 2008)

	total households	$100,000 or more	$100,000– $119,999	$120,000– $149,999	$150,000 or more
Lottery and gambling losses	5.1%	6.3%	7.2%	5.5%	6.1%
Personal taxes	54.7	69.5	67.8	72.4	69.0

Source: Bureau of Labor Statistics, unpublished data from the 2008 Consumer Expenditure Survey

Table 3.12 Amount High-Income Buyers Spent on Financial Products and Services, Average Week, 2008

(average amount spent by high-income households buying financial products and services during the average week, by before-tax income of household, 2008)

	total households	$100,000 or more	$100,000– $119,999	$120,000– $149,999	$150,000 or more
Lottery and gambling losses	$22.96	$15.17	$16.78	$17.60	$11.78
Personal taxes	4,172.14	12,774.60	4,962.08	9,157.02	23,667.22

Source: Calculations by New Strategist based on the Bureau of Labor Statistics' 2008 Consumer Expenditure Survey

Table 3.13 Percent Buying Financial Products and Services by Household Type, <u>Average Quarter</u>, 2008

(percent of households buying financial products and services during the average quarter, by type of household, 2008)

	total married couples	married couples, no children	married couples with children				single parent, at least one child <18	single person
			total	oldest child under 6	oldest child 6 to 17	oldest child 18 or older		
FINANCIAL, PERCENT BUYING	**44.6%**	**46.3%**	**43.5%**	**39.2%**	**44.5%**	**44.1%**	**31.4%**	**33.1%**
Lottery and gambling losses	12.2	14.3	10.4	6.9	10.4	12.4	7.7	9.9
Legal fees	2.2	2.0	2.2	2.5	2.3	1.8	4.4	1.9
Funeral expenses	1.1	1.5	0.7	0.4	0.6	1.1	0.6	0.5
Safe deposit box rental	2.7	3.9	1.6	0.6	1.6	2.4	1.0	2.2
Checking accounts, other bank service charges	11.8	10.4	13.1	14.0	14.0	10.9	9.8	9.9
Cemetery lots, vaults, and maintenance fees	0.6	0.9	0.4	0.2	0.3	0.9	0.1	0.6
Accounting fees	6.3	6.8	5.9	5.7	6.0	5.8	5.3	4.0
Finance charges, except mortgage and vehicles	7.1	5.8	8.3	8.3	7.9	9.0	6.3	4.9
Dating services	–	–	–	–	–	–	0.4	0.2
Vacation clubs	0.5	0.5	0.5	0.8	0.4	0.4	0.2	0.1
Expenses for other properties	7.1	9.3	5.1	2.9	5.3	6.3	1.0	3.1
Occupational expenses	7.9	7.1	8.7	6.7	8.9	9.7	3.9	4.3
Credit card memberships	0.7	0.9	0.5	0.5	0.5	0.4	0.6	0.6
Shopping club membership fees	4.8	4.7	4.7	4.8	4.6	4.8	2.5	1.6
CASH CONTRIBUTIONS, PERCENT SPENDING	**59.0**	**61.9**	**57.6**	**54.3**	**56.5**	**61.3**	**34.6**	**44.7**
Support for college students	4.2	4.6	4.0	0.6	2.6	8.6	2.0	1.5
Alimony expenditures	0.2	0.2	0.2	0.1	0.2	0.1	0.1	0.3
Child support expenditures	2.4	1.3	3.3	5.5	3.4	1.8	3.7	2.8
Gifts to members of other households of stocks, bonds, and mutual funds	0.3	0.5	0.2	0.3	0.2	0.1	–	0.2
Cash contributions to charities and other organizations	20.3	24.4	17.5	16.7	17.3	18.3	6.2	15.9
Cash contributions to church, religious organizations	36.7	37.3	36.8	30.6	36.2	41.4	18.6	23.0
Cash contributions to educational institutions	2.8	2.9	2.8	2.2	3.4	2.3	1.2	1.5
Cash contributions to political organizations	3.1	4.0	2.5	2.2	2.5	2.7	0.9	1.9
Other cash gifts	20.1	22.8	17.7	16.5	17.1	19.4	11.9	15.3
INSURANCE/PENSIONS, PERCENT BUYING	**90.9**	**81.4**	**98.6**	**99.2**	**98.9**	**97.8**	**86.6**	**67.8**
Life and other personal insurance	**36.0**	**35.4**	**36.9**	**29.0**	**38.0**	**39.8**	**20.5**	**15.9**
Life, endowment, annuity, other personal insurance	35.0	34.3	35.9	27.5	37.1	39.0	20.0	15.1
Other nonhealth insurance	2.5	2.7	2.4	2.5	2.2	2.8	1.5	1.4
Pensions and Social Security	**87.3**	**73.9**	**98.2**	**99.2**	**98.8**	**96.7**	**85.6**	**61.9**
Deductions for government retirement	3.7	3.2	4.3	3.5	3.9	5.4	1.6	1.8
Deductions for railroad retirement	0.3	0.2	0.4	0.4	0.3	0.3	–	0.1
Deductions for private pensions	14.0	12.2	16.2	18.1	16.4	14.9	8.5	6.7
Nonpayroll deposit to retirement plans	10.1	10.6	10.2	11.1	10.9	8.3	4.7	5.4
Deductions for Social Security	87.0	73.2	98.2	99.2	98.8	96.7	85.4	61.5
PERSONAL TAXES, PERCENT SPENDING	**69.6**	**67.8**	**71.8**	**74.3**	**72.1**	**69.7**	**64.7**	**56.5**
Federal income taxes	**56.0**	**52.2**	**59.9**	**63.8**	**61.7**	**54.6**	**53.6**	**40.8**
Federal income tax deducted	27.9	23.5	32.2	34.0	33.1	29.6	24.0	17.7
Additional federal income tax paid	11.5	15.8	8.2	6.1	7.3	11.1	4.3	9.1
Federal income tax refunds (percent receiving)	38.1	30.8	44.5	50.7	47.1	36.4	44.0	27.2
2008 tax stimulus (percent receiving)	**22.6**	**22.3**	**22.9**	**22.9**	**22.0**	**24.6**	**19.7**	**18.0**
State and local income taxes	**39.1**	**37.1**	**41.4**	**44.1**	**42.1**	**38.5**	**32.9**	**27.1**
State and local income tax deducted	19.7	17.6	22.0	22.6	22.3	21.1	14.2	12.4
Additional state and local income tax paid	9.3	11.6	7.4	5.8	7.2	8.7	4.3	6.1
State and local income tax refunds (percent receiving)	24.3	20.5	28.2	32.2	28.8	24.7	24.4	16.9
Other taxes	**19.6**	**22.5**	**17.5**	**16.1**	**17.4**	**18.7**	**13.0**	**15.5**

Note: "–" means sample is too small to make a reliable estimate.
Source: Bureau of Labor Statistics, unpublished data from the 2008 Consumer Expenditure Survey

Table 3.14 Amount Buyers Spent on Financial Products and Services by Household Type, <u>Average Quarter</u>, 2008

(average amount spent by households buying financial products and services during the average quarter, by type of household, 2008)

	total married couples	married couples, no children	married couples with children			single parent, at least one child <18	single person
			total	oldest child under 6	oldest child 6 to 17	oldest child 18 or older		
FINANCIAL, AMOUNT SPENT	**$524.55**	**$487.15**	**$542.96**	**$427.30**	**$533.30**	**$620.77**	**$481.62**	**$416.70**
Lottery and gambling losses	132.17	136.72	108.60	54.08	98.37	141.36	87.87	150.71
Legal fees	1,576.60	1,625.00	1,580.41	600.60	1,728.04	2,082.43	1,746.07	1,722.58
Funeral expenses	1,650.70	1,396.21	2,106.34	1,104.65	2,048.39	2,372.38	806.97	1,978.06
Safe deposit box rental	42.74	41.14	46.47	25.88	49.36	46.19	36.27	42.35
Checking accounts, other bank service charges	50.02	46.50	51.24	47.29	54.46	47.19	57.59	38.98
Cemetery lots, vaults, and maintenance fees	1,158.33	1,204.71	1,013.07	128.26	168.00	1,543.33	125.00	431.58
Accounting fees	319.90	330.66	319.90	210.65	294.10	429.25	247.27	257.83
Finance charges, except mortgage and vehicles	784.54	658.72	871.57	827.48	829.50	960.01	420.45	614.67
Dating services	–	–	–	–	–	–	92.68	65.00
Vacation clubs	611.73	482.29	776.53	503.85	1,191.67	386.63	420.31	425.00
Expenses for other properties	734.69	573.72	903.50	1,025.60	1,059.08	642.56	787.14	772.75
Occupational expenses	212.21	216.45	215.19	287.58	211.16	191.72	162.31	182.37
Credit card memberships	68.94	64.67	76.02	50.00	94.00	60.80	62.92	55.51
Shopping club membership fees	57.53	57.50	56.89	60.36	58.71	51.78	47.61	54.65
CASH CONTRIBUTIONS, AMOUNT SPENT	**966.35**	**1,042.12**	**909.29**	**629.69**	**937.31**	**1,012.15**	**535.49**	**735.09**
Support for college students	910.62	957.73	863.21	245.83	807.42	917.85	597.08	992.86
Alimony expenditures	3,725.00	2,867.71	5,576.47	2,414.29	6,853.26	2,344.64	1,067.86	4,272.66
Child support expenditures	1,520.85	1,890.80	1,423.72	1,406.70	1,456.54	1,349.59	1,530.36	1,680.46
Gifts to members of other households of stocks, bonds, and mutual funds	3,037.88	3,711.11	966.67	56.73	1,507.14	252.78	–	536.67
Cash contributions to charities and other organizations	294.36	329.36	254.51	197.46	266.06	266.65	220.94	182.60
Cash contributions to church, religious organizations	768.09	753.61	792.75	581.41	881.09	753.10	344.16	435.34
Cash contributions to educational institutions	544.68	360.10	737.50	108.03	618.99	1,385.67	333.26	654.11
Cash contributions to political organizations	202.59	194.80	206.18	122.02	255.31	165.36	132.35	153.48
Other cash gifts	572.06	747.07	384.60	271.27	281.86	597.77	270.55	719.54
INSURANCE AND PENSIONS, AMOUNT SPENT	**2,153.05**	**2,089.99**	**2,227.11**	**1,987.80**	**2,315.58**	**2,217.44**	**834.29**	**965.70**
Life and other personal insurance	**344.23**	**377.79**	**314.70**	**248.34**	**323.66**	**328.84**	**169.20**	**169.96**
Life, endowment, annuity, other personal insurance	340.53	375.91	308.86	248.37	318.43	318.56	160.04	170.14
Other nonhealth insurance	191.67	173.71	212.55	145.02	222.36	234.78	171.90	98.72
Pensions and Social Security	**2,100.04**	**2,119.96**	**2,118.39**	**1,916.37**	**2,194.29**	**2,107.80**	**804.02**	**1,015.13**
Deductions for government retirement	852.31	806.88	887.18	942.23	826.67	938.88	675.96	860.60
Deductions for railroad retirement	1,518.00	2,490.63	1,085.00	1,179.88	869.85	1,446.88	–	1,470.00
Deductions for private pensions	1,596.69	1,741.03	1,529.17	1,394.47	1,668.10	1,363.15	668.59	984.14
Nonpayroll deposit to retirement plans	1,818.68	2,182.02	1,507.46	1,249.33	1,678.90	1,325.75	910.55	1,416.19
Deductions for Social Security	1,599.56	1,493.65	1,666.96	1,483.31	1,696.84	1,726.25	677.12	761.45
PERSONAL TAXES, AMOUNT SPENT	**917.55**	**1,052.74**	**884.42**	**470.19**	**1,031.21**	**885.80**	**−210.40**	**533.32**
Federal income taxes	**1,145.10**	**1,296.87**	**1,096.27**	**690.17**	**1,210.94**	**1,155.49**	**−50.66**	**702.94**
Federal income tax deducted	2,477.14	2,437.28	2,584.41	2,084.64	2,905.34	2,306.63	1,104.54	1,652.56
Additional federal income tax paid	1,869.77	1,645.75	2,295.60	1,906.23	3,009.27	1,617.82	1,269.76	976.27
Federal income tax refunds	−698.30	−502.35	−818.55	−762.19	−921.08	−635.56	−788.62	−344.90
2008 tax stimulus	**−1,181.26**	**−979.16**	**−1,354.74**	**−1,312.26**	**−1,475.91**	**−1,192.27**	**−836.82**	**−504.27**
State and local income taxes	**491.63**	**471.54**	**529.90**	**370.28**	**604.83**	**497.57**	**117.64**	**264.49**
State and local income tax deducted	950.48	878.11	1,023.52	841.19	1,148.03	912.67	405.62	568.51
Additional state and local income tax paid	463.60	425.97	550.44	400.09	695.75	402.41	224.77	280.69
State and local income tax refunds	−156.68	−142.97	−165.09	−155.77	−179.17	−143.91	−116.62	−93.68
Other taxes	**371.23**	**361.42**	**394.81**	**282.11**	**382.13**	**472.53**	**131.13**	**216.90**

Note: "−" means sample is too small to make a reliable estimate. Negative amounts are money received.
Source: Calculations by New Strategist based on the Bureau of Labor Statistics' 2008 Consumer Expenditure Survey

Table 3.15 Percent Buying Financial Products and Services by Type of Household, <u>Average Week</u>, 2008

(percent of households buying financial products and services during the average week, by type of household, 2008)

| | total married couples | married couples, no children | married couples with children | | | | single parent, at least one child <18 | single person |
			total	oldest child under 6	oldest child 6 to 17	oldest child 18 or older		
Lottery and gambling losses	5.9%	7.0%	4.9%	3.3%	4.7%	6.2%	2.6%	4.6%
Personal taxes	59.6	54.1	64.2	69.0	64.4	60.6	56.8	47.3

Source: Bureau of Labor Statistics, unpublished data from the 2008 Consumer Expenditure Survey

Table 3.16 Amount Buyers Spent on Financial Products and Services by Type of Household, <u>Average Week</u>, 2008

(average amount spent by households buying financial products and services during the average week, by type of household, 2008)

| | total married couples | married couples, no children | married couples with children | | | | single parent, at least one child <18 | single person |
			total	oldest child under 6	oldest child 6 to 17	oldest child 18 or older		
Lottery and gambling losses	$21.55	$20.80	$19.59	$7.69	$15.17	$29.22	$22.66	$18.57
Personal taxes	5,478.60	5,946.25	5,740.17	4,720.61	6,830.34	4,411.54	55.29	3,300.38

Source: Calculations by New Strategist based on the Bureau of Labor Statistics' 2008 Consumer Expenditure Survey

Table 3.17 Percent Buying Financial Products and Services by Race and Hispanic Origin, <u>Average Quarter</u>, 2008

(percent of households buying financial products and services during the average quarter, by race and Hispanic origin of householder, 2008)

	total households	Asian	black	Hispanic	non-Hispanic white and other
FINANCIAL, PERCENT BUYING	**39.6%**	**30.0%**	**31.7%**	**30.3%**	**42.2%**
Lottery and gambling losses	11.5	6.5	10.4	9.6	12.0
Legal fees	2.3	2.1	1.7	1.8	2.5
Funeral expenses	0.9	0.8	0.7	0.9	0.9
Safe deposit box rental	2.2	2.5	0.5	0.5	2.8
Checking accounts, other bank service charges	11.2	8.1	11.0	7.9	11.8
Cemetery lots, vaults, and maintenance fees	0.6	0.2	0.2	0.5	0.7
Accounting fees	5.3	4.7	3.0	4.5	5.8
Finance charges, except mortgage and vehicles	6.2	4.6	5.9	5.7	6.4
Dating services	0.1	–	–	0.0	0.1
Vacation clubs	0.3	–	0.2	0.1	0.4
Expenses for other properties	5.1	1.7	2.9	2.4	5.9
Occupational expenses	6.2	6.2	4.5	4.6	6.8
Credit card memberships	0.7	0.6	0.3	0.4	0.8
Shopping club membership fees	3.3	4.3	2.5	2.7	3.6
CASH CONTRIBUTIONS, PERCENT SPENDING	**50.8**	**39.9**	**45.3**	**39.2**	**53.5**
Support for college students	2.9	1.9	2.2	0.9	3.3
Alimony expenditures	0.3	0.3	0.1	0.3	0.3
Child support expenditures	3.0	0.9	3.9	3.5	2.7
Gifts to members of other households of stocks, bonds, mutual funds	0.2	–	0.1	0.0	0.3
Cash contributions to charities and other organizations	17.0	10.7	7.4	6.6	20.1
Cash contributions to church, religious organizations	29.1	21.4	34.1	21.2	29.5
Cash contributions to educational institutions	2.1	1.4	0.6	0.8	2.5
Cash contributions to political organizations	2.4	0.6	1.7	0.6	2.8
Other cash gifts	17.4	14.7	9.4	14.9	19.1
INSURANCE/PENSIONS, PERCENT BUYING	**84.0**	**86.9**	**83.2**	**89.7**	**83.3**
Life and other personal insurance	**27.3**	**20.4**	**28.6**	**14.1**	**29.1**
Life, endowment, annuity, other personal insurance	26.4	19.7	27.5	13.6	28.2
Other nonhealth insurance	2.0	0.9	2.1	0.5	2.2
Pensions and Social Security	**80.1**	**85.8**	**77.7**	**88.7**	**79.2**
Deductions for government retirement	2.7	2.7	1.9	1.3	3.1
Deductions for railroad retirement	0.1	–	0.1	0.1	0.2
Deductions for private pensions	11.0	8.5	6.3	6.7	12.4
Nonpayroll deposit to retirement plans	7.9	7.2	3.3	3.8	9.2
Deductions for Social Security	79.8	85.6	77.6	88.6	78.8
PERSONAL TAXES, PERCENT SPENDING	**64.8**	**53.1**	**56.7**	**60.1**	**66.8**
Federal income taxes	**50.8**	**39.8**	**39.8**	**50.3**	**52.6**
Federal income tax deducted	24.5	20.3	19.6	26.2	25.1
Additional federal income tax paid	9.8	6.8	4.8	5.2	11.3
Federal income tax refunds (percent receiving)	35.4	26.8	29.4	37.8	36.0
2008 tax stimulus (percent receiving)	**21.0**	**17.1**	**19.8**	**18.4**	**21.6**
State and local income taxes	**34.6**	**27.4**	**25.6**	**25.3**	**37.4**
State and local income tax deducted	17.2	14.9	13.5	13.4	18.5
Additional state and local income tax paid	7.5	5.6	2.8	3.0	8.9
State and local income tax refunds (percent receiving)	21.8	14.4	16.9	16.7	23.4
Other taxes	**17.4**	**9.0**	**17.6**	**7.6**	**18.8**

Note: "Asian" and "black" include Hispanics and non-Hispanics who identify themselves as being of the respective race alone. "Hispanic" includes people of any race who identify themselves as Hispanic. "Other" includes people who identify themselves as non-Hispanic and as Alaska Native, American Indian, Asian (who are also included in the Asian column), or Native Hawaiian or other Pacific Islander as well as non-Hispanics reporting more than one race. "–" means sample is too small to make a reliable estimate.
Source: Bureau of Labor Statistics, unpublished data from the 2008 Consumer Expenditure Survey

Table 3.18 Amount Buyers Spent on Financial Products and Services by Race and Hispanic Origin, <u>Average Quarter</u>, 2008

(average amount spent by households buying financial products and services during the average quarter, by race and Hispanic origin of householder, 2008)

	total households	Asian	black	Hispanic	non-Hispanic white and other
FINANCIAL, AMOUNT SPENT	**$500.53**	**$533.40**	**$442.59**	**$462.18**	**$511.30**
Lottery and gambling losses	139.20	212.44	171.40	114.50	137.36
Legal fees	1,543.75	1,906.07	1,021.49	905.54	1,668.00
Funeral expenses	1,663.24	866.67	2,000.00	1,704.31	1,600.00
Safe deposit box rental	41.82	54.37	42.13	56.11	41.58
Checking accounts, other bank service charges	47.59	34.79	45.05	47.99	47.85
Cemetery lots, vaults, and maintenance fees	868.10	386.76	237.50	845.11	886.94
Accounting fees	291.18	240.74	271.13	188.20	304.94
Finance charges, except mortgage and vehicles	722.27	706.65	781.94	732.04	715.25
Dating services	65.00	–	–	25.00	70.83
Vacation clubs	587.10	–	228.13	380.56	623.61
Expenses for other properties	842.06	2,017.81	721.43	1,259.60	825.85
Occupational expenses	202.92	224.60	169.16	183.30	208.73
Credit card memberships	64.39	57.03	79.31	63.57	62.99
Shopping club membership fees	56.59	68.06	53.24	57.06	56.93
CASH CONTRIBUTIONS, AMOUNT SPENT	**854.42**	**730.04**	**646.49**	**644.61**	**905.05**
Support for college students	907.87	1,451.30	562.17	1,056.46	939.51
Alimony expenditures	3,764.42	1,504.81	1,292.86	2,037.50	4,320.37
Child support expenditures	1,568.81	1,189.52	1,427.38	1,494.63	1,611.49
Gifts to members of other households of stocks, bonds, and mutual funds	2,434.09	–	1,964.29	450.00	2,423.21
Cash contributions to charities and other organizations	248.28	271.12	148.55	207.73	256.16
Cash contributions to church, religious organizations	640.06	422.12	500.62	252.06	707.63
Cash contributions to educational institutions	555.12	2,779.04	579.37	2,962.83	441.50
Cash contributions to political organizations	184.81	585.89	161.98	181.85	187.81
Other cash gifts	586.48	594.88	355.32	632.76	599.36
INSURANCE AND PENSIONS, AMOUNT SPENT	**1,668.37**	**1,944.20**	**1,062.00**	**1,148.90**	**1,848.58**
Life and other personal insurance	**289.92**	**406.31**	**222.44**	**206.78**	**306.60**
Life, endowment, annuity, other personal insurance	286.88	414.83	217.50	209.07	303.57
Other nonhealth insurance	169.70	148.06	171.48	119.50	170.66
Pensions and Social Security	**1,651.12**	**1,872.27**	**1,054.87**	**1,129.87**	**1,831.35**
Deductions for government retirement	839.43	991.76	662.83	536.52	875.16
Deductions for railroad retirement	1,526.79	–	785.71	1,230.56	1,589.06
Deductions for private pensions	1,376.25	2,149.62	905.72	943.01	1,449.58
Nonpayroll deposit to retirement plans	1,670.32	1,481.82	838.73	1,247.49	1,742.95
Deductions for Social Security	1,271.57	1,507.72	930.17	996.97	1,371.22
PERSONAL TAXES, AMOUNT SPENT	**690.09**	**1,125.15**	**105.82**	**150.56**	**842.82**
Federal income taxes	**894.74**	**1,385.18**	**338.28**	**363.12**	**1,037.90**
Federal income tax deducted	2,120.94	3,102.90	1,483.45	1,488.79	2,299.44
Additional federal income tax paid	1,508.11	1,190.50	741.79	615.04	1,623.45
Federal income tax refunds	−604.23	−596.07	−653.45	−634.62	−592.66
2008 tax stimulus	**−932.50**	**−1,007.90**	**−807.36**	**−974.26**	**−945.69**
State and local income taxes	**391.90**	**628.90**	**227.89**	**244.81**	**425.28**
State and local income tax deducted	793.11	1,195.98	546.75	588.54	843.90
Additional state and local income tax paid	377.96	369.54	121.24	138.28	403.11
State and local income tax refunds	−135.41	−185.05	−110.32	−126.28	−139.31
Other taxes	**307.33**	**521.95**	**150.84**	**325.36**	**329.16**

Note: "Asian" and "black" include Hispanics and non-Hispanics who identify themselves as being of the respective race alone. "Hispanic" includes people of any race who identify themselves as Hispanic. "Other" includes people who identify themselves as non-Hispanic and as Alaska Native, American Indian, Asian (who are also included in the Asian column), or Native Hawaiian or other Pacific Islander as well as non-Hispanics reporting more than one race. "–" means sample is too small to make a reliable estimate. Negative amounts are money received.

Source: Bureau of Labor Statistics, unpublished data from the 2008 Consumer Expenditure Survey

Table 3.19 Percent Buying Financial Products and Services by Race and Hispanic Origin, <u>Average Week</u>, 2008

(percent of households buying financial products and services during the average week, by race and Hispanic origin of householder, 2008)

	total households	Asian	black	Hispanic	non-Hispanic white and other
Lottery and gambling losses	5.1%	3.8%	3.1%	3.2%	5.7%
Personal taxes	54.7	40.2	50.5	50.0	56.1

Note: "Asian" and "black" include Hispanics and non-Hispanics who identify themselves as being of the respective race alone. "Hispanic" includes people of any race who identify themselves as Hispanic. "Other" includes people who identify themselves as non-Hispanic and as Alaska Native, American Indian, Asian (who are also included in the Asian column), or Native Hawaiian or other Pacific Islander as well as non-Hispanics reporting more than one race.
Source: Bureau of Labor Statistics, unpublished data from the 2008 Consumer Expenditure Survey

Table 3.20 Amount Buyers Spent on Financial Products and Services by Race and Hispanic Origin, <u>Average Week</u>, 2008

(average amount spent by households buying financial products and services during the average week, by race and Hispanic origin of householder, 2008)

	total households	Asian	black	Hispanic	non-Hispanic white and other
Lottery and gambling losses	$22.96	$72.00	$21.94	$18.27	$23.47
Personal taxes	4,172.14	6,174.25	921.45	1,276.01	4,979.44

Note: "Asian" and "black" include Hispanics and non-Hispanics who identify themselves as being of the respective race alone. "Hispanic" includes people of any race who identify themselves as Hispanic. "Other" includes people who identify themselves as non-Hispanic and as Alaska Native, American Indian, Asian (who are also included in the Asian column), or Native Hawaiian or other Pacific Islander as well as non-Hispanics reporting more than one race.
Source: Calculations by New Strategist based on the Bureau of Labor Statistics' 2008 Consumer Expenditure Survey

Table 3.21 Percent Buying Financial Products and Services by Region, Average Quarter, 2008

(percent of households buying financial products and services during the average quarter, by region of residence, 2008)

	total households	Northeast	Midwest	South	West
FINANCIAL, PERCENT BUYING	**39.6%**	**41.8%**	**42.5%**	**36.0%**	**40.5%**
Lottery and gambling losses	11.5	16.2	12.5	9.7	9.7
Legal fees	2.3	2.5	2.1	2.2	2.6
Funeral expenses	0.9	0.8	0.7	1.0	0.9
Safe deposit box rental	2.2	1.9	2.8	2.0	2.3
Checking accounts, other bank service charges	11.2	10.8	12.8	10.0	11.9
Cemetery lots, vaults, and maintenance fees	0.6	0.4	0.5	0.8	0.5
Accounting fees	5.3	5.4	5.7	4.6	6.0
Finance charges, except mortgage and vehicles	6.2	5.9	6.6	6.0	6.6
Dating services	0.1	0.1	0.1	0.1	0.2
Vacation clubs	0.3	0.3	0.2	0.3	0.4
Expenses for other properties	5.1	4.2	4.8	6.4	4.0
Occupational expenses	6.2	8.0	7.9	3.9	6.9
Credit card memberships	0.7	0.9	0.4	0.5	1.1
Shopping club membership fees	3.3	3.0	2.7	3.0	4.8
CASH CONTRIBUTIONS, PERCENT SPENDING	**50.8**	**50.0**	**53.6**	**50.6**	**49.0**
Support for college students	2.9	3.3	3.2	3.0	2.0
Alimony expenditures	0.3	0.4	0.2	0.2	0.3
Child support expenditures	3.0	2.6	2.9	3.1	3.0
Gifts to members of other households of stocks, bonds, mutual funds	0.2	0.4	0.3	0.1	0.2
Cash contributions to charities and other organizations	17.0	19.7	18.5	15.3	15.9
Cash contributions to church, religious organizations	29.1	27.1	30.6	31.2	25.6
Cash contributions to educational institutions	2.1	2.5	2.5	1.4	2.4
Cash contributions to political organizations	2.4	2.3	2.9	1.8	3.0
Other cash gifts	17.4	18.7	21.2	15.5	15.8
INSURANCE AND PENSIONS, PERCENT BUYING	**84.0**	**82.1**	**84.5**	**84.1**	**84.9**
Life and other personal insurance	**27.3**	**26.6**	**29.2**	**30.4**	**21.0**
Life, endowment, annuity, other personal insurance	26.4	25.8	28.3	29.6	19.9
Other nonhealth insurance	2.0	1.8	2.2	2.1	1.7
Pensions and Social Security	**80.1**	**78.4**	**80.6**	**79.1**	**82.6**
Deductions for government retirement	2.7	2.5	3.0	2.7	2.7
Deductions for railroad retirement	0.1	0.0	0.2	0.2	0.0
Deductions for private pensions	11.0	10.9	12.2	11.1	9.7
Nonpayroll deposit to retirement plans	7.9	9.4	9.3	5.9	8.3
Deductions for Social Security	79.8	78.3	80.3	78.8	82.2
PERSONAL TAXES, PERCENT SPENDING	**64.8**	**62.7**	**65.4**	**67.6**	**61.5**
Federal income taxes	**50.8**	**48.9**	**52.5**	**51.3**	**49.7**
Federal income tax deducted	24.5	24.4	23.6	26.1	23.1
Additional federal income tax paid	9.8	8.8	9.5	9.5	11.4
Federal income tax refunds (percent receiving)	35.4	34.5	36.8	36.0	33.5
2008 tax stimulus (percent receiving)	**21.0**	**21.4**	**22.1**	**20.9**	**19.9**
State and local income taxes	**34.6**	**41.1**	**44.0**	**24.2**	**36.4**
State and local income tax deducted	17.2	22.9	20.2	11.6	18.6
Additional state and local income tax paid	7.5	10.7	9.0	4.6	8.1
State and local income tax refunds (percent receiving)	21.8	22.9	29.4	15.8	22.9
Other taxes	**17.4**	**16.3**	**13.8**	**25.9**	**8.2**

Source: Bureau of Labor Statistics, unpublished data from the 2008 Consumer Expenditure Survey

Table 3.22 Amount Buyers Spent on Financial Products and Services by Region, Average Quarter, 2008

(average amount spent by households buying financial products and services during the average quarter, by region of residence, 2008)

	total households	Northeast	Midwest	South	West
FINANCIAL, AMOUNT SPENT	**$500.53**	**$581.04**	**$411.79**	**$463.74**	**$580.88**
Lottery and gambling losses	139.20	169.24	131.13	97.75	175.91
Legal fees	1,543.75	1,581.40	1,424.53	1,097.58	2,221.26
Funeral expenses	1,663.24	2,914.24	1,252.40	1,382.11	1,575.58
Safe deposit box rental	41.82	58.29	35.92	41.50	38.74
Checking accounts, other bank service charges	47.59	38.35	44.28	49.52	55.57
Cemetery lots, vaults, and maintenance fees	868.10	1,914.29	544.12	717.95	823.96
Accounting fees	291.18	359.56	231.53	255.44	344.13
Finance charges, except mortgage and vehicles	722.27	812.73	640.64	721.18	740.20
Dating services	65.00	52.08	80.56	65.00	76.67
Vacation clubs	587.10	473.33	572.50	711.76	480.77
Expenses for other properties	842.06	1,300.42	760.51	631.66	1,090.92
Occupational expenses	202.92	182.37	184.50	234.82	215.19
Credit card memberships	64.39	52.65	58.13	74.48	66.59
Shopping club membership fees	56.59	53.83	50.92	51.58	66.30
CASH CONTRIBUTIONS, AMOUNT SPENT	**854.42**	**743.26**	**794.51**	**861.79**	**1,004.03**
Support for college students	907.87	666.99	823.84	1,051.16	1,022.63
Alimony expenditures	3,764.42	3,826.79	8,213.33	3,448.91	1,776.79
Child support expenditures	1,568.81	1,801.92	1,624.57	1,440.38	1,559.87
Gifts to members of other households of stocks, bonds, and mutual funds	2,434.09	1,797.62	854.00	932.69	7,143.42
Cash contributions to charities and other organizations	248.28	228.11	232.60	227.28	320.84
Cash contributions to church, religious organizations	640.06	408.27	592.68	650.16	882.13
Cash contributions to educational institutions	555.12	621.44	302.74	560.22	764.92
Cash contributions to political organizations	184.81	264.29	123.86	226.22	153.51
Other cash gifts	586.48	542.61	482.12	650.55	672.07
INSURANCE AND PENSIONS, AMOUNT SPENT	**1,668.37**	**1,822.53**	**1,642.29**	**1,533.94**	**1,787.28**
Life and other personal insurance	**289.92**	**361.61**	**262.30**	**263.95**	**315.24**
Life, endowment, annuity, other personal insurance	286.88	357.99	257.48	259.54	319.43
Other nonhealth insurance	169.70	206.88	169.12	167.06	143.97
Pensions and Social Security	**1,651.12**	**1,787.59**	**1,627.91**	**1,528.94**	**1,756.89**
Deductions for government retirement	839.43	818.11	878.73	765.47	926.96
Deductions for railroad retirement	1,526.79	1,000.00	1,922.62	1,334.78	625.00
Deductions for private pensions	1,376.25	1,487.56	1,205.43	1,319.06	1,598.28
Nonpayroll deposit to retirement plans	1,670.32	1,412.65	1,545.68	1,674.92	2,049.61
Deductions for Social Security	1,271.57	1,386.44	1,233.13	1,194.29	1,339.65
PERSONAL TAXES, AMOUNT SPENT	**690.09**	**900.11**	**485.50**	**514.03**	**1,050.20**
Federal income taxes	**894.74**	**1,000.69**	**636.57**	**798.61**	**1,250.48**
Federal income tax deducted	2,120.94	2,399.69	1,887.24	1,909.54	2,511.84
Additional federal income tax paid	1,508.11	1,432.80	1,191.05	1,296.05	2,117.52
Federal income tax refunds	−604.23	−645.65	−607.50	−587.78	−593.65
2008 tax stimulus	**−932.50**	**−885.76**	**−950.85**	**−936.40**	**−946.99**
State and local income taxes	**391.90**	**439.64**	**297.56**	**380.06**	**477.62**
State and local income tax deducted	793.11	796.84	708.92	821.79	854.33
Additional state and local income tax paid	377.96	308.26	220.66	370.50	641.71
State and local income tax refunds	−135.41	−152.61	−109.92	−130.80	−159.88
Other taxes	**307.33**	**514.16**	**450.71**	**159.23**	**475.46**

Note: Negative amounts are money received.
Source: Calculations by New Strategist based on the Bureau of Labor Statistics' 2008 Consumer Expenditure Survey

Table 3.23 Percent Buying Financial Products and Services by Region, Average Week, 2008

(percent of households buying financial products and services during the average week, by region of residence, 2008)

	total households	Northeast	Midwest	South	West
Lottery and gambling losses	5.1%	7.4%	5.6%	4.2%	4.4%
Personal taxes	54.7	51.6	51.6	61.5	49.6

Source: Bureau of Labor Statistics, unpublished data from the 2008 Consumer Expenditure Survey

Table 3.24 Amount Buyers Spent on Financial Products and Services by Region, Average Week, 2008

(average amount spent by households buying financial products and services during the average week, by region of residence, 2008)

	total households	Northeast	Midwest	South	West
Lottery and gambling losses	$22.96	$14.40	$20.18	$25.00	$35.86
Personal taxes	4,172.14	6,227.12	3,251.18	3,628.40	4,468.12

Source: Calculations by New Strategist based on the Bureau of Labor Statistics' 2008 Consumer Expenditure Survey

Table 3.25 Percent Buying Financial Products and Services by Education, <u>Average Quarter</u>, 2008

(percent of households buying financial products and services during the average quarter, by highest level of education of householder, 2008)

	total households	less than high school graduate	high school graduate	some college	associate's degree	college graduate total	bachelor's degree	master's, professional, doctorate
FINANCIAL, PERCENT BUYING	**39.6%**	**24.6%**	**38.4%**	**42.1%**	**43.5%**	**45.0%**	**44.0%**	**46.9%**
Lottery and gambling losses	11.5	9.3	13.4	13.2	12.0	9.6	10.3	8.5
Legal fees	2.3	1.2	2.2	2.4	2.7	2.8	2.9	2.7
Funeral expenses	0.9	0.8	1.0	0.8	0.8	0.8	0.6	1.2
Safe deposit box rental	2.2	1.0	2.0	1.8	2.7	3.2	2.9	3.8
Checking accounts, other bank service charges	11.2	5.0	9.5	13.3	13.5	13.5	13.5	13.7
Cemetery lots, vaults, and maintenance fees	0.6	0.7	0.6	0.8	0.4	0.4	0.3	0.6
Accounting fees	5.3	3.1	4.9	5.1	6.3	6.7	6.4	7.2
Finance charges, except mortgage and vehicles	6.2	3.4	5.7	7.3	6.5	7.2	7.8	6.2
Dating services	0.1	0.0	0.1	0.1	0.1	0.2	0.2	0.2
Vacation clubs	0.3	0.0	0.2	0.2	0.7	0.6	0.6	0.5
Expenses for other properties	5.1	3.1	4.3	4.7	5.8	6.9	6.3	8.0
Occupational expenses	6.2	2.5	5.8	6.1	8.2	8.0	7.1	9.5
Credit card memberships	0.7	0.2	0.5	0.6	0.7	1.1	1.0	1.4
Shopping club membership fees	3.3	1.1	2.7	3.6	4.1	4.7	4.7	4.7
CASH CONTRIBUTIONS, PERCENT SPENDING	**50.8**	**37.8**	**46.9**	**49.9**	**55.4**	**60.1**	**57.9**	**64.0**
Support for college students	2.9	0.7	2.1	2.5	2.9	5.0	4.4	6.0
Alimony expenditures	0.3	0.1	0.3	0.1	0.4	0.4	0.4	0.3
Child support expenditures	3.0	2.6	3.5	3.5	4.5	1.8	1.9	1.6
Gifts to members of other households of stocks, bonds, and mutual funds	0.2	0.1	0.2	0.3	0.3	0.3	0.3	0.2
Cash contributions to charities and other organizations	17.0	8.0	12.9	16.6	18.4	25.0	22.3	29.9
Cash contributions to church, religious organizations	29.1	22.2	26.9	28.4	29.5	34.9	34.0	36.6
Cash contributions to educational institutions	2.1	0.4	0.8	1.6	1.9	4.4	3.6	5.8
Cash contributions to political organizations	2.4	0.5	1.2	1.6	2.3	5.1	4.1	7.0
Other cash gifts	17.4	12.5	17.1	17.2	18.3	20.2	20.0	20.7
INSURANCE/PENSIONS, PERCENT BUYING	**84.0**	**70.6**	**81.0**	**85.7**	**88.6**	**90.6**	**90.6**	**90.7**
Life and other personal insurance	**27.3**	**16.9**	**26.7**	**26.5**	**33.1**	**31.9**	**31.0**	**33.6**
Life, endowment, annuity, other personal insurance	26.4	16.3	26.0	25.6	32.2	30.7	30.0	31.9
Other nonhealth insurance	2.0	1.1	1.7	1.9	1.8	2.8	2.2	3.7
Pensions and Social Security	**80.1**	**63.8**	**76.6**	**82.1**	**84.1**	**88.5**	**88.7**	**88.1**
Deductions for government retirement	2.7	0.7	1.6	2.6	2.9	4.8	4.1	6.0
Deductions for railroad retirement	0.1	0.0	0.2	0.2	0.1	0.1	0.1	0.2
Deductions for private pensions	11.0	3.2	8.9	10.9	13.0	16.2	15.8	16.9
Nonpayroll deposit to retirement plans	7.9	1.4	5.0	6.6	7.7	14.6	12.0	19.2
Deductions for Social Security	79.8	63.6	76.3	81.9	84.0	88.2	88.6	87.4
PERSONAL TAXES, PERCENT SPENDING	**64.8**	**53.2**	**63.7**	**65.9**	**71.6**	**68.7**	**68.3**	**69.4**
Federal income taxes	**50.8**	**36.2**	**47.9**	**54.0**	**57.9**	**56.0**	**55.4**	**57.1**
Federal income tax deducted	24.5	16.9	22.4	26.1	28.5	27.8	28.0	27.3
Additional federal income tax paid	9.8	4.9	7.4	9.7	11.1	14.1	12.6	16.7
Federal income tax refunds (percent receiving)	35.4	26.3	34.2	38.5	40.9	36.8	37.4	35.7
2008 tax stimulus (percent receiving)	**21.0**	**18.5**	**22.1**	**20.9**	**24.0**	**20.4**	**21.3**	**18.8**
State and local income taxes	**34.6**	**21.2**	**32.5**	**36.0**	**39.4**	**40.6**	**39.9**	**41.9**
State and local income tax deducted	17.2	10.6	15.7	18.0	19.9	20.5	20.7	20.2
Additional state and local income tax paid	7.5	2.6	5.9	7.8	9.0	10.7	9.4	13.1
State and local income tax refunds (percent receiving)	21.8	14.0	21.1	23.4	25.2	24.3	24.8	23.2
Other taxes	**17.4**	**13.6**	**17.0**	**16.7**	**20.2**	**19.2**	**19.0**	**19.4**

Source: Bureau of Labor Statistics, unpublished data from the 2008 Consumer Expenditure Survey

Table 3.26 Amount Buyers Spent on Financial Products and Services by Education, <u>Average Quarter</u>, 2008

(average amount spent by households buying financial products and services during the average quarter, by highest level of education of householder, 2008)

	total households	less than high school graduate	high school graduate	some college	associate's degree	college graduate total	bachelor's degree	master's, professional, doctorate
FINANCIAL, AMOUNT SPENT	**$500.53**	**$314.21**	**$450.46**	**$448.75**	**$431.79**	**$647.13**	**$656.21**	**$632.06**
Lottery and gambling losses	139.20	156.32	184.33	123.77	109.87	103.32	91.27	129.51
Legal fees	1,543.75	576.23	1,510.23	1,481.22	1,182.48	1,932.57	2,314.14	1,211.21
Funeral expenses	1,663.24	1,125.95	1,515.05	2,177.47	961.67	1,892.17	1,411.07	2,312.60
Safe deposit box rental	41.82	34.11	37.69	40.98	50.56	43.32	41.87	45.47
Checking accounts, other bank service charges	47.59	45.33	47.06	47.08	49.67	48.06	46.06	51.56
Cemetery lots, vaults, and maintenance fees	868.10	978.77	1,181.58	766.88	1,070.24	462.21	412.88	509.43
Accounting fees	291.18	178.91	216.70	251.22	304.86	384.93	335.53	463.74
Finance charges, except mortgage and vehicles	722.27	448.17	681.97	700.45	717.51	833.69	829.54	845.45
Dating services	65.00	100.00	62.50	60.71	66.07	71.88	79.69	54.41
Vacation clubs	587.10	275.00	660.94	439.71	499.63	625.85	458.20	982.41
Expenses for other properties	842.06	378.66	607.62	556.33	585.88	1,295.05	1,402.64	1,139.64
Occupational expenses	202.92	151.49	178.44	210.61	199.51	223.84	184.94	276.83
Credit card memberships	64.39	80.88	57.78	56.35	52.82	70.50	72.63	68.53
Shopping club membership fees	56.59	55.09	49.43	51.76	57.55	62.71	57.30	72.30
CASH CONTRIBUTIONS, AMOUNT SPENT	**854.42**	**512.51**	**679.14**	**774.85**	**739.53**	**1,166.99**	**1,024.11**	**1,398.86**
Support for college students	907.87	697.89	501.06	652.31	1,063.82	1,143.04	1,082.53	1,220.42
Alimony expenditures	3,764.42	920.00	4,648.44	2,773.21	3,848.75	3,625.71	3,495.51	3,927.68
Child support expenditures	1,568.81	1,166.70	1,383.16	1,512.25	1,589.85	2,227.06	1,963.66	2,806.72
Gifts to members of other households of stocks, bonds, and mutual funds	2,434.09	102.78	438.04	7,517.00	989.42	1,027.00	981.73	1,082.29
Cash contributions to charities and other organizations	248.28	142.06	155.22	154.92	186.11	368.94	332.12	418.56
Cash contributions to church, religious organizations	640.06	340.02	477.76	668.82	571.12	847.36	842.64	855.01
Cash contributions to educational institutions	555.12	77.33	137.50	246.25	196.79	778.42	375.98	1,221.23
Cash contributions to political organizations	184.81	66.15	76.29	182.45	147.82	218.43	173.97	265.52
Other cash gifts	586.48	561.72	549.30	428.39	433.66	766.83	550.18	1,143.63
INSURANCE/PENSIONS, AMOUNT SPENT	**1,668.37**	**790.71**	**1,240.65**	**1,442.54**	**1,618.28**	**2,526.82**	**2,275.12**	**2,977.80**
Life and other personal insurance	**289.92**	**210.00**	**222.42**	**255.88**	**270.36**	**388.87**	**367.87**	**423.62**
Life, endowment, annuity, other personal insurance	286.88	210.89	220.90	252.99	268.82	383.91	365.93	414.19
Other nonhealth insurance	169.70	104.13	110.90	152.96	159.46	225.63	182.14	273.98
Pensions and Social Security	**1,651.12**	**819.64**	**1,234.45**	**1,422.29**	**1,598.72**	**2,446.90**	**2,193.89**	**2,904.27**
Deductions for government retirement	839.43	529.85	538.12	692.18	593.49	1,059.51	1,001.23	1,130.13
Deductions for railroad retirement	1,526.79	337.50	1,731.25	1,714.71	852.27	1,291.07	1,573.08	765.28
Deductions for private pensions	1,376.25	554.84	892.18	1,085.18	1,334.44	1,848.80	1,602.31	2,261.95
Nonpayroll deposit to retirement plans	1,670.32	525.00	1,528.67	1,619.27	1,068.18	1,887.51	1,806.73	1,977.60
Deductions for Social Security	1,271.57	777.15	1,018.72	1,124.57	1,274.17	1,746.31	1,619.73	1,976.33
PERSONAL TAXES, AMOUNT SPENT	**690.09**	**−21.82**	**180.91**	**385.86**	**652.01**	**1,616.53**	**1,212.12**	**2,330.91**
Federal income taxes	**894.74**	**199.03**	**416.34**	**572.77**	**823.49**	**1,739.26**	**1,369.85**	**2,382.60**
Federal income tax deducted	2,120.94	931.86	1,420.68	1,666.98	1,980.46	3,353.23	2,831.91	4,311.38
Additional federal income tax paid	1,508.11	990.62	994.63	979.40	1,612.48	2,085.89	1,719.24	2,585.54
Federal income tax refunds	−604.23	−510.03	−563.37	−572.39	−650.99	−679.88	−672.15	−694.52
2008 tax stimulus	**−932.50**	**−774.62**	**−893.63**	**−983.55**	**−924.27**	**−1,005.80**	**−1,011.32**	**−994.88**
State and local income taxes	**391.90**	**178.67**	**218.06**	**296.00**	**377.61**	**638.97**	**536.94**	**813.16**
State and local income tax deducted	793.11	406.93	514.49	641.85	733.27	1,200.02	1,046.76	1,482.97
Additional state and local income tax paid	377.96	319.96	213.93	251.16	499.31	502.22	425.21	601.24
State and local income tax refunds	−135.41	−95.84	−108.38	−123.27	−165.59	−166.45	−170.95	−157.74
Other taxes	**307.33**	**160.63**	**251.43**	**265.68**	**310.57**	**429.71**	**372.85**	**529.46**

Note: Negative amounts are money received.
Source: Calculations by New Strategist based on the Bureau of Labor Statistics' 2008 Consumer Expenditure Survey

Table 3.27 Percent Buying Financial Products and Services by Education, <u>Average Week</u>, 2008

(percent of households buying financial products and services during the average week, by highest level of education of householder, 2008)

	total households	less than high school graduate	high school graduate	some college	associate's degree	college graduate total	bachelor's degree	master's, professional, doctorate
Lottery and gambling losses	5.1%	3.1%	6.1%	5.3%	5.1%	5.1%	5.7%	4.0%
Personal taxes	54.7	43.0	49.4	58.7	63.6	59.3	58.2	61.3

Source: Bureau of Labor Statistics, unpublished data from the 2008 Consumer Expenditure Survey

Table 3.28 Amount Buyers Spent on Financial Products and Services by Education, <u>Average Week</u>, 2008

(average amount spent by households buying financial products and services during the average week, by highest level of education of householder, 2008)

	total households	less than high school graduate	high school graduate	some college	associate's degree	college graduate total	bachelor's degree	master's, professional, doctorate
Lottery and gambling losses	$22.96	$13.64	$24.79	$34.02	$19.18	$16.05	$18.39	$9.25
Personal taxes	4,172.14	1,877.88	1,630.09	2,771.66	3,275.54	8,271.58	6,374.11	11,628.08

Source: Calculations by New Strategist based on the Bureau of Labor Statistics' 2008 Consumer Expenditure Survey

CHAPTER 4

Food and Alcoholic Beverages Buyers, 2008

Groceries are one of the largest household expense categories, and they draw most households into the marketplace on a weekly basis. At the top of the Food and Alcohol Buyers' Top 10 List is milk, purchased by 54 percent of households during an average week of 2008. Fresh fruits and vegetables, bread, cheese, and eggs also make it onto the top 10 list, as do snack foods. Lunch at fast-food restaurants is the only food-away-from-home category that makes the top 10 list, with 42 percent of households spending on this item during an average week. Alcoholic beverages do not appear on the top 10 list.

Quarterly spending

Most data on food and alcohol buying is collected on a weekly (diary survey) rather than quarterly (interview survey) basis. During the average quarter of 2008, some 78 percent of households bought local restaurant meals, 12 percent bought restaurant meals on trips, and 37 percent bought alcoholic beverages. Those who bought alcoholic beverages spent an average of $220 during the quarter on beer, wine, and other types of alcoholic beverages.

Weekly spending

During the average week of 2008, 83 percent of households bought groceries, with the purchasers spending an average of $86. Fresh milk is the individual food item that attracts the largest share of households on a weekly basis (54 percent). During the average week, a substantial 72 percent of households buy restaurant or carry-out meals. Lunch at fast-food restaurants ranks fifth on the Top 10 list, attracting 42 percent of households. Those who bought lunches at fast-food restaurants spent $17.66 on them during the average week. The alcoholic beverage that attracts the largest share of buyers on a weekly basis is beer. During the average week of 2008, 11 percent of households purchased beer for home consumption.

Food and Alcohol Buyers' Top 10

(food and alcohol categories bought by the largest percentage of households during an average quarter, 2008)

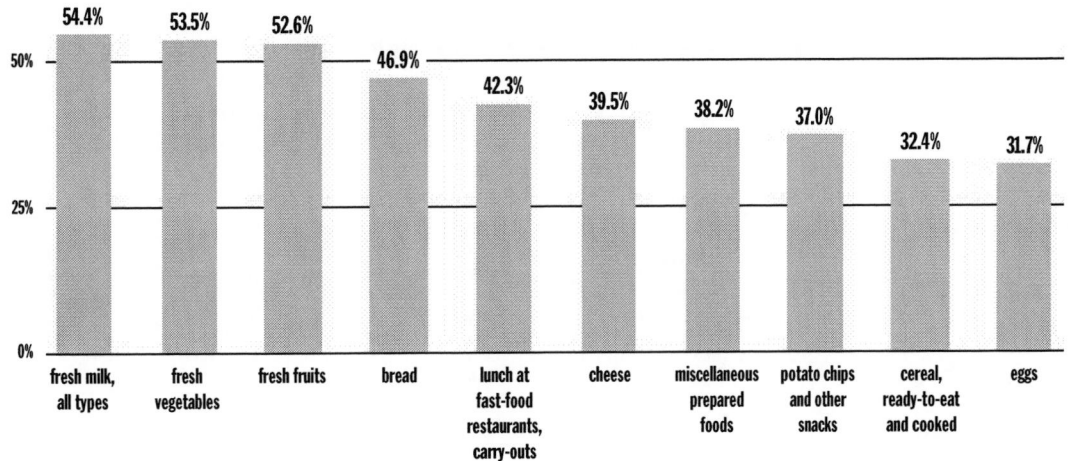

Table 4.1 Percent Buying Food and Alcohol, <u>Average Quarter</u>, 2008

(percent of households buying food and alcohol during the average quarter, by age of householder, 2008)

	total households	under 25	25 to 34	35 to 44	45 to 54	55 to 64	65 to 74	75+
FOOD, PERCENT BUYING	**99.5%**	**98.0%**	**99.6%**	**99.7%**	**99.8%**	**99.6%**	**99.7%**	**98.7%**
Groceries	**99.0**	**95.7**	**99.0**	**99.5**	**99.5**	**99.4**	**99.4**	**98.4**
Food and nonalcoholic beverages	99.0	95.5	99.0	99.5	99.5	99.4	99.3	98.4
Groceries purchased on trips	10.6	7.3	9.4	12.1	12.6	12.8	9.6	4.5
Food away from home	**81.8**	**85.5**	**86.6**	**86.9**	**84.4**	**79.6**	**75.7**	**64.7**
Meals at restaurants, carry-outs, etc.	78.5	82.9	83.7	82.7	81.3	75.9	73.0	62.2
Food or board at school	1.0	1.6	0.5	1.3	2.0	0.8	0.2	0.1
Catered affairs	1.9	1.2	2.0	2.2	2.5	1.9	1.2	0.5
Restaurant meals on trips	23.7	18.2	22.6	24.4	27.3	27.2	24.1	13.6
School lunches	9.2	1.6	8.3	23.6	12.8	2.2	1.0	0.5
Meals as pay	1.7	3.7	2.7	2.1	1.6	1.0	0.2	0.4
ALCOHOL, PERCENT BUYING	**37.0**	**41.0**	**41.7**	**39.9**	**40.8**	**37.2**	**29.2**	**19.93**
Consumed at home	**31.8**	**35.1**	**36.2**	**34.4**	**35.3**	**32.4**	**23.9**	**16.46**
Consumed away from home	**23.8**	**29.1**	**28.6**	**25.5**	**25.5**	**23.8**	**18.0**	**10.38**
Alcoholic beverages at restaurants, bars	17.4	23.6	22.7	18.6	18.2	16.5	11.7	6.79
Alcoholic beverages purchased on trips	11.8	10.2	12.6	12.4	13.1	13.9	10.3	5.24

Source: Bureau of Labor Statistics, unpublished data from the 2008 Consumer Expenditure Survey

Table 4.2 Amount Buyers Spent on Food and Alcohol, <u>Average Quarter</u>, 2008

(average amount spent by households buying food and alcohol during the average quarter, by age of householder, 2008)

	total households	under 25	25 to 34	35 to 44	45 to 54	55 to 64	65 to 74	75+
FOOD, AMOUNT SPENT	**$1,790.19**	**$1,280.67**	**$1,767.03**	**$2,142.56**	**$2,043.72**	**$1,810.25**	**$1,521.99**	**$1,176.01**
Groceries	**1,215.51**	**842.43**	**1,178.60**	**1,467.39**	**1,362.71**	**1,221.72**	**1,066.01**	**856.00**
Food and nonalcoholic beverages	1,203.56	840.36	1,170.43	1,454.54	1,348.99	1,203.19	1,052.47	849.83
Groceries purchased on trips	115.42	51.13	89.55	105.79	113.33	143.75	147.38	135.38
Food Away from home	**705.92**	**524.63**	**684.41**	**778.84**	**808.36**	**739.76**	**605.02**	**493.12**
Meals at restaurants, carry-outs, etc.	594.49	467.40	608.38	646.57	647.99	605.89	528.50	449.77
Food or board at school	858.58	705.90	219.81	755.19	987.25	1,326.92	239.06	412.50
Catered affairs	926.61	558.27	628.66	617.73	1,176.29	1,469.40	647.97	733.17
Restaurant meals on trips	251.13	121.30	189.71	250.44	276.88	305.27	258.14	242.38
School lunches	192.71	171.47	144.60	207.11	202.58	153.56	138.68	168.98
Meals as pay	440.66	490.64	555.63	414.69	329.11	383.00	258.33	368.57
ALCOHOL, AMOUNT SPENT	**220.32**	**256.48**	**234.35**	**215.50**	**220.10**	**221.37**	**191.58**	**177.72**
Consumed at home	**145.28**	**160.64**	**134.56**	**152.69**	**150.36**	**151.84**	**126.33**	**115.92**
Consumed away from home	**148.68**	**168.20**	**171.12**	**131.40**	**144.50**	**139.17**	**142.85**	**157.39**
Alcoholic beverages at restaurants, bars	145.91	184.72	172.46	127.68	138.13	122.03	140.08	149.96
Alcoholic beverages purchased on trips	85.07	52.71	77.35	79.11	89.23	93.57	90.45	117.46

Source: Calculations by New Strategist based on the Bureau of Labor Statistics' 2008 Consumer Expenditure Survey

Table 4.3 Percent Buying Food and Alcohol by Age, <u>Average Week</u>, 2008

(percent of households buying food and alcohol during the average week, by age of householder, 2008)

	total households	under 25	25 to 34	35 to 44	45 to 54	55 to 64	65 to 74	75+
FOOD, PERCENT BUYING	**89.4%**	**87.4%**	**90.3%**	**91.6%**	**90.0%**	**88.7%**	**88.9%**	**85.4%**
• GROCERIES	**82.9**	**71.9**	**82.4**	**86.4**	**84.2**	**82.7**	**84.4**	**80.6**
Cereals and bakery products	**70.9**	**53.0**	**69.1**	**75.3**	**73.1**	**71.1**	**74.4**	**69.1**
Cereals and cereal products	46.5	33.5	47.0	51.6	50.7	44.0	44.9	41.4
Flour	4.4	1.3	3.9	5.9	4.5	4.7	5.3	2.8
Prepared flour mixes	8.5	5.0	8.3	10.1	9.7	8.5	6.9	6.8
Ready-to-eat and cooked cereals	32.4	22.8	32.4	37.7	35.8	28.1	31.8	28.8
Rice	10.1	7.4	10.9	12.4	11.4	8.7	9.0	6.5
Pasta, cornmeal, and other cereal products	19.9	14.5	20.1	23.3	23.4	19.0	16.4	14.8
Bakery products	65.7	48.9	63.0	70.1	68.2	66.4	69.6	62.8
Bread	46.9	33.1	43.8	51.0	50.0	49.4	46.8	43.4
White bread	32.7	23.4	30.9	37.4	34.5	34.4	29.8	29.1
Bread, other than white	39.8	28.0	36.0	42.5	43.4	43.3	40.1	35.6
Crackers and cookies	31.7	21.0	28.6	34.2	35.5	30.9	33.9	31.2
Cookies	21.3	13.9	18.7	22.9	23.0	21.6	23.6	21.0
Crackers	18.5	12.6	16.5	20.8	22.1	16.9	18.8	16.4
Frozen and refrigerated bakery products	12.4	8.5	11.0	15.8	14.4	10.8	11.9	10.1
Other bakery products	39.7	24.8	35.9	44.7	43.8	39.6	41.8	35.7
Biscuits and rolls	26.5	14.5	24.1	31.1	30.8	26.0	26.8	20.6
Cakes and cupcakes	12.4	7.2	11.4	14.6	14.5	12.3	10.9	10.9
Bread and cracker products	4.2	2.0	4.6	4.6	4.2	4.6	4.7	3.0
Sweetrolls, coffee cakes, doughnuts	11.2	5.9	8.8	11.7	11.9	11.9	13.5	12.9
Pies, tarts, turnovers	6.5	3.3	4.9	8.6	7.3	6.4	6.6	5.7
Meats, poultry, fish, and eggs	**66.2**	**49.3**	**62.9**	**71.8**	**69.0**	**68.5**	**66.9**	**62.1**
Beef	34.1	25.0	32.4	39.5	37.3	34.3	31.7	27.2
Ground beef	22.7	16.3	21.1	28.2	25.3	21.3	20.7	17.4
Roast	6.5	4.6	5.1	7.1	8.0	7.3	6.5	4.6
Chuck roast	2.4	1.7	1.6	2.7	3.2	2.5	2.4	1.9
Round roast	1.3	1.0	1.0	1.5	1.5	1.8	1.2	0.9
Other roast	4.1	2.6	3.4	4.3	5.0	4.6	3.9	3.2
Steak	12.9	8.7	12.6	14.5	15.2	13.2	12.1	7.9
Round steak	5.2	4.0	6.2	6.2	5.7	4.8	4.5	2.4
Sirloin steak	5.6	3.8	6.2	6.3	6.5	5.5	5.1	2.5
Other steak	9.8	6.1	9.5	11.4	11.3	9.9	9.0	6.5
Other beef	5.3	3.9	4.7	6.0	6.4	5.3	4.7	4.4
Pork	32.5	21.8	29.8	36.5	35.9	33.4	32.9	27.8
Bacon	12.2	7.5	10.8	14.6	14.0	11.6	12.2	10.4
Pork chops	8.0	5.5	7.2	8.7	9.9	7.8	7.6	5.9
Ham	9.9	8.3	8.3	12.1	10.9	9.7	10.0	7.9
Ham, not canned	9.7	8.3	8.2	11.8	10.7	9.4	9.7	7.6
Canned ham	0.3	–	0.2	0.5	0.4	0.3	0.3	0.2
Sausage	11.9	6.9	10.8	13.4	13.8	11.8	12.5	9.2
Other pork	8.6	5.3	7.2	10.1	8.8	9.7	9.4	7.1
Other meats	31.0	23.0	28.3	35.5	34.8	29.4	31.4	25.9
Frankfurters	11.1	9.0	11.7	14.0	12.7	9.3	10.0	6.9
Lunch meats (cold cuts)	24.8	17.0	21.4	28.4	28.6	24.2	26.2	20.4
Bologna, liverwurst, salami	11.3	7.3	8.6	13.0	13.5	11.6	12.4	9.3
Other lunch meats	20.6	14.0	18.1	24.0	23.8	19.6	21.1	16.7
Lamb, organ meats, and others	2.1	1.3	1.7	2.3	2.3	2.3	1.8	2.7
Lamb and organ meats	1.8	1.0	1.6	1.9	1.8	1.8	1.6	2.5
Mutton, goat, and game	0.4	0.4	0.2	0.4	0.5	0.6	0.2	0.2

	total households	under 25	25 to 34	35 to 44	45 to 54	55 to 64	65 to 74	75+
Poultry	31.0%	24.1%	30.7%	36.2%	35.2%	30.2%	27.8%	21.2%
Fresh and frozen chicken	26.6	21.2	26.7	31.5	30.4	24.8	22.6	18.9
Fresh and frozen whole chicken	10.8	8.1	11.0	13.6	12.6	10.0	7.7	8.0
Fresh and frozen chicken parts	24.5	20.0	25.1	29.2	27.8	22.7	20.9	16.3
Other poultry	9.5	6.1	8.4	10.8	11.2	10.3	9.6	5.4
Fish and seafood	22.1	13.4	19.1	24.1	25.7	22.6	21.8	20.7
Canned fish and seafood	7.9	4.8	6.4	7.8	9.7	8.6	7.5	8.4
Fresh fish and shellfish	10.3	6.1	8.5	12.2	11.8	10.6	9.7	9.2
Frozen fish and shellfish	8.7	5.2	8.2	9.0	10.5	8.5	9.3	7.5
Eggs	31.7	22.0	28.6	36.2	34.0	32.5	31.2	28.9
Dairy products	**69.0**	**51.6**	**66.8**	**73.5**	**71.8**	**69.5**	**70.6**	**67.1**
Fresh milk and cream	57.0	41.6	55.4	62.8	60.2	56.8	56.3	53.5
Fresh milk, all types	54.4	40.4	52.9	60.2	57.6	53.4	53.5	50.8
Cream	13.6	6.3	12.6	16.7	15.6	13.5	12.9	11.0
Other dairy products	53.2	36.5	50.6	56.6	57.3	54.3	55.0	49.9
Butter	11.7	6.0	9.7	12.4	14.1	12.9	12.9	9.6
Cheese	39.5	25.8	37.5	44.1	43.8	40.4	37.8	34.1
Ice cream and related products	21.7	14.0	19.0	24.3	24.8	21.3	23.3	18.9
Miscellaneous dairy products	21.0	13.9	19.9	23.9	23.3	21.2	20.2	17.6
Fruits and vegetables	**70.7**	**52.0**	**66.9**	**73.9**	**73.7**	**71.8**	**74.7**	**71.9**
Fresh fruits	52.6	34.0	46.6	55.1	56.8	54.0	57.7	54.4
Apples	19.0	12.7	18.0	22.7	21.7	18.1	17.6	15.2
Bananas	33.7	19.9	27.8	34.6	36.9	35.1	38.1	38.2
Oranges	11.8	7.9	10.7	13.3	13.4	11.5	11.8	10.5
Citrus fruits, excluding oranges	16.6	9.5	15.3	19.1	19.8	15.5	17.3	13.4
Other fresh fruits	34.2	20.2	30.8	37.7	37.8	34.1	35.8	33.6
Fresh vegetables	53.5	34.3	49.3	57.1	57.7	55.3	55.2	53.2
Potatoes	20.5	10.1	18.2	22.2	22.6	22.8	22.0	18.5
Lettuce	20.1	12.1	17.9	22.3	23.3	21.3	18.6	17.9
Tomatoes	22.4	12.9	20.4	26.6	24.8	21.4	22.4	21.1
Other fresh vegetables	44.1	28.5	40.3	47.2	48.7	45.6	45.0	42.7
Processed fruits	39.3	29.9	37.7	42.4	42.4	36.9	40.0	39.4
Frozen fruits and fruit juices	5.0	2.5	3.9	6.7	6.2	4.7	4.3	4.6
Frozen orange juice	2.3	1.1	1.8	3.6	2.3	2.4	1.3	2.6
Frozen fruits	2.1	0.8	1.7	2.5	2.9	2.0	2.5	1.1
Frozen fruit juices, excluding orange	1.4	1.1	1.1	1.8	1.8	1.2	0.7	1.5
Canned fruits	12.4	8.1	11.3	12.6	14.0	11.4	14.5	13.6
Dried fruits	4.8	2.6	3.6	5.2	5.6	4.4	5.4	5.9
Fresh fruit juice	8.7	4.9	7.2	9.9	10.2	7.9	9.3	9.0
Canned and bottled fruit juice	25.8	22.2	26.5	29.1	28.5	23.7	22.3	22.0
Processed vegetables	39.9	28.6	39.3	43.2	43.0	40.2	38.4	37.2
Frozen vegetables	17.2	11.1	16.0	20.2	20.4	16.5	15.5	13.5
Canned and dried vegetables and juices	33.5	24.5	33.0	36.2	35.8	33.7	32.0	31.0
Canned beans	12.0	7.4	10.9	13.4	13.0	12.5	11.4	12.0
Canned corn	7.1	5.8	7.5	7.7	7.6	7.0	6.0	6.7
Canned miscellaneous vegetables	15.8	8.3	13.2	16.9	18.7	16.7	16.5	14.2
Dried peas	0.3	0.1	0.2	0.5	0.4	0.3	0.1	0.6
Dried beans	2.5	2.5	2.6	3.2	2.7	2.2	2.2	1.8
Dried miscellaneous vegetables	6.3	4.0	7.1	6.8	7.4	6.0	5.9	4.0
Fresh and canned vegetable juices	8.9	8.1	10.2	10.6	8.7	8.2	7.4	7.1
Sugar and other sweets	**41.4**	**29.3**	**39.7**	**47.0**	**44.6**	**40.2**	**43.5**	**34.3**
Candy and chewing gum	30.6	20.8	29.1	35.5	33.4	30.3	31.2	23.7
Sugar	11.8	9.2	11.0	14.5	13.4	10.6	11.3	9.2
Artificial sweeteners	2.2	0.9	1.6	2.6	2.4	2.5	3.0	1.8
Jams, preserves, other sweets	13.7	9.5	13.1	15.8	14.9	13.2	14.6	10.8

	total households	under 25	25 to 34	35 to 44	45 to 54	55 to 64	65 to 74	75+
Fats and oils	**34.3%**	**23.2%**	**31.5%**	**37.4%**	**37.8%**	**34.6%**	**36.6%**	**30.4%**
Margarine	6.9	3.4	4.5	7.0	7.7	6.6	9.8	8.7
Fats and oils	12.7	9.0	11.3	15.4	13.8	12.2	12.4	11.1
Salad dressings	14.6	9.3	13.4	15.6	17.4	14.8	15.0	11.2
Nondairy cream and imitation milk	9.3	4.9	8.6	9.8	10.9	9.8	10.7	7.2
Peanut butter	7.0	5.5	6.7	7.5	8.4	6.7	6.6	5.3
Miscellaneous foods	**68.0**	**54.0**	**67.0**	**72.4**	**71.3**	**67.8**	**68.6**	**63.7**
Frozen prepared foods	27.4	20.8	29.8	33.1	29.7	24.0	22.7	22.3
Frozen meals	16.7	12.3	16.6	19.7	19.0	14.7	14.2	15.1
Other frozen prepared foods	17.7	14.0	20.8	22.3	19.3	14.4	13.9	11.9
Canned and packaged soups	21.1	12.7	19.8	22.5	22.7	20.7	22.6	22.1
Potato chips, nuts, and other snacks	41.1	31.6	39.8	47.2	46.6	41.1	37.2	30.1
Potato chips and other snacks	37.0	29.6	36.9	43.5	42.3	35.5	32.0	25.0
Nuts	12.8	7.1	10.9	13.0	16.0	14.8	12.3	9.5
Condiments and seasonings	42.7	30.6	42.0	47.9	48.2	41.3	40.9	34.4
Salt, spices, and other seasonings	19.1	13.3	19.5	21.6	22.7	18.4	17.2	13.3
Olives, pickles, relishes	8.7	4.5	6.9	10.3	9.9	9.5	8.9	6.8
Sauces and gravies	28.1	21.5	29.6	33.7	32.5	25.6	23.5	18.8
Baking needs and miscellaneous products	15.1	9.8	13.0	16.5	18.1	14.9	15.7	13.0
Other canned/packaged prepared foods	46.6	36.6	46.1	53.8	49.2	44.9	44.1	40.2
Prepared salads	16.5	11.2	13.8	18.7	18.8	16.8	17.5	14.6
Prepared desserts	9.0	6.1	8.6	9.9	9.7	8.4	9.6	9.1
Baby food	4.4	3.9	7.7	5.7	4.0	2.8	2.4	1.9
Miscellaneous prepared foods	38.2	29.3	38.4	46.4	41.1	35.8	33.7	29.8
Nonalcoholic beverages	**57.4**	**47.9**	**57.7**	**66.1**	**63.2**	**53.6**	**52.9**	**44.1**
Cola	31.5	27.7	32.3	38.6	36.0	29.0	25.4	19.7
Other carbonated drinks	26.3	23.6	27.8	32.3	29.9	22.8	21.7	16.0
Tea	13.6	10.4	11.6	16.9	16.1	12.8	12.3	10.2
Coffee	12.5	5.7	10.9	12.8	14.0	15.0	13.1	11.1
Roasted coffee	11.7	5.4	10.6	12.0	13.2	14.0	12.0	10.3
Instant and freeze-dried coffee	9.8	4.1	8.3	9.7	11.0	11.9	10.8	9.8
Noncarbonated fruit-flavored drinks	11.8	9.8	12.1	16.5	13.6	8.5	10.1	7.0
Other nonalcoholic beverages and ice	6.4	7.0	5.8	8.0	7.8	5.5	6.1	2.6
Bottled water	20.8	16.2	21.9	25.9	24.8	17.5	17.9	11.2
Sports drinks	7.5	6.3	7.5	10.7	10.4	5.1	4.8	3.1
• MEALS AT RESTAURANTS, CARRY-OUTS	**72.4**	**73.7**	**77.4**	**77.5**	**74.8**	**71.3**	**65.4**	**55.6**
Lunch	**54.9**	**53.3**	**61.1**	**60.7**	**57.2**	**54.7**	**45.0**	**38.3**
At fast-food restaurants*	42.3	42.9	49.7	47.6	44.2	42.5	31.8	23.5
At full-service restaurants	21.2	12.7	22.0	21.7	21.6	23.4	21.3	20.0
At vending machines, mobile vendors	4.4	4.7	6.3	5.1	5.0	3.5	2.0	1.6
At employer and school cafeterias	10.6	9.2	10.0	17.1	14.7	7.9	3.1	3.2
Dinner	**47.2**	**50.3**	**53.3**	**51.9**	**51.6**	**44.1**	**38.4**	**28.6**
At fast-food restaurants*	29.9	34.7	35.7	36.0	35.0	24.5	18.2	14.2
At full-service restaurants	27.7	25.2	29.6	27.6	29.6	29.6	27.4	19.1
At vending machines, mobile vendors	0.9	1.0	1.4	0.9	1.0	0.6	0.7	0.2
At employer and school cafeterias	1.3	4.6	1.2	1.4	1.5	0.8	0.5	0.6
Snacks and nonalcoholic beverages	**35.0**	**37.9**	**42.7**	**41.7**	**38.1**	**31.7**	**24.4**	**14.5**
At fast-food restaurants*	24.9	25.5	29.1	30.2	27.3	22.8	18.8	10.8
At full-service restaurants	5.6	6.2	7.2	5.8	6.0	5.4	3.9	2.8
At vending machines, mobile vendors	13.6	16.9	18.0	17.3	15.9	10.8	6.2	3.9
At employer and school cafeterias	2.9	3.7	3.1	4.3	3.4	2.5	1.2	0.8

	total households	under 25	25 to 34	35 to 44	45 to 54	55 to 64	65 to 74	75+
Breakfast and brunch	**30.2%**	**26.1%**	**31.7%**	**33.7%**	**34.7%**	**30.0%**	**27.9%**	**15.8%**
At fast-food restaurants*	22.1	18.3	25.2	25.8	25.9	21.5	17.4	9.2
At full-service restaurants	9.9	6.6	8.2	8.7	10.4	12.4	13.0	8.3
At vending machines, mobile vendors	2.2	2.2	2.6	3.1	3.0	1.6	1.2	0.4
At employer and school cafeterias	3.1	4.1	3.1	4.4	4.2	2.5	1.4	0.6
ALCOHOL, PERCENT BUYING	**24.5**	**24.7**	**27.0**	**26.6**	**27.2**	**27.0**	**18.9**	**10.9**
Consumed at home	**16.4**	**15.9**	**16.6**	**18.7**	**18.9**	**18.0**	**12.8**	**7.5**
Beer and ale	11.3	12.2	13.1	14.0	12.8	11.5	6.4	3.4
Whiskey	0.6	0.7	0.3	0.2	0.6	1.4	0.6	0.3
Wine	6.9	4.8	5.2	7.0	8.6	8.0	7.8	4.0
Other alcoholic beverages	2.2	2.2	1.6	2.4	2.3	2.9	1.6	1.5
Consumed away from home (except on trips)	**13.2**	**13.6**	**15.7**	**13.1**	**15.1**	**15.2**	**9.5**	**4.5**
Beer and ale at restaurants, bars	8.8	10.1	11.2	9.2	10.3	9.4	5.5	1.9
Wine at restaurants, bars	4.1	2.6	4.2	3.9	4.2	5.5	4.3	2.0
Other alcoholic beverages at restaurants, bars	5.3	5.8	7.4	5.1	6.4	5.7	2.4	1.7

* The category fast-food restaurants also includes take-out, delivery, concession stands, buffets, and cafeterias other than employer and school.
Note: "–" means sample is too small to make a reliable estimate.
Source: Bureau of Labor Statistics, unpublished data from the 2008 Consumer Expenditure Survey

Table 4.4 Amount Buyers Spent on Food and Alcohol by Age, <u>Average Week</u>, 2008

(average amount spent by households buying food and alcohol during the average week, by age of householder, 2008)

	total households	under 25	25 to 34	35 to 44	45 to 54	55 to 64	65 to 74	75+
FOOD, AMOUNT SPENT	$127.99	$92.15	$124.76	$151.75	$149.96	$125.12	$108.04	$84.50
• GROCERIES	85.73	61.96	78.38	99.27	100.42	84.59	76.67	63.06
Cereals and bakery products	13.75	10.19	12.64	15.85	15.80	13.30	12.24	10.84
Cereals and cereal products	7.01	5.89	6.90	7.94	7.69	6.63	6.06	5.51
Flour	3.39	3.20	3.60	3.54	3.53	2.98	3.39	4.26
Prepared flour mixes	2.72	1.99	2.40	2.67	3.00	3.16	2.32	2.36
Ready-to-eat and cooked cereals	5.59	4.95	5.36	6.31	6.06	5.23	4.69	4.73
Rice	4.87	4.61	5.70	4.37	4.82	4.84	4.78	4.63
Pasta, cornmeal, and other cereal products	2.96	2.55	2.74	3.01	3.17	3.32	2.81	2.24
Bakery products	9.88	7.02	8.72	11.16	11.20	9.85	9.17	8.31
Bread	4.05	3.54	3.63	4.28	4.30	4.17	3.99	3.66
White bread	2.17	1.97	2.04	2.33	2.23	2.12	2.18	2.10
Bread, other than white	2.99	2.50	2.64	3.06	3.18	3.07	3.04	2.75
Crackers and cookies	4.95	4.38	4.80	5.14	5.44	4.96	4.70	4.20
Cookies	4.23	3.60	4.11	4.28	4.62	4.27	4.02	3.91
Crackers	3.62	3.34	3.65	3.75	3.95	3.61	3.41	3.05
Frozen and refrigerated bakery products	4.03	3.07	3.83	4.25	4.17	3.99	4.11	3.95
Other bakery products	6.35	4.36	5.91	7.20	6.79	6.37	5.79	5.37
Biscuits and rolls	3.59	2.84	3.33	3.73	3.80	3.70	3.24	3.50
Cakes and cupcakes	6.19	4.60	6.30	7.45	6.37	5.84	5.87	3.93
Bread and cracker products	2.14	1.97	1.98	2.17	2.36	2.38	2.15	1.64
Sweetrolls, coffee cakes, doughnuts	3.75	3.03	3.64	4.09	3.94	3.61	3.55	3.71
Pies, tarts, turnovers	4.30	3.34	3.85	4.52	4.12	4.68	4.97	4.07
Meats, poultry, fish, and eggs	24.59	22.36	22.69	27.17	28.38	23.72	22.46	17.83
Beef	13.48	12.71	12.62	13.99	14.95	13.63	12.48	10.87
Ground beef	7.63	8.09	7.26	7.83	8.07	8.13	7.02	5.92
Roast	11.49	10.31	10.35	11.80	12.13	12.35	10.86	10.15
Chuck roast	7.92	8.98	6.29	8.55	8.15	8.13	8.68	8.60
Round roast	9.02	12.37	8.08	9.52	9.40	9.04	7.44	6.52
Other roast	10.81	7.78	9.97	11.06	11.52	12.06	10.77	7.86
Steak	13.05	11.10	13.13	13.83	13.17	12.20	12.11	15.57
Round steak	4.82	4.80	4.65	5.46	4.58	4.39	4.65	7.14
Sirloin steak	7.90	7.43	7.07	7.74	7.95	8.30	7.30	12.20
Other steak	10.13	8.18	9.59	10.31	10.76	9.37	9.90	11.54
Other beef	8.10	11.08	8.09	7.79	8.98	8.30	6.81	5.52
Pork	9.62	9.55	8.82	10.31	10.04	9.56	10.09	7.82
Bacon	4.59	4.12	4.46	4.33	4.70	4.85	4.93	4.61
Pork chops	7.67	8.00	7.81	8.47	7.71	7.55	7.41	5.92
Ham	6.44	5.42	6.27	6.28	6.59	6.51	7.92	5.48
Ham, not canned	6.48	5.42	6.21	6.27	6.64	6.61	7.97	5.65
Canned ham	3.33	–	6.67	4.35	2.50	3.45	6.45	0.00
Sausage	4.56	4.65	3.99	4.93	4.84	4.50	4.57	4.22
Other pork	8.96	10.36	8.84	9.55	9.01	9.05	8.56	7.28
Other meats	6.62	5.53	6.19	7.00	7.29	6.66	6.21	5.48
Frankfurters	3.50	2.99	3.33	3.72	3.63	3.67	3.70	3.04
Lunch meats (cold cuts)	5.72	5.23	5.09	5.84	6.40	5.82	5.35	4.96
Bologna, liverwurst, salami	3.09	2.86	2.90	3.24	3.41	3.26	2.90	2.57
Other lunch meats	5.16	4.85	4.65	5.16	5.77	5.26	4.89	4.61
Lamb, organ meats, and others	11.37	8.21	15.79	13.22	10.92	9.44	10.50	7.52
Lamb and organ meats	10.11	7.14	10.32	13.16	9.78	8.79	10.49	8.00
Mutton, goat, and game	16.67	8.33	50.00	14.63	15.56	10.91	10.53	6.25

	total households	under 25	25 to 34	35 to 44	45 to 54	55 to 64	65 to 74	75+
Poultry	$9.88	$8.92	$9.51	$10.47	$10.67	$9.71	$9.06	$8.13
Fresh and frozen chicken	9.19	8.59	9.18	9.70	9.75	8.91	8.40	7.26
Fresh and frozen whole chicken	5.81	5.07	5.66	6.42	6.01	5.58	5.87	4.89
Fresh and frozen chicken parts	7.36	7.06	7.30	7.51	7.95	7.26	6.94	6.08
Other poultry	6.56	5.38	5.62	6.74	7.06	6.99	6.36	6.48
Fish and seafood	11.16	12.81	10.48	11.56	11.78	10.93	10.85	9.56
Canned fish and seafood	4.05	3.33	3.26	4.24	4.11	4.80	3.85	3.45
Fresh fish and shellfish	12.67	17.82	12.62	12.92	13.46	11.81	11.19	10.31
Frozen fish and shellfish	9.64	8.99	8.83	9.78	9.95	9.45	10.67	9.85
Eggs	3.10	2.91	3.11	3.18	3.21	3.11	2.95	2.84
Dairy products	**11.98**	**9.53**	**11.37**	**13.54**	**13.56**	**11.61**	**11.06**	**8.85**
Fresh milk and cream	5.67	5.04	5.69	6.55	6.11	5.18	5.05	4.41
Fresh milk, all types	5.30	4.83	5.39	6.10	5.66	4.83	4.65	4.13
Cream	2.57	2.37	2.31	2.64	2.69	2.67	2.63	2.36
Other dairy products	9.45	7.73	8.79	10.31	10.56	9.44	9.06	7.17
Butter	3.50	3.15	3.11	3.71	3.47	3.72	3.49	3.44
Cheese	6.54	5.70	6.33	6.71	7.26	6.54	6.43	4.90
Ice cream and related products	5.35	5.01	4.99	5.44	5.64	5.36	5.58	4.87
Miscellaneous dairy products	4.19	3.39	4.18	4.64	4.21	4.11	3.97	3.75
Fruits and vegetables	**17.86**	**13.67**	**16.73**	**19.62**	**20.32**	**18.26**	**15.87**	**14.20**
Fresh fruits	8.12	6.47	8.06	9.06	8.88	8.19	7.07	6.33
Apples	4.05	3.64	3.96	4.19	4.28	4.19	3.70	3.43
Bananas	1.84	1.71	1.94	2.00	1.98	1.85	1.57	1.54
Oranges	4.06	3.28	3.66	4.20	4.10	4.85	3.99	3.44
Citrus fruits, excluding oranges	2.11	2.01	2.09	2.10	2.22	2.33	1.91	1.64
Other fresh fruits	5.97	4.75	5.85	6.33	6.33	6.12	5.65	5.17
Fresh vegetables	7.61	6.35	7.27	8.00	8.30	8.17	6.83	6.15
Potatoes	3.56	3.47	3.62	3.55	3.63	3.56	3.41	3.19
Lettuce	2.54	2.40	2.29	2.56	2.75	2.68	2.37	2.12
Tomatoes	3.17	3.41	3.00	3.19	3.27	3.59	2.73	2.70
Other fresh vegetables	4.83	3.86	4.72	5.02	5.18	5.20	4.40	4.03
Processed fruits	5.70	5.02	5.25	5.96	6.35	5.78	5.28	4.95
Frozen fruits and fruit juices	4.37	3.16	4.16	4.17	4.39	4.66	4.92	3.70
Frozen orange juice	3.48	2.86	3.28	3.35	3.56	3.40	3.76	3.53
Frozen fruits	5.19	4.76	4.60	5.12	5.21	5.61	5.69	3.64
Frozen fruit juices, excluding orange	2.14	1.80	1.75	1.64	2.78	2.50	2.74	2.72
Canned fruits	3.22	3.21	3.01	2.87	3.35	3.43	3.32	3.17
Dried fruits	3.14	3.04	2.77	3.46	3.20	2.76	2.94	2.72
Fresh fruit juice	4.03	3.91	3.73	4.16	4.40	3.91	3.56	3.67
Canned and bottled fruit juice	4.38	3.96	4.23	4.50	4.63	4.56	4.18	3.90
Processed vegetables	5.13	4.27	4.78	5.56	5.72	5.10	4.87	4.17
Frozen vegetables	3.84	3.15	3.69	4.00	3.98	3.88	3.81	3.33
Canned and dried vegetables and juices	4.16	3.56	3.94	4.39	4.58	4.18	4.01	3.51
Canned beans	2.34	2.03	2.20	2.54	2.54	2.33	2.02	2.01
Canned corn	1.82	1.73	1.73	1.81	2.09	1.72	1.68	1.63
Canned miscellaneous vegetables	2.60	2.04	2.43	2.54	2.94	2.63	2.72	2.32
Dried peas	3.03	0.00	0.00	2.13	2.44	3.33	0.00	1.75
Dried beans	3.16	3.54	3.53	2.84	2.96	2.78	2.79	1.65
Dried miscellaneous vegetables	3.01	3.03	2.83	3.09	2.96	3.33	3.05	2.72
Fresh and canned vegetable juices	3.14	2.71	2.84	3.29	3.21	3.29	3.50	3.54
Sugar and other sweets	**6.02**	**5.18**	**4.98**	**6.27**	**6.42**	**6.45**	**5.86**	**5.98**
Candy and chewing gum	5.04	4.61	4.05	5.11	5.24	5.42	5.16	5.49
Sugar	2.87	2.72	2.99	3.03	2.84	2.84	2.58	2.73
Artificial sweeteners	5.43	4.35	5.00	5.49	6.61	5.67	5.76	4.92
Jams, preserves, other sweets	3.50	2.94	2.91	3.54	3.82	3.79	3.21	3.81

	total households	under 25	25 to 34	35 to 44	45 to 54	55 to 64	65 to 74	75+
Fats and oils	**$5.86**	**$5.00**	**$5.69**	**$6.07**	**$6.24**	**$5.93**	**$5.58**	**$5.26**
Margarine	2.48	2.36	2.22	2.44	2.46	2.58	2.15	2.77
Fats and oils	5.99	4.87	5.85	6.11	6.31	6.23	5.80	5.57
Salad dressings	3.57	3.32	3.35	3.52	3.73	3.80	3.67	3.39
Nondairy cream and imitation milk	3.32	3.09	4.07	3.27	3.30	3.18	2.98	2.80
Peanut butter	3.58	3.07	3.45	3.72	3.57	3.76	3.46	3.04
Miscellaneous foods	**19.22**	**16.02**	**19.54**	**22.58**	**21.48**	**18.04**	**15.83**	**13.34**
Frozen prepared foods	9.85	9.43	9.26	10.54	10.97	9.43	9.28	7.76
Frozen meals	8.39	7.50	7.52	8.42	9.55	8.37	8.41	7.48
Other frozen prepared foods	7.34	7.45	7.27	8.20	7.52	7.21	6.63	5.05
Canned and packaged soups	4.17	3.72	3.74	4.05	4.41	4.44	3.98	4.70
Potato chips, nuts, and other snacks	6.56	4.91	5.93	7.05	7.19	6.86	6.32	5.22
Potato chips and other snacks	5.36	4.29	5.05	6.12	5.79	5.35	4.82	3.64
Nuts	5.65	3.94	4.58	5.24	5.69	6.23	6.61	6.98
Condiments and seasonings	5.55	4.73	5.14	5.97	6.07	5.86	4.89	4.13
Salt, spices, and other seasonings	2.93	2.93	2.83	2.92	3.17	3.05	2.50	2.64
Olives, pickles, relishes	3.00	2.69	2.59	3.10	3.23	3.25	2.93	2.50
Sauces and gravies	3.70	3.11	3.55	3.80	3.88	4.11	3.66	2.77
Baking needs and miscellaneous products	3.32	2.64	2.93	3.83	3.49	3.36	2.94	2.93
Other canned/packaged prepared foods	9.48	8.83	10.99	10.70	9.67	8.48	7.90	6.77
Prepared salads	4.23	3.67	4.14	4.18	4.46	4.47	3.89	3.84
Prepared desserts	2.77	2.64	2.43	2.92	2.78	3.09	2.72	2.84
Baby food	15.07	20.88	19.61	16.87	11.59	8.57	7.66	6.84
Miscellaneous prepared foods	7.28	6.08	7.16	7.89	7.75	7.09	6.77	5.88
Nonalcoholic beverages	**11.49**	**9.88**	**10.33**	**12.55**	**12.92**	**11.50**	**10.37**	**9.04**
Cola	5.04	4.26	4.40	5.37	5.19	5.58	5.00	4.57
Other carbonated drinks	3.73	3.86	3.53	3.68	3.84	3.82	3.73	3.50
Tea	4.56	3.76	4.23	4.26	5.10	5.09	4.16	4.13
Coffee	7.87	6.30	7.71	7.89	8.09	7.96	7.87	7.77
Roasted coffee	5.63	4.49	5.47	5.84	5.86	5.57	5.50	5.14
Instant and freeze-dried coffee	3.26	2.68	3.14	3.29	3.28	3.36	3.42	3.38
Noncarbonated fruit-flavored drinks	4.56	3.77	3.81	4.96	4.62	3.88	4.77	6.54
Other nonalcoholic beverages and ice	4.22	6.00	4.15	3.89	4.62	3.85	3.95	4.21
Bottled water	5.69	4.63	5.24	5.84	6.46	5.77	4.97	4.92
Sports drinks	5.59	5.60	4.82	6.00	5.80	5.74	4.56	3.58
• MEALS AT RESTAURANTS, CARRY-OUTS	**59.96**	**48.84**	**62.14**	**68.81**	**67.42**	**57.51**	**47.81**	**38.42**
Lunch	**27.09**	**22.23**	**27.10**	**30.91**	**30.00**	**25.13**	**23.01**	**20.02**
At fast-food restaurants*	17.66	16.38	18.38	19.84	18.76	16.47	14.32	11.69
At full-service restaurants	26.77	26.73	26.82	28.55	28.90	24.45	25.82	23.20
At vending machines, mobile vendors	4.14	3.59	4.74	4.35	3.98	3.67	3.59	1.92
At employer and school cafeterias	14.64	13.51	12.26	16.95	16.45	11.25	7.77	7.91
Dinner	**43.83**	**34.24**	**42.32**	**47.10**	**46.92**	**45.75**	**39.66**	**37.66**
At fast-food restaurants*	22.01	18.98	23.61	24.64	22.47	20.26	16.98	16.26
At full-service restaurants	49.95	39.17	46.40	55.69	54.41	51.20	43.91	43.85
At vending machines, mobile vendors	6.90	5.77	11.11	5.81	6.86	3.28	7.25	0.00
At employer and school cafeterias	13.53	16.16	21.95	11.43	12.41	7.32	8.70	11.86
Snacks and nonalcoholic beverages	**9.76**	**10.00**	**10.49**	**11.36**	**10.02**	**8.14**	**6.75**	**6.74**
At fast-food restaurants*	8.55	8.18	9.61	10.11	8.79	6.98	6.22	4.64
At full-service restaurants	11.15	14.63	12.22	11.68	11.26	8.38	7.97	13.03
At vending machines, mobile vendors	3.89	3.73	3.72	4.28	4.02	4.09	2.43	2.58
At employer and school cafeterias	4.45	4.88	4.19	6.28	3.25	3.98	2.50	2.56

	total households	under 25	25 to 34	35 to 44	45 to 54	55 to 64	65 to 74	75+
Breakfast and brunch	**$14.70**	**$12.05**	**$14.19**	**$15.92**	**$14.99**	**$14.94**	**$14.54**	**$12.33**
At fast-food restaurants*	10.04	8.30	10.23	11.46	10.46	8.93	9.37	6.44
At full-service restaurants	19.47	16.72	19.71	22.21	20.25	19.15	18.15	16.22
At vending machines, mobile vendors	3.13	4.55	3.07	3.61	3.29	3.09	1.65	0.00
At employer and school cafeterias	7.03	10.32	7.42	8.20	6.68	5.26	2.88	1.79
ALCOHOL, AMOUNT SPENT	**31.71**	**33.23**	**32.25**	**30.65**	**32.34**	**33.72**	**30.99**	**21.02**
Consumed at home	**28.77**	**26.42**	**25.38**	**27.18**	**29.21**	**33.87**	**32.73**	**22.02**
Beer and ale	20.80	20.52	20.77	20.54	19.94	23.16	21.47	13.82
Whiskey	37.29	48.48	33.33	52.17	30.91	41.13	27.12	26.47
Wine	24.45	17.15	20.31	22.25	26.65	27.31	27.55	22.11
Other alcoholic beverages	22.12	24.88	20.86	21.99	21.55	21.65	30.49	14.38
Consumed away from home (except on trips)	**23.05**	**29.48**	**28.48**	**23.26**	**21.82**	**19.82**	**17.77**	**13.88**
Beer and ale at restaurants, bars	15.66	21.61	18.60	15.58	15.47	11.88	12.59	9.14
Wine at restaurants, bars	16.95	21.79	19.00	17.39	14.69	17.39	15.42	14.72
Other alcoholic beverages at restaurants, bars	18.23	21.80	21.65	18.52	16.77	16.34	13.64	10.00

* The category fast-food restaurants also includes take-out, delivery, concession stands, buffets, and cafeterias other than employer and school.
Note: "–" means sample is too small to make a reliable estimate.
Source: Calculations by New Strategist based on the Bureau of Labor Statistics' 2008 Consumer Expenditure Survey

Table 4.5 Percent Buying Food and Alcohol by Household Income, <u>Average Quarter</u>, 2008

(percent of households buying food and alcohol during the average quarter, by before-tax income of household, 2008)

	total households	under $20,000	$20,000– $39,999	$40,000– $49,999	$50,000– $69,999	$70,000– $79,999	$80,000– $99,999	$100,000 or more
FOOD, PERCENT BUYING	**99.5%**	**98.1%**	**99.6%**	**100.0%**	**100.0%**	**100.0%**	**100.0%**	**99.9%**
Groceries	**99.0**	**96.8**	**99.2**	**99.4**	**99.8**	**99.9**	**99.9**	**99.9**
Food and nonalcoholic beverages	99.0	96.8	99.1	99.4	99.8	99.9	99.9	99.9
Groceries purchased on trips	10.6	4.1	6.6	9.3	11.9	12.8	15.4	19.7
Food away from home	**81.8**	**63.0**	**75.7**	**85.1**	**88.2**	**91.5**	**93.4**	**95.4**
Meals at restaurants, carry-outs, etc.	78.5	59.8	72.5	80.8	84.5	88.5	89.8	93.0
Food or board at school	1.0	0.7	0.3	0.6	0.6	1.5	1.3	2.5
Catered affairs	1.9	0.8	0.9	1.1	2.1	2.8	2.3	4.1
Restaurant meals on trips	23.7	11.2	15.7	21.2	24.8	28.8	33.0	42.5
School lunches	9.2	1.6	4.7	7.9	10.8	15.5	15.6	17.9
Meals as pay	1.7	1.5	1.6	1.4	1.9	2.2	1.9	1.6
ALCOHOL, PERCENT BUYING	**37.0**	**20.8**	**27.6**	**36.2**	**41.2**	**44.0**	**47.1**	**57.4**
Consumed at home	**31.8**	**17.8**	**24.0**	**31.5**	**34.9**	**39.1**	**39.8**	**49.2**
Consumed away from home	**23.8**	**11.3**	**14.6**	**21.6**	**25.9**	**27.6**	**31.6**	**44.3**
Alcoholic beverages at restaurants, bars	17.4	8.1	10.4	15.9	19.0	20.3	22.6	32.7
Alcoholic beverages purchased on trips	11.8	4.7	6.7	9.6	11.7	13.0	16.6	24.9

Source: Bureau of Labor Statistics, unpublished data from the 2008 Consumer Expenditure Survey

Table 4.6 Amount Buyers Spent on Food and Alcohol by Household Income, <u>Average Quarter</u>, 2008

(average amount spent by households buying food and alcohol during the average quarter, by before-tax income of household, 2008)

	total households	under $20,000	$20,000– $39,999	$40,000– $49,999	$50,000– $69,999	$70,000– $79,999	$80,000– $99,999	$100,000 or more
FOOD, AMOUNT SPENT	**$1,790.19**	**$1,056.07**	**$1,401.40**	**$1,617.77**	**$1,836.34**	**$2,007.96**	**$2,226.60**	**$2,889.75**
Groceries	**1,215.51**	**815.23**	**1,039.03**	**1,150.80**	**1,263.02**	**1,351.37**	**1,470.93**	**1,716.08**
Food and nonalcoholic beverages	1,203.56	811.35	1,032.70	1,142.50	1,251.77	1,337.56	1,453.02	1,689.01
Groceries purchased on trips	115.42	95.98	109.24	93.91	94.23	108.27	120.72	137.39
Food away from home	**705.92**	**389.13**	**481.32**	**556.09**	**652.42**	**718.54**	**810.46**	**1,230.84**
Meals at restaurants, carry-outs, etc.	594.49	357.98	443.01	507.50	574.16	594.77	676.11	936.64
Food or board at school	858.58	894.06	239.75	283.20	565.68	587.18	635.63	1,224.02
Catered affairs	926.61	258.44	422.88	297.94	480.10	650.09	862.50	1,588.15
Restaurant meals on trips	251.13	143.10	166.35	176.54	195.12	218.69	253.37	376.74
School lunches	192.71	159.53	136.22	163.50	183.12	205.54	187.70	223.19
Meals as pay	440.66	361.61	408.81	574.26	450.53	434.13	463.90	510.78
ALCOHOL, AMOUNT SPENT	**220.32**	**181.28**	**174.54**	**204.29**	**188.29**	**210.35**	**214.16**	**293.04**
Consumed at home	**145.28**	**133.35**	**121.41**	**130.78**	**132.25**	**137.10**	**143.26**	**180.50**
Consumed away from home	**148.68**	**125.91**	**130.58**	**151.75**	**121.44**	**141.31**	**139.11**	**179.42**
Alcoholic beverages at restaurants, bars	145.91	140.87	142.04	164.50	126.75	149.80	138.06	154.03
Alcoholic beverages purchased on trips	85.07	57.26	64.00	69.17	62.05	65.22	76.77	116.90

Source: Calculations by New Strategist based on the Bureau of Labor Statistics' 2008 Consumer Expenditure Survey

Table 4.7 Percent Buying Food and Alcohol by Household Income, <u>Average Week,</u> 2008

(percent of households buying food and alcohol during the average week, by before-tax income of household, 2008)

	total households	under $20,000	$20,000–$39,999	$40,000–$49,999	$50,000–$69,999	$70,000–$79,999	$80,000–$99,999	$100,000 or more
FOOD, PERCENT BUYING	**89.4%**	**82.2%**	**86.7%**	**87.9%**	**91.6%**	**93.0%**	**94.5%**	**96.2%**
• GROCERIES	**82.9**	**75.6**	**79.6**	**80.5**	**86.0**	**85.9**	**89.0**	**90.0**
Cereals and bakery products	**70.9**	**62.6**	**66.3**	**68.6**	**73.1**	**75.2**	**79.5**	**79.9**
Cereals and cereal products	46.5	37.5	41.7	43.5	47.7	53.2	54.8	57.1
Flour	4.4	3.5	3.9	5.0	4.8	4.9	4.6	5.2
Prepared flour mixes	8.5	4.8	7.4	7.7	8.6	10.8	11.3	12.1
Ready-to-eat and cooked cereals	32.4	25.7	28.8	29.9	33.6	37.7	37.3	40.6
Rice	10.1	7.8	8.7	10.0	11.2	11.7	12.2	12.0
Pasta, cornmeal, and other cereal products	19.9	14.2	15.8	18.8	20.0	26.2	26.5	27.0
Bakery products	65.7	56.6	60.9	64.1	68.0	69.0	75.1	75.2
Bread	46.9	39.0	43.0	44.3	48.5	52.4	54.5	55.4
White bread	32.7	28.2	31.4	31.1	34.1	35.3	36.2	36.2
Bread, other than white	39.8	30.9	35.0	37.8	41.1	46.1	48.7	49.6
Crackers and cookies	31.7	23.1	28.0	29.2	34.1	35.5	40.0	40.2
Cookies	21.3	15.3	18.7	20.1	22.9	24.5	26.3	27.0
Crackers	18.5	12.5	15.8	16.8	18.2	21.0	26.1	25.4
Frozen and refrigerated bakery products	12.4	8.2	9.8	13.9	13.4	15.9	16.4	15.7
Other bakery products	39.7	28.6	34.8	36.4	42.5	42.5	52.2	50.7
Biscuits and rolls	26.5	16.3	20.7	24.6	29.3	29.1	38.4	37.2
Cakes and cupcakes	12.4	8.8	11.4	11.2	12.4	14.6	15.7	16.2
Bread and cracker products	4.2	2.8	3.1	3.8	4.2	5.2	6.1	6.2
Sweetrolls, coffee cakes, doughnuts	11.2	8.1	10.6	9.2	11.2	12.8	16.3	13.4
Pies, tarts, turnovers	6.5	4.3	4.8	6.2	6.3	9.3	9.2	9.2
Meats, poultry, fish, and eggs	**66.2**	**55.7**	**62.9**	**64.4**	**69.5**	**67.9**	**74.9**	**75.4**
Beef	34.1	25.5	31.9	32.5	34.7	37.7	40.4	42.3
Ground beef	22.7	16.9	21.4	21.0	23.8	23.6	27.4	27.9
Roast	6.5	3.8	5.6	7.1	6.9	7.5	8.8	8.6
Chuck roast	2.4	1.5	1.9	3.1	2.7	1.7	3.5	3.1
Round roast	1.3	1.0	0.9	1.6	1.6	0.8	1.8	1.8
Other roast	4.1	2.4	3.6	3.9	3.9	6.0	5.0	5.6
Steak	12.9	8.1	11.5	11.4	13.1	15.6	15.5	18.4
Round steak	5.2	3.2	4.9	4.6	5.9	5.6	6.7	6.7
Sirloin steak	5.6	3.0	5.1	4.4	5.8	8.3	6.8	7.9
Other steak	9.8	5.8	9.0	7.8	10.0	11.4	12.5	14.2
Other beef	5.3	4.8	4.9	4.7	5.1	5.6	5.6	6.8
Pork	32.5	25.5	30.5	32.9	34.0	35.9	38.1	37.5
Bacon	12.2	9.1	10.5	13.6	12.4	12.3	14.7	15.7
Pork chops	8.0	5.7	7.4	9.3	7.5	9.0	9.5	9.8
Ham	9.9	7.7	9.1	9.5	11.3	11.9	12.2	10.8
Ham, not canned	9.7	7.5	8.9	9.3	10.8	11.9	11.9	10.7
Canned ham	0.3	0.2	0.2	0.3	0.6	0.1	0.3	0.3
Sausage	11.9	8.8	10.8	11.7	12.4	13.4	14.7	14.3
Other pork	8.6	6.3	8.1	8.3	9.3	10.0	10.4	9.8
Other meats	31.0	23.0	29.0	30.2	32.0	33.5	37.8	37.5
Frankfurters	11.1	8.2	10.3	12.2	10.8	13.6	13.4	13.1
Lunch meats (cold cuts)	24.8	18.0	22.7	24.2	25.9	27.0	30.9	30.9
Bologna, liverwurst, salami	11.3	8.6	10.7	11.9	11.9	11.9	13.5	13.1
Other lunch meats	20.6	13.6	18.6	20.5	21.3	22.3	26.8	26.6
Lamb, organ meats, and others	2.1	1.6	1.9	1.3	2.6	2.1	2.6	2.7
Lamb and organ meats	1.8	1.3	1.8	1.1	1.9	1.8	2.3	2.4
Mutton, goat, and game	0.4	0.3	0.2	0.3	0.8	0.4	0.3	0.4

	total households	under $20,000	$20,000–$39,999	$40,000–$49,999	$50,000–$69,999	$70,000–$79,999	$80,000–$99,999	$100,000 or more
Poultry	31.0%	24.0%	27.6%	29.1%	31.5%	34.3%	40.0%	38.2%
Fresh and frozen chicken	26.6	21.2	23.9	24.8	27.3	28.4	33.1	32.5
Fresh and frozen whole chicken	10.8	8.6	9.9	9.3	11.3	10.5	13.2	13.9
Fresh and frozen chicken parts	24.5	19.5	21.5	22.8	25.3	26.3	30.7	30.3
Other poultry	9.5	6.0	7.4	8.8	9.8	10.2	14.5	13.2
Fish and seafood	22.1	15.5	20.3	19.2	21.8	24.9	28.0	29.6
Canned fish and seafood	7.9	5.4	7.7	7.7	7.8	8.9	10.9	9.4
Fresh fish and shellfish	10.3	6.4	9.3	8.0	9.9	12.1	12.9	15.6
Frozen fish and shellfish	8.7	6.7	7.3	7.8	8.4	9.8	11.1	12.0
Eggs	31.7	25.3	28.7	32.6	32.2	32.3	37.1	38.8
Dairy products	**69.0**	**58.9**	**64.2**	**66.6**	**71.4**	**72.6**	**78.3**	**79.8**
Fresh milk and cream	57.0	46.2	53.6	54.2	58.7	61.2	65.8	67.8
Fresh milk, all types	54.4	44.0	51.3	52.1	55.1	58.7	62.8	64.8
Cream	13.6	7.7	10.8	12.3	13.9	16.1	19.4	20.8
Other dairy products	53.2	41.4	46.9	50.5	55.2	58.3	63.9	67.4
Butter	11.7	8.4	10.1	9.0	12.0	12.3	16.1	16.6
Cheese	39.5	28.2	33.1	38.2	40.4	44.8	49.7	53.5
Ice cream and related products	21.7	15.0	18.4	21.6	23.7	24.7	25.6	28.9
Miscellaneous dairy products	21.0	14.7	16.0	19.1	20.3	25.0	28.0	31.5
Fruits and vegetables	**70.7**	**60.5**	**66.4**	**66.0**	**74.4**	**72.5**	**80.5**	**81.8**
Fresh fruits	52.6	41.7	47.3	47.0	54.7	55.9	63.5	66.6
Apples	19.0	12.5	15.6	16.3	18.8	22.7	23.7	29.0
Bananas	33.7	26.3	30.0	28.0	34.8	35.3	40.7	45.0
Oranges	11.8	8.2	10.0	10.7	12.6	13.7	14.5	16.2
Citrus fruits, excluding oranges	16.6	11.2	14.5	14.1	17.1	17.0	21.7	23.9
Other fresh fruits	34.2	24.0	29.4	31.0	35.5	37.5	43.7	46.7
Fresh vegetables	53.5	41.4	48.7	48.8	56.2	56.4	65.4	66.6
Potatoes	20.5	14.7	19.0	18.0	20.8	22.6	26.9	26.3
Lettuce	20.1	13.6	17.4	18.0	19.6	20.5	27.6	28.7
Tomatoes	22.4	15.7	19.4	21.3	23.1	23.9	28.2	30.6
Other fresh vegetables	44.1	33.5	39.0	39.2	46.6	46.3	54.4	57.6
Processed fruits	39.3	31.1	35.0	35.9	39.8	42.6	48.5	49.9
Frozen fruits and fruit juices	5.0	2.8	4.0	5.3	5.6	4.7	6.9	7.6
Frozen orange juice	2.3	1.4	1.9	2.3	3.0	2.1	2.9	3.0
Frozen fruits	2.1	0.9	1.6	2.4	2.1	2.0	3.1	3.7
Frozen fruit juices, excluding orange	1.4	1.1	1.0	1.3	1.9	1.1	1.4	2.1
Canned fruits	12.4	10.0	10.9	12.2	11.7	12.5	15.2	16.5
Dried fruits	4.8	3.5	4.1	4.5	4.4	5.7	5.1	7.3
Fresh fruit juice	8.7	5.3	6.9	8.8	8.7	10.8	12.1	12.5
Canned and bottled fruit juice	25.8	19.6	21.8	23.2	27.2	27.8	32.5	34.4
Processed vegetables	39.9	31.2	36.6	38.2	41.9	44.5	46.7	48.5
Frozen vegetables	17.2	11.5	14.1	16.4	17.6	24.0	21.7	23.1
Canned and dried vegetables and juices	33.5	26.3	31.2	32.1	35.2	37.6	38.3	39.9
Canned beans	12.0	8.8	10.6	11.3	12.5	13.3	15.1	15.2
Canned corn	7.1	5.8	7.0	6.9	7.2	7.8	7.9	8.3
Canned miscellaneous vegetables	15.8	10.5	13.4	15.0	17.5	18.6	19.5	20.8
Dried peas	0.3	0.1	0.2	0.4	0.3	0.9	0.7	0.4
Dried beans	2.5	2.2	2.9	2.5	2.3	3.4	3.4	1.9
Dried miscellaneous vegetables	6.3	4.1	6.0	6.9	6.5	7.4	7.8	7.4
Fresh and canned vegetable juices	8.9	6.9	8.9	7.8	8.3	10.3	9.8	11.5
Sugar and other sweets	**41.4**	**32.0**	**37.8**	**40.4**	**43.2**	**43.8**	**49.5**	**50.7**
Candy and chewing gum	30.6	21.6	26.8	30.1	33.2	32.9	38.5	38.7
Sugar	11.8	10.0	11.3	13.1	12.6	11.1	12.9	12.9
Artificial sweeteners	2.2	1.8	1.6	2.1	2.2	3.1	3.2	2.9
Jams, preserves, other sweets	13.7	9.8	11.9	11.4	13.8	15.0	17.7	19.3

	total households	under $20,000	$20,000–$39,999	$40,000–$49,999	$50,000–$69,999	$70,000–$79,999	$80,000–$99,999	$100,000 or more
Fats and oils	34.3%	27.2%	30.9%	32.5%	35.9%	37.3%	43.4%	40.9%
Margarine	6.9	6.0	6.8	6.2	6.5	6.4	8.1	8.1
Fats and oils	12.7	11.0	11.8	11.6	12.6	13.8	15.4	14.7
Salad dressings	14.6	10.1	12.3	15.3	14.7	17.0	19.7	18.6
Nondairy cream and imitation milk	9.3	6.5	7.8	8.1	10.8	10.8	12.7	11.7
Peanut butter	7.0	5.0	5.1	7.5	6.8	8.2	9.4	10.0
Miscellaneous foods	68.0	56.3	64.0	66.5	71.1	72.9	77.4	78.1
Frozen prepared foods	27.4	20.5	24.4	26.4	28.5	31.7	33.3	34.3
Frozen meals	16.7	12.6	14.9	15.9	16.2	20.4	20.1	21.4
Other frozen prepared foods	17.7	12.6	15.4	17.2	19.0	20.2	21.7	22.8
Canned and packaged soups	21.1	15.2	19.2	21.7	20.1	24.1	26.4	27.0
Potato chips, nuts, and other snacks	41.1	29.2	36.1	39.7	43.8	48.5	52.1	51.5
Potato chips and other snacks	37.0	25.7	32.1	34.9	40.1	43.3	47.8	46.7
Nuts	12.8	8.1	10.2	12.8	13.0	16.8	17.0	17.6
Condiments and seasonings	42.7	29.5	37.5	39.5	47.4	48.3	53.2	54.9
Salt, spices, and other seasonings	19.1	13.2	15.6	18.0	21.2	23.7	22.5	26.1
Olives, pickles, relishes	8.7	4.9	7.1	8.4	10.0	10.6	11.0	12.0
Sauces and gravies	28.1	18.2	23.9	26.7	30.5	34.3	37.0	36.9
Baking needs and miscellaneous products	15.1	9.6	12.0	14.5	17.0	18.9	20.9	19.6
Other canned/packaged prepared foods	46.6	35.2	41.3	46.4	49.4	52.9	54.8	57.9
Prepared salads	16.5	10.5	12.8	16.5	18.0	20.1	21.0	23.6
Prepared desserts	9.0	5.4	7.6	7.9	11.3	13.2	11.1	11.0
Baby food	4.4	2.6	2.9	4.0	5.1	5.7	5.7	6.8
Miscellaneous prepared foods	38.2	28.1	34.1	39.0	38.6	43.3	47.0	47.8
Nonalcoholic beverages	57.4	47.9	53.0	55.2	60.8	63.1	64.7	66.3
Cola	31.5	25.0	29.3	30.0	33.1	37.3	38.1	36.0
Other carbonated drinks	26.3	20.3	23.7	24.9	27.4	29.2	32.7	31.9
Tea	13.6	9.7	12.3	12.8	13.6	16.4	16.4	17.8
Coffee	12.5	10.3	10.9	10.4	13.2	11.3	14.4	17.0
Roasted coffee	11.7	9.7	10.2	9.6	12.6	10.5	13.7	16.0
Instant and freeze-dried coffee	9.8	8.2	9.1	8.6	10.4	8.3	11.0	12.8
Noncarbonated fruit-flavored drinks	11.8	9.6	10.9	12.5	11.1	15.1	14.1	13.6
Other nonalcoholic beverages and ice	6.4	3.9	5.4	8.3	6.7	5.5	9.8	7.8
Bottled water	20.8	13.8	17.3	20.8	21.5	25.8	26.0	28.2
Sports drinks	7.5	4.1	6.0	6.0	8.6	9.7	12.1	10.2
• MEALS AT RESTAURANTS, CARRY-OUTS	72.4	53.6	66.0	71.8	78.1	81.1	82.8	88.7
Lunch	54.9	36.5	47.0	50.8	59.8	64.4	66.8	74.5
At fast-food restaurants*	42.3	27.0	36.7	38.0	45.4	48.1	53.4	58.6
At full-service restaurants	21.2	12.1	15.2	18.1	21.4	26.3	26.8	36.5
At vending machines, mobile vendors	4.4	2.5	3.7	4.0	5.0	6.0	5.4	5.9
At employer and school cafeterias	10.6	4.6	6.0	8.6	11.7	13.5	15.4	20.2
Dinner	47.2	29.4	39.5	46.2	50.1	58.1	56.9	66.5
At fast-food restaurants*	29.9	18.8	25.6	29.6	31.6	36.8	37.3	40.5
At full-service restaurants	27.7	14.5	20.8	26.0	27.7	35.4	35.0	46.7
At vending machines, mobile vendors	0.9	0.5	1.1	1.0	1.1	1.3	0.7	0.7
At employer and school cafeterias	1.3	1.3	0.8	1.8	2.3	1.4	1.1	1.2
Snacks and nonalcoholic beverages	35.0	21.9	28.0	34.9	40.1	40.6	43.1	48.1
At fast-food restaurants*	24.9	14.7	19.0	24.1	26.7	28.2	33.4	37.7
At full-service restaurants	5.6	2.6	5.0	5.7	7.0	5.4	7.2	7.5
At vending machines, mobile vendors	13.6	8.9	10.8	14.3	16.3	15.9	17.5	17.2
At employer and school cafeterias	2.9	2.0	2.0	2.7	3.1	3.9	4.6	4.0

	total households	under $20,000	$20,000–$39,999	$40,000–$49,999	$50,000–$69,999	$70,000–$79,999	$80,000–$99,999	$100,000 or more
Breakfast and brunch	**30.2%**	**18.1%**	**25.2%**	**29.0%**	**32.2%**	**34.8%**	**37.6%**	**44.2%**
At fast-food restaurants*	22.1	12.5	17.8	21.1	22.9	26.9	28.7	33.8
At full-service restaurants	9.9	5.5	8.7	9.2	10.8	10.5	11.8	14.6
At vending machines, mobile vendors	2.2	1.4	1.8	2.3	3.0	2.7	2.4	2.9
At employer and school cafeterias	3.1	2.3	1.7	2.7	3.7	3.9	3.9	5.1
ALCOHOL, PERCENT BUYING	**24.5**	**13.4**	**18.3**	**23.1**	**25.8**	**28.9**	**31.1**	**40.2**
Consumed at home	**16.4**	**9.6**	**12.6**	**15.2**	**18.3**	**19.8**	**20.4**	**25.2**
Beer and ale	11.3	6.4	9.6	12.0	13.3	12.9	12.6	15.6
Whiskey	0.6	0.5	0.2	0.3	0.9	0.6	0.5	1.1
Wine	6.9	3.1	3.7	4.7	7.0	8.8	10.6	14.0
Other alcoholic beverages	2.2	1.6	1.7	0.9	2.2	1.8	3.3	3.8
Consumed away from home (except on trips)	**13.2**	**5.9**	**9.0**	**12.8**	**12.4**	**16.2**	**17.0**	**25.1**
Beer and ale at restaurants, bars	8.8	3.7	5.9	9.7	8.6	11.9	10.7	16.1
Wine at restaurants, bars	4.1	1.7	1.9	3.2	3.3	4.9	6.3	9.4
Other alcoholic beverages at restaurants, bars	5.3	1.8	3.8	4.5	5.3	7.5	6.6	10.3

* The category fast-food restaurants also includes take-out, delivery, concession stands, buffets, and cafeterias other than employer and school.
Source: Bureau of Labor Statistics, unpublished data from the 2008 Consumer Expenditure Survey

Table 4.8 Amount Buyers Spent on Food and Alcohol by Household Income, Average Week, 2008

(average amount spent by households buying food and alcohol during the average week, by before-tax income of household, 2008)

	total households	under $20,000	$20,000–$39,999	$40,000–$49,999	$50,000–$69,999	$70,000–$79,999	$80,000–$99,999	$100,000 or more
FOOD, AMOUNT SPENT	**$127.99**	**$117.71**	**$86.80**	**$106.49**	**$112.92**	**$143.19**	**$164.57**	**$199.42**
• GROCERIES	**85.73**	**90.25**	**62.96**	**76.12**	**78.97**	**95.27**	**107.79**	**119.33**
Cereals and bakery products	**13.75**	**15.22**	**10.01**	**11.88**	**12.26**	**15.17**	**17.36**	**18.45**
Cereals and cereal products	7.01	9.13	5.42	6.49	6.58	7.37	7.98	8.30
Flour	3.39	5.20	3.19	3.02	3.82	2.87	3.74	3.45
Prepared flour mixes	2.72	3.21	2.23	2.84	2.60	2.97	2.82	2.97
Ready-to-eat and cooked cereals	5.59	7.16	4.38	5.18	5.19	5.91	6.78	6.47
Rice	4.87	8.01	4.12	4.79	4.32	4.11	4.11	5.35
Pasta, cornmeal, and other cereal products	2.96	4.14	2.24	2.80	2.56	2.90	3.21	3.45
Bakery products	9.88	10.76	7.17	8.41	8.67	10.84	12.57	13.29
Bread	4.05	5.04	3.22	3.84	3.77	4.07	4.52	4.97
White bread	2.17	2.89	1.83	2.08	2.12	2.13	2.29	2.54
Bread, other than white	2.99	3.73	2.31	2.74	2.67	2.99	3.35	3.67
Crackers and cookies	4.95	6.11	3.72	4.30	4.45	5.35	5.88	6.17
Cookies	4.23	5.29	3.29	3.67	3.74	4.17	4.98	5.27
Crackers	3.62	4.80	2.72	3.15	3.28	4.20	3.94	4.17
Frozen and refrigerated bakery products	4.03	5.67	3.16	3.31	3.74	4.15	4.51	4.53
Other bakery products	6.35	7.76	4.70	5.35	5.66	6.60	7.46	8.00
Biscuits and rolls	3.59	4.72	2.72	3.08	3.22	3.54	3.91	4.30
Cakes and cupcakes	6.19	7.74	4.58	5.46	5.20	5.13	7.53	8.01
Bread and cracker products	2.14	3.33	1.73	2.26	2.08	2.32	2.15	2.27
Sweetrolls, coffee cakes, doughnuts	3.75	4.90	3.01	3.27	3.79	3.67	4.06	4.24
Pies, tarts, turnovers	4.30	6.02	3.45	4.24	4.19	4.50	4.56	4.89
Meats, poultry, fish, and eggs	**24.59**	**27.96**	**19.57**	**23.47**	**23.70**	**26.94**	**28.05**	**31.12**
Beef	13.48	16.56	10.71	13.42	13.75	13.35	14.34	16.68
Ground beef	7.63	9.82	6.11	7.06	8.49	7.81	7.96	8.68
Roast	11.49	16.39	9.19	11.56	11.66	9.81	11.66	13.43
Chuck roast	7.92	12.38	6.65	7.53	8.17	7.60	7.67	8.31
Round roast	9.02	8.92	6.99	7.77	8.13	6.67	11.48	10.50
Other roast	10.81	15.45	8.99	12.24	11.63	9.32	11.24	12.50
Steak	13.05	17.66	10.60	13.53	12.72	13.06	13.55	15.42
Round steak	4.82	7.72	3.84	5.28	5.65	5.33	4.21	5.38
Sirloin steak	7.90	11.45	6.15	8.29	10.27	8.45	6.87	8.84
Other steak	10.13	13.17	7.93	9.68	9.52	9.15	10.81	12.55
Other beef	8.10	9.95	7.47	9.82	8.47	7.37	8.60	9.45
Pork	9.62	12.35	8.01	9.14	9.43	9.74	10.76	10.74
Bacon	4.59	6.41	3.95	4.44	4.72	4.23	4.62	5.02
Pork chops	7.67	11.20	6.77	8.13	7.32	8.04	7.81	7.87
Ham	6.44	8.10	5.82	6.13	6.08	6.20	7.33	6.88
Ham, not canned	6.48	8.12	5.84	6.13	6.24	6.20	7.40	6.82
Canned ham	3.33	1.78	5.52	6.25	3.23	0.00	3.23	4.00
Sausage	4.56	6.24	3.83	4.58	4.79	4.10	4.97	5.03
Other pork	8.96	11.97	7.10	8.14	7.69	9.55	10.34	10.27
Other meats	6.62	8.17	5.14	6.46	6.42	6.54	7.07	7.95
Frankfurters	3.50	4.82	2.78	3.10	3.85	3.32	3.59	4.12
Lunch meats (cold cuts)	5.72	7.20	4.47	5.36	5.66	5.66	6.06	6.87
Bologna, liverwurst, salami	3.09	4.06	2.53	2.96	3.02	2.93	2.97	3.65
Other lunch meats	5.16	6.72	4.02	4.82	4.87	5.34	5.45	6.17
Lamb, organ meats, and others	11.37	11.74	10.26	17.39	7.46	10.19	12.89	11.76
Lamb and organ meats	10.11	9.35	10.31	17.96	7.48	9.55	13.42	11.06
Mutton, goat, and game	16.67	24.44	5.06	6.25	11.54	12.82	8.00	14.63

	total households	under $20,000	$20,000– $39,999	$40,000– $49,999	$50,000– $69,999	$70,000– $79,999	$80,000– $99,999	$100,000 or more
Poultry	$9.88	$13.22	$8.33	$9.41	$9.38	$9.63	$10.06	$11.20
Fresh and frozen chicken	9.19	12.63	7.72	8.91	8.75	9.25	9.26	10.19
Fresh and frozen whole chicken	5.81	7.71	5.18	5.84	5.07	5.44	5.75	6.31
Fresh and frozen chicken parts	7.36	10.39	6.15	7.09	7.49	7.84	7.55	8.03
Other poultry	6.56	8.19	6.15	6.57	6.22	6.58	6.47	7.33
Fish and seafood	11.16	13.88	9.24	10.72	10.29	13.16	11.59	12.95
Canned fish and seafood	4.05	6.11	2.97	3.50	3.52	3.93	4.42	4.81
Fresh fish and shellfish	12.67	15.77	10.86	13.05	13.00	16.82	13.15	13.18
Frozen fish and shellfish	9.64	12.28	8.78	9.41	8.58	9.16	9.63	11.15
Eggs	3.10	4.35	2.64	3.01	3.19	3.12	3.13	3.30
Dairy products	**11.98**	**13.94**	**8.88**	**10.79**	**10.71**	**12.82**	**14.77**	**16.00**
Fresh milk and cream	5.67	7.51	4.54	5.50	5.23	5.68	6.78	6.77
Fresh milk, all types	5.30	7.26	4.31	5.21	4.85	5.25	6.23	6.14
Cream	2.57	3.54	2.03	2.32	2.52	2.42	2.84	2.94
Other dairy products	9.45	11.37	6.95	8.47	8.51	10.00	11.11	12.12
Butter	3.50	4.91	2.93	3.50	3.44	3.02	3.97	3.74
Cheese	6.54	7.93	5.07	5.85	5.71	6.75	7.44	8.07
Ice cream and related products	5.35	7.25	4.25	5.10	4.99	5.56	5.86	5.99
Miscellaneous dairy products	4.19	6.20	3.16	3.78	3.78	4.29	4.50	4.79
Fruits and vegetables	**17.86**	**19.57**	**13.50**	**15.98**	**16.20**	**19.50**	**20.98**	**24.07**
Fresh fruits	8.12	9.10	6.34	7.52	7.43	8.57	8.63	10.44
Apples	4.05	5.19	3.22	3.89	4.42	4.05	4.02	4.59
Bananas	1.84	2.52	1.53	1.72	1.89	1.82	1.82	2.09
Oranges	4.06	5.05	3.59	4.15	3.82	3.71	3.94	4.38
Citrus fruits, excluding oranges	2.11	2.79	1.66	1.99	1.85	2.23	2.26	2.34
Other fresh fruits	5.97	7.39	4.88	5.89	5.06	6.21	6.25	7.30
Fresh vegetables	7.61	9.23	5.93	7.07	6.91	7.62	8.63	9.73
Potatoes	3.56	5.23	3.05	3.47	3.50	3.55	3.83	3.69
Lettuce	2.54	3.13	1.93	2.33	2.34	2.59	2.69	3.10
Tomatoes	3.17	4.18	2.52	2.79	3.05	3.23	3.27	3.59
Other fresh vegetables	4.83	5.89	3.78	4.54	4.26	4.73	5.42	6.13
Processed fruits	5.70	6.87	4.32	4.93	5.48	5.82	6.35	6.92
Frozen fruits and fruit juices	4.37	5.08	3.72	4.25	4.14	4.65	4.66	4.50
Frozen orange juice	3.48	3.51	3.31	3.91	2.99	3.86	3.10	3.73
Frozen fruits	5.19	7.30	4.32	5.13	5.00	4.90	5.88	4.93
Frozen fruit juices, excluding orange	2.14	2.24	1.67	2.29	2.29	2.80	2.78	2.86
Canned fruits	3.22	4.31	2.67	2.91	2.79	3.84	3.49	3.46
Dried fruits	3.14	4.28	2.44	3.07	2.68	3.66	3.52	3.30
Fresh fruit juice	4.03	5.12	3.18	3.81	4.09	3.90	4.38	4.41
Canned and bottled fruit juice	4.38	5.82	3.47	3.97	4.05	4.14	4.71	5.09
Processed vegetables	5.13	6.50	4.29	5.09	4.89	5.80	5.77	5.82
Frozen vegetables	3.84	5.15	3.20	3.83	3.91	4.00	3.83	4.11
Canned and dried vegetables and juices	4.16	5.46	3.58	4.20	3.83	4.31	4.86	4.69
Canned beans	2.34	3.28	1.88	2.35	2.48	2.26	2.39	2.50
Canned corn	1.82	2.95	1.65	1.70	1.88	1.66	1.65	1.81
Canned miscellaneous vegetables	2.60	3.57	2.33	2.76	2.27	2.58	3.02	2.98
Dried peas	3.03	–	–	0.00	2.70	1.18	1.52	2.50
Dried beans	3.16	4.45	2.78	3.64	2.44	2.39	4.12	2.66
Dried miscellaneous vegetables	3.01	4.12	2.55	2.88	2.89	2.85	3.35	3.25
Fresh and canned vegetable juices	3.14	4.37	2.68	3.32	2.68	3.88	3.49	3.47
Sugar and other sweets	**6.02**	**7.34**	**4.60**	**5.39**	**5.75**	**6.12**	**6.63**	**7.70**
Candy and chewing gum	5.04	5.87	3.90	4.44	4.82	5.14	5.35	6.67
Sugar	2.87	4.45	2.48	2.85	2.82	2.71	2.70	2.78
Artificial sweeteners	5.43	7.63	4.56	5.85	5.31	5.88	5.97	6.25
Jams, preserves, other sweets	3.50	4.55	2.87	3.37	3.34	3.39	3.83	3.99

	total households	under $20,000	$20,000– $39,999	$40,000– $49,999	$50,000– $69,999	$70,000– $79,999	$80,000– $99,999	$100,000 or more
Fats and oils	**$5.86**	**$8.34**	**$4.76**	**$5.66**	**$5.73**	**$6.01**	**$6.11**	**$6.65**
Margarine	2.48	3.66	2.10	2.51	2.25	2.51	2.47	2.34
Fats and oils	5.99	8.24	5.13	6.04	5.61	6.10	6.04	6.96
Salad dressings	3.57	5.15	3.00	3.42	3.66	3.52	3.71	3.86
Nondairy cream and imitation milk	3.32	5.32	2.64	3.08	3.09	3.07	3.32	3.58
Peanut butter	3.58	4.98	2.81	3.35	3.45	3.80	3.85	3.70
Miscellaneous foods	**19.22**	**20.82**	**13.42**	**16.04**	**18.01**	**22.04**	**23.27**	**26.05**
Frozen prepared foods	9.85	12.53	7.96	9.18	9.47	10.40	10.88	11.46
Frozen meals	8.39	10.34	7.14	8.01	8.45	8.96	8.45	9.61
Other frozen prepared foods	7.34	9.97	5.71	6.71	6.73	7.26	8.85	8.21
Canned and packaged soups	4.17	5.68	3.53	4.33	3.87	4.78	4.40	4.52
Potato chips, nuts, and other snacks	6.56	7.35	4.69	5.69	6.02	6.70	7.52	8.51
Potato chips and other snacks	5.36	5.97	3.74	4.64	4.99	5.45	6.13	6.89
Nuts	5.65	7.36	4.85	5.43	5.09	5.31	5.78	6.58
Condiments and seasonings	5.55	7.02	3.87	4.57	5.34	5.87	6.03	6.81
Salt, spices, and other seasonings	2.93	4.06	2.23	2.58	2.83	2.70	3.20	3.41
Olives, pickles, relishes	3.00	3.93	2.48	2.85	2.50	2.74	2.99	3.66
Sauces and gravies	3.70	4.68	2.74	3.30	3.53	3.88	3.86	4.60
Baking needs and miscellaneous products	3.32	4.69	2.27	2.56	3.03	3.02	3.55	3.62
Other canned/packaged prepared foods	9.48	11.29	6.78	7.75	8.92	10.47	11.14	12.21
Prepared salads	4.23	5.89	3.32	3.46	3.93	4.38	4.39	5.09
Prepared desserts	2.77	4.14	2.13	2.43	2.77	3.19	2.53	3.17
Baby food	15.07	16.02	10.91	12.90	14.14	18.07	18.15	16.84
Miscellaneous prepared foods	7.28	9.47	5.40	6.08	6.95	7.26	8.11	9.15
Nonalcoholic beverages	**11.49**	**13.40**	**8.80**	**10.38**	**10.66**	**12.23**	**13.49**	**14.64**
Cola	5.04	6.75	4.00	4.75	4.57	5.14	5.23	6.06
Other carbonated drinks	3.73	4.76	3.14	3.70	3.58	3.46	4.16	4.27
Tea	4.56	5.81	3.53	4.05	4.46	4.83	4.64	5.39
Coffee	7.87	10.20	6.49	7.44	7.14	8.29	8.78	8.81
Roasted coffee	5.63	7.40	4.39	4.97	4.99	6.29	6.21	6.50
Instant and freeze-dried coffee	3.26	4.29	2.82	3.13	3.04	3.24	3.74	3.61
Noncarbonated fruit-flavored drinks	4.56	5.40	3.71	4.42	4.65	5.29	4.34	5.29
Other nonalcoholic beverages and ice	4.22	5.05	3.44	3.83	4.73	3.99	4.59	4.99
Bottled water	5.69	7.83	4.29	4.95	5.15	5.22	6.24	6.99
Sports drinks	5.59	7.83	4.35	5.15	4.52	6.99	5.47	6.20
• MEALS AT RESTAURANTS, CARRY-OUTS	**59.96**	**52.72**	**38.04**	**46.60**	**49.67**	**63.21**	**71.93**	**95.35**
Lunch	**27.09**	**27.35**	**18.05**	**21.58**	**24.04**	**27.70**	**30.48**	**38.30**
At fast-food restaurants*	17.66	19.69	13.21	15.51	17.62	19.18	19.07	21.17
At full-service restaurants	26.77	31.24	19.28	22.01	23.98	24.53	27.66	33.93
At vending machines, mobile vendors	4.14	6.68	3.31	4.03	5.03	4.69	3.87	3.41
At employer and school cafeterias	14.64	14.20	9.63	13.47	11.42	13.83	16.61	17.60
Dinner	**43.83**	**43.91**	**29.75**	**34.66**	**33.89**	**43.21**	**50.23**	**63.42**
At fast-food restaurants*	22.01	25.84	17.84	19.92	19.74	22.45	24.21	26.46
At full-service restaurants	49.95	53.83	33.74	39.68	36.64	46.84	55.49	67.02
At vending machines, mobile vendors	6.90	3.16	5.88	8.06	12.24	6.92	9.46	10.14
At employer and school cafeterias	13.53	24.88	12.12	15.89	8.00	12.06	7.55	7.44
Snacks and nonalcoholic beverages	**9.76**	**9.80**	**7.33**	**8.91**	**10.22**	**9.01**	**11.39**	**12.18**
At fast-food restaurants*	8.55	9.29	6.66	8.26	8.08	8.18	9.84	10.32
At full-service restaurants	11.15	11.44	7.57	8.50	15.72	9.06	10.28	14.84
At vending machines, mobile vendors	3.89	4.22	2.97	3.34	4.83	4.46	3.66	3.90
At employer and school cafeterias	4.45	4.88	4.32	4.85	1.85	3.85	5.47	4.74

	total households	under $20,000	$20,000–$39,999	$40,000–$49,999	$50,000–$69,999	$70,000–$79,999	$80,000–$99,999	$100,000 or more
Breakfast and brunch	**$14.70**	**$16.85**	**$11.13**	**$13.03**	**$14.68**	**$13.41**	**$15.24**	**$18.08**
At fast-food restaurants*	10.04	12.50	8.57	9.61	9.96	9.27	10.30	11.94
At full-service restaurants	19.47	21.95	13.54	16.83	19.09	17.62	21.49	24.01
At vending machines, mobile vendors	3.13	3.72	2.77	3.98	4.44	4.46	2.89	2.78
At employer and school cafeterias	7.03	10.78	3.42	3.74	10.29	5.61	4.59	7.47
ALCOHOL, AMOUNT SPENT	**31.71**	**36.45**	**23.35**	**28.53**	**28.97**	**31.54**	**33.02**	**38.42**
Consumed at home	**28.77**	**33.47**	**20.71**	**24.54**	**22.98**	**27.33**	**31.50**	**37.14**
Beer and ale	20.80	29.45	16.92	20.43	17.11	21.83	20.57	24.07
Whiskey	37.29	36.42	19.26	23.81	20.00	22.41	34.04	56.64
Wine	24.45	25.14	16.72	17.54	26.07	22.95	27.60	28.93
Other alcoholic beverages	22.12	25.79	18.16	24.18	18.60	24.86	22.87	24.80
Consumed away from home (except on trips)	**23.05**	**28.60**	**18.66**	**22.16**	**24.96**	**22.80**	**22.56**	**24.21**
Beer and ale at restaurants, bars	15.66	23.51	12.47	13.96	17.70	14.01	15.67	15.84
Wine at restaurants, bars	16.95	24.01	14.16	16.09	12.54	17.86	15.64	18.70
Other alcoholic beverages at restaurants, bars	18.23	22.06	17.83	22.22	23.89	15.58	17.68	17.07

* The category fast-food restaurants also includes take-out, delivery, concession stands, buffets, and cafeterias other than employer and school.
Note: "–" means sample is too small to make a reliable estimate.
Source: Calculations by New Strategist based on the Bureau of Labor Statistics' 2008 Consumer Expenditure Survey

Table 4.9 Percent of High-Income Households Buying Food and Alcohol, Average Quarter, 2008

(percent of high-income households buying food and alcohol during the average quarter, by before-tax income of household, 2008)

	total households	$100,000 or more	$100,000–$119,999	$120,000–$149,999	$150,000 or more
FOOD, PERCENT BUYING	**99.5%**	**99.9%**	**99.9%**	**100.0%**	**99.9%**
Groceries	**99.0**	**99.9**	**99.7**	**100.0**	**99.9**
Food and nonalcoholic beverages	99.0	99.9	99.7	100.0	99.9
Groceries purchased on trips	10.6	19.7	15.6	19.2	23.3
Food away from home	**81.8**	**95.4**	**94.1**	**95.8**	**96.2**
Meals at restaurants, carry-outs, etc.	78.5	93.0	91.3	92.8	94.3
Food or board at school	1.0	2.5	1.8	1.4	3.9
Catered affairs	1.9	4.1	3.0	4.6	4.6
Restaurant meals on trips	23.7	42.5	35.6	40.8	49.3
School lunches	9.2	17.9	18.0	19.5	16.8
Meals as pay	1.7	1.6	1.3	2.0	1.6
ALCOHOL, PERCENT BUYING	**37.0**	**57.4**	**52.6**	**54.6**	**63.2**
Consumed at home	**31.8**	**49.2**	**45.8**	**45.6**	**54.4**
Consumed away from home	**23.8**	**44.3**	**37.8**	**40.4**	**52.1**
Alcoholic beverages at restaurants, bars	17.4	32.7	28.3	28.1	39.3
Alcoholic beverages purchased on trips	11.8	24.9	19.6	22.8	30.5

Source: Bureau of Labor Statistics, unpublished data from the 2008 Consumer Expenditure Survey

Table 4.10 Amount High-Income Buyers Spent on Food and Alcohol, Average Quarter, 2008

(average amount spent by high-income households buying food and alcohol during the average quarter, by before-tax household income of household, 2008)

	total households	$100,000 or more	$100,000–$119,999	$120,000–$149,999	$150,000 or more
FOOD, AMOUNT SPENT	**$1,790.19**	**$2,889.75**	**$2,438.88**	**$2,737.84**	**$3,360.48**
Groceries	**1,215.51**	**1,716.08**	**1,551.32**	**1,695.00**	**1,865.11**
Food and nonalcoholic beverages	1,203.56	1,689.01	1,535.02	1,670.32	1,827.66
Groceries purchased on trips	115.42	137.39	104.33	128.69	160.29
Food away from home	**705.92**	**1,230.84**	**945.45**	**1,088.90**	**1,553.48**
Meals at restaurants, carry-outs, etc.	594.49	936.64	752.72	871.37	1,125.39
Food or board at school	858.58	1,224.02	748.91	903.15	1,478.96
Catered affairs	926.61	1,588.15	1,511.74	680.17	2,234.55
Restaurant meals on trips	251.13	376.74	280.21	335.85	456.45
School lunches	192.71	223.19	210.05	234.18	226.41
Meals as pay	440.66	510.78	488.08	401.79	614.60
ALCOHOL, AMOUNT SPENT	**220.32**	**293.04**	**241.54**	**262.47**	**345.70**
Consumed at home	**145.28**	**180.50**	**155.78**	**172.05**	**202.35**
Consumed away from home	**148.68**	**179.42**	**147.44**	**160.52**	**208.10**
Alcoholic beverages at restaurants, bars	145.91	154.03	128.08	148.42	171.99
Alcoholic beverages purchased on trips	85.07	116.90	99.15	101.34	133.95

Source: Calculations by New Strategist based on the Bureau of Labor Statistics' 2008 Consumer Expenditure Survey

Table 4.11 Percent of High-Income Households Buying Food and Alcohol, <u>Average Week</u>, 2008

(percent of high-income households buying food and alcohol during the average week, by before-tax income of household, 2008)

	total households	$100,000 or more	$100,000– $119,999	$120,000– $149,999	$150,000 or more
FOOD, PERCENT BUYING	**89.4%**	**96.2%**	**96.0%**	**97.0%**	**95.8%**
• GROCERIES	**82.9**	**90.0**	**90.3**	**92.0**	**88.1**
Cereals and bakery products	**70.9**	**79.9**	**80.8**	**81.8**	**77.5**
Cereals and cereal products	46.5	57.1	57.5	58.1	55.9
Flour	4.4	5.2	5.2	5.5	5.1
Prepared flour mixes	8.5	12.1	13.0	10.9	12.2
Ready-to-eat and cooked cereals	32.4	40.6	41.1	41.1	39.8
Rice	10.1	12.0	11.0	13.1	12.1
Pasta, cornmeal, and other cereal products	19.9	27.0	27.4	26.8	26.7
Bakery products	65.7	75.2	75.4	77.7	73.2
Bread	46.9	55.4	55.9	55.0	55.1
White bread	32.7	36.2	38.5	35.6	34.4
Bread, other than white	39.8	49.6	50.1	48.9	49.7
Crackers and cookies	31.7	40.2	38.2	41.4	41.4
Cookies	21.3	27.0	26.6	28.2	26.4
Crackers	18.5	25.4	23.8	27.2	25.9
Frozen and refrigerated bakery products	12.4	15.7	16.9	16.6	13.8
Other bakery products	39.7	50.7	49.7	55.3	48.3
Biscuits and rolls	26.5	37.2	36.2	41.2	35.1
Cakes and cupcakes	12.4	16.2	17.5	16.3	14.8
Bread and cracker products	4.2	6.2	7.2	5.3	5.8
Sweetrolls, coffee cakes, doughnuts	11.2	13.4	12.5	15.0	13.2
Pies, tarts, turnovers	6.5	9.2	9.5	10.7	7.8
Meats, poultry, fish, and eggs	**66.2**	**75.4**	**74.5**	**77.8**	**74.4**
Beef	34.1	42.3	43.1	43.9	40.1
Ground beef	22.7	27.9	29.6	29.4	24.9
Roast	6.5	8.6	8.2	9.8	8.0
Chuck roast	2.4	3.1	3.9	4.0	1.6
Round roast	1.3	1.8	1.6	2.7	1.3
Other roast	4.1	5.6	4.3	6.5	6.2
Steak	12.9	18.4	19.4	17.4	18.2
Round steak	5.2	6.7	6.9	5.8	7.2
Sirloin steak	5.6	7.9	7.0	8.1	8.8
Other steak	9.8	14.2	14.5	14.0	13.9
Other beef	5.3	6.8	7.3	7.4	5.7
Pork	32.5	37.5	38.3	37.1	37.1
Bacon	12.2	15.7	15.7	15.0	16.3
Pork chops	8.0	9.8	10.5	8.8	9.9
Ham	9.9	10.8	10.6	10.4	11.1
Ham, not canned	9.7	10.7	10.5	10.4	11.1
Canned ham	0.3	0.3	0.4	0.2	0.2
Sausage	11.9	14.3	14.8	15.3	13.0
Other pork	8.6	9.8	10.5	9.0	9.8
Other meats	31.0	37.5	37.5	39.9	35.6
Frankfurters	11.1	13.1	13.4	13.8	12.3
Lunch meats (cold cuts)	24.8	30.9	31.4	31.9	29.5
Bologna, liverwurst, salami	11.3	13.1	13.2	14.2	12.3
Other lunch meats	20.6	26.6	27.0	27.8	25.2
Lamb, organ meats, and others	2.1	2.7	2.3	2.6	3.2
Lamb and organ meats	1.8	2.4	2.1	2.2	2.7
Mutton, goat, and game	0.4	0.4	0.2	0.4	0.6

	total households	$100,000 or more	$100,000–$119,999	$120,000–$149,999	$150,000 or more
Poultry	31.0%	38.2%	37.1%	39.4%	38.4%
Fresh and frozen chicken	26.6	32.5	31.4	33.7	32.6
Fresh and frozen whole chicken	10.8	13.9	13.5	14.3	14.2
Fresh and frozen chicken parts	24.5	30.3	30.0	31.0	30.0
Other poultry	9.5	13.2	14.1	13.1	12.4
Fish and seafood	22.1	29.6	29.9	28.4	30.2
Canned fish and seafood	7.9	9.4	9.6	9.5	9.0
Fresh fish and shellfish	10.3	15.6	15.8	14.0	16.5
Frozen fish and shellfish	8.7	12.0	10.8	12.1	13.2
Eggs	31.7	38.8	40.4	39.9	36.3
Dairy products	**69.0**	**79.8**	**79.6**	**82.1**	**78.4**
Fresh milk and cream	57.0	67.8	66.6	71.1	66.5
Fresh milk, all types	54.4	64.8	64.3	68.5	62.4
Cream	13.6	20.8	20.4	21.4	20.6
Other dairy products	53.2	67.4	67.4	69.1	66.2
Butter	11.7	16.6	16.8	17.8	15.4
Cheese	39.5	53.5	53.5	54.3	52.9
Ice cream and related products	21.7	28.9	29.1	29.5	28.1
Miscellaneous dairy products	21.0	31.5	29.9	32.7	32.4
Fruits and vegetables	**70.7**	**81.8**	**82.5**	**83.2**	**80.1**
Fresh fruits	52.6	66.6	63.2	68.9	68.2
Apples	19.0	29.0	27.2	29.3	30.5
Bananas	33.7	45.0	44.0	44.5	46.5
Oranges	11.8	16.2	15.6	17.4	16.0
Citrus fruits, excluding oranges	16.6	23.9	20.1	26.7	25.6
Other fresh fruits	34.2	46.7	43.6	47.2	49.5
Fresh vegetables	53.5	66.6	65.2	67.6	67.2
Potatoes	20.5	26.3	25.5	27.3	26.3
Lettuce	20.1	28.7	26.1	29.0	31.0
Tomatoes	22.4	30.6	28.1	31.1	32.8
Other fresh vegetables	44.1	57.6	54.8	59.3	59.2
Processed fruits	39.3	49.9	51.8	50.9	47.1
Frozen fruits and fruit juices	5.0	7.6	9.0	7.2	6.3
Frozen orange juice	2.3	3.0	4.3	2.4	2.0
Frozen fruits	2.1	3.7	3.7	3.4	3.8
Frozen fruit juices, excluding orange	1.4	2.1	2.5	2.5	1.4
Canned fruits	12.4	16.5	17.8	15.2	16.2
Dried fruits	4.8	7.3	6.7	8.6	6.9
Fresh fruit juice	8.7	12.5	11.2	12.1	14.1
Canned and bottled fruit juice	25.8	34.4	36.1	34.4	32.5
Processed vegetables	39.9	48.5	51.0	50.6	44.3
Frozen vegetables	17.2	23.1	25.2	22.5	21.5
Canned and dried vegetables and juices	33.5	39.9	40.9	42.3	37.0
Canned beans	12.0	15.2	15.6	15.1	14.8
Canned corn	7.1	8.3	8.9	8.2	7.8
Canned miscellaneous vegetables	15.8	20.8	20.8	21.9	19.8
Dried peas	0.3	0.4	0.4	1.0	–
Dried beans	2.5	1.9	1.8	1.8	2.0
Dried miscellaneous vegetables	6.3	7.4	7.2	8.8	6.5
Fresh and canned vegetable juices	8.9	11.5	13.1	11.8	9.7
Sugar and other sweets	**41.4**	**50.7**	**51.8**	**52.2**	**48.2**
Candy and chewing gum	30.6	38.7	38.1	41.0	37.5
Sugar	11.8	12.9	15.1	12.9	10.8
Artificial sweeteners	2.2	2.9	3.0	3.6	2.2
Jams, preserves, other sweets	13.7	19.3	21.5	18.5	17.7

	total households	$100,000 or more	$100,000– $119,999	$120,000– $149,999	$150,000 or more
Fats and oils	**34.3%**	**40.9%**	**42.6%**	**41.3%**	**38.8%**
Margarine	6.9	8.1	9.3	9.0	6.3
Fats and oils	12.7	14.7	16.3	13.7	13.7
Salad dressings	14.6	18.6	19.8	16.9	18.8
Nondairy cream and imitation milk	9.3	11.7	12.0	10.1	12.8
Peanut butter	7.0	10.0	9.5	11.3	9.6
Miscellaneous foods	**68.0**	**78.1**	**78.5**	**82.6**	**74.3**
Frozen prepared foods	27.4	34.3	36.6	37.5	29.5
Frozen meals	16.7	21.4	22.2	23.7	18.8
Other frozen prepared foods	17.7	22.8	25.6	23.6	19.2
Canned and packaged soups	21.1	27.0	29.4	27.1	24.5
Potato chips, nuts, and other snacks	41.1	51.5	50.7	54.8	49.8
Potato chips and other snacks	37.0	46.7	46.1	50.3	44.6
Nuts	12.8	17.6	16.8	15.2	20.5
Condiments and seasonings	42.7	54.9	54.0	58.4	53.1
Salt, spices, and other seasonings	19.1	26.1	25.0	27.2	26.3
Olives, pickles, relishes	8.7	12.0	11.5	13.3	11.6
Sauces and gravies	28.1	36.9	37.2	38.4	35.5
Baking needs and miscellaneous products	15.1	19.6	19.0	21.0	19.3
Other canned/packaged prepared foods	46.6	57.9	57.3	61.4	55.7
Prepared salads	16.5	23.6	25.5	22.9	22.2
Prepared desserts	9.0	11.0	10.7	11.5	11.0
Baby food	4.4	6.8	6.6	8.1	6.0
Miscellaneous prepared foods	38.2	47.8	46.2	50.6	47.2
Nonalcoholic beverages	**57.4**	**66.3**	**67.5**	**65.6**	**65.8**
Cola	31.5	36.0	36.8	37.9	33.8
Other carbonated drinks	26.3	31.9	32.8	34.5	28.9
Tea	13.6	17.8	17.4	17.5	18.5
Coffee	12.5	17.0	16.5	18.4	16.5
Roasted coffee	11.7	16.0	15.5	17.3	15.6
Instant and freeze-dried coffee	9.8	12.8	12.3	12.9	13.1
Noncarbonated fruit-flavored drinks	11.8	13.6	13.9	15.0	12.2
Other nonalcoholic beverages and ice	6.4	7.8	7.2	8.1	8.2
Bottled water	20.8	28.2	26.9	25.0	32.0
Sports drinks	7.5	10.2	10.8	9.4	10.1
• MEALS AT RESTAURANTS, CARRY-OUTS	**72.4**	**88.7**	**86.0**	**90.0**	**90.4**
Lunch	**54.9**	**74.5**	**70.6**	**77.3**	**76.3**
At fast-food restaurants*	42.3	58.6	56.4	59.8	59.8
At full-service restaurants	21.2	36.5	31.4	37.6	40.8
At vending machines, mobile vendors	4.4	5.9	7.2	6.7	3.8
At employer and school cafeterias	10.6	20.2	19.9	21.2	19.8
Dinner	**47.2**	**66.5**	**61.7**	**68.3**	**70.1**
At fast-food restaurants*	29.9	40.5	38.0	43.6	40.7
At full-service restaurants	27.7	46.7	41.0	48.2	51.4
At vending machines, mobile vendors	0.9	0.7	0.7	0.9	0.6
At employer and school cafeterias	1.3	1.2	1.0	1.8	1.0
Snacks and nonalcoholic beverages	**35.0**	**48.1**	**44.7**	**52.9**	**48.0**
At fast-food restaurants*	24.9	37.7	33.8	40.1	39.8
At full-service restaurants	5.6	7.5	6.8	8.8	7.2
At vending machines, mobile vendors	13.6	17.2	17.7	21.8	13.1
At employer and school cafeterias	2.9	4.0	3.6	5.1	3.6

	total households	$100,000 or more	$100,000– $119,999	$120,000– $149,999	$150,000 or more
Breakfast and brunch	**30.2%**	**44.2%**	**41.0%**	**45.3%**	**46.6%**
At fast-food restaurants*	22.1	33.8	31.5	33.9	36.0
At full-service restaurants	9.9	14.6	14.0	15.1	14.8
At vending machines, mobile vendors	2.2	2.9	4.8	1.7	1.8
At employer and school cafeterias	3.1	5.1	3.6	6.6	5.4
ALCOHOL, PERCENT BUYING	**24.5**	**40.2**	**36.5**	**40.6**	**43.7**
Consumed at home	**16.4**	**25.2**	**25.3**	**25.0**	**25.4**
Beer and ale	11.3	15.6	16.5	15.3	14.9
Whiskey	0.6	1.1	1.1	1.3	1.0
Wine	6.9	14.0	13.4	12.9	15.4
Other alcoholic beverages	2.2	3.8	3.3	3.4	4.5
Consumed away from home (except on trips)	**13.2**	**25.1**	**20.8**	**26.5**	**28.4**
Beer and ale at restaurants, bars	8.8	16.1	14.1	17.4	17.2
Wine at restaurants, bars	4.1	9.4	6.6	11.0	11.1
Other alcoholic beverages at restaurants, bars	5.3	10.3	7.3	11.2	12.8

* The category fast-food restaurants also includes take-out, delivery, concession stands, buffets, and cafeterias other than employer and school.
Source: Bureau of Labor Statistics, unpublished data from the 2008 Consumer Expenditure Survey

Table 4.12 Amount High-Income Buyers Spent on Food and Alcohol, Average Week, 2008

(average amount spent by high-income households buying food and alcohol during the average week, by before-tax income of household, 2008)

	total households	$100,000 or more	$100,000–$119,999	$120,000–$149,999	$150,000 or more
FOOD, AMOUNT SPENT	**$127.99**	**$199.42**	**$178.17**	**$196.92**	**$223.37**
• GROCERIES	**85.73**	**119.33**	**113.44**	**118.27**	**126.42**
Cereals and bakery products	**13.75**	**18.45**	**17.69**	**18.41**	**19.30**
Cereals and cereal products	7.01	8.30	8.32	8.19	8.39
Flour	3.39	3.45	3.65	3.84	2.97
Prepared flour mixes	2.72	2.97	2.69	2.93	3.20
Ready-to-eat and cooked cereals	5.59	6.47	6.67	6.20	6.54
Rice	4.87	5.35	5.71	5.87	4.48
Pasta, cornmeal, and other cereal products	2.96	3.45	3.18	3.43	3.75
Bakery products	9.88	13.29	12.62	13.23	14.05
Bread	4.05	4.97	4.96	4.54	5.30
White bread	2.17	2.54	2.55	2.33	2.73
Bread, other than white	2.99	3.67	3.55	3.42	4.00
Crackers and cookies	4.95	6.17	5.63	6.07	6.74
Cookies	4.23	5.27	4.71	5.21	5.87
Crackers	3.62	4.17	3.79	3.83	4.84
Frozen and refrigerated bakery products	4.03	4.53	4.15	5.08	4.49
Other bakery products	6.35	8.00	7.83	8.01	8.15
Biscuits and rolls	3.59	4.30	3.84	4.51	4.56
Cakes and cupcakes	6.19	8.01	7.93	8.46	7.70
Bread and cracker products	2.14	2.27	2.49	2.27	2.08
Sweetrolls, coffee cakes, doughnuts	3.75	4.24	3.99	4.00	4.63
Pies, tarts, turnovers	4.30	4.89	4.55	4.41	5.91
Meats, poultry, fish, and eggs	**24.59**	**31.12**	**30.53**	**29.50**	**33.04**
Beef	13.48	16.68	15.82	15.73	18.47
Ground beef	7.63	8.68	8.20	8.46	9.41
Roast	11.49	13.43	12.64	12.00	15.75
Chuck roast	7.92	8.31	8.91	7.46	8.64
Round roast	9.02	10.50	11.39	8.49	11.94
Other roast	10.81	12.50	11.29	9.94	15.53
Steak	13.05	15.42	13.98	14.53	17.63
Round steak	4.82	5.38	5.39	4.15	5.96
Sirloin steak	7.90	8.84	7.18	8.52	10.47
Other steak	10.13	12.55	12.66	11.47	13.34
Other beef	8.10	9.45	8.88	9.57	10.35
Pork	9.62	10.74	10.79	10.50	10.88
Bacon	4.59	5.02	5.15	5.05	4.90
Pork chops	7.67	7.87	7.93	7.77	7.89
Ham	6.44	6.88	6.95	7.18	6.66
Ham, not canned	6.48	6.82	6.84	7.18	6.57
Canned ham	3.33	4.00	2.70	5.88	5.56
Sausage	4.56	5.03	5.53	4.77	4.78
Other pork	8.96	10.27	8.92	10.83	11.35
Other meats	6.62	7.95	7.37	7.67	8.87
Frankfurters	3.50	4.12	4.42	4.06	3.81
Lunch meats (cold cuts)	5.72	6.87	6.15	6.93	7.66
Bologna, liverwurst, salami	3.09	3.65	3.34	3.59	4.08
Other lunch meats	5.16	6.17	5.49	6.12	6.98
Lamb, organ meats, and others	11.37	11.76	10.82	10.69	13.35
Lamb and organ meats	10.11	11.06	8.65	11.16	13.55
Mutton, goat, and game	16.67	14.63	30.43	10.53	9.84

	total households	$100,000 or more	$100,000–$119,999	$120,000–$149,999	$150,000 or more
Poultry	$9.88	$11.20	$11.10	$11.05	$11.43
Fresh and frozen chicken	9.19	10.19	10.19	9.72	10.58
Fresh and frozen whole chicken	5.81	6.31	5.94	6.30	6.56
Fresh and frozen chicken parts	7.36	8.03	7.97	7.69	8.39
Other poultry	6.56	7.33	6.58	8.17	7.56
Fish and seafood	11.16	12.95	12.02	12.15	14.55
Canned fish and seafood	4.05	4.81	4.56	4.54	5.25
Fresh fish and shellfish	12.67	13.18	12.27	12.55	14.44
Frozen fish and shellfish	9.64	11.15	11.29	10.44	11.56
Eggs	3.10	3.30	3.29	3.26	3.34
Dairy products	**11.98**	**16.00**	**15.14**	**15.92**	**16.92**
Fresh milk and cream	5.67	6.77	6.68	6.66	6.95
Fresh milk, all types	5.30	6.14	6.05	5.99	6.40
Cream	2.57	2.94	2.74	2.99	3.11
Other dairy products	9.45	12.12	11.28	12.07	13.06
Butter	3.50	3.74	3.80	3.61	3.77
Cheese	6.54	8.07	7.21	8.31	8.79
Ice cream and related products	5.35	5.99	5.77	5.66	6.47
Miscellaneous dairy products	4.19	4.79	4.75	4.62	4.91
Fruits and vegetables	**17.86**	**24.07**	**22.04**	**22.93**	**27.16**
Fresh fruits	8.12	10.44	10.11	9.23	11.70
Apples	4.05	4.59	4.88	4.20	4.62
Bananas	1.84	2.09	2.16	1.93	2.11
Oranges	4.06	4.38	4.49	4.08	4.57
Citrus fruits, excluding oranges	2.11	2.34	2.14	2.33	2.58
Other fresh fruits	5.97	7.30	6.86	6.22	8.52
Fresh vegetables	7.61	9.73	8.57	9.26	11.29
Potatoes	3.56	3.69	3.65	3.70	3.76
Lettuce	2.54	3.10	3.02	2.82	3.32
Tomatoes	3.17	3.59	3.24	3.60	3.90
Other fresh vegetables	4.83	6.13	5.40	5.59	7.23
Processed fruits	5.70	6.92	6.36	6.98	7.51
Frozen fruits and fruit juices	4.37	4.50	4.54	4.75	4.42
Frozen orange juice	3.48	3.73	3.71	4.64	3.03
Frozen fruits	5.19	4.93	4.90	5.00	4.72
Frozen fruit juices, excluding orange	2.14	2.86	2.82	2.45	2.08
Canned fruits	3.22	3.46	3.32	3.22	3.72
Dried fruits	3.14	3.30	3.00	3.71	3.34
Fresh fruit juice	4.03	4.41	3.92	4.32	4.91
Canned and bottled fruit juice	4.38	5.09	4.57	5.44	5.38
Processed vegetables	5.13	5.82	5.70	5.72	6.01
Frozen vegetables	3.84	4.11	3.89	4.26	4.19
Canned and dried vegetables and juices	4.16	4.69	4.72	4.59	4.76
Canned beans	2.34	2.50	2.50	2.45	2.50
Canned corn	1.82	1.81	1.79	1.95	1.93
Canned miscellaneous vegetables	2.60	2.98	2.93	2.96	3.08
Dried peas	3.03	2.50	2.63	3.13	–
Dried beans	3.16	2.66	2.84	3.28	1.96
Dried miscellaneous vegetables	3.01	3.25	3.19	3.19	3.41
Fresh and canned vegetable juices	3.14	3.47	3.44	3.04	3.82
Sugar and other sweets	**6.02**	**7.70**	**7.35**	**7.89**	**7.90**
Candy and chewing gum	5.04	6.67	6.45	6.52	7.05
Sugar	2.87	2.78	2.78	2.72	2.79
Artificial sweeteners	5.43	6.25	6.04	6.63	5.88
Jams, preserves, other sweets	3.50	3.99	3.48	4.61	4.19

	total households	$100,000 or more	$100,000– $119,999	$120,000– $149,999	$150,000 or more
Fats and oils	**$5.86**	**$6.65**	**$6.45**	**$6.42**	**$7.09**
Margarine	2.48	2.34	2.16	2.45	2.55
Fats and oils	5.99	6.96	6.19	7.24	7.75
Salad dressings	3.57	3.86	3.98	3.73	3.94
Nondairy cream and imitation milk	3.32	3.58	3.58	3.88	3.37
Peanut butter	3.58	3.70	3.49	3.73	3.75
Miscellaneous foods	**19.22**	**26.05**	**24.48**	**26.30**	**27.54**
Frozen prepared foods	9.85	11.46	11.26	12.22	10.96
Frozen meals	8.39	9.61	9.23	10.28	9.46
Other frozen prepared foods	7.34	8.21	8.12	9.05	7.55
Canned and packaged soups	4.17	4.52	4.49	4.07	4.93
Potato chips, nuts, and other snacks	6.56	8.51	7.84	7.94	9.66
Potato chips and other snacks	5.36	6.89	6.33	6.62	7.69
Nuts	5.65	6.58	6.26	6.72	6.74
Condiments and seasonings	5.55	6.81	6.44	6.62	7.38
Salt, spices, and other seasonings	2.93	3.41	3.32	3.45	3.42
Olives, pickles, relishes	3.00	3.66	3.47	3.69	3.89
Sauces and gravies	3.70	4.60	4.32	4.38	5.10
Baking needs and miscellaneous products	3.32	3.62	3.43	3.57	3.90
Other canned/packaged prepared foods	9.48	12.21	11.01	12.73	13.06
Prepared salads	4.23	5.09	4.87	4.98	5.41
Prepared desserts	2.77	3.17	2.98	3.12	3.38
Baby food	15.07	16.84	15.05	17.55	17.98
Miscellaneous prepared foods	7.28	9.15	8.10	9.62	9.83
Nonalcoholic beverages	**11.49**	**14.64**	**13.86**	**15.47**	**14.82**
Cola	5.04	6.06	6.45	5.76	5.84
Other carbonated drinks	3.73	4.27	4.09	4.53	4.25
Tea	4.56	5.39	4.89	5.21	5.99
Coffee	7.87	8.81	8.30	9.67	8.55
Roasted coffee	5.63	6.50	6.21	7.41	5.98
Instant and freeze-dried coffee	3.26	3.61	3.34	3.87	3.58
Noncarbonated fruit-flavored drinks	4.56	5.29	5.24	4.87	5.74
Other nonalcoholic beverages and ice	4.22	4.99	4.45	5.44	5.11
Bottled water	5.69	6.99	6.44	7.85	6.94
Sports drinks	5.59	6.20	5.72	6.07	6.75
• MEALS AT RESTAURANTS, CARRY-OUTS	**59.96**	**95.35**	**79.89**	**91.41**	**113.60**
Lunch	**27.09**	**38.30**	**35.05**	**36.53**	**42.80**
At fast-food restaurants*	17.66	21.17	19.31	21.54	22.66
At full-service restaurants	26.77	33.93	31.68	31.14	37.73
At vending machines, mobile vendors	4.14	3.41	4.17	2.98	2.08
At employer and school cafeterias	14.64	17.60	18.05	16.16	18.38
Dinner	**43.83**	**63.42**	**51.60**	**58.86**	**77.61**
At fast-food restaurants*	22.01	26.46	25.61	24.72	28.72
At full-service restaurants	49.95	67.02	53.60	60.71	82.69
At vending machines, mobile vendors	6.90	10.14	9.09	6.59	18.18
At employer and school cafeterias	13.53	7.44	8.91	6.25	9.28
Snacks and nonalcoholic beverages	**9.76**	**12.18**	**12.00**	**11.68**	**12.74**
At fast-food restaurants*	8.55	10.32	10.47	10.21	10.28
At full-service restaurants	11.15	14.84	14.37	11.85	18.12
At vending machines, mobile vendors	3.89	3.90	3.79	3.86	3.96
At employer and school cafeterias	4.45	4.74	5.00	3.93	5.29

	total households	$100,000 or more	$100,000–$119,999	$120,000–$149,999	$150,000 or more
Breakfast and brunch	**$14.70**	**$18.08**	**$16.45**	**$17.05**	**$20.34**
At fast-food restaurants*	10.04	11.94	10.99	11.24	13.29
At full-service restaurants	19.47	24.01	21.32	22.66	27.73
At vending machines, mobile vendors	3.13	2.78	2.72	1.16	4.40
At employer and school cafeterias	7.03	7.47	4.96	7.12	9.39
ALCOHOL, AMOUNT SPENT	**31.71**	**38.42**	**36.05**	**38.42**	**40.45**
Consumed at home	**28.77**	**37.14**	**34.65**	**36.18**	**40.45**
Beer and ale	20.80	24.07	26.14	24.14	21.60
Whiskey	37.29	56.64	71.93	51.59	45.10
Wine	24.45	28.93	22.00	29.91	34.48
Other alcoholic beverages	22.12	24.80	20.92	23.32	28.32
Consumed away from home (except on trips)	**23.05**	**24.21**	**21.07**	**24.88**	**26.11**
Beer and ale at restaurants, bars	15.66	15.84	15.41	16.27	15.90
Wine at restaurants, bars	16.95	18.70	15.96	18.69	20.41
Other alcoholic beverages at restaurants, bars	18.23	17.07	16.09	15.25	18.91

The category fast-food restaurants also includes take-out, delivery, concession stands, buffets, and cafeterias other than employer and school.
Note: "–" means sample is too small to make a reliable estimate.
Source: Calculations by New Strategist based on the Bureau of Labor Statistics' 2008 Consumer Expenditure Survey

Table 4.13 Percent Buying Food and Alcohol by Household Type, <u>Average Quarter</u>, 2008

(percent of households buying food and alcohol during the average quarter, by type of household, 2008)

	total married couples	married couples, no children	married couples with children				single parent, at least one child <18	single person
			total	oldest child under 6	oldest child 6 to 17	oldest child 18 or older		
FOOD, PERCENT BUYING	99.9%	99.9%	99.9%	100.0%	99.9%	99.9%	99.1%	98.8%
Groceries	99.9	99.8	99.9	99.9	99.9	99.9	98.9	97.5
Food and nonalcoholic beverages	99.8	99.8	99.9	99.9	99.9	99.9	98.9	97.4
Groceries purchased on trips	13.7	13.9	14.2	13.1	15.0	13.4	7.6	7.1
Food away from home	86.6	85.0	88.6	87.4	90.3	86.3	78.6	74.9
Meals at restaurants, carry-outs, etc.	83.1	82.3	84.6	85.7	85.3	82.7	73.8	72.2
Food or board at school	1.4	0.8	2.0	0.4	2.0	2.9	1.5	0.5
Catered affairs	2.6	2.1	2.8	2.6	3.0	2.8	1.0	0.9
Restaurant meals on trips	29.5	31.7	28.7	27.0	29.8	27.8	15.8	18.2
School lunches	14.1	0.0	26.7	4.6	41.1	15.2	21.8	0.0
Meals as pay	1.3	1.0	1.6	1.4	1.8	1.3	1.8	2.1
ALCOHOL, PERCENT BUYING	40.2	41.5	40.5	43.4	42.2	35.7	23.2	34.2
Consumed at home	34.4	35.5	34.8	38.7	36.5	29.3	18.9	29.2
Consumed away from home	25.9	28.3	25.0	25.8	26.4	22.4	14.1	22.9
Alcoholic beverages at restaurants, bars	18.0	19.9	17.5	18.5	18.8	14.8	9.1	17.9
Alcoholic beverages purchased on trips	14.0	16.0	12.9	12.9	13.4	12.2	7.0	10.1

Source: Bureau of Labor Statistics, unpublished data from the 2008 Consumer Expenditure Survey

Table 4.14 Amount Buyers Spent on Food and Alcohol by Household Type, <u>Average Quarter</u>, 2008

(average amount spent by households buying food and alcohol during the average quarter, by type of household, 2008)

	total married couples	married couples, no children	married couples with children				single parent, at least one child <18	single person
			total	oldest child under 6	oldest child 6 to 17	oldest child 18 or older		
FOOD, AMOUNT SPENT	$2,209.23	$1,912.88	$2,442.67	$2,002.04	$2,551.52	$2,517.08	$1,663.13	$1,089.88
Groceries	1,489.35	1,235.68	1,673.22	1,427.08	1,745.40	1,695.18	1,221.49	709.93
Food and nonalcoholic beverages	1,472.38	1,217.41	1,656.37	1,414.49	1,727.41	1,677.78	1,214.74	704.16
Groceries purchased on trips	126.64	136.34	118.69	95.81	119.82	129.84	87.88	87.68
Food away from home	832.08	797.06	869.10	658.52	893.15	952.70	559.76	513.21
Meals at restaurants, carry-outs, etc.	674.33	655.22	690.12	577.68	704.06	734.59	476.52	464.90
Food or board at school	992.63	1,394.41	881.69	231.55	606.34	1,266.38	192.74	900.98
Catered affairs	1,112.70	1,447.30	981.43	687.35	619.09	1,793.59	406.12	443.75
Restaurant meals on trips	288.16	294.17	285.87	187.05	295.18	325.59	195.65	172.21
School lunches	194.33	250.00	194.30	90.84	194.87	210.19	193.64	25.00
Meals as pay	403.38	395.30	411.23	540.47	387.16	387.30	475.14	416.59
ALCOHOL, AMOUNT SPENT	217.60	229.18	209.41	190.10	217.57	206.66	156.16	217.69
Consmed at home	153.16	150.93	154.92	143.29	159.35	154.50	116.35	126.43
Consumed away from home	134.19	146.72	123.28	105.00	127.42	127.35	101.35	164.06
Alcoholic beverages at restaurants, bars	122.46	128.55	115.58	95.46	121.71	116.96	106.57	168.23
Alcoholic beverages purchased on trips	90.65	99.75	81.92	72.29	80.22	91.18	66.20	73.10

Source: Calculations by New Strategist based on the Bureau of Labor Statistics' 2008 Consumer Expenditure Survey

Table 4.15 Percent Buying Food and Alcohol by Household Type, <u>Average Week</u>, 2008

(percent of households buying food and alcohol during the average week, by type of household, 2008)

| | total married couples | married couples, no children | married couples with children | | | single parent, at least one child <18 | single person |
			total	oldest child under 6	oldest child 6 to 17	oldest child 18 or older		
FOOD, PERCENT BUYING	**91.7%**	**88.9%**	**93.7%**	**94.0%**	**93.3%**	**94.1%**	**89.0%**	**85.2%**
• GROCERIES	**87.4**	**84.4**	**89.5**	**88.9**	**89.6**	**89.8**	**81.4**	**75.0**
Cereals and bakery products	**78.4**	**74.1**	**81.5**	**77.7**	**82.4**	**82.2**	**67.8**	**58.4**
Cereals and cereal products	55.0	48.0	60.1	54.2	62.0	60.4	47.1	31.3
Flour	5.7	5.1	5.9	4.8	5.7	6.9	4.6	2.1
Prepared flour mixes	11.1	8.5	12.9	10.7	13.6	13.2	7.2	3.8
Ready-to-eat and cooked cereals	38.8	32.1	44.3	38.0	46.3	44.7	34.4	21.1
Rice	12.3	9.3	14.1	10.4	15.5	13.9	10.6	5.4
Pasta, cornmeal, and other cereal products	24.9	19.8	28.7	26.3	29.6	28.7	21.5	10.7
Bakery products	73.7	68.8	77.2	71.4	78.7	78.3	62.4	52.6
Bread	54.8	50.1	58.2	51.7	59.3	60.2	43.1	34.3
White bread	38.3	33.4	41.2	35.3	42.8	42.3	34.8	21.8
Bread, other than white	47.5	43.8	49.7	43.3	50.3	52.7	32.4	28.9
Crackers and cookies	38.7	33.7	42.7	34.9	44.4	44.6	29.5	20.7
Cookies	25.9	21.7	29.0	21.9	29.7	32.3	18.3	13.1
Crackers	23.4	20.0	26.6	21.2	28.4	26.6	17.8	11.1
Frozen and refrigerated bakery products	15.4	12.3	17.6	13.6	20.4	15.2	14.1	7.1
Other bakery products	47.6	41.3	52.4	42.9	53.8	55.9	36.5	26.9
Biscuits and rolls	33.5	27.6	38.4	29.4	40.7	40.1	20.9	16.0
Cakes and cupcakes	15.1	12.3	17.0	11.0	17.6	19.6	13.4	7.3
Bread and cracker products	5.6	4.6	6.3	5.1	6.6	6.5	3.1	1.8
Sweetrolls, coffee cakes, doughnuts	13.9	12.4	14.9	9.0	15.8	17.0	8.0	7.2
Pies, tarts, turnovers	8.0	5.8	9.5	7.4	10.5	9.2	6.2	3.6
Meats, poultry, fish, and eggs	**74.2**	**70.4**	**76.5**	**70.7**	**77.3**	**78.7**	**61.5**	**52.7**
Beef	41.0	35.2	45.1	38.3	45.9	48.0	33.7	20.9
Ground beef	27.8	21.8	32.2	26.4	33.6	33.3	25.3	12.4
Roast	8.5	7.6	9.0	5.2	8.7	11.9	4.5	3.3
Chuck roast	3.1	2.9	3.2	1.5	3.0	4.5	1.5	1.1
Round roast	1.8	1.6	1.9	1.7	1.3	3.1	0.7	0.7
Other roast	5.3	4.8	5.5	3.2	5.7	6.8	2.5	2.2
Steak	15.6	13.2	17.4	13.8	17.6	19.2	12.6	7.5
Round steak	6.2	5.2	6.9	6.8	6.8	7.2	5.4	2.9
Sirloin steak	6.7	5.3	7.7	6.2	7.9	8.4	5.9	3.1
Other steak	11.6	9.9	12.7	10.6	13.3	13.0	9.3	5.7
Other beef	6.4	5.4	7.0	3.3	7.1	9.0	6.7	2.8
Pork	38.5	34.8	40.8	33.4	41.4	44.4	30.8	20.4
Bacon	15.1	13.0	16.5	11.7	17.6	17.5	11.5	6.3
Pork chops	9.6	7.9	10.8	6.5	11.2	12.6	7.5	4.5
Ham	11.7	10.2	12.2	9.1	12.4	13.8	9.5	6.1
Ham, not canned	11.5	9.9	12.1	9.0	12.3	13.5	9.3	5.9
Canned ham	0.3	0.3	0.3	0.1	0.3	0.4	0.5	0.2
Sausage	14.1	11.6	15.6	13.5	15.7	16.9	13.5	6.5
Other pork	10.9	9.7	11.1	9.5	11.4	11.5	5.9	4.3
Other meats	37.0	32.6	40.4	31.3	41.7	43.9	31.0	19.6
Frankfurters	13.4	10.1	15.7	11.7	17.1	15.8	13.3	5.7
Lunch meats (cold cuts)	30.1	27.1	32.8	24.1	33.5	37.3	23.9	15.3
Bologna, liverwurst, salami	13.9	12.9	15.0	9.9	15.3	17.8	10.1	6.6
Other lunch meats	25.3	22.5	27.6	19.1	28.3	32.0	19.5	12.4
Lamb, organ meats, and others	2.7	2.5	2.6	1.1	2.6	3.5	1.7	1.3
Lamb and organ meats	2.3	2.2	2.1	0.8	2.2	2.8	1.1	1.1
Mutton, goat, and game	0.4	0.3	0.5	0.3	0.4	0.9	0.6	0.2

	total married couples	married couples, no children	married couples with children				single parent, at least one child <18	single person
			total	oldest child under 6	oldest child 6 to 17	oldest child 18 or older		
Poultry	36.8%	31.1%	40.6%	34.4%	42.3%	41.3%	30.3%	19.0%
Fresh and frozen chicken	31.1	25.6	34.8	30.2	36.6	34.4	26.7	16.3
Fresh and frozen whole chicken	13.0	10.1	14.9	10.3	16.7	14.5	11.4	6.5
Fresh and frozen chicken parts	28.7	23.6	32.2	27.9	34.0	31.6	24.4	14.8
Other poultry	12.0	10.2	13.2	9.9	13.2	15.3	9.0	4.9
Fish and seafood	26.5	24.2	27.9	22.2	29.8	28.1	19.0	14.6
Canned fish and seafood	9.6	8.9	9.7	7.1	10.6	9.9	6.9	5.1
Fresh fish and shellfish	12.7	11.6	13.6	10.8	14.3	14.0	8.0	6.3
Frozen fish and shellfish	10.7	9.4	11.2	8.7	11.7	11.9	8.0	5.1
Eggs	37.5	33.0	40.2	33.8	41.2	42.6	30.8	20.8
Dairy products	**76.9**	**73.7**	**79.4**	**75.8**	**81.0**	**78.9**	**65.5**	**57.0**
Fresh milk and cream	65.4	60.2	69.4	63.4	71.8	69.1	57.3	43.5
Fresh milk, all types	62.5	56.7	67.2	61.8	69.3	66.8	54.7	41.0
Cream	17.7	15.3	19.3	16.8	19.8	20.1	11.4	7.8
Other dairy products	61.8	58.3	64.4	61.0	65.9	63.8	46.2	40.9
Butter	14.5	13.1	15.5	11.1	15.4	18.2	9.1	7.4
Cheese	47.4	43.3	50.5	46.3	52.3	50.2	34.1	27.1
Ice cream and related products	26.5	24.3	28.5	23.3	30.3	28.8	21.3	13.5
Miscellaneous dairy products	26.4	23.1	28.9	28.4	29.1	29.0	17.1	13.7
Fruits and vegetables	**78.3**	**75.6**	**80.0**	**75.2**	**80.5**	**82.1**	**64.6**	**59.1**
Fresh fruits	61.5	58.5	63.6	58.0	64.6	65.5	41.3	40.5
Apples	23.6	19.1	27.2	24.3	29.1	25.7	15.0	12.0
Bananas	40.9	38.7	42.4	40.1	41.6	45.4	23.7	24.2
Oranges	15.2	12.7	17.2	16.4	17.3	17.4	7.8	7.2
Citrus fruits, excluding oranges	20.8	18.3	22.7	20.5	21.9	25.3	13.4	10.1
Other fresh fruits	42.0	38.0	44.7	41.8	45.2	45.5	25.9	23.5
Fresh vegetables	62.6	60.1	64.1	58.1	64.2	67.7	45.0	39.5
Potatoes	25.3	24.1	25.9	22.2	26.3	27.7	16.1	12.8
Lettuce	25.4	22.8	27.1	21.9	27.7	29.3	14.7	12.1
Tomatoes	27.5	25.1	28.8	25.7	29.0	30.4	16.8	14.1
Other fresh vegetables	52.5	49.3	54.5	47.7	55.0	57.9	35.3	31.5
Processed fruits	45.9	39.7	50.8	48.8	52.1	49.8	39.0	28.1
Frozen fruits and fruit juices	6.5	5.3	7.5	5.4	7.7	8.6	4.3	2.9
Frozen orange juice	2.7	1.9	3.5	1.6	4.2	3.5	2.3	1.5
Frozen fruits	2.9	2.6	3.1	3.2	2.7	3.7	1.2	1.0
Frozen fruit juices, excluding orange	1.8	1.3	2.2	1.7	2.2	2.7	1.5	0.9
Canned fruits	14.7	12.9	15.9	14.2	16.2	16.5	10.7	8.7
Dried fruits	6.1	5.4	6.5	7.7	6.3	6.2	3.0	3.3
Fresh fruit juice	10.7	9.0	12.2	11.2	11.6	13.7	6.7	5.1
Canned and bottled fruit juice	30.5	23.8	35.9	34.2	37.6	33.8	29.0	16.7
Processed vegetables	47.1	42.4	50.3	44.7	51.8	51.3	37.6	27.3
Frozen vegetables	21.0	18.2	22.9	17.6	23.9	24.7	17.0	10.3
Canned and dried vegetables and juices	39.9	35.3	42.9	38.0	44.2	43.8	31.4	22.0
Canned beans	14.7	13.1	15.5	11.7	16.4	16.4	11.0	6.9
Canned corn	8.1	6.9	8.9	6.5	9.3	9.8	7.9	4.2
Canned miscellaneous vegetables	19.8	17.5	20.8	16.4	21.2	22.8	11.5	9.2
Dried peas	0.5	0.3	0.6	0.6	0.4	0.9	–	0.1
Dried beans	3.5	2.2	4.3	3.0	4.5	4.6	1.6	1.2
Dried miscellaneous vegetables	7.8	7.1	8.1	5.8	8.9	8.2	6.7	3.5
Fresh and canned vegetable juices	10.9	8.4	13.0	14.0	13.7	11.1	10.5	5.3
Sugar and other sweets	**48.9**	**42.4**	**53.7**	**45.6**	**55.9**	**55.0**	**41.5**	**27.4**
Candy and chewing gum	36.7	31.2	40.7	31.1	43.1	42.5	31.3	18.8
Sugar	13.9	11.0	15.9	12.1	16.3	17.8	11.9	6.9
Artificial sweeteners	2.7	2.3	3.0	2.0	2.8	3.8	1.1	1.6
Jams, preserves, other sweets	17.3	13.8	20.0	16.7	21.8	18.8	12.0	7.6

	total married couples	married couples, no children	married couples with children				single parent, at least one child <18	single person
			total	oldest child under 6	oldest child 6 to 17	oldest child 18 or older		
Fats and oils	**41.2%**	**37.9%**	**43.5%**	**33.8%**	**44.9%**	**47.2%**	**35.2%**	**22.2%**
Margarine	8.0	7.7	8.1	6.0	7.3	10.9	6.8	5.0
Fats and oils	15.4	12.8	16.8	11.9	16.8	20.0	13.7	6.8
Salad dressings	18.0	16.1	19.3	12.5	20.4	21.6	14.0	8.6
Nondairy cream and imitation milk	11.7	11.0	12.6	8.8	13.6	13.3	9.4	5.6
Peanut butter	8.9	7.6	10.3	8.7	12.1	7.9	5.0	4.1
Miscellaneous foods	**75.0**	**71.0**	**77.9**	**77.9**	**78.6**	**76.6**	**66.6**	**56.2**
Frozen prepared foods	30.4	23.9	35.7	31.5	38.1	34.1	30.7	20.0
Frozen meals	18.3	15.2	21.0	16.3	22.6	21.1	18.4	12.6
Other frozen prepared foods	20.1	14.7	24.7	21.8	25.9	24.6	21.2	11.3
Canned and packaged soups	25.2	23.1	26.2	19.8	27.5	28.0	18.6	14.4
Potato chips, nuts, and other snacks	49.0	43.5	53.4	47.7	55.7	52.9	42.9	26.5
Potato chips and other snacks	44.7	37.8	50.2	44.4	52.5	50.0	39.1	22.3
Nuts	15.6	15.0	15.9	12.5	16.2	17.6	11.7	8.3
Condiments and seasonings	51.1	46.0	54.9	51.0	56.4	54.8	43.6	27.4
Salt, spices, and other seasonings	24.2	19.9	27.0	21.7	27.8	29.1	18.5	10.7
Olives, pickles, relishes	10.7	9.9	11.2	8.5	12.3	10.9	7.9	4.8
Sauces and gravies	34.6	29.0	38.7	34.5	40.4	38.4	29.8	15.3
Baking needs and miscellaneous products	18.5	16.4	19.9	17.4	21.6	18.4	10.3	9.3
Other canned/packaged prepared foods	54.5	47.7	60.0	61.7	60.9	57.2	43.0	33.3
Prepared salads	19.5	18.9	20.4	15.9	20.8	22.5	11.8	11.9
Prepared desserts	11.2	9.6	12.2	8.7	13.7	11.9	7.5	5.3
Baby food	6.0	2.6	8.7	22.2	6.2	4.5	4.6	1.3
Miscellaneous prepared foods	45.3	37.2	51.8	48.0	54.0	50.1	37.0	25.1
Nonalcoholic beverages	**63.9**	**56.0**	**70.0**	**63.1**	**72.0**	**70.8**	**61.4**	**42.9**
Cola	36.8	29.8	41.6	34.8	42.6	44.1	33.9	19.8
Other carbonated drinks	31.2	24.3	36.1	29.5	37.6	37.6	30.9	14.8
Tea	16.1	12.5	18.9	12.8	18.7	23.3	13.7	8.2
Coffee	15.2	15.2	15.7	12.8	15.6	17.6	8.5	9.0
Roasted coffee	14.3	14.4	14.7	12.5	14.4	16.6	8.2	8.5
Instant and freeze-dried coffee	11.9	12.5	11.7	9.1	11.3	14.0	6.3	7.5
Noncarbonated fruit-flavored drinks	13.7	8.8	17.1	10.6	19.2	17.5	15.3	6.3
Other nonalcoholic beverages and ice	7.7	6.1	9.1	5.9	10.3	9.0	8.0	3.0
Bottled water	24.2	19.0	28.5	20.5	30.2	30.5	24.5	12.3
Sports drinks	9.2	6.1	11.8	7.6	12.3	13.7	9.3	3.8
• MEALS AT RESTAURANTS, CARRY-OUTS	**77.3**	**73.0**	**81.0**	**77.6**	**82.2**	**80.9**	**71.1**	**64.4**
Lunch	**60.8**	**54.9**	**66.3**	**63.5**	**67.7**	**65.5**	**52.6**	**45.9**
At fast-food restaurants*	47.4	41.4	52.7	53.0	52.0	53.7	42.8	32.8
At full-service restaurants	24.4	24.4	25.1	24.2	25.4	25.0	11.7	19.1
At vending machines, mobile vendors	4.8	3.7	5.6	4.3	6.7	4.6	5.1	3.2
At employer and school cafeterias	13.4	5.9	20.2	9.3	25.9	16.9	13.5	6.0
Dinner	**52.5**	**47.7**	**57.2**	**55.5**	**58.0**	**56.9**	**43.0**	**38.1**
At fast-food restaurants*	33.3	25.5	40.6	39.5	41.1	40.5	32.3	21.7
At full-service restaurants	31.7	32.7	31.3	28.5	30.9	33.9	18.2	24.2
At vending machines, mobile vendors	0.9	0.8	0.9	0.2	0.9	1.2	0.9	0.8
At employer and school cafeterias	1.2	0.9	1.5	0.8	1.7	1.4	0.2	1.7
Snacks and nonalcoholic beverages	39.5	32.8	45.5	45.4	47.6	41.9	34.4	27.5
At fast-food restaurants*	**29.5**	**23.8**	**34.8**	**36.8**	**35.8**	**31.8**	**21.5**	**18.5**
At full-service restaurants	6.1	5.2	6.7	5.0	7.3	6.7	3.8	4.8
At vending machines, mobile vendors	15.1	10.9	18.7	16.6	20.4	17.1	17.4	10.0
At employer and school cafeterias	3.3	2.5	4.1	3.0	4.8	3.6	2.8	2.4

	total married couples	married couples, no children	married couples with children				single parent, at least one child <18	single person
			total	oldest child under 6	oldest child 6 to 17	oldest child 18 or older		
Breakfast and brunch	**33.9%**	**29.7%**	**37.4%**	**37.9%**	**37.7%**	**36.5%**	**24.1%**	**26.1%**
At fast-food restaurants*	25.1	20.2	29.3	31.9	28.6	28.8	18.6	18.2
At full-service restaurants	11.3	12.2	10.1	7.1	9.8	12.5	5.3	9.1
At vending machines, mobile vendors	2.5	1.5	3.3	2.3	3.9	2.8	2.6	1.5
At employer and school cafeterias	3.3	2.1	4.2	3.8	4.7	3.7	3.4	2.6
ALCOHOL, PERCENT BUYING	**27.2**	**28.2**	**26.7**	**26.0**	**27.1**	**26.6**	**16.0**	**21.3**
Consumed at home	**18.3**	**18.2**	**18.3**	**17.4**	**18.9**	**17.8**	**11.1**	**13.8**
Beer and ale	12.1	11.3	12.7	12.6	13.1	12.0	7.3	9.5
Whiskey	0.7	1.0	0.5	0.4	0.2	1.1	0.2	0.4
Wine	8.6	9.1	8.3	7.1	8.8	8.1	4.6	5.2
Other alcoholic beverages	2.4	2.5	2.3	1.0	2.5	2.8	1.3	1.8
Consumed away from home (except on trips)	**14.3**	**15.6**	**13.7**	**13.5**	**13.5**	**14.2**	**7.3**	**12.6**
Beer and ale at restaurants, bars	9.4	10.1	9.1	9.8	8.9	9.1	3.7	8.4
Wine at restaurants, bars	5.0	5.9	4.4	3.4	4.6	4.7	2.2	3.6
Other alcoholic beverages at restaurants, bars	5.8	6.4	5.5	5.3	5.0	6.3	3.2	4.8

The category fast-food restaurants also includes take-out, delivery, concession stands, buffets, and cafeterias other than employer and school.

Note: "–" means sample is too small to make a reliable estimate.

Source: Bureau of Labor Statistics, unpublished data from the 2008 Consumer Expenditure Survey

Table 4.16 Amount Buyers Spent on Food and Alcohol by Household Type, Average Week, 2008

(average amount spent by households buying food and alcohol during the average week, by type of household, 2008)

	total married couples	married couples, no children	married couples with children total	oldest child under 6	oldest child 6 to 17	oldest child 18 or older	single parent, at least one child <18	single person
FOOD, AMOUNT SPENT	**$158.16**	**$132.81**	**$177.94**	**$146.13**	**$184.65**	**$186.25**	**$103.38**	**$76.71**
• GROCERIES	**104.23**	**87.43**	**116.22**	**95.95**	**120.06**	**122.17**	**75.18**	**49.99**
Cereals and bakery products	**16.21**	**13.39**	**18.17**	**14.25**	**19.01**	**19.02**	**12.72**	**8.63**
Cereals and cereal products	7.66	6.48	8.42	7.60	8.53	8.69	7.18	4.95
Flour	3.67	3.37	3.74	3.37	4.01	3.49	3.24	2.91
Prepared flour mixes	2.79	2.72	2.78	2.71	2.73	3.03	3.21	2.36
Ready-to-eat and cooked cereals	6.06	5.36	6.57	6.25	6.65	6.61	5.63	4.22
Rice	4.73	4.72	4.48	4.82	4.13	4.98	4.34	4.04
Pasta, cornmeal, and other cereal products	3.05	2.78	3.27	3.05	3.28	3.35	2.80	2.62
Bakery products	11.52	9.90	12.61	9.76	13.17	13.26	8.40	6.63
Bread	4.45	4.03	4.61	4.08	4.60	4.92	3.45	3.21
White bread	2.32	2.10	2.42	2.24	2.48	2.44	2.07	1.74
Bread, other than white	3.24	3.01	3.38	3.03	3.32	3.66	2.38	2.49
Crackers and cookies	5.30	4.96	5.60	4.84	5.63	5.93	4.00	4.11
Cookies	4.43	4.37	4.51	3.56	4.54	4.83	3.55	3.75
Crackers	3.89	3.60	4.10	4.28	4.08	4.02	2.97	3.24
Frozen and refrigerated bakery products	4.22	4.06	4.31	3.76	4.51	4.21	4.33	3.69
Other bakery products	7.06	6.33	7.45	6.18	7.85	7.41	5.38	4.77
Biscuits and rolls	3.82	3.66	3.96	3.36	4.01	4.19	2.88	3.00
Cakes and cupcakes	6.90	6.18	7.32	7.43	7.79	6.48	6.03	4.79
Bread and cracker products	2.14	2.16	2.06	2.17	1.96	2.45	1.60	2.19
Sweetrolls, coffee cakes, doughnuts	3.95	3.96	3.90	3.78	4.00	3.76	3.25	3.46
Pies, tarts, turnovers	4.51	4.30	4.41	5.44	4.29	4.14	3.70	4.41
Meats, poultry, fish, and eggs	**27.80**	**23.80**	**30.20**	**22.47**	**31.01**	**33.21**	**23.82**	**15.37**
Beef	14.44	13.17	15.09	11.93	15.00	16.87	12.30	10.12
Ground beef	8.07	7.60	8.20	6.93	8.30	8.64	7.06	6.11
Roast	12.03	11.65	12.39	11.95	12.31	12.49	9.73	10.33
Chuck roast	8.36	7.96	8.49	5.37	9.24	7.95	9.21	6.48
Round roast	9.55	7.98	10.58	12.73	9.16	10.78	8.22	7.58
Other roast	11.28	10.79	11.55	10.22	11.82	11.76	9.49	10.19
Steak	13.43	12.69	14.06	13.45	13.61	15.03	11.39	11.36
Round steak	4.97	4.61	5.20	4.55	4.99	5.98	4.28	4.81
Sirloin steak	8.22	7.56	8.56	6.67	7.95	10.42	6.81	7.01
Other steak	10.75	10.36	11.16	10.82	10.65	12.18	8.57	8.36
Other beef	8.66	8.04	8.92	7.95	8.85	9.35	7.36	6.12
Pork	10.23	9.67	10.23	9.00	10.54	10.29	9.36	7.30
Bacon	4.78	4.85	4.73	4.19	4.60	5.14	4.36	4.13
Pork chops	7.73	7.12	8.00	7.85	8.19	7.78	7.96	6.89
Ham	6.76	7.42	6.16	5.70	6.39	6.09	6.50	5.62
Ham, not canned	6.81	7.45	6.14	5.78	6.32	6.16	6.47	5.56
Canned ham	3.13	3.23	3.45	0.00	3.45	2.44	4.44	5.88
Sausage	4.77	4.41	4.73	4.58	4.53	5.22	4.52	4.02
Other pork	9.38	9.33	9.46	9.28	10.07	8.49	9.37	7.53
Other meats	7.22	6.89	7.44	5.92	7.57	7.92	5.65	5.16
Frankfurters	3.74	3.66	3.88	4.02	3.85	3.87	2.79	3.17
Lunch meats (cold cuts)	6.05	5.77	6.24	5.35	6.16	6.75	5.26	4.83
Bologna, liverwurst, salami	3.24	3.18	3.26	2.92	3.32	3.32	3.16	2.75
Other lunch meats	5.42	5.10	5.64	5.23	5.45	6.04	4.82	4.52
Lamb, organ meats, and others	12.50	12.90	13.51	8.26	16.86	10.26	7.69	7.03
Lamb and organ meats	11.30	11.11	12.80	7.79	16.59	9.09	7.41	6.42
Mutton, goat, and game	18.18	25.00	14.00	12.50	18.92	12.94	8.20	10.53

	total married couples	married couples, no children	married couples with children				single parent, at least one child <18	single person
			total	oldest child under 6	oldest child 6 to 17	oldest child 18 or older		
Poultry	$10.37	$9.54	$10.85	$9.12	$10.94	$11.62	$10.80	$7.84
Fresh and frozen chicken	9.62	8.81	10.01	8.59	10.14	10.62	10.34	7.32
Fresh and frozen whole chicken	6.17	5.93	6.26	5.72	6.06	6.90	6.30	4.63
Fresh and frozen chicken parts	7.63	7.00	7.93	7.20	7.95	8.35	8.36	6.03
Other poultry	6.91	7.05	6.97	5.47	6.97	7.57	5.68	6.11
Fish and seafood	11.50	10.48	12.02	10.29	11.81	13.20	9.10	9.88
Canned fish and seafood	4.17	3.81	4.21	3.40	4.23	4.47	3.19	3.89
Fresh fish and shellfish	12.56	11.30	13.35	12.00	13.34	13.98	10.54	12.12
Frozen fish and shellfish	9.86	9.45	10.10	8.63	9.94	11.00	8.28	9.41
Eggs	3.26	3.00	3.38	3.01	3.42	3.45	2.89	2.70
Dairy products	**14.00**	**11.88**	**15.59**	**14.20**	**16.01**	**15.65**	**10.56**	**7.91**
Fresh milk and cream	6.32	5.13	7.16	7.22	7.32	6.84	5.20	4.04
Fresh milk, all types	5.84	4.73	6.64	6.68	6.81	6.29	4.99	3.83
Cream	2.66	2.62	2.64	2.68	2.68	2.64	2.10	2.43
Other dairy products	10.73	9.72	11.51	10.15	11.71	11.96	8.56	6.72
Butter	3.59	3.60	3.62	3.24	3.76	3.57	2.74	3.24
Cheese	7.24	6.73	7.60	6.91	7.66	7.88	5.73	5.05
Ice cream and related products	5.69	5.59	5.78	5.32	5.81	5.94	5.02	4.59
Miscellaneous dairy products	4.43	4.07	4.71	4.90	4.72	4.52	3.98	3.74
Fruits and vegetables	**21.08**	**18.62**	**22.84**	**21.93**	**22.83**	**23.37**	**13.64**	**11.86**
Fresh fruits	9.24	8.18	10.06	10.49	10.06	9.84	6.39	5.78
Apples	4.29	4.13	4.48	4.41	4.50	4.55	3.47	3.49
Bananas	1.95	1.76	2.12	2.02	2.09	2.18	1.56	1.49
Oranges	4.35	4.56	4.19	3.48	4.44	4.21	3.09	3.45
Citrus fruits, excluding oranges	2.21	2.02	2.34	2.39	2.33	2.29	1.94	1.78
Other fresh fruits	6.56	6.20	6.81	7.51	6.73	6.52	4.79	4.76
Fresh vegetables	8.56	8.24	8.69	8.57	8.68	8.79	5.87	5.75
Potatoes	3.68	3.49	3.78	3.38	4.00	3.53	3.60	3.04
Lettuce	2.68	2.68	2.70	2.24	2.78	2.73	2.18	2.14
Tomatoes	3.41	3.42	3.37	3.47	3.17	3.58	2.50	2.69
Other fresh vegetables	5.38	5.33	5.32	6.00	5.15	5.29	3.74	3.93
Processed fruits	6.17	5.47	6.59	6.54	6.30	7.20	4.69	4.70
Frozen fruits and fruit juices	4.64	4.53	4.66	4.24	4.58	5.00	3.25	3.81
Frozen orange juice	3.66	3.16	3.68	1.85	3.79	3.42	2.59	2.74
Frozen fruits	5.44	5.32	5.45	4.97	5.13	6.15	3.25	4.81
Frozen fruit juices, excluding orange	2.29	2.31	2.23	1.72	1.82	3.02	2.72	2.33
Canned fruits	3.41	3.32	3.45	3.79	3.21	3.58	2.44	3.10
Dried fruits	3.14	3.14	3.37	3.50	3.19	3.21	2.36	3.01
Fresh fruit juice	4.12	3.55	4.44	4.18	4.49	4.52	3.41	3.70
Canned and bottled fruit juice	4.63	4.29	4.77	4.91	4.49	5.18	3.90	3.89
Processed vegetables	5.58	5.12	5.83	5.01	5.84	6.24	4.52	3.96
Frozen vegetables	4.00	3.80	4.18	4.04	4.10	4.38	3.36	3.51
Canned and dried vegetables and juices	4.49	4.19	4.59	4.06	4.62	4.84	3.64	3.32
Canned beans	2.46	2.21	2.57	2.40	2.50	2.80	2.37	2.02
Canned corn	1.84	1.75	2.02	1.70	1.93	2.26	1.91	1.66
Canned miscellaneous vegetables	2.68	2.75	2.65	2.69	2.64	2.72	2.26	2.29
Dried peas	2.00	3.23	1.75	1.56	2.63	2.30	–	0.00
Dried beans	3.14	2.79	2.81	2.37	3.08	2.81	1.89	2.42
Dried miscellaneous vegetables	3.09	3.12	3.08	3.46	3.02	3.16	2.38	2.88
Fresh and canned vegetable juices	3.39	3.44	3.23	2.79	3.28	3.59	2.47	3.00
Sugar and other sweets	**6.59**	**6.44**	**6.72**	**5.44**	**6.99**	**6.91**	**4.75**	**4.78**
Candy and chewing gum	5.51	5.62	5.53	4.70	5.92	5.20	3.80	4.30
Sugar	2.94	2.74	3.01	2.98	2.89	3.21	2.95	2.61
Artificial sweeteners	5.93	6.96	5.76	4.59	5.30	6.58	3.60	5.63
Jams, preserves, other sweets	3.65	3.78	3.61	3.41	3.45	4.14	3.25	3.03

	total married couples	married couples, no children	married couples with children				single parent, at least one child <18	single person
			total	oldest child under 6	oldest child 6 to 17	oldest child 18 or older		
Fats and oils	**$6.20**	**$5.84**	**$6.37**	**$6.07**	**$6.28**	**$6.69**	**$5.00**	**$4.92**
Margarine	2.49	2.58	2.35	2.66	2.34	2.40	2.34	2.41
Fats and oils	6.31	6.16	6.37	7.15	6.03	6.60	4.84	5.29
Salad dressings	3.72	3.72	3.68	3.77	3.62	3.79	3.44	3.27
Nondairy cream and imitation milk	3.32	3.26	3.33	3.07	3.24	3.45	3.20	3.74
Peanut butter	3.70	3.42	3.71	3.43	3.80	3.92	3.21	3.19
Miscellaneous foods	**21.98**	**18.11**	**25.11**	**25.54**	**25.42**	**24.23**	**18.24**	**12.45**
Frozen prepared foods	10.25	9.73	10.61	9.18	10.70	11.23	9.81	8.55
Frozen meals	8.51	8.55	8.52	7.54	8.67	8.70	7.75	8.29
Other frozen prepared foods	7.75	6.99	8.08	7.61	8.19	8.14	7.47	6.04
Canned and packaged soups	4.29	4.45	4.23	4.44	3.89	4.72	3.82	4.02
Potato chips, nuts, and other snacks	7.27	6.83	7.66	6.16	8.25	7.43	5.95	4.91
Potato chips and other snacks	5.84	5.15	6.35	5.11	6.96	5.94	5.20	3.89
Nuts	6.03	6.79	5.65	5.35	5.80	5.46	4.37	5.21
Condiments and seasonings	6.04	5.59	6.30	5.90	6.44	6.26	4.20	4.27
Salt, spices, and other seasonings	3.06	3.02	3.07	3.68	3.13	2.72	2.27	2.71
Olives, pickles, relishes	3.18	3.33	3.13	3.43	3.09	3.11	2.79	2.71
Sauces and gravies	4.02	3.87	4.11	3.97	4.04	4.35	3.02	3.07
Baking needs and miscellaneous products	3.35	3.24	3.42	3.15	3.47	3.43	2.82	3.01
Other canned/packaged prepared foods	10.38	8.28	11.85	16.48	10.85	10.59	9.43	6.70
Prepared salads	4.41	4.29	4.56	5.04	4.27	4.75	3.81	3.78
Prepared desserts	2.85	3.02	2.78	2.30	2.78	3.03	2.66	2.63
Baby food	15.83	9.20	17.92	24.36	13.01	10.07	13.13	7.58
Miscellaneous prepared foods	7.71	6.89	8.27	7.75	8.42	8.31	7.60	5.85
Nonalcoholic beverages	**12.91**	**11.60**	**13.69**	**10.58**	**13.70**	**15.45**	**10.28**	**8.04**
Cola	5.44	5.40	5.48	4.46	5.64	5.76	4.52	4.14
Other carbonated drinks	3.94	3.95	3.93	3.15	3.86	4.46	3.14	2.90
Tea	4.80	4.65	4.80	4.63	4.49	5.37	4.03	4.17
Coffee	8.09	8.05	8.17	9.96	7.69	8.19	8.22	7.43
Roasted coffee	5.80	5.63	5.93	7.22	5.76	5.60	6.11	5.19
Instant and freeze-dried coffee	3.37	3.29	3.51	4.06	3.28	3.64	3.00	3.08
Noncarbonated fruit-flavored drinks	4.82	4.45	4.91	5.36	4.95	4.56	3.39	4.60
Other nonalcoholic beverages and ice	4.41	4.40	4.51	4.44	4.37	4.77	3.61	4.01
Bottled water	6.06	5.62	6.21	5.45	6.17	6.62	5.31	4.64
Sports drinks	5.77	5.74	5.67	4.99	5.86	5.56	4.84	5.31
• MEALS AT RESTAURANTS, CARRY-OUTS	**69.91**	**60.75**	**77.36**	**66.92**	**78.83**	**81.09**	**43.27**	**43.31**
Lunch	**30.53**	**26.50**	**32.98**	**28.71**	**34.10**	**33.55**	**21.95**	**20.58**
At fast-food restaurants*	18.98	16.49	20.39	19.89	20.07	21.25	15.77	14.10
At full-service restaurants	29.76	28.51	29.48	26.45	29.94	30.43	23.07	20.72
At vending machines, mobile vendors	3.72	3.51	3.90	3.93	4.47	2.63	3.31	5.61
At employer and school cafeterias	15.87	10.83	17.34	11.76	18.29	16.67	14.38	11.52
Dinner	**49.51**	**47.62**	**51.38**	**43.20**	**51.78**	**55.77**	**31.54**	**33.60**
At fast-food restaurants*	24.21	20.10	26.31	24.06	27.09	26.30	18.83	15.47
At full-service restaurants	55.94	53.24	58.89	50.44	60.03	61.52	40.83	37.70
At vending machines, mobile vendors	7.69	9.09	9.41	20.83	10.47	5.74	4.65	3.75
At employer and school cafeterias	10.57	9.89	11.56	5.13	14.94	6.94	5.00	18.18
Snacks and nonalcoholic beverages	**10.36**	**8.50**	**11.53**	**9.76**	**12.07**	**11.70**	**8.84**	**8.41**
At fast-food restaurants*	9.13	7.60	10.28	9.12	10.86	9.91	8.61	6.83
At full-service restaurants	10.54	9.40	10.33	7.97	11.03	10.39	9.42	13.02
At vending machines, mobile vendors	3.98	3.76	4.06	3.02	4.03	4.73	4.14	3.39
At employer and school cafeterias	4.85	3.56	5.37	5.61	5.03	6.42	3.57	3.75

	total married couples	married couples, no children	married couples with children				single parent, at least one child <18	single person
			total	oldest child under 6	oldest child 6 to 17	oldest child 18 or older		
Breakfast and brunch	**$15.86**	**$14.46**	**$16.42**	**$14.11**	**$15.77**	**$19.14**	**$10.87**	**$12.74**
At fast-food restaurants*	10.61	8.68	11.48	11.46	11.45	11.54	7.92	8.99
At full-service restaurants	21.33	19.80	22.94	19.21	21.65	26.00	17.04	15.55
At vending machines, mobile vendors	3.25	2.05	3.64	3.98	3.55	3.89	2.72	2.61
At employer and school cafeterias	7.23	5.21	8.29	6.28	8.80	8.65	4.73	7.95
ALCOHOL, AMOUNT SPENT	**31.73**	**33.18**	**30.39**	**28.64**	**28.47**	**34.91**	**21.07**	**31.08**
Consumed at home	**30.47**	**32.75**	**28.53**	**26.66**	**26.46**	**33.65**	**17.81**	**25.54**
Beer and ale	21.25	21.33	20.57	18.30	20.17	22.92	13.72	18.82
Whiskey	40.00	39.58	36.73	58.54	29.41	35.14	41.18	30.23
Wine	25.41	28.12	23.10	24.96	20.34	27.56	14.44	24.47
Other alcoholic beverages	22.13	23.23	22.17	33.67	20.88	21.91	19.05	19.02
Consumed away from home (except on trips)	**21.43**	**21.85**	**21.15**	**20.80**	**20.06**	**23.24**	**19.15**	**24.45**
Beer and ale at restaurants, bars	13.57	13.23	13.58	13.46	13.39	14.05	12.57	17.32
Wine at restaurants, bars	16.67	17.57	15.91	18.51	15.40	15.78	15.98	17.50
Other alcoholic beverages at restaurants, bars	16.52	15.81	17.58	16.45	16.10	20.22	17.59	20.79

* The category fast-food restaurants also includes take-out, delivery, concession stands, buffets, and cafeterias other than employer and school.
Note: "–" means sample is too small to make a reliable estimate.
Source: Calculations by New Strategist based on the Bureau of Labor Statistics' 2008 Consumer Expenditure Survey

Table 4.17 Percent Buying Food and Alcohol by Race and Hispanic Origin, <u>Average Quarter</u>, 2008

(percent of households buying food and alcohol during the average quarter, by race and Hispanic origin of householder, 2008)

	total households	Asian	black	Hispanic	non-Hispanic white and other
FOOD, PERCENT BUYING	99.5%	99.3%	99.3%	99.5%	99.5%
Groceries	99.0	98.2	98.7	99.1	99.1
Food and nonalcoholic beverages	99.0	98.1	98.7	99.1	99.0
Groceries purchased on trips	10.6	8.9	4.6	7.1	12.0
Food away from home	81.8	84.3	72.4	75.6	84.1
Meals at restaurants, carry-outs, etc.	78.5	80.3	70.0	71.7	80.8
Food or board at school	1.0	0.7	0.6	0.8	1.2
Catered affairs	1.9	1.6	1.1	1.8	2.0
Restaurant meals on trips	23.7	24.9	11.6	14.9	26.9
School lunches	9.2	9.7	7.8	7.7	9.6
Meals as pay	1.7	2.3	0.8	2.2	1.7
ALCOHOL, PERCENT BUYING	37.0	29.5	20.4	26.0	41.3
Consumed at home	31.8	23.2	17.6	22.3	35.5
Consumed away from home	23.8	19.2	10.5	13.3	27.4
Alcoholic beverages at restaurants, bars	17.4	14.1	7.5	9.1	20.2
Alcoholic beverages purchased on trips	11.8	8.8	4.4	6.4	13.7

Note: "Asian" and "black" include Hispanics and non-Hispanics who identify themselves as being of the respective race alone. "Hispanic" includes people of any race who identify themselves as Hispanic. "Other" includes people who identify themselves as non-Hispanic and as Alaska Native, American Indian, Asian (who are also included in the Asian column), or Native Hawaiian or other Pacific Islander as well as non-Hispanics reporting more than one race.
Source: Bureau of Labor Statistics, unpublished data from the 2008 Consumer Expenditure Survey

Table 4.18 Amount Buyers Spent on Food and Alcohol by Race and Hispanic Origin, <u>Average Quarter</u>, 2008

(average amount spent by households buying food and alcohol during the average quarter, by race and Hispanic origin of householder, 2008)

	total households	Asian	black	Hispanic	non-Hispanic white and other
FOOD, AMOUNT SPENT	$1,790.19	$1,982.69	$1,436.25	$1,845.77	$1,837.99
Groceries	1,215.51	1,314.32	1,058.17	1,320.77	1,224.71
Food and nonalcoholic beverages	1,203.56	1,303.89	1,054.65	1,311.72	1,211.11
Groceries purchased on trips	115.42	137.57	75.11	125.98	116.94
Food away from home	705.92	804.31	526.93	697.70	731.56
Meals at restaurants, carry-outs, etc.	594.49	690.66	479.49	611.37	608.15
Food or board at school	858.58	693.28	297.73	1,474.67	829.13
Catered affairs	926.61	877.64	578.10	863.83	963.13
Restaurant meals on trips	251.13	289.32	161.66	248.98	257.37
School lunches	192.71	174.59	204.56	181.36	192.54
Meals as pay	440.66	714.71	446.30	507.85	425.88
ALCOHOL, AMOUNT SPENT	220.32	226.68	170.51	194.56	226.56
Consumed at home	145.28	141.31	126.42	137.80	147.41
Consumed away from home	148.68	178.02	119.48	149.47	150.39
Alcoholic beverages at restaurants, bars	145.91	192.68	136.68	149.81	146.23
Alcoholic beverages purchased on trips	85.07	79.06	52.15	97.62	85.90

Note: "Asian" and "black" include Hispanics and non-Hispanics who identify themselves as being of the respective race alone. "Hispanic" includes people of any race who identify themselves as Hispanic. "Other" includes people who identify themselves as non-Hispanic and as Alaska Native, American Indian, Asian (who are also included in the Asian column), or Native Hawaiian or other Pacific Islander as well as non-Hispanics reporting more than one race.
Source: Calculations by New Strategist based on the Bureau of Labor Statistics' 2008 Consumer Expenditure Survey

Table 4.19 Percent Buying Food and Alcohol by Race and Hispanic Origin, <u>Average Week</u>, 2008

(percent of households buying food and alcohol during the average week, by race and Hispanic origin of householder, 2008)

	total households	Asian	black	Hispanic	non-Hispanic white and other
FOOD, PERCENT BUYING	**89.4%**	**87.7%**	**87.2%**	**91.2%**	**89.6%**
• GROCERIES	**82.9**	**81.9**	**78.2**	**85.5**	**83.3**
Cereals and bakery products	**70.9**	**68.7**	**64.1**	**73.1**	**71.6**
Cereals and cereal products	46.5	46.4	43.1	51.6	46.3
Flour	4.4	5.5	4.8	5.8	4.2
Prepared flour mixes	8.5	4.6	7.1	6.7	9.0
Ready-to-eat and cooked cereals	32.4	22.8	30.7	35.1	32.3
Rice	10.1	16.7	10.6	16.3	9.1
Pasta, cornmeal, and other cereal products	19.9	19.1	16.5	19.9	20.5
Bakery products	65.7	58.1	58.1	66.9	66.7
Bread	46.9	38.6	41.3	50.0	47.3
White bread	32.7	25.8	30.5	38.3	32.1
Bread, other than white	39.8	32.2	31.4	41.4	40.9
Crackers and cookies	31.7	24.0	25.7	30.9	32.8
Cookies	21.3	16.9	18.3	22.8	21.5
Crackers	18.5	13.1	12.9	16.4	19.7
Frozen and refrigerated bakery products	12.4	8.2	9.7	10.0	13.2
Other bakery products	39.7	34.1	30.0	37.0	41.6
Biscuits and rolls	26.5	20.4	17.3	22.2	28.5
Cakes and cupcakes	12.4	13.0	10.9	11.3	12.9
Bread and cracker products	4.2	3.6	2.7	3.8	4.5
Sweetrolls, coffee cakes, doughnuts	11.2	8.1	8.2	12.1	11.5
Pies, tarts, turnovers	6.5	4.9	4.3	4.9	7.1
Meats, poultry, fish, and eggs	**66.2**	**65.8**	**62.5**	**72.0**	**65.9**
Beef	34.1	30.2	32.2	42.1	33.2
Ground beef	22.7	17.3	23.3	26.4	22.0
Roast	6.5	5.4	5.6	7.8	6.5
Chuck roast	2.4	1.4	2.4	3.0	2.3
Round roast	1.3	0.9	0.8	1.9	1.3
Other roast	4.1	3.9	3.5	4.3	4.1
Steak	12.9	12.0	10.2	19.1	12.4
Round steak	5.2	4.6	4.4	9.9	4.6
Sirloin steak	5.6	5.2	3.9	8.6	5.4
Other steak	9.8	9.2	8.1	13.4	9.5
Other beef	5.3	6.4	6.1	9.3	4.6
Pork	32.5	30.7	33.7	38.1	31.6
Bacon	12.2	8.5	13.4	13.5	11.8
Pork chops	8.0	7.2	9.2	9.7	7.5
Ham	9.9	8.9	7.9	14.8	9.5
Ham, not canned	9.7	8.6	7.6	14.5	9.4
Canned ham	0.3	0.6	0.3	0.5	0.3
Sausage	11.9	9.6	13.9	12.6	11.4
Other pork	8.6	13.9	8.9	11.1	8.2
Other meats	31.0	22.7	25.3	34.2	31.4
Frankfurters	11.1	9.8	10.2	14.7	10.7
Lunch meats (cold cuts)	24.8	16.2	19.6	26.3	25.4
Bologna, liverwurst, salami	11.3	7.4	9.1	11.3	11.7
Other lunch meats	20.6	13.6	16.0	21.2	21.2
Lamb, organ meats, and others	2.1	1.8	1.9	2.7	2.1
Lamb and organ meats	1.8	1.8	1.6	2.3	1.7
Mutton, goat, and game	0.4	–	0.3	0.4	0.4

	total households	Asian	black	Hispanic	non-Hispanic white and other
Poultry	31.0%	33.7%	36.0%	40.7%	28.8%
Fresh and frozen chicken	26.6	30.7	31.8	37.9	24.1
Fresh and frozen whole chicken	10.8	14.2	12.0	18.6	9.5
Fresh and frozen chicken parts	24.5	27.5	29.5	33.7	22.3
Other poultry	9.5	7.1	10.7	6.9	9.6
Fish and seafood	22.1	33.6	20.9	25.0	21.8
Canned fish and seafood	7.9	6.3	6.5	8.7	8.0
Fresh fish and shellfish	10.3	21.9	10.4	12.2	9.9
Frozen fish and shellfish	8.7	15.0	8.1	10.0	8.6
Eggs	31.7	28.9	30.0	40.3	30.6
Dairy products	**69.0**	**61.1**	**57.0**	**71.3**	**70.5**
Fresh milk and cream	57.0	50.8	44.7	61.6	58.2
Fresh milk, all types	54.4	48.2	43.3	59.8	55.2
Cream	13.6	8.2	7.1	11.9	14.8
Other dairy products	53.2	38.7	40.0	51.3	55.5
Butter	11.7	6.9	8.6	8.6	12.7
Cheese	39.5	20.6	26.5	38.9	41.6
Ice cream and related products	21.7	16.0	15.5	18.8	23.1
Miscellaneous dairy products	21.0	16.9	13.9	20.6	22.2
Fruits and vegetables	**70.7**	**73.1**	**63.2**	**75.1**	**71.2**
Fresh fruits	52.6	54.9	39.4	59.3	53.6
Apples	19.0	19.8	12.9	21.5	19.6
Bananas	33.7	32.4	22.9	40.1	34.4
Oranges	11.8	16.1	8.0	15.9	11.8
Citrus fruits, excluding oranges	16.6	18.8	9.8	29.6	15.8
Other fresh fruits	34.2	38.5	21.5	42.8	34.9
Fresh vegetables	53.5	61.4	41.6	60.3	54.3
Potatoes	20.5	18.9	15.3	22.9	21.0
Lettuce	20.1	20.5	12.8	24.9	20.5
Tomatoes	22.4	27.2	15.1	33.2	22.0
Other fresh vegetables	44.1	56.2	33.8	49.9	44.9
Processed fruits	39.3	33.0	36.6	43.3	39.2
Frozen fruits and fruit juices	5.0	2.5	3.1	3.9	5.5
Frozen orange juice	2.3	1.4	1.7	1.9	2.5
Frozen fruits	2.1	0.7	0.9	1.6	2.4
Frozen fruit juices, excluding orange	1.4	0.5	1.2	1.0	1.5
Canned fruits	12.4	8.1	10.2	10.9	13.0
Dried fruits	4.8	4.0	3.1	4.1	5.2
Fresh fruit juice	8.7	5.7	7.1	9.0	8.9
Canned and bottled fruit juice	25.8	23.1	27.4	31.6	24.8
Processed vegetables	39.9	33.2	35.8	43.6	40.0
Frozen vegetables	17.2	12.0	15.4	13.1	18.0
Canned and dried vegetables and juices	33.5	28.3	28.8	40.4	33.1
Canned beans	12.0	10.0	9.7	13.5	12.1
Canned corn	7.1	4.3	7.0	7.9	7.0
Canned miscellaneous vegetables	15.8	12.2	10.7	14.8	16.7
Dried peas	0.3	0.2	0.2	0.4	0.3
Dried beans	2.5	1.4	2.1	7.5	1.9
Dried miscellaneous vegetables	6.3	7.5	4.7	9.2	6.1
Fresh and canned vegetable juices	8.9	6.1	9.6	11.4	8.5
Sugar and other sweets	**41.4**	**33.9**	**36.2**	**42.5**	**42.1**
Candy and chewing gum	30.6	25.5	24.0	29.3	31.8
Sugar	11.8	11.0	14.5	16.8	10.7
Artificial sweeteners	2.2	1.7	1.8	2.1	2.3
Jams, preserves, other sweets	13.7	10.0	9.8	12.4	14.5

	total households	Asian	black	Hispanic	non-Hispanic white and other
Fats and oils	**34.3%**	**26.0%**	**28.5%**	**36.5%**	**34.9%**
Margarine	6.9	3.9	6.0	5.5	7.2
Fats and oils	12.7	13.0	14.0	20.2	11.4
Salad dressings	14.6	8.8	11.4	14.3	15.2
Nondairy cream and imitation milk	9.3	6.2	4.1	8.4	10.3
Peanut butter	7.0	3.2	4.5	4.9	7.7
Miscellaneous foods	**68.0**	**62.6**	**58.0**	**69.3**	**69.4**
Frozen prepared foods	27.4	20.4	21.5	23.2	28.9
Frozen meals	16.7	11.6	12.8	13.7	17.7
Other frozen prepared foods	17.7	13.8	14.1	14.2	18.8
Canned and packaged soups	21.1	15.4	15.0	18.4	22.4
Potato chips, nuts, and other snacks	41.1	34.1	33.2	39.0	42.6
Potato chips and other snacks	37.0	29.2	31.2	36.0	38.0
Nuts	12.8	12.5	7.7	10.8	13.8
Condiments and seasonings	42.7	38.3	34.4	45.0	43.7
Salt, spices, and other seasonings	19.1	24.1	15.7	26.4	18.6
Olives, pickles, relishes	8.7	5.4	5.4	7.5	9.3
Sauces and gravies	28.1	24.3	24.0	28.8	28.7
Baking needs and miscellaneous products	15.1	10.9	10.8	12.4	16.2
Other canned/packaged prepared foods	46.6	41.0	34.3	51.2	47.9
Prepared salads	16.5	11.0	11.6	11.4	18.1
Prepared desserts	9.0	6.5	4.7	9.3	9.7
Baby food	4.4	3.1	3.7	5.5	4.3
Miscellaneous prepared foods	38.2	35.9	27.8	46.0	38.6
Nonalcoholic beverages	**57.4**	**51.3**	**53.5**	**65.2**	**56.8**
Cola	31.5	20.6	29.1	39.3	30.8
Other carbonated drinks	26.3	15.7	25.4	31.9	25.6
Tea	13.6	13.8	11.9	14.8	13.7
Coffee	12.5	11.1	6.4	13.3	13.2
Roasted coffee	11.7	10.5	6.0	12.2	12.5
Instant and freeze-dried coffee	9.8	7.3	5.1	10.2	10.5
Noncarbonated fruit-flavored drinks	11.8	8.1	15.8	17.6	10.4
Other nonalcoholic beverages and ice	6.4	5.7	5.2	7.4	6.4
Bottled water	20.8	24.4	18.6	27.0	20.2
Sports drinks	7.5	5.5	6.0	10.2	7.4
• MEALS AT RESTAURANTS, CARRY-OUTS	**72.4**	**72.2**	**65.3**	**69.6**	**73.8**
Lunch	**54.9**	**56.3**	**46.7**	**52.1**	**56.5**
At fast-food restaurants*	42.3	45.1	38.9	41.2	42.9
At full-service restaurants	21.2	21.9	10.8	17.9	23.3
At vending machines, mobile vendors	4.4	2.9	3.8	6.7	4.1
At employer and school cafeterias	10.6	12.9	9.3	8.1	11.1
Dinner	**47.2**	**48.7**	**42.2**	**44.7**	**48.3**
At fast-food restaurants*	29.9	30.8	30.8	31.4	29.6
At full-service restaurants	27.7	29.3	17.5	22.0	30.2
At vending machines, mobile vendors	0.9	0.4	0.4	1.6	0.8
At employer and school cafeterias	1.3	0.7	1.3	0.8	1.4
Snacks and nonalcoholic beverages	**35.0**	**28.5**	**29.1**	**30.3**	**36.5**
At fast-food restaurants*	24.9	20.8	17.1	19.2	26.9
At full-service restaurants	5.6	3.9	4.9	4.9	5.8
At vending machines, mobile vendors	13.6	10.5	14.5	14.0	13.4
At employer and school cafeterias	2.9	4.3	2.3	2.3	3.1

	total households	Asian	black	Hispanic	non-Hispanic white and other
Breakfast and brunch	**30.2%**	**28.6%**	**26.4%**	**31.8%**	**30.6%**
At fast-food restaurants*	22.1	21.8	20.4	24.3	22.1
At full-service restaurants	9.9	7.2	6.6	10.5	10.3
At vending machines, mobile vendors	2.2	1.8	2.5	4.2	1.9
At employer and school cafeterias	3.1	2.5	3.3	3.8	3.0
ALCOHOL, PERCENT BUYING	**24.5**	**18.5**	**15.0**	**17.6**	**26.9**
Consumed at home	**16.4**	**11.2**	**11.6**	**12.4**	**17.7**
Beer and ale	11.3	8.6	8.7	10.3	11.8
Whiskey	0.6	0.1	0.2	0.3	0.7
Wine	6.9	3.7	3.8	3.5	7.8
Other alcoholic beverages	2.2	0.5	1.2	1.3	2.4
Consumed away from home (except on trips)	**13.2**	**9.8**	**5.8**	**7.7**	**15.1**
Beer and ale at restaurants, bars	8.8	5.1	3.5	5.8	10.1
Wine at restaurants, bars	4.1	4.0	1.4	1.7	4.8
Other alcoholic beverages at restaurants, bars	5.3	5.5	2.3	3.0	6.1

* The category fast-food restaurants also includes take-out, delivery, concession stands, buffets, and cafeterias other than employer and school.
Note: "Asian" and "black" include Hispanics and non-Hispanics who identify themselves as being of the respective race alone. "Hispanic" includes people of any race who identify themselves as Hispanic. "Other" includes people who identify themselves as non-Hispanic and as Alaska Native, American Indian, Asian (who are also included in the Asian column), or Native Hawaiian or other Pacific Islander as well as non-Hispanics reporting more than one race. "–" means sample is too small to make a reliable estimate.
Source: Bureau of Labor Statistics, unpublished data from the 2008 Consumer Expenditure Survey

Table 4.20 Amount Buyers Spent on Food and Alcohol by Race and Hispanic Origin, <u>Average Week</u>, 2008

(average amount spent by households buying food and alcohol during the average week, by race and Hispanic origin of householder, 2008)

	total households	Asian	black	Hispanic	non-Hispanic white and other
FOOD, AMOUNT SPENT	**$127.99**	**$143.51**	**$96.98**	**$130.87**	**$132.17**
• GROCERIES	**85.73**	**91.38**	**69.14**	**90.07**	**87.44**
Cereals and bakery products	**13.75**	**15.73**	**11.48**	**13.40**	**14.11**
Cereals and cereal products	7.01	10.62	6.61	7.09	7.07
Flour	3.39	3.97	2.70	3.77	3.61
Prepared flour mixes	2.72	2.82	2.12	2.39	2.79
Ready-to-eat and cooked cereals	5.59	5.31	5.44	5.44	5.61
Rice	4.87	15.38	4.42	5.22	4.84
Pasta, cornmeal, and other cereal products	2.96	4.24	2.61	2.67	3.02
Bakery products	9.88	10.12	7.74	9.15	10.26
Bread	4.05	5.01	3.46	4.18	4.10
White bread	2.17	2.71	2.20	2.33	2.15
Bread, other than white	2.99	3.79	2.42	2.90	3.06
Crackers and cookies	4.95	4.83	4.12	4.37	5.15
Cookies	4.23	4.21	3.72	3.60	4.41
Crackers	3.62	3.44	2.94	3.23	3.76
Frozen and refrigerated bakery products	4.03	4.13	3.40	3.80	4.10
Other bakery products	6.35	7.18	5.59	6.25	6.45
Biscuits and rolls	3.59	4.02	2.95	3.29	3.69
Cakes and cupcakes	6.19	7.90	5.81	7.68	6.07
Bread and cracker products	2.14	1.65	2.22	2.10	2.23
Sweetrolls, coffee cakes, doughnuts	3.75	3.83	3.40	3.63	3.82
Pies, tarts, turnovers	4.30	4.67	4.69	3.91	4.38
Meats, poultry, fish, and eggs	**24.59**	**29.53**	**26.09**	**27.74**	**23.87**
Beef	13.48	12.73	12.44	14.01	13.57
Ground beef	7.63	6.92	7.64	7.30	7.72
Roast	11.49	10.54	10.32	11.11	11.69
Chuck roast	7.92	10.56	8.05	8.22	8.15
Round roast	9.02	8.89	7.23	9.09	8.96
Other roast	10.81	8.55	9.46	10.39	10.95
Steak	13.05	12.30	11.17	12.05	13.54
Round steak	4.82	5.03	4.31	4.94	4.97
Sirloin steak	7.90	7.95	6.35	6.28	8.36
Other steak	10.13	9.06	8.66	9.50	10.39
Other beef	8.10	9.36	8.31	8.57	8.03
Pork	9.62	12.10	9.92	9.62	9.60
Bacon	4.59	4.59	4.34	4.08	4.74
Pork chops	7.67	10.32	8.89	8.14	7.44
Ham	6.44	6.85	5.94	5.74	6.71
Ham, not canned	6.48	6.78	6.04	5.74	6.74
Canned ham	3.33	5.45	3.33	4.35	3.57
Sausage	4.56	4.17	4.96	4.44	4.56
Other pork	8.96	11.34	8.84	8.30	9.18
Other meats	6.62	6.12	6.50	5.61	6.79
Frankfurters	3.50	3.18	3.22	3.06	3.72
Lunch meats (cold cuts)	5.72	5.91	4.91	4.56	5.97
Bologna, liverwurst, salami	3.09	3.38	2.86	2.82	3.17
Other lunch meats	5.16	5.28	4.37	4.15	5.42
Lamb, organ meats, and others	11.37	6.52	18.52	10.07	10.19
Lamb and organ meats	10.11	6.52	17.18	9.87	9.36
Mutton, goat, and game	16.67	–	32.00	11.11	15.79

	total households	Asian	black	Hispanic	non-Hispanic white and other
Poultry	$9.88	$10.68	$10.15	$10.11	$9.76
Fresh and frozen chicken	9.19	10.27	9.41	9.85	8.96
Fresh and frozen whole chicken	5.81	6.82	5.65	6.84	5.57
Fresh and frozen chicken parts	7.36	7.92	7.83	7.30	7.30
Other poultry	6.56	6.34	6.17	5.63	6.75
Fish and seafood	11.16	17.40	13.22	11.70	10.72
Canned fish and seafood	4.05	5.71	5.06	3.78	3.98
Fresh fish and shellfish	12.67	16.32	14.40	13.71	12.17
Frozen fish and shellfish	9.64	12.91	11.73	9.30	9.40
Eggs	3.10	3.57	3.03	3.60	3.04
Dairy products	**11.98**	**10.24**	**8.88**	**11.57**	**12.42**
Fresh milk and cream	5.67	6.52	5.01	6.07	5.69
Fresh milk, all types	5.30	6.43	4.80	5.76	5.29
Cream	2.57	2.58	2.10	2.53	2.63
Other dairy products	9.45	7.62	7.05	8.79	9.79
Butter	3.50	3.19	3.13	3.03	3.55
Cheese	6.54	5.33	4.82	6.36	6.71
Ice cream and related products	5.35	5.67	4.63	4.89	5.50
Miscellaneous dairy products	4.19	4.19	3.96	4.18	4.20
Fruits and vegetables	**17.86**	**22.42**	**13.59**	**20.18**	**18.09**
Fresh fruits	8.12	10.74	6.27	9.20	8.15
Apples	4.05	5.50	3.72	3.62	4.14
Bananas	1.84	2.66	1.83	2.35	1.77
Oranges	4.06	5.52	3.25	4.03	4.15
Citrus fruits, excluding oranges	2.11	2.28	1.95	2.13	2.09
Other fresh fruits	5.97	6.83	5.17	5.74	6.08
Fresh vegetables	7.61	11.55	6.01	7.86	7.77
Potatoes	3.56	3.91	3.60	3.45	3.57
Lettuce	2.54	4.68	2.35	2.09	2.58
Tomatoes	3.17	4.34	2.58	3.32	3.19
Other fresh vegetables	4.83	7.48	3.73	4.65	4.99
Processed fruits	5.70	5.46	5.14	6.15	5.69
Frozen fruits and fruit juices	4.37	3.67	3.50	4.85	4.36
Frozen orange juice	3.48	4.32	3.01	4.15	3.27
Frozen fruits	5.19	2.99	4.35	5.13	5.02
Frozen fruit juices, excluding orange	2.14	1.85	1.64	2.88	2.01
Canned fruits	3.22	2.72	2.93	2.93	3.23
Dried fruits	3.14	4.46	2.62	2.72	3.10
Fresh fruit juice	4.03	4.20	3.93	4.76	3.95
Canned and bottled fruit juice	4.38	4.59	4.09	5.06	4.28
Processed vegetables	5.13	4.82	4.86	5.30	5.15
Frozen vegetables	3.84	3.33	4.08	3.75	3.82
Canned and dried vegetables and juices	4.16	4.25	3.90	4.50	4.13
Canned beans	2.34	2.29	2.57	2.75	2.23
Canned corn	1.82	1.39	1.86	1.89	1.85
Canned miscellaneous vegetables	2.60	2.86	2.43	2.29	2.70
Dried peas	3.03	0.00	0.00	2.38	2.94
Dried beans	3.16	2.13	2.83	4.01	2.67
Dried miscellaneous vegetables	3.01	3.59	2.78	3.06	3.10
Fresh and canned vegetable juices	3.14	3.95	2.72	3.24	3.19
Sugar and other sweets	**6.02**	**7.14**	**4.29**	**5.51**	**6.30**
Candy and chewing gum	5.04	6.20	3.04	4.40	5.35
Sugar	2.87	3.09	3.10	3.09	2.80
Artificial sweeteners	5.43	6.67	4.44	5.37	5.63
Jams, preserves, other sweets	3.50	3.90	2.87	3.38	3.59

	total households	Asian	black	Hispanic	non-Hispanic white and other
Fats and oils	**$5.86**	**$7.64**	**$5.51**	**$6.57**	**$5.78**
Margarine	2.48	2.28	2.32	2.19	2.50
Fats and oils	5.99	9.88	5.63	6.08	6.07
Salad dressings	3.57	3.28	3.17	3.65	3.63
Nondairy cream and imitation milk	3.32	3.73	3.14	4.27	3.22
Peanut butter	3.58	3.13	3.12	3.27	3.65
Miscellaneous foods	**19.22**	**18.39**	**14.89**	**16.88**	**20.12**
Frozen prepared foods	9.85	9.52	8.69	8.75	10.13
Frozen meals	8.39	8.56	7.42	7.39	8.63
Other frozen prepared foods	7.34	6.90	6.51	7.09	7.47
Canned and packaged soups	4.17	4.62	3.54	3.32	4.33
Potato chips, nuts, and other snacks	6.56	7.18	5.23	5.47	6.87
Potato chips and other snacks	5.36	5.57	4.45	4.64	5.58
Nuts	5.65	6.58	4.57	4.26	5.86
Condiments and seasonings	5.55	6.34	4.91	4.60	5.77
Salt, spices, and other seasonings	2.93	4.07	2.67	2.54	3.06
Olives, pickles, relishes	3.00	2.80	2.60	2.81	3.11
Sauces and gravies	3.70	3.91	3.51	3.05	3.84
Baking needs and miscellaneous products	3.32	3.21	2.68	2.58	3.47
Other canned/packaged prepared foods	9.48	9.67	8.15	9.48	9.63
Prepared salads	4.23	4.17	3.54	3.52	4.37
Prepared desserts	2.77	2.62	2.14	2.80	2.79
Baby food	15.07	11.11	15.30	18.65	14.55
Miscellaneous prepared foods	7.28	8.19	6.18	6.90	7.46
Nonalcoholic beverages	**11.49**	**11.85**	**9.38**	**11.33**	**11.79**
Cola	5.04	5.05	3.96	4.43	5.33
Other carbonated drinks	3.73	3.62	2.92	3.51	3.87
Tea	4.56	5.43	3.88	4.18	4.68
Coffee	7.87	7.69	6.89	6.60	8.09
Roasted coffee	5.63	5.36	4.85	4.91	5.76
Instant and freeze-dried coffee	3.26	3.98	2.77	2.76	3.43
Noncarbonated fruit-flavored drinks	4.56	4.34	4.30	4.03	4.71
Other nonalcoholic beverages and ice	4.22	5.40	3.45	3.77	4.51
Bottled water	5.69	8.04	5.60	5.52	5.73
Sports drinks	5.59	4.33	5.38	5.28	5.56
• MEALS AT RESTAURANTS, CARRY-OUTS	**59.96**	**70.64**	**46.62**	**60.78**	**61.68**
Lunch	**27.09**	**31.55**	**21.36**	**28.69**	**27.60**
At fast-food restaurants*	17.66	20.59	15.60	20.00	17.60
At full-service restaurants	26.77	28.44	24.79	28.48	26.74
At vending machines, mobile vendors	4.14	2.43	2.36	7.50	3.66
At employer and school cafeterias	14.64	17.01	12.47	13.56	15.02
Dinner	**43.83**	**55.07**	**34.14**	**41.53**	**45.48**
At fast-food restaurants*	22.01	22.93	22.70	23.15	21.70
At full-service restaurants	49.95	66.84	40.92	50.18	50.76
At vending machines, mobile vendors	6.90	33.33	2.33	11.88	6.02
At employer and school cafeterias	13.53	5.80	21.60	10.53	13.29
Snacks and nonalcoholic beverages	**9.76**	**9.47**	**7.83**	**10.71**	**9.89**
At fast-food restaurants*	8.55	8.22	7.09	9.93	8.58
At full-service restaurants	11.15	11.22	8.15	10.12	11.65
At vending machines, mobile vendors	3.89	3.80	3.79	4.72	3.72
At employer and school cafeterias	4.45	3.76	4.89	7.73	4.19

	total households	Asian	black	Hispanic	non-Hispanic white and other
Breakfast and brunch	**$14.70**	**$12.93**	**$14.34**	**$17.44**	**$14.33**
At fast-food restaurants*	10.04	8.35	9.18	12.28	9.79
At full-service restaurants	19.47	22.22	25.26	19.98	18.89
At vending machines, mobile vendors	3.13	6.52	2.40	5.21	2.62
At employer and school cafeterias	7.03	6.43	5.45	6.81	7.36
ALCOHOL, AMOUNT SPENT	**31.71**	**28.24**	**25.08**	**29.68**	**32.45**
Consumed at home	**28.77**	**25.69**	**23.02**	**27.96**	**29.44**
Beer and ale	20.80	21.87	18.74	22.63	20.79
Whiskey	37.29	28.57	123.53	61.29	33.33
Wine	24.45	21.64	13.87	17.51	25.70
Other alcoholic beverages	22.12	37.25	24.59	26.98	21.31
Consumed away from home (except on trips)	**23.05**	**24.11**	**19.03**	**22.88**	**23.28**
Beer and ale at restaurants, bars	15.66	13.45	10.76	16.03	15.92
Wine at restaurants, bars	16.95	15.63	17.86	13.53	17.05
Other alcoholic beverages at restaurants, bars	18.23	19.23	20.26	19.80	18.00

The category fast-food restaurants also includes take-out, delivery, concession stands, buffets, and cafeterias other than employer and school.
Note: "Asian" and "black" include Hispanics and non-Hispanics who identify themselves as being of the respective race alone. "Hispanic" includes people of any race who identify themselves as Hispanic. "Other" includes people who identify themselves as non-Hispanic and as Alaska Native, American Indian, Asian (who are also included in the Asian column), or Native Hawaiian or other Pacific Islander as well as non-Hispanics reporting more than one race. "–" means sample is too small to make a reliable estimate.
Source: Calculations by New Strategist based on the Bureau of Labor Statistics' 2008 Consumer Expenditure Survey

Table 4.21 Percent Buying Food and Alcohol by Region, <u>Average Quarter</u>, 2008

(percent of households buying food and alcohol during the average quarter, by region of residence, 2008)

	total households	Northeast	Midwest	South	West
FOOD, PERCENT BUYING	**99.5%**	**99.3%**	**99.3%**	**99.7%**	**99.5%**
Groceries	**99.0**	**98.8**	**98.7**	**99.3**	**99.2**
Food and nonalcoholic beverages	99.0	98.7	98.7	99.3	99.1
Groceries purchased on trips	10.6	10.3	11.2	8.6	13.4
Food away from home	**81.8**	**78.4**	**84.0**	**81.0**	**83.5**
Meals at restaurants, carry-outs, etc.	78.5	74.7	80.3	78.5	79.9
Food or board at school	1.0	1.1	1.6	0.8	0.7
Catered affairs	1.9	2.4	2.1	1.4	1.9
Restaurant meals on trips	23.7	21.8	25.5	20.5	28.4
School lunches	9.2	8.7	10.5	9.2	8.2
Meals as pay	1.7	1.8	1.8	1.0	2.6
ALCOHOL, PERCENT BUYING	**37.0**	**40.2**	**40.8**	**31.1**	**39.9**
Consumed at home	**31.8**	**35.3**	**35.1**	**26.9**	**33.4**
Consumed away from home	**23.8**	**26.0**	**27.4**	**18.7**	**26.3**
Alcoholic beverages at restaurants, bars	17.4	20.0	20.6	13.5	18.1
Alcoholic beverages purchased on trips	11.8	11.8	13.0	9.1	14.8

Source: Bureau of Labor Statistics, unpublished data from the 2008 Consumer Expenditure Survey

Table 4.22 Amount Buyers Spent on Food and Alcohol by Region, <u>Average Quarter</u>, 2008

(average amount spent by households buying food and alcohol during the average quarter, by region of residence, 2008)

	total households	Northeast	Midwest	South	West
FOOD, AMOUNT SPENT	**$1,790.19**	**$1,889.15**	**$1,602.61**	**$1,768.29**	**$1,937.05**
Groceries	**1,215.51**	**1,279.97**	**1,087.06**	**1,205.32**	**1,310.26**
Food and nonalcoholic beverages	1,203.56	1,266.71	1,075.83	1,195.73	1,295.28
Groceries purchased on trips	115.42	131.49	101.07	113.49	119.45
Food away from home	**705.92**	**779.59**	**617.45**	**698.58**	**752.13**
Meals at restaurants, carry-outs, etc.	594.49	640.72	517.48	605.22	621.17
Food or board at school	858.58	935.55	656.33	856.40	1,226.76
Catered affairs	926.61	1,480.25	517.87	850.88	919.19
Restaurant meals on trips	251.13	286.86	219.06	242.41	268.33
School lunches	192.71	199.42	193.35	189.75	191.60
Meals as pay	440.66	437.50	328.29	416.24	536.48
ALCOHOL, AMOUNT SPENT	**220.32**	**234.40**	**209.40**	**209.62**	**233.51**
Consumed at home	**145.28**	**146.16**	**129.27**	**147.24**	**159.23**
Consumed away from home	**148.68**	**164.35**	**146.00**	**137.02**	**152.21**
Alcoholic beverages at restaurants, bars	145.91	155.48	145.90	134.15	151.48
Alcoholic beverages purchased on trips	85.07	98.99	76.74	83.08	85.48

Source: Calculations by New Strategist based on the Bureau of Labor Statistics' 2008 Consumer Expenditure Survey

Table 4.23 Percent Buying Food and Alcohol by Region, <u>Average Week</u>, 2008

(percent of households buying food and alcohol during the average week, by region of residence, 2008)

	total households	Northeast	Midwest	South	West
FOOD, PERCENT BUYING	**89.4%**	**90.3%**	**90.0%**	**88.3%**	**89.9%**
• GROCERIES	**82.9**	**83.4**	**83.1**	**81.5**	**84.5**
Cereals and bakery products	**70.9**	**72.5**	**70.9**	**70.4**	**70.4**
Cereals and cereal products	46.5	49.9	47.1	45.6	44.5
Flour	4.4	3.9	4.7	4.1	5.1
Prepared flour mixes	8.5	8.3	8.8	8.8	7.6
Ready-to-eat and cooked cereals	32.4	34.7	34.3	31.4	30.1
Rice	10.1	11.8	8.4	10.2	10.2
Pasta, cornmeal, and other cereal products	19.9	22.5	20.8	18.6	19.2
Bakery products	65.7	67.1	65.6	65.3	65.3
Bread	46.9	48.1	46.4	47.0	46.4
White bread	32.7	32.6	31.0	34.3	31.8
Bread, other than white	39.8	41.1	38.0	39.4	41.3
Crackers and cookies	31.7	34.3	32.2	31.0	30.4
Cookies	21.3	24.0	20.5	20.9	20.4
Crackers	18.5	18.8	20.1	18.2	17.2
Frozen and refrigerated bakery products	12.4	12.2	13.7	12.3	11.5
Other bakery products	39.7	43.0	40.5	37.8	39.1
Biscuits and rolls	26.5	31.2	28.8	23.3	25.4
Cakes and cupcakes	12.4	14.4	12.7	12.6	10.3
Bread and cracker products	4.2	6.0	4.2	3.6	3.8
Sweetrolls, coffee cakes, doughnuts	11.2	10.7	11.7	10.7	11.9
Pies, tarts, turnovers	6.5	7.0	6.1	6.8	6.1
Meats, poultry, fish, and eggs	**66.2**	**67.5**	**64.9**	**66.0**	**66.9**
Beef	34.1	34.3	33.4	34.6	33.6
Ground beef	22.7	22.7	23.6	23.8	19.9
Roast	6.5	6.4	6.0	6.6	7.0
Chuck roast	2.4	2.0	2.3	2.4	2.8
Round roast	1.3	1.5	0.9	1.3	1.7
Other roast	4.1	3.5	3.8	4.5	4.2
Steak	12.9	13.5	11.2	12.7	14.2
Round steak	5.2	4.8	4.0	5.4	6.4
Sirloin steak	5.6	5.4	4.5	5.9	6.3
Other steak	9.8	10.3	8.3	10.0	10.5
Other beef	5.3	5.5	4.7	5.1	6.1
Pork	32.5	32.2	31.3	34.0	31.6
Bacon	12.2	11.5	11.8	13.2	11.5
Pork chops	8.0	8.4	8.3	8.1	7.0
Ham	9.9	10.0	9.6	10.3	9.6
Ham, not canned	9.7	9.8	9.4	10.1	9.4
Canned ham	0.3	0.3	0.3	0.3	0.2
Sausage	11.9	11.0	11.2	12.9	11.5
Other pork	8.6	8.6	7.9	8.4	9.7
Other meats	31.0	32.7	31.8	30.3	29.7
Frankfurters	11.1	11.0	11.2	11.4	10.8
Lunch meats (cold cuts)	24.8	26.8	26.3	24.0	23.1
Bologna, liverwurst, salami	11.3	12.6	11.7	11.6	9.6
Other lunch meats	20.6	21.5	22.5	19.6	19.4
Lamb, organ meats, and others	2.1	2.5	1.7	1.9	2.6
Lamb and organ meats	1.8	2.1	1.3	1.7	2.2
Mutton, goat, and game	0.4	0.3	0.4	0.3	0.4

	total households	Northeast	Midwest	South	West
Poultry	31.0%	34.6%	27.6%	31.0%	31.4%
Fresh and frozen chicken	26.6	29.4	23.4	26.6	27.5
Fresh and frozen whole chicken	10.8	12.3	8.6	11.4	11.0
Fresh and frozen chicken parts	24.5	26.5	21.5	24.5	25.6
Other poultry	9.5	11.1	8.8	9.5	8.7
Fish and seafood	22.1	25.9	19.9	20.6	23.4
Canned fish and seafood	7.9	9.4	7.7	7.7	7.3
Fresh fish and shellfish	10.3	13.5	8.7	8.3	12.5
Frozen fish and shellfish	8.7	9.8	7.9	8.8	8.5
Eggs	31.7	31.2	30.7	31.8	32.7
Dairy products	**69.0**	**71.9**	**69.2**	**66.0**	**71.1**
Fresh milk and cream	57.0	60.4	58.5	54.3	57.2
Fresh milk, all types	54.4	57.5	56.0	52.4	53.4
Cream	13.6	14.7	14.0	11.5	15.6
Other dairy products	53.2	55.7	54.0	49.8	55.9
Butter	11.7	14.0	11.9	10.2	12.2
Cheese	39.5	41.9	41.8	36.4	40.0
Ice cream and related products	21.7	22.6	22.5	20.3	22.4
Miscellaneous dairy products	21.0	24.5	22.2	17.5	22.6
Fruits and vegetables	**70.7**	**72.7**	**69.5**	**67.9**	**74.9**
Fresh fruits	52.6	55.0	51.9	48.2	58.4
Apples	19.0	20.8	19.2	16.4	21.6
Bananas	33.7	35.5	32.8	30.9	37.6
Oranges	11.8	13.4	11.9	9.7	13.9
Citrus fruits, excluding oranges	16.6	17.0	13.2	14.7	22.9
Other fresh fruits	34.2	35.3	33.8	30.2	40.1
Fresh vegetables	53.5	55.8	51.7	49.4	59.9
Potatoes	20.5	22.0	20.0	19.3	21.8
Lettuce	20.1	21.6	21.4	16.8	22.9
Tomatoes	22.4	22.8	20.2	20.7	27.2
Other fresh vegetables	44.1	48.4	41.1	39.5	51.3
Processed fruits	39.3	44.6	39.1	36.7	39.3
Frozen fruits and fruit juices	5.0	4.5	6.6	4.0	5.5
Frozen orange juice	2.3	1.3	3.1	1.8	3.0
Frozen fruits	2.1	2.2	2.7	1.8	2.1
Frozen fruit juices, excluding orange	1.4	1.5	2.0	1.0	1.3
Canned fruits	12.4	13.1	13.6	11.7	11.9
Dried fruits	4.8	5.4	5.3	4.2	4.7
Fresh fruit juice	8.7	11.7	8.7	7.0	9.0
Canned and bottled fruit juice	25.8	30.9	23.4	25.0	25.4
Processed vegetables	39.9	41.0	41.2	39.1	39.1
Frozen vegetables	17.2	19.2	18.7	16.5	15.1
Canned and dried vegetables and juices	33.5	33.8	33.9	33.0	33.5
Canned beans	12.0	12.4	11.8	13.2	9.8
Canned corn	7.1	6.5	6.7	8.0	6.7
Canned miscellaneous vegetables	15.8	15.8	16.9	15.9	14.4
Dried peas	0.3	0.4	0.4	0.3	0.4
Dried beans	2.5	2.2	2.0	2.6	3.2
Dried miscellaneous vegetables	6.3	6.8	6.7	5.4	7.0
Fresh and canned vegetable juices	8.9	8.9	8.7	8.6	9.7
Sugar and other sweets	**41.4**	**41.5**	**43.2**	**39.7**	**42.2**
Candy and chewing gum	30.6	31.0	34.0	27.5	31.8
Sugar	11.8	12.4	11.0	12.7	10.9
Artificial sweeteners	2.2	2.3	2.2	2.4	1.9
Jams, preserves, other sweets	13.7	14.7	13.8	13.0	13.9

	total households	Northeast	Midwest	South	West
Fats and oils	**34.3%**	**36.1%**	**34.2%**	**34.0%**	**33.6%**
Margarine	6.9	7.3	7.3	6.8	6.2
Fats and oils	12.7	14.0	11.7	12.5	12.9
Salad dressings	14.6	15.5	14.4	14.1	14.8
Nondairy cream and imitation milk	9.3	8.8	9.6	9.1	9.9
Peanut butter	7.0	7.5	8.0	6.7	5.9
Miscellaneous foods	**68.0**	**67.4**	**68.6**	**66.3**	**70.7**
Frozen prepared foods	27.4	27.6	31.3	25.9	25.8
Frozen meals	16.7	17.6	18.0	15.8	16.1
Other frozen prepared foods	17.7	17.4	21.6	16.6	16.0
Canned and packaged soups	21.1	22.8	22.7	19.2	21.1
Potato chips, nuts, and other snacks	41.1	42.0	44.3	38.9	40.9
Potato chips and other snacks	37.0	38.3	40.4	35.3	35.1
Nuts	12.8	13.8	13.8	10.5	14.5
Condiments and seasonings	42.7	43.4	43.7	40.9	44.2
Salt, spices, and other seasonings	19.1	20.3	19.2	17.6	20.6
Olives, pickles, relishes	8.7	9.9	9.0	8.2	8.1
Sauces and gravies	28.1	29.2	28.6	26.8	28.9
Baking needs and miscellaneous products	15.1	15.2	17.0	14.3	14.3
Other canned/packaged prepared foods	46.6	44.5	47.3	44.5	51.1
Prepared salads	16.5	18.8	16.5	15.0	17.3
Prepared desserts	9.0	9.6	10.2	7.8	9.4
Baby food	4.4	5.8	4.3	3.7	4.3
Miscellaneous prepared foods	38.2	35.5	39.4	35.9	42.9
Nonalcoholic beverages	**57.4%**	**57.6**	**55.1**	**57.8**	**58.8**
Cola	31.5	28.7	31.5	33.7	30.4
Other carbonated drinks	26.3	26.0	26.0	25.9	27.4
Tea	13.6	17.2	12.2	13.0	13.0
Coffee	12.5	14.0	11.1	12.9	11.8
Roasted coffee	11.7	13.0	10.2	12.4	11.1
Instant and freeze-dried coffee	9.8	10.7	8.5	10.7	9.1
Noncarbonated fruit-flavored drinks	11.8	12.7	10.9	11.5	12.7
Other nonalcoholic beverages and ice	6.4	5.6	6.8	5.9	7.5
Bottled water	20.8	23.0	18.5	19.4	23.3
Sports drinks	7.5	6.2	7.2	7.2	9.4
• MEALS AT RESTAURANTS, CARRY-OUTS	**72.4**	**71.4**	**71.8**	**72.3**	**73.8**
Lunch	**54.9**	**53.5**	**53.6**	**55.7**	**55.9**
At fast-food restaurants*	42.3	41.2	39.6	43.9	43.1
At full-service restaurants	21.2	19.1	19.1	22.3	23.2
At vending machines, mobile vendors	4.4	4.5	4.9	4.3	3.8
At employer and school cafeterias	10.6	12.5	11.7	9.8	9.0
Dinner	**47.2**	**44.9**	**48.2**	**48.4**	**46.0**
At fast-food restaurants*	29.9	27.5	31.8	30.9	28.3
At full-service restaurants	27.7	27.9	26.1	28.6	27.8
At vending machines, mobile vendors	0.9	0.5	1.1	0.8	1.1
At employer and school cafeterias	1.3	0.9	2.1	1.1	1.3
Snacks and nonalcoholic beverages	**35.0**	**35.1**	**36.3**	**32.8**	**36.9**
At fast-food restaurants*	24.9	25.8	24.9	21.8	29.2
At full-service restaurants	5.6	6.4	6.1	5.0	5.2
At vending machines, mobile vendors	13.6	12.0	16.4	14.3	11.2
At employer and school cafeterias	2.9	3.9	3.7	2.3	2.4

	total households	Northeast	Midwest	South	West
Breakfast and brunch	**30.2%**	**34.1%**	**30.1%**	**28.8%**	**29.4%**
At fast-food restaurants*	22.1	26.4	20.1	21.9	21.0
At full-service restaurants	9.9	10.4	10.5	8.7	10.8
At vending machines, mobile vendors	2.2	2.6	2.5	2.0	2.1
At employer and school cafeterias	3.1	3.6	4.0	2.7	2.5
ALCOHOL, PERCENT BUYING	**24.5**	**23.4**	**26.7**	**22.4**	**26.6**
Consumed at home	**16.4**	**14.3**	**16.8**	**16.1**	**18.4**
Beer and ale	11.3	9.3	12.1	11.7	11.5
Whiskey	0.6	0.5	0.6	0.6	0.6
Wine	6.9	6.6	6.1	6.2	9.0
Other alcoholic beverages	2.2	2.3	2.2	1.8	2.7
Consumed away from home (except on trips)	**13.2**	**13.2**	**15.8**	**11.0**	**14.1**
Beer and ale at restaurants, bars	8.8	8.4	10.9	7.5	9.2
Wine at restaurants, bars	4.1	5.2	4.3	3.2	4.3
Other alcoholic beverages at restaurants, bars	5.3	5.6	6.4	4.3	5.6

* The category fast-food restaurants also includes take-out, delivery, concession stands, buffets, and cafeterias other than employer and school.
Source: Bureau of Labor Statistics, unpublished data from the 2008 Consumer Expenditure Survey

Table 4.24 Amount Buyers Spent on Food and Alcohol by Region, Average Week, 2008

(average amount spent by households buying food and alcohol during the average week, by region of residence, 2008)

	total households	Northeast	Midwest	South	West
FOOD, AMOUNT SPENT	**$127.99**	**$135.75**	**$117.63**	**$124.29**	**$137.89**
• GROCERIES	**85.73**	**91.46**	**80.63**	**81.49**	**92.76**
Cereals and bakery products	**13.75**	**15.36**	**13.10**	**12.91**	**14.43**
Cereals and cereal products	7.01	7.52	6.69	6.42	7.86
Flour	3.39	3.30	3.80	2.96	3.93
Prepared flour mixes	2.72	2.76	2.61	2.49	3.15
Ready-to-eat and cooked cereals	5.59	5.65	5.37	5.44	5.99
Rice	4.87	6.17	3.95	4.03	5.69
Pasta, cornmeal, and other cereal products	2.96	3.15	2.74	2.58	3.60
Bakery products	9.88	11.01	9.35	9.40	10.19
Bread	4.05	4.32	3.69	3.79	4.57
White bread	2.17	2.39	2.07	2.01	2.36
Bread, other than white	2.99	3.14	2.84	2.77	3.31
Crackers and cookies	4.95	5.10	4.71	4.84	5.24
Cookies	4.23	4.54	4.11	4.11	4.28
Crackers	3.62	3.51	3.39	3.52	4.24
Frozen and refrigerated bakery products	4.03	3.94	3.80	3.98	4.51
Other bakery products	6.35	7.14	5.90	6.26	6.20
Biscuits and rolls	3.59	3.95	3.27	3.52	3.66
Cakes and cupcakes	6.19	6.88	5.50	6.36	6.04
Bread and cracker products	2.14	2.17	2.16	1.95	2.10
Sweetrolls, coffee cakes, doughnuts	3.75	3.82	3.51	3.82	3.96
Pies, tarts, turnovers	4.30	4.45	4.11	3.97	5.27
Meats, poultry, fish, and eggs	**24.59**	**26.23**	**22.21**	**24.58**	**25.53**
Beef	13.48	13.16	12.84	13.52	14.42
Ground beef	7.63	7.28	7.51	7.77	7.85
Roast	11.49	11.06	11.46	11.31	12.05
Chuck roast	7.92	7.92	7.83	7.95	8.16
Round roast	9.02	9.27	7.78	7.63	10.78
Other roast	10.81	11.46	11.44	10.29	10.19
Steak	13.05	12.41	12.87	13.11	13.66
Round steak	4.82	4.35	5.69	4.46	5.19
Sirloin steak	7.90	8.60	8.52	7.58	7.30
Other steak	10.13	9.71	10.00	9.84	10.88
Other beef	8.10	8.55	8.32	7.78	8.09
Pork	9.62	9.21	9.26	9.82	10.04
Bacon	4.59	4.52	4.48	4.55	4.87
Pork chops	7.67	7.40	7.09	8.26	7.76
Ham	6.44	6.02	6.75	6.38	6.69
Ham, not canned	6.48	6.00	6.83	6.45	6.71
Canned ham	3.33	3.85	3.03	2.94	4.35
Sausage	4.56	4.09	4.45	4.81	4.70
Other pork	8.96	9.01	7.86	9.44	9.18
Other meats	6.62	7.61	6.13	6.37	6.60
Frankfurters	3.50	3.71	3.40	3.51	3.61
Lunch meats (cold cuts)	5.72	6.56	5.40	5.55	5.45
Bologna, liverwurst, salami	3.09	3.50	2.92	3.02	3.22
Other lunch meats	5.16	6.15	4.84	5.00	4.89
Lamb, organ meats, and others	11.37	13.06	9.04	10.82	12.06
Lamb and organ meats	10.11	13.15	8.59	9.64	9.22
Mutton, goat, and game	16.67	12.50	10.53	15.63	23.26

	total households	Northeast	Midwest	South	West
Poultry	$9.88	$10.24	$9.43	$9.75	$10.16
Fresh and frozen chicken	9.19	9.43	8.69	9.08	9.49
Fresh and frozen whole chicken	5.81	6.90	5.48	5.18	6.27
Fresh and frozen chicken parts	7.36	7.24	7.24	7.42	7.51
Other poultry	6.56	6.93	6.51	6.42	6.66
Fish and seafood	11.16	12.36	9.25	11.13	11.69
Canned fish and seafood	4.05	4.04	3.65	4.05	4.37
Fresh fish and shellfish	12.67	13.32	10.52	13.66	12.45
Frozen fish and shellfish	9.64	10.43	8.09	9.79	10.24
Eggs	3.10	3.15	2.77	2.95	3.64
Dairy products	**11.98**	**12.33**	**11.69**	**11.44**	**12.79**
Fresh milk and cream	5.67	5.58	5.27	5.71	6.11
Fresh milk, all types	5.30	5.15	4.93	5.37	5.73
Cream	2.57	2.78	2.29	2.51	2.81
Other dairy products	9.45	9.88	9.27	8.94	10.01
Butter	3.50	3.36	3.36	3.44	3.76
Cheese	6.54	6.69	6.17	6.24	7.22
Ice cream and related products	5.35	5.22	5.21	5.46	5.54
Miscellaneous dairy products	4.19	4.28	3.87	4.13	4.47
Fruits and vegetables	**17.86**	**19.17**	**16.35**	**16.42**	**20.33**
Fresh fruits	8.12	8.48	7.38	7.53	9.30
Apples	4.05	3.98	4.12	3.84	4.36
Bananas	1.84	1.92	1.62	1.75	2.13
Oranges	4.06	4.12	3.86	4.14	4.10
Citrus fruits, excluding oranges	2.11	2.24	1.97	2.05	2.18
Other fresh fruits	5.97	6.32	5.27	5.82	6.53
Fresh vegetables	7.61	8.22	6.52	7.06	8.87
Potatoes	3.56	3.50	3.31	3.67	3.57
Lettuce	2.54	2.64	2.29	2.38	2.75
Tomatoes	3.17	3.29	2.93	3.00	3.45
Other fresh vegetables	4.83	5.15	3.97	4.46	5.75
Processed fruits	5.70	5.86	5.47	5.42	6.19
Frozen fruits and fruit juices	4.37	3.98	4.24	4.21	4.88
Frozen orange juice	3.48	2.99	3.55	2.72	3.97
Frozen fruits	5.19	4.48	4.91	5.65	5.29
Frozen fruit juices, excluding orange	2.14	2.63	2.02	1.96	2.99
Canned fruits	3.22	3.06	3.09	3.24	3.20
Dried fruits	3.14	2.95	2.81	2.86	3.65
Fresh fruit juice	4.03	4.03	3.80	4.01	4.24
Canned and bottled fruit juice	4.38	4.54	4.10	4.16	4.85
Processed vegetables	5.13	5.08	4.91	5.21	5.29
Frozen vegetables	3.84	3.65	3.42	4.18	3.90
Canned and dried vegetables and juices	4.16	4.09	4.07	4.10	4.44
Canned beans	2.34	2.26	2.20	2.42	2.45
Canned corn	1.82	1.84	1.64	1.88	1.93
Canned miscellaneous vegetables	2.60	2.66	2.61	2.58	2.72
Dried peas	3.03	2.70	2.70	0.00	2.78
Dried beans	3.16	3.20	3.59	2.65	2.81
Dried miscellaneous vegetables	3.01	2.94	2.84	2.98	3.41
Fresh and canned vegetable juices	3.14	3.28	3.09	2.78	3.82
Sugar and other sweets	**6.02**	**6.22**	**6.18**	**5.49**	**6.44**
Candy and chewing gum	5.04	5.00	5.33	4.54	5.45
Sugar	2.87	2.83	2.83	2.90	2.76
Artificial sweeteners	5.43	6.01	4.63	5.51	6.19
Jams, preserves, other sweets	3.50	3.61	3.19	3.30	4.09

	total households	Northeast	Midwest	South	West
Fats and oils	**$5.86**	**$6.07**	**$5.50**	**$5.59**	**$6.46**
Margarine	2.48	2.60	2.48	2.37	2.42
Fats and oils	5.99	6.64	5.47	5.59	6.54
Salad dressings	3.57	3.41	3.47	3.49	3.98
Nondairy cream and imitation milk	3.32	3.30	2.82	3.29	3.83
Peanut butter	3.58	3.34	3.49	3.56	3.73
Miscellaneous foods	**19.22**	**19.48**	**19.24**	**18.11**	**20.70**
Frozen prepared foods	9.85	9.11	9.66	10.22	10.18
Frozen meals	8.39	8.02	7.96	8.79	8.65
Other frozen prepared foods	7.34	6.34	7.38	7.61	7.75
Canned and packaged soups	4.17	4.12	3.79	4.02	4.87
Potato chips, nuts, and other snacks	6.56	6.47	6.46	6.33	7.14
Potato chips and other snacks	5.36	5.04	5.30	5.36	5.75
Nuts	5.65	5.75	5.21	5.43	6.12
Condiments and seasonings	5.55	5.67	5.38	5.26	6.02
Salt, spices, and other seasonings	2.93	3.00	2.76	2.84	3.16
Olives, pickles, relishes	3.00	2.94	3.10	2.93	3.11
Sauces and gravies	3.70	3.70	3.60	3.55	4.08
Baking needs and miscellaneous products	3.32	3.15	2.99	3.22	4.07
Other canned/packaged prepared foods	9.48	10.13	8.70	8.90	10.57
Prepared salads	4.23	4.20	4.06	4.14	4.51
Prepared desserts	2.77	3.01	2.44	2.83	2.99
Baby food	15.07	14.21	15.55	17.38	12.67
Miscellaneous prepared foods	7.28	7.36	6.34	6.89	8.60
Nonalcoholic beverages	**11.49**	**11.75**	**11.00**	**11.06**	**12.40**
Cola	5.04	4.73	5.02	5.13	5.21
Other carbonated drinks	3.73	3.65	3.88	3.59	3.84
Tea	4.56	4.53	4.61	4.54	4.60
Coffee	7.87	7.48	8.03	7.35	9.01
Roasted coffee	5.63	5.44	5.89	5.01	6.56
Instant and freeze-dried coffee	3.26	3.27	3.42	3.09	3.63
Noncarbonated fruit-flavored drinks	4.56	5.22	3.75	4.09	5.37
Other nonalcoholic beverages and ice	4.22	4.63	4.27	3.93	4.77
Bottled water	5.69	6.04	5.02	5.57	6.13
Sports drinks	5.59	5.14	5.29	5.82	5.52
• MEALS AT RESTAURANTS, CARRY-OUTS	**59.96**	**64.75**	**54.19**	**59.94**	**61.77**
Lunch	**27.09**	**27.59**	**24.39**	**28.23**	**27.41**
At fast-food restaurants*	17.66	19.10	16.67	17.18	18.25
At full-service restaurants	26.77	25.26	23.14	30.12	25.50
At vending machines, mobile vendors	4.14	3.99	4.50	3.04	5.50
At employer and school cafeterias	14.64	15.18	15.59	13.52	14.73
Dinner	**43.83**	**50.36**	**38.82**	**42.44**	**46.24**
At fast-food restaurants*	22.01	22.46	21.24	22.52	21.57
At full-service restaurants	49.95	58.60	44.53	46.76	53.16
At vending machines, mobile vendors	6.90	5.77	6.60	6.33	10.19
At employer and school cafeterias	13.53	11.36	11.43	12.50	20.47
Snacks and nonalcoholic beverages	**9.76**	**10.81**	**8.93**	**8.99**	**10.91**
At fast-food restaurants*	8.55	8.90	7.80	7.83	9.90
At full-service restaurants	11.15	14.44	8.18	11.67	10.73
At vending machines, mobile vendors	3.89	3.58	4.02	3.93	3.85
At employer and school cafeterias	4.45	3.63	3.77	4.35	6.78

	total households	Northeast	Midwest	South	West
Breakfast and brunch	**$14.70**	**$14.83**	**$12.99**	**$14.31**	**$16.93**
At fast-food restaurants*	10.04	10.56	8.44	10.06	11.02
At full-service restaurants	19.47	18.63	17.97	19.49	21.63
At vending machines, mobile vendors	3.13	4.28	2.44	2.48	4.25
At employer and school cafeterias	7.03	6.48	6.73	6.23	9.88
ALCOHOL, AMOUNT SPENT	**31.71**	**33.59**	**29.57**	**30.83**	**33.76**
Consumed at home	**28.77**	**32.89**	**26.06**	**27.79**	**30.03**
Beer and ale	20.80	22.82	20.55	19.90	21.08
Whiskey	37.29	44.68	23.44	48.39	27.59
Wine	24.45	28.03	21.98	23.18	25.55
Other alcoholic beverages	22.12	22.17	18.89	23.46	22.47
Consumed away from home (except on trips)	**23.05**	**23.90**	**22.24**	**21.96**	**24.75**
Beer and ale at restaurants, bars	15.66	14.68	17.52	14.97	15.31
Wine at restaurants, bars	16.95	17.47	15.19	17.08	18.22
Other alcoholic beverages at restaurants, bars	18.23	17.91	15.09	17.59	22.99

The category fast-food restaurants also includes take-out, delivery, concession stands, buffets, and cafeterias other than employer and school.
Source: Calculations by New Strategist based on the Bureau of Labor Statistics' 2008 Consumer Expenditure Survey

Table 4.25 Percent Buying Food and Alcohol by Education, Average Quarter, 2008

(percent of households buying food and alcohol during the average quarter, by highest level of education of householder, 2008)

	total households	less than high school graduate	high school graduate	some college	associate's degree	college graduate total	bachelor's degree	master's, professional, doctorate
FOOD, PERCENT BUYING	99.5%	99.0%	99.6%	99.1%	99.9%	99.8%	99.7%	99.9%
Groceries	99.0	98.5	99.2	98.2	99.8	99.6	99.5	99.6
Food and nonalcoholic beverages	99.0	98.5	99.1	98.1	99.8	99.5	99.5	99.6
Groceries purchased on trips	10.6	4.0	6.9	10.9	11.2	16.6	14.5	20.3
Food away from home	81.8	64.3	77.2	84.6	85.4	91.4	90.0	93.8
Meals at restaurants, carry-outs, etc.	78.5	61.2	73.4	80.9	81.5	89.0	87.7	91.2
Food or board at school	1.0	0.4	0.7	1.3	0.8	1.5	1.5	1.6
Catered affairs	1.9	0.8	1.5	1.6	2.1	2.9	2.8	3.0
Restaurant meals on trips	23.7	9.7	16.8	23.6	25.1	36.4	32.7	43.1
School lunches	9.2	4.5	8.3	9.1	12.6	11.3	11.9	10.2
Meals as pay	1.7	1.3	1.8	1.9	1.4	1.7	1.7	1.6
ALCOHOL, PERCENT BUYING	37.0	19.3	29.6	39.1	39.4	50.1	49.0	52.1
Consumed at home	31.8	17.0	26.1	33.2	35.2	42.2	41.8	42.9
Consumed away from home	23.8	8.2	15.5	25.0	24.5	37.7	36.0	40.8
Alcoholic beverages at restaurants, bars	17.4	5.9	11.0	18.0	18.6	27.9	26.8	29.8
Alcoholic beverages purchased on trips	11.8	3.2	6.9	11.6	12.4	20.4	18.8	23.2

Source: Bureau of Labor Statistics, unpublished data from the 2008 Consumer Expenditure Survey

Table 4.26 Amount Buyers Spent on Food and Alcohol by Education, Average Quarter, 2008

(average amount spent by households buying food and alcohol during the average quarter, by highest level of education of householder, 2008)

	total households	less than high school graduate	high school graduate	some college	associate's degree	college graduate total	bachelor's degree	master's, professional, doctorate
FOOD, AMOUNT SPENT	$1,790.19	$1,433.19	$1,594.35	$1,705.21	$1,825.73	$2,193.09	$2,086.80	$2,383.60
Groceries	1,215.51	1,117.80	1,156.10	1,152.76	1,226.90	1,359.27	1,324.24	1,422.03
Food and nonalcoholic beverages	1,203.56	1,113.81	1,148.75	1,141.85	1,215.07	1,338.76	1,306.23	1,397.09
Groceries purchased on trips	115.42	97.88	111.64	108.32	105.10	124.59	124.28	125.05
Food away from home	705.92	494.35	571.12	659.98	702.21	914.52	848.07	1,028.83
Meals at restaurants, carry-outs, etc.	594.49	469.38	508.61	566.16	596.26	719.11	682.13	782.93
Food or board at school	858.58	217.14	440.15	708.46	1,077.68	1,147.08	748.68	1,806.37
Catered affairs	926.61	307.44	587.41	947.98	684.69	1,213.81	1,070.68	1,448.50
Restaurant meals on trips	251.13	157.41	190.94	215.64	240.53	307.81	275.11	352.41
School lunches	192.71	151.39	195.42	191.89	182.55	203.47	202.71	205.13
Meals as pay	440.66	410.52	439.06	398.68	458.16	484.88	544.41	376.41
ALCOHOL, AMOUNT SPENT	220.32	192.74	195.13	213.59	216.19	243.77	236.54	255.92
Consumed at home	145.28	153.74	143.17	144.34	137.30	147.31	143.80	153.49
Consumed away from home	148.68	133.68	132.70	142.32	150.48	158.97	154.98	165.35
Alcoholic beverages at restaurants, bars	145.91	152.67	143.87	148.63	148.06	144.17	146.20	140.88
Alcoholic beverages purchased on trips	85.07	63.73	69.19	76.23	76.01	97.09	88.35	109.80

Source: Calculations by New Strategist based on the Bureau of Labor Statistics' 2008 Consumer Expenditure Survey

Table 4.27 Percent Buying Food and Alcohol by Education, Average Week, 2008

(percent of households buying food and alcohol during the average week, by highest level of education of householder, 2008)

	total households	less than high school graduate	high school graduate	some college	associate's degree	college graduate total	college graduate bachelor's degree	college graduate master's, professional, doctorate
FOOD, PERCENT BUYING	**89.4%**	**87.1%**	**89.2%**	**88.8%**	**90.7%**	**90.8%**	**91.3%**	**90.0%**
• **GROCERIES**	**82.9**	**82.1**	**82.7**	**81.3**	**84.8**	**84.2**	**84.4**	**83.8**
Cereals and bakery products	**70.9**	**69.5**	**71.5**	**68.8**	**74.9**	**71.5**	**71.2**	**72.0**
Cereals and cereal products	46.5	46.2	47.9	42.9	49.2	47.4	47.0	48.0
Flour	4.4	6.9	4.7	3.4	3.7	4.1	3.6	4.8
Prepared flour mixes	8.5	7.7	8.9	7.7	10.0	8.6	8.8	8.2
Ready-to-eat and cooked cereals	32.4	31.6	34.2	29.3	34.0	33.0	33.2	32.6
Rice	10.1	10.5	10.5	9.5	10.0	9.9	9.3	11.0
Pasta, cornmeal, and other cereal products	19.9	17.6	21.0	18.5	21.3	20.8	20.7	21.1
Bakery products	65.7	64.1	65.6	64.5	69.9	66.2	66.3	66.0
Bread	46.9	46.5	47.3	45.3	50.3	47.0	46.8	47.4
White bread	32.7	35.2	35.6	31.2	33.1	29.8	29.9	29.5
Bread, other than white	39.8	36.6	38.5	38.5	45.5	41.9	41.0	43.4
Crackers and cookies	31.7	30.1	30.9	31.8	32.4	33.1	33.2	33.0
Cookies	21.3	21.3	21.2	21.3	22.8	20.8	20.6	21.1
Crackers	18.5	15.7	18.0	18.2	18.0	20.7	20.7	20.7
Frozen and refrigerated bakery products	12.4	9.5	13.9	12.3	12.6	12.4	12.7	12.0
Other bakery products	39.7	35.3	38.0	39.8	45.5	41.4	41.7	40.9
Biscuits and rolls	26.5	19.7	25.5	26.3	30.9	29.2	29.9	28.1
Cakes and cupcakes	12.4	12.5	12.6	12.1	14.4	11.9	11.4	12.9
Bread and cracker products	4.2	3.4	3.9	4.5	4.7	4.5	4.8	3.9
Sweetrolls, coffee cakes, doughnuts	11.2	11.6	11.5	10.7	12.6	10.8	10.8	10.6
Pies, tarts, turnovers	6.5	5.4	6.2	7.3	8.3	6.1	6.6	5.3
Meats, poultry, fish, and eggs	**66.2**	**66.3**	**67.5**	**63.6**	**67.9**	**66.6**	**66.3**	**67.2**
Beef	34.1	36.4	34.7	33.8	35.5	32.1	33.2	30.2
Ground beef	22.7	24.9	24.7	22.0	24.4	19.8	20.9	17.7
Roast	6.5	6.0	6.3	6.8	5.9	7.0	7.3	6.4
Chuck roast	2.4	2.8	2.1	2.4	2.3	2.6	2.6	2.6
Round roast	1.3	1.2	1.4	1.4	1.1	1.4	1.6	1.0
Other roast	4.1	3.0	3.9	4.7	3.5	4.4	4.7	4.0
Steak	12.9	12.6	12.2	12.8	15.0	13.0	12.9	13.3
Round steak	5.2	5.9	4.6	5.2	6.1	5.2	5.0	5.6
Sirloin steak	5.6	4.8	5.1	6.3	6.3	5.7	5.6	5.7
Other steak	9.8	9.1	9.5	9.5	12.1	9.9	9.6	10.3
Other beef	5.3	7.8	5.2	4.9	4.9	4.8	5.0	4.3
Pork	32.5	35.5	34.7	30.1	36.2	29.9	29.7	30.2
Bacon	12.2	13.5	13.4	10.9	14.5	10.8	11.0	10.5
Pork chops	8.0	8.5	8.7	7.7	8.9	7.0	6.8	7.3
Ham	9.9	12.3	10.5	9.5	10.4	8.5	8.3	8.9
Ham, not canned	9.7	11.7	10.3	9.3	10.2	8.4	8.3	8.7
Canned ham	0.3	0.7	0.3	0.3	0.2	0.2	0.1	0.4
Sausage	11.9	13.3	12.6	11.2	13.1	10.6	10.7	10.5
Other pork	8.6	10.3	8.6	7.9	9.7	7.9	8.4	7.1
Other meats	31.0	31.7	31.9	29.8	33.6	29.8	29.6	30.3
Frankfurters	11.1	13.7	11.9	10.6	12.1	9.4	9.7	8.7
Lunch meats (cold cuts)	24.8	24.9	25.5	23.3	27.9	24.4	23.7	25.6
Bologna, liverwurst, salami	11.3	13.2	12.4	9.8	11.9	10.5	10.4	10.8
Other lunch meats	20.6	18.1	21.1	19.9	23.6	20.8	20.3	21.7
Lamb, organ meats, and others	2.1	3.0	2.1	2.0	2.1	1.9	1.7	2.3
Lamb and organ meats	1.8	2.7	1.6	1.7	1.9	1.6	1.3	2.2
Mutton, goat, and game	0.4	0.3	0.5	0.3	0.3	0.3	0.4	0.2

	total households	less than high school graduate	high school graduate	some college	associate's degree	college graduate		
						total	bachelor's degree	master's, professional, doctorate
Poultry	31.0%	30.5%	30.5%	29.8%	34.6%	31.4%	31.1%	32.1%
Fresh and frozen chicken	26.6	27.8	26.5	25.7	28.9	26.1	25.6	27.0
Fresh and frozen whole chicken	10.8	11.8	10.5	10.2	12.2	10.8	10.9	10.7
Fresh and frozen chicken parts	24.5	25.2	24.5	23.3	26.6	24.3	24.0	24.8
Other poultry	9.5	7.6	9.3	8.7	10.9	10.7	11.0	10.1
Fish and seafood	22.1	19.5	21.5	20.8	22.3	24.7	24.1	25.8
Canned fish and seafood	7.9	6.7	8.5	7.7	9.1	7.8	7.5	8.4
Fresh fish and shellfish	10.3	8.7	9.4	9.7	8.9	12.6	12.1	13.6
Frozen fish and shellfish	8.7	7.7	9.2	7.7	8.1	9.7	9.3	10.6
Eggs	31.7	33.2	32.4	29.2	31.9	32.0	31.9	32.2
Dairy products	**69.0**	**66.5**	**68.1**	**66.5**	**73.0**	**71.5**	**71.2**	**72.1**
Fresh milk and cream	57.0	56.1	56.3	55.0	60.8	58.5	58.6	58.2
Fresh milk, all types	54.4	53.9	54.0	52.0	58.7	55.4	55.2	55.6
Cream	13.6	11.4	12.1	13.7	15.4	15.4	15.0	16.0
Other dairy products	53.2	45.4	51.6	51.5	58.8	58.0	57.2	59.5
Butter	11.7	8.9	11.7	11.3	12.2	13.3	13.0	13.8
Cheese	39.5	33.0	38.3	38.4	46.2	42.3	41.3	44.2
Ice cream and related products	21.7	17.4	21.6	21.9	22.9	23.3	23.3	23.2
Miscellaneous dairy products	21.0	16.0	18.8	19.6	24.0	25.5	24.2	28.0
Fruits and vegetables	**70.7**	**67.4**	**70.1**	**68.3**	**74.3**	**73.7**	**72.6**	**75.6**
Fresh fruits	52.6	48.9	49.1	50.0	57.0	58.2	56.7	61.0
Apples	19.0	15.9	17.0	17.1	22.1	22.9	21.9	24.7
Bananas	33.7	31.7	30.8	32.5	37.5	36.9	35.2	40.1
Oranges	11.8	12.1	10.6	10.1	11.6	14.2	13.9	14.6
Citrus fruits, excluding oranges	16.6	16.1	13.8	14.7	18.3	20.5	19.7	22.2
Other fresh fruits	34.2	31.0	30.2	31.9	38.2	39.9	38.5	42.7
Fresh vegetables	53.5	50.3	52.1	50.1	57.3	57.7	57.3	58.4
Potatoes	20.5	19.4	20.6	19.2	21.4	21.7	21.4	22.3
Lettuce	20.1	18.7	19.1	18.7	21.0	22.5	22.2	23.0
Tomatoes	22.4	21.8	21.5	19.9	23.6	25.2	24.6	26.2
Other fresh vegetables	44.1	41.0	41.4	41.4	47.0	49.3	48.7	50.5
Processed fruits	39.3	35.1	37.4	38.2	42.2	43.0	41.8	45.2
Frozen fruits and fruit juices	5.0	3.6	4.7	4.8	5.2	6.2	6.0	6.6
Frozen orange juice	2.3	2.0	2.6	2.2	2.2	2.3	2.2	2.5
Frozen fruits	2.1	1.0	1.8	2.1	2.0	3.1	3.0	3.2
Frozen fruit juices, excluding orange	1.4	1.3	1.3	1.2	1.6	1.7	1.7	1.6
Canned fruits	12.4	10.6	12.2	11.7	15.0	13.3	12.7	14.5
Dried fruits	4.8	4.5	4.1	4.1	4.6	6.2	5.7	7.1
Fresh fruit juice	8.7	7.3	8.0	7.7	10.4	10.2	9.8	10.8
Canned and bottled fruit juice	25.8	23.8	23.9	25.8	28.6	27.6	27.6	27.7
Processed vegetables	39.9	39.1	40.5	38.4	40.8	40.8	39.8	42.5
Frozen vegetables	17.2	13.0	17.3	17.2	18.3	18.6	17.7	20.4
Canned and dried vegetables and juices	33.5	34.7	34.7	31.6	34.1	33.0	32.3	34.2
Canned beans	12.0	11.1	13.4	11.6	12.6	11.1	10.5	12.3
Canned corn	7.1	7.6	7.9	7.1	7.7	6.1	5.6	7.2
Canned miscellaneous vegetables	15.8	14.3	16.7	15.1	16.0	16.0	15.7	16.6
Dried peas	0.3	0.3	0.2	0.4	0.4	0.4	0.3	0.6
Dried beans	2.5	4.9	2.3	2.1	2.3	2.1	2.1	2.0
Dried miscellaneous vegetables	6.3	6.9	7.1	5.5	5.6	6.2	6.2	6.0
Fresh and canned vegetable juices	8.9	9.2	8.8	8.4	9.7	9.1	9.2	9.0
Sugar and other sweets	**41.4**	**41.0**	**40.9**	**40.4**	**43.2**	**42.2**	**42.4**	**42.0**
Candy and chewing gum	30.6	28.3	29.5	30.2	33.1	32.2	32.8	30.9
Sugar	11.8	15.0	12.8	11.0	13.5	9.6	9.7	9.3
Artificial sweeteners	2.2	2.5	1.9	2.0	2.8	2.4	2.4	2.4
Jams, preserves, other sweets	13.7	11.8	13.9	13.7	14.9	14.2	14.0	14.5

	total households	less than high school graduate	high school graduate	some college	associate's degree	college graduate		
						total	bachelor's degree	master's, professional, doctorate
Fats and oils	**34.3%**	**34.6%**	**34.8%**	**33.8%**	**37.7%**	**33.1%**	**32.8%**	**33.7%**
Margarine	6.9	7.6	8.0	6.3	7.2	5.8	6.1	5.1
Fats and oils	12.7	16.4	13.0	12.1	12.5	11.2	11.0	11.6
Salad dressings	14.6	13.2	14.9	14.6	17.2	14.2	13.7	15.0
Nondairy cream and imitation milk	9.3	7.8	9.3	9.3	11.4	9.5	10.2	8.0
Peanut butter	7.0	5.3	7.1	7.0	7.8	7.4	6.8	8.4
Miscellaneous foods	**68.0**	**62.7**	**66.9**	**66.4**	**73.0**	**71.2**	**70.4**	**72.6**
Frozen prepared foods	27.4	22.2	27.7	28.3	29.5	28.2	27.9	29.0
Frozen meals	16.7	13.1	16.7	16.8	17.9	17.9	16.4	20.6
Other frozen prepared foods	17.7	14.7	18.2	18.1	18.9	18.0	18.2	17.6
Canned and packaged soups	21.1	18.0	21.1	20.2	24.1	22.3	22.4	22.0
Potato chips, nuts, and other snacks	41.1	34.0	39.9	41.3	46.1	43.9	43.5	44.6
Potato chips and other snacks	37.0	31.1	36.5	37.5	42.3	38.1	37.7	38.7
Nuts	12.8	9.1	11.6	12.1	14.2	15.6	15.8	15.4
Condiments and seasonings	42.7	39.2	42.4	41.3	45.1	45.0	44.9	45.2
Salt, spices, and other seasonings	19.1	19.4	18.8	17.7	19.4	20.4	19.6	21.9
Olives, pickles, relishes	8.7	7.1	8.5	8.7	9.4	9.2	9.1	9.4
Sauces and gravies	28.1	24.5	28.9	27.9	29.9	28.8	29.6	27.3
Baking needs and miscellaneous products	15.1	12.6	15.6	13.9	15.8	16.4	16.2	16.8
Other canned/packaged prepared foods	46.6	43.2	44.3	45.9	51.7	49.4	48.3	51.6
Prepared salads	16.5	10.1	16.5	16.9	17.1	19.1	18.3	20.6
Prepared desserts	9.0	7.6	9.6	8.8	9.5	9.3	8.8	10.0
Baby food	4.4	4.3	4.3	4.1	4.1	4.8	5.0	4.5
Miscellaneous prepared foods	38.2	37.7	36.4	37.3	42.4	39.5	38.6	41.0
Nonalcoholic beverages	**57.4**	**57.1**	**57.1**	**56.3**	**62.4**	**57.0**	**56.9**	**57.1**
Cola	31.5	34.3	33.7	31.5	32.8	28.0	27.8	28.2
Other carbonated drinks	26.3	28.2	26.8	26.5	28.7	24.0	25.2	21.9
Tea	13.6	13.3	14.4	12.7	15.1	13.2	13.0	13.4
Coffee	12.5	12.5	11.4	11.3	13.2	14.2	13.4	15.7
Roasted coffee	11.7	11.3	10.9	10.5	12.1	13.6	12.8	15.0
Instant and freeze-dried coffee	9.8	10.4	9.2	8.8	10.6	10.8	10.4	11.4
Noncarbonated fruit-flavored drinks	11.8	13.2	12.6	11.7	14.4	9.9	10.6	8.6
Other nonalcoholic beverages and ice	6.4	5.4	6.3	7.1	6.9	6.3	6.4	6.2
Bottled water	20.8	17.3	20.2	20.2	23.7	22.4	22.5	22.3
Sports drinks	7.5	6.2	7.4	7.1	10.3	7.8	8.1	7.1
• MEALS AT RESTAURANTS, CARRY-OUTS	**72.4**	**58.2**	**68.4**	**75.0**	**76.3**	**79.3**	**79.1**	**79.7**
Lunch	**54.9**	**40.0**	**49.3**	**56.6**	**61.8**	**63.5**	**63.1**	**64.1**
At fast-food restaurants*	42.3	31.9	38.1	44.0	48.3	47.6	47.4	48.1
At full-service restaurants	21.2	11.9	16.6	20.7	24.0	29.3	27.8	31.9
At vending machines, mobile vendors	4.4	3.1	5.2	4.3	5.0	4.1	4.4	3.4
At employer and school cafeterias	10.6	5.8	8.3	10.5	13.3	14.2	14.8	13.1
Dinner	**47.2**	**32.1**	**42.6**	**49.3**	**50.4**	**55.7**	**56.4**	**54.4**
At fast-food restaurants*	29.9	21.5	28.1	33.3	32.1	32.2	33.6	29.6
At full-service restaurants	27.7	15.2	23.0	27.3	29.8	37.6	36.8	39.3
At vending machines, mobile vendors	0.9	1.1	1.1	0.8	0.6	0.7	0.7	0.8
At employer and school cafeterias	1.3	0.8	1.2	1.5	1.8	1.5	1.5	1.4
Snacks and nonalcoholic beverages	**35.0**	**23.8**	**29.8**	**37.5**	**39.6**	**41.4**	**41.5**	**41.2**
At fast-food restaurants*	24.9	14.5	21.0	26.4	28.8	31.0	30.9	31.2
At full-service restaurants	5.6	4.2	5.0	5.3	5.8	6.8	6.8	6.7
At vending machines, mobile vendors	13.6	11.2	12.1	15.2	14.4	14.7	15.3	13.7
At employer and school cafeterias	2.9	1.6	2.4	2.9	3.7	3.8	3.5	4.2

	total households	less than high school graduate	high school graduate	some college	associate's degree	college graduate		
						total	bachelor's degree	master's, professional, doctorate
Breakfast and brunch	**30.2%**	**21.8%**	**28.1%**	**31.2%**	**35.2%**	**33.7%**	**33.5%**	**34.2%**
At fast-food restaurants*	22.1	16.1	20.2	22.2	27.1	25.1	25.0	25.2
At full-service restaurants	9.9	8.0	9.9	10.1	11.3	10.1	9.9	10.4
At vending machines, mobile vendors	2.2	1.9	2.8	2.1	2.6	1.9	2.1	1.5
At employer and school cafeterias	3.1	1.9	2.4	3.7	4.0	3.7	3.3	4.5
ALCOHOL, PERCENT BUYING	**24.5**	**11.7**	**20.9**	**24.3**	**25.7**	**33.5**	**33.1**	**34.3**
Consumed at home	**16.4**	**8.9**	**14.4**	**16.7**	**17.6**	**21.2**	**20.8**	**22.0**
Beer and ale	11.3	7.4	11.2	11.6	12.6	12.6	13.1	11.8
Whiskey	0.6	0.1	0.5	0.5	0.5	1.0	1.2	0.6
Wine	6.9	2.2	3.7	6.7	7.4	12.0	11.0	13.8
Other alcoholic beverages	2.2	0.6	1.6	2.3	2.3	3.3	3.2	3.4
Consumed away from home (except on trips)	**13.2**	**4.1**	**10.6**	**12.4**	**14.4**	**20.1**	**20.3**	**19.7**
Beer and ale at restaurants, bars	8.8	2.6	7.4	8.4	10.4	12.8	13.4	11.6
Wine at restaurants, bars	4.1	1.0	2.5	3.3	3.7	7.7	7.7	7.8
Other alcoholic beverages at restaurants, bars	5.3	1.6	4.0	5.5	6.0	7.9	8.0	7.7

The category fast-food restaurants also includes take-out, delivery, concession stands, buffets, and cafeterias other than employer and school.
Source: Bureau of Labor Statistics, unpublished data from the 2008 Consumer Expenditure Survey

Table 4.28 Amount Buyers Spent on Food and Alcohol by Education, <u>Average Week</u>, 2008

(average amount spent by households buying food and alcohol during the average week, by highest level of education of householder, 2008)

	total households	less than high school graduate	high school graduate	some college	associate's degree	college graduate total	bachelor's degree	master's, professional, doctorate
FOOD, AMOUNT SPENT	**$127.99**	**$100.56**	**$113.88**	**$123.39**	**$139.70**	**$152.86**	**$148.86**	**$160.42**
• GROCERIES	**85.73**	**74.49**	**80.36**	**83.31**	**90.63**	**96.00**	**93.89**	**99.96**
Cereals and bakery products	**13.75**	**11.99**	**12.90**	**13.29**	**13.88**	**15.63**	**15.44**	**15.99**
Cereals and cereal products	7.01	6.65	6.60	6.60	7.16	7.81	7.70	7.97
Flour	3.39	4.06	3.23	3.20	2.96	3.46	3.58	3.31
Prepared flour mixes	2.72	2.34	2.58	2.74	2.41	3.04	2.96	3.06
Ready-to-eat and cooked cereals	5.59	5.20	5.20	5.39	5.86	6.16	6.27	5.92
Rice	4.87	5.06	4.36	4.41	4.80	5.56	4.94	6.35
Pasta, cornmeal, and other cereal products	2.96	2.51	2.57	2.71	3.33	3.51	3.39	3.71
Bakery products	9.88	8.20	9.24	9.78	9.81	11.29	11.11	11.64
Bread	4.05	3.72	3.70	3.96	4.08	4.55	4.36	4.89
White bread	2.17	2.19	2.05	2.08	2.15	2.38	2.28	2.54
Bread, other than white	2.99	2.62	2.65	2.96	2.94	3.42	3.31	3.60
Crackers and cookies	4.95	4.02	4.63	4.85	4.76	5.77	5.66	6.01
Cookies	4.23	3.42	3.96	4.22	4.00	5.01	5.00	5.03
Crackers	3.62	3.06	3.28	3.53	3.51	4.25	4.11	4.48
Frozen and refrigerated bakery products	4.03	3.47	3.96	3.90	3.74	4.58	4.49	4.68
Other bakery products	6.35	5.63	6.14	6.28	6.17	6.89	6.89	6.88
Biscuits and rolls	3.59	3.25	3.29	3.53	3.59	3.93	3.95	3.91
Cakes and cupcakes	6.19	5.60	5.70	6.14	5.57	7.31	7.29	7.30
Bread and cracker products	2.14	2.04	2.34	1.98	2.11	2.22	2.29	2.30
Sweetrolls, coffee cakes, doughnuts	3.75	3.37	3.58	3.92	3.66	4.09	4.26	3.67
Pies, tarts, turnovers	4.30	3.54	4.33	4.39	4.11	4.73	4.42	5.63
Meats, poultry, fish, and eggs	**24.59**	**24.30**	**23.92**	**23.99**	**25.64**	**25.42**	**25.48**	**25.32**
Beef	13.48	12.54	13.34	13.13	14.04	14.23	14.45	13.83
Ground beef	7.63	7.47	7.50	7.69	7.92	7.74	7.75	7.71
Roast	11.49	11.91	11.62	10.41	10.94	12.29	13.15	10.71
Chuck roast	7.92	8.96	7.80	7.88	8.66	7.81	8.20	7.45
Round roast	9.02	9.24	8.03	7.86	8.33	10.79	11.80	8.25
Other roast	10.81	11.63	11.76	8.80	9.89	11.34	11.83	10.33
Steak	13.05	10.79	13.21	12.98	13.52	13.90	14.20	13.43
Round steak	4.82	4.96	4.55	5.05	4.95	5.01	5.23	4.82
Sirloin steak	7.90	6.51	7.72	7.95	7.95	8.50	9.06	7.73
Other steak	10.13	8.34	10.67	9.50	10.16	10.85	11.12	10.37
Other beef	8.10	8.32	8.72	7.77	7.96	7.79	7.57	8.00
Pork	9.62	9.90	9.50	9.81	9.28	9.63	9.82	9.26
Bacon	4.59	4.36	4.62	4.61	4.42	4.81	4.82	4.78
Pork chops	7.67	8.36	7.40	7.70	7.40	7.88	7.66	8.31
Ham	6.44	6.17	6.37	6.20	6.85	6.82	7.00	6.73
Ham, not canned	6.48	6.34	6.41	6.22	6.85	6.88	6.88	6.77
Canned ham	3.33	2.74	4.00	3.85	4.76	5.00	0.00	2.63
Sausage	4.56	4.52	4.45	4.90	4.49	4.62	4.97	3.99
Other pork	8.96	8.28	9.39	9.21	7.91	9.32	9.20	9.52
Other meats	6.62	6.09	6.30	6.44	6.79	7.28	7.14	7.47
Frankfurters	3.50	3.15	3.36	3.49	3.55	4.06	4.01	4.13
Lunch meats (cold cuts)	5.72	4.53	5.44	5.80	5.95	6.36	6.36	6.32
Bologna, liverwurst, salami	3.09	2.87	2.98	3.06	3.27	3.42	3.28	3.61
Other lunch meats	5.16	4.14	4.85	5.27	5.37	5.72	5.76	5.67
Lamb, organ meats, and others	11.37	12.46	10.73	10.20	8.96	12.70	12.43	12.33
Lamb and organ meats	10.11	12.55	6.96	9.52	8.06	12.74	12.70	12.44
Mutton, goat, and game	16.67	11.54	20.75	14.29	15.38	11.76	13.95	11.11

	total households	less than high school graduate	high school graduate	some college	associate's degree	college graduate total	bachelor's degree	master's, professional, doctorate
Poultry	$9.88	$9.82	$9.84	$9.24	$9.91	$10.38	$10.40	$10.37
Fresh and frozen chicken	9.19	9.00	9.18	8.46	9.28	9.77	9.77	9.73
Fresh and frozen whole chicken	5.81	6.25	5.84	5.39	5.68	6.01	5.80	6.33
Fresh and frozen chicken parts	7.36	6.96	7.42	6.95	7.43	7.83	7.79	7.85
Other poultry	6.56	6.71	6.26	6.70	6.99	6.65	6.55	6.96
Fish and seafood	11.16	10.10	10.43	11.22	10.47	12.28	11.77	13.16
Canned fish and seafood	4.05	3.43	4.01	3.79	3.63	4.63	4.55	4.55
Fresh fish and shellfish	12.67	12.56	11.62	13.05	13.20	12.97	12.63	13.67
Frozen fish and shellfish	9.64	8.41	8.83	9.91	10.42	10.57	10.24	10.95
Eggs	3.10	3.38	2.93	3.01	3.16	3.19	3.16	3.23
Dairy products	**11.98**	**10.28**	**10.89**	**11.66**	**12.86**	**13.62**	**13.33**	**14.15**
Fresh milk and cream	5.67	5.72	5.34	5.36	5.94	6.07	6.13	5.98
Fresh milk, all types	5.30	5.45	5.00	5.00	5.51	5.65	5.76	5.46
Cream	2.57	2.36	2.56	2.55	2.47	2.73	2.73	2.76
Other dairy products	9.45	7.98	8.54	9.35	9.82	10.68	10.32	11.32
Butter	3.50	3.47	3.25	3.45	3.60	3.70	3.63	3.76
Cheese	6.54	5.61	5.73	6.45	6.82	7.49	7.19	8.01
Ice cream and related products	5.35	5.30	5.05	5.47	5.10	5.67	5.75	5.56
Miscellaneous dairy products	4.19	3.43	4.00	3.78	4.21	4.74	4.63	4.97
Fruits and vegetables	**17.86**	**15.79**	**15.73**	**17.03**	**18.10**	**21.14**	**20.65**	**22.02**
Fresh fruits	8.12	7.16	7.11	7.70	8.25	9.50	9.35	9.79
Apples	4.05	3.65	3.76	3.80	4.35	4.42	4.49	4.29
Bananas	1.84	1.89	1.75	1.84	1.84	1.92	1.93	1.89
Oranges	4.06	3.62	3.86	4.07	3.97	4.45	4.53	4.24
Citrus fruits, excluding oranges	2.11	2.05	1.89	2.11	1.97	2.29	2.24	2.30
Other fresh fruits	5.97	4.97	5.40	5.90	5.85	6.81	6.66	7.08
Fresh vegetables	7.61	6.96	6.77	7.33	7.08	8.96	8.73	9.36
Potatoes	3.56	3.81	3.44	3.54	3.27	3.60	3.51	3.77
Lettuce	2.54	2.19	2.31	2.36	2.52	2.93	2.93	2.91
Tomatoes	3.17	2.99	2.93	3.06	3.10	3.46	3.37	3.59
Other fresh vegetables	4.83	4.15	4.20	4.66	4.47	5.80	5.69	5.98
Processed fruits	5.70	5.07	5.19	5.68	5.91	6.28	6.22	6.39
Frozen fruits and fruit juices	4.37	3.90	3.62	4.56	4.41	4.70	4.53	4.87
Frozen orange juice	3.48	3.57	2.73	3.59	4.50	3.49	3.23	3.56
Frozen fruits	5.19	3.96	4.55	5.80	4.59	5.21	5.37	5.56
Frozen fruit juices, excluding orange	2.14	2.24	1.54	2.61	2.45	2.41	2.34	3.18
Canned fruits	3.22	3.01	2.96	3.09	3.67	3.38	3.31	3.39
Dried fruits	3.14	2.69	2.69	2.94	2.81	3.40	3.52	3.39
Fresh fruit juice	4.03	3.84	3.87	3.76	3.95	4.33	4.27	4.44
Canned and bottled fruit juice	4.38	3.86	4.14	4.53	4.13	4.75	4.64	4.92
Processed vegetables	5.13	4.76	5.11	5.05	5.36	5.32	5.27	5.41
Frozen vegetables	3.84	3.23	3.81	3.77	4.15	3.98	3.96	4.02
Canned and dried vegetables and juices	4.16	4.15	4.07	4.08	4.19	4.34	4.33	4.33
Canned beans	2.34	2.34	2.16	2.32	2.54	2.43	2.48	2.28
Canned corn	1.82	1.84	1.91	1.84	1.69	1.80	1.80	1.68
Canned miscellaneous vegetables	2.60	2.38	2.52	2.58	2.87	2.82	2.75	2.95
Dried peas	3.03	0.00	5.00	2.86	2.63	2.38	2.94	1.75
Dried beans	3.16	3.70	2.61	2.42	3.03	2.88	2.80	3.05
Dried miscellaneous vegetables	3.01	3.03	2.82	2.73	2.67	3.58	3.70	3.16
Fresh and canned vegetable juices	3.14	3.03	3.08	3.23	2.90	3.29	3.27	3.43
Sugar and other sweets	**6.02**	**4.95**	**5.57**	**5.69**	**6.09**	**7.08**	**7.22**	**6.82**
Candy and chewing gum	5.04	3.78	4.58	4.67	4.93	6.22	6.33	5.96
Sugar	2.87	3.39	2.96	2.63	2.58	2.82	2.78	2.89
Artificial sweeteners	5.43	5.24	5.88	6.09	5.40	5.39	5.39	5.79
Jams, preserves, other sweets	3.50	2.72	3.24	3.51	3.30	4.16	4.08	4.20

	total households	less than high school graduate	high school graduate	some college	associate's degree	college graduate total	bachelor's degree	master's, professional, doctorate
Fats and oils	**$5.86**	**$5.76**	**$5.75**	**$5.70**	**$5.75**	**$6.16**	**$6.19**	**$6.12**
Margarine	2.48	2.36	2.51	2.37	2.36	2.43	2.29	2.55
Fats and oils	5.99	5.68	5.63	5.85	5.70	6.86	6.81	6.98
Salad dressings	3.57	3.49	3.56	3.50	3.73	3.75	3.73	3.72
Nondairy cream and imitation milk	3.32	3.21	3.22	3.33	2.98	3.59	3.71	3.25
Peanut butter	3.58	3.19	3.37	3.58	3.84	3.67	3.68	3.69
Miscellaneous foods	**19.22**	**14.91**	**17.78**	**19.90**	**19.38**	**21.70**	**21.02**	**22.88**
Frozen prepared foods	9.85	8.10	9.75	9.55	10.13	10.76	9.91	12.36
Frozen meals	8.39	6.42	8.07	8.40	8.46	9.34	8.65	10.38
Other frozen prepared foods	7.34	6.51	7.43	7.14	7.82	7.62	7.36	8.19
Canned and packaged soups	4.17	3.50	3.89	4.16	4.60	4.54	4.60	4.45
Potato chips, nuts, and other snacks	6.56	5.33	5.84	6.99	6.55	7.31	7.24	7.45
Potato chips and other snacks	5.36	4.57	4.66	5.87	5.42	5.88	5.91	5.83
Nuts	5.65	4.31	5.45	5.69	5.16	6.21	5.84	6.90
Condiments and seasonings	5.55	4.61	5.16	5.59	5.47	6.22	6.10	6.45
Salt, spices, and other seasonings	2.93	2.52	2.67	3.16	2.68	3.29	3.22	3.46
Olives, pickles, relishes	3.00	2.52	2.82	2.97	2.98	3.37	3.41	3.18
Sauces and gravies	3.70	3.11	3.46	3.59	3.87	4.24	4.09	4.51
Baking needs and miscellaneous products	3.32	2.93	2.88	3.52	3.16	3.71	3.64	3.82
Other canned/packaged prepared foods	9.48	7.64	8.69	9.77	8.83	10.87	10.65	11.28
Prepared salads	4.23	3.46	3.76	4.26	3.91	4.81	4.86	4.81
Prepared desserts	2.77	2.51	2.61	2.84	2.42	3.03	3.05	3.10
Baby food	15.07	11.29	14.59	15.82	17.23	16.04	14.86	18.16
Miscellaneous prepared foods	7.28	6.00	6.45	7.57	6.97	8.42	8.18	8.81
Nonalcoholic beverages	**11.49**	**10.27**	**11.31**	**11.45**	**11.75**	**12.14**	**12.24**	**11.95**
Cola	5.04	4.63	5.17	4.99	5.15	5.15	5.14	5.14
Other carbonated drinks	3.73	3.40	3.59	4.11	3.62	3.70	3.61	3.83
Tea	4.56	3.82	4.57	4.16	4.24	5.25	5.46	4.84
Coffee	7.87	7.14	7.14	7.71	7.53	8.89	8.89	8.94
Roasted coffee	5.63	4.96	4.87	5.53	5.55	6.42	6.34	6.54
Instant and freeze-dried coffee	3.26	3.19	3.04	3.30	3.02	3.63	3.65	3.68
Noncarbonated fruit-flavored drinks	4.56	3.78	3.98	4.36	6.27	5.06	5.02	5.34
Other nonalcoholic beverages and ice	4.22	3.69	3.99	4.67	3.49	4.76	5.16	4.07
Bottled water	5.69	5.42	5.65	5.45	5.45	6.02	6.04	5.92
Sports drinks	5.59	4.18	5.15	6.08	5.24	6.06	6.04	6.22
• MEALS AT RESTAURANTS, CARRY-OUTS	**59.96**	**45.45**	**51.37**	**55.78**	**65.30**	**73.20**	**71.64**	**76.09**
Lunch	**27.09**	**25.38**	**24.25**	**25.06**	**28.38**	**30.65**	**29.93**	**31.96**
At fast-food restaurants*	17.66	18.44	17.38	16.84	18.84	17.86	17.47	18.59
At full-service restaurants	26.77	29.25	22.89	25.42	25.65	29.32	29.21	29.56
At vending machines, mobile vendors	4.14	4.79	5.62	3.29	4.03	2.95	3.39	1.76
At employer and school cafeterias	14.64	10.90	14.94	13.21	15.70	15.69	15.72	15.60
Dinner	**43.83**	**32.84**	**37.92**	**40.71**	**45.45**	**52.65**	**50.71**	**56.41**
At fast-food restaurants*	22.01	21.61	22.09	20.83	23.12	22.65	23.13	21.67
At full-service restaurants	49.95	37.82	42.05	47.25	51.28	57.84	55.81	61.35
At vending machines, mobile vendors	6.90	6.42	8.26	5.33	10.94	6.85	4.23	12.00
At employer and school cafeterias	13.53	11.39	15.97	13.33	8.94	15.17	18.79	6.57
Snacks and nonalcoholic beverages	**9.76**	**9.57**	**9.76**	**8.90**	**10.23**	**10.32**	**10.21**	**10.50**
At fast-food restaurants*	8.55	8.05	8.49	8.20	8.59	8.99	8.86	9.20
At full-service restaurants	11.15	11.61	9.98	9.74	14.19	11.95	11.42	13.00
At vending machines, mobile vendors	3.89	5.01	3.95	3.69	4.25	3.46	3.67	2.99
At employer and school cafeterias	4.45	4.32	6.22	3.08	4.03	4.27	4.56	4.06

	total households	less than high school graduate	high school graduate	some college	associate's degree	college graduate total	bachelor's degree	master's, professional, doctorate
Breakfast and brunch	**$14.70**	**$15.90**	**$14.71**	**$13.72**	**$15.00**	**$14.92**	**$14.89**	**$14.98**
At fast-food restaurants*	10.04	11.37	9.99	9.66	9.72	10.04	9.79	10.47
At full-service restaurants	19.47	17.63	18.97	17.97	19.79	21.83	22.56	20.56
At vending machines, mobile vendors	3.13	4.23	3.18	3.30	3.88	2.69	2.43	2.65
At employer and school cafeterias	7.03	7.81	6.28	7.12	7.85	7.01	7.06	7.06
ALCOHOL, AMOUNT SPENT	**31.71**	**25.64**	**28.25**	**30.33**	**32.58**	**35.25**	**34.99**	**35.72**
Consumed at home	**28.77**	**24.10**	**24.84**	**27.83**	**27.03**	**33.18**	**32.40**	**34.59**
Beer and ale	20.80	22.30	20.64	22.39	20.14	19.51	19.66	19.40
Whiskey	37.29	33.33	48.15	46.94	25.00	30.93	26.50	46.67
Wine	24.45	17.49	18.03	20.39	22.52	29.13	27.77	31.25
Other alcoholic beverages	22.12	16.36	21.34	20.70	19.57	24.09	25.31	21.87
Consumed away from home (except on trips)	**23.05**	**20.49**	**22.04**	**22.11**	**25.21**	**23.78**	**23.86**	**23.65**
Beer and ale at restaurants, bars	15.66	15.53	17.25	14.69	18.74	14.73	15.18	13.68
Wine at restaurants, bars	16.95	13.54	13.71	15.85	13.66	18.94	18.23	20.21
Other alcoholic beverages at restaurants, bars	18.23	18.63	17.66	17.70	19.70	18.27	17.69	19.35

The category fast-food restaurants also includes take-out, delivery, concession stands, buffets, and cafeterias other than employer and school.
Source: Calculations by New Strategist based on the Bureau of Labor Statistics' 2008 Consumer Expenditure Survey

CHAPTER 5

Buyers of Gifts for People in Other Households, 2008

The Consumer Expenditure Survey collects data on gifts bought only for people in other households, not for people within households. Consequently, the percentage of households that buy gifts and the amount households spend on gifts are greatly understated. Much of the multi-household gift spending is for family members living elsewhere, such as adult children and grandchildren.

Quarterly spending

During the average quarter of 2008, 28 percent of households purchased gifts for people in other households, spending an average of $831 on those gifts during the quarter. A substantial 15 percent of households purchased clothes for people in other households, the figure peaking at 19 percent among householders aged 55 to 64. Only 2 percent of households gave gifts of education to people in other households during the average quarter of 2008, but the figure reached 5 percent among householders aged 45 to 54. At $3,603 on average, the amount spent on gifts of education during the average quarter far surpassed spending on any other type of gift.

Weekly spending

During the average week of 2008, 18 percent of households purchased gifts for people in other households. The buyers spent an average of $51 on the item(s). During the average week, 9 percent of households bought gifts of apparel and 5 percent bought gifts of food. Those who gave gifts of apparel spent an average of $47 on the items. The most popular apparel categories are clothes for infants, many being purchased by grandparents.

Top Gift Categories

(gifts for people in other households bought by the largest percentage of households during an average week, 2008)

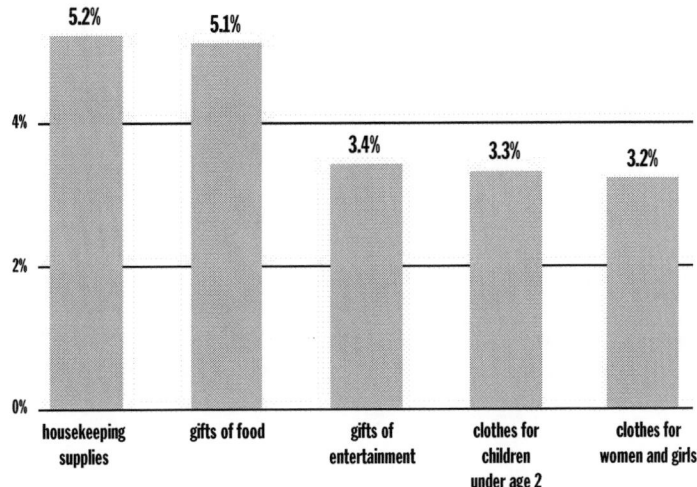

Table 5.1 Percent Buying Gifts for People in Other Households by Age, Average Quarter, 2008

(percent of households buying gifts of products or services for people in other households during the average quarter, by age of householder, 2008)

GIFTS, PERCENT BUYING	total households	under 25	25 to 34	35 to 44	45 to 54	55 to 64	65 to 74	75+
	27.6%	20.4%	24.6%	23.9%	32.4%	35.3%	29.4%	19.8%
Housing	9.3	6.8	7.3	7.1	11.8	12.7	9.7	7.6
Household textiles	2.0	0.9	1.4	1.5	2.7	2.7	2.3	1.8
Appliances and miscellaneous housewares	1.7	0.6	1.1	1.1	2.5	2.6	1.4	1.0
Major appliances	0.4	0.1	0.2	0.4	0.5	0.6	0.3	0.2
Small appliances and miscellaneous housewares	1.3	0.5	1.0	0.8	2.1	2.1	1.2	0.9
Miscellaneous household equipment	4.2	3.5	3.5	3.3	4.8	6.1	4.7	3.0
Other housing	3.0	2.7	1.9	2.1	4.6	4.0	2.6	2.5
Apparel and services	15.2	10.8	14.6	13.9	17.8	19.2	15.3	8.7
Males, aged 2 and over	3.9	2.0	2.5	3.1	5.3	5.7	4.4	2.4
Females, aged 2 and over	4.9	2.3	3.4	3.7	6.2	7.5	6.0	2.8
Children under age 2	8.5	6.8	9.6	8.5	9.5	10.0	7.4	4.0
Other apparel products and services	3.7	2.1	2.9	3.5	4.5	5.1	4.1	1.7
Jewelry and watches	1.7	1.3	1.7	1.7	1.7	2.0	1.8	0.9
All other apparel products and services	2.2	0.8	1.5	2.0	3.1	3.3	2.6	0.8
Transportation	4.5	2.6	2.8	4.0	5.6	6.6	5.2	2.9
Health care	1.0	–	0.3	0.7	2.0	1.4	0.7	0.7
Entertainment	8.5	5.0	6.4	7.2	9.4	13.2	10.5	4.6
Toys, games, arts and crafts, and tricycles	5.2	2.9	3.5	4.4	5.5	8.6	7.0	3.1
Other entertainment	4.1	2.3	3.4	3.4	5.0	6.1	4.7	1.8
Education	2.2	0.3	0.6	1.4	5.1	3.2	1.5	1.0
All other gifts	4.7	2.9	3.4	3.6	5.7	6.6	5.7	3.5

Note: "–" means sample is too small to make a reliable estimate.
Source: Bureau of Labor Statistics, unpublished data from the 2008 Consumer Expenditure Survey

Table 5.2 Amount Buyers Spent on Gifts for People in Other Households by Age, <u>Average Quarter</u>, 2008

(average amount spent by households buying gifts of products or services for people in other households during the average quarter, by age of householder, 2008)

	total households	under 25	25 to 34	35 to 44	45 to 54	55 to 64	65 to 74	75+
GIFTS, AMOUNT SPENT	$830.84	$296.96	$348.38	$596.94	$1,248.53	$1,037.94	$766.98	$784.16
Housing	401.21	220.90	232.13	311.53	555.52	467.26	352.84	312.42
Household textiles	82.09	37.50	59.42	56.17	96.98	84.96	107.13	80.03
Appliances and miscellaneous housewares	186.97	189.09	104.82	187.28	168.18	235.00	217.66	184.95
Major appliances	441.67	860.00	172.06	378.29	389.29	536.48	539.52	671.67
Small appliances and miscellaneous housewares	111.57	40.00	93.04	90.58	110.85	134.48	123.08	101.99
Miscellaneous household equipment	149.82	68.02	87.00	137.04	207.24	147.41	174.05	138.72
Other housing	866.53	423.97	628.42	708.78	1,047.14	1,035.52	796.88	633.46
Apparel and services	192.34	138.81	193.81	164.40	204.86	212.27	202.37	172.74
Males, aged 2 and over	164.57	115.74	117.76	136.89	184.91	191.58	143.28	179.38
Females, aged 2 and over	171.81	115.28	126.79	130.98	190.06	181.32	209.16	184.34
Children under age 2	94.20	103.42	102.82	92.26	93.36	86.91	92.14	94.49
Other apparel products and services	175.96	143.99	390.10	168.56	134.19	147.83	131.17	106.32
Jewelry and watches	259.88	181.87	607.98	237.93	173.84	192.28	170.20	126.86
All other apparel products and services	94.59	74.70	77.20	91.41	96.84	107.28	91.18	77.85
Transportation	547.15	565.37	380.46	424.18	562.88	550.72	607.70	963.78
Health care	515.00	–	221.00	229.29	348.97	540.69	385.92	2,401.84
Entertainment	220.30	144.64	173.48	212.10	237.85	224.83	248.39	247.26
Toys, games, arts and crafts, and tricycles	156.53	129.31	131.09	134.69	163.07	172.27	172.19	146.60
Other entertainment	257.00	152.08	196.28	271.37	268.11	242.68	302.10	380.34
Education	3,602.60	1,017.31	1,614.55	1,851.80	3,779.31	4,434.64	3,788.78	3,885.82
All other gifts	520.82	181.68	237.95	872.66	503.17	441.82	677.47	517.71

Note: "–" means sample is too small to make a reliable estimate.
Source: Calculations by New Strategist based on the Bureau of Labor Statistics' 2008 Consumer Expenditure Survey

Table 5.3 Percent Buying Gifts for People in Other Households by Age, Average Week, 2008

(percent of households buying gifts of products or services for people in other households during the average week, by age of householder, 2008)

GIFTS, PERCENT BUYING	total households	under 25	25 to 34	35 to 44	45 to 54	55 to 64	65 to 74	75+
	18.1%	13.5%	17.9%	18.6%	19.9%	20.5%	18.6%	12.4%
Food	5.1	2.3	4.7	5.0	5.5	7.0	5.6	3.3
Housing	7.4	3.4	6.1	6.8	9.1	9.5	7.8	5.6
Housekeeping supplies	5.2	3.1	4.4	5.0	6.4	6.3	5.0	4.2
Laundry and cleaning supplies	0.5	0.7	0.2	0.8	0.6	0.5	0.6	0.1
Other household products	1.5	0.8	1.1	1.4	2.5	1.5	1.3	0.6
Postage and stationery	4.1	2.5	3.6	3.9	4.7	5.1	3.8	3.7
Household textiles	0.7	0.2	0.6	0.4	1.2	0.9	0.6	0.3
Appliances and miscellaneous housewares	0.9	0.4	0.7	0.8	1.3	0.9	1.0	0.5
Major appliances	0.1	–	0.1	–	0.1	0.0	–	0.1
Small appliances and miscellaneous housewares	0.8	0.4	0.6	0.8	1.2	0.9	1.0	0.4
Miscellaneous household equipment	2.8	1.0	2.0	2.3	4.0	4.0	3.4	1.6
Other housing	0.1	–	–	0.1	0.1	0.2	–	–
Apparel and services	8.6	7.5	9.5	9.7	9.3	8.5	7.7	4.7
Males, aged 2 and over	2.1	1.6	1.2	2.5	2.4	2.3	2.9	1.2
Females, aged 2 and over	3.2	2.4	2.3	2.8	4.2	3.8	3.8	2.0
Children under age 2	3.3	3.7	5.7	4.4	2.6	2.1	2.1	1.0
Other apparel products and services	2.2	1.1	1.8	2.4	2.4	2.5	2.5	1.3
Transportation	0.1	0.1	0.1	0.0	0.2	0.1	–	0.1
Health care	0.4	0.1	0.3	0.5	0.6	0.5	0.5	0.1
Entertainment	3.4	1.7	3.2	3.3	4.0	4.7	4.3	1.2
Education	1.0	0.3	1.0	0.7	1.1	1.4	1.5	0.4
All other gifts	2.6	2.9	2.0	2.3	3.3	3.2	2.7	1.5

Note: "–" means sample is too small to make a reliable estimate.
Source: Bureau of Labor Statistics, unpublished data from the 2008 Consumer Expenditure Survey

Table 5.4 Amount Buyers Spent on Gifts for People in Other Households by Age, <u>Average Week</u>, 2008

(average amount spent by households buying gifts of products or services for people in other households during the average week, by age of householder, 2008)

	total households	under 25	25 to 34	35 to 44	45 to 54	55 to 64	65 to 74	75+
GIFTS, AMOUNT SPENT	$51.38	$43.26	$43.01	$44.75	$64.72	$52.69	$61.32	$30.97
Food	19.77	28.02	18.90	17.96	22.02	17.55	22.82	18.40
Housing	27.58	23.55	28.60	17.28	39.58	25.21	28.48	14.87
Housekeeping supplies	11.75	16.56	11.39	8.40	13.19	10.90	16.17	7.95
Laundry and cleaning supplies	5.77	4.05	4.35	4.88	5.36	12.96	5.45	0.00
Other household products	12.33	22.89	12.38	5.84	15.75	8.44	19.84	7.27
Postage and stationery	9.54	11.84	10.08	7.89	8.97	9.36	14.06	7.57
Household textiles	32.35	8.33	23.33	14.29	52.54	26.09	21.67	24.24
Appliances and miscellaneous housewares	31.76	13.89	48.65	14.47	42.06	32.95	17.89	26.09
Major appliances	80.00	–	107.69	–	71.43	50.00	–	83.33
Small appliances and miscellaneous housewares	28.05	13.89	33.87	14.47	37.90	30.68	17.89	17.50
Miscellaneous household equipment	31.80	22.00	37.56	24.14	39.49	26.75	33.33	19.23
Other housing	37.50	–	–	30.00	36.36	54.55	–	–
Apparel and services	46.90	38.07	37.68	44.52	55.72	44.94	68.27	27.08
Males, aged 2 and over	37.80	34.76	28.69	38.10	41.60	34.93	48.45	19.33
Females, aged 2 and over	44.79	30.13	28.76	43.48	54.89	44.88	52.00	30.61
Children under age 2	28.13	34.22	29.95	26.70	27.73	24.41	27.49	18.95
Other apparel products and services	40.93	23.68	45.90	39.34	47.93	32.11	53.04	20.61
Transportation	20.00	0.00	28.57	0.00	11.11	28.57	–	20.00
Health care	11.90	0.00	9.68	9.62	15.52	13.46	11.11	0.00
Entertainment	36.05	50.59	26.67	33.03	37.22	41.19	38.59	26.72
Education	10.20	6.06	5.00	7.04	13.76	9.86	15.07	10.26
All other gifts	32.82	22.26	26.73	31.62	35.26	36.16	27.04	53.79

Note: "–" means sample is too small to make a reliable estimate.
Source: Calculations by New Strategist based on the Bureau of Labor Statistics' 2008 Consumer Expenditure Survey

Table 5.5 Percent Buying Gifts for People in Other Households by Household Income, <u>Average Quarter</u>, 2008

(percent of households buying gifts of products or services for people in other households during the average quarter, by before-tax income of household, 2008)

GIFTS, PERCENT BUYING	total households	under $20,000	$20,000– $39,999	$40,000– $49,999	$50,000– $69,999	$70,000– $79,999	$80,000– $99,999	$100,000 or more
GIFTS, PERCENT BUYING	**27.6%**	**17.6%**	**23.6%**	**26.3%**	**30.2%**	**32.3%**	**33.8%**	**38.6%**
Housing	**9.3**	**6.0**	**7.8**	**8.7**	**10.3**	**10.2**	**11.5**	**13.3**
Household textiles	2.0	1.2	1.7	1.4	2.5	2.4	2.5	3.0
Appliances and miscellaneous housewares	1.7	0.6	1.3	1.2	2.2	2.0	2.3	2.7
Major appliances	0.4	0.1	0.4	0.1	0.4	0.3	0.4	0.8
Small appliances and miscellaneous housewares	1.3	0.5	1.0	1.1	1.9	1.7	1.9	2.0
Miscellaneous household equipment	4.2	2.3	3.5	4.7	4.7	5.1	5.5	5.9
Other housing	3.0	2.6	2.6	2.5	2.6	2.9	3.0	4.9
Apparel and services	**15.2**	**9.3**	**13.3**	**14.0**	**16.8**	**18.0**	**18.5**	**21.0**
Males, aged 2 and over	3.9	1.9	3.4	3.4	4.5	4.5	4.7	5.7
Females, aged 2 and over	4.9	2.5	4.4	4.1	5.5	5.7	6.2	7.1
Children under age 2	8.5	5.4	7.3	7.8	8.9	10.6	10.3	12.1
Other apparel products and services	3.7	1.9	3.1	3.6	4.2	4.3	4.1	5.7
Jewelry and watches	1.7	0.9	1.4	1.7	1.9	2.0	2.1	2.4
All other apparel products and services	2.2	1.0	1.8	2.1	2.6	2.4	2.5	3.8
Transportation	**4.5**	**1.7**	**2.8**	**4.0**	**5.2**	**5.9**	**5.9**	**8.2**
Health care	**1.0**	**0.4**	**0.9**	**0.7**	**0.7**	**0.8**	**1.2**	**2.0**
Entertainment	**8.5**	**4.4**	**6.5**	**7.8**	**9.1**	**11.0**	**10.7**	**13.5**
Toys, games, arts and crafts, and tricycles	5.2	3.0	4.6	4.9	5.8	6.6	6.6	7.2
Other entertainment	4.1	1.7	2.7	3.5	4.4	5.7	5.1	7.6
Education	**2.2**	**0.6**	**0.9**	**0.9**	**1.9**	**2.9**	**3.4**	**6.0**
All other gifts	**4.7**	**2.2**	**3.2**	**4.3**	**5.7**	**5.8**	**6.1**	**7.7**

Source: Bureau of Labor Statistics, unpublished data from the 2008 Consumer Expenditure Survey

Table 5.6 Amount Buyers Spent on Gifts for People in Other Households by Household Income, <u>Average Quarter</u>, 2008

(average amount spent by households buying gifts of products or services for people in other households during the average quarter, by before-tax income of household, 2008)

	total households	under $20,000	$20,000– $39,999	$40,000– $49,999	$50,000– $69,999	$70,000– $79,999	$80,000– $99,999	$100,000 or more
GIFTS, AMOUNT SPENT	$830.84	$436.08	$419.12	$646.68	$586.62	$664.71	$793.36	$1,647.43
Housing	401.21	265.97	299.30	327.53	266.59	386.80	334.92	694.40
Household textiles	82.09	63.21	83.93	65.76	78.08	71.09	79.25	101.10
Appliances and miscellaneous housewares	186.97	111.82	156.64	108.27	133.15	150.00	157.24	294.33
Major appliances	441.67	428.80	323.01	309.62	298.03	586.21	234.76	588.92
Small appliances and miscellaneous housewares	111.57	62.36	84.99	82.46	98.93	73.80	136.59	160.05
Miscellaneous household equipment	149.82	96.87	82.24	148.15	111.11	146.56	151.82	251.31
Other housing	866.53	471.22	663.98	780.59	682.94	955.79	819.65	1,343.88
Apparel and services	192.34	166.44	151.20	185.60	178.39	186.28	191.40	252.66
Males, aged 2 and over	164.57	127.86	130.08	128.64	139.97	156.07	165.40	229.80
Females, aged 2 and over	171.81	119.08	147.85	160.84	141.30	194.24	195.49	218.51
Children under age 2	94.20	90.37	76.68	89.46	89.89	90.69	98.71	113.41
Other apparel products and services	175.96	252.71	112.70	221.09	186.91	135.71	131.74	191.28
Jewelry and watches	259.88	434.62	149.16	353.80	289.12	177.51	169.95	253.68
All other apparel products and services	94.59	61.56	70.72	88.39	92.06	93.13	76.93	125.86
Transportation	547.15	387.24	546.13	778.96	347.94	484.53	392.48	695.05
Health care	515.00	761.70	199.18	245.71	1,306.76	207.41	393.91	542.00
Entertainment	220.30	141.09	180.46	189.97	170.19	210.45	227.46	311.18
Toys, games, arts and crafts, and tricycles	156.53	104.53	131.59	180.80	132.97	139.20	172.56	204.84
Other entertainment	257.00	186.70	208.21	175.94	176.81	243.84	255.21	360.06
Education	3,602.60	2,554.36	1,333.77	5,101.06	2,476.06	2,230.95	3,138.69	4,635.64
All other gifts	520.82	501.58	396.99	405.35	439.71	231.80	400.41	772.36

Source: Calculations by New Strategist based on the Bureau of Labor Statistics' 2008 Consumer Expenditure Survey

Table 5.7 Percent Buying Gifts for People in Other Households by Household Income, <u>Average Week</u>, 2008

(percent of households buying gifts of products or services for people in other households during the average week, by before-tax income of household, 2008)

	total households	under $20,000	$20,000– $39,999	$40,000– $49,999	$50,000– $69,999	$70,000– $79,999	$80,000– $99,999	$100,000 or more
GIFTS, PERCENT BUYING	**18.1%**	**11.3%**	**14.7%**	**16.4%**	**20.9%**	**19.2%**	**21.7%**	**26.8%**
Food	**5.1**	**2.8**	**4.2**	**4.8**	**6.3**	**5.0**	**5.2**	**8.2**
Housing	**7.4**	**3.2**	**5.4**	**5.8**	**8.5**	**8.1**	**9.8**	**13.1**
Housekeeping supplies	5.2	2.1	3.6	4.2	6.6	5.9	6.8	9.1
Laundry and cleaning supplies	0.5	0.4	0.5	0.1	0.4	0.3	0.7	1.1
Other household products	1.5	0.8	0.9	1.2	1.2	1.7	1.7	3.2
Postage and stationery	4.1	1.3	2.7	3.4	5.6	4.7	5.7	7.0
Household textiles	0.7	0.4	0.4	0.4	0.5	1.1	0.8	1.5
Appliances and miscellaneous housewares	0.9	0.3	0.5	0.5	0.9	0.9	1.0	2.0
Major appliances	0.1	–	0.1	–	0.1	–	–	0.2
Small appliances and miscellaneous housewares	0.8	0.3	0.4	0.5	0.8	0.9	1.0	1.9
Miscellaneous household equipment	2.8	1.1	2.1	1.9	2.8	2.9	3.4	5.9
Other housing	0.1	0.0	0.1	0.1	0.1	0.1	0.2	0.1
Apparel and services	**8.6**	**5.4**	**7.4**	**7.8**	**9.7**	**8.9**	**9.9**	**12.1**
Males, aged 2 and over	2.1	1.4	1.8	1.9	2.1	2.0	2.6	3.2
Females, aged 2 and over	3.2	1.9	3.0	2.8	3.5	2.9	3.6	4.5
Children under age 2	3.3	1.9	2.4	2.8	3.8	3.7	3.8	5.4
Other apparel products and services	2.2	1.3	2.1	2.1	2.2	1.9	2.5	3.0
Transportation	**0.1**	**–**	**0.1**	**–**	**0.1**	**0.1**	**0.3**	**0.2**
Health care	**0.4**	**0.4**	**0.3**	**0.4**	**0.4**	**0.4**	**0.5**	**0.6**
Entertainment	**3.4**	**2.2**	**2.5**	**3.0**	**3.7**	**4.0**	**4.8**	**5.3**
Education	**1.0**	**0.3**	**0.6**	**1.2**	**0.9**	**1.2**	**1.8**	**1.7**
All other gifts	**2.6**	**2.6**	**2.3**	**2.2**	**2.8**	**1.9**	**2.6**	**3.4**

Note: "–" means sample is too small to make a reliable estimate.
Source: Bureau of Labor Statistics, unpublished data from the 2008 Consumer Expenditure Survey

Table 5.8 Amount Buyers Spent on Gifts for People in Other Households by Household Income, <u>Average Week</u>, 2008

(average amount spent by households buying gifts of products or services for people in other households during the average week, by before-tax income of household, 2008)

	total households	under $20,000	$20,000–$39,999	$40,000–$49,999	$50,000–$69,999	$70,000–$79,999	$80,000–$99,999	$100,000 or more
GIFTS, AMOUNT SPENT	$51.38	$47.57	$44.62	$39.32	$45.81	$44.74	$42.40	$51.61
Food	19.77	14.00	19.22	24.42	16.13	18.16	16.53	18.16
Housing	27.58	25.17	20.45	22.38	21.50	21.88	30.09	23.38
Housekeeping supplies	11.75	15.37	8.75	12.74	10.35	10.94	12.18	9.53
Laundry and cleaning supplies	5.77	11.94	3.42	25.00	4.88	5.13	10.34	5.97
Other household products	12.33	17.81	8.05	20.69	6.50	12.12	6.47	10.40
Postage and stationery	9.54	10.50	8.35	7.99	10.32	9.09	12.34	7.53
Household textiles	32.35	17.06	26.91	27.91	10.64	19.05	51.38	9.64
Appliances and miscellaneous housewares	31.76	4.62	23.28	25.49	34.88	24.07	21.18	21.36
Major appliances	80.00	–	39.08	–	20.00	66.67	–	–
Small appliances and miscellaneous housewares	28.05	4.62	15.88	25.49	35.37	21.57	21.18	21.36
Miscellaneous household equipment	31.80	31.73	25.55	24.23	26.79	26.63	32.30	37.28
Other housing	37.50	26.67	29.24	57.14	75.00	60.00	57.14	26.09
Apparel and services	46.90	43.45	40.26	32.95	42.14	40.32	38.88	52.32
Males, aged 2 and over	37.80	34.95	31.78	20.21	36.59	32.00	41.12	50.00
Females, aged 2 and over	44.79	38.64	33.62	29.64	46.59	37.86	39.12	39.61
Children under age 2	28.13	23.48	29.18	17.61	23.68	24.62	25.07	41.91
Other apparel products and services	40.93	47.70	34.39	41.35	36.49	38.95	30.37	34.25
Transportation	20.00	–	11.00	–	14.29	16.67	9.09	10.71
Health care	11.90	10.25	10.70	11.90	14.63	13.16	10.53	5.88
Entertainment	36.05	37.47	35.82	26.26	39.40	35.64	19.14	33.82
Education	10.20	11.41	12.68	9.48	10.64	10.14	9.02	5.65
All other gifts	32.82	43.49	28.51	20.81	35.82	31.73	24.35	38.78

Note: "–" means sample is too small to make a reliable estimate.
Source: Calculations by New Strategist based on the Bureau of Labor Statistics' 2008 Consumer Expenditure Survey

Table 5.9 Percent of High-Income Households Buying Gifts for People in Other Households, <u>Average Quarter</u>, 2008

(percent of high-income households buying gifts of products or services for people in other households during the average quarter, by before-tax income of household, 2008)

	total households	$100,000 or more	$100,000– $119,999	$120,000– $149,999	$150,000 or more
GIFTS, PERCENT BUYING	**27.6%**	**38.6%**	**35.8%**	**36.3%**	**42.6%**
Housing	**9.3**	**13.3**	**11.6**	**11.5**	**15.8**
Household textiles	2.0	3.0	3.2	2.3	3.2
Appliances and miscellaneous housewares	1.7	2.7	2.5	1.8	3.5
Major appliances	0.4	0.8	0.4	0.7	1.2
Small appliances and miscellaneous housewares	1.3	2.0	2.2	1.3	2.4
Miscellaneous household equipment	4.2	5.9	5.2	5.7	6.6
Other housing	3.0	4.9	3.6	3.3	7.1
Apparel and services	**15.2**	**21.0**	**19.8**	**20.9**	**22.0**
Males, aged 2 and over	3.9	5.7	5.0	5.3	6.5
Females, aged 2 and over	4.9	7.1	6.3	5.5	8.8
Children under age 2	8.5	12.1	12.6	12.8	11.2
Other apparel products and services	3.7	5.7	4.4	5.5	6.8
Jewelry and watches	1.7	2.4	1.3	2.7	3.1
All other apparel products and services	2.2	3.8	3.3	3.3	4.6
Transportation	**4.5**	**8.2**	**6.8**	**7.4**	**10.0**
Health care	**1.0**	**2.0**	**1.2**	**1.8**	**2.9**
Entertainment	**8.5**	**13.5**	**12.3**	**10.9**	**16.3**
Toys, games, arts and crafts, and tricycles	5.2	7.2	7.0	5.9	8.4
Other entertainment	4.1	7.6	6.2	6.0	9.8
Education	**2.2**	**6.0**	**4.3**	**4.6**	**8.3**
All other gifts	**4.7**	**7.7**	**6.4**	**6.0**	**9.8**

Source: Bureau of Labor Statistics, unpublished data from the 2008 Consumer Expenditure Survey

Table 5.10 Amount High-Income Buyers Spent on Gifts for People in Other Households, <u>Average Quarter</u>, 2008

(average amount spent by high-income households buying gifts of products or services for people in other households during the average quarter, by before-tax income of household, 2008)

	total households	$100,000 or more	$100,000–$119,999	$120,000–$149,999	$150,000 or more
GIFTS, AMOUNT SPENT	**$830.84**	**$1,647.43**	**$928.47**	**$1,005.43**	**$2,505.72**
Housing	**401.21**	**694.40**	**441.59**	**380.16**	**998.13**
Household textiles	82.09	101.10	93.20	73.28	120.36
Appliances and miscellaneous housewares	186.97	294.33	201.73	158.70	396.30
Major appliances	441.67	588.92	342.07	187.69	810.81
Small appliances and miscellaneous housewares	111.57	160.05	163.89	127.88	168.14
Miscellaneous household equipment	149.82	251.31	150.67	174.43	359.88
Other housing	866.53	1,343.88	984.14	879.14	1,641.54
Apparel and services	**192.34**	**252.66**	**201.14**	**196.83**	**325.64**
Males, aged 2 and over	164.57	229.80	168.25	196.97	286.46
Females, aged 2 and over	171.81	218.51	202.91	175.00	245.44
Children under age 2	94.20	113.41	101.61	99.71	134.63
Other apparel products and services	175.96	191.28	134.21	153.64	241.73
Jewelry and watches	259.88	253.68	197.69	191.67	308.20
All other apparel products and services	94.59	125.86	100.84	100.84	152.64
Transportation	**547.15**	**695.05**	**752.06**	**521.16**	**748.18**
Health care	**515.00**	**542.00**	**412.30**	**723.44**	**510.47**
Entertainment	**220.30**	**311.18**	**244.47**	**282.04**	**365.89**
Toys, games, arts and crafts, and tricycles	156.53	204.84	195.29	201.92	213.05
Other entertainment	257.00	360.06	265.26	316.67	427.38
Education	**3,602.60**	**4,635.64**	**2,170.98**	**2,633.19**	**6,420.41**
All other gifts	**520.82**	**772.36**	**518.09**	**875.79**	**867.28**

Source: Calculations by New Strategist based on the Bureau of Labor Statistics' 2008 Consumer Expenditure Survey

Table 5.11 Percent of High-Income Households Buying Gifts for People in Other Households, <u>Average Week</u>, 2008

(percent of high-income households buying gifts of products or services for people in other households during the average week, by before-tax income of household, 2008)

	total households	$100,000 or more	$100,000–$119,999	$120,000–$149,999	$150,000 or more
GIFTS, PERCENT BUYING	**18.1%**	**26.8%**	**26.3%**	**27.5%**	**26.9%**
Food	**5.1**	**8.2**	**8.9**	**8.7**	**7.0**
Housing	**7.4**	**13.1**	**13.8**	**11.9**	**13.5**
Housekeeping supplies	5.2	9.1	10.5	8.3	8.4
Laundry and cleaning supplies	0.5	1.1	1.3	1.2	0.7
Other household products	1.5	3.2	3.1	3.0	3.3
Postage and stationery	4.1	7.0	8.6	5.8	6.4
Household textiles	0.7	1.5	1.3	0.9	2.2
Appliances and miscellaneous housewares	0.9	2.0	2.2	1.9	1.9
Major appliances	0.1	0.2	0.3	0.1	0.1
Small appliances and miscellaneous housewares	0.8	1.9	2.1	1.8	1.9
Miscellaneous household equipment	2.8	5.9	5.0	5.6	7.0
Other housing	0.1	0.1	0.1	0.2	–
Apparel and services	**8.6**	**12.1**	**12.2**	**12.5**	**11.9**
Males, aged 2 and over	2.1	3.2	3.0	3.0	3.6
Females, aged 2 and over	3.2	4.5	4.9	3.5	4.8
Children under age 2	3.3	5.4	5.7	5.9	4.6
Other apparel products and services	2.2	3.0	2.7	3.3	3.1
Transportation	**0.1**	**0.2**	**0.2**	**0.3**	**0.1**
Health care	**0.4**	**0.6**	**0.6**	**0.5**	**0.6**
Entertainment	**3.4**	**5.3**	**4.2**	**5.6**	**6.3**
Education	**1.0**	**1.7**	**0.9**	**1.9**	**2.3**
All other gifts	**2.6**	**3.4**	**2.4**	**4.6**	**3.6**

Note: "–" means sample is too small to make a reliable estimate.
Source: Bureau of Labor Statistics, unpublished data from the 2008 Consumer Expenditure Survey

Table 5.12 Amount High-Income Buyers Spent on Gifts for People in Other Households, <u>Average Week</u>, 2008

(average amount spent by high-income households buying gifts of products or services for people in other households during the average week, by before-tax income of household, 2008)

	total households	$100,000 or more	$100,000–$119,999	$120,000–$149,999	$150,000 or more
GIFTS, AMOUNT SPENT	**$51.38**	**$68.80**	**$57.38**	**$68.33**	**$80.71**
Food	**19.77**	**24.91**	**21.33**	**25.77**	**28.65**
Housing	**27.58**	**38.36**	**30.84**	**37.13**	**47.06**
Housekeeping supplies	11.75	13.82	13.66	15.48	12.63
Laundry and cleaning supplies	5.77	6.67	7.87	6.45	2.99
Other household products	12.33	15.24	14.52	13.58	17.58
Postage and stationery	9.54	10.13	10.29	13.77	7.22
Household textiles	32.35	49.66	49.23	28.41	56.48
Appliances and miscellaneous housewares	31.76	43.72	42.86	26.34	59.26
Major appliances	80.00	120.00	132.00	77.78	100.00
Small appliances and miscellaneous housewares	28.05	36.27	28.71	23.73	53.44
Miscellaneous household equipment	31.80	36.56	24.10	42.25	42.06
Other housing	37.50	20.00	25.00	23.81	–
Apparel and services	**46.90**	**62.60**	**51.81**	**62.28**	**74.20**
Males, aged 2 and over	37.80	45.03	26.00	52.82	56.51
Females, aged 2 and over	44.79	65.85	59.63	66.86	72.08
Children under age 2	28.13	30.47	25.27	38.71	28.76
Other apparel products and services	40.93	51.49	43.07	46.79	63.26
Transportation	**20.00**	**27.78**	**50.00**	**7.41**	**10.00**
Health care	**11.90**	**12.50**	**20.69**	**7.84**	**10.34**
Entertainment	**36.05**	**42.67**	**42.24**	**47.93**	**39.14**
Education	**10.20**	**12.65**	**10.23**	**9.63**	**15.65**
All other gifts	**32.82**	**35.09**	**24.07**	**31.73**	**46.35**

Note: "–" means sample is too small to make a reliable estimate.
Source: Calculations by New Strategist based on the Bureau of Labor Statistics' 2008 Consumer Expenditure Survey

Table 5.13 Percent Buying Gifts for People in Other Households by Household Type, Average Quarter, 2008

(percent of households buying gifts of products or services for people in other households during the average quarter, by type of household, 2008)

| | total married couples | married couples, no children | married couples with children | | | | single parent, at least one child <18 | single person |
			total	oldest child under 6	oldest child 6 to 17	oldest child 18 or older		
GIFTS, PERCENT BUYING	**31.5%**	**36.9%**	**27.7%**	**26.9%**	**25.6%**	**31.9%**	**21.2%**	**24.1%**
Housing	**10.3**	**12.7**	**8.5**	**7.0**	**7.9**	**10.5**	**7.4**	**8.8**
Household textiles	2.4	3.0	1.9	1.7	1.5	2.8	1.5	1.5
Appliances and miscellaneous housewares	2.1	2.6	1.6	0.9	1.4	2.6	0.8	1.2
Major appliances	0.5	0.5	0.4	0.2	0.3	0.6	0.0	0.2
Small appliances and miscellaneous housewares	1.7	2.1	1.3	0.7	1.1	2.0	0.8	1.0
Miscellaneous household equipment	4.5	5.6	3.8	3.6	3.5	4.3	2.7	4.5
Other housing	3.3	4.0	2.8	1.7	2.7	3.5	2.7	3.0
Apparel and services	**17.8**	**20.2**	**16.1**	**17.7**	**14.7**	**17.5**	**11.6**	**11.6**
Males, aged 2 and over	4.5	6.6	2.9	2.5	2.6	3.7	2.4	3.4
Females, aged 2 and over	5.6	7.5	4.2	3.2	3.7	5.7	2.9	4.5
Children under age 2	10.7	10.3	11.0	13.2	10.3	11.0	6.9	4.7
Other apparel products and services	4.0	5.1	3.0	2.4	2.4	4.4	2.4	3.7
Jewelry and watches	1.6	2.0	1.4	1.4	1.3	1.5	1.4	1.9
All other apparel products and services	2.6	3.5	1.9	1.4	1.3	3.3	1.4	1.9
Transportation	**5.4**	**7.0**	**4.2**	**2.9**	**3.9**	**5.4**	**3.0**	**3.9**
Health care	**1.1**	**1.5**	**0.8**	**0.1**	**0.9**	**1.0**	**0.6**	**0.9**
Entertainment	**9.8**	**13.1**	**7.3**	**6.3**	**6.5**	**9.5**	**3.9**	**7.7**
Toys, games, arts and crafts, and tricycles	6.2	8.8	4.5	3.5	3.7	6.4	1.8	4.5
Other entertainment	4.5	5.8	3.5	3.3	3.2	4.2	2.3	3.9
Education	**3.2**	**3.6**	**2.9**	**0.1**	**2.5**	**5.2**	**1.6**	**1.2**
All other gifts	**5.3**	**7.4**	**3.8**	**2.8**	**3.6**	**5.0**	**3.0**	**4.5**

Source: Bureau of Labor Statistics, unpublished data from the 2008 Consumer Expenditure Survey

Table 5.14 Amount Buyers Spent on Gifts for People in Other Households by Household Type, <u>Average Quarter</u>, 2008

(average amount spent by households buying gifts of products or services for people in other households during the average quarter, by type of household, 2008)

	total married couples	married couples, no children	married couples with children				single parent, at least one child <18	single person
			total	oldest child under 6	oldest child 6 to 17	oldest child 18 or older		
GIFTS, AMOUNT SPENT	**$995.11**	**$1,069.38**	**$936.72**	**$310.82**	**$875.55**	**$1,335.55**	**$445.19**	**$684.91**
Housing	**449.03**	**463.87**	**442.20**	**227.24**	**525.73**	**419.40**	**312.11**	**341.51**
Household textiles	82.99	81.41	86.46	51.16	83.39	102.22	53.25	86.35
Appliances and miscellaneous housewares	204.49	225.78	150.92	278.74	118.20	153.79	83.84	163.33
Major appliances	473.94	604.41	304.17	900.00	211.11	268.22	393.75	503.75
Small appliances and miscellaneous housewares	120.15	127.10	105.00	93.28	94.32	116.87	67.95	94.31
Miscellaneous household equipment	180.55	176.08	191.47	132.76	247.36	141.67	77.38	119.43
Other housing	974.01	1,030.04	957.25	462.13	1,118.89	879.47	721.40	706.33
Apparel and services	**187.09**	**205.97**	**166.59**	**138.16**	**147.14**	**211.80**	**173.67**	**220.08**
Males, aged 2 and over	175.39	175.19	171.99	156.87	169.43	182.10	133.79	147.54
Females, aged 2 and over	177.71	192.03	163.13	106.13	152.10	194.29	127.18	165.79
Children under age 2	95.82	91.08	96.62	115.97	86.08	99.93	99.20	76.45
Other apparel products and services	131.01	122.37	143.33	75.42	115.98	190.95	270.76	261.99
Jewelry and watches	158.23	149.11	161.40	66.85	133.93	250.82	390.10	408.98
All other apparel products and services	100.29	95.51	109.64	65.15	85.85	136.08	65.38	90.85
Transportation	**579.95**	**614.54**	**509.29**	**716.13**	**304.71**	**698.48**	**190.71**	**478.16**
Health care	**449.10**	**551.16**	**301.95**	**46.43**	**334.07**	**255.21**	**363.60**	**760.83**
Entertainment	**245.13**	**241.51**	**251.12**	**198.93**	**259.56**	**261.43**	**139.85**	**183.36**
Toys, games, arts and crafts, and tricycles	173.64	173.40	168.79	152.57	157.41	185.46	102.99	127.38
Other entertainment	289.69	281.30	309.30	220.71	340.50	309.14	157.86	213.36
Education	**3,873.67**	**3,990.22**	**3,991.26**	**47.92**	**3,994.80**	**4,032.01**	**1,865.03**	**3,910.78**
All other gifts	**591.28**	**548.44**	**669.32**	**321.93**	**506.20**	**983.72**	**226.66**	**460.22**

Note: "–" means sample is too small to make a reliable estimate.
Source: Calculations by New Strategist based on the Bureau of Labor Statistics' 2008 Consumer Expenditure Survey

Table 5.15 Percent Buying Gifts for People in Other Households by Type of Household, <u>Average Week</u>, 2008

(percent of households buying gifts of products or services for people in other households during the average week, by type of household, 2008)

| | total married couples | married couples, no children | married couples with children | | | | single parent, at least one child <18 | single person |
			total	oldest child under 6	oldest child 6 to 17	oldest child 18 or older		
GIFTS, PERCENT BUYING	**21.8%**	**21.2%**	**22.9%**	**28.0%**	**22.3%**	**17.8%**	**15.5%**	**13.6%**
Food	**6.2**	**6.7**	**6.0**	**6.3**	**6.6**	**3.9**	**3.3**	**4.4**
Housing	**9.7**	**10.2**	**9.5**	**10.5**	**9.3**	**7.7**	**4.6**	**5.2**
Housekeeping supplies	6.9	6.9	7.2	8.1	7.2	5.5	2.9	3.6
Laundry and cleaning supplies	0.7	0.6	0.7	0.8	0.8	0.6	0.2	0.4
Other household products	2.1	2.0	2.2	2.1	2.3	1.9	0.9	0.8
Postage and stationery	5.5	5.5	5.7	6.9	5.5	4.3	2.4	2.7
Household textiles	0.9	1.1	0.8	0.8	0.5	0.3	0.7	0.4
Appliances and miscellaneous housewares	1.3	1.4	1.2	1.4	1.2	0.5	0.3	0.4
Major appliances	0.1	0.1	0.1	0.2	–	–	0.2	0.0
Small appliances and miscellaneous housewares	1.2	1.4	1.2	1.2	1.2	0.5	0.1	0.4
Miscellaneous household equipment	3.9	4.2	3.5	3.7	3.2	4.2	2.1	1.7
Other housing	0.1	0.1	0.1	–	0.2	–	–	0.1
Apparel and services	**10.2**	**8.8**	**11.6**	**17.6**	**10.2**	**10.1**	**9.6**	**5.4**
Males, aged 2 and over	2.3	2.3	2.4	3.9	1.4	1.7	2.4	1.7
Females, aged 2 and over	3.4	4.0	3.0	3.4	2.7	3.1	2.9	2.9
Children under age 2	4.4	2.7	5.9	11.4	5.5	5.5	4.4	0.9
Other apparel products and services	2.5	2.4	2.5	1.7	2.4	2.6	2.6	1.4
Transportation	**0.2**	**0.2**	**0.1**	**0.2**	**0.0**	**–**	**–**	**0.0**
Health care	**0.5**	**0.6**	**0.4**	**0.7**	**0.2**	**0.4**	**0.4**	**0.3**
Entertainment	**4.3**	**4.6**	**4.4**	**4.5**	**4.7**	**2.5**	**2.3**	**2.6**
Education	**1.3**	**1.3**	**1.3**	**1.4**	**1.2**	**1.4**	**0.4**	**0.6**
All other gifts	**2.9**	**3.2**	**2.8**	**2.5**	**2.9**	**2.8**	**2.3**	**2.4**

Note: "–" means sample is too small to make a reliable estimate.
Source: Bureau of Labor Statistics, unpublished data from the 2008 Consumer Expenditure Survey

Table 5.16 Amount Buyers Spent on Gifts for People in Other Households by Type of Household, <u>Average Week</u>, 2008

(average amount spent by households buying gifts of products or services for people in other households during the average week, by type of household, 2008)

| | total married couples | married couples, no children | married couples with children | | | | single parent, at least one child <18 | single person |
			total	oldest child under 6	oldest child 6 to 17	oldest child 18 or older		
GIFTS, AMOUNT SPENT	**$54.01**	**$60.60**	**$49.35**	**$39.46**	**$47.27**	**$61.79**	**$56.14**	**$44.25**
Food	**21.07**	**23.63**	**17.70**	**13.43**	**17.33**	**21.94**	**16.06**	**16.25**
Housing	**29.96**	**31.83**	**29.29**	**20.40**	**30.50**	**33.66**	**29.41**	**19.62**
Housekeeping supplies	11.24	11.98	11.02	10.31	11.58	10.30	16.72	11.76
Laundry and cleaning supplies	4.48	4.69	5.71	5.26	6.02	4.88	5.00	10.53
Other household products	13.04	13.93	12.56	6.73	11.79	16.84	15.22	10.39
Postage and stationery	8.76	9.52	8.45	9.37	9.26	6.37	13.75	11.03
Household textiles	39.08	37.14	43.04	8.54	57.41	46.72	12.33	27.78
Appliances and miscellaneous housewares	33.60	36.23	29.84	29.71	27.35	32.56	83.87	11.36
Major appliances	66.67	75.00	40.00	26.67	–	66.67	81.25	100.00
Small appliances and miscellaneous housewares	31.15	31.62	29.17	30.89	27.35	30.89	92.86	11.36
Miscellaneous household equipment	34.02	35.07	35.51	21.93	40.43	36.86	24.76	24.70
Other housing	44.44	45.45	37.50	–	37.50	–	–	50.00
Apparel and services	**47.80**	**55.29**	**43.91**	**31.58**	**42.24**	**60.41**	**54.90**	**42.27**
Males, aged 2 and over	39.66	35.06	45.64	25.90	35.00	69.14	34.43	31.18
Females, aged 2 and over	50.44	57.22	45.95	33.43	43.28	57.76	44.56	35.15
Children under age 2	29.12	34.34	26.95	24.12	29.01	27.76	41.63	20.22
Other apparel products and services	38.78	36.67	41.53	40.46	43.44	38.74	49.23	38.85
Transportation	**13.33**	**19.05**	**8.33**	**4.35**	**0.00**	**5.26**	**–**	**50.00**
Health care	**10.87**	**10.71**	**12.50**	**6.85**	**25.00**	**6.52**	**5.13**	**15.15**
Entertainment	**35.03**	**37.94**	**30.96**	**32.21**	**29.32**	**33.89**	**41.48**	**39.02**
Education	**9.77**	**9.09**	**9.02**	**4.26**	**6.50**	**16.55**	**13.89**	**9.52**
All other gifts	**33.67**	**38.41**	**31.77**	**36.36**	**26.30**	**39.85**	**23.11**	**34.02**

Note: "–" means sample is too small to make a reliable estimate.
Source: Calculations by New Strategist based on the Bureau of Labor Statistics' 2008 Consumer Expenditure Survey

Table 5.17 Percent Buying Gifts for People in Other Households by Race and Hispanic Origin, Average Quarter, 2008

(percent of households buying gifts of products or services for people in other households during the average quarter, by race and Hispanic origin of householder, 2008)

GIFTS, PERCENT BUYING	total households	Asian	black	Hispanic	non-Hispanic white and other
	27.6%	20.4%	19.4%	20.8%	30.0%
Housing	**9.3**	**5.5**	**6.2**	**5.5**	**10.4**
Household textiles	2.0	0.8	1.3	0.9	2.3
Appliances and miscellaneous housewares	1.7	1.0	0.7	0.8	1.9
Major appliances	0.4	0.2	0.2	0.2	0.4
Small appliances and miscellaneous housewares	1.3	0.8	0.6	0.6	1.6
Miscellaneous household equipment	4.2	2.7	2.4	2.1	4.9
Other housing	3.0	1.8	2.7	2.1	3.2
Apparel and services	**15.2**	**11.0**	**11.3**	**13.5**	**16.0**
Males, aged 2 and over	3.9	3.3	2.3	2.5	4.3
Females, aged 2 and over	4.9	3.3	3.1	3.1	5.4
Children under age 2	8.5	5.8	7.1	9.1	8.6
Other apparel products and services	3.7	2.8	2.5	2.5	4.0
Jewelry and watches	1.7	1.7	0.9	1.0	1.9
All other apparel products and services	2.2	1.5	1.8	1.7	2.4
Transportation	**4.5**	**3.7**	**2.0**	**2.6**	**5.2**
Health care	**1.0**	**0.6**	**0.3**	**0.6**	**1.1**
Entertainment	**8.5**	**5.4**	**4.5**	**4.6**	**9.7**
Toys, games, arts and crafts, and tricycles	5.2	3.0	3.1	2.8	5.9
Other entertainment	4.1	2.7	1.8	2.2	4.7
Education	**2.2**	**2.1**	**1.4**	**1.1**	**2.5**
All other gifts	**4.7**	**4.0**	**2.3**	**2.6**	**5.3**

Note: "Asian" and "black" include Hispanics and non-Hispanics who identify themselves as being of the respective race alone. "Hispanic" includes people of any race who identify themselves as Hispanic. "Other" includes people who identify themselves as non-Hispanic and as Alaska Native, American Indian, Asian (who are also included in the Asian column), or Native Hawaiian or other Pacific Islander as well as non-Hispanics reporting more than one race.
Source: Bureau of Labor Statistics, unpublished data from the 2008 Consumer Expenditure Survey

Table 5.18 Amount Buyers Spent on Gifts for People in Other Households by Race and Hispanic Origin, <u>Average Quarter</u>, 2008

(average amount spent by households buying gifts of products or services for people in other households during the average quarter, by race and Hispanic origin of householder, 2008)

	total households	Asian	black	Hispanic	non-Hispanic white and other
GIFTS, AMOUNT SPENT	$830.84	$1,069.98	$649.06	$596.66	$873.47
Housing	401.21	503.26	451.94	288.09	405.10
Household textiles	82.09	77.53	87.41	76.60	81.91
Appliances and miscellaneous housewares	186.97	127.89	129.73	202.30	189.25
Major appliances	441.67	338.33	185.53	486.36	454.88
Small appliances and miscellaneous housewares	111.57	89.56	101.25	85.45	113.29
Miscellaneous household equipment	149.82	138.33	124.69	117.98	153.70
Other housing	866.53	1,249.43	851.95	533.82	899.38
Apparel and services	192.34	251.85	208.83	185.32	191.36
Males, aged 2 and over	164.57	136.50	157.35	195.38	162.27
Females, aged 2 and over	171.81	207.11	179.21	186.56	169.60
Children under age 2	94.20	106.28	132.64	103.20	87.78
Other apparel products and services	175.96	365.40	199.70	196.36	171.51
Jewelry and watches	259.88	546.99	387.78	283.33	248.55
All other apparel products and services	94.59	69.48	88.76	134.97	90.55
Transportation	547.15	1,114.54	356.09	242.61	581.93
Health care	515.00	364.29	327.27	232.66	547.05
Entertainment	220.30	223.93	199.72	221.70	221.89
Toys, games, arts and crafts, and tricycles	156.53	234.87	143.75	155.69	157.75
Other entertainment	257.00	179.03	254.07	265.81	256.46
Education	3,602.60	4,140.21	2,776.65	2,912.27	3,704.27
All other gifts	520.82	424.19	648.18	977.48	477.20

Note: "Asian" and "black" include Hispanics and non-Hispanics who identify themselves as being of the respective race alone. "Hispanic" includes people of any race who identify themselves as Hispanic. "Other" includes people who identify themselves as non-Hispanic and as Alaska Native, American Indian, Asian (who are also included in the Asian column), or Native Hawaiian or other Pacific Islander as well as non-Hispanics reporting more than one race.
Source: Calculations by New Strategist based on the Bureau of Labor Statistics' 2008 Consumer Expenditure Survey

Table 5.19 Percent Buying Gifts for People in Other Households by Race and Hispanic Origin, Average Week, 2008

(percent of households buying gifts of products or services for people in other households during the average week, by race and Hispanic origin of householder, 2008)

GIFTS, PERCENT BUYING	total households	Asian	black	Hispanic	non-Hispanic white and other
	18.1%	12.1%	12.4%	15.3%	19.4%
Food	5.1	3.0	2.4	2.3	5.9
Housing	7.4	4.0	2.2	3.5	8.7
Housekeeping supplies	5.2	2.1	1.4	2.5	6.2
Laundry and cleaning supplies	0.5	0.4	0.1	0.3	0.6
Other household products	1.5	1.0	0.5	0.8	1.7
Postage and stationery	4.1	1.1	1.1	1.8	4.9
Household textiles	0.7	0.3	0.4	0.1	0.8
Appliances and miscellaneous housewares	0.9	0.7	–	0.7	1.0
Major appliances	0.1	–	–	0.1	0.1
Small appliances and miscellaneous housewares	0.8	0.7	–	0.6	1.0
Miscellaneous household equipment	2.8	1.9	0.8	1.5	3.3
Other housing	0.1	–	0.1	0.1	0.1
Apparel and services	8.6	4.9	8.3	10.8	8.3
Males, aged 2 and over	2.1	1.1	2.0	2.1	2.1
Females, aged 2 and over	3.2	1.6	2.8	3.4	3.2
Children under age 2	3.3	1.7	3.5	4.7	3.0
Other apparel products and services	2.2	1.0	2.3	3.2	2.0
Transportation	0.1	0.2	–	–	0.1
Health care	0.4	0.6	0.2	0.1	0.5
Entertainment	3.4	2.6	1.8	2.2	3.9
Education	1.0	0.8	0.3	0.2	1.2
All other gifts	2.6	2.7	2.1	1.3	2.9

Note: "Asian" and "black" include Hispanics and non-Hispanics who identify themselves as being of the respective race alone. "Hispanic" includes people of any race who identify themselves as Hispanic. "Other" includes people who identify themselves as non-Hispanic and as Alaska Native, American Indian, Asian (who are also included in the Asian column), or Native Hawaiian or other Pacific Islander as well as non-Hispanics reporting more than one race. "–" means sample is too small to make a reliable estimate.
Source: Bureau of Labor Statistics, unpublished data from the 2008 Consumer Expenditure Survey

Table 5.20 Amount Buyers Spent on Gifts for People in Other Households by Race and Hispanic Origin, <u>Average Week</u>, 2008

(average amount spent by households buying gifts of products or services for people in other households during the average week, by race and Hispanic origin of householder, 2008)

	total households	Asian	black	Hispanic	non-Hispanic white and other
GIFTS, AMOUNT SPENT	**$51.38**	**$55.86**	**$48.47**	**$44.20**	**$52.42**
Food	**19.77**	**25.58**	**15.42**	**19.91**	**20.07**
Housing	**27.58**	**33.59**	**19.18**	**28.41**	**27.78**
Housekeeping supplies	11.75	13.62	13.33	13.04	11.53
Laundry and cleaning supplies	5.77	16.22	0.00	6.25	6.45
Other household products	12.33	11.88	6.12	13.33	12.87
Postage and stationery	9.54	8.85	14.29	12.00	9.20
Household textiles	32.35	11.76	10.81	9.09	34.57
Appliances and miscellaneous housewares	31.76	41.43	–	29.41	32.00
Major appliances	80.00	–	–	16.67	100.00
Small appliances and miscellaneous housewares	28.05	41.43	–	29.03	27.84
Miscellaneous household equipment	31.80	37.31	23.17	28.77	32.13
Other housing	37.50	–	10.00	33.33	50.00
Apparel and services	**46.90**	**34.41**	**44.07**	**37.98**	**48.79**
Males, aged 2 and over	37.80	33.96	24.26	25.48	41.90
Females, aged 2 and over	44.79	36.77	40.00	40.90	46.08
Children under age 2	28.13	25.75	29.91	21.23	29.04
Other apparel products and services	40.93	35.71	42.61	36.96	41.21
Transportation	**20.00**	**6.25**	–	–	**15.38**
Health care	**11.90**	**25.81**	**8.70**	**22.22**	**12.00**
Entertainment	**36.05**	**76.72**	**47.54**	**38.81**	**34.88**
Education	**10.20**	**3.66**	**4.00**	**4.35**	**10.83**
All other gifts	32.82	28.68	33.50	25.40	33.10

Note: "Asian" and "black" include Hispanics and non-Hispanics who identify themselves as being of the respective race alone. "Hispanic" includes people of any race who identify themselves as Hispanic. "Other" includes people who identify themselves as non-Hispanic and as Alaska Native, American Indian, Asian (who are also included in the Asian column), or Native Hawaiian or other Pacific Islander as well as non-Hispanics reporting more than one race. "–" means sample is too small to make a reliable estimate.
Source: Calculations by New Strategist based on the Bureau of Labor Statistics' 2008 Consumer Expenditure Survey

Table 5.21 Percent Buying Gifts for People in Other Households by Region, Average Quarter, 2008

(percent of households buying gifts of products or services for people in other households during the average quarter, by region of residence, 2008)

GIFTS, PERCENT BUYING	total households	Northeast	Midwest	South	West
	27.6%	**27.2%**	**30.8%**	**25.6%**	**28.0%**
Housing	**9.3**	**10.1**	**10.7**	**8.5**	**8.7**
Household textiles	2.0	1.9	2.3	1.9	1.9
Appliances and miscellaneous housewares	1.7	1.4	2.1	1.7	1.5
Major appliances	0.4	0.3	0.3	0.4	0.4
Small appliances and miscellaneous housewares	1.3	1.1	1.8	1.3	1.1
Miscellaneous household equipment	4.2	5.2	5.3	3.2	4.1
Other housing	3.0	3.2	3.0	3.2	2.8
Apparel and services	**15.2**	**14.7**	**16.2**	**14.6**	**15.4**
Males, aged 2 and over	3.9	4.0	4.8	3.5	3.4
Females, aged 2 and over	4.9	5.4	5.5	4.4	4.4
Children under age 2	8.5	7.3	8.9	8.5	9.1
Other apparel products and services	3.7	4.0	3.7	3.4	3.8
Jewelry and watches	1.7	1.9	1.9	1.4	1.8
All other apparel products and services	2.2	2.3	2.1	2.3	2.3
Transportation	**4.5**	**3.9**	**4.5**	**4.1**	**5.7**
Health care	**1.0**	**0.8**	**1.1**	**0.9**	**1.0**
Entertainment	**8.5**	**8.5**	**10.3**	**7.7**	**7.8**
Toys, games, arts and crafts, and tricycles	5.2	5.2	6.7	4.9	4.1
Other entertainment	4.1	4.1	4.7	3.6	4.2
Education	**2.2**	**2.6**	**2.6**	**2.1**	**1.8**
All other gifts	**4.7**	**4.4**	**5.1**	**3.9**	**5.7**

Source: Bureau of Labor Statistics, unpublished data from the 2008 Consumer Expenditure Survey

Table 5.22 Amount Buyers Spent on Gifts for People in Other Households by Region, <u>Average Quarter</u>, 2008

(average amount spent by households buying gifts of products or services for people in other households during the average quarter, by region of residence, 2008)

	total households	Northeast	Midwest	South	West
GIFTS, AMOUNT SPENT	**$830.84**	**$1,109.36**	**$696.18**	**$767.46**	**$853.34**
Housing	**401.21**	**443.53**	**337.30**	**407.52**	**431.19**
Household textiles	82.09	97.41	66.88	82.85	87.37
Appliances and miscellaneous housewares	186.97	201.98	126.09	210.91	218.28
Major appliances	441.67	292.97	297.58	519.51	541.67
Small appliances and miscellaneous housewares	111.57	168.47	94.80	101.69	110.45
Miscellaneous household equipment	149.82	161.56	132.76	123.60	194.23
Other housing	866.53	1,004.57	831.46	809.92	877.30
Apparel and services	**192.34**	**206.22**	**191.62**	**184.27**	**194.64**
Males, aged 2 and over	164.57	186.35	143.32	147.84	201.24
Females, aged 2 and over	171.81	189.38	146.97	167.29	192.60
Children under age 2	94.20	98.09	80.06	97.64	100.63
Other apparel products and services	175.96	132.10	243.55	176.10	146.49
Jewelry and watches	259.88	173.54	385.70	279.89	173.00
All other apparel products and services	94.59	86.73	84.13	94.80	109.91
Transportation	**547.15**	**435.26**	**459.81**	**625.49**	**592.30**
Health care	**515.00**	**214.87**	**370.98**	**480.62**	**921.29**
Entertainment	**220.30**	**216.25**	**208.43**	**226.47**	**230.61**
Toys, games, arts and crafts, and tricycles	156.53	159.66	137.52	160.11	178.93
Other entertainment	257.00	248.16	260.25	265.38	247.99
Education	**3,602.60**	**5,653.97**	**2,611.07**	**3,053.29**	**3,647.71**
All other gifts	**520.82**	**570.92**	**427.89**	**456.78**	**645.99**

Source: Calculations by New Strategist based on the Bureau of Labor Statistics' 2008 Consumer Expenditure Survey

Table 5.23 Percent Buying Gifts for People in Other Households by Region, <u>Average Week</u>, 2008

(percent of households buying gifts of products or services for people in other households during the average week, by region of residence, 2008)

GIFTS, PERCENT BUYING	total households	Northeast	Midwest	South	West
GIFTS, PERCENT BUYING	**18.1%**	**17.3%**	**19.9%**	**17.8%**	**17.6%**
Food	**5.1**	**4.2**	**6.4**	**4.5**	**5.6**
Housing	**7.4**	**6.3**	**9.1**	**6.5**	**7.9**
Housekeeping supplies	5.2	4.2	6.6	4.3	6.0
Laundry and cleaning supplies	0.5	0.4	0.5	0.5	0.7
Other household products	1.5	1.0	1.9	1.2	1.8
Postage and stationery	4.1	3.3	5.3	3.5	4.5
Household textiles	0.7	0.3	0.8	0.8	0.7
Appliances and miscellaneous housewares	0.9	0.6	0.9	0.9	1.0
Major appliances	0.1	0.0	0.1	0.1	0.0
Small appliances and miscellaneous housewares	0.8	0.6	0.8	0.8	1.0
Miscellaneous household equipment	2.8	2.4	3.5	2.4	3.2
Other housing	0.1	0.1	0.1	0.1	0.0
Apparel and services	**8.6**	**8.4**	**8.6**	**9.1**	**7.8**
Males, aged 2 and over	2.1	2.1	2.0	2.4	1.8
Females, aged 2 and over	3.2	3.3	2.8	3.6	2.7
Children under age 2	3.3	3.4	3.3	3.3	3.2
Other apparel products and services	2.2	2.1	2.3	2.2	1.9
Transportation	**0.1**	**0.1**	**0.2**	**0.1**	**0.1**
Health care	**0.4**	**0.5**	**0.2**	**0.5**	**0.5**
Entertainment	**3.4**	**3.0**	**3.3**	**3.6**	**3.8**
Education	**1.0**	**1.0**	**1.4**	**0.7**	**1.1**
All other gifts	**2.6**	**2.2**	**2.4**	**2.7**	**3.1**

Source: Bureau of Labor Statistics, unpublished data from the 2008 Consumer Expenditure Survey

Table 5.24 Amount Buyers Spent on Gifts for People in Other Households by Region, <u>Average Week</u>, 2008

(average amount spent by households buying gifts of products or services for people in other households during the average week, by region of residence, 2008)

	total households	Northeast	Midwest	South	West
GIFTS, AMOUNT SPENT	**$51.38**	**$54.82**	**$46.83**	**$49.66**	**$56.49**
Food	**19.77**	**22.46**	**18.27**	**19.82**	**19.82**
Housing	**27.58**	**26.31**	**24.01**	**26.39**	**33.96**
Housekeeping supplies	11.75	10.66	12.07	9.70	14.09
Laundry and cleaning supplies	5.77	4.65	8.00	6.67	6.94
Other household products	12.33	13.73	11.46	9.92	15.64
Postage and stationery	9.54	8.59	10.13	7.78	11.50
Household textiles	32.35	21.88	24.05	28.75	57.58
Appliances and miscellaneous housewares	31.76	43.10	32.18	35.29	21.15
Major appliances	80.00	100.00	137.50	80.00	33.33
Small appliances and miscellaneous housewares	28.05	42.86	22.22	31.33	20.79
Miscellaneous household equipment	31.80	34.84	25.22	29.22	39.31
Other housing	37.50	50.00	66.67	38.46	33.33
Apparel and services	**46.90**	**59.31**	**46.96**	**41.71**	**45.29**
Males, aged 2 and over	37.80	42.45	36.87	31.78	47.16
Females, aged 2 and over	44.79	62.20	47.84	36.36	42.44
Children under age 2	28.13	31.29	31.90	24.77	26.67
Other apparel products and services	40.93	47.12	39.48	41.63	35.94
Transportation	**20.00**	**11.11**	**14.29**	**28.57**	**0.00**
Health care	**11.90**	**6.52**	**21.05**	**9.43**	**19.57**
Entertainment	**36.05**	**34.78**	**31.80**	**38.20**	**37.11**
Education	**10.20**	**10.20**	**7.86**	**8.96**	**14.15**
All other gifts	**32.82**	**33.02**	**29.75**	**34.56**	**32.46**

Source: Calculations by New Strategist based on the Bureau of Labor Statistics' 2008 Consumer Expenditure Survey

Table 5.25 Percent Buying Gifts for People in Other Households by Education, <u>Average Quarter</u>, 2008

(percent of households buying gifts of products or services for people in other households during the average quarter, by highest level of education of householder, 2008)

	total households	less than high school graduate	high school graduate	some college	associate's degree	college graduate total	bachelor's degree	master's, professional, doctorate
GIFTS, PERCENT BUYING	**27.6%**	**18.2%**	**23.9%**	**28.7%**	**30.3%**	**34.1%**	**32.8%**	**36.3%**
Housing	**9.3**	**6.0**	**7.7**	**9.3**	**11.3**	**11.9**	**11.1**	**13.4**
Household textiles	2.0	1.4	1.5	2.2	2.3	2.6	2.3	3.1
Appliances and miscellaneous housewares	1.7	0.8	1.1	1.6	2.4	2.4	2.2	2.8
Major appliances	0.4	0.2	0.3	0.3	0.5	0.5	0.5	0.6
Small appliances and miscellaneous housewares	1.3	0.6	0.9	1.3	1.9	2.0	1.8	2.3
Miscellaneous household equipment	4.2	2.1	3.7	4.1	5.4	5.5	4.9	6.6
Other housing	3.0	2.3	2.3	3.0	3.4	4.0	3.8	4.3
Apparel and services	**15.2**	**10.5**	**13.9**	**15.3**	**16.4**	**18.0**	**17.8**	**18.5**
Males, aged 2 and over	3.9	2.1	3.6	4.0	4.1	4.9	4.7	5.1
Females, aged 2 and over	4.9	2.6	4.5	5.0	5.1	6.2	5.8	6.8
Children under age 2	8.5	7.2	7.8	8.4	9.6	9.5	9.6	9.3
Other apparel products and services	3.7	2.1	3.0	3.7	3.8	5.0	4.9	5.1
Jewelry and watches	1.7	0.8	1.2	1.6	1.7	2.6	2.6	2.7
All other apparel products and services	2.2	1.4	2.0	2.4	2.2	2.7	2.6	2.9
Transportation	**4.5**	**1.4**	**3.1**	**4.8**	**5.1**	**6.8**	**5.5**	**9.1**
Health care	**1.0**	**0.4**	**0.7**	**1.0**	**0.9**	**1.4**	**1.2**	**1.8**
Entertainment	**8.5**	**4.3**	**6.8**	**9.3**	**8.6**	**11.3**	**10.4**	**12.8**
Toys, games, arts and crafts, and tricycles	5.2	3.2	4.4	5.7	5.6	6.4	6.1	6.9
Other entertainment	4.1	1.4	3.1	4.5	4.4	5.9	5.1	7.2
Education	**2.2**	**0.7**	**1.3**	**2.1**	**2.2**	**3.9**	**3.5**	**4.5**
All other gifts	**4.7**	**1.8**	**3.3**	**5.1**	**4.7**	**7.0**	**5.6**	**9.4**

Source: Bureau of Labor Statistics, unpublished data from the 2008 Consumer Expenditure Survey

Table 5.26 Amount Buyers Spent on Gifts for People in Other Households by Education, Average Quarter, 2008

(average amount spent by households buying gifts of products or services for people in other households during the average quarter, by highest level of education of householder, 2008)

| | | | | | | college graduate | | |
	total households	less than high school graduate	high school graduate	some college	associate's degree	total	bachelor's degree	master's, professional, doctorate
GIFTS, AMOUNT SPENT	**$830.84**	**$379.98**	**$500.73**	**$705.93**	**$674.99**	**$1,279.44**	**$1,049.86**	**$1,652.29**
Housing	**401.21**	**323.83**	**272.98**	**353.52**	**315.88**	**547.37**	**467.81**	**665.38**
Household textiles	82.09	79.60	78.57	78.46	69.78	89.83	79.17	104.38
Appliances and miscellaneous housewares	186.97	169.55	128.90	179.30	189.77	214.40	144.14	314.82
Major appliances	441.67	481.25	229.63	385.34	416.04	562.50	241.30	1,013.11
Small appliances and miscellaneous housewares	111.57	62.07	90.23	130.58	118.17	115.40	114.21	116.59
Miscellaneous household equipment	149.82	231.64	97.83	178.47	111.92	160.51	134.62	195.24
Other housing	866.53	516.63	632.26	712.80	690.51	1,222.42	1,048.10	1,508.47
Apparel and services	**192.34**	**171.06**	**164.62**	**199.74**	**173.78**	**218.16**	**207.20**	**237.20**
Males, aged 2 and over	164.57	142.23	151.33	185.44	172.35	162.50	145.78	190.68
Females, aged 2 and over	171.81	167.87	157.13	189.91	149.70	176.13	149.91	217.10
Children under age 2	94.20	107.18	90.77	94.84	83.96	94.50	95.05	93.49
Other apparel products and services	175.96	148.17	111.05	155.71	154.66	233.72	247.44	209.92
Jewelry and watches	259.88	224.67	148.53	207.80	230.99	338.69	383.37	260.41
All other apparel products and services	94.59	94.58	79.42	104.56	91.14	98.35	80.78	127.34
Transportation	**547.15**	**722.48**	**480.10**	**442.26**	**394.55**	**648.57**	**687.25**	**606.24**
Health care	**515.00**	**513.41**	**202.65**	**381.07**	**540.96**	**711.44**	**856.65**	**520.88**
Entertainment	**220.30**	**144.07**	**205.51**	**237.06**	**198.78**	**237.59**	**236.96**	**238.41**
Toys, games, arts and crafts, and tricycles	156.53	130.12	184.39	161.65	149.23	145.23	153.28	132.50
Other entertainment	257.00	142.15	186.70	284.40	203.49	299.49	302.21	296.22
Education	**3,602.60**	**1,127.65**	**2,004.51**	**2,484.45**	**3,239.08**	**4,818.85**	**3,764.67**	**6,281.72**
All other gifts	**520.82**	**289.49**	**454.20**	**531.55**	**330.00**	**613.58**	**587.41**	**642.28**

Source: Calculations by New Strategist based on the Bureau of Labor Statistics' 2008 Consumer Expenditure Survey

Table 5.27 Percent Buying Gifts for People in Other Households by Education, <u>Average Week</u>, 2008

(percent of households buying gifts of products or services for people in other households during the average week, by highest level of education of householder, 2008)

GIFTS, PERCENT BUYING	total households	less than high school graduate	high school graduate	some college	associate's degree	college graduate total	bachelor's degree	master's, professional, doctorate
	18.1%	11.4%	14.8%	18.1%	20.3%	23.7%	23.5%	24.2%
Food	5.1	2.1	4.2	5.1	4.6	7.5	7.8	7.1
Housing	7.4	2.4	5.3	7.3	8.6	11.2	11.2	11.2
Housekeeping supplies	5.2	1.6	3.7	4.9	6.3	8.1	8.0	8.4
Laundry and cleaning supplies	0.5	0.3	0.6	0.3	0.7	0.7	0.6	0.8
Other household products	1.5	0.7	0.9	1.2	1.9	2.4	2.6	2.1
Postage and stationery	4.1	0.9	3.0	4.0	5.0	6.4	6.0	7.1
Household textiles	0.7	0.3	0.6	0.7	0.3	1.1	1.0	1.2
Appliances and miscellaneous housewares	0.9	0.1	0.5	0.8	1.0	1.5	1.4	1.7
Major appliances	0.1	–	0.1	0.0	0.1	0.1	0.1	0.1
Small appliances and miscellaneous housewares	0.8	0.1	0.5	0.8	0.9	1.5	1.3	1.7
Miscellaneous household equipment	2.8	0.7	2.0	3.0	2.7	4.5	4.8	4.0
Other housing	0.1	–	0.0	0.1	0.1	0.2	0.1	0.3
Apparel and services	8.6	7.6	7.8	8.0	9.9	9.7	10.0	9.2
Males, aged 2 and over	2.1	1.8	1.6	2.0	2.7	2.5	2.7	2.2
Females, aged 2 and over	3.2	2.6	2.9	3.5	3.3	3.5	3.3	3.7
Children under age 2	3.3	3.2	2.9	2.8	4.1	3.8	3.8	3.7
Other apparel products and services	2.2	2.5	2.4	1.8	2.1	2.0	2.4	1.4
Transportation	0.1	–	0.1	0.0	0.1	0.2	0.2	0.3
Health care	0.4	0.4	0.3	0.5	0.9	0.4	0.3	0.6
Entertainment	3.4	1.1	2.9	3.5	4.4	4.8	4.8	4.7
Education	1.0	0.0	0.5	1.0	1.0	1.8	1.5	2.6
All other gifts	2.6	1.7	2.6	2.2	3.5	3.1	2.9	3.6

Note: "–" means sample is too small to make a reliable estimate.
Source: Bureau of Labor Statistics, unpublished data from the 2008 Consumer Expenditure Survey

Table 5.28 Amount Buyers Spent on Gifts for People in Other Households by Education, <u>Average Week</u>, 2008

(average amount spent by households buying gifts of products or services for people in other households during the average week, by highest level of education of householder, 2008)

	total households	less than high school graduate	high school graduate	some college	associate's degree	college graduate total	bachelor's degree	master's, professional, doctorate
GIFTS, AMOUNT SPENT	**$51.38**	**$50.48**	**$51.69**	**$46.09**	**$48.13**	**$55.37**	**$53.98**	**$57.92**
Food	**19.77**	**12.62**	**17.97**	**17.98**	**22.39**	**22.18**	**21.59**	**23.23**
Housing	**27.58**	**24.15**	**21.09**	**28.57**	**24.68**	**30.90**	**27.69**	**36.69**
Housekeeping supplies	11.75	12.66	9.43	11.22	11.22	12.82	11.18	15.61
Laundry and cleaning supplies	5.77	8.00	3.57	6.45	9.46	5.71	6.25	6.17
Other household products	12.33	5.71	11.36	16.39	6.28	14.11	14.01	14.29
Postage and stationery	9.54	15.91	7.80	8.21	10.32	10.34	8.19	13.48
Household textiles	32.35	12.00	20.00	55.22	21.21	31.82	37.86	23.58
Appliances and miscellaneous housewares	31.76	22.22	22.64	27.27	42.42	35.33	31.21	42.51
Major appliances	80.00	–	40.00	100.00	80.00	125.00	150.00	50.00
Small appliances and miscellaneous housewares	28.05	22.22	18.75	23.38	40.43	30.14	23.88	39.52
Miscellaneous household equipment	31.80	46.48	25.25	31.56	32.85	32.74	28.21	43.25
Other housing	37.50	–	100.00	20.00	42.86	38.89	46.15	28.57
Apparel and services	**46.90**	**51.18**	**48.01**	**43.59**	**34.24**	**50.41**	**51.71**	**47.99**
Males, aged 2 and over	37.80	40.56	39.02	43.00	23.70	37.80	39.56	33.94
Females, aged 2 and over	44.79	53.05	45.26	41.16	35.56	46.96	46.39	47.83
Children under age 2	28.13	28.62	29.31	20.00	21.65	33.87	35.54	30.65
Other apparel products and services	40.93	35.20	39.92	36.07	33.02	51.23	50.00	54.93
Transportation	**20.00**	**–**	**14.29**	**0.00**	**16.67**	**20.83**	**36.84**	**8.82**
Health care	**11.90**	**14.63**	**15.38**	**8.33**	**9.20**	**12.82**	**11.11**	**15.87**
Entertainment	**36.05**	**43.40**	**35.44**	**30.37**	**42.79**	**37.05**	**36.19**	**38.09**
Education	**10.20**	**0.00**	**12.00**	**13.27**	**11.54**	**8.15**	**6.90**	**8.91**
All other gifts	**32.82**	**29.52**	**34.62**	**28.18**	**31.07**	**35.03**	**27.68**	**45.86**

Note: "–" means sample is too small to make a reliable estimate.
Source: Calculations by New Strategist based on the Bureau of Labor Statistics' 2008 Consumer Expenditure Survey

CHAPTER 6

Health Care Buyers, 2008

Spending on health care has grown sharply over the past few years as health care costs soared and employers shifted more expenses onto their employees. Between 2000 and 2008, out-of-pocket spending on health care by the average household rose 15 percent, after adjusting for inflation.

Quarterly spending

During the average quarter of 2008, 78 percent of households had out-of-pocket health care expenditures, the buyers devoting an average of $904 to health care during the quarter. Number one on the Health Care Buyers' Top 10 list is health insurance. Sixty-three percent of households had out-of-pocket health insurance expenses during the average quarter of 2008, and those that did spent $656 for coverage. Among householders aged 65 or older, an even larger 90 percent had out-of-pocket health insurance expenses during the average quarter because of Medicare's required co-payments. In contrast, among householders under age 25, only one in four had out-of-pocket expenditures for health insurance because many do not have coverage.

Weekly spending

The diary portion of the Consumer Expenditure Survey captures spending on only a few health care items—prescription drugs, nonprescription drugs, vitamins, and topicals and dressings. During the average week of 2008, 18 percent of households spent on prescription drugs, with the purchasers spending an average of $13.54 on the item(s).

Health Care Buyers' Top 10

(health care categories bought by the largest percentage of households during an average quarter, 2008)

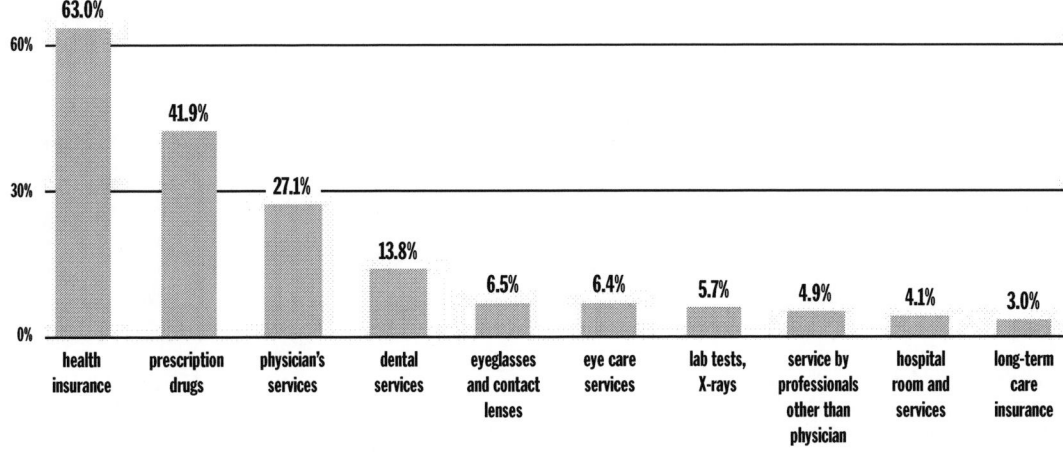

Table 6.1 Percent Spending Out-of-Pocket on Health Care by Age, <u>Average Quarter</u>, 2008

(percent of households with out-of-pocket health care expenses during the average quarter, by age of householder, 2008)

	total households	under 25	25 to 34	35 to 44	45 to 54	55 to 64	65 to 74	75+
HEALTH CARE, PERCENT BUYING	77.9%	41.5%	64.9%	75.3%	80.6%	84.0%	94.7%	96.6%
Health insurance	**63.0**	**25.3**	**49.3**	**56.8**	**62.7**	**66.3**	**89.6**	**92.5**
Commercial health insurance	14.3	5.4	14.6	15.5	17.9	17.5	11.1	7.6
Traditional fee-for-service health plan (not BCBS)	4.0	1.3	3.6	3.5	4.2	4.9	4.8	4.8
Preferred-provider health plan (not BCBS)	10.4	4.2	11.1	12.0	13.9	13.0	6.3	2.9
Blue Cross, Blue Shield	20.4	10.1	19.5	21.8	23.7	23.6	17.5	16.7
Traditional fee-for-service health plan	3.4	1.7	2.1	2.9	4.2	4.1	3.4	4.8
Preferred-provider health plan	8.9	3.9	9.0	10.3	11.9	10.8	5.7	2.8
Health maintenance organization	6.3	3.9	7.6	7.5	7.2	7.2	4.2	2.7
Commercial Medicare supplement	1.7	0.2	0.8	0.9	0.4	1.2	4.4	6.6
Other BCBS health insurance	0.7	0.6	0.6	0.7	0.9	1.1	0.6	0.4
Health maintenance plans (HMOs)	13.4	6.6	12.3	16.1	15.4	16.0	11.7	8.4
Medicare payments	22.2	1.6	2.0	3.9	7.2	17.9	80.0	86.3
Medicare prescription drug premium	7.3	0.2	0.7	1.4	2.5	5.6	25.3	30.1
Commercial Medicare supplements/ other health insurance	11.3	5.4	8.7	9.3	10.5	10.8	17.3	19.9
Commercial Medicare supplement (not BCBS)	4.7	3.2	2.3	1.8	2.0	2.7	13.1	16.5
Other health insurance (not BCBS)	7.0	2.4	6.4	7.6	8.7	8.4	6.0	4.6
Long-term care insurance	3.0	0.6	1.5	2.0	3.1	4.4	5.8	3.8
Medical services	**41.6**	**19.8**	**34.9**	**42.2**	**48.0**	**48.9**	**43.6**	**38.7**
Physician's services	27.1	11.9	23.0	28.1	32.3	33.2	25.9	22.5
Dental services	13.8	3.8	9.4	14.9	17.2	16.1	15.5	13.1
Eye care services	6.4	2.5	4.6	5.8	7.5	7.8	7.7	7.7
Service by professionals other than physician	4.9	1.7	4.1	4.6	6.0	5.8	5.0	4.7
Lab tests, X-rays	5.7	2.3	4.1	4.8	7.1	8.9	5.4	4.1
Hospital room and services	4.1	2.1	4.0	4.4	4.6	4.8	3.8	3.5
Care in convalescent or nursing home	0.1	0.1	0.0	0.0	0.0	0.2	0.2	0.5
Other medical services	1.6	0.4	1.0	1.5	1.5	2.3	2.3	1.5
Prescription drugs	**41.9**	**16.1**	**27.1**	**35.6**	**43.7**	**52.3**	**58.9**	**58.4**
Medical supplies	**7.9**	**2.8**	**5.8**	**8.0**	**9.6**	**9.3**	**8.9**	**8.2**
Eyeglasses and contact lenses	6.5	2.5	5.4	7.3	8.3	7.5	6.6	4.1
Hearing aids	0.3	0.2	0.0	0.1	0.1	0.1	0.5	1.8
Medical equipment for general use	0.6	0.1	0.3	0.4	0.6	0.9	0.8	1.0
Supportive, convalescent medical equipment	0.5	0.0	0.1	0.2	0.6	0.6	0.7	1.1
Rental of medical equipment	0.3	0.1	0.1	0.2	0.2	0.5	0.3	0.4
Rental of supportive, convalescent medical equipment	0.2	–	0.1	0.2	0.2	0.3	0.3	0.6

Note: "–" means sample is too small to make a reliable estimate.
Source: Bureau of Labor Statistics, unpublished data from the 2008 Consumer Expenditure Survey

Table 6.2 Amount Buyers Spent Out-of-Pocket on Health Care by Age, <u>Average Quarter</u>, 2008

(average amount spent by households with out-of-pocket health care expenses during the average quarter, by age of householder, 2008)

	total households	under 25	25 to 34	35 to 44	45 to 54	55 to 64	65 to 74	75+
HEALTH CARE, AMOUNT SPENT	$903.63	$371.04	$634.61	$781.17	$854.50	$1,069.01	$1,207.34	$1,092.01
Health insurance	656.00	385.10	497.94	590.30	607.59	733.36	809.81	751.79
Commercial health insurance	559.10	369.46	465.30	554.84	591.18	610.97	561.15	606.83
Traditional fee-for-service health plan (not BCBS)	544.84	366.79	477.00	566.17	623.45	518.57	498.86	586.70
Preferred-provider health plan (not BCBS)	554.96	352.84	455.20	550.10	573.40	628.57	600.63	611.07
Blue Cross, Blue Shield	584.93	360.57	499.71	574.13	562.23	749.71	590.20	550.22
Traditional fee-for-service health plan	591.49	234.52	435.92	607.67	531.25	821.30	642.37	512.89
Preferred-provider health plan	604.49	409.94	525.53	579.11	574.89	764.37	633.27	596.39
Health maintenance organization	560.29	368.11	488.64	551.61	545.16	722.36	491.65	628.01
Commercial Medicare supplement	492.21	350.00	405.72	541.67	494.77	467.39	515.30	495.16
Other BCBS health insurance	231.08	176.23	156.64	276.89	181.18	283.26	308.20	217.68
Health maintenance plans (HMOs)	505.32	356.93	429.54	534.83	512.49	530.92	571.59	457.86
Medicare payments	380.94	345.54	330.53	373.29	328.29	324.29	405.62	389.11
Medicare prescription drug premium	197.37	88.24	210.29	169.64	161.39	187.12	204.39	203.05
Commercial Medicare supplements/ other health insurance	287.94	220.56	193.27	190.99	236.67	198.79	436.44	465.61
Commercial Medicare supplement (not BCBS)	471.88	311.71	437.61	411.11	539.95	403.49	476.95	512.20
Other health insurance (not BCBS)	145.15	82.38	101.21	135.95	162.67	127.35	217.70	184.34
Long-term care insurance	498.92	80.36	180.37	174.49	325.48	632.88	714.22	787.11
Medical services	434.15	180.84	338.60	414.58	436.20	518.86	489.70	461.86
Physician's services	168.00	106.19	164.49	172.84	162.93	194.39	170.98	130.52
Dental services	461.46	235.25	264.26	385.51	456.61	531.43	665.34	527.93
Eye care services	139.89	92.16	145.65	123.96	123.76	176.50	140.25	138.26
Service by professionals other than physician	291.29	132.18	261.64	318.71	299.96	331.64	257.50	256.69
Lab tests, X-rays	236.51	167.92	287.02	250.68	214.66	260.75	212.90	168.77
Hospital room and services	611.92	241.94	547.86	669.22	700.33	787.24	343.85	400.79
Care in convalescent or nursing home	4,143.18	205.00	1,762.50	1,587.50	816.67	1,173.33	5,084.72	6,609.18
Other medical services	325.00	148.21	401.26	349.19	242.95	345.33	373.89	281.68
Prescription drugs	212.20	103.29	136.47	170.01	169.50	252.55	299.47	258.95
Medical supplies	261.02	147.49	193.88	219.61	253.52	281.50	320.35	362.50
Eyeglasses and contact lenses	230.03	152.11	183.88	209.30	234.62	276.13	260.48	223.37
Hearing aids	1,041.13	98.61	575.00	718.75	1,148.08	2,035.71	1,523.11	829.03
Medical equipment for general use	185.09	103.13	386.54	108.57	304.92	116.19	74.04	187.50
Supportive, convalescent medical equipment	156.52	106.25	105.36	123.75	186.16	78.57	223.57	178.77
Rental of medical equipment	153.85	50.00	61.36	144.57	245.00	211.70	66.91	94.74
Rental of supportive, convalescent medical equipment	157.95	–	150.00	190.48	36.25	84.62	278.13	197.95

Note: "–" means sample is too small to make a reliable estimate.
Source: Calculations by New Strategist based on the Bureau of Labor Statistics' 2008 Consumer Expenditure Survey

Table 6.3 Percent Spending Out-of-Pocket on Health Care by Age, Average Week, 2008

(percent of households with out-of-pocket health care expenses during the average week, by age of householder, 2008)

	total households	under 25	25 to 34	35 to 44	45 to 54	55 to 64	65 to 74	75+
Prescription drugs	18.0%	10.3%	13.5%	17.0%	19.3%	20.1%	23.9%	20.1%
Nonprescription drugs	15.6	9.1	11.6	15.2	17.3	17.5	20.1	16.2
Nonprescription vitamins	4.2	1.2	2.7	3.2	4.1	5.1	7.3	6.8
Topicals and dressings	8.4	6.2	7.2	8.8	9.2	8.7	9.7	7.3

Source: Bureau of Labor Statistics, unpublished data from the 2008 Consumer Expenditure Survey

Table 6.4 Amount Buyers Spent Out-of-Pocket on Health Care by Age, Average Week, 2008

(average amount spent by households with out-of-pocket health care expenses during the average week, by age of householder, 2008)

	total households	under 25	25 to 34	35 to 44	45 to 54	55 to 64	65 to 74	75+
Prescription drugs	$13.54	$9.34	$9.64	$12.16	$13.45	$17.77	$13.96	$14.49
Nonprescription drugs	10.71	8.59	8.25	10.12	10.48	13.52	10.43	11.33
Nonprescription vitamins	17.92	15.00	12.50	16.77	19.27	24.02	16.89	15.54
Topicals and dressings	7.05	5.15	5.81	6.15	8.40	8.64	6.20	7.22

Source: Calculations by New Strategist based on the Bureau of Labor Statistics' 2008 Consumer Expenditure Survey

Table 6.5 Percent Spending Out-of-Pocket on Health Care by Household Income, <u>Average Quarter</u>, 2008

(percent of households with out-of-pocket health care expenses during the average quarter, by before-tax income of household, 2008)

	total households	under $20,000	$20,000–$39,999	$40,000–$49,999	$50,000–$69,999	$70,000–$79,999	$80,000–$99,999	$100,000 or more
HEALTH CARE, PERCENT BUYING	**77.9%**	**62.0%**	**73.3%**	**78.4%**	**82.0%**	**87.5%**	**88.0%**	**90.3%**
Health insurance	**63.0**	**46.6**	**59.6**	**65.9**	**66.9**	**71.9**	**72.2**	**74.4**
Commercial health insurance	14.3	4.9	10.1	13.8	17.5	22.1	19.8	22.8
Traditional fee-for-service health plan (not BCBS)	4.0	2.2	3.5	4.6	3.8	5.7	6.7	4.9
Preferred-provider health plan (not BCBS)	10.4	2.8	6.7	9.3	14.0	16.8	13.3	18.2
Blue Cross, Blue Shield	20.4	8.2	16.4	23.6	23.4	26.4	28.2	29.7
Traditional fee-for-service health plan	3.4	1.8	3.2	4.2	3.4	4.1	4.4	4.2
Preferred-provider health plan	8.9	2.1	6.0	8.7	10.4	11.5	13.9	15.9
Health maintenance organization	6.3	2.7	4.9	8.0	7.9	8.9	8.3	8.5
Commercial Medicare supplement	1.7	1.6	2.1	2.3	1.6	2.0	1.6	1.0
Other BCBS health insurance	0.7	0.2	0.5	1.5	0.9	0.9	0.7	1.2
Health maintenance plans (HMOs)	13.4	5.1	11.4	14.8	16.0	18.2	17.5	19.4
Medicare payments	22.2	33.5	31.2	21.9	17.0	12.2	13.4	9.8
Medicare prescription drug premium	7.3	12.1	10.3	7.2	5.2	3.6	3.1	3.1
Commercial Medicare supplements/ other health insurance	11.3	6.5	11.3	12.0	12.0	13.9	13.8	13.7
Commercial Medicare supplement (not BCBS)	4.7	4.3	7.2	5.2	4.5	3.7	4.3	2.6
Other health insurance (not BCBS)	7.0	2.5	4.6	7.1	8.0	10.9	9.9	11.4
Long-term care insurance	3.0	1.0	2.3	2.1	3.3	3.2	3.1	6.3
Medical services	**41.6**	**23.4**	**34.6**	**40.4**	**45.9**	**53.3**	**51.4**	**60.0**
Physician's services	27.1	14.0	22.3	25.1	30.5	37.0	35.0	39.6
Dental services	13.8	5.4	9.4	12.6	14.7	18.1	19.3	25.0
Eye care services	6.4	3.3	5.1	5.9	7.0	8.9	8.6	9.8
Service by professionals other than physician	4.9	2.7	4.0	4.7	5.3	5.7	6.4	7.2
Lab tests, X-rays	5.7	2.6	4.8	6.1	6.3	7.6	7.3	8.2
Hospital room and services	4.1	2.4	3.3	3.7	4.9	5.3	6.1	5.4
Care in convalescent or nursing home	0.1	0.2	0.2	0.0	0.1	–	0.0	0.1
Other medical services	1.6	1.2	1.4	1.7	1.7	1.8	1.3	2.0
Prescription drugs	**41.9**	**33.8**	**39.4**	**39.4**	**42.9**	**45.4**	**48.3**	**51.0**
Medical supplies	**7.9**	**4.1**	**6.2**	**7.0**	**8.1**	**11.0**	**10.9**	**12.5**
Eyeglasses and contact lenses	6.5	3.0	4.7	5.2	6.9	9.5	9.1	11.1
Hearing aids	0.3	0.4	0.3	0.3	0.3	0.2	0.3	0.2
Medical equipment for general use	0.6	0.3	0.6	0.8	0.7	0.6	0.6	0.6
Supportive, convalescent medical equipment	0.5	0.3	0.6	0.3	0.5	0.5	0.6	0.5
Rental of medical equipment	0.3	0.2	0.3	0.4	0.2	0.2	0.6	0.2
Rental of supportive, convalescent medical equipment	0.2	0.1	0.3	0.2	0.3	0.2	0.3	0.2

Note: "–" means sample is too small to make a reliable estimate.
Source: Bureau of Labor Statistics, unpublished data from the 2008 Consumer Expenditure Survey

Table 6.6 Amount Buyers Spent Out-of-Pocket on Health Care by Household Income, <u>Average Quarter</u>, 2008

(average amount spent by households with out-of-pocket health care expenses during the average quarter, by before-tax income of household, 2008)

	total households	under $20,000	$20,000– $39,999	$40,000– $49,999	$50,000– $69,999	$70,000– $79,999	$80,000– $99,999	$100,000 or more
HEALTH CARE, AMOUNT SPENT	$903.63	$620.10	$814.26	$830.86	$937.20	$956.10	$996.71	$1,167.96
Health insurance	**656.00**	**544.79**	**622.89**	**610.09**	**646.41**	**645.90**	**710.03**	**780.21**
Commercial health insurance	559.10	510.36	470.30	466.74	557.16	562.31	623.32	622.97
Traditional fee-for-service health plan (not BCBS)	544.84	562.79	471.29	436.55	596.99	672.85	566.46	575.15
Preferred-provider health plan (not BCBS)	554.96	514.77	462.16	479.70	531.98	513.00	640.37	626.19
Blue Cross, Blue Shield	584.93	629.79	464.62	480.43	556.65	565.07	603.83	722.73
Traditional fee-for-service health plan	591.49	673.62	532.82	453.49	569.19	445.33	566.78	792.61
Preferred-provider health plan	604.49	634.75	464.44	501.67	541.63	553.28	626.17	734.64
Health maintenance organization	560.29	640.82	413.10	475.82	544.33	613.92	593.45	659.12
Commercial Medicare supplement	492.21	473.27	462.26	435.94	587.65	431.19	499.53	580.79
Other BCBS health insurance	231.08	758.74	198.49	170.13	206.76	421.35	108.82	256.03
Health maintenance plans (HMOs)	505.32	443.23	408.91	423.94	480.89	473.06	618.10	610.18
Medicare payments	380.94	329.19	409.88	417.41	409.63	399.28	395.89	380.22
Medicare prescription drug premium	197.37	156.91	202.05	263.14	215.25	200.77	214.69	247.28
Commercial Medicare supplements/ other health insurance	287.94	319.89	352.73	327.55	272.25	247.36	259.48	220.83
Commercial Medicare supplement (not BCBS)	471.88	393.97	467.16	582.92	510.22	457.11	510.06	439.37
Other health insurance (not BCBS)	145.15	158.56	131.97	126.70	120.87	160.56	140.26	165.81
Long-term care insurance	498.92	612.71	540.88	569.62	439.75	472.05	501.20	479.91
Medical services	**434.15**	**319.45**	**354.96**	**349.34**	**465.48**	**466.88**	**461.83**	**535.78**
Physician's services	168.00	112.73	142.20	139.21	183.63	170.20	168.15	207.69
Dental services	461.46	378.33	454.98	430.18	416.31	412.31	441.27	532.16
Eye care services	139.89	150.41	106.36	121.16	144.75	147.90	145.94	157.48
Service by professionals other than physician	291.29	180.17	207.79	291.68	371.23	279.82	240.55	370.96
Lab tests, X-rays	236.51	226.77	217.36	182.63	236.56	214.17	198.69	296.78
Hospital room and services	611.92	426.51	513.99	345.38	645.65	1,072.85	724.71	654.58
Care in convalescent or nursing home	4,143.18	4,613.91	2,562.36	9,181.25	8,795.00	–	1,462.50	404.17
Other medical services	325.00	228.68	226.13	214.70	679.88	484.44	495.28	192.52
Prescription drugs	**212.20**	**154.52**	**223.02**	**228.51**	**233.18**	**215.12**	**205.69**	**229.62**
Medical supplies	**261.02**	**243.35**	**243.04**	**257.33**	**276.04**	**233.95**	**252.77**	**289.87**
Eyeglasses and contact lenses	230.03	191.50	197.21	248.80	232.58	209.81	215.58	262.07
Hearing aids	1,041.13	509.30	1,145.11	762.50	1,451.47	891.67	1,682.26	1,710.23
Medical equipment for general use	185.09	1,174.48	133.48	63.25	93.75	127.05	122.54	328.13
Supportive, convalescent medical equipment	156.52	126.38	165.66	290.44	126.09	252.88	121.55	83.80
Rental of medical equipment	153.85	54.94	131.40	151.43	156.25	463.04	161.40	159.52
Rental of supportive, convalescent medical equipment	157.95	218.25	132.49	230.56	42.31	205.95	138.33	161.76

Note: "–" means sample is too small to make a reliable estimate.
Source: Calculations by New Strategist based on the Bureau of Labor Statistics' 2008 Consumer Expenditure Survey

Table 6.7 Percent Spending Out-of-Pocket on Health Care by Household Income, <u>Average Week</u>, 2008

(percent of households with out-of-pocket health care expenses during the average week, by before-tax income of household, 2008)

	total households	under $20,000	$20,000– $39,999	$40,000– $49,999	$50,000– $69,999	$70,000– $79,999	$80,000– $99,999	$100,000 or more
Prescription drugs	18.0%	13.1%	16.6%	16.7%	19.5%	19.4%	20.2%	22.9%
Nonprescription drugs	15.6	11.5	14.1	15.0	17.0	15.7	18.0	20.0
Nonprescription vitamins	4.2	2.4	4.4	3.4	4.4	5.5	4.7	5.7
Topicals and dressings	8.4	5.5	7.4	6.9	7.9	8.9	12.7	11.7

Source: Bureau of Labor Statistics, unpublished data from the 2008 Consumer Expenditure Survey

Table 6.8 Amount Buyers Spent Out-of-Pocket on Health Care by Household Income, <u>Average Week</u>, 2008

(average amount spent by households with out-of-pocket health care expenses during the average week, by before-tax income of household, 2008)

	total households	under $20,000	$20,000– $39,999	$40,000– $49,999	$50,000– $69,999	$70,000– $79,999	$80,000– $99,999	$100,000 or more
Prescription drugs	$13.54	$11.51	$13.96	$13.80	$12.44	$12.66	$13.63	$15.40
Nonprescription drugs	10.71	9.18	10.96	11.17	9.84	9.47	10.21	12.37
Nonprescription vitamins	17.92	19.09	17.77	18.02	17.08	17.67	19.53	18.52
Topicals and dressings	7.05	9.75	5.56	4.96	6.62	5.93	6.44	8.82

Source: Calculations by New Strategist based on the Bureau of Labor Statistics' 2008 Consumer Expenditure Survey

Table 6.9 Percent of High-Income Households Spending Out-of-Pocket on Health Care, Average Quarter, 2008

(percent of high-income households with out-of-pocket health care expenses during the average quarter, by before-tax income of household, 2008)

	total households	$100,000 or more	$100,000– $119,999	$120,000– $149,999	$150,000 or more
HEALTH CARE, PERCENT BUYING	**77.9%**	**90.3%**	**89.3%**	**91.2%**	**90.6%**
Health insurance	**63.0**	**74.4**	**73.9**	**75.5**	**74.1**
Commercial health insurance	14.3	22.8	19.9	25.0	23.7
Traditional fee-for-service health plan (not BCBS)	4.0	4.9	4.6	6.1	4.3
Preferred-provider health plan (not BCBS)	10.4	18.2	15.4	19.8	19.5
Blue Cross, Blue Shield	20.4	29.7	29.5	30.1	29.5
Traditional fee-for-service health plan	3.4	4.2	5.7	3.8	3.3
Preferred-provider health plan	8.9	15.9	14.8	16.0	16.8
Health maintenance organization	6.3	8.5	8.2	9.5	8.0
Commercial Medicare supplement	1.7	1.0	1.1	0.7	1.0
Other BCBS health insurance	0.7	1.2	1.2	1.1	1.2
Health maintenance plans (HMOs)	13.4	19.4	19.7	19.2	19.2
Medicare payments	22.2	9.8	11.0	9.0	9.3
Medicare prescription drug premium	7.3	3.1	3.7	2.5	3.1
Commercial Medicare supplements/other health insurance	11.3	13.7	14.5	13.5	13.2
Commercial Medicare supplement (not BCBS)	4.7	2.6	3.5	1.7	2.5
Other health insurance (not BCBS)	7.0	11.4	11.5	11.9	10.9
Long-term care insurance	3.0	6.3	6.7	6.4	6.0
Medical services	**41.6**	**60.0**	**57.5**	**60.8**	**61.5**
Physician's services	27.1	39.6	37.3	41.6	40.2
Dental services	13.8	25.0	23.6	25.9	25.6
Eye care services	6.4	9.8	9.4	9.9	10.1
Service by professionals other than physician	4.9	7.2	5.9	7.3	8.2
Lab tests, X-rays	5.7	8.2	8.5	7.6	8.5
Hospital room and services	4.1	5.4	5.5	5.4	5.3
Care in convalescent or nursing home	0.1	0.1	0.1	0.1	0.0
Other medical services	1.6	2.0	2.6	1.4	2.1
Prescription drugs	**41.9**	**51.0**	**48.7**	**52.0**	**52.1**
Medical supplies	**7.9**	**12.5**	**12.4**	**11.5**	**13.2**
Eyeglasses and contact lenses	6.5	11.1	11.0	10.3	11.8
Hearing aids	0.3	0.2	0.2	0.3	0.2
Medical equipment for general use	0.6	0.6	0.7	0.5	0.8
Supportive, convalescent medical equipment	0.5	0.5	0.7	0.4	0.5
Rental of medical equipment	0.3	0.2	0.3	0.2	0.1
Rental of supportive, convalescent medical equipment	0.2	0.2	0.2	0.2	0.2

Source: Bureau of Labor Statistics, unpublished data from the 2008 Consumer Expenditure Survey

Table 6.10 Amount High-Income Buyers Spent Out-of-Pocket on Health Care, <u>Average Quarter</u>, 2008

(average amount spent by high-income households with out-of-pocket health care expenses during the average quarter, by before-tax income of household, 2008)

	total households	$100,000 or more	$100,000– $119,999	$120,000– $149,999	$150,000 or more
HEALTH CARE, AMOUNT SPENT	**$903.63**	**$1,167.96**	**$1,059.70**	**$1,117.79**	**$1,288.82**
Health insurance	**656.00**	**780.21**	**710.85**	**738.23**	**865.12**
Commercial health insurance	559.10	622.97	587.66	596.55	665.88
Traditional fee-for-service health plan (not BCBS)	544.84	575.15	483.62	614.56	618.20
Preferred-provider health plan (not BCBS)	554.96	626.19	615.98	566.61	672.73
Blue Cross, Blue Shield	584.93	722.73	638.36	671.06	826.82
Traditional fee-for-service health plan	591.49	792.61	813.03	778.13	779.64
Preferred-provider health plan	604.49	734.64	579.49	660.61	892.35
Health maintenance organization	560.29	659.12	603.01	614.64	742.31
Commercial Medicare supplement	492.21	580.79	462.83	851.39	551.29
Other BCBS health insurance	231.08	256.03	159.62	280.84	318.18
Health maintenance plans (HMOs)	505.32	610.18	555.94	570.68	681.41
Medicare payments	380.94	380.22	388.15	384.40	370.22
Medicare prescription drug premium	197.37	247.28	254.10	244.88	242.87
Commercial Medicare supplements/other health insurance	287.94	220.83	220.97	221.74	220.00
Commercial Medicare supplement (not BCBS)	471.88	439.37	427.56	448.03	449.50
Other health insurance (not BCBS)	145.15	165.81	148.97	188.63	163.66
Long-term care insurance	498.92	479.91	399.25	396.61	612.56
Medical services	**434.15**	**535.78**	**485.16**	**521.39**	**584.06**
Physician's services	168.00	207.69	153.54	195.35	257.36
Dental services	461.46	532.16	541.54	491.28	552.56
Eye care services	139.89	157.48	148.30	138.48	176.73
Service by professionals other than physician	291.29	370.96	263.87	395.03	419.31
Lab tests, X-rays	236.51	296.78	270.51	270.41	333.98
Hospital room and services	611.92	654.58	610.31	730.86	640.67
Care in convalescent or nursing home	4,143.18	404.17	316.67	721.43	275.00
Other medical services	325.00	192.52	292.77	408.51	-6.46
Prescription drugs	**212.20**	**229.62**	**224.05**	**221.24**	**239.49**
Medical supplies	**261.02**	**289.87**	**271.06**	**257.67**	**322.95**
Eyeglasses and contact lenses	230.03	262.07	246.76	230.17	292.08
Hearing aids	1,041.13	1,710.23	2,088.24	217.59	2,517.71
Medical equipment for general use	185.09	328.13	276.87	897.83	127.33
Supportive, convalescent medical equipment	156.52	83.80	64.73	103.95	96.94
Rental of medical equipment	153.85	159.52	131.67	326.14	23.21
Rental of supportive, convalescent medical equipment	157.95	161.76	25.00	111.25	295.59

Source: Calculations by New Strategist based on the Bureau of Labor Statistics' 2008 Consumer Expenditure Survey

Table 6.11 Percent of High-Income Households Spending Out-of-Pocket on Health Care, Average Week, 2008

(percent of high-income households with out-of-pocket health care expenses during the average week, by before-tax income of household, 2008)

	total households	$100,000 or more	$100,000– $119,999	$120,000– $149,999	$150,000 or more
Prescription drugs	18.0%	22.9%	22.3%	24.5%	22.2%
Nonprescription drugs	15.6	20.0	19.5	21.4	19.3
Nonprescription vitamins	4.2	5.7	5.4	5.6	6.0
Topicals and dressings	8.4	11.7	10.6	12.6	12.1

Source: Bureau of Labor Statistics, unpublished data from the 2008 Consumer Expenditure Survey

Table 6.12 Amount High-Income Buyers Spent Out-of-Pocket on Health Care, Average Week, 2008

(average amount spent by high-income households with out-of-pocket health care expenses during the average week, by before-tax income of household, 2008)

	total households	$100,000 or more	$100,000– $119,999	$120,000– $149,999	$150,000 or more
Prescription drugs	$13.54	$15.40	$15.41	$14.44	$16.20
Nonprescription drugs	10.71	12.37	12.45	12.00	12.65
Nonprescription vitamins	17.92	18.52	18.66	17.38	19.07
Topicals and dressings	7.05	8.82	6.70	7.28	11.85

Source: Calculations by New Strategist based on the Bureau of Labor Statistics' 2008 Consumer Expenditure Survey

Table 6.13 Percent Spending Out-of-Pocket on Health Care by Type of Household, <u>Average Quarter</u>, 2008

(percent of households with out-of-pocket health care expenses during the average quarter, by type of householder, 2008)

	total married couples	married couples, no children	married couples with children				single parent, at least one child <18	single person
			total	oldest child under 6	oldest child 6 to 17	oldest child 18 or older		
HEALTH CARE, PERCENT BUYING	**85.6%**	**90.0%**	**82.2%**	**77.8%**	**82.1%**	**85.0%**	**56.9%**	**70.6%**
Health insurance	**69.7**	**77.1**	**63.5**	**58.9**	**62.6**	**67.9**	**39.5**	**57.7**
Commercial health insurance	17.7	17.6	18.3	17.8	18.5	18.4	10.1	9.9
Traditional fee-for-service health plan (not BCBS)	4.9	5.8	4.1	4.1	3.8	4.4	2.1	2.9
Preferred-provider health plan (not BCBS)	13.1	12.1	14.5	14.1	14.7	14.3	8.1	7.0
Blue Cross, Blue Shield	24.1	23.9	24.7	24.1	24.6	25.3	14.6	15.2
Traditional fee-for-service health plan	4.0	4.7	3.4	2.4	3.5	3.9	1.0	2.9
Preferred-provider health plan	11.3	10.3	12.7	11.5	13.3	12.5	7.0	5.6
Health maintenance organization	7.2	6.4	7.8	10.0	6.7	8.2	6.3	4.5
Commercial Medicare supplement	1.6	2.5	0.9	0.4	0.9	1.2	0.3	1.9
Other BCBS health insurance	1.0	1.2	0.7	0.6	0.7	0.8	0.5	0.5
Health maintenance plans (HMOs)	16.0	14.8	17.2	15.4	17.2	18.2	8.6	9.9
Medicare payments	20.7	36.1	5.3	0.6	2.0	13.9	3.0	28.4
Medicare prescription drug premium	6.3	11.2	1.4	–	0.3	4.1	0.6	10.4
Commercial Medicare supplements/ other health insurance	12.6	15.4	10.6	10.5	10.0	11.5	7.4	9.8
Commercial Medicare supplement (not BCBS)	4.5	7.1	2.2	2.1	1.6	3.2	1.7	5.3
Other health insurance (not BCBS)	8.6	9.2	8.5	8.5	8.6	8.4	5.9	4.8
Long-term care insurance	3.7	5.0	2.5	1.8	2.6	2.8	1.1	2.4
Medical services	**52.0**	**51.2**	**53.9**	**52.7**	**54.4**	**53.6**	**30.4**	**29.3**
Physician's services	35.1	33.6	36.9	39.9	36.4	35.9	19.8	17.4
Dental services	18.7	18.3	19.8	12.7	22.3	19.8	9.8	8.1
Eye care services	8.4	8.8	8.4	5.7	8.8	9.3	3.4	4.4
Service by professionals other than physician	5.9	6.3	5.9	5.7	5.5	6.8	3.3	3.6
Lab tests, X-rays	7.2	8.0	6.8	6.4	6.6	7.5	4.7	3.4
Hospital room and services	5.5	5.5	5.8	7.4	5.5	5.4	3.3	2.2
Care in convalescent or nursing home	0.1	0.2	0.0	–	–	0.0	0.1	0.2
Other medical services	1.7	1.8	1.8	1.6	1.9	1.8	1.7	1.3
Prescription drugs	**49.2**	**55.9**	**43.6**	**38.4**	**42.0**	**49.7**	**27.0**	**34.6**
Medical supplies	**10.2**	**10.0**	**10.7**	**6.4**	**11.4**	**12.0**	**6.4**	**5.2**
Eyeglasses and contact lenses	8.6	7.9	9.6	5.8	10.4	10.5	5.7	3.7
Hearing aids	0.3	0.5	0.2	0.1	0.1	0.3	0.3	0.4
Medical equipment for general use	0.7	0.9	0.5	0.4	0.4	0.8	0.5	0.5
Supportive, convalescent medical equipment	0.5	0.7	0.4	0.2	0.5	0.5	0.2	0.5
Rental of medical equipment	0.3	0.3	0.2	0.3	0.3	0.1	0.2	0.3
Rental of supportive, convalescent medical equipment	0.2	0.3	0.2	0.1	0.3	0.2	0.1	0.2

Note: "–" means sample is too small to make a reliable estimate.
Source: Bureau of Labor Statistics, unpublished data from the 2008 Consumer Expenditure Survey

Table 6.14 Amount Buyers Spent Out-of-Pocket on Health Care by Type of Household, <u>Average Quarter</u>, 2008

(average amount spent by households with out-of-pocket health care expenses during the average quarter, by type of household, 2008)

	total married couples	married couples, no children	married couples with children			single parent, at least one child <18	single person
			total	oldest child under 6	oldest child 6 to 17	oldest child 18 or older		
HEALTH CARE, AMOUNT SPENT	**$1,104.62**	**$1,251.88**	**$980.52**	**$785.78**	**$977.50**	**$1,091.87**	**$624.49**	**$604.09**
Health insurance	**783.85**	**856.89**	**718.05**	**642.03**	**705.71**	**777.04**	**505.91**	**463.47**
Commercial health insurance	637.83	619.42	657.95	591.25	667.78	679.13	507.82	396.07
Traditional fee-for-service health plan (not BCBS)	616.24	604.12	629.00	480.37	632.03	707.97	650.96	410.29
Preferred-provider health plan (not BCBS)	635.60	616.45	656.98	606.65	673.95	656.48	470.84	386.14
Blue Cross, Blue Shield	696.31	714.46	685.01	614.99	714.13	675.92	529.90	392.12
Traditional fee-for-service health plan	709.21	729.20	721.93	531.67	826.21	627.95	467.42	394.86
Preferred-provider health plan	689.92	707.54	681.31	594.26	700.02	696.00	564.26	434.58
Health maintenance organization	685.47	715.86	660.99	614.65	702.00	636.78	489.06	340.95
Commercial Medicare supplement	601.68	600.71	528.30	932.93	528.57	445.45	510.58	404.90
Other BCBS health insurance	274.21	270.21	283.80	267.67	289.58	278.53	263.24	125.00
Health maintenance plans (HMOs)	595.47	578.42	628.24	612.93	629.70	633.52	482.68	329.57
Medicare payments	466.59	484.12	414.94	569.92	376.41	420.99	425.17	289.16
Medicare prescription drug premium	251.42	263.91	221.17	–	229.63	219.62	244.92	146.11
Commercial Medicare supplements/ other health insurance	305.04	353.87	237.76	239.46	204.06	287.57	184.01	278.54
Commercial Medicare supplement (not BCBS)	554.54	554.24	565.02	780.85	425.16	605.42	420.29	398.54
Other health insurance (not BCBS)	158.78	164.26	150.12	107.51	158.06	161.86	110.93	123.04
Long-term care insurance	535.48	701.24	305.97	104.71	198.82	550.36	89.64	501.16
Medical services	**480.76**	**529.66**	**447.11**	**326.11**	**475.07**	**468.83**	**362.27**	**329.60**
Physician's services	181.87	196.85	173.25	150.39	184.36	169.00	170.81	116.11
Dental services	464.17	488.66	425.37	270.62	430.65	474.47	381.39	452.26
Eye care services	146.82	168.42	129.68	142.08	123.00	136.01	74.70	145.15
Service by professionals other than physician	314.30	337.16	306.39	271.05	301.01	330.26	169.97	259.71
Lab tests, X-rays	257.80	277.25	243.50	243.00	267.43	207.11	220.48	206.54
Hospital room and services	684.24	675.46	696.74	480.96	775.32	735.54	461.69	408.67
Care in convalescent or nursing home	5,113.89	5,609.72	975.00	–	–	812.50	1,372.22	3,895.83
Other medical services	454.19	572.03	355.80	178.07	424.07	325.97	259.17	56.39
Prescription drugs	**245.98**	**293.37**	**188.53**	**126.03**	**175.89**	**235.62**	**123.40**	**146.77**
Medical supplies	**279.15**	**307.49**	**253.42**	**206.93**	**251.25**	**271.55**	**193.00**	**218.68**
Eyeglasses and contact lenses	241.08	261.04	223.14	211.05	213.20	243.80	178.53	213.17
Hearing aids	1,177.94	1,093.98	1,155.26	28.57	796.43	1,572.79	337.04	617.86
Medical equipment for general use	263.60	190.88	424.49	106.25	981.25	72.12	84.38	85.56
Supportive, convalescent medical equipment	166.98	216.43	94.05	98.33	97.83	88.24	296.67	112.50
Rental of medical equipment	193.75	160.00	266.30	55.00	266.13	662.50	110.94	71.43
Rental of supportive, convalescent medical equipment	222.92	255.17	185.87	335.71	227.59	59.78	206.82	100.00

Note: "–" means sample is too small to make a reliable estimate.
Source: Calculations by New Strategist based on the Bureau of Labor Statistics' 2008 Consumer Expenditure Survey

Table 6.15 Percent Spending Out-of-Pocket on Health Care by Type of Household, <u>Average Week</u>, 2008

(percent of households with out-of-pocket health care expenses during the average week, by type of householder, 2008)

| | total married couples | married couples, no children | married couples with children | | | | single parent, at least one child <18 | single person |
			total	oldest child under 6	oldest child 6 to 17	oldest child 18 or older		
Prescription drugs	22.2%	22.3%	21.4%	21.6%	19.7%	24.2%	12.9%	12.3%
Nonprescription drugs	19.4	18.9	19.1	18.1	17.6	22.3	11.5	10.4
Nonprescription vitamins	5.3	6.5	4.3	4.4	3.6	5.2	2.3	3.2
Topicals and dressings	10.3	10.0	10.3	11.5	9.2	11.6	7.7	5.3

Source: Bureau of Labor Statistics, unpublished data from the 2008 Consumer Expenditure Survey

Table 6.16 Amount Buyers Spent Out-of-Pocket on Health Care by Type of Household, <u>Average Week</u>, 2008

(average amount spent by households with out-of-pocket health care expenses during the average week, by type of household, 2008)

| | total married couples | married couples, no children | married couples with children | | | | single parent, at least one child <18 | single person |
			total	oldest child under 6	oldest child 6 to 17	oldest child 18 or older		
Prescription drugs	$13.58	$15.09	$12.44	$9.88	$11.91	$14.62	$12.28	$14.53
Nonprescription drugs	10.80	11.99	9.87	7.80	9.89	10.92	9.50	11.40
Nonprescription vitamins	17.52	16.97	18.35	16.33	16.76	21.37	20.87	18.87
Topicals and dressings	7.01	7.43	6.69	5.91	7.17	6.47	6.49	7.58

Source: Calculations by New Strategist based on the Bureau of Labor Statistics' 2008 Consumer Expenditure Survey

Table 6.17 Percent Spending Out-of-Pocket on Health Care by Race and Hispanic Origin, <u>Average Quarter</u>, 2008

(percent of households with out-of-pocket health care expenses during the average quarter, by race and Hispanic origin of householder, 2008)

	total households	Asian	black	Hispanic	non-Hispanic white and other
HEALTH CARE, PERCENT BUYING	**77.9%**	**67.5%**	**64.5%**	**58.8%**	**82.8%**
Health insurance	**63.0**	**55.1**	**51.4**	**41.8**	**68.0**
Commercial health insurance	14.3	12.1	10.4	7.9	15.9
Traditional fee-for-service health plan (not BCBS)	4.0	2.6	2.6	2.6	4.5
Preferred-provider health plan (not BCBS)	10.4	9.7	7.8	5.3	11.6
Blue Cross, Blue Shield	20.4	15.1	15.6	9.3	22.8
Traditional fee-for-service health plan	3.4	2.1	3.2	0.8	3.8
Preferred-provider health plan	8.9	5.7	5.6	3.4	10.2
Health maintenance organization	6.3	5.9	6.1	4.6	6.6
Commercial Medicare supplement	1.7	1.0	0.8	0.4	2.0
Other BCBS health insurance	0.7	0.6	0.4	0.2	0.9
Health maintenance plans (HMOs)	13.4	18.5	11.5	12.7	13.9
Medicare payments	22.2	11.7	17.3	11.6	24.6
Medicare prescription drug premium	7.3	3.6	6.5	4.3	7.9
Commercial Medicare supplements/other health insurance	11.3	8.0	5.6	5.4	13.0
Commercial Medicare supplement (not BCBS)	4.7	2.7	2.6	2.2	5.5
Other health insurance (not BCBS)	7.0	5.4	3.0	3.5	8.1
Long-term care insurance	3.0	2.2	1.5	1.2	3.5
Medical services	**41.6**	**30.8**	**25.2**	**28.0**	**46.2**
Physician's services	27.1	19.6	17.6	18.2	30.0
Dental services	13.8	9.9	5.8	7.6	16.0
Eye care services	6.4	4.6	3.6	3.8	7.3
Service by professionals other than physician	4.9	2.6	1.7	3.1	5.6
Lab tests, X-rays	5.7	3.4	2.1	3.6	6.5
Hospital room and services	4.1	1.8	1.9	3.1	4.6
Care in convalescent or nursing home	0.1	–	0.0	0.0	0.1
Other medical services	1.6	1.1	0.6	1.1	1.8
Prescription drugs	**41.9**	**26.0**	**30.2**	**25.0**	**46.3**
Medical supplies	**7.9**	**6.0**	**4.1**	**5.5**	**8.9**
Eyeglasses and contact lenses	6.5	5.5	3.4	4.8	7.3
Hearing aids	0.3	0.3	0.1	0.1	0.4
Medical equipment for general use	0.6	0.1	0.2	0.2	0.7
Supportive, convalescent medical equipment	0.5	0.1	0.2	0.2	0.5
Rental of medical equipment	0.3	0.0	0.2	0.1	0.3
Rental of supportive, convalescent medical equipment	0.2	–	0.1	0.2	0.3

Note: "Asian" and "black" include Hispanics and non-Hispanics who identify themselves as being of the respective race alone. "Hispanic" includes people of any race who identify themselves as Hispanic. "Other" includes people who identify themselves as non-Hispanic and as Alaska Native, American Indian, Asian (who are also included in the Asian column), or Native Hawaiian or other Pacific Islander as well as non-Hispanics reporting more than one race. "–" means sample is too small to make a reliable estimate.
Source: Bureau of Labor Statistics, unpublished data from the 2008 Consumer Expenditure Survey

Table 6.18 Amount Buyers Spent Out-of-Pocket on Health Care by Race and Hispanic Origin, Average Quarter, 2008

(average amount spent by households with out-of-pocket health care expenses during the average quarter, by race and Hispanic origin of householder, 2008)

	total households	Asian	black	Hispanic	non-Hispanic white and other
HEALTH CARE, AMOUNT SPENT	**$903.63**	**$774.90**	**$590.96**	**$616.57**	**$973.17**
Health insurance	**656.00**	**646.99**	**493.89**	**488.09**	**691.31**
Commercial health insurance	559.10	566.17	490.06	491.09	571.44
Traditional fee-for-service health plan (not BCBS)	544.84	587.60	582.44	473.65	547.70
Preferred-provider health plan (not BCBS)	554.96	549.41	458.32	499.62	569.71
Blue Cross, Blue Shield	584.93	687.00	457.91	469.99	606.06
Traditional fee-for-service health plan	591.49	666.39	452.46	536.25	610.63
Preferred-provider health plan	604.49	809.43	474.01	484.60	622.52
Health maintenance organization	560.29	543.43	442.30	449.24	589.61
Commercial Medicare supplement	492.21	835.64	345.73	409.66	504.66
Other BCBS health insurance	231.08	517.37	276.97	153.13	231.25
Health maintenance plans (HMOs)	505.32	510.61	384.80	425.83	532.95
Medicare payments	380.94	453.41	334.94	384.38	385.77
Medicare prescription drug premium	197.37	180.85	180.73	169.10	202.11
Commercial Medicare supplements/other health insurance	287.94	228.89	246.97	244.90	293.71
Commercial Medicare supplement (not BCBS)	471.88	459.44	386.93	358.95	485.64
Other health insurance (not BCBS)	145.15	110.04	123.10	158.45	145.68
Long-term care insurance	498.92	556.05	228.31	212.80	533.26
Medical services	**434.15**	**334.80**	**290.56**	**363.33**	**452.91**
Physician's services	168.00	192.85	97.47	139.21	177.18
Dental services	461.46	354.46	578.99	415.13	457.52
Eye care services	139.89	94.33	110.08	177.00	139.22
Service by professionals other than physician	291.29	350.77	249.85	235.06	297.91
Lab tests, X-rays	236.51	199.49	252.83	189.99	239.64
Hospital room and services	611.92	362.64	414.45	589.25	626.94
Care in convalescent or nursing home	4,143.18	–	1,600.00	1,700.00	4,191.07
Other medical services	325.00	341.97	144.92	514.58	318.61
Prescription drugs	**212.20**	**170.31**	**158.15**	**177.18**	**220.75**
Medical supplies	**261.02**	**321.05**	**164.79**	**224.82**	**271.16**
Eyeglasses and contact lenses	230.03	217.64	168.20	230.36	233.93
Hearing aids	1,041.13	2,180.47	197.73	100.00	1,100.00
Medical equipment for general use	185.09	13.89	137.50	105.88	188.21
Supportive, convalescent medical equipment	156.52	136.36	100.00	233.33	154.17
Rental of medical equipment	153.85	-18.75	148.61	328.57	142.24
Rental of supportive, convalescent medical equipment	157.95	–	81.25	13.33	169.23

Note: "Asian" and "black" include Hispanics and non-Hispanics who identify themselves as being of the respective race alone. "Hispanic" includes people of any race who identify themselves as Hispanic. "Other" includes people who identify themselves as non-Hispanic and as Alaska Native, American Indian, Asian (who are also included in the Asian column), or Native Hawaiian or other Pacific Islander as well as non-Hispanics reporting more than one race. "–" means sample is too small to make a reliable estimate.
Source: Calculations by New Strategist based on the Bureau of Labor Statistics' 2008 Consumer Expenditure Survey

Table 6.19 Percent Spending Out-of-Pocket on Health Care by Race and Hispanic Origin, <u>Average Week</u>, 2008

(percent of households with out-of-pocket health care expenses during the average week, by race and Hispanic origin of householder, 2008)

	total households	Asian	black	Hispanic	non-Hispanic white and other
Prescription drugs	18.0%	15.6%	12.4%	16.5%	19.0%
Nonprescription drugs	15.6	12.6	11.3	14.8	16.4
Nonprescription vitamins	4.2	3.8	1.6	2.9	4.8
Topicals and dressings	8.4	5.2	5.0	8.0	8.9

Note: "Asian" and "black" include Hispanics and non-Hispanics who identify themselves as being of the respective race alone. "Hispanic" includes people of any race who identify themselves as Hispanic. "Other" includes people who identify themselves as non-Hispanic and as Alaska Native, American Indian, Asian (who are also included in the Asian column), or Native Hawaiian or other Pacific Islander as well as non-Hispanics reporting more than one race.
Source: Bureau of Labor Statistics, unpublished data from the 2008 Consumer Expenditure Survey

Table 6.20 Amount Buyers Spent Out-of-Pocket on Health Care by Race and Hispanic Origin, <u>Average Week</u>, 2008

(average amount spent by households with out-of-pocket health care expenses during the average week, by race and Hispanic origin of householder, 2008)

	total households	Asian	black	Hispanic	non-Hispanic white and other
Prescription drugs	$13.54	$14.92	$9.34	$11.29	$14.23
Nonprescription drugs	10.71	10.01	7.60	9.52	11.17
Nonprescription vitamins	17.92	28.01	18.99	15.31	18.26
Topicals and dressings	7.05	7.66	3.57	6.28	7.50

Note: "Asian" and "black" include Hispanics and non-Hispanics who identify themselves as being of the respective race alone. "Hispanic" includes people of any race who identify themselves as Hispanic. "Other" includes people who identify themselves as non-Hispanic and as Alaska Native, American Indian, Asian (who are also included in the Asian column), or Native Hawaiian or other Pacific Islander as well as non-Hispanics reporting more than one race.
Source: Calculations by New Strategist based on the Bureau of Labor Statistics' 2008 Consumer Expenditure Survey

Table 6.21 Percent Spending Out-of-Pocket on Health Care by Region, Average Quarter, 2008

(percent of households with out-of-pocket health care expenses during the average quarter, by region of residence, 2008)

	total households	Northeast	Midwest	South	West
HEALTH CARE, PERCENT BUYING	**77.9%**	**79.8%**	**80.9%**	**76.3%**	**75.6%**
Health insurance	**63.0**	**66.4**	**65.0**	**62.5**	**59.0**
Commercial health insurance	14.3	11.4	16.2	14.5	14.4
Traditional fee-for-service health plan (not BCBS)	4.0	5.0	4.3	3.3	4.1
Preferred-provider health plan (not BCBS)	10.4	6.5	11.9	11.4	10.6
Blue Cross, Blue Shield	20.4	24.3	21.6	21.2	14.6
Traditional fee-for-service health plan	3.4	3.9	3.2	3.9	2.2
Preferred-provider health plan	8.9	7.9	10.5	9.2	7.5
Health maintenance organization	6.3	9.9	5.6	6.6	3.7
Commercial Medicare supplement	1.7	2.6	2.0	1.4	1.2
Other BCBS health insurance	0.7	0.8	0.9	0.7	0.6
Health maintenance plans (HMOs)	13.4	15.6	13.4	10.7	16.2
Medicare payments	22.2	24.7	21.3	23.0	19.7
Medicare prescription drug premium	7.3	7.0	8.0	7.8	6.2
Commercial Medicare supplements/other health insurance	11.3	11.9	12.8	10.7	10.1
Commercial Medicare supplement (not BCBS)	4.7	5.5	5.1	4.6	4.0
Other health insurance (not BCBS)	7.0	6.8	8.1	6.7	6.4
Long-term care insurance	3.0	3.2	2.9	3.0	3.1
Medical services	**41.6**	**43.9**	**43.7**	**38.7**	**42.3**
Physician's services	27.1	29.8	26.7	26.2	26.8
Dental services	13.8	15.1	15.1	11.7	14.7
Eye care services	6.4	7.0	7.7	5.7	5.8
Service by professionals other than physician	4.9	4.8	5.6	4.0	5.5
Lab tests, X-rays	5.7	5.7	6.0	5.3	6.0
Hospital room and services	4.1	3.8	5.4	3.7	3.9
Care in convalescent or nursing home	0.1	0.1	0.2	0.1	0.1
Other medical services	1.6	1.5	1.7	1.3	1.9
Prescription drugs	**41.9**	**43.1**	**44.8**	**41.8**	**38.1**
Medical supplies	**7.9**	**8.6**	**9.1**	**7.1**	**7.6**
Eyeglasses and contact lenses	6.5	7.1	7.6	5.8	6.1
Hearing aids	0.3	0.3	0.4	0.2	0.4
Medical equipment for general use	0.6	0.6	0.6	0.6	0.5
Supportive, convalescent medical equipment	0.5	0.3	0.6	0.5	0.4
Rental of medical equipment	0.3	0.4	0.1	0.2	0.3
Rental of supportive, convalescent medical equipment	0.2	0.2	0.2	0.1	0.3

Source: Bureau of Labor Statistics, unpublished data from the 2008 Consumer Expenditure Survey

Table 6.22 Amount Buyers Spent Out-of-Pocket on Health Care by Region, <u>Average Quarter</u>, 2008

(average amount spent by households with out-of-pocket health care expenses during the average quarter, by region of residence, 2008)

	total households	Northeast	Midwest	South	West
HEALTH CARE, AMOUNT SPENT	**$903.63**	**$905.34**	**$894.46**	**$882.80**	**$946.48**
Health insurance	**656.00**	**662.23**	**665.32**	**636.59**	**672.99**
Commercial health insurance	559.10	525.88	574.78	543.42	587.98
Traditional fee-for-service health plan (not BCBS)	544.84	567.07	563.23	518.27	540.57
Preferred-provider health plan (not BCBS)	554.96	481.39	576.05	541.10	593.06
Blue Cross, Blue Shield	584.93	617.74	550.43	563.21	643.50
Traditional fee-for-service health plan	591.49	653.49	519.44	546.95	738.66
Preferred-provider health plan	604.49	627.48	579.93	591.10	648.07
Health maintenance organization	560.29	606.50	535.47	524.96	599.93
Commercial Medicare supplement	492.21	513.75	463.39	530.00	436.74
Other BCBS health insurance	231.08	231.55	203.74	197.92	348.64
Health maintenance plans (HMOs)	505.32	498.65	487.95	496.34	534.95
Medicare payments	380.94	371.30	388.71	383.03	378.52
Medicare prescription drug premium	197.37	193.07	211.33	179.67	218.04
Commercial Medicare supplements/other health insurance	287.94	273.52	307.71	294.34	265.93
Commercial Medicare supplement (not BCBS)	471.88	397.59	557.69	495.00	401.73
Other health insurance (not BCBS)	145.15	156.22	135.11	134.27	166.69
Long-term care insurance	498.92	451.11	557.08	460.64	543.69
Medical services	**434.15**	**394.21**	**408.31**	**419.80**	**517.43**
Physician's services	168.00	145.80	162.32	169.90	191.29
Dental services	461.46	514.35	365.05	446.78	536.78
Eye care services	139.89	114.79	136.72	149.25	154.24
Service by professionals other than physician	291.29	263.58	234.86	289.57	374.68
Lab tests, X-rays	236.51	168.17	244.45	281.27	218.80
Hospital room and services	611.92	455.87	551.68	650.00	768.85
Care in convalescent or nursing home	4,143.18	3,179.55	3,940.28	2,752.50	8,217.86
Other medical services	325.00	32.83	298.79	307.28	557.51
Prescription drugs	**212.20**	**200.60**	**197.81**	**224.86**	**217.96**
Medical supplies	**261.02**	**274.42**	**266.61**	**274.36**	**222.10**
Eyeglasses and contact lenses	230.03	248.88	237.12	222.13	214.14
Hearing aids	1,041.13	991.18	1,145.95	2,031.25	174.39
Medical equipment for general use	185.09	119.74	148.05	199.55	269.71
Supportive, convalescent medical equipment	156.52	113.33	127.63	182.35	171.88
Rental of medical equipment	153.85	181.55	111.54	135.23	172.58
Rental of supportive, convalescent medical equipment	157.95	246.74	87.50	189.29	131.82

Source: Calculations by New Strategist based on the Bureau of Labor Statistics' 2008 Consumer Expenditure Survey

Table 6.23 Percent Spending Out-of-Pocket on Health Care by Region, <u>Average Week</u>, 2008

(percent of households with out-of-pocket health care expenses during the average week, by region of residence, 2008)

	total households	Northeast	Midwest	South	West
Prescription drugs	18.0%	16.1%	16.2%	19.5%	18.8%
Nonprescription drugs	15.6	14.0	14.1	17.4	15.5
Nonprescription vitamins	4.2	3.7	4.0	4.0	5.3
Topicals and dressings	8.4	8.1	8.4	8.4	8.5

Source: Bureau of Labor Statistics, unpublished data from the 2008 Consumer Expenditure Survey

Table 6.24 Amount Buyers Spent Out-of-Pocket on Health Care by Region, <u>Average Week</u>, 2008

(average amount spent by households with out-of-pocket health care expenses during the average week, by region of residence, 2008)

	total households	Northeast	Midwest	South	West
Prescription drugs	$13.54	$13.27	$14.25	$11.93	$15.81
Nonprescription drugs	10.71	10.49	10.88	9.92	11.97
Nonprescription vitamins	17.92	17.91	19.50	14.90	20.83
Topicals and dressings	7.05	7.80	7.03	6.41	7.76

Source: Calculations by New Strategist based on the Bureau of Labor Statistics' 2008 Consumer Expenditure Survey

Table 6.25 Percent Spending Out-of-Pocket on Health Care by Education, <u>Average Quarter</u>, 2008

(percent of households with out-of-pocket health care expenses during the average quarter, by highest level of education of householder, 2008)

						college graduate		
	total households	less than high school graduate	high school graduate	some college	associate's degree	total	bachelor's degree	master's, professional, doctorate
HEALTH CARE, PERCENT BUYING	77.9%	66.4%	78.1%	73.9%	83.0%	84.9%	83.1%	88.2%
Health insurance	**63.0**	**52.2**	**64.3**	**57.6**	**67.7**	**69.9**	**67.4**	**74.4**
Commercial health insurance	14.3	7.1	12.6	13.4	15.8	19.7	19.3	20.4
Traditional fee-for-service health plan (not BCBS)	4.0	3.0	3.8	3.8	5.2	4.5	4.3	5.0
Preferred-provider health plan (not BCBS)	10.4	4.1	8.9	9.8	11.0	15.4	15.1	15.9
Blue Cross, Blue Shield	20.4	11.4	18.9	20.1	22.9	25.6	25.0	26.5
Traditional fee-for-service health plan	3.4	2.4	3.3	3.3	3.7	3.9	3.7	4.3
Preferred-provider health plan	8.9	3.2	7.4	8.7	9.5	12.9	13.3	12.2
Health maintenance organization	6.3	3.6	6.2	6.5	7.9	7.3	6.9	7.9
Commercial Medicare supplement	1.7	2.3	1.8	1.7	1.7	1.3	1.2	1.5
Other BCBS health insurance	0.7	0.5	0.6	0.6	0.8	1.1	0.8	1.6
Health maintenance plans (HMOs)	13.4	8.8	13.3	12.6	16.1	15.7	15.1	16.7
Medicare payments	22.2	32.5	27.8	17.9	19.5	16.2	15.2	18.0
Medicare prescription drug premium	7.3	12.3	8.6	6.1	5.7	5.2	5.1	5.3
Commercial Medicare supplements/ other health insurance	11.3	6.8	12.0	10.1	13.3	13.0	12.2	14.6
Commercial Medicare supplement (not BCBS)	4.7	4.1	6.7	3.6	4.9	4.1	4.3	3.7
Other health insurance (not BCBS)	7.0	2.9	5.9	6.9	8.9	9.3	8.1	11.5
Long-term care insurance	3.0	0.6	2.4	2.9	3.4	4.7	3.9	6.2
Medical services	**41.6**	**27.3**	**37.5**	**41.1**	**46.1**	**51.4**	**49.2**	**55.3**
Physician's services	27.1	17.9	24.5	26.8	29.9	33.3	32.0	35.7
Dental services	13.8	5.8	11.4	13.4	15.0	19.8	18.3	22.5
Eye care services	6.4	3.5	6.0	6.2	6.6	8.4	8.0	9.2
Service by professionals other than physician	4.9	2.8	4.1	4.9	5.4	6.3	6.0	6.9
Lab tests, X-rays	5.7	3.3	4.8	6.0	6.5	7.1	6.5	8.2
Hospital room and services	4.1	3.3	3.8	4.4	5.3	4.2	4.2	4.4
Care in convalescent or nursing home	0.1	0.1	0.1	0.1	0.2	0.1	0.1	0.1
Other medical services	1.6	1.1	1.1	1.3	2.2	2.1	1.9	2.5
Prescription drugs	**41.9**	**35.7**	**42.6**	**40.1**	**45.2**	**44.8**	**43.0**	**48.0**
Medical supplies	**7.9**	**4.6**	**7.0**	**7.7**	**8.9**	**10.3**	**10.0**	**11.0**
Eyeglasses and contact lenses	6.5	3.2	5.5	6.5	7.0	8.9	8.5	9.7
Hearing aids	0.3	0.4	0.2	0.3	0.5	0.3	0.3	0.2
Medical equipment for general use	0.6	0.5	0.6	0.4	0.8	0.7	0.6	0.8
Supportive, convalescent medical equipment	0.5	0.4	0.5	0.3	0.6	0.6	0.7	0.4
Rental of medical equipment	0.3	0.2	0.2	0.3	0.4	0.3	0.3	0.1
Rental of supportive, convalescent medical equipment	0.2	0.2	0.2	0.3	0.3	0.2	0.2	0.2

Source: Bureau of Labor Statistics, unpublished data from the 2008 Consumer Expenditure Survey

Table 6.26 Amount Buyers Spent Out-of-Pocket on Health Care by Education, <u>Average Quarter</u>, 2008

(average amount spent by households with out-of-pocket health care expenses during the average quarter, by highest level of education of householder, 2008)

	total households	less than high school graduate	high school graduate	some college	associate's degree	college graduate total	bachelor's degree	master's, professional, doctorate
HEALTH CARE, AMOUNT SPENT	$903.63	$712.55	$832.20	$892.98	$899.06	$1,045.15	$984.82	$1,147.11
Health insurance	656.00	576.60	612.98	646.82	653.71	727.07	701.87	768.01
Commercial health insurance	559.10	523.40	488.04	548.33	628.38	592.83	552.06	662.40
Traditional fee-for-service health plan (not BCBS)	544.84	535.53	498.68	547.41	570.25	572.52	561.21	591.15
Preferred-provider health plan (not BCBS)	554.96	506.63	477.96	538.06	639.13	589.96	546.93	664.11
Blue Cross, Blue Shield	584.93	465.88	525.50	586.41	545.17	660.91	647.50	683.31
Traditional fee-for-service health plan	591.49	481.22	542.42	584.37	591.33	665.86	609.01	755.24
Preferred-provider health plan	604.49	402.50	555.51	607.82	525.71	671.79	648.95	716.15
Health maintenance organization	560.29	485.81	483.04	564.34	556.32	635.85	651.52	612.55
Commercial Medicare supplement	492.21	486.67	458.02	480.65	492.73	553.65	479.75	668.62
Other BCBS health insurance	231.08	112.23	307.08	198.73	127.11	259.72	265.79	257.01
Health maintenance plans (HMOs)	505.32	420.67	471.81	498.26	534.52	548.95	533.19	574.25
Medicare payments	380.94	374.45	382.97	382.11	378.65	384.24	383.89	384.66
Medicare prescription drug premium	197.37	208.57	188.95	178.48	170.18	222.43	218.04	229.62
Commercial Medicare supplements/ other health insurance	287.94	331.90	317.23	282.54	275.49	260.20	265.01	252.66
Commercial Medicare supplement (not BCBS)	471.88	450.00	440.01	476.40	499.23	514.66	521.12	500.33
Other health insurance (not BCBS)	145.15	134.71	143.90	168.48	136.98	136.83	120.20	157.91
Long-term care insurance	498.92	716.67	391.29	368.51	360.34	626.48	593.59	663.77
Medical services	434.15	329.67	381.84	437.49	431.90	494.42	467.59	537.21
Physician's services	168.00	135.21	149.12	157.79	155.54	198.84	185.84	219.70
Dental services	461.46	360.29	430.27	467.64	482.38	484.00	446.08	539.17
Eye care services	139.89	124.36	120.23	127.88	171.50	154.22	128.82	193.61
Service by professionals other than physician	291.29	253.62	256.48	285.80	216.96	343.85	359.92	319.40
Lab tests, X-rays	236.51	192.17	244.88	224.87	243.14	247.55	247.01	248.18
Hospital room and services	611.92	686.36	585.30	651.30	527.56	606.19	655.20	521.32
Care in convalescent or nursing home	4,143.18	762.50	1,753.57	4,944.23	3,222.22	7,522.50	9,741.67	4,063.46
Other medical services	325.00	289.09	386.28	317.91	344.26	304.93	263.74	362.85
Prescription drugs	212.20	204.65	221.89	217.55	177.83	214.51	206.12	228.04
Medical supplies	261.02	192.99	252.42	261.14	268.70	279.45	265.11	302.85
Eyeglasses and contact lenses	230.03	207.47	226.41	216.28	243.19	240.10	225.29	263.40
Hearing aids	1,041.13	87.50	1,247.73	1,364.52	573.89	1,515.00	1,305.88	2,057.61
Medical equipment for general use	185.09	115.22	218.15	139.74	220.89	188.08	135.59	259.87
Supportive, convalescent medical equipment	156.52	119.29	88.78	103.91	287.93	198.66	209.85	165.13
Rental of medical equipment	153.85	343.75	169.74	122.50	129.61	101.00	97.66	111.54
Rental of supportive, convalescent medical equipment	157.95	95.00	169.57	174.11	142.97	150.00	157.89	134.38

Source: Calculations by New Strategist based on the Bureau of Labor Statistics' 2008 Consumer Expenditure Survey

Table 6.27 Percent Spending Out-of-Pocket on Health Care by Education, <u>Average Week</u>, 2008

(percent of households with out-of-pocket health care expenses during the average week, by highest level of education of householder, 2008)

	total households	less than high school graduate	high school graduate	some college	associate's degree	college graduate total	college graduate bachelor's degree	college graduate master's, professional, doctorate
Prescription drugs	18.0%	15.3%	16.6%	18.0%	20.0%	19.9%	19.6%	20.4%
Nonprescription drugs	15.6	14.0	14.5	15.9	17.6	16.5	16.1	17.2
Nonprescription vitamins	4.2	2.8	3.6	3.6	4.6	5.9	5.8	6.0
Topicals and dressings	8.4	7.2	7.4	8.0	9.4	9.8	10.0	9.4

Source: Bureau of Labor Statistics, unpublished data from the 2008 Consumer Expenditure Survey

Table 6.28 Amount Buyers Spent Out-of-Pocket on Health Care by Education, <u>Average Week</u>, 2008

(average amount spent by households with out-of-pocket health care expenses during the average week, by highest level of education of householder, 2008)

	total households	less than high school graduate	high school graduate	some college	associate's degree	college graduate total	college graduate bachelor's degree	college graduate master's, professional, doctorate
Prescription drugs	$13.54	$11.86	$12.45	$12.79	$13.93	$15.36	$14.78	$16.45
Nonprescription drugs	10.71	9.08	10.08	9.79	11.72	12.14	11.95	12.43
Nonprescription vitamins	17.92	19.57	16.57	20.73	15.72	17.97	16.61	20.33
Topicals and dressings	7.05	6.10	6.39	6.88	6.16	8.36	7.89	9.32

Source: Calculations by New Strategist based on the Bureau of Labor Statistics' 2008 Consumer Expenditure Survey

CHAPTER 7

Housing Buyers: Household Services, Supplies, and Furnishings, 2008

Between 2000 and 2008, average household spending on furnishings declined 16 percent, after adjusting for inflation, despite near record levels of homeownership. In contrast, spending on household services grew during those years. Behind these diverging trends is the growing importance of Internet service, which now ranks first among household services, supplies, and furnishings categories in the percentage of households spending on it during an average quarter.

Quarterly spending

During the average quarter of 2008, the 54 percent majority of households bought computer information services, making it the most common household service. The percentage of households buying computer information services ranges from a high of 63 percent among 35-to-44-year-olds to a low of 26 percent among householders aged 75 or older. The buyers paid an average of $102 during the quarter for Internet service. Householders aged 25 to 44 are most likely to spend on day care centers, 11 to 12 percent having done so during the average quarter of 2008. The percentage of households that paid for gardening and lawn care service during the average quarter rises with age from just 2 percent of householders under age 25 to a high of 23 percent among householders aged 75 or older.

Weekly spending

During the average week of 2008, 54 percent of households bought housekeeping supplies. Seven percent of households purchased lawn and garden supplies during the average week, the figure peaking at 10 percent among householders aged 65 to 74. Householders aged 65 to 74 are also the ones most likely to buy postage during the average week, 12 percent doing so and the purchasers spending an average of $19.

Household Services, Supplies, and Furnishings Buyers' Top 10

*(household services, supplies, and furnishings categories bought by the largest
percentage of households during an average quarter, 2008)*

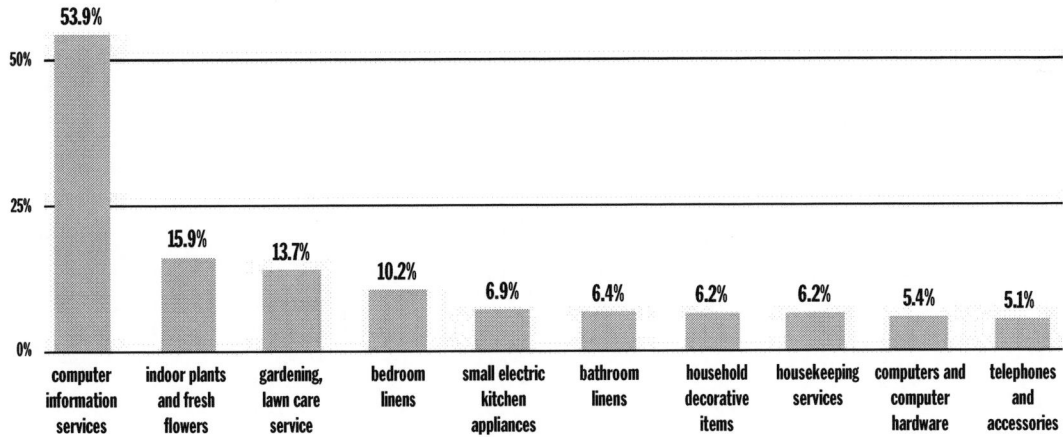

Table 7.1 Percent Buying Household Services, Furnishings, and Equipment by Age, <u>Average Quarter</u>, 2008

(percent of households buying household services, furnishings, and equipment during the average quarter, by age of householder, 2008)

	total households	under 25	25 to 34	35 to 44	45 to 54	55 to 64	65 to 74	75+
HOUSEHOLD SERVICES, PERCENT BUYING	**65.9%**	**47.6%**	**68.0%**	**72.3%**	**70.2%**	**69.9%**	**59.3%**	**53.4%**
Personal services	**7.3**	**4.0**	**16.2**	**14.2**	**4.4**	**1.8**	**1.2**	**2.8**
Babysitting and child care in own home	1.6	0.5	3.1	4.2	1.2	0.2	0.1	–
Babysitting and child care in someone else's home	1.1	1.2	3.1	1.7	0.5	0.1	0.1	–
Care for elderly, invalids, handicapped, etc.	0.4	–	0.0	0.1	0.4	0.5	0.4	2.4
Day care centers, nurseries, and preschools	5.0	2.4	11.7	10.6	2.9	1.0	0.4	0.3
Other household services	**64.4**	**45.6**	**63.9**	**70.4**	**69.3**	**69.6**	**59.0**	**52.6**
Housekeeping services	6.2	0.7	2.5	5.4	6.2	8.5	7.2	12.7
Gardening, lawn care service	13.7	2.1	8.3	11.7	13.9	17.6	19.0	23.0
Water-softening service	1.4	1.1	1.1	1.8	1.2	1.8	1.8	1.3
Nonclothing laundry and dry cleaning, sent out	0.6	0.2	0.5	0.5	0.5	0.9	0.9	0.5
Nonclothing laundry and dry cleaning, coin-operated	3.5	6.0	4.9	3.3	3.1	3.1	2.4	2.7
Termite and pest control services	3.6	0.7	2.2	3.8	3.4	5.1	5.2	4.1
Home security system service fee	4.6	0.5	3.5	5.9	5.0	6.0	4.6	3.6
Other home services	2.0	0.3	1.3	1.6	2.3	2.5	2.7	3.4
Termite and pest control products	2.5	0.4	1.7	2.5	2.2	3.5	3.7	3.3
Moving, storage, and freight express	2.1	1.4	2.2	2.0	2.5	2.5	1.9	1.2
Appliance repair, including at service center	2.5	0.5	1.4	2.3	3.3	3.2	3.1	2.5
Reupholstering and furniture repair	0.5	0.2	0.3	0.5	0.6	0.8	0.8	0.4
Repairs and rentals of lawn and garden equipment, hand and power tools, etc.	1.2	0.1	0.8	1.2	1.5	1.4	1.8	1.1
Appliance rental	0.2	0.1	0.2	0.4	0.2	0.1	0.3	–
Rental of office equipment for nonbusiness use	0.0	–	0.1	0.0	–	0.0	0.1	–
Repair of computer systems for nonbusiness use	0.8	0.6	0.5	0.9	0.9	1.0	0.8	0.3
Computer information services	53.9	37.0	56.8	62.9	61.5	59.0	45.5	26.2
Installation of computer	0.1	0.1	0.1	–	0.1	0.1	0.1	–
HOUSEHOLD FURNISHINGS AND EQUIPMENT, PERCENT BUYING	**52.7**	**49.8**	**53.2**	**55.1**	**56.1**	**55.7**	**50.0**	**39.0**
Household textiles	**19.3**	**18.4**	**19.7**	**20.4**	**20.6**	**20.3**	**18.9**	**12.7**
Bathroom linens	6.4	7.4	7.0	6.7	7.3	6.3	5.7	3.1
Bedroom linens	10.2	10.3	10.8	11.4	11.4	10.1	9.0	5.7
Kitchen and dining room linens	1.7	1.7	1.7	1.7	2.1	1.6	2.1	0.9
Curtains and draperies	2.4	2.4	3.2	3.2	2.3	2.1	2.1	0.7
Slipcovers and decorative pillows	1.2	1.1	1.4	1.3	1.3	1.4	1.2	0.8
Sewing materials for household items	3.4	1.9	2.7	2.3	3.4	5.1	4.7	3.9
Other linens	0.5	0.4	0.4	0.4	0.5	0.6	0.3	0.4
Furniture	**10.2**	**12.5**	**12.7**	**10.8**	**10.3**	**9.8**	**8.5**	**4.6**
Mattresses and springs	1.7	1.6	2.2	1.8	1.8	1.6	1.1	1.3
Other bedroom furniture	1.9	2.3	2.9	2.3	1.9	1.8	1.2	0.5
Sofas	2.2	4.0	2.8	2.8	2.0	1.5	1.3	0.9
Living room chairs	1.7	2.4	1.7	1.8	1.7	1.6	1.6	1.3
Living room tables	1.4	2.4	1.7	1.6	1.4	1.2	0.9	0.7
Kitchen and dining room furniture	1.2	1.3	1.5	1.2	1.2	1.3	0.8	0.4
Infants' furniture	0.8	2.0	1.4	0.7	0.5	0.7	0.4	0.1
Outdoor furniture	1.5	0.5	1.5	1.8	1.7	1.7	1.3	0.6
Wall units, cabinets, and other furniture	2.7	4.1	3.7	2.9	2.8	2.2	2.2	1.1
Floor coverings	**3.0**	**2.7**	**2.7**	**3.4**	**3.4**	**3.1**	**2.7**	**1.7**
Wall-to-wall carpeting	0.3	0.2	0.2	0.4	0.3	0.4	0.4	0.3
Floor coverings, nonpermanent	2.6	2.6	2.5	3.1	3.1	2.7	2.3	1.4
Major appliances	**8.2**	**7.9**	**8.0**	**9.1**	**8.4**	**9.0**	**7.1**	**5.7**
Dishwashers (built-in), garbage disposals, range hoods (renter)	0.1	0.2	0.1	0.1	0.0	0.0	–	0.0
Dishwashers (built-in), garbage disposals, range hoods (owner)	0.6	0.2	0.3	0.8	0.8	1.0	0.6	0.4

	total consumer units	under 25	25 to 34	35 to 44	45 to 54	55 to 64	65 to 74	75+
Refrigerators, freezers (renter)	0.4%	1.0%	0.7%	0.4%	0.3%	0.2%	0.1%	0.2%
Refrigerators, freezers (owner)	1.3	0.6	1.3	1.5	1.2	1.9	1.1	1.1
Washing machines (renter)	0.4	1.0	0.7	0.4	0.2	0.4	0.2	0.2
Washing machines (owner)	1.0	0.4	0.6	1.3	1.3	1.2	0.8	0.9
Clothes dryers (renter)	0.3	0.6	0.5	0.3	0.2	0.2	0.1	0.2
Clothes dryers (owner)	0.9	0.5	0.4	1.1	1.0	1.0	0.7	0.8
Cooking stoves, ovens (renter)	0.1	0.1	0.3	0.2	0.1	0.0	0.1	0.1
Cooking stoves, ovens (owner)	0.7	0.4	0.4	0.7	0.9	0.7	0.9	0.4
Microwave ovens (renter)	0.7	2.6	1.3	0.7	0.5	0.3	0.1	0.1
Microwave ovens (owner)	1.0	0.4	0.7	1.1	1.2	1.3	0.9	0.8
Window air conditioners (renter)	0.2	0.2	0.3	0.1	0.1	0.2	0.1	0.1
Window air conditioners (owner)	0.3	0.2	0.1	0.2	0.5	0.4	0.3	0.2
Electric floor-cleaning equipment	2.4	2.3	2.6	2.7	2.2	2.6	2.1	1.6
Sewing machines	0.3	0.1	0.2	0.3	0.2	0.5	0.5	0.1
Small appliances and misc. housewares	**16.1**	**17.9**	**17.6**	**16.6**	**17.2**	**17.1**	**13.6**	**9.4**
Housewares	9.9	12.0	11.9	11.0	10.6	9.9	7.3	4.3
Plastic dinnerware	2.5	3.2	3.6	3.1	2.5	2.0	1.8	0.8
China and other dinnerware	2.5	4.0	3.2	2.4	2.8	2.4	1.6	1.0
Flatware	1.4	2.5	1.7	1.5	1.6	1.2	1.1	0.4
Glassware	1.9	2.7	2.2	2.4	1.9	2.0	1.6	0.6
Silver serving pieces	0.1	0.0	0.1	0.1	0.0	0.1	0.1	0.1
Other serving pieces	0.7	1.0	0.7	0.5	0.8	0.7	0.4	0.5
Nonelectric cookware	3.5	4.5	3.9	3.4	3.7	3.8	2.2	2.2
Small appliances	8.1	8.3	8.0	7.5	8.8	9.5	7.6	5.9
Small electric kitchen appliances	6.9	6.8	6.8	6.4	7.4	8.1	6.6	5.0
Portable heating and cooling equipment	1.5	1.7	1.6	1.3	1.8	1.6	1.4	1.1
Miscellaneous household equipment	**35.8**	**32.8**	**36.4**	**37.3**	**39.5**	**38.7**	**32.9**	**24.4**
Window coverings	1.7	1.2	2.0	2.0	1.9	1.7	1.6	0.8
Infants' equipment	0.6	1.4	1.4	0.5	0.4	0.4	0.2	0.1
Outdoor equipment	1.2	0.8	1.3	1.4	1.6	1.1	1.1	0.2
Lamps and lighting fixtures	3.5	4.2	3.9	3.5	3.6	3.5	3.4	1.6
Clocks and other household decorative items	6.2	7.2	6.7	6.3	6.9	6.1	5.7	3.1
Telephones and accessories	5.1	5.1	5.7	6.1	6.1	4.5	3.4	2.3
Lawn and garden equipment	2.3	0.8	2.1	2.7	2.8	2.9	2.4	1.1
Power tools	2.1	1.1	2.0	2.2	2.6	2.6	1.9	0.5
Office furniture for home use	0.7	0.7	0.9	0.8	0.4	0.7	0.8	0.2
Hand tools	1.7	1.4	2.0	1.8	1.8	2.0	1.4	0.9
Indoor plants and fresh flowers	15.9	8.9	13.3	15.5	17.6	20.2	17.3	13.5
Closet and storage items	1.3	1.8	2.2	1.2	1.4	1.3	0.9	0.5
Rental of furniture	0.2	0.5	0.3	0.3	0.1	0.1	0.0	–
Luggage	1.4	0.8	1.3	1.9	1.7	1.7	1.0	0.6
Computers and computer hardware, nonbusiness use	5.4	5.2	6.3	5.9	6.5	5.5	4.3	1.9
Computer software and accessories, nonbusiness use	4.5	3.8	4.5	4.8	5.5	5.1	3.9	2.1
Personal digital assistants	0.3	0.2	0.4	0.4	0.5	0.2	0.1	0.1
Internet services away from home	0.8	1.3	0.7	1.1	0.9	0.6	0.7	0.3
Telephone answering devices	0.2	0.1	0.2	0.1	0.3	0.3	0.2	0.1
Business equipment for home use	0.6	0.7	0.5	0.7	0.7	0.5	0.7	0.6
Smoke alarms (owner)	0.4	0.2	0.4	0.3	0.5	0.5	0.6	0.4
Smoke alarms (renter)	0.1	0.1	0.2	0.2	0.1	0.1	0.1	–
Other household appliances (owner)	1.0	0.2	0.7	0.9	1.1	1.5	1.5	1.1
Other household appliances (renter)	0.3	0.7	0.5	0.3	0.2	0.4	0.1	0.3

Note: "–" means sample is too small to make a reliable estimate.
Source: Bureau of Labor Statistics, unpublished data from the 2008 Consumer Expenditure Survey

Table 7.2 Amount Buyers Spent on Household Services, Furnishings, and Equipment by Age, <u>Average Quarter</u>, 2008

(average amount spent by households buying household services, furnishings, and equipment during the average quarter, by age of householder, 2008)

	total households	under 25	25 to 34	35 to 44	45 to 54	55 to 64	65 to 74	75+
HOUSEHOLD SERVICES, AMOUNT SPENT	**$377.80**	**$170.88**	**$417.87**	**$475.42**	**$341.48**	**$314.13**	**$315.89**	**$483.06**
Personal services	**1,312.33**	**887.53**	**1,110.93**	**1,348.24**	**1,417.10**	**985.53**	**1,763.11**	**3,186.88**
Babysitting and child care in own home	717.33	350.48	516.19	728.82	1,196.98	510.94	350.00	–
Babysitting and child care in someone else's home	838.68	602.85	876.61	836.48	514.29	380.00	4,409.09	–
Care for elderly, invalids, handicapped, etc.	3,063.64	–	450.00	210.00	3,338.51	1,648.37	3,096.25	3,603.93
Day care centers, nurseries, and preschools	1,224.95	1,071.37	1,165.71	1,378.43	1,185.10	642.60	563.95	649.04
Other household services	**238.01**	**101.56**	**163.08**	**216.22**	**255.22**	**290.41**	**280.74**	**317.98**
Housekeeping services	483.17	147.69	422.47	542.82	584.10	488.59	416.41	393.04
Gardening, lawn care service	210.43	118.69	127.17	184.50	224.08	251.79	210.37	222.01
Water-softening service	85.49	93.46	66.89	84.71	96.82	80.65	92.80	85.80
Nonclothing laundry and dry cleaning, sent out	46.61	17.19	38.68	46.00	60.00	52.93	36.24	36.70
Nonclothing laundry and dry cleaning, coin-operated	23.87	21.97	26.95	29.15	24.76	19.35	19.60	15.11
Termite and pest control services	132.02	132.64	96.46	121.41	143.13	138.95	126.60	159.11
Home security system service fee	118.21	92.19	111.06	112.31	112.97	127.22	120.54	139.13
Other home services	236.76	48.28	198.00	216.30	245.04	293.80	190.95	243.14
Termite and pest control products	27.46	24.40	22.40	22.31	29.00	31.29	25.41	33.86
Moving, storage, and freight express	571.50	259.97	383.45	437.24	555.47	666.12	1,010.71	890.65
Appliance repair, including at service center	178.73	91.49	166.43	167.56	187.92	181.90	184.10	183.94
Reupholstering and furniture repair	288.21	45.45	167.97	160.56	280.83	433.12	255.72	504.29
Repairs and rentals of lawn and garden equipment, hand and power tools, etc.	148.94	179.55	81.33	155.51	142.59	151.67	165.33	203.24
Appliance rental	115.00	35.71	125.00	149.34	77.63	110.42	88.89	–
Rental of office equipment for nonbusiness use	412.50	–	150.00	600.00	–	825.00	203.13	–
Repair of computer systems for nonbusiness use	219.41	419.76	112.26	211.78	287.92	146.50	204.63	283.59
Computer information services	101.76	85.54	104.21	104.58	103.86	103.15	94.53	92.62
Installation of computer	130.56	132.50	53.57	–	179.55	102.27	230.36	–
HOUSEHOLD FURNISHINGS AND EQUIPMENT, AMOUNT SPENT	**579.71**	**397.29**	**550.21**	**638.80**	**631.20**	**642.16**	**519.15**	**416.89**
Household textiles	**118.75**	**69.54**	**96.66**	**119.82**	**133.81**	**137.77**	**137.82**	**88.83**
Bathroom linens	48.76	31.90	44.14	53.93	46.72	53.75	54.88	54.46
Bedroom linens	101.56	72.94	98.91	102.25	109.27	108.21	101.96	89.65
Kitchen and dining room linens	29.22	22.69	21.06	30.99	29.98	38.36	28.23	30.34
Curtains and draperies	215.25	58.81	87.50	187.38	318.53	288.89	401.09	157.09
Slipcovers and decorative pillows	59.07	39.86	44.79	59.92	81.20	65.74	42.65	54.55
Sewing materials for household items	77.05	29.59	47.09	66.52	73.58	109.94	87.02	60.10
Other linens	68.33	30.77	44.51	81.82	65.50	79.74	79.03	78.85
Furniture	**930.73**	**570.09**	**814.31**	**1,138.10**	**979.66**	**1,024.90**	**746.01**	**1,021.07**
Mattresses and springs	775.44	672.98	599.65	786.05	822.74	991.10	660.14	835.16
Other bedroom furniture	894.72	431.94	768.82	965.82	1,065.03	1,071.09	880.74	492.71
Sofas	1,131.63	563.80	1,050.09	1,252.35	1,273.61	1,249.84	1,174.42	1,449.73
Living room chairs	534.02	244.19	381.50	659.23	601.36	566.26	514.22	687.31
Living room tables	304.11	125.84	200.87	564.81	287.32	289.87	217.98	265.49
Kitchen and dining room furniture	744.02	484.16	648.86	791.94	642.80	1,060.69	574.69	1,056.58
Infants' furniture	271.75	252.11	310.07	267.28	221.50	255.51	355.23	50.00
Outdoor furniture	318.49	89.71	341.33	293.78	380.35	296.78	306.73	237.28
Wall units, cabinets, and other furniture	402.83	168.40	274.13	533.33	401.87	579.26	463.14	391.89
Floor coverings	**376.52**	**75.74**	**239.65**	**336.59**	**375.37**	**490.81**	**448.52**	**810.30**
Wall-to-wall carpeting	2,008.33	257.81	1,420.65	1,731.41	2,004.17	2,077.27	2,058.13	3,753.13
Floor coverings, nonpermanent	166.57	61.27	105.22	155.52	213.76	229.61	169.02	100.74
Major appliances	**618.68**	**323.80**	**526.65**	**651.02**	**674.05**	**707.29**	**649.61**	**572.77**
Dishwashers (built-in), garbage disposals, range hoods (renter)	440.00	398.33	383.33	820.00	450.00	975.00	–	283.33
Dishwashers (built-in), garbage disposals, range hoods (owner)	561.11	457.81	355.47	541.45	630.19	636.62	405.42	514.02

	total consumer units	under 25	25 to 34	35 to 44	45 to 54	55 to 64	65 to 74	75+
Refrigerators, freezers (renter)	$474.32	$322.79	$526.76	$430.56	$454.46	$683.33	$355.00	$571.05
Refrigerators, freezers (owner)	942.56	717.24	934.14	935.10	1,122.41	909.05	847.20	833.10
Washing machines (renter)	386.59	250.50	454.29	455.11	320.83	356.94	321.05	456.67
Washing machines (owner)	706.75	357.95	706.45	700.39	769.92	750.65	604.32	614.83
Clothes dryers (renter)	323.21	179.66	369.50	403.03	214.06	307.29	57.14	454.41
Clothes dryers (owner)	680.81	349.50	658.72	709.43	756.97	712.13	534.93	634.81
Cooking stoves, ovens (renter)	406.25	208.33	430.77	438.10	250.00	437.50	178.13	454.17
Cooking stoves, ovens (owner)	1,116.54	631.41	1,022.37	1,126.09	1,056.76	1,228.08	1,372.53	789.74
Microwave ovens (renter)	96.74	81.23	94.25	107.31	114.62	99.22	92.86	71.43
Microwave ovens (owner)	196.25	122.67	160.82	195.76	188.43	200.57	223.63	258.23
Window air conditioners (renter)	218.33	215.00	191.13	244.23	234.38	223.61	213.89	450.00
Window air conditioners (owner)	319.83	237.50	181.82	276.19	314.58	354.27	445.31	271.88
Electric floor-cleaning equipment	169.20	155.90	137.84	169.69	177.97	174.05	227.78	151.55
Sewing machines	454.46	250.00	107.95	523.21	312.50	482.08	746.57	85.71
Small appliances and misc. housewares	**86.99**	**56.23**	**74.32**	**82.58**	**99.78**	**103.25**	**79.21**	**95.68**
Housewares	73.66	55.47	65.59	67.91	83.58	88.60	70.07	71.54
Plastic dinnerware	27.85	16.07	31.04	32.21	28.64	25.25	22.57	23.03
China and other dinnerware	81.93	53.23	65.48	75.32	92.92	101.26	102.22	105.67
Flatware	64.18	33.07	64.31	63.51	65.61	108.55	40.35	47.86
Glassware	33.29	25.37	32.68	28.40	32.41	36.48	55.16	24.58
Silver serving pieces	54.17	200.00	81.25	60.00	25.00	68.75	12.50	18.75
Other serving pieces	46.54	20.96	33.33	48.15	48.36	71.88	55.71	39.13
Nonelectric cookware	77.17	49.55	65.91	80.63	93.48	86.68	69.31	60.14
Small appliances	82.47	41.36	66.19	82.89	94.14	94.44	74.67	99.79
Small electric kitchen appliances	70.55	41.53	60.70	74.84	89.70	73.83	61.38	52.02
Portable heating and cooling equipment	121.85	34.88	75.79	110.98	92.04	184.75	120.99	303.41
Miscellaneous household equipment	**313.29**	**231.33**	**297.82**	**320.91**	**352.70**	**341.11**	**306.54**	**200.54**
Window coverings	304.65	109.48	219.26	253.83	292.58	259.91	675.31	539.33
Infants' equipment	149.18	125.88	157.22	192.50	90.70	201.25	78.41	163.64
Outdoor equipment	234.32	72.56	179.07	240.36	223.09	421.43	168.20	150.00
Lamps and lighting fixtures	95.43	48.10	71.52	87.92	108.29	140.36	84.66	114.18
Clocks and other household decorative items	142.22	93.61	130.42	125.59	127.71	240.40	115.56	130.56
Telephones and accessories	118.38	122.73	134.82	116.80	129.13	105.09	89.82	75.00
Lawn and garden equipment	489.38	300.31	376.34	621.90	583.24	437.29	339.17	358.41
Power tools	218.29	167.86	209.95	191.06	211.10	296.78	156.87	203.72
Office furniture for home use	301.54	89.24	327.45	292.67	273.26	388.46	314.94	353.13
Hand tools	91.52	89.58	106.34	101.54	77.87	116.88	44.16	35.88
Indoor plants and fresh flowers	88.93	43.96	77.23	82.81	103.26	98.92	86.95	79.75
Closet and storage items	67.91	41.90	71.05	69.83	70.56	64.00	104.44	37.04
Rental of furniture	338.89	306.52	324.24	373.15	342.86	318.75	37.50	–
Luggage	109.57	84.87	105.08	119.63	100.15	118.83	113.59	86.21
Computers and computer hardware, nonbusiness use	703.00	705.30	613.92	661.16	796.82	685.68	797.26	628.63
Computer software and accessories, nonbusiness use	129.79	133.73	129.22	126.36	132.64	134.47	119.78	128.59
Personal digital assistants	234.17	197.37	292.44	193.24	236.70	191.25	293.75	190.00
Internet services away from home	88.58	69.47	108.21	89.91	90.76	77.87	81.15	111.61
Telephone answering devices	61.11	57.69	41.67	91.67	71.55	62.50	58.33	58.33
Business equipment for home use	91.53	71.13	53.00	83.46	118.12	87.50	110.07	104.09
Smoke alarms (owner)	61.31	32.14	86.05	40.52	101.63	42.65	25.79	48.65
Smoke alarms (renter)	43.18	21.43	33.82	76.67	29.17	42.86	22.73	–
Other household appliances (owner)	190.69	46.43	152.74	251.45	137.39	205.34	212.41	210.14
Other household appliances (renter)	109.09	35.07	184.24	130.56	67.71	85.81	19.44	150.00

Note: "–" means sample is too small to make a reliable estimate.
Source: Calculations by New Strategist based on the Bureau of Labor Statistics' 2008 Consumer Expenditure Survey

Table 7.3 Percent Buying Housekeeping Supplies, Furnishings, and Equipment by Age, <u>Average Week</u>, 2008

(percent of households buying housekeeping supplies, furnishings, and equipment during the average week, by age of householder, 2008)

	total households	under 25	25 to 34	35 to 44	45 to 54	55 to 64	65 to 74	75+
HOUSEKEEPING SUPPLIES, PERCENT BUYING	53.9%	33.6%	51.9%	57.0%	56.6%	55.9%	58.7%	50.8%
Laundry and cleaning supplies	28.3	17.5	26.7	32.6	30.5	29.2	29.3	22.9
Soaps and detergents	20.1	12.2	19.9	23.2	22.3	19.7	19.5	16.6
Other laundry cleaning products	18.0	11.5	16.2	21.2	19.2	19.0	19.5	12.8
Other household products	40.4	23.3	38.3	43.2	43.3	41.9	44.2	37.0
Cleansing and toilet tissue, paper towels, and napkins	24.8	12.9	23.4	26.7	27.8	24.7	27.4	23.1
Miscellaneous household products	25.7	15.5	24.4	29.2	27.8	26.0	27.2	20.6
Lawn and garden supplies	6.6	3.5	3.9	5.5	7.4	9.2	9.5	6.0
Postage and stationery	22.8	11.0	21.0	22.1	24.2	26.0	26.0	23.8
Stationery, stationery supplies, giftwrap	17.4	8.3	17.2	17.5	18.6	19.7	18.4	17.0
Postage	8.5	3.5	6.0	7.2	9.1	10.5	12.1	10.9
Delivery services	0.5	0.2	0.3	0.3	0.9	0.5	0.5	0.4
HOUSEHOLD FURNISHINGS AND EQUIPMENT, PERCENT BUYING	30.5	20.0	29.1	32.5	32.8	34.0	33.0	21.8
Household textiles	6.2	3.5	5.8	6.3	7.7	7.2	6.8	3.2
Bathroom linens	3.0	1.9	2.4	3.3	3.5	3.3	3.4	1.5
Bedroom linens	2.6	1.6	2.8	2.1	3.4	2.7	2.7	1.3
Kitchen and dining room linens	1.3	0.6	1.2	1.3	1.6	2.0	1.2	0.6
Slipcovers and decorative pillows	0.3	–	0.2	0.1	0.5	0.3	0.2	0.2
Outdoor furniture	0.4	–	0.5	0.3	0.6	0.6	0.3	–
Floor coverings, nonpermanent	1.2	0.6	1.0	1.3	1.6	1.3	1.1	1.0
Major appliances	0.7	0.5	1.1	0.6	0.7	0.6	0.5	0.4
Electric floor-cleaning equipment	0.5	0.4	0.9	0.4	0.6	0.3	0.2	0.3
Miscellaneous household appliances	0.2	0.1	0.1	0.1	0.2	0.4	–	0.1
Housewares	8.1	5.3	8.0	9.3	8.6	9.7	7.7	4.5
China and other dinnerware	1.3	1.4	1.6	1.7	1.1	1.4	0.9	0.6
Glassware	1.9	1.3	1.6	2.2	2.0	2.3	1.9	0.9
Nonelectric cookware	2.2	1.1	1.6	2.4	3.0	2.5	2.1	1.4
Tableware, nonelectric kitchenware	4.3	2.5	4.7	4.6	4.4	4.9	4.5	2.3
Miscellaneous household equipment	24.3	15.9	23.4	26.0	26.5	27.0	26.4	16.9
Infants' equipment	1.2	1.0	2.7	1.3	1.0	0.7	0.6	0.1
Laundry and cleaning equipment	4.9	3.5	4.4	5.8	5.2	5.4	5.0	3.3
Outdoor equipment	1.3	0.4	1.3	1.0	1.6	1.6	1.9	1.1
Lamps and lighting fixtures	1.3	0.6	0.6	1.6	1.5	1.7	1.9	0.8
Clocks and other household decorative items	8.0	3.7	8.0	8.8	8.8	9.1	8.8	4.9
Telephones and accessories	1.2	0.8	1.3	1.5	1.2	1.5	1.2	0.5
Lawn and garden equipment	2.0	1.2	1.8	2.0	2.1	2.5	2.0	2.0
Power tools	1.3	1.1	0.8	1.3	1.7	1.7	1.6	0.6
Hand tools	1.8	0.9	1.5	2.0	2.2	1.9	2.2	1.0
Indoor plants and fresh flowers	4.2	2.3	3.3	3.9	4.9	5.3	4.7	4.1
Closet and storage items	2.4	1.5	2.2	3.0	2.6	2.8	2.1	1.3
Other hardware	0.8	1.4	0.6	1.2	1.1	0.5	0.9	0.2
Miscellaneous household equipment and parts	4.9	3.5	4.3	6.2	5.3	5.6	4.9	2.4
Luggage	0.8	0.4	0.8	1.0	1.1	0.6	0.5	0.2

Note: "–" means sample is too small to make a reliable estimate.
Source: Bureau of Labor Statistics, unpublished data from the 2008 Consumer Expenditure Survey

Table 7.4 Amount Buyers Spent on Housekeeping Supplies, Furnishings, and Equipment by Age, <u>Average Week</u>, 2008

(average amount spent by households buying housekeeping supplies, furnishings, and equipment during the average week, by age of householder, 2008)

	total households	under 25	25 to 34	35 to 44	45 to 54	55 to 64	65 to 74	75+
HOUSEKEEPING SUPPLIES, AMOUNT SPENT	**$23.35**	**$17.34**	**$22.04**	**$22.41**	**$25.98**	**$25.56**	**$24.49**	**$18.37**
Laundry and cleaning supplies	**10.03**	**9.15**	**10.84**	**10.49**	**10.46**	**10.08**	**8.90**	**7.65**
Soaps and detergents	7.75	6.70	8.28	8.23	7.99	7.70	7.19	5.80
Other laundry cleaning products	7.13	6.78	7.67	7.14	7.36	7.47	6.21	6.16
Other household products	**16.70**	**12.72**	**14.79**	**16.08**	**19.43**	**18.37**	**16.53**	**13.12**
Cleansing and toilet tissue, paper towels, and napkins	8.09	7.75	7.57	7.99	8.44	8.45	8.31	7.27
Miscellaneous household products	11.07	10.23	9.45	10.99	13.07	11.76	10.52	8.54
Lawn and garden supplies	28.81	11.01	40.20	29.14	32.93	27.78	22.58	23.71
Postage and stationery	**13.16**	**11.41**	**13.69**	**10.98**	**12.80**	**14.05**	**17.17**	**11.44**
Stationery, stationery supplies, giftwrap	9.00	6.15	11.66	7.56	8.17	9.22	11.44	6.94
Postage	15.85	21.49	14.41	14.53	15.53	16.29	18.83	13.67
Delivery services	16.33	5.00	6.25	18.75	19.32	21.57	16.67	11.36
HOUSEHOLD FURNISHINGS AND EQUIPMENT, AMOUNT SPENT	**52.23**	**33.68**	**46.62**	**47.79**	**69.51**	**53.18**	**48.74**	**37.33**
Household textiles	**29.33**	**14.08**	**29.31**	**22.03**	**40.10**	**29.22**	**25.63**	**23.91**
Bathroom linens	14.24	12.17	15.42	14.41	15.01	12.69	16.57	8.50
Bedroom linens	47.06	14.65	42.05	36.02	63.05	53.11	36.19	44.00
Kitchen and dining room linens	9.09	4.69	6.84	8.66	9.49	8.63	15.25	6.25
Slipcovers and decorative pillows	36.00	–	26.09	23.08	48.08	24.00	20.00	25.00
Outdoor furniture	**138.46**	**–**	**258.33**	**41.38**	**123.33**	**96.61**	**171.88**	**–**
Floor coverings, nonpermanent	**98.37**	**56.25**	**24.49**	**37.31**	**234.36**	**66.93**	**79.28**	**16.16**
Major appliances	**94.03**	**16.67**	**100.00**	**144.64**	**95.77**	**53.97**	**144.68**	**36.11**
Electric floor-cleaning equipment	110.64	11.36	107.53	158.14	114.29	66.67	223.53	46.15
Miscellaneous household appliances	33.33	30.00	30.00	28.57	14.29	44.44	–	9.09
Housewares	**17.10**	**7.56**	**13.00**	**11.99**	**18.93**	**21.84**	**25.58**	**17.92**
China and other dinnerware	16.28	5.93	7.64	11.18	21.30	21.99	44.19	24.19
Glassware	18.38	5.60	11.04	8.76	26.53	22.08	32.45	6.82
Nonelectric cookware	12.39	5.71	13.38	10.29	10.44	13.06	18.22	18.88
Tableware, nonelectric kitchenware	13.35	7.57	11.30	10.58	13.01	19.96	13.25	14.66
Miscellaneous household equipment	**41.31**	**32.68**	**34.92**	**43.82**	**47.68**	**43.57**	**38.23**	**32.11**
Infants' equipment	33.61	18.75	28.10	54.62	29.81	22.86	50.00	10.00
Laundry and cleaning equipment	6.33	4.60	5.63	6.42	7.49	6.54	5.77	4.28
Outdoor equipment	47.01	175.68	32.84	42.27	34.15	92.95	20.21	34.58
Lamps and lighting fixtures	42.42	7.81	41.82	25.15	50.66	42.77	56.15	62.03
Clocks and other household decorative items	30.46	17.71	31.19	24.77	40.32	29.20	31.81	17.28
Telephones and accessories	68.85	28.21	63.36	101.37	55.74	75.00	37.07	70.83
Lawn and garden equipment	63.32	33.61	30.73	85.64	65.57	52.24	70.56	95.90
Power tools	39.85	42.86	27.38	63.16	42.69	25.00	40.25	22.03
Hand tools	17.78	93.26	17.65	17.50	14.29	11.70	17.04	9.47
Indoor plants and fresh flowers	21.28	27.31	17.07	18.78	21.86	26.04	20.47	17.04
Closet and storage items	18.49	6.54	27.93	27.70	13.28	14.44	10.48	6.06
Other hardware	38.10	30.15	25.86	20.87	70.00	42.59	22.22	21.05
Miscellaneous household equipment and parts	17.61	11.33	13.18	14.29	23.22	20.28	19.22	11.98
Luggage	32.00	17.07	26.25	26.80	42.98	34.55	20.00	31.58

Note: "–" means sample is too small to make a reliable estimate.
Source: Calculations by New Strategist based on the Bureau of Labor Statistics' 2008 Consumer Expenditure Survey

Table 7.5 Percent Buying Household Services, Furnishings, and Equipment by Household Income, <u>Average Quarter</u>, 2008

(percent of households buying household services, furnishings, and equipment during the average quarter, by before-tax income of household, 2008)

	total households	under $20,000	$20,000–$39,999	$40,000–$49,999	$50,000–$69,999	$70,000–$79,999	$80,000–$99,999	$100,000 or more
HOUSEHOLD SERVICES, PERCENT BUYING	**65.9%**	**41.7%**	**54.4%**	**65.0%**	**73.6%**	**79.8%**	**82.7%**	**90.1%**
Personal services	**7.3**	**2.5**	**4.5**	**5.2**	**8.2**	**9.7**	**12.4**	**13.5**
Babysitting and child care in own home	1.6	0.3	0.7	1.1	1.2	1.6	3.0	4.3
Babysitting and child care in someone else's home	1.1	0.5	0.8	0.9	1.5	1.2	2.0	1.3
Care for elderly, invalids, handicapped, etc.	0.4	0.5	0.5	0.2	0.4	0.2	0.4	0.5
Day care centers, nurseries, and preschools	5.0	1.3	2.6	3.6	5.7	8.1	8.6	9.7
Other household services	**64.4**	**40.4**	**52.7**	**63.3**	**71.5**	**78.6**	**80.7**	**89.1**
Housekeeping services	6.2	3.4	3.3	2.9	3.7	4.8	6.5	17.0
Gardening, lawn care service	13.7	7.4	10.0	10.6	12.6	14.8	15.9	27.2
Water-softening service	1.4	1.0	1.0	1.5	1.9	2.2	1.9	1.7
Nonclothing laundry and dry cleaning, sent out	0.6	0.2	0.4	0.7	0.6	0.9	0.8	1.1
Nonclothing laundry and dry cleaning, coin-operated	3.5	5.6	3.6	4.3	3.3	2.1	3.0	1.4
Termite and pest control services	3.6	1.6	2.4	2.6	3.7	4.2	4.7	7.4
Home security system service fee	4.6	1.6	2.9	1.9	4.0	5.7	5.7	11.3
Other home services	2.0	0.7	1.2	2.0	2.4	2.2	3.8	3.5
Termite and pest control products	2.5	1.3	1.8	1.6	2.9	2.2	2.9	5.1
Moving, storage, and freight express	2.1	1.1	1.9	2.0	2.1	1.8	2.7	3.3
Appliance repair, including at service center	2.5	1.0	1.5	2.7	2.7	3.1	3.1	4.6
Reupholstering and furniture repair	0.5	0.3	0.3	0.5	0.6	0.4	0.8	1.0
Repairs and rentals of lawn and garden equipment, hand and power tools, etc.	1.2	0.5	1.0	0.9	1.2	0.9	1.9	2.1
Appliance rental	0.2	0.3	0.2	0.3	0.2	0.3	0.2	0.0
Rental of office equipment for nonbusiness use	0.0	0.0	0.0	–	0.0	–	0.1	–
Repair of computer systems for nonbusiness use	0.8	0.3	0.5	0.8	0.8	1.2	1.2	1.3
Computer information services	53.9	26.2	40.8	53.3	63.1	71.3	72.3	80.7
Installation of computer	0.1	0.1	0.1	0.1	0.1	0.1	0.0	0.2
HOUSEHOLD FURNISHINGS AND EQUIPMENT, PERCENT BUYING	**52.7**	**37.3**	**45.7**	**50.6**	**57.1**	**60.8**	**64.3**	**68.5**
Household textiles	**19.3**	**13.4**	**17.2**	**18.0**	**21.6**	**22.2**	**23.1**	**24.7**
Bathroom linens	6.4	4.9	6.0	6.3	7.4	7.3	6.9	7.7
Bedroom linens	10.2	6.8	8.5	9.2	11.4	12.0	13.8	13.7
Kitchen and dining room linens	1.7	1.4	1.5	1.5	1.6	1.5	1.8	2.6
Curtains and draperies	2.4	1.3	2.2	2.3	3.2	3.0	2.2	3.3
Slipcovers and decorative pillows	1.2	1.1	0.9	1.0	1.0	1.5	1.6	1.9
Sewing materials for household items	3.4	2.3	3.3	3.1	3.6	4.1	4.0	4.4
Other linens	0.5	0.3	0.3	0.4	0.5	0.5	0.7	0.6
Furniture	**10.2**	**6.4**	**8.2**	**9.5**	**10.2**	**12.4**	**12.2**	**15.5**
Mattresses and springs	1.7	1.1	1.2	1.7	1.9	1.7	2.1	2.7
Other bedroom furniture	1.9	1.3	1.6	1.6	2.2	1.8	2.6	3.0
Sofas	2.2	1.6	2.0	1.5	2.1	3.4	2.4	2.9
Living room chairs	1.7	1.3	1.4	1.3	1.8	2.3	2.2	2.2
Living room tables	1.4	1.0	1.2	1.5	1.2	1.4	1.6	2.2
Kitchen and dining room furniture	1.2	0.9	1.0	0.9	1.1	0.9	1.1	2.1
Infants' furniture	0.8	0.6	0.6	1.0	0.6	1.4	0.8	1.0
Outdoor furniture	1.5	0.5	0.9	1.4	1.6	1.4	2.3	2.9
Wall units, cabinets, and other furniture	2.7	1.6	2.5	2.6	2.7	3.7	3.0	4.1
Floor coverings	**3.0**	**1.9**	**2.2**	**2.8**	**3.4**	**3.5**	**3.4**	**4.5**
Wall-to-wall carpeting (owner)	0.3	0.2	0.2	0.2	0.4	0.4	0.4	0.5
Floor coverings, nonpermanent	2.6	1.6	1.9	2.5	3.0	3.1	3.1	4.1
Major appliances	**8.2**	**5.5**	**7.5**	**6.9**	**8.6**	**8.8**	**9.8**	**11.4**
Dishwashers (built-in), garbage disposals, range hoods (renter)	0.1	0.0	0.0	0.1	0.0	0.1	–	0.1
Dishwashers (built-in), garbage disposals, range hoods (owner)	0.6	0.1	0.3	0.4	0.5	0.8	1.1	1.6

	total households	under $20,000	$20,000– $39,999	$40,000– $49,999	$50,000– $69,999	$70,000– $79,999	$80,000– $99,999	$100,000 or more
Refrigerators, freezers (renter)	0.4%	0.5%	0.6%	0.5%	0.2%	0.2%	0.3%	0.2%
Refrigerators, freezers (owner)	1.3	0.5	1.0	0.8	1.7	1.8	1.6	2.3
Washing machines (renter)	0.4	0.6	0.5	0.6	0.5	0.3	0.2	0.1
Washing machines (owner)	1.0	0.4	0.6	0.7	1.0	1.2	1.8	1.9
Clothes dryers (renter)	0.3	0.3	0.3	0.5	0.3	0.3	0.2	0.1
Clothes dryers (owner)	0.9	0.3	0.7	0.5	0.9	0.7	1.2	1.8
Cooking stoves, ovens (renter)	0.1	0.1	0.3	0.2	0.1	0.1	–	0.1
Cooking stoves, ovens (owner)	0.7	0.3	0.4	0.4	0.6	1.1	1.1	1.3
Microwave ovens (renter)	0.7	1.0	1.0	1.0	0.7	0.4	0.3	0.1
Microwave ovens (owner)	1.0	0.4	0.9	0.5	1.2	1.2	1.6	1.6
Window air conditioners (renter)	0.2	0.2	0.2	0.1	0.2	0.1	0.1	0.1
Window air conditioners (owner)	0.3	0.1	0.2	0.1	0.6	0.5	0.4	0.3
Electric floor-cleaning equipment	2.4	1.4	2.0	2.5	2.3	2.1	3.1	3.7
Sewing machines	0.3	0.2	0.3	0.1	0.4	0.4	0.4	0.3
Small appliances and misc. housewares	**16.1**	**12.3**	**14.1**	**15.7**	**16.6**	**18.7**	**18.7**	**20.6**
Housewares	9.9	7.5	8.5	9.3	10.2	12.6	11.2	13.1
Plastic dinnerware	2.5	2.3	2.2	2.5	2.2	3.6	2.6	3.3
China and other dinnerware	2.5	1.8	2.3	2.4	2.6	3.2	2.2	3.4
Flatware	1.4	1.5	1.4	1.1	1.4	1.3	1.5	1.6
Glassware	1.9	1.5	1.6	1.8	2.1	1.9	2.2	2.7
Silver serving pieces	0.1	0.0	0.1	0.1	0.0	–	0.1	0.1
Other serving pieces	0.7	0.5	0.5	0.4	0.7	0.6	0.6	1.1
Nonelectric cookware	3.5	2.6	3.1	2.8	3.9	3.9	4.0	4.4
Small appliances	8.1	6.2	7.2	7.9	8.7	8.5	9.8	10.1
Small electric kitchen appliances	6.9	5.1	6.2	6.7	7.5	7.2	8.6	8.5
Portable heating and cooling equipment	1.5	1.3	1.3	1.7	1.5	1.7	1.6	1.8
Miscellaneous household equipment	**35.8**	**21.4**	**28.4**	**33.7**	**39.3**	**43.5**	**48.2**	**51.9**
Window coverings	1.7	1.1	1.2	1.5	1.9	2.4	2.4	2.4
Infants' equipment	0.6	0.4	0.4	1.0	0.7	1.1	0.8	0.6
Outdoor equipment	1.2	0.5	0.8	1.1	1.1	2.0	2.1	1.9
Lamps and lighting fixtures	3.5	2.5	2.5	3.3	3.7	3.6	4.0	5.2
Clocks and other household decorative items	6.2	3.6	4.2	6.3	6.1	8.8	8.2	9.7
Telephones and accessories	5.1	3.0	3.8	5.1	5.5	6.2	6.0	7.9
Lawn and garden equipment	2.3	0.9	1.9	1.8	2.9	3.6	3.6	3.4
Power tools	2.1	0.7	1.4	2.0	2.5	3.4	2.8	3.3
Office furniture for home use	0.7	0.3	0.4	0.4	0.7	1.0	0.7	1.3
Hand tools	1.7	0.8	1.3	1.8	2.4	2.1	2.3	2.3
Indoor plants and fresh flowers	15.9	7.8	11.9	15.0	17.1	19.4	21.7	25.9
Closet and storage items	1.3	0.8	1.0	1.4	1.4	1.6	1.7	2.1
Rental of furniture	0.2	0.2	0.2	0.4	0.2	0.2	0.1	0.1
Luggage	1.4	0.5	0.8	1.0	1.5	1.6	2.0	3.1
Computers and computer hardware, nonbusiness use	5.4	2.8	3.3	5.2	6.5	6.8	6.9	9.2
Computer software and accessories, nonbusiness use	4.5	2.5	3.2	3.4	5.0	5.3	6.3	7.8
Personal digital assistants	0.3	0.1	0.1	0.1	0.4	0.5	0.3	0.7
Internet services away from home	0.8	0.4	0.6	0.7	0.9	0.8	1.3	1.2
Telephone answering devices	0.2	0.1	0.1	0.1	0.2	0.1	0.3	0.4
Business equipment for home use	0.6	0.4	0.4	0.6	0.5	0.9	1.2	0.8
Smoke alarms (owner)	0.4	0.2	0.4	0.3	0.4	0.7	0.7	0.6
Smoke alarms (renter)	0.1	0.1	0.1	0.1	0.1	0.2	0.1	0.1
Other household appliances (owner)	1.0	0.5	1.0	0.8	0.9	1.1	1.9	1.5
Other household appliances (renter)	0.3	0.5	0.4	0.3	0.4	0.1	0.4	0.1

Note: "–" means sample is too small to make a reliable estimate.
Source: Bureau of Labor Statistics, unpublished data from the 2008 Consumer Expenditure Survey

Table 7.6 Amount Buyers Spent on Household Services, Furnishings, and Equipment by Household Income, <u>Average Quarter</u>, 2008

(average amount spent by households buying household services, furnishings, and equipment during the average quarter, by before-tax income of household, 2008)

	total households	under $20,000	$20,000–$39,999	$40,000–$49,999	$50,000–$69,999	$70,000–$79,999	$80,000–$99,999	$100,000 or more
HOUSEHOLD SERVICES, AMOUNT SPENT	**$377.80**	**$209.76**	**$240.10**	**$238.47**	**$319.25**	**$343.47**	**$413.45**	**$658.77**
Personal services	**1,312.33**	**867.18**	**953.62**	**941.02**	**1,208.46**	**1,144.60**	**1,163.43**	**1,795.94**
Babysitting and child care in own home	717.33	576.85	374.52	133.49	663.33	308.75	499.67	1,017.97
Babysitting and child care in someone else's home	838.68	531.23	655.52	575.29	824.17	824.58	869.80	1,119.69
Care for elderly, invalids, handicapped, etc.	3,063.64	1,733.30	1,884.92	6,285.00	4,541.48	4,151.25	939.53	4,695.31
Day care centers, nurseries, and preschools	1,224.95	592.77	906.44	796.41	982.76	1,097.11	1,255.43	1,662.67
Other household services	**238.01**	**161.22**	**167.91**	**168.21**	**190.01**	**207.07**	**244.41**	**394.34**
Housekeeping services	483.17	348.42	296.15	356.70	398.29	425.88	481.75	590.26
Gardening, lawn care service	210.43	190.52	155.07	142.54	169.90	177.33	200.03	284.13
Water-softening service	85.49	77.12	80.71	105.82	81.41	89.86	82.03	88.62
Nonclothing laundry and dry cleaning, sent out	46.61	30.14	48.30	27.27	29.17	42.35	29.01	70.23
Nonclothing laundry and dry cleaning, coin-operated	23.87	20.89	27.57	21.32	22.00	21.38	30.22	28.82
Termite and pest control services	132.02	141.27	119.52	157.59	137.50	85.36	157.59	132.21
Home security system service fee	118.21	118.10	111.20	108.38	112.59	125.26	110.75	124.00
Other home services	236.76	150.37	178.23	229.04	257.17	170.00	230.84	287.50
Termite and pest control products	27.46	28.64	25.91	29.56	26.39	20.16	31.63	28.20
Moving, storage, and freight express	571.50	558.40	477.89	343.62	434.59	733.70	689.31	699.85
Appliance repair, including at service center	178.73	123.85	189.69	162.78	163.28	223.20	167.89	193.75
Reupholstering and furniture repair	288.21	268.27	218.03	297.40	161.29	147.30	276.28	393.25
Repairs and rentals of lawn and garden equipment, hand and power tools, etc.	148.94	183.94	138.59	135.90	116.19	141.21	136.04	168.87
Appliance rental	115.00	127.54	145.32	121.21	59.78	74.17	143.33	25.00
Rental of office equipment for nonbusiness use	412.50	122.70	371.37	–	187.50	–	975.00	–
Repair of computer systems for nonbusiness use	219.41	331.19	155.69	167.76	147.32	291.39	246.90	251.37
Computer information services	101.76	85.98	92.39	96.20	100.69	102.02	104.73	114.82
Installation of computer	130.56	78.22	130.16	230.77	116.67	88.89	118.75	113.33
HOUSEHOLD FURNISHINGS AND EQUIPMENT, AMOUNT SPENT	**579.71**	**339.29**	**376.43**	**458.03**	**533.84**	**627.07**	**628.50**	**945.71**
Household textiles	**118.75**	**72.91**	**87.64**	**89.98**	**103.18**	**115.58**	**127.95**	**194.46**
Bathroom linens	48.76	36.48	39.96	44.96	47.91	51.00	60.79	62.48
Bedroom linens	101.56	76.06	88.55	85.75	99.21	101.07	102.75	133.08
Kitchen and dining room linens	29.22	21.35	21.66	18.00	28.35	31.68	40.34	40.18
Curtains and draperies	215.25	59.35	94.89	107.97	111.35	145.35	275.00	519.33
Slipcovers and decorative pillows	59.07	35.04	40.83	51.77	67.35	66.16	52.83	83.76
Sewing materials for household items	77.05	57.62	64.70	67.81	69.02	88.75	70.60	110.06
Other linens	68.33	31.84	63.32	31.88	58.02	71.23	113.18	81.75
Furniture	**930.73**	**587.20**	**634.90**	**687.83**	**838.15**	**1,022.33**	**936.12**	**1,398.26**
Mattresses and springs	775.44	487.70	643.62	666.08	771.91	945.49	696.10	1,016.60
Other bedroom furniture	894.72	582.85	654.24	790.22	926.26	1,218.30	752.35	1,173.33
Sofas	1,131.63	679.74	685.02	1,050.51	966.27	1,406.07	1,418.52	1,721.17
Living room chairs	534.02	254.09	301.36	445.42	497.96	632.73	562.44	902.17
Living room tables	304.11	166.41	161.90	214.55	189.88	377.92	304.03	542.66
Kitchen and dining room furniture	744.02	527.44	394.68	569.72	563.79	386.54	826.43	1,223.93
Infants' furniture	271.75	233.07	172.63	120.45	400.85	173.15	351.90	407.25
Outdoor furniture	318.49	104.41	166.85	151.07	247.47	157.39	251.52	544.44
Wall units, cabinets, and other furniture	402.83	182.95	320.03	328.54	267.87	352.57	414.05	675.24
Floor coverings	**376.52**	**372.10**	**171.47**	**318.19**	**281.47**	**431.38**	**295.97**	**577.78**
Wall-to-wall carpeting	2,008.33	2,048.25	1,194.32	2,038.64	1,504.55	2,489.10	1,275.00	2,640.69
Floor coverings, nonpermanent	166.57	102.95	72.88	163.39	102.42	166.18	149.76	299.08
Major appliances	**618.68**	**391.37**	**431.66**	**512.12**	**629.25**	**698.92**	**741.89**	**857.64**
Dishwashers (built-in), garbage disposals, range hoods (renter)	440.00	197.61	211.77	115.00	425.00	450.00	–	675.00
Dishwashers (built-in), garbage disposals, range hoods (owner)	561.11	415.21	300.77	569.51	489.90	425.96	624.55	654.14

	total households	under $20,000	$20,000– $39,999	$40,000– $49,999	$50,000– $69,999	$70,000– $79,999	$80,000– $99,999	$100,000 or more
Refrigerators, freezers (renter)	$474.32	$415.07	$362.17	$748.33	$223.86	$835.00	$606.25	$786.76
Refrigerators, freezers (owner)	942.56	667.74	783.24	755.52	859.16	1,002.12	1,068.43	1,124.56
Washing machines (renter)	386.59	284.39	404.35	384.82	475.96	615.15	198.68	567.86
Washing machines (owner)	706.75	733.82	530.11	626.01	689.29	681.91	678.98	819.28
Clothes dryers (renter)	323.21	262.46	323.99	311.46	345.83	682.58	165.79	409.38
Clothes dryers (owner)	680.81	573.14	520.08	500.46	698.26	477.61	814.05	785.77
Cooking stoves, ovens (renter)	406.25	382.31	319.53	642.65	214.29	833.33	–	435.00
Cooking stoves, ovens (owner)	1,116.54	1,072.07	995.50	705.00	1,170.63	1,100.00	1,141.27	1,164.09
Microwave ovens (renter)	96.74	107.41	78.91	110.42	67.50	221.62	158.09	96.43
Microwave ovens (owner)	196.25	121.37	153.83	237.50	189.78	135.48	224.36	242.33
Window air conditioners (renter)	218.33	174.45	191.60	283.93	216.30	190.00	254.17	283.33
Window air conditioners (owner)	319.83	132.46	323.78	562.50	373.75	241.04	307.64	308.62
Electric floor-cleaning equipment	169.20	110.66	138.68	144.66	208.19	188.76	187.22	193.65
Sewing machines	454.46	215.60	260.70	1,820.45	466.07	349.38	242.57	744.83
Small appliances and misc. housewares	**86.99**	**64.30**	**69.48**	**73.60**	**85.89**	**83.44**	**92.16**	**122.47**
Housewares	73.66	51.06	62.13	63.36	75.39	70.42	79.05	99.62
Plastic dinnerware	27.85	17.12	21.27	31.87	27.88	32.73	27.65	39.00
China and other dinnerware	81.93	69.21	61.68	66.04	83.78	75.40	68.26	119.47
Flatware	64.18	28.22	60.77	90.95	71.72	37.21	79.93	92.74
Glassware	33.29	18.52	29.76	31.18	34.54	32.53	39.01	43.54
Silver serving pieces	54.17	58.73	29.51	27.27	112.50	–	89.29	45.45
Other serving pieces	46.54	28.31	40.61	46.71	58.68	46.72	36.48	57.88
Nonelectric cookware	77.17	52.32	59.69	63.47	70.03	102.40	109.85	98.87
Small appliances	82.47	66.65	62.80	71.42	75.26	78.53	85.18	121.08
Small electric kitchen appliances	70.55	47.82	48.06	60.06	68.83	57.65	73.26	115.25
Portable heating and cooling equipment	121.85	141.30	117.61	95.56	94.54	152.86	130.10	133.75
Miscellaneous household equipment	**313.29**	**193.57**	**208.49**	**281.34**	**302.81**	**313.33**	**331.92**	**451.03**
Window coverings	304.65	105.33	204.18	160.00	182.86	272.36	416.63	557.99
Infants' equipment	149.18	90.12	91.33	168.00	178.26	119.86	147.08	214.22
Outdoor equipment	234.32	164.94	149.78	148.39	127.86	189.87	207.07	408.33
Lamps and lighting fixtures	95.43	53.60	66.32	63.38	78.77	86.08	165.73	134.26
Clocks and other household decorative items	142.22	90.82	83.08	122.26	131.96	117.49	135.68	219.19
Telephones and accessories	118.38	78.84	99.72	94.44	112.41	119.40	127.54	155.16
Lawn and garden equipment	489.38	245.35	444.60	508.33	530.57	355.15	754.64	472.87
Power tools	218.29	185.73	212.79	195.98	248.22	162.65	204.82	235.92
Office furniture for home use	301.54	175.63	152.01	190.70	215.75	318.95	225.35	485.32
Hand tools	91.52	75.80	110.01	87.43	84.28	73.58	76.52	103.53
Indoor plants and fresh flowers	88.93	60.27	63.08	69.66	74.16	87.88	90.15	127.26
Closet and storage items	67.91	34.40	48.65	56.87	52.59	62.66	98.69	96.43
Rental of furniture	338.89	251.48	521.97	365.85	352.50	427.63	266.67	41.67
Luggage	109.57	85.84	72.43	82.52	92.67	131.44	83.54	140.83
Computers and computer hardware, nonbusiness use	703.00	596.71	496.06	733.24	695.53	689.73	651.88	847.82
Computer software and accessories, nonbusiness use	129.79	124.14	127.45	95.89	108.38	130.43	116.77	157.78
Personal digital assistants	234.17	247.00	197.99	161.36	161.59	265.82	228.79	275.00
Internet services away from home	88.58	52.59	70.92	89.23	87.23	85.71	86.94	113.91
Telephone answering devices	61.11	63.16	43.21	50.00	61.90	20.83	74.04	74.34
Business equipment for home use	91.53	60.05	55.56	71.31	72.64	80.75	127.61	136.01
Smoke alarms (owner)	61.31	28.46	30.84	161.29	35.14	169.18	42.80	47.66
Smoke alarms (renter)	43.18	35.12	77.15	34.62	28.57	26.25	38.64	50.00
Other household appliances (owner)	190.69	92.47	158.73	206.91	201.37	179.59	145.81	265.83
Other household appliances (renter)	109.09	138.94	38.26	153.57	136.31	37.50	111.43	141.67

Note: "–" means sample is too small to make a reliable estimate.
Source: Calculations by New Strategist based on the Bureau of Labor Statistics' 2008 Consumer Expenditure Survey

Table 7.7 Percent Buying Housekeeping Supplies, Furnishings, and Equipment by Household Income, <u>Average Week</u>, 2008

(percent of households buying housekeeping supplies, furnishings, and equipment during the average week, by before-tax income of household, 2008)

	total households	under $20,000	$20,000–$39,999	$40,000–$49,999	$50,000–$69,999	$70,000–$79,999	$80,000–$99,999	$100,000 or more
HOUSEKEEPING SUPPLIES, PERCENT BUYING	**53.9%**	**42.6%**	**49.9%**	**50.7%**	**57.6%**	**49.7%**	**56.0%**	**60.8%**
Laundry and cleaning supplies	**28.3**	**21.4**	**26.9**	**25.9**	**30.1**	**26.0**	**30.5**	**33.8**
Soaps and detergents	20.1	16.2	19.6	18.6	20.6	18.7	20.5	23.3
Other laundry cleaning products	18.0	12.9	15.7	16.5	20.0	16.0	19.8	23.3
Other household products	**40.4**	**32.1**	**37.2**	**37.7**	**42.4**	**37.0**	**40.9**	**45.7**
Cleansing and toilet tissue, paper towels, and napkins	24.8	21.2	24.1	22.5	27.1	23.8	23.2	27.0
Miscellaneous household products	25.7	17.7	21.9	24.7	25.5	22.0	28.2	30.9
Lawn and garden supplies	6.6	4.0	5.4	6.6	6.5	5.4	6.2	9.2
Postage and stationery	**22.8**	**14.7**	**19.8**	**21.1**	**23.8**	**19.5**	**23.6**	**27.4**
Stationery, stationery supplies, giftwrap	17.4	10.8	14.2	15.7	18.3	14.4	18.7	22.4
Postage	8.5	5.7	8.0	8.0	8.8	7.6	8.3	9.3
Delivery services	0.5	0.1	0.4	0.4	0.2	0.3	0.5	1.1
HOUSEHOLD FURNISHINGS AND EQUIPMENT, PERCENT BUYING	**30.5**	**18.8**	**25.2**	**27.1**	**31.6**	**25.1**	**34.3**	**40.9**
Household textiles	**6.2**	**4.2**	**5.2**	**5.4**	**6.2**	**5.2**	**7.2**	**7.6**
Bathroom linens	3.0	2.0	2.9	2.5	2.9	2.6	3.3	3.8
Bedroom linens	2.6	1.6	1.9	2.5	2.5	2.1	2.9	2.5
Kitchen and dining room linens	1.3	0.9	0.8	1.0	1.2	1.0	1.7	1.7
Slipcovers and decorative pillows	0.3	0.1	0.1	–	0.5	0.2	0.3	0.3
Outdoor furniture	**0.4**	**0.2**	**0.2**	**0.5**	**0.3**	**0.2**	**0.4**	**0.9**
Floor coverings, nonpermanent	**1.2**	**0.7**	**0.6**	**0.8**	**1.5**	**0.9**	**1.1**	**1.7**
Major appliances	**0.7**	**0.3**	**0.4**	**0.9**	**0.9**	**0.6**	**0.4**	**0.7**
Electric floor-cleaning equipment	0.5	0.1	0.2	0.5	0.7	0.4	0.4	0.6
Miscellaneous household appliances	0.2	0.1	0.1	0.3	0.2	0.1	0.1	0.1
Housewares	**8.1**	**4.1**	**6.9**	**7.6**	**8.1**	**6.5**	**7.5**	**11.2**
China and other dinnerware	1.3	0.5	1.0	1.6	1.2	1.0	2.2	1.5
Glassware	1.9	0.7	1.6	1.5	1.7	1.4	1.4	2.4
Nonelectric cookware	2.2	1.4	1.7	1.7	2.4	1.8	1.4	2.7
Tableware, nonelectric kitchenware	4.3	2.3	3.5	4.5	3.9	3.4	3.6	6.0
Miscellaneous household equipment	**24.3**	**13.7**	**19.3**	**21.2**	**25.8**	**19.5**	**28.0**	**34.2**
Infants' equipment	1.2	0.7	0.6	0.7	1.3	0.8	1.6	2.3
Laundry and cleaning equipment	4.9	3.4	3.4	3.8	5.4	3.9	5.2	6.6
Outdoor equipment	1.3	0.5	1.3	0.7	1.5	1.0	1.0	2.3
Lamps and lighting fixtures	1.3	0.8	1.0	1.4	1.4	1.1	0.9	2.1
Clocks and other household decorative items	8.0	3.7	6.2	7.0	8.4	6.1	7.5	10.5
Telephones and accessories	1.2	0.8	1.0	1.1	1.3	1.0	1.0	1.9
Lawn and garden equipment	2.0	1.2	1.3	2.7	2.1	1.7	2.1	2.5
Power tools	1.3	0.6	1.2	1.3	1.4	1.1	1.6	2.0
Hand tools	1.8	1.0	1.3	2.1	1.7	1.4	2.6	2.6
Indoor plants and fresh flowers	4.2	1.7	3.0	2.7	4.0	2.8	5.1	6.0
Closet and storage items	2.4	1.1	1.5	2.5	2.2	1.7	2.9	4.5
Other hardware	0.8	0.5	0.6	0.9	0.7	0.6	1.3	1.4
Miscellaneous household equipment and parts	4.9	2.7	3.4	4.5	5.8	3.9	6.0	7.9
Luggage	0.8	0.3	0.5	0.6	0.9	0.6	1.3	1.0

Source: Bureau of Labor Statistics, unpublished data from the 2008 Consumer Expenditure Survey

Table 7.8 Amount Buyers Spent on Housekeeping Supplies, Furnishings, and Equipment by Household Income, <u>Average Week</u>, 2008

(average amount spent by households buying housekeeping supplies, furnishings, and equipment during the average week, by before-tax income of household, 2008)

	total households	under $20,000	$20,000– $39,999	$40,000– $49,999	$50,000– $69,999	$70,000– $79,999	$80,000– $99,999	$100,000 or more
HOUSEKEEPING SUPPLIES, AMOUNT SPENT	**$23.35**	**$16.34**	**$18.35**	**$20.21**	**$21.01**	**$25.00**	**$28.43**	**$33.87**
Laundry and cleaning supplies	**10.03**	**9.00**	**8.66**	**9.74**	**9.53**	**11.30**	**10.90**	**11.95**
Soaps and detergents	7.75	7.04	7.00	8.02	7.28	8.58	8.28	8.84
Other laundry cleaning products	7.13	6.16	6.11	6.31	6.79	8.47	7.48	8.81
Other household products	**16.70**	**10.75**	**11.68**	**13.69**	**14.93**	**17.27**	**20.40**	**26.63**
Cleansing and toilet tissue, paper towels, and napkins	8.09	6.63	7.28	7.99	7.49	7.62	9.71	10.01
Miscellaneous household products	11.07	7.81	7.72	8.63	11.47	12.34	14.04	14.69
Lawn and garden supplies	28.81	16.33	16.50	18.55	21.05	29.01	25.87	53.09
Postage and stationery	**13.16**	**10.80**	**12.60**	**12.12**	**12.21**	**14.77**	**15.52**	**14.47**
Stationery, stationery supplies, giftwrap	9.00	5.55	7.48	7.07	9.24	11.66	10.61	10.94
Postage	15.85	16.75	17.03	17.50	13.24	15.15	17.98	14.70
Delivery services	16.33	37.92	14.06	11.63	21.74	11.54	18.35	16.67
HOUSEHOLD FURNISHINGS AND EQUIPMENT, AMOUNT SPENT	**52.23**	**31.26**	**31.73**	**51.72**	**56.47**	**44.65**	**54.79**	**76.13**
Household textiles	**29.33**	**22.12**	**23.25**	**24.17**	**26.67**	**26.63**	**24.90**	**43.82**
Bathroom linens	14.24	12.93	12.78	14.17	11.50	16.26	15.92	17.39
Bedroom linens	47.06	35.40	39.60	36.18	39.92	39.30	38.00	68.39
Kitchen and dining room linens	9.09	6.34	6.73	6.00	9.68	10.00	9.36	11.07
Slipcovers and decorative pillows	36.00	10.17	25.81	–	40.43	34.48	61.29	32.61
Outdoor furniture	**138.46**	**38.26**	**65.18**	**112.00**	**125.00**	**422.73**	**103.49**	**157.53**
Floor coverings, nonpermanent	**98.37**	**20.94**	**28.88**	**34.94**	**279.08**	**47.66**	**82.56**	**72.57**
Major appliances	**94.03**	**163.18**	**51.42**	**42.39**	**80.68**	**55.81**	**132.86**	**132.14**
Electric floor-cleaning equipment	110.64	96.60	45.28	54.17	86.36	63.89	157.14	143.88
Miscellaneous household appliances	33.33	2.60	29.95	23.33	59.09	0.00	25.00	20.00
Housewares	**17.10**	**8.60**	**12.82**	**14.38**	**15.40**	**13.92**	**21.59**	**23.57**
China and other dinnerware	16.28	6.69	14.08	23.60	20.87	11.98	8.44	20.90
Glassware	18.38	6.20	18.21	9.66	15.66	13.14	29.96	20.43
Nonelectric cookware	12.39	8.04	7.80	8.38	11.16	9.22	24.45	14.06
Tableware, nonelectric kitchenware	13.35	7.43	9.15	9.47	12.21	13.09	15.19	19.61
Miscellaneous household equipment	**41.31**	**27.22**	**27.19**	**46.34**	**36.23**	**33.98**	**42.89**	**59.77**
Infants' equipment	33.61	18.25	24.63	11.27	31.01	19.75	18.67	60.80
Laundry and cleaning equipment	6.33	5.61	4.87	5.59	6.12	5.42	6.82	7.76
Outdoor equipment	47.01	24.68	22.64	66.22	39.73	32.69	61.47	65.02
Lamps and lighting fixtures	42.42	30.01	32.43	35.92	43.36	57.61	32.20	60.11
Clocks and other household decorative items	30.46	16.32	22.87	48.58	21.92	24.83	37.00	36.91
Telephones and accessories	68.85	57.65	46.00	44.04	57.60	85.58	50.26	117.86
Lawn and garden equipment	63.32	70.43	31.64	43.22	57.89	33.49	51.79	105.39
Power tools	39.85	31.13	42.65	41.79	43.38	44.17	36.22	38.50
Hand tools	17.78	11.28	11.99	38.76	15.48	9.41	17.97	19.10
Indoor plants and fresh flowers	21.28	17.15	16.17	19.56	17.22	19.46	26.39	25.00
Closet and storage items	18.49	7.32	9.43	9.13	10.09	15.81	10.31	39.95
Other hardware	38.10	13.51	14.64	54.02	108.96	38.06	19.72	35.38
Miscellaneous household equipment and parts	17.61	9.30	13.57	14.61	18.23	14.96	21.65	22.38
Luggage	32.00	22.98	36.14	35.00	12.36	58.14	34.62	33.62

Note: "–" means sample is too small to make a reliable estimate.
Source: Calculations by New Strategist based on the Bureau of Labor Statistics' 2008 Consumer Expenditure Survey

Table 7.9 Percent of High-Income Households Buying Household Services, Furnishings, and Equipment, Average Quarter, 2008

(percent of high-income households buying household services, furnishings, and equipment during the average quarter, by before-tax income of household, 2008)

	total households	$100,000 or more	$100,000–$119,999	$120,000–$149,999	$150,000 or more
HOUSEHOLD SERVICES, PERCENT BUYING	**65.9%**	**90.1%**	**87.6%**	**89.5%**	**92.6%**
Personal services	**7.3**	**13.5**	**12.9**	**13.3**	**14.2**
Babysitting and child care in own home	1.6	4.3	2.8	3.9	5.9
Babysitting and child care in someone else's home	1.1	1.3	1.8	1.0	1.0
Care for elderly, invalids, handicapped, etc.	0.4	0.5	0.4	0.3	0.7
Day care centers, nurseries, and preschools	5.0	9.7	9.6	9.7	9.8
Other household services	**64.4**	**89.1**	**86.2**	**88.7**	**91.7**
Housekeeping services	6.2	17.0	7.8	13.4	26.9
Gardening, lawn care service	13.7	27.2	19.9	26.1	33.8
Water-softening service	1.4	1.7	1.6	1.5	1.8
Nonclothing laundry and dry cleaning, sent out	0.6	1.1	0.7	0.9	1.5
Nonclothing laundry and dry cleaning, coin-operated	3.5	1.4	1.3	1.7	1.4
Termite and pest control services	3.6	7.4	6.8	6.9	8.3
Home security system service fee	4.6	11.3	7.4	10.3	15.1
Other home services	2.0	3.5	2.3	3.2	4.6
Termite and pest control products	2.5	5.1	4.4	5.0	5.7
Moving, storage, and freight express	2.1	3.3	3.5	2.7	3.6
Appliance repair, including at service center	2.5	4.6	4.0	4.4	5.1
Reupholstering and furniture repair	0.5	1.0	0.7	0.6	1.5
Repairs and rentals of lawn and garden equipment, hand and power tools, etc.	1.2	2.1	2.6	2.2	1.7
Appliance rental	0.2	0.0	–	0.0	–
Rental of office equipment for nonbusiness use	0.0	–	–	–	–
Repair of computer systems for nonbusiness use	0.8	1.3	1.2	1.5	1.2
Computer information services	53.9	80.7	78.6	80.7	82.3
Installation of computer	0.1	0.2	0.2	0.1	0.1
HOUSEHOLD FURNISHINGS AND EQUIPMENT, PERCENT BUYING	**52.7**	**68.5**	**65.6**	**67.2**	**71.7**
Household textiles	**19.3**	**24.7**	**24.7**	**24.7**	**24.6**
Bathroom linens	6.4	7.7	8.1	7.5	7.4
Bedroom linens	10.2	13.7	13.6	12.9	14.4
Kitchen and dining room linens	1.7	2.6	3.1	2.0	2.5
Curtains and draperies	2.4	3.3	3.0	3.5	3.3
Slipcovers and decorative pillows	1.2	1.9	1.8	2.3	1.8
Sewing materials for household items	3.4	4.4	4.8	4.7	3.8
Other linens	0.5	0.6	0.7	0.7	0.5
Furniture	**10.2**	**15.5**	**14.7**	**13.0**	**17.8**
Mattresses and springs	1.7	2.7	2.6	1.8	3.3
Other bedroom furniture	1.9	3.0	3.0	2.5	3.3
Sofas	2.2	2.9	2.9	2.3	3.2
Living room chairs	1.7	2.2	1.6	1.7	3.0
Living room tables	1.4	2.2	2.1	1.7	2.6
Kitchen and dining room furniture	1.2	2.1	1.9	1.9	2.5
Infants' furniture	0.8	1.0	0.8	1.0	1.2
Outdoor furniture	1.5	2.9	2.6	2.7	3.2
Wall units, cabinets, and other furniture	2.7	4.1	3.9	4.1	4.3
Floor coverings	**3.0**	**4.5**	**4.5**	**3.9**	**4.9**
Wall-to-wall carpeting	0.3	0.5	0.6	0.5	0.5
Floor coverings, nonpermanent	2.6	4.1	4.0	3.5	4.6
Major appliances	**8.2**	**11.4**	**10.6**	**12.0**	**11.7**
Dishwashers (built-in), garbage disposals, range hoods (renter)	0.1	0.1	–	0.2	0.1
Dishwashers (built-in), garbage disposals, range hoods (owner)	0.6	1.6	1.1	2.1	1.7

	total households	$100,000 or more	$100,000– $119,999	$120,000– $149,999	$150,000 or more
Refrigerators, freezers (renter)	0.4%	0.2%	0.3%	0.2%	0.1%
Refrigerators, freezers (owner)	1.3	2.3	2.1	1.9	2.7
Washing machines (renter)	0.4	0.1	0.1	0.1	0.0
Washing machines (owner)	1.0	1.9	1.7	1.6	2.2
Clothes dryers (renter)	0.3	0.1	0.1	0.1	0.0
Clothes dryers (owner)	0.9	1.8	1.9	1.5	2.0
Cooking stoves, ovens (renter)	0.1	0.1	–	0.1	0.1
Cooking stoves, ovens (owner)	0.7	1.3	0.9	1.2	1.6
Microwave ovens (renter)	0.7	0.1	0.1	0.2	0.1
Microwave ovens (owner)	1.0	1.6	1.1	1.8	1.9
Window air conditioners (renter)	0.2	0.1	0.1	0.1	0.1
Window air conditioners (owner)	0.3	0.3	0.2	0.4	0.3
Electric floor-cleaning equipment	2.4	3.7	3.6	4.0	3.5
Sewing machines	0.3	0.3	0.2	0.3	0.4
Small appliances and misc. housewares	**16.1**	**20.6**	**19.4**	**20.2**	**21.8**
Housewares	9.9	13.1	12.4	12.1	14.2
Plastic dinnerware	2.5	3.3	2.8	3.6	3.4
China and other dinnerware	2.5	3.4	2.7	2.4	4.7
Flatware	1.4	1.6	1.8	1.2	1.6
Glassware	1.9	2.7	2.1	2.7	3.1
Silver serving pieces	0.1	0.1	0.3	–	0.0
Other serving pieces	0.7	1.1	1.4	1.0	0.9
Nonelectric cookware	3.5	4.4	4.4	4.6	4.4
Small appliances	8.1	10.1	9.4	10.4	10.5
Small electric kitchen appliances	6.9	8.5	7.3	8.7	9.3
Portable heating and cooling equipment	1.5	1.8	2.3	1.8	1.4
Miscellaneous household equipment	**35.8**	**51.9**	**48.2**	**51.4**	**55.2**
Window coverings	1.7	2.4	2.2	2.7	2.4
Infants' equipment	0.6	0.6	0.6	0.7	0.5
Outdoor equipment	1.2	1.9	1.0	2.2	2.4
Lamps and lighting fixtures	3.5	5.2	4.5	5.5	5.7
Clocks and other household decorative items	6.2	9.7	9.2	9.6	10.2
Telephones and accessories	5.1	7.9	7.1	8.8	7.8
Lawn and garden equipment	2.3	3.4	3.3	3.7	3.3
Power tools	2.1	3.3	3.8	2.7	3.2
Office furniture for home use	0.7	1.3	1.3	0.8	1.5
Hand tools	1.7	2.3	2.7	2.1	2.1
Indoor plants and fresh flowers	15.9	25.9	23.3	24.8	28.7
Closet and storage items	1.3	2.1	1.6	2.4	2.3
Rental of furniture	0.2	0.1	0.1	0.2	0.1
Luggage	1.4	3.1	2.7	3.6	3.0
Computers and computer hardware, nonbusiness use	5.4	9.2	8.9	9.1	9.5
Computer software and accessories, nonbusiness use	4.5	7.8	7.6	8.3	7.7
Personal digital assistants	0.3	0.7	0.7	0.4	0.9
Internet services away from home	0.8	1.2	1.1	1.1	1.4
Telephone answering devices	0.2	0.4	0.1	0.4	0.6
Business equipment for home use	0.6	0.8	0.8	0.6	1.1
Smoke alarms (owner)	0.4	0.6	0.7	0.7	0.5
Smoke alarms (renter)	0.1	0.1	–	–	0.2
Other household appliances (owner)	1.0	1.5	1.7	1.4	1.4
Other household appliances (renter)	0.3	0.1	0.1	0.1	0.1

Note: "–" means sample is too small to make a reliable estimate.
Source: Bureau of Labor Statistics, unpublished data from the 2008 Consumer Expenditure Survey

Table 7.10 Amount High-Income Buyers Spent on Household Services, Furnishings, and Equipment, <u>Average Quarter</u>, 2008

(average amount spent by high-income households buying household services, furnishings, and equipment during the average quarter, by before-tax income of household, 2008)

	total households	$100,000 or more	$100,000– $119,999	$120,000– $149,999	$150,000 or more
HOUSEHOLD SERVICES, AMOUNT SPENT	**$377.80**	**$658.77**	**$423.96**	**$562.56**	**$902.84**
Personal services	**1,312.33**	**1,795.94**	**1,189.08**	**1,493.25**	**2,435.63**
Babysitting and child care in own home	717.33	1,017.97	363.52	604.40	1,450.55
Babysitting and child care in someone else's home	838.68	1,119.69	789.34	1,001.72	1,720.62
Care for elderly, invalids, handicapped, etc.	3,063.64	4,695.31	2,144.23	1,216.67	6,867.65
Day care centers, nurseries, and preschools	1,224.95	1,662.67	1,248.57	1,659.12	1,999.74
Other household services	**238.01**	**394.34**	**253.24**	**344.01**	**535.34**
Housekeeping services	483.17	590.26	501.60	463.66	653.42
Gardening, lawn care service	210.43	284.13	181.53	253.43	349.31
Water-softening service	85.49	88.62	96.86	73.69	91.35
Nonclothing laundry and dry cleaning, sent out	46.61	70.23	37.67	57.14	87.66
Nonclothing laundry and dry cleaning, coin-operated	23.87	28.82	21.00	28.47	34.40
Termite and pest control services	132.02	132.21	128.17	147.30	126.71
Home security system service fee	118.21	124.00	114.47	128.35	125.83
Other home services	236.76	287.50	385.73	239.98	269.58
Termite and pest control products	27.46	28.20	24.94	26.99	31.03
Moving, storage, and freight express	571.50	699.85	405.12	1,166.06	695.74
Appliance repair, including at service center	178.73	193.75	149.25	278.27	173.68
Reupholstering and furniture repair	288.21	393.25	338.18	230.45	458.50
Repairs and rentals of lawn and garden equipment, hand and power tools, etc.	148.94	168.87	148.54	151.85	209.16
Appliance rental	115.00	25.00	–	41.67	–
Rental of office equipment for nonbusiness use	412.50	–	–	–	–
Repair of computer systems for nonbusiness use	219.41	251.37	185.69	183.95	364.41
Computer information services	101.76	114.82	108.10	111.89	121.99
Installation of computer	130.56	113.33	130.43	52.50	140.00
HOUSEHOLD FURNISHINGS AND EQUIPMENT, AMOUNT SPENT	**579.71**	**945.71**	**711.08**	**797.16**	**1,214.30**
Household textiles	**118.75**	**194.46**	**151.90**	**137.89**	**267.03**
Bathroom linens	48.76	62.48	53.57	49.80	79.03
Bedroom linens	101.56	133.08	112.99	121.57	155.54
Kitchen and dining room linens	29.22	40.18	32.48	35.51	50.20
Curtains and draperies	215.25	519.33	376.01	248.30	812.61
Slipcovers and decorative pillows	59.07	83.76	44.72	48.89	143.89
Sewing materials for household items	77.05	110.06	84.15	78.17	162.40
Other linens	68.33	81.75	101.84	59.59	80.77
Furniture	**930.73**	**1,398.26**	**990.34**	**1,290.08**	**1,725.72**
Mattresses and springs	775.44	1,016.60	784.07	1,069.75	1,151.08
Other bedroom furniture	894.72	1,173.33	967.99	1,046.33	1,398.70
Sofas	1,131.63	1,721.17	1,282.57	1,580.33	2,110.60
Living room chairs	534.02	902.17	588.57	819.53	1,076.26
Living room tables	304.11	542.66	337.86	222.04	814.71
Kitchen and dining room furniture	744.02	1,223.93	682.75	1,000.27	1,662.25
Infants' furniture	271.75	407.25	192.28	277.48	606.74
Outdoor furniture	318.49	544.44	376.62	578.29	637.11
Wall units, cabinets, and other furniture	402.83	675.24	446.99	767.93	784.53
Floor coverings	**376.52**	**577.78**	**516.39**	**533.77**	**646.65**
Wall-to-wall carpeting	2,008.33	2,640.69	2,655.74	2,465.10	2,676.09
Floor coverings, nonpermanent	166.57	299.08	176.38	219.09	427.29
Major appliances	**618.68**	**857.64**	**641.93**	**744.01**	**1,095.92**
Dishwashers (built-in), garbage disposals, range hoods (renter)	440.00	675.00	–	270.45	1,390.63
Dishwashers (built-in), garbage disposals, range hoods (owner)	561.11	654.14	563.32	578.90	759.58

	total households	$100,000 or more	$100,000– $119,999	$120,000– $149,999	$150,000 or more
Refrigerators, freezers (renter)	$474.32	$786.76	$755.17	$647.50	$1,335.00
Refrigerators, freezers (owner)	942.56	1,124.56	801.18	1,254.76	1,274.91
Washing machines (renter)	386.59	567.86	365.38	875.00	1,016.67
Washing machines (owner)	706.75	819.28	767.84	798.48	862.39
Clothes dryers (renter)	323.21	409.38	373.08	720.00	443.75
Clothes dryers (owner)	680.81	785.77	676.18	742.67	891.92
Cooking stoves, ovens (renter)	406.25	435.00	–	370.83	436.11
Cooking stoves, ovens (owner)	1,116.54	1,164.09	655.38	1,205.34	1,388.05
Microwave ovens (renter)	96.74	96.43	129.55	84.38	80.00
Microwave ovens (owner)	196.25	242.33	176.59	246.96	270.62
Window air conditioners (renter)	218.33	283.33	125.00	365.91	305.00
Window air conditioners (owner)	319.83	308.62	346.88	257.56	333.06
Electric floor-cleaning equipment	169.20	193.65	161.80	154.71	250.57
Sewing machines	454.46	744.83	392.71	69.23	1,277.14
Small appliances and misc. housewares	**86.99**	**122.47**	**98.07**	**103.15**	**152.11**
Housewares	73.66	99.62	80.83	91.22	117.76
Plastic dinnerware	27.85	39.00	21.59	37.29	51.99
China and other dinnerware	81.93	119.47	99.91	88.67	138.89
Flatware	64.18	92.74	92.96	104.41	87.10
Glassware	33.29	43.54	37.86	30.04	54.50
Silver serving pieces	54.17	45.45	44.64	–	62.50
Other serving pieces	46.54	57.88	43.17	64.66	70.43
Nonelectric cookware	77.17	98.87	80.83	105.59	109.08
Small appliances	82.47	121.08	96.34	94.09	156.85
Small electric kitchen appliances	70.55	115.25	81.05	84.77	156.12
Portable heating and cooling equipment	121.85	133.75	137.00	132.22	130.03
Miscellaneous household equipment	**313.29**	**451.03**	**358.76**	**396.44**	**550.76**
Window coverings	304.65	557.99	275.89	531.60	789.24
Infants' equipment	149.18	214.22	185.17	190.07	270.74
Outdoor equipment	234.32	408.33	306.13	272.35	522.02
Lamps and lighting fixtures	95.43	134.26	133.15	98.28	157.68
Clocks and other household decorative items	142.22	219.19	181.28	212.81	251.08
Telephones and accessories	118.38	155.16	150.53	135.72	173.43
Lawn and garden equipment	489.38	472.87	243.48	325.34	770.23
Power tools	218.29	235.92	201.53	232.85	272.55
Office furniture for home use	301.54	485.32	545.54	229.63	531.49
Hand tools	91.52	103.53	53.65	104.56	156.34
Indoor plants and fresh flowers	88.93	127.26	107.25	110.19	150.44
Closet and storage items	67.91	96.43	70.47	82.85	120.26
Rental of furniture	338.89	41.67	62.50	26.47	70.00
Luggage	109.57	140.83	122.63	135.60	159.00
Computers and computer hardware, nonbusiness use	703.00	847.82	670.47	689.68	1,086.35
Computer software and accessories, nonbusiness use	129.79	157.78	112.93	162.12	191.54
Personal digital assistants	234.17	275.00	278.04	228.75	289.52
Internet services away from home	88.58	113.91	92.59	146.71	109.55
Telephone answering devices	61.11	74.34	27.27	74.39	80.08
Business equipment for home use	91.53	136.01	113.82	239.11	109.05
Smoke alarms (owner)	61.31	47.66	42.81	44.57	54.17
Smoke alarms (renter)	43.18	50.00	–	–	51.47
Other household appliances (owner)	190.69	265.83	175.00	475.54	217.88
Other household appliances (renter)	109.09	141.67	325.00	179.17	42.50

Note: "–" means sample is too small to make a reliable estimate.
Source: Calculations by New Strategist based on the Bureau of Labor Statistics' 2008 Consumer Expenditure Survey

Table 7.11 Percent of High-Income Households Buying Housekeeping Supplies, Furnishings, and Equipment, Average Week, 2008

(percent of high-income households buying housekeeping supplies, furnishings, and equipment during the average week, by before-tax income of household, 2008)

	total households	$100,000 or more	$100,000–$119,999	$120,000–$149,999	$150,000 or more
HOUSEKEEPING SUPPLIES, PERCENT BUYING	**53.9%**	**66.2%**	**65.0%**	**69.0%**	**65.2%**
Laundry and cleaning supplies	**28.3**	**34.1**	**34.8**	**36.9**	**31.3**
Soaps and detergents	20.1	24.0	25.8	24.9	21.3
Other laundry cleaning products	18.0	22.3	20.7	25.4	21.4
Other household products	**40.4**	**50.7**	**51.0**	**51.6**	**49.7**
Cleansing and toilet tissue, paper towels, and napkins	24.8	28.7	28.7	27.6	29.5
Miscellaneous household products	25.7	36.7	39.3	36.1	34.5
Lawn and garden supplies	6.6	9.9	9.0	8.7	11.6
Postage and stationery	**22.8**	**33.3**	**32.6**	**33.1**	**34.3**
Stationery, stationery supplies, giftwrap	17.4	26.5	26.5	27.7	25.7
Postage	8.5	12.0	10.8	11.4	13.8
Delivery services	0.5	0.9	0.8	0.6	1.3
HOUSEHOLD FURNISHINGS AND EQUIPMENT, PERCENT BUYING	**30.5**	**45.0**	**42.3**	**45.1**	**47.6**
Household textiles	**6.2**	**9.5**	**8.3**	**9.2**	**10.9**
Bathroom linens	3.0	3.9	3.7	4.0	4.1
Bedroom linens	2.6	4.5	3.1	4.7	5.7
Kitchen and dining room linens	1.3	2.4	2.2	2.3	2.9
Slipcovers and decorative pillows	0.3	0.5	0.2	0.5	0.8
Outdoor furniture	**0.4**	**0.7**	**0.4**	**1.1**	**0.8**
Floor coverings, nonpermanent	**1.2**	**2.4**	**2.2**	**2.4**	**2.6**
Major appliances	**0.7**	**1.1**	**1.0**	**1.3**	**1.1**
Electric floor-cleaning equipment	0.5	1.0	0.8	1.0	1.1
Miscellaneous household appliances	0.2	0.3	0.2	0.3	0.3
Housewares	**8.1**	**13.3**	**12.5**	**12.5**	**14.9**
China and other dinnerware	1.3	2.0	2.6	1.8	1.6
Glassware	1.9	3.7	3.9	2.6	4.4
Nonelectric cookware	2.2	3.8	3.2	3.1	4.9
Tableware, nonelectric kitchenware	4.3	7.2	6.4	7.3	8.1
Miscellaneous household equipment	**24.3**	**37.2**	**34.0**	**37.8**	**40.2**
Infants' equipment	1.2	2.0	1.7	1.8	2.4
Laundry and cleaning equipment	4.9	7.9	7.7	7.0	8.8
Outdoor equipment	1.3	2.2	2.2	1.8	2.5
Lamps and lighting fixtures	1.3	1.9	1.3	1.9	2.5
Clocks and other household decorative items	8.0	14.4	13.2	13.8	16.2
Telephones and accessories	1.2	1.7	1.7	0.9	2.3
Lawn and garden equipment	2.0	3.0	3.0	1.8	3.9
Power tools	1.3	1.9	1.7	1.9	2.1
Hand tools	1.8	2.7	2.7	3.3	2.2
Indoor plants and fresh flowers	4.2	8.7	6.9	7.7	11.4
Closet and storage items	2.4	3.8	3.5	3.8	4.3
Other hardware	0.8	1.3	1.1	1.6	1.3
Miscellaneous household equipment and parts	4.9	7.2	7.1	7.6	7.1
Luggage	0.8	1.2	1.0	1.4	1.2

Source: Bureau of Labor Statistics, unpublished data from the 2008 Consumer Expenditure Survey

Table 7.12 Amount High-Income Buyers Spent on Housekeeping Supplies, Furnishings, and Equipment, <u>Average Week</u>, 2008

(average amount spent by high-income households buying housekeeping supplies, furnishings, and equipment during the average week, by before-tax income of household, 2008)

	total households	$100,000 or more	$100,000–$119,999	$120,000–$149,999	$150,000 or more
HOUSEKEEPING SUPPLIES, AMOUNT SPENT	**$23.35**	**$33.87**	**$33.95**	**$30.55**	**$36.51**
Laundry and cleaning supplies	**10.03**	**11.95**	**10.98**	**12.32**	**12.77**
Soaps and detergents	7.75	8.84	8.13	9.23	9.48
Other laundry cleaning products	7.13	8.81	8.34	8.83	9.27
Other household products	**16.70**	**26.63**	**27.75**	**22.38**	**28.93**
Cleansing and toilet tissue, paper towels, and napkins	8.09	10.01	9.85	10.11	10.12
Miscellaneous household products	11.07	14.69	15.02	11.54	16.85
Lawn and garden supplies	28.81	53.09	59.73	52.58	48.06
Postage and stationery	**13.16**	**14.47**	**12.55**	**15.16**	**15.84**
Stationery, stationery supplies, giftwrap	9.00	10.94	9.15	10.87	12.93
Postage	15.85	14.70	14.06	16.32	14.18
Delivery services	16.33	16.67	18.52	24.14	11.90
HOUSEHOLD FURNISHINGS AND EQUIPMENT, AMOUNT SPENT	**52.23**	**76.13**	**65.14**	**71.13**	**89.88**
Household textiles	**29.33**	**43.82**	**32.69**	**40.07**	**55.04**
Bathroom linens	14.24	17.39	13.78	22.39	16.79
Bedroom linens	47.06	68.39	64.86	51.61	81.31
Kitchen and dining room linens	9.09	11.07	5.94	9.73	15.44
Slipcovers and decorative pillows	36.00	32.61	17.65	35.42	36.00
Outdoor furniture	**138.46**	**157.53**	**152.63**	**209.09**	**103.70**
Floor coverings, nonpermanent	**98.37**	**72.57**	**57.53**	**49.79**	**102.75**
Major appliances	**94.03**	**132.14**	**172.55**	**103.10**	**119.09**
Electric floor-cleaning equipment	110.64	143.88	210.98	114.42	115.45
Miscellaneous household appliances	33.33	20.00	15.00	32.00	17.24
Housewares	**17.10**	**23.57**	**17.79**	**21.19**	**30.17**
China and other dinnerware	16.28	20.90	13.73	18.23	35.40
Glassware	18.38	20.43	20.46	11.28	24.83
Nonelectric cookware	12.39	14.06	8.33	12.94	18.35
Tableware, nonelectric kitchenware	13.35	19.61	12.60	22.31	23.62
Miscellaneous household equipment	**41.31**	**59.77**	**55.71**	**53.91**	**67.64**
Infants' equipment	33.61	60.80	33.53	27.47	100.84
Laundry and cleaning equipment	6.33	7.76	5.86	9.91	8.11
Outdoor equipment	47.01	65.02	44.64	46.70	94.09
Lamps and lighting fixtures	42.42	60.11	43.85	95.29	48.37
Clocks and other household decorative items	30.46	36.91	30.25	51.16	33.02
Telephones and accessories	68.85	117.86	163.31	79.35	95.11
Lawn and garden equipment	63.32	105.39	110.51	41.48	123.35
Power tools	39.85	38.50	42.42	36.79	36.41
Hand tools	17.78	19.10	23.22	21.32	12.04
Indoor plants and fresh flowers	21.28	25.00	24.31	19.95	28.23
Closet and storage items	18.49	39.95	44.96	62.40	20.71
Other hardware	38.10	35.38	29.73	36.08	39.37
Miscellaneous household equipment and parts	17.61	22.38	16.53	23.41	27.82
Luggage	32.00	33.62	27.27	25.00	47.86

Source: Calculations by New Strategist based on the Bureau of Labor Statistics' 2008 Consumer Expenditure Survey

Table 7.13 Percent Buying Household Services, Furnishings, and Equipment by Household Type, <u>Average Quarter</u>, 2008

(percent of households buying household services, furnishings, and equipment during the average quarter, by type of household, 2008)

	total married couples	married couples, no children	married couples with children				single parent, at least one child <18	single person
			total	oldest child under 6	oldest child 6 to 17	oldest child 18 or older		
HOUSEHOLD SERVICES, PERCENT BUYING	**75.7%**	**72.3%**	**79.3%**	**80.0%**	**80.4%**	**77.2%**	**61.9%**	**51.9%**
Personal services	**10.6**	**0.9**	**19.4**	**44.6**	**20.3**	**2.7**	**15.3**	**1.0**
Babysitting and child care in own home	2.7	0.0	5.3	12.1	5.8	0.4	3.0	–
Babysitting and child care in someone else's home	1.5	–	2.7	5.8	2.9	0.5	3.1	0.0
Care for elderly, invalids, handicapped, etc.	0.4	0.5	0.2	0.1	0.1	0.3	–	0.7
Day care centers, nurseries, and preschools	7.5	0.3	14.1	34.1	14.4	1.6	10.6	0.2
Other household services	**74.0**	**72.1**	**76.5**	**72.9**	**77.5**	**76.8**	**56.4**	**51.6**
Housekeeping services	7.2	8.1	6.6	7.1	7.1	5.5	3.2	6.2
Gardening, lawn care service	15.6	18.3	13.6	11.0	14.6	13.2	8.3	13.4
Water-softening service	1.7	1.6	1.7	1.3	1.8	2.0	1.0	1.1
Nonclothing laundry and dry cleaning, sent out	0.7	1.0	0.5	0.4	0.5	0.6	0.2	0.5
Nonclothing laundry and dry cleaning, coin-operated	2.0	1.9	2.0	2.7	2.0	1.6	4.5	5.3
Termite and pest control services	5.0	5.6	4.8	4.4	5.3	4.1	2.2	2.0
Home security system service fee	6.3	6.3	6.6	6.2	7.4	5.5	2.2	2.8
Other home services	2.5	2.8	2.3	2.5	2.3	2.3	1.5	1.7
Termite and pest control products	3.6	3.9	3.4	3.2	3.8	2.8	1.3	1.4
Moving, storage, and freight express	2.1	2.2	1.9	2.1	1.7	2.2	1.5	1.9
Appliance repair, including at service center	3.3	3.2	3.5	1.8	3.9	3.7	2.1	1.3
Reupholstering and furniture repair	0.7	0.9	0.5	0.3	0.5	0.6	0.2	0.3
Repairs and rentals of lawn and garden equipment, hand and power tools, etc.	1.7	1.8	1.5	1.3	1.4	1.9	0.1	0.7
Appliance rental	0.2	0.1	0.2	0.2	0.1	0.3	0.4	0.1
Rental of office equipment for nonbusiness use	0.0	–	0.0	0.1	–	0.1	0.1	0.0
Repair of computer systems for nonbusiness use	1.0	1.0	1.1	0.6	1.2	1.1	0.5	0.5
Computer information services	65.6	61.0	70.4	65.9	71.3	71.4	48.4	36.7
Installation of computer	0.1	0.1	0.1	–	0.1	0.2	0.1	0.1
HOUSEHOLD FURNISHINGS AND EQUIPMENT, PERCENT BUYING	**60.1**	**59.8**	**61.2**	**63.6**	**62.1**	**58.1**	**46.6**	**41.7**
Household textiles	**22.3**	**21.4**	**23.0**	**26.0**	**22.7**	**21.9**	**19.7**	**14.1**
Bathroom linens	7.0	6.3	7.5	8.6	7.2	7.4	8.3	4.7
Bedroom linens	12.0	11.2	12.6	16.2	11.8	11.8	10.7	7.1
Kitchen and dining room linens	2.0	1.8	2.4	2.1	2.3	2.8	1.4	1.3
Curtains and draperies	2.9	2.5	3.1	3.9	3.3	2.4	3.5	1.4
Slipcovers and decorative pillows	1.5	1.3	1.6	2.0	1.6	1.6	1.4	0.9
Sewing materials for household items	4.4	4.9	3.9	4.1	3.8	3.9	1.4	2.5
Other linens	0.6	0.6	0.5	0.5	0.6	0.3	0.3	0.3
Furniture	**12.2**	**11.3**	**13.2**	**17.3**	**13.0**	**11.3**	**8.4**	**7.0**
Mattresses and springs	2.0	1.8	2.1	2.4	2.1	2.1	1.2	1.2
Other bedroom furniture	2.4	2.0	2.8	3.2	3.1	1.9	1.9	1.0
Sofas	2.5	1.8	3.1	3.9	3.2	2.4	2.5	1.7
Living room chairs	2.0	2.0	2.0	2.9	1.6	2.2	1.4	1.5
Living room tables	1.5	1.3	1.7	2.5	1.4	1.7	1.8	1.3
Kitchen and dining room furniture	1.3	1.2	1.5	2.8	1.3	1.1	1.4	0.9
Infants' furniture	1.0	0.7	1.1	3.8	0.7	0.2	1.0	0.2
Outdoor furniture	2.0	2.0	2.2	2.2	2.2	2.2	0.9	0.7
Wall units, cabinets, and other furniture	3.1	2.9	3.4	3.4	3.5	3.2	2.8	2.2
Floor coverings	**3.8**	**3.6**	**4.2**	**5.1**	**4.2**	**3.6**	**3.1**	**1.8**
Wall-to-wall carpeting	0.5	0.4	0.5	0.8	0.4	0.6	0.2	0.2
Floor coverings, nonpermanent	3.4	3.2	3.7	4.4	3.9	3.0	2.9	1.6
Major appliances	**9.7**	**9.0**	**10.3**	**10.2**	**10.1**	**10.6**	**8.1**	**5.3**
Dishwashers (built-in), garbage disposals, range hoods (renter)	0.1	0.0	0.1	0.2	0.1	–	0.0	0.0
Dishwashers (built-in), garbage disposals, range hoods (owner)	1.0	1.0	1.0	0.8	1.0	1.1	0.3	0.2

	total married couples	married couples, no children	married couples with children				single parent, at least one child <18	single person
			total	oldest child under 6	oldest child 6 to 17	oldest child 18 or older		
Refrigerators, freezers (renter)	0.3%	0.2%	0.4%	0.9%	0.3%	0.1%	0.5%	0.4%
Refrigerators, freezers (owner)	1.9	1.9	1.9	2.0	2.0	1.7	0.5	0.6
Washing machines (renter)	0.3	0.2	0.3	0.8	0.2	0.2	1.1	0.3
Washing machines (owner)	1.4	1.2	1.7	1.7	1.5	2.0	0.7	0.5
Clothes dryers (renter)	0.2	0.2	0.2	0.5	0.1	0.1	0.7	0.2
Clothes dryers (owner)	1.2	1.2	1.3	1.2	1.3	1.3	0.6	0.4
Cooking stoves, ovens (renter)	0.1	0.0	0.1	0.4	0.0	0.1	0.5	0.1
Cooking stoves, ovens (owner)	0.9	1.0	0.9	0.6	0.8	1.1	0.3	0.2
Microwave ovens (renter)	0.4	0.3	0.4	1.0	0.3	0.2	1.2	0.9
Microwave ovens (owner)	1.4	1.3	1.5	0.7	1.4	2.0	0.6	0.5
Window air conditioners (renter)	0.2	0.1	0.1	0.2	0.2	–	0.1	0.1
Window air conditioners (owner)	0.4	0.4	0.4	0.6	0.3	0.7	0.3	0.1
Electric floor-cleaning equipment	2.7	2.6	3.0	3.1	3.1	2.6	2.4	1.8
Sewing machines	0.4	0.3	0.4	0.3	0.4	0.5	0.3	0.2
Small appliances and misc. housewares	**18.1**	**17.5**	**18.5**	**18.1**	**19.3**	**17.3**	**15.4**	**12.4**
Housewares	11.2	10.1	12.2	12.0	12.9	11.3	10.7	7.3
Plastic dinnerware	2.9	1.9	3.7	4.7	3.8	3.0	3.1	1.9
China and other dinnerware	2.8	2.7	2.7	2.5	3.0	2.3	2.3	1.9
Flatware	1.5	1.2	1.7	1.6	2.0	1.2	1.6	1.3
Glassware	2.1	2.2	1.9	1.3	2.2	1.7	2.1	1.4
Silver serving pieces	0.1	0.1	0.0	–	–	0.0	0.1	0.1
Other serving pieces	0.8	0.7	0.8	0.8	0.8	0.9	1.0	0.4
Nonelectric cookware	3.8	3.6	4.0	4.7	3.8	4.0	3.3	2.7
Small appliances	9.1	9.2	8.9	8.1	9.2	8.8	6.8	6.7
Small electric kitchen appliances	7.7	8.0	7.3	6.6	7.7	7.2	5.9	5.6
Portable heating and cooling equipment	1.6	1.4	1.9	1.9	1.9	1.9	1.2	1.3
Miscellaneous household equipment	**42.9**	**42.9**	**43.9**	**46.7**	**44.7**	**40.9**	**28.7**	**26.8**
Window coverings	2.1	2.0	2.2	2.3	2.4	1.9	1.6	1.2
Infants' equipment	0.8	0.5	1.0	3.3	0.6	0.1	0.9	0.2
Outdoor equipment	1.6	1.6	1.7	2.0	1.5	1.8	1.0	0.6
Lamps and lighting fixtures	3.9	3.9	3.9	5.0	4.1	3.1	3.1	2.8
Clocks and other household decorative items	7.5	7.6	7.6	9.0	8.0	6.1	4.9	4.4
Telephones and accessories	5.9	4.7	6.9	6.9	7.3	6.4	6.4	3.3
Lawn and garden equipment	3.3	3.5	3.2	3.5	3.1	3.2	1.4	1.0
Power tools	2.9	2.9	2.9	2.6	2.9	3.1	0.5	1.2
Office furniture for home use	0.8	0.9	0.7	0.8	0.9	0.5	0.5	0.4
Hand tools	2.2	2.2	2.2	2.8	1.9	2.3	0.7	1.2
Indoor plants and fresh flowers	20.2	22.3	19.6	19.7	19.0	20.6	9.9	11.2
Closet and storage items	1.5	1.3	1.7	2.7	1.4	1.4	1.5	1.0
Rental of furniture	0.2	0.1	0.2	0.3	0.3	0.1	0.4	0.1
Luggage	1.7	1.7	1.8	1.1	1.8	2.2	1.1	1.2
Computers and computer hardware, nonbusiness use	6.6	6.2	7.2	7.0	7.0	7.6	3.8	3.8
Computer software and accessories, nonbusiness use	5.8	5.8	6.1	5.7	6.4	5.7	3.1	3.4
Personal digital assistants	0.4	0.3	0.5	0.5	0.6	0.4	0.3	0.2
Internet services away from home	0.9	0.7	1.0	0.6	1.3	0.8	0.6	0.6
Telephone answering devices	0.2	0.2	0.2	0.0	0.2	0.4	0.0	0.2
Business equipment for home use	0.8	0.8	0.9	0.5	1.0	0.8	0.7	0.4
Smoke alarms (owner)	0.6	0.5	0.6	0.6	0.7	0.5	0.2	0.3
Smoke alarms (renter)	0.1	0.1	0.1	0.2	0.0	0.2	0.2	0.1
Other household appliances (owner)	1.4	1.5	1.3	0.9	1.3	1.4	0.5	0.6
Other household appliances (renter)	0.3	0.3	0.2	0.5	0.2	0.2	0.4	0.5

Note: "–" means sample is too small to make a reliable estimate.
Source: Bureau of Labor Statistics, unpublished data from the 2008 Consumer Expenditure Survey

Table 7.14 Amount Buyers Spent on Household Services, Furnishings, and Equipment by Household Type, <u>Average Quarter</u>, 2008

(average amount spent by households buying household services, furnishings, and equipment during the average quarter, by type of household, 2008)

	total married couples	married couples, no children	married couples with children total	oldest child under 6	oldest child 6 to 17	oldest child 18 or older	single parent, at least one child <18	single person
HOUSEHOLD SERVICES, AMOUNT SPENT	**$431.98**	**$301.37**	**$540.60**	**$1,060.38**	**$512.52**	**$270.58**	**$442.42**	**$246.00**
Personal services	**1,275.09**	**2,142.39**	**1,234.32**	**1,525.30**	**1,047.39**	**788.82**	**1,107.47**	**1,895.36**
Babysitting and child care in own home	686.05	400.00	678.21	1,040.03	420.83	522.09	985.38	–
Babysitting and child care in someone else's home	864.63	–	858.36	909.89	883.62	250.00	627.86	375.00
Care for elderly, invalids, handicapped, etc.	2,773.57	3,795.00	952.94	479.17	912.50	1,037.50	–	2,256.82
Day care centers, nurseries, and preschools	1,250.83	616.18	1,266.60	1,464.97	1,127.94	877.97	1,136.38	1,403.26
Other household services	**259.47**	**274.71**	**248.63**	**230.85**	**256.71**	**244.62**	**184.95**	**211.69**
Housekeeping services	562.45	489.34	629.93	518.39	670.52	624.73	568.35	326.73
Gardening, lawn care service	237.64	244.08	235.15	161.93	239.92	262.30	174.40	159.79
Water-softening service	86.83	70.86	84.77	37.21	86.51	99.62	67.89	70.64
Nonclothing laundry and dry cleaning, sent out	41.44	38.11	46.00	60.26	37.76	51.72	110.87	51.56
Nonclothing laundry and dry cleaning, coin-operated	26.76	21.08	28.11	35.22	25.63	26.42	36.23	16.81
Termite and pest control services	120.29	128.65	110.79	90.60	111.17	122.49	144.98	158.54
Home security system service fee	117.47	116.04	116.93	117.21	105.75	142.40	103.69	127.57
Other home services	218.18	209.57	225.00	225.40	233.66	208.08	278.31	250.29
Termite and pest control products	26.75	27.81	24.93	19.92	24.21	29.82	25.60	29.17
Moving, storage, and freight express	539.30	608.18	505.95	806.67	445.66	410.47	429.55	732.16
Appliance repair, including at service center	187.46	207.28	165.26	192.17	161.42	163.91	127.01	152.26
Reupholstering and furniture repair	302.46	412.23	131.50	205.56	125.93	117.24	66.67	334.38
Repairs and rentals of lawn and garden equipment, hand and power tools, etc.	141.36	154.17	127.14	82.03	114.54	161.83	107.69	178.04
Appliance rental	112.50	85.71	122.06	145.45	236.11	49.07	134.66	84.62
Rental of office equipment for nonbusiness use	450.00	–	591.67	140.00	–	1,060.00	425.00	350.00
Repair of computer systems for nonbusiness use	215.75	221.32	228.30	186.11	226.28	247.32	165.10	270.65
Computer information services	103.49	100.47	105.45	107.90	104.79	105.26	99.35	94.57
Installation of computer	183.33	213.89	90.63	–	116.67	73.44	59.09	90.00
HOUSEHOLD FURNISHINGS AND EQUIPMENT, AMOUNT SPENT	**697.36**	**657.00**	**736.73**	**763.35**	**720.28**	**749.76**	**420.80**	**379.83**
Household textiles	**138.41**	**142.43**	**136.84**	**110.14**	**160.77**	**112.96**	**94.11**	**88.97**
Bathroom linens	51.36	52.41	50.70	43.07	51.91	54.01	40.81	45.80
Bedroom linens	110.59	109.12	111.80	95.53	120.61	109.97	94.73	83.38
Kitchen and dining room linens	32.02	36.73	28.75	18.15	32.83	27.53	18.31	25.75
Curtains and draperies	284.45	320.30	285.53	146.69	401.82	138.51	83.62	130.40
Slipcovers and decorative pillows	70.72	75.37	70.27	87.44	79.03	42.95	59.55	41.13
Sewing materials for household items	82.97	94.64	66.99	38.58	74.60	72.01	43.57	70.96
Other linens	75.89	90.95	62.76	25.48	73.28	62.12	100.74	37.93
Furniture	**1,052.99**	**988.94**	**1,111.14**	**1,082.80**	**1,106.00**	**1,147.24**	**831.95**	**692.56**
Mattresses and springs	828.73	907.30	774.77	687.50	782.78	817.50	619.07	609.03
Other bedroom furniture	949.69	948.37	960.16	841.22	949.20	1,119.90	715.49	780.53
Sofas	1,345.53	1,392.66	1,326.48	1,119.04	1,412.58	1,334.39	862.05	785.63
Living room chairs	639.29	603.05	657.96	719.79	657.76	607.31	403.65	340.20
Living room tables	403.21	307.81	474.41	883.87	341.20	316.03	175.00	185.23
Kitchen and dining room furniture	964.18	1,019.96	962.25	1,034.44	815.58	1,135.84	495.96	425.54
Infants' furniture	300.52	285.56	317.89	336.84	244.85	547.50	147.22	143.18
Outdoor furniture	351.10	318.97	378.51	312.27	378.79	416.67	194.66	232.25
Wall units, cabinets, and other furniture	470.68	489.01	469.70	314.05	482.08	542.88	303.67	281.86
Floor coverings	**431.68**	**493.33**	**406.98**	**396.21**	**376.95**	**477.32**	**236.28**	**237.71**
Wall-to-wall carpeting	2,109.04	2,478.41	2,034.80	1,728.75	2,210.00	2,077.82	2,618.06	1,413.24
Floor coverings, nonpermanent	184.33	208.70	168.19	115.32	202.12	137.92	89.60	114.17
Major appliances	**737.85**	**742.61**	**751.05**	**800.91**	**733.93**	**751.51**	**402.22**	**414.45**
Dishwashers (built-in), garbage disposals, range hoods (renter)	541.67	275.00	632.14	1,118.75	293.75	–	108.33	200.00
Dishwashers (built-in), garbage disposals, range hoods (owner)	537.76	523.21	570.34	568.67	560.89	590.79	450.96	606.25

	total married couples	married couples, no children	married couples with children				single parent, at least one child <18	single person
			total	oldest child under 6	oldest child 6 to 17	oldest child 18 or older		
Refrigerators, freezers (renter)	$556.25	$575.00	$572.14	$611.21	$554.55	$545.83	$487.77	$473.08
Refrigerators, freezers (owner)	998.67	943.55	1,070.03	1,122.32	991.21	1,182.75	851.89	764.17
Washing machines (renter)	433.04	400.00	410.16	412.95	464.29	304.76	394.39	343.55
Washing machines (owner)	748.06	772.29	746.84	752.40	775.17	711.93	648.93	606.38
Clothes dryers (renter)	369.74	345.83	293.06	401.89	197.22	138.46	375.70	247.92
Clothes dryers (owner)	726.64	696.58	750.78	746.67	786.17	697.07	533.62	489.53
Cooking stoves, ovens (renter)	325.00	691.67	270.00	276.39	200.00	266.67	440.38	500.00
Cooking stoves, ovens (owner)	1,223.39	1,178.75	1,318.68	1,646.61	1,370.48	1,164.22	718.38	882.61
Microwave ovens (renter)	97.92	93.97	81.76	74.51	95.19	73.53	58.33	113.86
Microwave ovens (owner)	213.31	213.65	222.93	214.93	207.37	245.69	115.45	163.30
Window air conditioners (renter)	255.00	287.50	201.79	195.83	201.32	–	135.71	205.36
Window air conditioners (owner)	310.00	286.11	323.86	188.64	270.37	432.58	250.96	413.46
Electric floor-cleaning equipment	193.70	210.02	174.92	178.59	180.66	160.93	113.66	119.20
Sewing machines	602.70	518.18	573.13	118.97	559.38	754.26	130.15	160.94
Small appliances and misc. housewares	**96.82**	**96.19**	**98.79**	**79.33**	**94.10**	**119.91**	**57.08**	**72.71**
Housewares	81.23	84.22	78.19	51.33	78.15	95.49	48.08	59.12
Plastic dinnerware	31.01	32.72	30.19	24.58	29.11	37.54	21.74	19.47
China and other dinnerware	92.90	102.21	88.24	53.19	92.75	100.98	59.96	60.71
Flatware	74.50	66.80	76.47	35.67	75.37	109.15	36.81	42.60
Glassware	37.38	38.50	36.64	24.63	36.82	41.42	28.54	29.50
Silver serving pieces	35.00	35.00	50.00	–	–	50.00	85.00	47.50
Other serving pieces	50.00	47.86	53.70	26.60	70.07	43.82	21.88	35.47
Nonelectric cookware	89.16	83.93	91.17	55.53	87.90	121.18	48.72	60.86
Small appliances	92.76	91.29	97.47	100.90	87.42	113.67	54.14	70.61
Small electric kitchen appliances	81.30	74.28	91.49	102.19	75.91	114.22	47.66	56.28
Portable heating and cooling equipment	130.83	175.18	103.17	74.60	119.58	90.89	73.72	117.05
Miscellaneous household equipment	**359.20**	**347.42**	**363.54**	**327.39**	**355.99**	**402.31**	**205.44**	**231.77**
Window coverings	374.88	478.52	321.15	335.51	343.01	266.75	116.05	256.78
Infants' equipment	175.97	256.38	154.47	193.20	83.06	157.14	148.63	50.00
Outdoor equipment	262.04	274.35	266.47	274.26	248.99	284.13	125.25	110.83
Lamps and lighting fixtures	116.71	117.91	112.02	80.31	124.08	114.58	49.60	75.90
Clocks and other household decorative items	150.43	171.40	130.64	127.06	132.93	128.67	116.35	136.38
Telephones and accessories	125.17	117.17	131.02	146.02	118.90	144.69	110.61	95.72
Lawn and garden equipment	534.42	443.66	584.27	288.60	763.99	473.91	135.79	421.68
Power tools	238.72	222.49	241.84	205.99	208.68	312.91	159.38	161.74
Office furniture for home use	379.57	341.09	467.91	793.00	420.98	315.87	143.63	189.20
Hand tools	108.03	105.41	106.71	139.62	98.40	94.43	22.26	63.98
Indoor plants and fresh flowers	97.21	94.85	97.37	76.05	94.17	114.60	67.00	73.59
Closet and storage items	74.32	69.44	81.06	70.68	87.94	81.16	45.29	56.31
Rental of furniture	370.00	300.00	442.05	384.09	491.00	327.27	255.71	215.00
Luggage	111.98	116.97	111.52	88.06	95.88	140.16	99.34	109.50
Computers and computer hardware, nonbusiness use	756.81	747.25	739.00	720.40	716.05	785.99	575.07	596.83
Computer software and accessories, nonbusiness use	131.60	123.46	136.80	149.82	132.63	137.13	82.92	121.07
Personal digital assistants	241.46	306.25	209.38	243.62	188.64	245.71	242.59	227.78
Internet services away from home	96.07	93.24	98.75	93.75	97.40	103.27	57.46	65.95
Telephone answering devices	63.16	55.88	72.62	200.00	98.44	54.49	108.33	63.24
Business equipment for home use	107.19	116.36	105.00	91.00	102.91	115.33	59.33	58.55
Smoke alarms (owner)	70.91	37.24	100.83	44.92	83.46	170.37	41.18	42.24
Smoke alarms (renter)	34.09	32.50	38.64	33.70	12.50	51.47	162.50	29.17
Other household appliances (owner)	218.38	197.15	239.29	167.82	168.22	377.30	130.56	153.07
Other household appliances (renter)	141.67	140.44	151.14	190.63	108.82	150.00	52.63	102.08

Note: "–" means sample is too small to make a reliable estimate.
Source: Calculations by New Strategist based on the Bureau of Labor Statistics' 2008 Consumer Expenditure Survey

Table 7.15 Percent Buying Housekeeping Supplies, Furnishings, and Equipment by Household Type, <u>Average Week</u>, 2008

(percent of households buying housekeeping supplies, furnishings, and equipment during the average week, by type of household, 2008)

	total married couples	married couples, no children	married couples with children				single parent, at least one child <18	single person
			total	oldest child under 6	oldest child 6 to 17	oldest child 18 or older		
HOUSEKEEPING SUPPLIES, PERCENT BUYING	**62.9%**	**59.6%**	**65.1%**	**63.5%**	**63.9%**	**68.0%**	**52.3%**	**40.8%**
Laundry and cleaning supplies	**34.3**	**29.9**	**37.5**	**32.7**	**36.7**	**42.1**	**28.9**	**18.4**
Soaps and detergents	24.4	20.2	27.3	23.9	27.3	29.4	23.0	12.2
Other laundry cleaning products	22.4	19.3	24.6	20.2	23.6	29.4	17.0	11.0
Other household products	**48.4**	**45.0**	**50.9**	**50.6**	**49.9**	**52.9**	**39.2**	**27.9**
Cleansing and toilet tissue, paper towels, and napkins	29.0	26.4	31.0	25.2	32.2	32.4	25.9	17.8
Miscellaneous household products	32.4	28.0	36.1	38.6	34.7	36.9	23.7	15.2
Lawn and garden supplies	8.9	9.3	8.4	7.9	7.2	11.0	3.9	3.8
Postage and stationery	**28.1**	**27.0**	**28.8**	**28.9**	**28.2**	**29.9**	**19.1**	**17.0**
Stationery, stationery supplies, giftwrap	22.3	20.8	23.7	24.7	23.3	23.8	14.6	11.4
Postage	10.1	10.9	9.0	8.3	8.3	10.7	6.8	7.5
Delivery services	0.7	0.7	0.6	0.7	0.4	0.8	0.3	0.3
HOUSEHOLD FURNISHINGS AND EQUIPMENT, PERCENT BUYING	**38.1**	**35.8**	**40.3**	**41.3**	**39.3**	**41.5**	**27.0**	**19.9**
Household textiles	**7.8**	**7.1**	**8.2**	**6.8**	**8.4**	**8.9**	**7.6**	**3.6**
Bathroom linens	3.5	3.0	3.6	2.6	3.8	3.8	3.4	1.8
Bedroom linens	3.2	2.8	3.5	3.7	3.4	3.6	3.6	1.4
Kitchen and dining room linens	1.9	2.1	1.7	1.3	1.9	1.7	0.9	0.7
Slipcovers and decorative pillows	0.4	0.3	0.4	–	0.3	0.8	0.2	0.2
Outdoor furniture	**0.6**	**0.5**	**0.7**	**0.7**	**0.8**	**0.5**	**0.1**	**0.3**
Floor coverings, nonpermanent	**1.7**	**1.5**	**1.9**	**1.6**	**1.9**	**2.2**	**0.9**	**0.5**
Major appliances	**0.6**	**0.4**	**0.8**	**1.1**	**0.8**	**0.7**	**0.9**	**0.7**
Electric floor-cleaning equipment	0.5	0.2	0.7	1.0	0.6	0.7	0.7	0.4
Miscellaneous household appliances	0.1	0.2	0.0	0.1	0.0	–	0.2	0.2
Housewares	**10.5**	**9.5**	**11.4**	**14.0**	**10.1**	**12.1**	**5.9**	**5.1**
China and other dinnerware	1.8	1.2	2.4	4.9	1.5	2.6	0.8	0.5
Glassware	2.5	2.0	2.9	2.0	3.1	3.0	1.4	1.0
Nonelectric cookware	2.7	2.4	2.9	2.6	2.2	4.3	1.4	1.6
Tableware, nonelectric kitchenware	5.5	5.5	5.6	8.0	5.0	5.1	3.2	2.7
Miscellaneous household equipment	**31.3**	**29.2**	**33.5**	**35.9**	**32.4**	**33.8**	**20.5**	**14.8**
Infants' equipment	1.7	0.6	2.5	8.5	1.3	0.8	1.1	0.3
Laundry and cleaning equipment	6.2	5.8	6.4	5.9	5.5	8.4	3.9	3.0
Outdoor equipment	1.7	2.2	1.5	2.0	1.3	1.4	0.5	0.8
Lamps and lighting fixtures	1.7	1.8	1.5	0.8	1.6	1.7	1.4	0.8
Clocks and other household decorative items	10.7	9.7	11.9	10.9	11.9	12.5	6.9	4.6
Telephones and accessories	1.5	1.3	1.7	1.4	1.3	2.6	2.1	0.7
Lawn and garden equipment	2.7	2.9	2.5	3.5	2.6	1.5	0.8	1.2
Power tools	1.8	1.8	1.8	1.6	1.5	2.3	0.9	0.7
Hand tools	2.3	2.2	2.5	3.0	2.4	2.1	2.1	1.2
Indoor plants and fresh flowers	5.8	6.1	5.7	4.6	5.4	6.9	1.8	2.5
Closet and storage items	3.3	2.8	3.6	3.5	3.7	3.5	2.6	1.1
Other hardware	1.1	1.0	1.2	1.2	1.1	1.3	0.8	0.4
Miscellaneous household equipment and parts	6.5	5.6	7.4	7.8	7.8	6.5	4.1	2.6
Luggage	0.8	0.7	1.0	0.9	0.9	1.4	1.0	0.6

Note: "–" means sample is too small to make a reliable estimate.
Source: Bureau of Labor Statistics, unpublished data from the 2008 Consumer Expenditure Survey

(average amount spent by households buying housekeeping supplies, furnishings, and equipment during the average week, by type of household, 2008)

	total married couples	married couples, no children	married couples with children				single parent, at least one child <18	single person
			total	oldest child under 6	oldest child 6 to 17	oldest child 18 or older		
HOUSEKEEPING SUPPLIES, AMOUNT SPENT	**$26.94**	**$25.25**	**$28.53**	**$29.40**	**$26.57**	**$31.32**	**$19.11**	**$16.36**
Laundry and cleaning supplies	**10.67**	**9.66**	**11.25**	**9.98**	**12.03**	**10.63**	**10.24**	**8.03**
Soaps and detergents	8.21	7.53	8.58	8.10	9.16	7.85	7.64	6.38
Other laundry cleaning products	7.42	7.09	7.63	6.54	8.11	7.38	7.05	6.38
Other household products	**19.71**	**17.93**	**21.47**	**23.67**	**18.53**	**25.05**	**11.24**	**10.80**
Cleansing and toilet tissue, paper towels, and napkins	8.70	8.19	8.98	9.14	9.09	8.77	7.45	6.48
Miscellaneous household products	12.39	11.86	13.09	10.97	11.47	17.20	8.32	7.74
Lawn and garden supplies	33.82	27.89	40.74	69.34	32.68	36.99	13.18	17.54
Postage and stationery	**13.31**	**15.19**	**11.87**	**11.86**	**11.79**	**11.93**	**13.82**	**12.86**
Stationery, stationery supplies, giftwrap	9.11	10.19	8.56	8.88	8.67	8.23	6.58	8.78
Postage	15.97	16.77	14.57	13.80	15.06	14.21	23.75	15.05
Delivery services	16.42	22.86	12.28	14.08	13.51	10.71	28.00	16.13
HOUSEHOLD FURNISHINGS AND EQUIPMENT, AMOUNT SPENT	**57.41**	**54.29**	**60.78**	**50.84**	**52.32**	**81.36**	**34.83**	**43.70**
Household textiles	**30.90**	**34.64**	**27.46**	**25.70**	**25.18**	**31.98**	**22.18**	**24.65**
Bathroom linens	14.37	17.67	13.09	12.36	15.40	9.19	13.82	15.47
Bedroom linens	51.27	60.14	41.79	37.13	36.72	53.09	31.74	35.56
Kitchen and dining room linens	8.47	8.21	9.41	4.76	8.99	11.52	8.79	11.43
Slipcovers and decorative pillows	38.89	26.67	44.74	–	40.74	49.38	4.76	33.33
Outdoor furniture	**112.73**	**84.78**	**105.88**	**65.71**	**142.67**	**49.06**	**25.00**	**137.50**
Floor coverings, nonpermanent	**117.86**	**35.81**	**186.24**	**33.97**	**57.84**	**453.70**	**27.59**	**31.48**
Major appliances	**103.17**	**116.28**	**103.66**	**20.35**	**132.89**	**131.51**	**89.66**	**92.54**
Electric floor-cleaning equipment	118.75	181.82	108.22	21.36	146.77	131.51	110.29	93.02
Miscellaneous household appliances	25.00	31.25	25.00	9.09	25.00	–	15.79	47.06
Housewares	**18.82**	**24.63**	**15.41**	**15.75**	**13.14**	**18.56**	**7.81**	**16.57**
China and other dinnerware	17.93	27.12	13.17	7.76	10.20	22.27	18.99	11.11
Glassware	18.78	30.61	12.59	8.72	11.82	15.93	3.55	25.96
Nonelectric cookware	14.71	18.07	12.89	20.54	11.87	11.06	5.56	9.88
Tableware, nonelectric kitchenware	14.36	17.79	12.68	13.91	10.76	14.23	5.97	13.24
Miscellaneous household equipment	**44.64**	**44.40**	**45.35**	**44.01**	**42.63**	**50.99**	**30.02**	**36.66**
Infants' equipment	32.74	78.33	24.80	26.79	22.48	19.28	29.82	42.42
Laundry and cleaning equipment	6.67	6.61	6.56	6.44	5.83	7.43	3.60	5.76
Outdoor equipment	47.13	46.30	50.68	55.50	32.33	78.52	41.30	28.92
Lamps and lighting fixtures	46.39	47.16	46.94	73.08	20.25	82.66	31.69	35.90
Clocks and other household decorative items	30.31	32.96	29.16	33.85	26.34	31.47	21.14	38.39
Telephones and accessories	81.88	50.79	102.96	62.41	147.29	78.29	53.33	56.72
Lawn and garden equipment	68.03	62.94	80.00	44.48	90.73	100.67	25.64	68.07
Power tools	37.22	37.08	39.89	38.27	47.06	31.76	52.87	49.32
Hand tools	19.91	14.41	24.90	54.39	19.67	10.33	14.63	11.11
Indoor plants and fresh flowers	22.43	22.81	20.49	25.93	21.04	17.44	15.56	21.83
Closet and storage items	21.65	20.85	23.35	14.41	25.40	25.57	10.85	8.26
Other hardware	46.30	34.34	55.65	31.36	21.50	122.83	13.16	21.05
Miscellaneous household equipment and parts	18.25	19.40	16.10	11.97	16.99	17.36	9.85	12.16
Luggage	36.90	41.54	36.54	11.11	30.00	54.74	46.08	22.03

Note: "–" means sample is too small to make a reliable estimate.
Source: Calculations by New Strategist based on the Bureau of Labor Statistics' 2008 Consumer Expenditure Survey

Table 7.17 Percent Buying Household Services, Furnishings, and Equipment by Race and Hispanic Origin, Average Quarter, 2008

(percent of households buying household services, furnishings, and equipment during the average quarter, by race and Hispanic origin of householder, 2008)

	total households	Asian	black	Hispanic	non-Hispanic white and other
HOUSEHOLD SERVICES, PERCENT BUYING	65.9%	73.1%	51.2%	54.9%	70.0%
Personal services	**7.3**	**6.2**	**6.3**	**8.8**	**7.3**
Babysitting and child care in own home	1.6	0.8	0.5	1.3	1.9
Babysitting and child care in someone else's home	1.1	0.7	0.9	2.2	0.9
Care for elderly, invalids, handicapped, etc.	0.4	0.0	0.1	0.3	0.5
Day care centers, nurseries, and preschools	5.0	5.0	5.0	5.3	4.9
Other household services	**64.4**	**71.8**	**49.2**	**51.5**	**68.8**
Housekeeping services	6.2	3.8	1.6	3.2	7.3
Gardening, lawn care service	13.7	16.2	6.7	9.0	15.6
Water-softening service	1.4	0.7	1.7	1.0	1.5
Nonclothing laundry and dry cleaning, sent out	0.6	0.5	0.2	0.4	0.7
Nonclothing laundry and dry cleaning, coin-operated	3.5	4.4	5.4	6.2	2.8
Termite and pest control services	3.6	1.5	1.7	2.4	4.1
Home security system service fee	4.6	5.2	5.4	2.6	4.8
Other home services	2.0	0.9	0.9	1.2	2.4
Termite and pest control products	2.5	0.8	1.1	1.9	2.9
Moving, storage, and freight express	2.1	1.2	1.4	0.9	2.3
Appliance repair, including at service center	2.5	1.3	1.8	1.5	2.7
Reupholstering and furniture repair	0.5	0.5	0.1	0.5	0.6
Repairs and rentals of lawn and garden equipment, hand and power tools, etc.	1.2	0.9	0.6	0.3	1.4
Appliance rental	0.2	0.0	0.2	0.3	0.2
Rental of office equipment for nonbusiness use	0.0	–	–	0.0	0.0
Repair of computer systems for nonbusiness use	0.8	0.2	0.6	0.8	0.8
Computer information services	53.9	63.6	39.0	41.3	58.2
Installation of computer	0.1	0.1	0.1	–	0.1
HOUSEHOLD FURNISHINGS AND EQUIPMENT, PERCENT BUYING	**52.7**	**47.8**	**38.8**	**46.3**	**55.9**
Household textiles	**19.3**	**14.8**	**16.5**	**17.8**	**20.0**
Bathroom linens	6.4	6.1	6.9	7.5	6.2
Bedroom linens	10.2	8.4	10.4	8.8	10.4
Kitchen and dining room linens	1.7	2.0	1.5	2.0	1.7
Curtains and draperies	2.4	1.4	2.5	2.7	2.4
Slipcovers and decorative pillows	1.2	1.0	0.9	1.2	1.3
Sewing materials for household items	3.4	1.1	0.9	1.8	4.1
Other linens	0.5	0.8	0.5	0.4	0.5
Furniture	**10.2**	**10.1**	**7.5**	**8.3**	**10.9**
Mattresses and springs	1.7	2.4	1.4	1.3	1.8
Other bedroom furniture	1.9	1.7	1.8	1.8	2.0
Sofas	2.2	2.2	2.2	2.1	2.2
Living room chairs	1.7	1.3	1.4	1.2	1.8
Living room tables	1.4	1.4	1.5	1.2	1.4
Kitchen and dining room furniture	1.2	1.0	0.8	1.0	1.3
Infants' furniture	0.8	0.8	0.7	0.9	0.8
Outdoor furniture	1.5	0.7	0.6	0.7	1.7
Wall units, cabinets, and other furniture	2.7	3.3	1.9	2.2	2.9
Floor coverings	**3.0**	**1.7**	**2.1**	**1.9**	**3.2**
Wall-to-wall carpeting	0.3	–	0.2	0.3	0.4
Floor coverings, nonpermanent	2.6	1.7	1.9	1.7	2.9
Major appliances	**8.2**	**7.1**	**6.4**	**7.7**	**8.5**
Dishwashers (built-in), garbage disposals, range hoods (renter)	0.1	–	–	0.1	0.1
Dishwashers (built-in), garbage disposals, range hoods (owner)	0.6	0.2	0.3	0.3	0.7

	total households	Asian	black	Hispanic	non-Hispanic white and other
Refrigerators, freezers (renter)	0.4%	0.8%	0.6%	0.5%	0.3%
Refrigerators, freezers (owner)	1.3	0.9	0.6	1.0	1.5
Washing machines (renter)	0.4	0.2	0.5	0.6	0.4
Washing machines (owner)	1.0	0.5	0.8	0.9	1.1
Clothes dryers (renter)	0.3	0.2	0.4	0.4	0.3
Clothes dryers (owner)	0.9	0.6	0.6	0.6	0.9
Cooking stoves, ovens (renter)	0.1	0.4	0.1	0.2	0.1
Cooking stoves, ovens (owner)	0.7	0.4	0.4	0.6	0.7
Microwave ovens (renter)	0.7	1.4	1.2	1.2	0.5
Microwave ovens (owner)	1.0	0.8	0.8	1.0	1.0
Window air conditioners (renter)	0.2	0.1	0.1	0.3	0.1
Window air conditioners (owner)	0.3	0.0	0.2	0.2	0.3
Electric floor-cleaning equipment	2.4	2.1	1.6	1.7	2.6
Sewing machines	0.3	0.3	0.1	0.2	0.3
Small appliances and misc. housewares	**16.1**	**14.6**	**11.8**	**16.2**	**16.7**
Housewares	9.9	9.4	7.5	9.9	10.3
Plastic dinnerware	2.5	1.6	2.6	2.4	2.5
China and other dinnerware	2.5	2.8	2.0	2.5	2.6
Flatware	1.4	1.4	1.1	1.9	1.4
Glassware	1.9	1.9	1.7	2.1	2.0
Silver serving pieces	0.1	0.2	0.0	0.0	0.1
Other serving pieces	0.7	0.2	0.5	0.6	0.7
Nonelectric cookware	3.5	4.2	2.1	3.6	3.6
Small appliances	8.1	7.4	5.7	8.5	8.5
Small electric kitchen appliances	6.9	6.4	4.4	7.2	7.2
Portable heating and cooling equipment	1.5	1.1	1.6	1.7	1.5
Miscellaneous household equipment	**35.8**	**32.4**	**21.8**	**27.4**	**39.4**
Window coverings	1.7	1.0	1.4	1.3	1.8
Infants' equipment	0.6	0.6	0.8	0.6	0.6
Outdoor equipment	1.2	0.6	0.7	1.0	1.3
Lamps and lighting fixtures	3.5	3.7	2.5	2.6	3.8
Clocks and other household decorative items	6.2	3.8	3.1	4.4	6.9
Telephones and accessories	5.1	5.2	4.5	4.1	5.3
Lawn and garden equipment	2.3	0.9	1.3	1.3	2.6
Power tools	2.1	1.2	0.9	1.3	2.4
Office furniture for home use	0.7	0.7	0.3	0.4	0.7
Hand tools	1.7	1.4	0.6	1.1	2.0
Indoor plants and fresh flowers	15.9	11.1	7.3	9.9	18.2
Closet and storage items	1.3	1.0	0.9	0.9	1.5
Rental of furniture	0.2	0.0	0.4	0.2	0.1
Luggage	1.4	1.9	0.8	1.1	1.6
Computers and computer hardware, nonbusiness use	5.4	7.1	2.6	3.7	6.1
Computer software and accessories, nonbusiness use	4.5	4.7	1.9	2.5	5.3
Personal digital assistants	0.3	0.1	0.1	0.2	0.4
Internet services away from home	0.8	0.8	0.6	0.9	0.9
Telephone answering devices	0.2	0.4	0.1	0.2	0.2
Business equipment for home use	0.6	0.4	0.4	0.4	0.7
Smoke alarms (owner)	0.4	0.4	0.2	0.2	0.5
Smoke alarms (renter)	0.1	–	0.1	0.1	0.1
Other household appliances (owner)	1.0	0.8	0.3	0.7	1.2
Other household appliances (renter)	0.3	0.5	0.3	0.3	0.3

Note: "Asian" and "black" include Hispanics and non-Hispanics who identify themselves as being of the respective race alone. "Hispanic" includes people of any race who identify themselves as Hispanic. "Other" includes people who identify themselves as non-Hispanic and as Alaska Native, American Indian, Asian (who are also included in the Asian column), or Native Hawaiian or other Pacific Islander as well as non-Hispanics reporting more than one race. "–" means sample is too small to make a reliable estimate.
Source: Bureau of Labor Statistics, unpublished data from the 2008 Consumer Expenditure Survey

Table 7.18 Amount Buyers Spent on Household Services, Furnishings, and Equipment by Race and Hispanic Origin, <u>Average Quarter,</u> 2008

(average amount spent by households buying household services, furnishings, and equipment during the average quarter, by race and Hispanic origin of householder, 2008)

	total households	Asian	black	Hispanic	non-Hispanic white and other
HOUSEHOLD SERVICES, AMOUNT SPENT	**$377.80**	**$317.35**	**$297.66**	**$362.64**	**$389.10**
Personal services	**1,312.33**	**1,690.11**	**1,112.54**	**1,147.49**	**1,372.76**
Babysitting and child care in own home	717.33	975.31	1,556.25	1,238.49	626.34
Babysitting and child care in someone else's home	838.68	1,284.62	787.78	883.86	825.82
Care for elderly, invalids, handicapped, etc.	3,063.64	3,350.00	403.57	1,340.00	3,324.51
Day care centers, nurseries, and preschools	1,224.95	1,763.26	1,076.98	1,156.63	1,264.91
Other household services	**238.01**	**177.70**	**168.10**	**191.73**	**250.98**
Housekeeping services	483.17	553.11	397.44	585.38	479.54
Gardening, lawn care service	210.43	133.63	183.32	191.65	213.70
Water-softening service	85.49	164.64	76.87	110.26	84.66
Nonclothing laundry and dry cleaning, sent out	46.61	59.80	16.18	47.86	47.83
Nonclothing laundry and dry cleaning, coin-operated	23.87	18.96	30.35	32.04	19.08
Termite and pest control services	132.02	169.87	154.26	123.03	131.57
Home security system service fee	118.21	137.52	107.62	133.56	118.97
Other home services	236.76	94.77	298.84	208.91	234.39
Termite and pest control products	27.46	41.98	32.73	28.01	27.09
Moving, storage, and freight express	571.50	625.00	373.25	295.43	607.91
Appliance repair, including at service center	178.73	163.09	156.22	173.68	181.59
Reupholstering and furniture repair	288.21	107.65	112.50	238.00	304.24
Repairs and rentals of lawn and garden equipment, hand and power tools, etc.	148.94	60.56	240.83	156.73	143.39
Appliance rental	115.00	37.50	104.55	94.44	119.74
Rental of office equipment for nonbusiness use	412.50	–	–	158.33	341.67
Repair of computer systems for nonbusiness use	219.41	110.42	95.91	129.11	243.44
Computer information services	101.76	96.31	100.28	101.73	101.96
Installation of computer	130.56	30.56	270.00	–	120.45
HOUSEHOLD FURNISHINGS AND EQUIPMENT, AMOUNT SPENT	**579.71**	**612.01**	**500.66**	**458.18**	**603.16**
Household textiles	**118.75**	**136.85**	**117.25**	**96.46**	**121.91**
Bathroom linens	48.76	39.87	49.56	46.47	48.99
Bedroom linens	101.56	115.98	112.78	108.24	99.02
Kitchen and dining room linens	29.22	38.81	31.85	30.03	28.78
Curtains and draperies	215.25	435.00	95.02	90.54	256.67
Slipcovers and decorative pillows	59.07	60.42	40.96	33.04	65.12
Sewing materials for household items	77.05	41.37	59.84	29.66	80.80
Other linens	68.33	40.63	87.00	54.88	66.67
Furniture	**930.73**	**961.49**	**1,054.73**	**756.06**	**937.81**
Mattresses and springs	775.44	872.60	760.39	761.84	775.98
Other bedroom furniture	894.72	815.61	1,084.29	615.30	904.52
Sofas	1,131.63	1,371.06	988.50	942.80	1,177.55
Living room chairs	534.02	362.21	495.21	380.67	555.77
Living room tables	304.11	265.56	222.99	187.91	332.57
Kitchen and dining room furniture	744.02	575.00	568.75	483.25	796.80
Infants' furniture	271.75	342.26	281.69	251.40	274.01
Outdoor furniture	318.49	186.23	216.81	156.69	334.36
Wall units, cabinets, and other furniture	402.83	402.41	440.72	321.27	408.76
Floor coverings	**376.52**	**210.61**	**252.23**	**198.97**	**406.97**
Wall-to-wall carpeting	2,008.33	–	1,431.52	843.75	2,225.71
Floor coverings, nonpermanent	166.57	210.61	109.34	77.54	180.34
Major appliances	**618.68**	**784.96**	**464.09**	**534.30**	**648.70**
Dishwashers (built-in), garbage disposals, range hoods (renter)	440.00	–	–	665.00	475.00
Dishwashers (built-in), garbage disposals, range hoods (owner)	561.11	1,550.00	423.21	438.79	573.99

	total households	Asian	black	Hispanic	non-Hispanic white and other
Refrigerators, freezers (renter)	$474.32	$899.67	$442.24	$451.02	$478.79
Refrigerators, freezers (owner)	942.56	1,219.68	801.98	1,008.85	944.90
Washing machines (renter)	386.59	866.67	257.29	450.91	394.74
Washing machines (owner)	706.75	1,121.20	598.40	622.35	728.30
Clothes dryers (renter)	323.21	693.06	217.68	357.86	340.00
Clothes dryers (owner)	680.81	1,242.86	639.83	612.11	695.43
Cooking stoves, ovens (renter)	406.25	687.21	385.42	512.50	356.82
Cooking stoves, ovens (owner)	1,116.54	1,938.51	972.56	765.95	1,170.00
Microwave ovens (renter)	96.74	118.01	87.08	123.53	91.20
Microwave ovens (owner)	196.25	204.43	175.33	155.41	204.57
Window air conditioners (renter)	218.33	406.25	167.31	196.32	245.83
Window air conditioners (owner)	319.83	393.75	515.48	426.19	291.94
Electric floor-cleaning equipment	169.20	197.25	86.50	222.51	172.38
Sewing machines	454.46	321.32	768.75	120.45	461.72
Small appliances and misc. housewares	**86.99**	**102.32**	**75.95**	**85.97**	**88.28**
Housewares	73.66	89.79	67.68	81.80	73.10
Plastic dinnerware	27.85	48.25	25.00	28.75	28.25
China and other dinnerware	81.93	92.20	60.59	69.38	86.38
Flatware	64.18	66.42	106.31	74.73	56.65
Glassware	33.29	27.67	32.12	25.49	34.62
Silver serving pieces	54.17	73.33	75.00	50.00	57.14
Other serving pieces	46.54	178.13	75.54	34.58	45.22
Nonelectric cookware	77.17	74.23	57.65	98.07	75.69
Small appliances	82.47	88.09	68.85	67.93	85.95
Small electric kitchen appliances	70.55	89.64	54.05	64.56	72.96
Portable heating and cooling equipment	121.85	77.86	98.57	67.88	133.72
Miscellaneous household equipment	**313.29**	**312.75**	**238.91**	**269.18**	**324.22**
Window coverings	304.65	132.58	151.11	119.29	342.66
Infants' equipment	149.18	147.41	143.83	211.82	141.53
Outdoor equipment	234.32	145.18	141.79	198.25	245.74
Lamps and lighting fixtures	95.43	209.50	68.32	80.39	99.93
Clocks and other household decorative items	142.22	141.27	127.87	150.97	142.60
Telephones and accessories	118.38	139.38	94.15	139.51	119.15
Lawn and garden equipment	489.38	243.21	374.81	733.08	479.17
Power tools	218.29	178.63	211.78	136.47	225.00
Office furniture for home use	301.54	78.26	133.00	151.16	326.35
Hand tools	91.52	92.04	80.36	71.53	93.94
Indoor plants and fresh flowers	88.93	65.70	77.25	85.54	89.93
Closet and storage items	67.91	32.91	58.78	86.17	67.12
Rental of furniture	338.89	83.33	366.67	243.75	341.07
Luggage	109.57	98.27	147.73	126.15	104.65
Computers and computer hardware, nonbusiness use	703.00	688.39	665.71	676.20	708.21
Computer software and accessories, nonbusiness use	129.79	125.32	117.14	113.25	131.70
Personal digital assistants	234.17	108.33	200.00	180.56	240.71
Internet services away from home	88.58	55.67	70.91	103.78	87.94
Telephone answering devices	61.11	53.05	95.00	58.33	62.50
Business equipment for home use	91.53	126.32	164.58	73.17	87.86
Smoke alarms (owner)	61.31	70.12	30.68	76.56	62.76
Smoke alarms (renter)	43.18	–	109.62	50.00	34.09
Other household appliances (owner)	190.69	426.23	63.46	83.33	203.13
Other household appliances (renter)	109.09	605.98	50.96	67.19	123.53

Note: "Asian" and "black" include Hispanics and non-Hispanics who identify themselves as being of the respective race alone. "Hispanic" includes people of any race who identify themselves as Hispanic. "Other" includes people who identify themselves as non-Hispanic and as Alaska Native, American Indian, Asian (who are also included in the Asian column), or Native Hawaiian or other Pacific Islander as well as non-Hispanics reporting more than one race. "–" means sample is too small to make a reliable estimate.
Source: Calculations by New Strategist based on the Bureau of Labor Statistics' 2008 Consumer Expenditure Survey

Table 7.19 Percent Buying Housekeeping Supplies, Furnishings, and Equipment by Race and Hispanic Origin, Average Week, 2008

(percent of households buying housekeeping supplies, furnishings, and equipment during the average week, by race and Hispanic origin of householder, 2008)

	total households	Asian	black	Hispanic	non-Hispanic white and other
HOUSEKEEPING SUPPLIES, PERCENT BUYING	53.9%	42.9%	47.7%	54.6%	54.7%
Laundry and cleaning supplies	28.3	19.9	29.3	32.1	27.6
Soaps and detergents	20.1	14.3	22.9	24.5	19.1
Other laundry cleaning products	18.0	11.7	17.2	21.1	17.7
Other household products	40.4	29.4	36.7	41.1	40.8
Cleansing and toilet tissue, paper towels, and napkins	24.8	14.6	24.8	27.7	24.5
Miscellaneous household products	25.7	19.2	20.8	24.2	26.6
Lawn and garden supplies	6.6	4.6	3.4	5.2	7.2
Postage and stationery	22.8	17.6	13.4	18.4	24.9
Stationery, stationery supplies, giftwrap	17.4	10.4	9.6	13.2	19.3
Postage	8.5	8.6	5.9	6.4	9.2
Delivery services	0.5	0.3	0.1	0.8	0.5
HOUSEHOLD FURNISHINGS AND EQUIPMENT, PERCENT BUYING	30.5	28.9	22.3	28.4	32.0
Household textiles	6.2	5.3	6.2	7.8	6.1
Bathroom linens	3.0	3.1	4.0	4.4	2.6
Bedroom linens	2.6	1.7	2.3	2.4	2.6
Kitchen and dining room linens	1.3	1.5	0.9	1.8	1.4
Slipcovers and decorative pillows	0.3	0.2	0.1	0.2	0.3
Outdoor furniture	0.4	0.3	0.1	0.2	0.5
Floor coverings, nonpermanent	1.2	1.0	1.2	0.9	1.3
Major appliances	0.7	0.8	0.4	0.4	0.7
Electric floor-cleaning equipment	0.5	0.5	0.2	0.3	0.5
Miscellaneous household appliances	0.2	0.2	0.1	0.1	0.2
Housewares	8.1	8.6	6.0	8.0	8.5
China and other dinnerware	1.3	1.2	1.2	1.7	1.2
Glassware	1.9	1.5	1.7	1.5	1.9
Nonelectric cookware	2.2	2.8	2.0	1.7	2.3
Tableware, nonelectric kitchenware	4.3	4.8	2.4	4.1	4.6
Miscellaneous household equipment	24.3	23.1	15.8	20.8	26.2
Infants' equipment	1.2	1.1	0.8	1.7	1.2
Laundry and cleaning equipment	4.9	3.8	3.7	5.1	5.1
Outdoor equipment	1.3	1.6	0.5	0.8	1.5
Lamps and lighting fixtures	1.3	2.2	0.7	0.6	1.5
Clocks and other household decorative items	8.0	5.7	4.5	6.0	8.9
Telephones and accessories	1.2	3.0	1.2	1.3	1.2
Lawn and garden equipment	2.0	2.1	1.3	1.6	2.2
Power tools	1.3	0.9	0.4	1.8	1.4
Hand tools	1.8	0.5	0.7	1.5	2.0
Indoor plants and fresh flowers	4.2	3.6	1.9	3.1	4.8
Closet and storage items	2.4	2.5	1.6	2.0	2.6
Other hardware	0.8	0.7	0.7	0.5	0.9
Miscellaneous household equipment and parts	4.9	5.3	2.5	4.7	5.3
Luggage	0.8	0.9	0.4	0.4	0.9

Note: "Asian" and "black" include Hispanics and non-Hispanics who identify themselves as being of the respective race alone. "Hispanic" includes people of any race who identify themselves as Hispanic. "Other" includes people who identify themselves as non-Hispanic and as Alaska Native, American Indian, Asian (who are also included in the Asian column), or Native Hawaiian or other Pacific Islander as well as non-Hispanics reporting more than one race.
Source: Bureau of Labor Statistics, unpublished data from the 2008 Consumer Expenditure Survey

Table 7.20 Amount Buyers Spent on Housekeeping Supplies, Furnishings, and Equipment by Race and Hispanic Origin, Average Week, 2008

(average amount spent by households buying housekeeping supplies, furnishings, and equipment during the average week, by race and Hispanic origin of householder, 2008)

	total households	Asian	black	Hispanic	non-Hispanic white and other
HOUSEKEEPING SUPPLIES, AMOUNT SPENT	**$23.35**	**$22.16**	**$18.58**	**$19.09**	**$24.60**
Laundry and cleaning supplies	**10.03**	**12.64**	**10.05**	**10.98**	**9.88**
Soaps and detergents	7.75	9.40	7.64	8.44	7.65
Other laundry cleaning products	7.13	10.12	6.98	6.94	7.20
Other household products	**16.70**	**15.70**	**11.85**	**11.80**	**18.06**
Cleansing and toilet tissue, paper towels, and napkins	8.09	11.79	7.41	7.73	8.22
Miscellaneous household products	11.07	11.02	8.74	8.90	11.65
Lawn and garden supplies	28.81	16.99	20.41	10.85	31.22
Postage and stationery	**13.16**	**13.50**	**11.62**	**11.13**	**13.51**
Stationery, stationery supplies, giftwrap	9.00	9.70	6.15	6.91	9.44
Postage	15.85	14.62	16.41	17.34	15.58
Delivery services	16.33	31.25	9.09	5.33	19.61
HOUSEHOLD FURNISHINGS AND EQUIPMENT, AMOUNT SPENT	**52.23**	**57.12**	**49.28**	**35.24**	**54.70**
Household textiles	**29.33**	**30.55**	**31.82**	**20.05**	**30.74**
Bathroom linens	14.24	12.30	13.53	13.32	14.62
Bedroom linens	47.06	52.30	56.47	34.60	47.51
Kitchen and dining room linens	9.09	14.86	10.47	6.29	9.63
Slipcovers and decorative pillows	36.00	62.50	37.50	18.18	35.71
Outdoor furniture	**138.46**	**60.61**	**580.00**	**195.00**	**117.02**
Floor coverings, nonpermanent	**98.37**	**35.92**	**28.81**	**27.27**	**115.63**
Major appliances	**94.03**	**89.47**	**102.38**	**35.90**	**98.65**
Electric floor-cleaning equipment	110.64	118.52	119.05	41.18	115.09
Miscellaneous household appliances	33.33	21.74	15.38	0.00	35.29
Housewares	**17.10**	**20.65**	**9.56**	**11.15**	**18.77**
China and other dinnerware	16.28	33.06	10.74	15.52	17.89
Glassware	18.38	14.09	7.60	4.76	21.35
Nonelectric cookware	12.39	11.59	5.08	7.51	13.60
Tableware, nonelectric kitchenware	13.35	17.86	8.33	10.24	14.22
Miscellaneous household equipment	**41.31**	**50.71**	**43.62**	**30.98**	**42.23**
Infants' equipment	33.61	26.17	22.37	37.06	33.90
Laundry and cleaning equipment	6.33	7.65	4.11	6.61	6.34
Outdoor equipment	47.01	28.93	48.15	46.99	47.06
Lamps and lighting fixtures	42.42	36.11	52.86	29.82	42.11
Clocks and other household decorative items	30.46	26.68	15.81	19.70	32.51
Telephones and accessories	68.85	34.34	147.11	43.94	60.33
Lawn and garden equipment	63.32	176.42	77.86	59.12	62.33
Power tools	39.85	58.06	75.00	27.78	41.43
Hand tools	17.78	8.00	26.03	38.00	15.35
Indoor plants and fresh flowers	21.28	16.11	15.54	10.65	22.53
Closet and storage items	18.49	28.40	20.50	10.00	19.22
Other hardware	38.10	30.99	134.33	15.22	29.35
Miscellaneous household equipment and parts	17.61	16.79	12.30	9.57	18.91
Luggage	32.00	72.34	10.26	21.62	33.72

Note: "Asian" and "black" include Hispanics and non-Hispanics who identify themselves as being of the respective race alone. "Hispanic" includes people of any race who identify themselves as Hispanic. "Other" includes people who identify themselves as non-Hispanic and as Alaska Native, American Indian, Asian (who are also included in the Asian column), or Native Hawaiian or other Pacific Islander as well as non-Hispanics reporting more than one race.
Source: Calculations by New Strategist based on the Bureau of Labor Statistics' 2008 Consumer Expenditure Survey

Table 7.21 Percent Buying Household Services, Furnishings, and Equipment by Region, <u>Average Quarter</u>, 2008

(percent of households buying household services, furnishings, and equipment during the average quarter, by region of residence, 2008)

	total households	Northeast	Midwest	South	West
HOUSEHOLD SERVICES, PERCENT BUYING	**65.9%**	**69.6%**	**66.3%**	**62.5%**	**67.9%**
Personal services	**7.3**	**7.6**	**7.5**	**7.1**	**7.1**
Babysitting and child care in own home	1.6	1.7	2.2	1.0	2.0
Babysitting and child care in someone else's home	1.1	1.1	1.0	1.0	1.3
Care for elderly, invalids, handicapped, etc.	0.4	0.5	0.5	0.4	0.5
Day care centers, nurseries, and preschools	5.0	5.1	5.1	5.2	4.4
Other household services	**64.4**	**68.1**	**64.9**	**60.8**	**66.6**
Housekeeping services	6.2	6.8	5.7	5.1	7.8
Gardening, lawn care service	13.7	13.5	11.1	13.4	17.3
Water-softening service	1.4	1.0	2.1	1.4	1.1
Nonclothing laundry and dry cleaning, sent out	0.6	0.6	0.6	0.5	0.8
Nonclothing laundry and dry cleaning, coin-operated	3.5	6.0	4.3	2.3	2.7
Termite and pest control services	3.6	1.9	1.5	5.5	4.3
Home security system service fee	4.6	3.3	3.0	6.3	4.6
Other home services	2.0	2.8	2.1	1.6	2.1
Termite and pest control products	2.5	1.4	1.0	3.6	3.3
Moving, storage, and freight express	2.1	1.6	1.8	1.9	3.1
Appliance repair, including at service center	2.5	2.5	3.1	2.1	2.5
Reupholstering and furniture repair	0.5	0.5	0.4	0.6	0.7
Repairs and rentals of lawn and garden equipment, hand and power tools, etc.	1.2	1.2	1.4	1.3	0.8
Appliance rental	0.2	0.3	0.2	0.2	0.1
Rental of office equipment for nonbusiness use	0.0	0.0	0.0	0.0	0.0
Repair of computer systems for nonbusiness use	0.8	0.8	0.8	0.7	0.9
Computer information services	53.9	57.6	54.2	50.1	56.7
Installation of computer	0.1	0.1	0.1	0.1	0.1
HOUSEHOLD FURNISHINGS AND EQUIPMENT, PERCENT BUYING	**52.7**	**53.8**	**54.9**	**48.9**	**55.6**
Household textiles	**19.3**	**19.2**	**21.1**	**17.7**	**20.0**
Bathroom linens	6.4	6.5	7.0	6.0	6.6
Bedroom linens	10.2	10.6	10.7	10.1	9.7
Kitchen and dining room linens	1.7	1.7	1.7	1.6	1.9
Curtains and draperies	2.4	2.7	2.5	2.3	2.3
Slipcovers and decorative pillows	1.2	1.0	1.3	1.3	1.3
Sewing materials for household items	3.4	2.7	4.5	2.2	4.8
Other linens	0.5	0.6	0.4	0.4	0.5
Furniture	**10.2**	**9.3**	**10.3**	**9.7**	**11.6**
Mattresses and springs	1.7	1.4	1.7	1.6	2.1
Other bedroom furniture	1.9	1.9	1.9	1.9	2.1
Sofas	2.2	1.9	2.1	2.3	2.2
Living room chairs	1.7	1.6	1.7	1.9	1.5
Living room tables	1.4	1.3	1.3	1.6	1.3
Kitchen and dining room furniture	1.2	1.0	1.1	1.1	1.5
Infants' furniture	0.8	0.7	0.7	0.6	1.1
Outdoor furniture	1.5	1.5	1.4	1.4	1.5
Wall units, cabinets, and other furniture	2.7	2.5	3.0	2.6	2.9
Floor coverings	**3.0**	**2.8**	**3.4**	**2.7**	**3.0**
Wall-to-wall carpeting	0.3	0.4	0.5	0.2	0.3
Floor coverings, nonpermanent	2.6	2.4	2.9	2.5	2.8
Major appliances	**8.2**	**8.0**	**8.2**	**7.9**	**8.6**
Dishwashers (built-in), garbage disposals, range hoods (renter)	0.1	0.0	0.1	0.0	0.1
Dishwashers (built-in), garbage disposals, range hoods (owner)	0.6	0.7	0.7	0.6	0.6

	total households	Northeast	Midwest	South	West
Refrigerators, freezers (renter)	0.4%	0.3%	0.3%	0.4%	0.5%
Refrigerators, freezers (owner)	1.3	1.4	1.6	1.2	1.2
Washing machines (renter)	0.4	0.3	0.3	0.5	0.6
Washing machines (owner)	1.0	0.8	1.0	1.1	1.1
Clothes dryers (renter)	0.3	0.2	0.1	0.4	0.4
Clothes dryers (owner)	0.9	0.7	0.9	0.9	0.9
Cooking stoves, ovens (renter)	0.1	0.2	0.1	0.1	0.1
Cooking stoves, ovens (owner)	0.7	0.7	0.7	0.7	0.5
Microwave ovens (renter)	0.7	0.8	0.6	0.7	0.8
Microwave ovens (owner)	1.0	0.9	0.9	1.2	0.9
Window air conditioners (renter)	0.2	0.3	0.1	0.1	0.1
Window air conditioners (owner)	0.3	0.5	0.2	0.3	0.2
Electric floor-cleaning equipment	2.4	2.3	2.5	2.0	2.8
Sewing machines	0.3	0.3	0.3	0.2	0.4
Small appliances and misc. housewares	**16.1**	**15.1**	**16.3**	**15.3**	**17.8**
Housewares	9.9	8.9	10.6	9.1	11.3
Plastic dinnerware	2.5	2.6	2.5	2.8	2.2
China and other dinnerware	2.5	2.1	2.8	2.2	3.0
Flatware	1.4	1.1	1.3	1.4	1.8
Glassware	1.9	1.7	2.2	1.8	2.2
Silver serving pieces	0.1	0.0	0.1	0.1	0.1
Other serving pieces	0.7	0.5	0.8	0.6	0.7
Nonelectric cookware	3.5	2.9	3.7	2.9	4.4
Small appliances	8.1	7.5	7.9	8.0	9.1
Small electric kitchen appliances	6.9	6.3	6.6	6.7	7.8
Portable heating and cooling equipment	1.5	1.4	1.6	1.5	1.5
Miscellaneous household equipment	**35.8**	**37.5**	**38.9**	**31.9**	**37.7**
Window coverings	1.7	1.9	1.7	1.7	1.5
Infants' equipment	0.6	0.7	0.7	0.5	0.6
Outdoor equipment	1.2	1.0	1.4	1.0	1.5
Lamps and lighting fixtures	3.5	3.7	3.7	3.0	3.7
Clocks and other household decorative items	6.2	5.9	7.7	5.0	6.7
Telephones and accessories	5.1	4.8	5.5	4.7	5.4
Lawn and garden equipment	2.3	1.8	2.8	2.5	2.0
Power tools	2.1	1.7	2.3	1.9	2.4
Office furniture for home use	0.7	0.4	0.7	0.6	0.9
Hand tools	1.7	1.4	2.0	1.2	2.5
Indoor plants and fresh flowers	15.9	19.4	17.6	13.1	15.9
Closet and storage items	1.3	1.5	1.5	1.1	1.4
Rental of furniture	0.2	0.3	0.1	0.3	0.1
Luggage	1.4	1.2	1.5	1.2	1.9
Computers and computer hardware, nonbusiness use	5.4	5.1	5.9	4.6	6.5
Computer software and accessories, nonbusiness use	4.5	4.6	4.9	3.8	5.4
Personal digital assistants	0.3	0.2	0.3	0.3	0.4
Internet services away from home	0.8	0.9	0.7	0.8	0.9
Telephone answering devices	0.2	0.2	0.1	0.2	0.2
Business equipment for home use	0.6	0.8	0.7	0.5	0.5
Smoke alarms (owner)	0.4	0.5	0.6	0.4	0.3
Smoke alarms (renter)	0.1	0.1	0.2	0.1	0.2
Other household appliances (owner)	1.0	1.1	1.1	0.8	1.2
Other household appliances (renter)	0.3	0.3	0.4	0.3	0.4

Source: Bureau of Labor Statistics, unpublished data from the 2008 Consumer Expenditure Survey

Table 7.22 Amount Buyers Spent on Household Services, Furnishings, and Equipment by Region, <u>Average Quarter</u>, 2008

(average amount spent by households buying household services, furnishings, and equipment during the average quarter, by region of residence, 2008)

	total households	Northeast	Midwest	South	West
HOUSEHOLD SERVICES, AMOUNT SPENT	**$377.80**	**$422.94**	**$325.02**	**$363.14**	**$414.60**
Personal services	**1,312.33**	**1,676.03**	**1,183.30**	**1,177.94**	**1,354.62**
Babysitting and child care in own home	717.33	962.86	376.58	618.81	1,012.13
Babysitting and child care in someone else's home	838.68	921.10	938.95	753.50	795.28
Care for elderly, invalids, handicapped, etc.	3,063.64	5,032.98	2,278.19	3,192.31	2,127.22
Day care centers, nurseries, and preschools	1,224.95	1,479.85	1,170.17	1,108.06	1,272.88
Other household services	**238.01**	**246.12**	**194.97**	**235.01**	**278.83**
Housekeeping services	483.17	529.24	403.27	483.47	510.44
Gardening, lawn care service	210.43	262.97	168.37	211.55	202.82
Water-softening service	85.49	166.83	81.60	62.50	78.13
Nonclothing laundry and dry cleaning, sent out	46.61	40.45	36.86	40.43	63.41
Nonclothing laundry and dry cleaning, coin-operated	23.87	28.28	16.86	26.75	23.32
Termite and pest control services	132.02	206.88	164.31	125.87	105.77
Home security system service fee	118.21	148.63	124.50	104.21	126.96
Other home services	236.76	280.62	217.77	217.61	229.83
Termite and pest control products	27.46	32.32	29.21	27.42	25.37
Moving, storage, and freight express	571.50	430.32	425.14	560.90	734.92
Appliance repair, including at service center	178.73	188.10	155.66	171.17	211.69
Reupholstering and furniture repair	288.21	375.51	337.82	285.00	215.15
Repairs and rentals of lawn and garden equipment, hand and power tools, etc.	148.94	162.39	132.22	164.68	124.68
Appliance rental	115.00	151.56	102.27	100.00	86.36
Rental of office equipment for nonbusiness use	412.50	200.00	612.50	137.50	150.00
Repair of computer systems for nonbusiness use	219.41	230.77	225.31	146.59	290.34
Computer information services	101.76	100.86	97.06	103.16	105.13
Installation of computer	130.56	82.14	196.88	84.38	172.92
HOUSEHOLD FURNISHINGS AND EQUIPMENT, AMOUNT SPENT	**579.71**	**595.93**	**556.38**	**575.89**	**595.76**
Household textiles	**118.75**	**113.44**	**107.00**	**122.39**	**130.58**
Bathroom linens	48.76	53.95	41.93	45.80	56.37
Bedroom linens	101.56	102.95	95.55	105.04	101.34
Kitchen and dining room linens	29.22	26.32	27.83	30.18	31.78
Curtains and draperies	215.25	150.93	170.77	223.13	315.79
Slipcovers and decorative pillows	59.07	60.15	47.66	57.56	73.64
Sewing materials for household items	77.05	65.99	84.00	84.05	70.40
Other linens	68.33	77.63	54.05	55.36	88.54
Furniture	**930.73**	**1,141.14**	**872.26**	**985.28**	**773.29**
Mattresses and springs	775.44	884.24	715.29	848.27	676.55
Other bedroom furniture	894.72	1,226.83	691.13	995.26	678.17
Sofas	1,131.63	1,509.13	1,105.41	1,049.04	1,017.79
Living room chairs	534.02	595.91	615.03	506.15	433.55
Living room tables	304.11	275.56	477.17	238.06	283.40
Kitchen and dining room furniture	744.02	730.77	674.34	790.95	759.73
Infants' furniture	271.75	433.45	219.64	265.73	227.88
Outdoor furniture	318.49	412.82	313.03	287.85	289.63
Wall units, cabinets, and other furniture	402.83	454.98	387.17	421.60	356.46
Floor coverings	**376.52**	**435.71**	**429.65**	**321.68**	**352.31**
Wall-to-wall carpeting	2,008.33	2,000.00	2,180.00	1,916.30	1,879.17
Floor coverings, nonpermanent	166.57	160.31	160.15	172.40	170.64
Major appliances	**618.68**	**645.53**	**614.11**	**566.37**	**681.77**
Dishwashers (built-in), garbage disposals, range hoods (renter)	440.00	250.00	450.00	258.33	829.17
Dishwashers (built-in), garbage disposals, range hoods (owner)	561.11	633.08	552.94	467.86	650.86

	total households	Northeast	Midwest	South	West
Refrigerators, freezers (renter)	$474.32	$360.34	$381.67	$411.90	$670.56
Refrigerators, freezers (owner)	942.56	961.48	900.96	821.49	1,183.26
Washing machines (renter)	386.59	435.71	375.00	316.15	461.61
Washing machines (owner)	706.75	818.90	642.45	634.49	815.09
Clothes dryers (renter)	323.21	339.06	271.15	286.11	373.21
Clothes dryers (owner)	680.81	774.62	627.30	610.44	790.96
Cooking stoves, ovens (renter)	406.25	298.81	286.36	459.09	520.00
Cooking stoves, ovens (owner)	1,116.54	1,374.25	1,094.01	923.90	1,239.81
Microwave ovens (renter)	96.74	92.11	96.61	88.26	111.08
Microwave ovens (owner)	196.25	204.62	193.82	177.35	236.47
Window air conditioners (renter)	218.33	222.50	158.33	256.25	227.08
Window air conditioners (owner)	319.83	289.50	397.06	320.97	323.75
Electric floor-cleaning equipment	169.20	165.28	194.28	171.89	147.44
Sewing machines	454.46	384.26	572.32	459.52	386.90
Small appliances and misc. housewares	**86.99**	**93.30**	**84.43**	**79.85**	**94.98**
Housewares	73.66	77.56	67.24	71.17	80.60
Plastic dinnerware	27.85	38.22	28.34	23.92	25.35
China and other dinnerware	81.93	97.22	63.91	93.75	76.99
Flatware	64.18	63.17	38.07	75.89	70.00
Glassware	33.29	42.65	29.05	31.64	33.49
Silver serving pieces	54.17	37.50	28.57	91.67	31.25
Other serving pieces	46.54	57.00	30.84	54.84	47.43
Nonelectric cookware	77.17	72.62	86.93	61.39	88.12
Small appliances	82.47	96.49	83.13	72.04	86.93
Small electric kitchen appliances	70.55	84.68	69.33	60.22	76.57
Portable heating and cooling equipment	121.85	132.50	127.34	110.20	124.83
Miscellaneous household equipment	**313.29**	**307.62**	**295.64**	**309.23**	**342.27**
Window coverings	304.65	224.87	181.25	323.27	509.06
Infants' equipment	149.18	180.07	100.00	143.27	194.30
Outdoor equipment	234.32	418.37	201.85	164.85	240.52
Lamps and lighting fixtures	95.43	88.55	98.38	89.85	105.91
Clocks and other household decorative items	142.22	173.47	114.72	144.76	148.70
Telephones and accessories	118.38	109.21	111.54	122.67	126.26
Lawn and garden equipment	489.38	554.97	622.13	469.76	282.95
Power tools	218.29	208.53	224.89	236.38	193.62
Office furniture for home use	301.54	246.79	317.50	287.90	329.41
Hand tools	91.52	98.54	93.63	83.40	92.96
Indoor plants and fresh flowers	88.93	103.15	82.49	83.73	88.85
Closet and storage items	67.91	84.42	60.76	71.93	56.60
Rental of furniture	338.89	389.29	140.00	311.54	370.83
Luggage	109.57	107.11	91.21	110.71	123.28
Computers and computer hardware, nonbusiness use	703.00	707.63	616.69	721.06	761.90
Computer software and accessories, nonbusiness use	129.79	126.63	114.04	135.12	141.14
Personal digital assistants	234.17	198.91	279.31	230.56	226.22
Internet services away from home	88.58	98.33	75.38	101.30	75.53
Telephone answering devices	61.11	64.58	43.18	60.53	84.38
Business equipment for home use	91.53	89.33	114.13	76.89	89.42
Smoke alarms (owner)	61.31	102.88	36.86	62.50	46.15
Smoke alarms (renter)	43.18	27.78	66.67	55.00	29.41
Other household appliances (owner)	190.69	221.14	160.36	117.47	278.39
Other household appliances (renter)	109.09	55.00	73.65	97.12	191.46

Source: Calculations by New Strategist based on the Bureau of Labor Statistics' 2008 Consumer Expenditure Survey

Table 7.23 Percent Buying Housekeeping Supplies, Furnishings, and Equipment by Region, <u>Average Week</u>, 2008

(percent of households buying housekeeping supplies, furnishings, and equipment during the average week, by region of residence, 2008)

	total households	Northeast	Midwest	South	West
HOUSEKEEPING SUPPLIES, PERCENT BUYING	**53.9%**	**53.1%**	**53.2%**	**55.3%**	**52.9%**
Laundry and cleaning supplies	**28.3**	**27.3**	**27.0**	**30.6**	**26.9**
Soaps and detergents	20.1	19.3	18.9	22.6	18.0
Other laundry cleaning products	18.0	17.1	17.1	19.5	17.1
Other household products	**40.4**	**39.5**	**40.1**	**42.1**	**38.5**
Cleansing and toilet tissue, paper towels, and napkins	24.8	26.2	24.2	25.9	22.6
Miscellaneous household products	25.7	24.5	26.3	26.2	25.1
Lawn and garden supplies	6.6	6.2	5.6	7.1	6.9
Postage and stationery	**22.8**	**22.3**	**24.0**	**21.3**	**24.5**
Stationery, stationery supplies, giftwrap	17.4	16.0	19.2	16.5	18.5
Postage	8.5	9.7	8.2	7.6	9.3
Delivery services	0.5	0.6	0.5	0.3	0.7
HOUSEHOLD FURNISHINGS AND EQUIPMENT, PERCENT BUYING	**30.5**	**29.2**	**29.2**	**30.7**	**32.5**
Household textiles	**6.2**	**6.0**	**5.1**	**6.6**	**7.0**
Bathroom linens	3.0	2.6	2.3	3.4	3.2
Bedroom linens	2.6	2.7	2.2	2.5	2.9
Kitchen and dining room linens	1.3	1.3	1.0	1.3	1.8
Slipcovers and decorative pillows	0.3	0.1	0.3	0.3	0.2
Outdoor furniture	**0.4**	**0.3**	**0.3**	**0.5**	**0.4**
Floor coverings, nonpermanent	**1.2**	**1.2**	**1.0**	**1.4**	**1.2**
Major appliances	**0.7**	**0.5**	**0.6**	**0.7**	**0.8**
Electric floor-cleaning equipment	0.5	0.4	0.4	0.5	0.6
Miscellaneous household appliances	0.2	0.1	0.2	0.1	0.2
Housewares	**8.1**	**6.6**	**7.1**	**8.5**	**9.9**
China and other dinnerware	1.3	0.9	0.9	1.6	1.5
Glassware	1.9	1.6	1.7	2.0	1.9
Nonelectric cookware	2.2	2.0	1.7	2.4	2.5
Tableware, nonelectric kitchenware	4.3	3.2	3.9	4.1	5.9
Miscellaneous household equipment	**24.3**	**23.4**	**23.9**	**24.3**	**25.6**
Infants' equipment	1.2	1.2	1.3	1.2	1.1
Laundry and cleaning equipment	4.9	4.4	4.6	4.9	5.6
Outdoor equipment	1.3	1.4	1.6	1.2	1.3
Lamps and lighting fixtures	1.3	0.8	1.3	1.4	1.6
Clocks and other household decorative items	8.0	7.8	7.2	8.4	8.4
Telephones and accessories	1.2	1.0	1.3	1.4	1.0
Lawn and garden equipment	2.0	1.7	2.0	2.0	2.2
Power tools	1.3	1.2	1.4	1.2	1.6
Hand tools	1.8	1.3	1.7	1.9	2.2
Indoor plants and fresh flowers	4.2	4.7	3.7	4.1	4.6
Closet and storage items	2.4	1.8	2.4	2.5	2.7
Other hardware	0.8	0.7	0.8	0.9	0.9
Miscellaneous household equipment and parts	4.9	4.7	5.4	4.8	4.9
Luggage	0.8	0.8	0.6	0.7	0.9

Source: Bureau of Labor Statistics, unpublished data from the 2008 Consumer Expenditure Survey

Table 7.24 Amount Buyers Spent on Housekeeping Supplies, Furnishings, and Equipment by Region, <u>Average Week</u>, 2008

(average amount spent by households buying housekeeping supplies, furnishings, and equipment during the average week, by region of residence, 2008)

	total households	Northeast	Midwest	South	West
HOUSEKEEPING SUPPLIES, AMOUNT SPENT	**$23.35**	**$24.07**	**$24.53**	**$22.45**	**$23.08**
Laundry and cleaning supplies	**10.03**	**10.00**	**9.65**	**9.84**	**10.83**
Soaps and detergents	7.75	7.86	7.41	7.52	8.46
Other laundry cleaning products	7.13	7.08	7.01	6.68	8.15
Other household products	**16.70**	**17.64**	**17.97**	**16.17**	**15.46**
Cleansing and toilet tissue, paper towels, and napkins	8.09	8.12	7.52	7.83	9.07
Miscellaneous household products	11.07	12.47	11.69	10.29	10.71
Lawn and garden supplies	28.81	29.08	41.28	29.11	17.49
Postage and stationery	**13.16**	**13.84**	**13.49**	**12.28**	**13.68**
Stationery, stationery supplies, giftwrap	9.00	10.40	9.89	7.71	9.05
Postage	15.85	13.96	15.10	16.62	17.08
Delivery services	16.33	11.48	20.00	19.35	14.93
HOUSEHOLD FURNISHINGS AND EQUIPMENT, AMOUNT SPENT	**52.23**	**44.64**	**48.16**	**56.61**	**54.88**
Household textiles	**29.33**	**24.25**	**27.10**	**31.06**	**32.05**
Bathroom linens	14.24	12.93	13.85	13.53	17.09
Bedroom linens	47.06	34.94	41.47	53.78	52.08
Kitchen and dining room linens	9.09	12.60	7.14	9.30	7.87
Slipcovers and decorative pillows	36.00	10.00	31.25	43.33	33.33
Outdoor furniture	**138.46**	**159.26**	**70.97**	**174.47**	**111.36**
Floor coverings, nonpermanent	**98.37**	**65.25**	**25.00**	**169.72**	**46.72**
Major appliances	**94.03**	**72.55**	**75.41**	**76.81**	**144.44**
Electric floor-cleaning equipment	110.64	78.38	95.00	70.21	178.13
Miscellaneous household appliances	33.33	25.00	36.84	42.86	10.53
Housewares	**17.10**	**18.45**	**19.66**	**13.81**	**18.99**
China and other dinnerware	16.28	27.91	17.44	16.56	11.11
Glassware	18.38	22.64	31.18	13.37	11.34
Nonelectric cookware	12.39	12.69	13.79	10.17	14.40
Tableware, nonelectric kitchenware	13.35	10.97	12.37	9.83	19.19
Miscellaneous household equipment	**41.31**	**36.41**	**41.65**	**41.42**	**44.52**
Infants' equipment	33.61	33.33	23.08	25.22	60.18
Laundry and cleaning equipment	6.33	6.15	6.11	6.28	6.46
Outdoor equipment	47.01	47.06	37.42	72.50	19.84
Lamps and lighting fixtures	42.42	46.99	50.75	35.77	42.33
Clocks and other household decorative items	30.46	23.43	33.56	25.48	41.22
Telephones and accessories	68.85	60.20	61.94	75.00	70.30
Lawn and garden equipment	63.32	42.26	73.33	72.06	54.34
Power tools	39.85	36.29	39.13	40.00	44.52
Hand tools	17.78	13.95	15.15	15.87	24.11
Indoor plants and fresh flowers	21.28	22.75	21.29	20.29	21.34
Closet and storage items	18.49	14.29	22.46	19.60	14.65
Other hardware	38.10	25.68	32.89	51.65	29.67
Miscellaneous household equipment and parts	17.61	25.48	17.16	14.26	17.11
Luggage	32.00	48.10	21.82	27.03	34.41

Source: Calculations by New Strategist based on the Bureau of Labor Statistics' 2008 Consumer Expenditure Survey

Table 7.25 Percent Buying Household Services, Furnishings, and Equipment by Education, <u>Average Quarter</u>, 2008

(percent of households buying household services, furnishings, and equipment during the average quarter, by highest level of education of householder, 2008)

	total households	less than high school graduate	high school graduate	some college	associate's degree	college graduate total	college graduate bachelor's degree	college graduate master's, professional, doctorate
HOUSEHOLD SERVICES, PERCENT BUYING	**65.9%**	**39.3%**	**58.1%**	**67.2%**	**75.0%**	**82.3%**	**80.6%**	**85.4%**
Personal services	**7.3**	**4.1**	**5.1**	**7.3**	**8.3**	**10.5**	**10.5**	**10.6**
Babysitting and child care in own home	1.6	0.7	0.7	1.0	1.9	3.3	3.0	3.9
Babysitting and child care in someone else's home	1.1	1.1	0.9	1.1	1.3	1.1	1.2	0.9
Care for elderly, invalids, handicapped, etc.	0.4	0.3	0.5	0.4	0.1	0.7	0.6	0.7
Day care centers, nurseries, and preschools	5.0	2.1	3.3	5.3	6.1	7.3	7.6	6.9
Other household services	**64.4**	**36.8**	**56.4**	**65.8**	**73.6**	**81.3**	**79.7**	**84.3**
Housekeeping services	6.2	1.9	3.4	5.3	4.5	11.8	9.6	15.8
Gardening, lawn care service	13.7	5.1	10.1	11.9	13.7	22.8	19.9	27.9
Water-softening service	1.4	1.4	1.4	1.2	1.5	1.7	1.7	1.7
Nonclothing laundry and dry cleaning, sent out	0.6	0.3	0.4	0.6	0.5	1.0	0.9	1.3
Nonclothing laundry and dry cleaning, coin-operated	3.5	4.7	3.3	3.8	3.3	3.0	3.3	2.6
Termite and pest control services	3.6	1.4	2.8	3.2	4.7	5.5	5.2	6.0
Home security system service fee	4.6	1.6	3.0	3.8	5.6	7.8	7.0	9.1
Other home services	2.0	1.1	1.4	1.9	2.5	3.1	3.0	3.3
Termite and pest control products	2.5	1.2	1.9	2.4	3.5	3.6	3.4	4.1
Moving, storage, and freight express	2.1	0.9	1.5	2.4	2.9	2.7	2.2	3.6
Appliance repair, including at service center	2.5	1.6	2.3	2.1	2.2	3.5	3.2	3.9
Reupholstering and furniture repair	0.5	0.2	0.5	0.3	0.4	1.0	0.8	1.3
Repairs and rentals of lawn and garden equipment, hand and power tools, etc.	1.2	0.6	1.0	1.2	1.0	1.7	1.7	1.6
Appliance rental	0.2	0.5	0.2	0.1	0.3	0.1	0.2	0.1
Rental of office equipment for nonbusiness use	0.0	0.0	0.0	0.0	0.0	–	–	–
Repair of computer systems for nonbusiness use	0.8	0.2	0.6	1.1	0.8	1.0	1.0	1.0
Computer information services	53.9	24.1	44.8	56.5	65.0	71.4	69.8	74.3
Installation of computer	0.1	–	0.1	0.1	0.1	0.1	0.1	0.2
HOUSEHOLD FURNISHINGS AND EQUIPMENT, PERCENT BUYING	**52.7**	**38.5**	**47.3**	**54.4**	**56.8**	**61.9**	**60.4**	**64.7**
Household textiles	**19.3**	**14.9**	**16.5**	**20.8**	**21.7**	**22.0**	**21.8**	**22.4**
Bathroom linens	6.4	5.5	5.6	7.4	6.6	6.9	6.9	6.9
Bedroom linens	10.2	7.3	8.9	11.3	11.0	11.8	11.6	12.2
Kitchen and dining room linens	1.7	1.1	1.4	1.6	2.0	2.3	2.4	2.1
Curtains and draperies	2.4	1.9	2.0	2.8	3.2	2.6	2.3	3.1
Slipcovers and decorative pillows	1.2	0.8	0.8	1.5	1.1	1.7	1.7	1.7
Sewing materials for household items	3.4	2.4	2.5	3.3	4.5	4.5	4.4	4.7
Other linens	0.5	0.3	0.3	0.5	1.0	0.5	0.5	0.4
Furniture	**10.2**	**6.5**	**8.4**	**10.9**	**10.6**	**12.9**	**12.3**	**13.9**
Mattresses and springs	1.7	1.1	1.6	1.5	1.8	2.2	2.4	1.9
Other bedroom furniture	1.9	1.4	1.8	2.3	1.9	2.1	2.1	2.2
Sofas	2.2	1.7	2.0	2.3	2.3	2.4	2.5	2.3
Living room chairs	1.7	1.1	1.4	1.9	1.6	2.1	2.2	2.0
Living room tables	1.4	0.8	1.1	1.6	1.6	1.8	1.6	2.1
Kitchen and dining room furniture	1.2	0.6	1.0	1.4	1.2	1.4	1.2	1.9
Infants' furniture	0.8	0.9	0.7	0.9	0.7	0.7	0.7	0.8
Outdoor furniture	1.5	0.5	1.2	1.5	1.7	2.1	1.9	2.5
Wall units, cabinets, and other furniture	2.7	1.4	1.9	2.8	3.0	4.0	3.8	4.5
Floor coverings	**3.0**	**1.9**	**2.5**	**3.1**	**3.3**	**3.6**	**3.5**	**3.8**
Wall-to-wall carpeting	0.3	0.2	0.3	0.3	0.3	0.4	0.4	0.6
Floor coverings, nonpermanent	2.6	1.7	2.2	2.8	3.1	3.2	3.2	3.4
Major appliances	**8.2**	**6.5**	**7.7**	**8.0**	**10.0**	**8.9**	**8.7**	**9.2**
Dishwashers (built-in), garbage disposals, range hoods (renter)	0.1	–	0.1	0.0	0.1	0.1	0.1	0.0
Dishwashers (built-in), garbage disposals, range hoods (owner)	0.6	0.2	0.6	0.5	0.6	1.0	0.9	1.1

	total households	less than high school graduate	high school graduate	some college	associate's degree	college graduate total	bachelor's degree	master's, professional, doctorate
Refrigerators, freezers (renter)	0.4%	0.4%	0.4%	0.6%	0.4%	0.2%	0.2%	0.1%
Refrigerators, freezers (owner)	1.3	0.9	1.1	1.2	1.4	1.8	1.6	2.0
Washing machines (renter)	0.4	0.5	0.4	0.5	0.4	0.3	0.3	0.3
Washing machines (owner)	1.0	0.6	1.0	1.0	1.2	1.1	1.0	1.4
Clothes dryers (renter)	0.3	0.2	0.3	0.4	0.2	0.3	0.2	0.3
Clothes dryers (owner)	0.9	0.7	0.8	0.7	1.2	1.0	0.9	1.1
Cooking stoves, ovens (renter)	0.1	0.2	0.2	0.1	0.1	0.1	0.0	0.1
Cooking stoves, ovens (owner)	0.7	0.4	0.6	0.5	0.9	0.9	0.8	0.9
Microwave ovens (renter)	0.7	0.9	0.8	0.8	0.7	0.4	0.5	0.3
Microwave ovens (owner)	1.0	0.6	1.0	0.8	1.0	1.4	1.3	1.4
Window air conditioners (renter)	0.2	0.2	0.2	0.2	0.1	0.1	0.0	0.1
Window air conditioners (owner)	0.3	0.3	0.3	0.3	0.4	0.3	0.3	0.3
Electric floor-cleaning equipment	2.4	1.6	2.0	2.4	3.3	2.7	2.7	2.7
Sewing machines	0.3	0.1	0.2	0.3	0.4	0.3	0.3	0.4
Small appliances and misc. housewares	**16.1**	**12.3**	**14.4**	**17.5**	**17.1**	**18.0**	**17.5**	**18.9**
Housewares	9.9	7.9	8.3	11.0	10.3	11.3	11.0	12.0
Plastic dinnerware	2.5	2.4	2.1	3.1	2.9	2.5	2.4	2.6
China and other dinnerware	2.5	1.8	1.9	2.9	2.5	3.1	2.8	3.5
Flatware	1.4	1.0	1.2	1.8	1.3	1.5	1.4	1.7
Glassware	1.9	1.6	1.6	2.1	1.8	2.3	2.1	2.6
Silver serving pieces	0.1	0.1	0.0	0.1	–	0.1	0.1	0.1
Other serving pieces	0.7	0.3	0.5	0.8	0.7	0.8	0.8	0.8
Nonelectric cookware	3.5	2.7	2.9	3.7	3.9	4.0	4.1	3.7
Small appliances	8.1	5.9	7.7	8.5	8.8	9.0	8.8	9.4
Small electric kitchen appliances	6.9	4.9	6.5	7.2	7.4	7.7	7.2	8.5
Portable heating and cooling equipment	1.5	1.3	1.6	1.5	1.6	1.5	1.7	1.3
Miscellaneous household equipment	**35.8**	**20.6**	**29.8**	**37.3**	**40.3**	**46.4**	**45.0**	**48.8**
Window coverings	1.7	0.9	1.6	1.9	2.2	2.0	1.9	2.1
Infants' equipment	0.6	0.4	0.5	0.9	0.6	0.6	0.6	0.7
Outdoor equipment	1.2	0.4	1.1	1.4	1.8	1.3	1.2	1.5
Lamps and lighting fixtures	3.5	2.0	2.6	3.5	3.8	4.8	4.5	5.3
Clocks and other household decorative items	6.2	3.0	4.7	6.4	7.0	8.7	8.3	9.4
Telephones and accessories	5.1	3.2	4.3	5.7	5.4	6.1	5.6	7.0
Lawn and garden equipment	2.3	1.6	2.2	2.3	2.9	2.7	2.5	3.1
Power tools	2.1	0.8	1.8	2.1	2.7	2.7	2.6	2.8
Office furniture for home use	0.7	0.1	0.3	0.8	1.0	1.0	1.0	1.1
Hand tools	1.7	0.9	1.2	1.9	2.5	2.1	2.1	2.3
Indoor plants and fresh flowers	15.9	8.2	12.9	15.1	18.5	22.2	20.8	24.7
Closet and storage items	1.3	0.5	0.8	1.3	1.6	2.1	2.1	2.2
Rental of furniture	0.2	0.3	0.2	0.2	0.1	0.1	0.1	0.1
Luggage	1.4	0.4	0.8	1.5	1.5	2.5	2.3	2.8
Computers and computer hardware, nonbusiness use	5.4	1.5	4.1	6.0	6.7	7.7	7.2	8.5
Computer software and accessories, nonbusiness use	4.5	1.1	2.5	5.4	5.6	7.1	7.0	7.3
Personal digital assistants	0.3	0.1	0.1	0.3	0.4	0.6	0.5	0.6
Internet services away from home	0.8	0.4	0.6	0.9	0.9	1.1	1.1	1.2
Telephone answering devices	0.2	0.1	0.1	0.2	0.2	0.3	0.2	0.3
Business equipment for home use	0.6	0.3	0.4	0.8	0.8	0.8	0.7	0.9
Smoke alarms (owner)	0.4	0.2	0.5	0.4	0.5	0.4	0.4	0.5
Smoke alarms (renter)	0.1	0.1	0.1	0.1	0.1	0.1	0.1	0.2
Other household appliances (owner)	1.0	0.4	1.0	1.0	1.2	1.4	1.3	1.4
Other household appliances (renter)	0.3	0.4	0.3	0.3	0.5	0.3	0.3	0.3

Note: "–" means sample is too small to make a reliable estimate.
Source: Bureau of Labor Statistics, unpublished data from the 2008 Consumer Expenditure Survey

Table 7.26 Amount Buyers Spent on Household Services, Furnishings, and Equipment by Education, <u>Average Quarter</u>, 2008

(average amount spent by households buying household services, furnishings, and equipment during the average quarter, by highest level of education of householder, 2008)

	total households	less than high school graduate	high school graduate	some college	associate's degree	college graduate total	bachelor's degree	master's, professional, doctorate
HOUSEHOLD SERVICES, AMOUNT SPENT	$377.80	$231.89	$292.24	$312.05	$318.29	$523.92	$451.14	$647.33
Personal services	1,312.33	815.98	1,307.68	1,046.41	990.55	1,633.07	1,372.15	2,097.70
Babysitting and child care in own home	717.33	666.78	455.07	749.74	344.84	832.06	570.60	1,195.13
Babysitting and child care in someone else's home	838.68	584.73	982.50	708.04	663.49	1,025.47	811.42	1,547.19
Care for elderly, invalids, handicapped, etc.	3,063.64	778.57	4,308.89	1,426.35	417.86	3,676.52	3,271.09	4,320.71
Day care centers, nurseries, and preschools	1,224.95	943.75	1,038.66	1,055.60	1,100.86	1,466.26	1,280.06	1,838.06
Other household services	238.01	156.80	183.16	202.68	212.60	318.89	275.34	392.84
Housekeeping services	483.17	345.70	383.53	370.45	396.86	569.04	508.75	634.76
Gardening, lawn care service	210.43	187.35	182.71	175.49	206.90	238.21	228.63	250.38
Water-softening service	85.49	79.53	97.12	78.36	97.09	79.49	81.10	76.67
Nonclothing laundry and dry cleaning, sent out	46.61	41.91	37.86	30.36	31.77	59.34	61.76	55.56
Nonclothing laundry and dry cleaning, coin-operated	23.87	24.78	28.65	22.24	24.70	19.90	20.59	18.22
Termite and pest control services	132.02	139.61	124.91	126.24	139.35	134.98	112.21	170.76
Home security system service fee	118.21	113.29	113.08	113.54	123.61	121.01	117.87	125.27
Other home services	236.76	254.69	216.85	206.81	230.39	256.49	243.83	276.44
Termite and pest control products	27.46	33.12	25.81	26.65	29.10	27.29	25.07	30.48
Moving, storage, and freight express	571.50	542.03	508.67	535.50	355.17	711.94	579.17	855.97
Appliance repair, including at service center	178.73	130.38	170.11	207.74	152.13	187.54	192.73	179.94
Reupholstering and furniture repair	288.21	198.61	221.88	112.50	189.74	378.32	391.46	364.58
Repairs and rentals of lawn and garden equipment, hand and power tools, etc.	148.94	103.75	178.61	129.23	133.50	156.78	157.74	155.56
Appliance rental	115.00	160.94	118.75	94.64	79.81	55.36	32.81	120.00
Rental of office equipment for nonbusiness use	412.50	237.50	137.50	681.25	116.67	–	–	–
Repair of computer systems for nonbusiness use	219.41	106.82	220.91	205.96	451.33	182.58	164.50	214.29
Computer information services	101.76	95.82	96.65	99.44	104.40	106.18	106.12	106.32
Installation of computer	130.56	–	127.78	100.00	315.63	118.75	128.13	106.25
HOUSEHOLD FURNISHINGS AND EQUIPMENT, AMOUNT SPENT	579.71	404.53	498.88	527.23	566.54	727.50	648.49	859.78
Household textiles	118.75	84.06	93.26	113.44	98.28	157.68	119.12	224.82
Bathroom linens	48.76	44.00	42.70	48.10	53.86	53.91	51.73	57.87
Bedroom linens	101.56	87.70	93.25	98.27	92.70	116.48	111.80	124.59
Kitchen and dining room linens	29.22	27.68	26.09	24.68	22.41	35.78	30.25	46.95
Curtains and draperies	215.25	64.18	112.18	195.55	103.25	403.43	143.67	740.40
Slipcovers and decorative pillows	59.07	46.75	56.40	53.02	54.28	68.64	63.92	77.34
Sewing materials for household items	77.05	62.91	60.87	67.17	61.22	99.00	88.04	117.28
Other linens	68.33	73.21	67.86	48.53	46.21	97.34	98.53	96.79
Furniture	930.73	777.40	856.16	773.46	891.37	1,124.09	1,004.36	1,316.75
Mattresses and springs	775.44	673.81	731.60	640.03	760.60	901.95	826.48	1,072.45
Other bedroom furniture	894.72	861.41	817.46	789.22	995.39	1,014.95	854.88	1,294.55
Sofas	1,131.63	896.86	982.49	944.38	1,235.62	1,412.91	1,250.30	1,722.64
Living room chairs	534.02	377.63	482.78	457.42	450.91	672.07	527.17	954.58
Living room tables	304.11	260.39	228.70	200.47	182.21	458.99	307.21	675.37
Kitchen and dining room furniture	744.02	517.67	508.25	662.41	519.56	1,067.02	842.03	1,325.00
Infants' furniture	271.75	197.13	286.43	226.72	314.73	336.62	268.18	426.83
Outdoor furniture	318.49	245.11	261.04	273.98	237.87	397.64	422.75	365.67
Wall units, cabinets, and other furniture	402.83	295.77	385.37	278.76	303.21	518.97	515.12	524.61
Floor coverings	376.52	415.21	366.63	260.27	286.64	477.00	452.14	517.12
Wall-to-wall carpeting	2,008.33	2,731.82	2,495.54	1,236.03	1,463.28	2,158.93	2,243.57	2,008.93
Floor coverings, nonpermanent	166.57	107.49	96.73	132.55	155.65	249.85	245.60	256.94
Major appliances	618.68	411.66	629.63	545.13	554.52	759.63	727.08	815.83
Dishwashers (built-in), garbage disposals, range hoods (renter)	440.00	–	615.00	312.50	211.11	665.00	287.50	2,066.67
Dishwashers (built-in), garbage disposals, range hoods (owner)	561.11	305.26	591.67	480.09	578.52	588.89	615.32	552.06

	total households	less than high school graduate	high school graduate	some college	associate's degree	college graduate total	bachelor's degree	master's, professional, doctorate
Refrigerators, freezers (renter)	$474.32	$466.46	$470.24	$396.43	$477.03	$626.39	$669.57	$430.56
Refrigerators, freezers (owner)	942.56	671.77	965.65	944.96	906.48	1,011.71	1,064.44	931.47
Washing machines (renter)	386.59	293.63	403.66	379.81	489.58	405.83	428.57	378.03
Washing machines (owner)	706.75	642.62	703.50	639.39	640.04	788.16	774.49	810.71
Clothes dryers (renter)	323.21	135.42	394.64	312.84	303.26	343.27	335.23	354.55
Clothes dryers (owner)	680.81	517.80	717.68	617.71	614.19	775.76	752.45	807.37
Cooking stoves, ovens (renter)	406.25	451.19	520.00	241.67	285.71	293.75	325.00	326.92
Cooking stoves, ovens (owner)	1,116.54	660.71	1,081.15	810.38	819.71	1,455.46	1,309.52	1,664.63
Microwave ovens (renter)	96.74	101.76	89.56	85.58	108.21	114.77	118.98	91.07
Microwave ovens (owner)	196.25	109.32	209.90	157.91	172.50	229.81	228.60	232.32
Window air conditioners (renter)	218.33	226.19	191.30	279.41	137.50	215.00	250.00	200.00
Window air conditioners (owner)	319.83	375.96	398.00	221.21	244.29	350.86	405.00	234.82
Electric floor-cleaning equipment	169.20	112.35	196.06	141.32	177.94	184.59	176.01	199.81
Sewing machines	454.46	128.85	504.17	590.91	768.90	234.85	239.17	224.36
Small appliances and misc. housewares	**86.99**	**76.75**	**75.92**	**82.75**	**86.96**	**101.54**	**90.49**	**119.93**
Housewares	73.66	75.82	65.27	67.33	72.70	83.27	75.27	96.36
Plastic dinnerware	27.85	23.83	24.05	23.71	27.85	36.74	29.31	48.86
China and other dinnerware	81.93	82.07	70.21	72.46	99.51	90.52	79.51	106.47
Flatware	64.18	40.20	55.74	67.36	62.22	75.66	65.07	92.37
Glassware	33.29	18.47	34.16	30.28	30.11	40.50	33.06	51.25
Silver serving pieces	54.17	20.00	33.33	39.29	–	70.45	83.33	60.71
Other serving pieces	46.54	59.38	43.63	35.76	47.26	54.06	45.25	69.21
Nonelectric cookware	77.17	112.13	72.61	65.48	64.16	80.38	78.95	83.33
Small appliances	82.47	57.45	71.64	83.06	83.15	98.25	86.59	117.89
Small electric kitchen appliances	70.55	53.02	52.68	70.35	75.60	88.17	71.69	113.43
Portable heating and cooling equipment	121.85	63.76	132.91	129.97	106.17	134.09	145.33	109.09
Miscellaneous household equipment	**313.29**	**236.75**	**266.96**	**302.46**	**315.08**	**362.68**	**327.17**	**421.41**
Window coverings	304.65	122.61	170.22	297.38	170.23	498.97	443.85	585.60
Infants' equipment	149.18	133.52	175.53	150.57	205.17	119.44	103.51	142.47
Outdoor equipment	234.32	204.55	192.76	200.36	173.46	317.86	211.09	480.74
Lamps and lighting fixtures	95.43	61.38	100.29	75.07	101.73	110.22	97.32	129.71
Clocks and other household decorative items	142.22	93.81	96.78	120.22	117.74	190.74	184.56	200.61
Telephones and accessories	118.38	102.13	112.44	114.29	123.38	127.79	129.32	125.85
Lawn and garden equipment	489.38	757.21	552.79	477.67	353.98	418.98	365.52	493.49
Power tools	218.29	209.57	242.57	160.16	307.21	210.30	190.99	242.05
Office furniture for home use	301.54	114.58	211.29	252.56	196.13	403.75	364.18	466.27
Hand tools	91.52	55.11	111.38	70.03	94.72	103.17	122.56	72.01
Indoor plants and fresh flowers	88.93	69.05	76.16	84.41	78.76	104.14	104.65	103.40
Closet and storage items	67.91	51.85	54.88	64.53	50.00	80.49	60.02	115.64
Rental of furniture	338.89	462.93	229.17	351.04	204.17	325.00	383.93	65.00
Luggage	109.57	76.39	90.33	98.79	91.03	125.20	108.48	150.09
Computers and computer hardware, nonbusiness use	703.00	918.99	628.19	679.24	722.65	725.65	658.77	827.93
Computer software and accessories, nonbusiness use	129.79	110.81	126.11	122.64	131.46	136.41	132.54	143.14
Personal digital assistants	234.17	205.00	180.00	238.71	336.59	218.75	204.81	236.33
Internet services away from home	88.58	87.50	98.28	73.84	76.90	96.90	101.79	87.50
Telephone answering devices	61.11	52.08	57.50	47.22	65.28	73.15	76.04	71.88
Business equipment for home use	91.53	56.03	80.81	94.14	87.50	104.33	97.50	113.24
Smoke alarms (owner)	61.31	37.50	72.50	92.05	39.00	39.20	39.10	39.35
Smoke alarms (renter)	43.18	41.07	38.64	77.50	10.00	36.36	36.11	34.38
Other household appliances (owner)	190.69	123.72	204.25	181.96	124.36	212.50	156.34	312.68
Other household appliances (renter)	109.09	104.38	97.22	92.42	30.09	193.52	257.69	91.07

Note: "–" means sample is too small to make a reliable estimate.
Source: Calculations by New Strategist based on the Bureau of Labor Statistics' 2008 Consumer Expenditure Survey

Table 7.27 Percent Buying Housekeeping Supplies, Furnishings, and Equipment by Education, <u>Average Week</u>, 2008

(percent of households buying housekeeping supplies, furnishings, and equipment during the average week, by highest level of education of householder, 2008)

	total households	less than high school graduate	high school graduate	some college	associate's degree	college graduate		master's, professional, doctorate
						total	bachelor's degree	
HOUSEKEEPING SUPPLIES, PERCENT BUYING	**53.9%**	**52.4%**	**50.4%**	**51.6%**	**57.3%**	**58.5%**	**58.5%**	**58.5%**
Laundry and cleaning supplies	**28.3**	**31.3**	**27.8**	**26.4**	**31.6**	**28.0**	**27.7**	**28.5**
Soaps and detergents	20.1	23.8	19.8	18.5	22.9	19.1	18.9	19.7
Other laundry cleaning products	18.0	20.5	17.4	17.2	19.1	17.5	17.8	16.9
Other household products	**40.4**	**41.1**	**37.7**	**39.7**	**42.6**	**42.3**	**42.5**	**42.1**
Cleansing and toilet tissue, paper towels, and napkins	24.8	25.9	24.8	24.9	26.5	23.9	24.6	22.5
Miscellaneous household products	25.7	24.7	22.4	25.4	28.8	28.3	28.0	28.8
Lawn and garden supplies	6.6	5.1	5.7	6.2	6.4	8.4	8.2	8.6
Postage and stationery	**22.8**	**16.5**	**19.2**	**22.1**	**23.3**	**29.4**	**29.1**	**30.0**
Stationery, stationery supplies, giftwrap	17.4	11.7	14.8	17.3	17.2	22.7	22.8	22.6
Postage	8.5	6.4	6.6	7.6	9.4	11.7	11.0	13.1
Delivery services	0.5	0.3	0.4	0.6	0.7	0.6	0.4	0.8
HOUSEHOLD FURNISHINGS AND EQUIPMENT, PERCENT BUYING	**30.5**	**22.8**	**26.1**	**30.2**	**34.0**	**37.2**	**35.8**	**39.7**
Household textiles	**6.2**	**5.5**	**6.0**	**6.5**	**5.6**	**6.8**	**6.4**	**7.5**
Bathroom linens	3.0	3.2	3.0	2.9	2.4	3.0	2.7	3.6
Bedroom linens	2.6	1.6	2.2	3.2	2.0	3.0	2.9	3.3
Kitchen and dining room linens	1.3	1.1	1.2	1.3	1.6	1.5	1.4	1.6
Slipcovers and decorative pillows	0.3	0.1	0.2	0.1	0.2	0.4	0.4	0.5
Outdoor furniture	**0.4**	**0.1**	**0.2**	**0.3**	**0.4**	**0.8**	**0.7**	**0.9**
Floor coverings, nonpermanent	**1.2**	**1.1**	**0.9**	**1.1**	**1.4**	**1.7**	**1.6**	**1.9**
Major appliances	**0.7**	**0.4**	**0.5**	**0.7**	**0.6**	**1.0**	**1.0**	**1.0**
Electric floor-cleaning equipment	0.5	0.2	0.3	0.6	0.3	0.7	0.7	0.8
Miscellaneous household appliances	0.2	0.2	0.1	0.2	0.2	0.2	0.2	0.2
Housewares	**8.1**	**5.7**	**5.9**	**7.9**	**9.7**	**11.0**	**11.2**	**10.6**
China and other dinnerware	1.3	0.9	1.2	1.3	1.2	1.6	1.6	1.5
Glassware	1.9	1.5	1.1	1.9	1.9	2.6	2.7	2.5
Nonelectric cookware	2.2	1.7	1.6	2.1	2.4	3.0	3.0	3.0
Tableware, nonelectric kitchenware	4.3	2.3	3.0	4.1	5.4	6.2	6.3	6.1
Miscellaneous household equipment	**24.3**	**16.5**	**19.6**	**25.2**	**27.8**	**30.6**	**29.4**	**33.0**
Infants' equipment	1.2	0.9	0.9	0.9	1.6	1.7	1.6	2.0
Laundry and cleaning equipment	4.9	4.4	4.3	4.6	4.5	6.1	5.8	6.7
Outdoor equipment	1.3	0.9	1.3	1.4	1.2	1.6	1.2	2.4
Lamps and lighting fixtures	1.3	0.9	1.0	1.6	1.3	1.7	1.6	1.7
Clocks and other household decorative items	8.0	4.3	6.0	8.7	9.3	10.7	10.7	10.5
Telephones and accessories	1.2	0.9	1.2	1.0	1.2	1.6	1.3	2.0
Lawn and garden equipment	2.0	1.1	1.4	2.1	2.4	2.8	2.7	2.9
Power tools	1.3	0.9	1.5	1.4	1.5	1.2	1.0	1.6
Hand tools	1.8	1.0	1.4	1.9	2.3	2.3	2.4	2.1
Indoor plants and fresh flowers	4.2	2.1	2.5	4.5	4.2	6.6	6.2	7.3
Closet and storage items	2.4	1.9	1.7	2.2	2.7	3.3	3.2	3.4
Other hardware	0.8	0.3	0.7	1.2	0.9	0.9	0.9	1.1
Miscellaneous household equipment and parts	4.9	3.4	3.7	5.2	6.1	6.2	6.1	6.4
Luggage	0.8	0.3	0.5	0.8	1.2	1.0	0.9	1.2

Source: Bureau of Labor Statistics, unpublished data from the 2008 Consumer Expenditure Survey

Table 7.28 Amount Buyers Spent on Housekeeping Supplies, Furnishings, and Equipment by Education, <u>Average Week</u>, 2008

(average amount spent by households buying housekeeping supplies, furnishings, and equipment during the average week, by highest level of education of householder, 2008)

	total households	less than high school graduate	high school graduate	some college	associate's degree	college graduate total	bachelor's degree	master's, professional, doctorate
HOUSEKEEPING SUPPLIES, AMOUNT SPENT	**$23.35**	**$20.99**	**$20.83**	**$22.29**	**$22.81**	**$27.23**	**$25.76**	**$29.98**
Laundry and cleaning supplies	**10.03**	**10.61**	**9.14**	**10.13**	**9.69**	**10.58**	**10.41**	**10.94**
Soaps and detergents	7.75	7.94	6.86	8.05	7.57	8.36	8.38	8.29
Other laundry cleaning products	7.13	7.01	6.84	6.91	6.92	7.78	7.31	8.80
Other household products	**16.70**	**14.48**	**15.11**	**15.36**	**16.60**	**20.00**	**19.29**	**21.34**
Cleansing and toilet tissue, paper towels, and napkins	8.09	6.98	7.55	7.79	8.01	9.34	9.15	9.80
Miscellaneous household products	11.07	8.21	10.26	10.74	11.82	12.90	12.10	14.36
Lawn and garden supplies	28.81	41.78	26.49	22.87	24.14	30.98	30.95	30.85
Postage and stationery	**13.16**	**10.47**	**11.85**	**12.33**	**12.66**	**15.31**	**13.80**	**18.05**
Stationery, stationery supplies, giftwrap	9.00	4.96	6.62	9.59	8.01	11.31	10.23	13.31
Postage	15.85	17.61	18.55	13.06	15.16	15.54	14.52	17.07
Delivery services	16.33	9.38	15.38	12.73	20.29	20.00	18.18	22.67
HOUSEHOLD FURNISHINGS AND EQUIPMENT, AMOUNT SPENT	**52.23**	**32.40**	**47.77**	**47.91**	**48.57**	**64.56**	**65.05**	**63.76**
Household textiles	**29.33**	**16.30**	**19.17**	**35.08**	**23.71**	**39.79**	**38.69**	**41.51**
Bathroom linens	14.24	11.84	12.00	14.43	19.75	16.44	16.23	16.67
Bedroom linens	47.06	28.30	29.49	53.31	34.48	61.26	61.46	60.37
Kitchen and dining room linens	9.09	5.50	5.83	8.46	8.28	12.75	10.49	16.88
Slipcovers and decorative pillows	36.00	0.00	29.17	35.71	20.00	40.91	27.91	60.87
Outdoor furniture	**138.46**	**22.22**	**160.87**	**138.71**	**152.63**	**134.67**	**137.88**	**127.96**
Floor coverings, nonpermanent	**98.37**	**29.63**	**304.44**	**39.05**	**19.71**	**65.48**	**76.58**	**48.40**
Major appliances	**94.03**	**55.56**	**82.00**	**144.44**	**46.43**	**86.32**	**69.47**	**116.84**
Electric floor-cleaning equipment	110.64	50.00	80.00	160.32	70.37	95.83	75.00	130.38
Miscellaneous household appliances	33.33	65.00	33.33	20.00	13.64	26.32	17.65	38.10
Housewares	**17.10**	**13.81**	**13.54**	**13.98**	**15.20**	**22.04**	**19.62**	**26.60**
China and other dinnerware	16.28	7.95	19.35	13.08	16.39	19.35	14.19	29.22
Glassware	18.38	28.77	12.73	13.40	18.04	20.23	19.70	21.60
Nonelectric cookware	12.39	6.47	8.64	8.78	10.04	18.24	17.23	20.61
Tableware, nonelectric kitchenware	13.35	7.93	9.46	12.25	12.52	16.75	14.94	20.30
Miscellaneous household equipment	**41.31**	**28.93**	**34.25**	**35.79**	**44.66**	**51.19**	**52.93**	**48.29**
Infants' equipment	33.61	31.82	24.42	19.15	21.38	49.12	60.65	32.00
Laundry and cleaning equipment	6.33	6.62	5.63	5.48	5.75	6.89	7.44	6.27
Outdoor equipment	47.01	27.66	37.30	36.30	45.90	66.26	51.24	80.17
Lamps and lighting fixtures	42.42	43.53	48.96	32.92	18.40	50.90	54.27	46.20
Clocks and other household decorative items	30.46	24.30	23.15	19.36	22.48	44.51	46.55	40.68
Telephones and accessories	68.85	51.76	61.79	39.39	35.48	100.64	123.48	72.77
Lawn and garden equipment	63.32	61.90	43.88	64.59	139.09	51.09	62.45	31.27
Power tools	39.85	30.11	49.67	37.50	46.00	33.33	35.00	31.21
Hand tools	17.78	12.87	11.81	11.92	42.92	18.50	21.70	12.21
Indoor plants and fresh flowers	21.28	13.21	21.60	18.76	16.71	24.58	23.71	26.19
Closet and storage items	18.49	8.42	9.77	24.07	43.40	15.85	14.64	18.48
Other hardware	38.10	6.25	30.43	55.28	16.47	36.96	36.47	38.68
Miscellaneous household equipment and parts	17.61	15.20	15.55	20.73	17.62	17.21	17.36	16.77
Luggage	32.00	19.23	28.85	27.27	31.67	36.89	23.66	56.67

Source: Calculations by New Strategist based on the Bureau of Labor Statistics' 2008 Consumer Expenditure Survey

CHAPTER 8

Housing Buyers: Shelter and Utilities, 2008

Americans spend more on shelter than on any other major category, an average of $10,183 per household in 2008. The average household boosted its spending on shelter by 14 percent between 2000 and 2008, after adjusting for inflation, and increased its spending on utilities by an even larger 17 percent.

Quarterly spending

Nearly every household spends on shelter and utilities. During an average quarter, electricity is the shelter and utility category on which the largest percentage of households spends money, with 92 percent doing so. Landline telephone service ranks second in popularity among shelter and utility categories, with 72 percent spending on residential phone service. Cellular phone service ranks fourth, with 60 percent of households spending on it and the buyers spending $270 during the quarter. Forty-one percent of households paid mortgage interest during the average quarter, and 31 percent paid rent.

Weekly spending

The weekly spending (diary) portion of the Consumer Expenditure Survey collects data on only a handful of shelter categories. During the average week of 2008, 35 percent of households paid fuel and utility bills. Twenty-two percent paid for phone service, spending an average of $104. The 18 percent of householders who paid an electricity bill during the average week of 2008 spent $140 on the service.

Household Services, Supplies, and Furnishings Buyers' Top 10

(household services, supplies, and furnishings categories bought by the largest percentage of households during an average quarter, 2008)

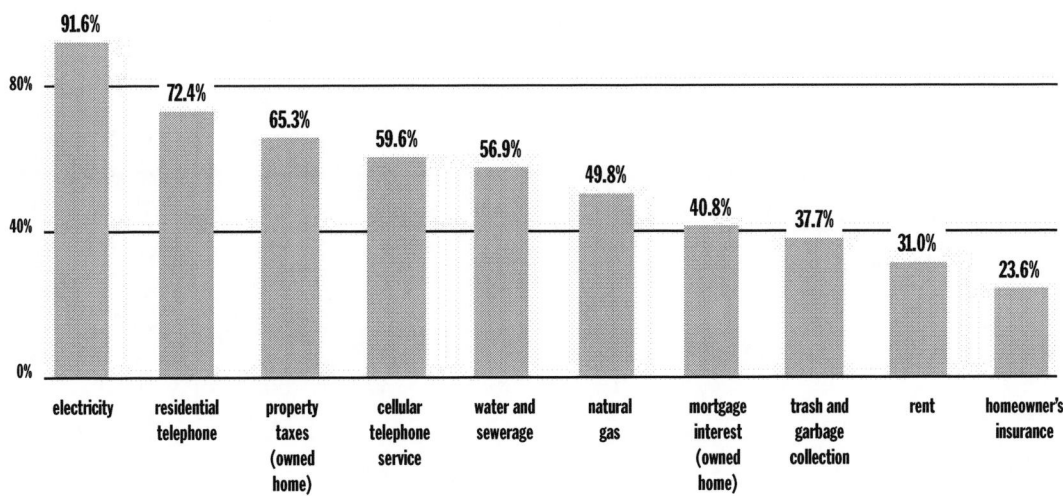

Table 8.1 Percent Buying Shelter and Utilities by Age, <u>Average Quarter</u>, 2008

(percent of households buying shelter and utilities during the average quarter, by age of householder, 2008)

	total households	under 25	25 to 34	35 to 44	45 to 54	55 to 64	65 to 74	75+
SHELTER, PERCENT BUYING	97.7%	86.2%	98.0%	98.8%	99.2%	98.8%	98.6%	97.1%
Owned dwellings	**66.7**	**15.2**	**47.1**	**67.4**	**76.3**	**81.2**	**80.6**	**75.3**
Mortgage interest and charges	43.7	10.9	41.1	58.2	58.1	49.3	32.6	13.3
Mortgage interest	40.8	10.7	40.8	57.0	54.8	43.3	26.6	10.7
Interest paid, home equity loan	4.2	0.5	3.2	5.1	5.7	5.9	3.7	1.3
Interest paid, home equity line of credit	5.5	0.5	2.8	5.4	8.5	7.6	6.5	2.4
Property taxes	65.3	14.9	46.2	66.8	74.9	79.5	78.1	72.1
Maintenance, repairs, insurance, other expenses	35.3	7.5	26.3	36.2	39.3	43.5	42.6	37.8
Homeowner's insurance	23.6	4.5	18.5	25.3	27.8	29.4	26.4	21.0
Ground rent	1.6	0.6	1.3	1.1	1.1	2.1	2.9	2.6
Maintenance and repair services	12.0	1.9	7.2	10.2	12.5	14.9	17.9	18.2
Painting and papering	1.0	0.1	0.4	0.8	1.2	1.6	1.4	1.5
Plumbing and water heating	3.4	0.7	2.4	2.4	3.3	3.9	4.9	6.9
Heat, air conditioning, electrical work	4.2	0.6	2.5	3.8	4.8	5.0	6.1	6.1
Roofing and gutters	1.0	0.3	0.4	0.7	1.3	1.1	1.8	2.1
Other repair and maintenance services	4.0	0.2	2.3	3.2	4.0	5.3	6.5	6.1
Repair, replacement of hard-surface flooring	0.6	–	0.4	0.5	0.6	0.7	0.8	1.0
Repair of built-in appliances	0.3	0.1	0.1	0.3	0.3	0.5	0.4	0.5
Maintenance and repair materials	4.9	1.8	4.3	5.2	5.7	6.7	5.3	2.9
Paints, wallpaper, and supplies	1.9	0.9	1.9	2.2	2.1	2.6	1.7	0.6
Tools, equipment for painting, wallpapering	1.9	0.9	1.9	2.2	2.1	2.6	1.7	0.6
Plumbing supplies and equipment	0.7	0.1	0.6	0.7	0.8	1.1	0.7	0.6
Electrical supplies, heating and cooling equipment	0.3	0.2	0.2	0.4	0.4	0.3	0.3	0.3
Hard-surface flooring, repair and replacement	0.3	0.1	0.3	0.3	0.3	0.3	0.4	0.1
Roofing and gutters	0.2	0.1	0.2	0.1	0.2	0.4	0.4	0.1
Plaster, paneling, siding, windows, doors, screens, awnings	0.6	0.1	0.7	0.6	0.8	0.9	0.5	0.3
Patio, walk, fence, driveway, masonry, brick, and stucco materials	0.4	–	0.4	0.4	0.4	0.5	0.4	0.1
Miscellaneous supplies and equipment	1.5	0.7	1.1	1.6	1.8	1.8	1.7	1.2
Property management and security	5.3	1.4	4.8	4.7	5.1	6.1	6.3	8.5
Property management	5.0	1.4	4.7	4.4	4.9	5.6	5.9	7.9
Management and upkeep services for security	1.3	0.1	0.8	0.8	1.0	1.8	1.9	2.7
Parking	2.4	0.9	2.4	1.6	2.1	2.6	3.4	4.1
Rented dwellings	**32.0**	**69.6**	**52.2**	**32.4**	**24.6**	**18.9**	**18.4**	**23.1**
Rent	31.0	68.7	51.0	31.7	23.4	17.9	17.6	21.9
Rent as pay	1.4	1.7	1.9	1.3	1.2	1.0	1.5	1.1
Maintenance, insurance, and other expenses	3.9	4.8	6.7	4.1	3.4	2.9	1.9	3.1
Tenant's insurance	2.9	3.4	5.5	3.1	2.2	2.0	1.5	2.1
Maintenance and repair services	0.5	0.4	0.5	0.4	0.5	0.5	0.3	0.9
Maintenance and repair materials	0.8	1.4	1.0	1.1	0.8	0.7	0.2	0.3
Other lodging	**18.8**	**8.9**	**14.0**	**18.2**	**24.3**	**24.5**	**20.4**	**12.1**
Owned vacation homes	5.5	0.4	1.7	4.2	7.2	9.1	8.6	4.9
Mortgage interest and charges	1.7	0.2	0.6	1.9	2.3	3.0	1.4	0.8
Property taxes	5.2	0.4	1.6	3.9	6.8	8.6	8.3	4.7
Maintenance, insurance, and other expenses	2.0	–	0.5	1.4	2.6	3.5	3.0	1.9
Housing while attending school	0.9	1.6	0.3	0.4	2.5	1.0	0.1	0.1
Lodging on trips	14.2	7.0	12.5	14.7	17.7	17.5	14.6	7.8

	total households	under 25	25 to 34	35 to 44	45 to 54	55 to 64	65 to 74	75+
UTILITIES, FUELS, AND PUBLIC SERVICES, PERCENT BUYING	97.7%	83.4%	98.3%	99.0%	99.2%	98.8%	99.0%	98.0%
Natural gas	49.8	30.3	46.5	52.2	53.7	54.1	50.2	48.1
Electricity	91.6	70.4	90.0	94.4	94.6	94.8	93.9	89.1
Fuel oil and other fuels	8.4	2.0	5.4	8.4	9.6	10.9	9.8	9.6
Fuel oil	3.4	0.4	1.7	3.4	3.7	4.4	4.1	5.2
Coal, wood, and other fuels	0.7	0.3	0.5	0.7	1.0	1.0	0.7	0.7
Bottled gas	4.7	1.3	3.3	4.7	5.4	6.2	5.5	4.4
Telephone services	92.8	67.2	92.2	94.5	95.3	96.0	95.9	94.8
Residential telephone and pay phones	72.4	20.1	50.5	72.2	79.9	84.9	89.2	91.9
Cellular phone service	59.6	56.3	69.6	68.2	66.3	58.6	47.4	27.2
Phone cards	4.7	3.9	5.5	5.7	5.1	3.8	3.9	3.0
Voice over IP	1.3	0.3	1.7	1.9	1.5	1.2	1.0	0.6
Water and other public services	62.6	30.1	54.9	67.0	68.3	69.0	66.9	62.8
Water and sewerage maintenance	56.9	27.4	50.8	60.9	61.9	62.1	60.8	56.1
Trash and garbage collection	37.7	18.7	32.9	40.8	40.5	43.0	39.7	36.0
Septic tank cleaning	0.4	0.0	0.2	0.4	0.5	0.5	0.4	0.3

Note: "–" means sample is too small to make a reliable estimate.
Source: Bureau of Labor Statistics, unpublished data from the 2008 Consumer Expenditure Survey

Table 8.2 Amount Buyers Spent on Shelter and Utilities by Age, <u>Average Quarter</u>, 2008

(average amount spent by households buying shelter and utilities during the average quarter, by age of householder, 2008)

	total households	under 25	25 to 34	35 to 44	45 to 54	55 to 64	65 to 74	75+
SHELTER, AMOUNT SPENT	**$2,605.44**	**$1,892.87**	**$2,789.55**	**$3,210.84**	**$2,932.29**	**$2,560.21**	**$1,846.57**	**$1,687.06**
Owned dwellings*	**2,533.50**	**2,279.47**	**3,116.69**	**3,360.88**	**2,821.22**	**2,274.31**	**1,654.21**	**1,320.29**
Mortgage interest and charges	2,189.04	2,096.69	2,526.15	2,659.46	2,126.61	1,834.23	1,407.17	1,293.89
Mortgage interest	2,193.23	2,079.60	2,437.00	2,600.44	2,087.06	1,899.53	1,513.22	1,438.93
Interest paid, home equity loan	616.21	807.61	804.95	586.04	632.97	567.30	504.96	539.76
Interest paid, home equity line of credit	640.11	611.98	612.27	682.93	670.69	634.77	587.33	457.17
Property taxes	673.15	474.26	572.94	735.64	729.28	718.11	596.94	574.71
Maintenance, repairs, insurance, other expenses	833.11	608.65	629.38	619.22	939.25	855.80	959.62	1,076.21
Homeowner's insurance	374.60	365.40	305.91	322.08	379.87	396.77	427.64	466.87
Ground rent	794.22	578.81	650.76	750.45	775.67	818.78	822.73	926.15
Maintenance and repair services	1,316.72	1,086.62	1,041.09	1,011.19	1,776.98	1,267.76	1,286.49	1,261.59
Painting and papering	1,773.54	200.00	1,185.71	1,876.52	1,736.89	1,629.91	2,948.39	1,083.10
Plumbing and water heating	403.35	192.03	254.75	314.20	589.52	397.14	393.21	386.79
Heat, air conditioning, electrical work	711.70	421.12	510.96	585.27	708.25	699.50	939.02	808.58
Roofing and gutters	2,324.52	1,154.31	2,574.29	2,648.57	3,150.00	2,350.71	1,195.00	2,121.26
Other repair and maintenance services	1,546.99	5,302.08	1,560.84	997.81	2,423.06	1,430.13	1,212.54	1,285.29
Repair, replacement of hard-surface flooring	1,600.91	–	1,641.89	1,444.27	1,971.93	1,480.00	1,491.25	1,393.75
Repair of built-in appliances	188.33	85.00	196.88	154.17	200.96	170.92	289.74	170.10
Maintenance and repair materials	359.67	208.33	393.69	350.86	345.46	441.54	306.89	206.03
Paints, wallpaper, and supplies	152.65	136.05	126.46	166.26	156.34	173.35	93.21	218.75
Tools, equipment for painting, wallpapering	16.40	14.53	13.62	17.83	16.83	18.58	9.97	23.33
Plumbing supplies and equipment	182.39	176.92	171.05	141.18	176.22	210.00	233.82	164.06
Electrical supplies, heating and cooling equipment	185.61	292.05	238.54	245.95	156.88	196.21	130.88	56.90
Hard-surface flooring, repair and replacement	885.58	12.50	868.97	1,147.22	659.17	989.52	927.03	193.75
Roofing and gutters	977.17	158.33	1,105.26	1,543.18	1,423.86	674.43	823.78	1,029.17
Plaster, paneling, siding, windows, doors, screens, awnings	564.52	75.00	693.57	554.55	442.67	810.64	222.50	131.90
Patio, walk, fence, driveway, masonry, brick, and stucco materials	94.44	–	64.29	79.17	92.86	108.65	172.44	19.64
Miscellaneous supplies and equipment	290.31	205.38	271.10	268.67	292.19	413.20	215.09	184.57
Property management and security	284.88	123.95	158.21	241.67	223.34	296.45	357.75	487.41
Property management	249.01	120.54	139.57	232.97	199.80	252.66	317.34	405.16
Management and upkeep services for security	213.00	125.00	130.36	142.43	171.91	204.37	207.26	346.70
Parking	93.51	52.45	54.15	91.72	70.79	90.02	81.29	183.52
Rented dwellings	**2,125.82**	**1,775.60**	**2,267.90**	**2,323.97**	**2,069.44**	**2,123.78**	**1,755.15**	**2,223.08**
Rent	2,108.22	1,752.09	2,256.24	2,282.47	2,080.13	2,077.38	1,713.98	2,255.76
Rent as pay	1,352.02	1,319.91	1,230.92	1,597.64	1,267.34	1,601.94	1,221.64	1,146.14
Maintenance, insurance, and other expenses	228.70	209.18	139.56	234.02	206.84	465.22	171.20	282.79
Tenant's insurance	95.42	52.80	81.65	117.62	91.41	113.73	82.38	131.80
Maintenance and repair services	773.94	1,321.05	284.62	840.28	644.68	1,478.65	344.70	671.51
Maintenance and repair materials	325.63	242.22	326.23	281.37	235.54	645.08	565.63	75.00
Other lodging	**926.58**	**581.38**	**584.74**	**851.45**	**1,016.97**	**1,150.81**	**799.34**	**1,079.62**
Owned vacation homes	1,373.72	1,355.77	1,247.06	1,530.08	1,323.57	1,597.88	869.68	1,605.49
Mortgage interest and charges	2,060.03	618.42	2,123.31	2,301.30	1,996.68	1,964.20	1,569.16	3,004.63
Property taxes	482.87	1,054.49	355.28	379.46	446.41	542.12	447.22	689.77
Maintenance, insurance, and other expenses	805.33	–	557.55	416.48	763.51	1,108.52	526.82	1,143.62
Housing while attending school	1,880.22	1,791.93	3,448.21	1,336.43	1,719.31	2,192.37	990.63	3,025.00
Lodging on trips	577.09	248.18	409.92	584.99	616.40	662.44	602.81	643.05

	total households	under 25	25 to 34	35 to 44	45 to 54	55 to 64	65 to 74	75+
UTILITIES, FUELS, AND PUBLIC SERVICES, AMOUNT SPENT	**$933.60**	**$561.83**	**$801.89**	**$1,043.53**	**$1,070.11**	**$1,005.61**	**$893.34**	**$782.53**
Natural gas	**266.79**	**174.18**	**215.39**	**281.69**	**290.14**	**278.85**	**274.88**	**273.28**
Electricity	**369.36**	**262.49**	**327.24**	**410.18**	**407.73**	**385.66**	**352.77**	**317.22**
Fuel oil and other fuels	**571.51**	**313.37**	**448.33**	**498.65**	**552.75**	**583.83**	**637.18**	**802.41**
Fuel oil	851.40	603.57	808.91	812.98	773.58	867.49	858.31	1,024.71
Coal, wood, and other fuels	414.86	62.04	216.84	488.64	452.72	406.77	573.16	371.53
Bottled gas	341.52	270.71	279.15	233.44	368.85	340.26	427.33	482.77
Telephone services	**303.44**	**272.27**	**303.60**	**347.88**	**356.89**	**298.95**	**246.97**	**181.43**
Residential telephone and pay phones	161.32	158.37	150.36	168.49	167.13	167.52	159.91	141.57
Cellular phone service	269.62	263.03	284.39	295.78	304.18	241.28	192.71	147.95
Phone cards	59.17	70.74	77.90	58.20	62.72	46.64	40.83	31.54
Voice over IP	116.17	96.88	103.44	122.33	119.05	125.21	110.19	118.75
Water and other public services	**178.03**	**139.19**	**162.46**	**190.90**	**185.27**	**183.93**	**173.43**	**164.62**
Water and sewerage maintenance	146.03	116.41	134.01	158.18	153.14	147.03	142.51	134.02
Trash and garbage collection	73.39	53.23	63.13	75.67	75.51	79.47	72.66	75.21
Septic tank cleaning	225.00	308.33	148.91	180.71	227.94	290.43	130.13	347.58

Amount does not include principal reduction, which is considered an asset.
Note: "–" means sample is too small to make a reliable estimate.
Source: Calculations by New Strategist based on the Bureau of Labor Statistics' 2008 Consumer Expenditure Survey

Table 8.3 Percent Buying Utilities and Fuels by Age, Average Week, 2008

(percent of households buying utilities and fuels during the average week, by age of householder, 2008)

	total households	under 25	25 to 34	35 to 44	45 to 54	55 to 64	65 to 74	75+
UTILITIES AND FUELS, PERCENT BUYING	**34.9%**	**24.0%**	**35.7%**	**36.2%**	**35.5%**	**37.6%**	**35.5%**	**32.2%**
Electricity and natural gas	**21.7**	**13.1**	**22.2**	**21.8**	**22.2**	**24.0**	**22.7**	**20.0**
Electricity	17.6	11.5	17.3	17.8	18.5	18.8	18.9	16.9
Natural gas	9.9	4.8	10.5	9.7	10.2	12.2	9.5	8.6
Fuel oil and other fuels	**5.5**	**3.2**	**4.7**	**6.1**	**6.5**	**6.2**	**5.3**	**4.1**
Fuel oil	1.3	1.3	0.6	1.3	1.3	1.5	1.6	1.4
Bottled and tank gas	1.9	0.6	1.8	2.0	2.2	1.9	2.1	1.6
Coal	0.5	0.3	0.3	0.8	0.5	0.4	0.5	0.1
Miscellaneous fuels	2.7	1.3	2.9	3.1	3.4	3.0	2.1	1.2
Telephone services	**22.4**	**14.4**	**22.7**	**23.5**	**23.0**	**23.6**	**23.2**	**21.0**

Source: Bureau of Labor Statistics, unpublished data from the 2008 Consumer Expenditure Survey

Table 8.4 Amount Buyers Spent on Utilities and Fuels by Age, Average Week, 2008

(average amount spent by households buying utilities and fuels during the average week, by age of householder, 2008)

	total households	under 25	25 to 34	35 to 44	45 to 54	55 to 64	65 to 74	75+
UTILITIES AND FUELS, AMOUNT SPENT	**$184.62**	**$164.34**	**$168.12**	**$209.62**	**$194.70**	**$187.25**	**$165.45**	**$164.57**
Electricity and natural gas	**158.61**	**164.30**	**145.87**	**177.68**	**167.73**	**156.01**	**138.56**	**147.15**
Electricity	139.80	149.18	135.33	159.35	144.09	134.72	125.49	118.27
Natural gas	97.78	91.18	84.51	106.79	102.83	99.67	82.37	110.61
Fuel oil and other fuels	**125.87**	**75.16**	**61.24**	**123.13**	**91.32**	**164.90**	**173.90**	**245.65**
Fuel oil	303.97	134.33	191.94	296.06	242.75	404.58	391.25	347.10
Bottled and tank gas	112.30	36.51	50.27	132.14	87.44	162.23	110.85	195.48
Coal	60.87	50.00	71.88	79.52	44.90	54.76	38.00	16.67
Miscellaneous fuels	25.93	18.32	18.12	17.74	15.82	27.70	15.17	190.24
Telephone services	**103.61**	**106.93**	**109.19**	**125.32**	**112.95**	**95.80**	**78.06**	**63.94**

Source: Calculations by New Strategist based on the Bureau of Labor Statistics' 2008 Consumer Expenditure Survey

Table 8.5 Percent Buying Shelter and Utilities by Household Income, Average Quarter, 2008

(percent of households buying shelter and utilities during the average quarter, by before-tax income of household, 2008)

	total households	under $20,000	$20,000–$39,999	$40,000–$49,999	$50,000–$69,999	$70,000–$79,999	$80,000–$99,999	$100,000 or more
SHELTER, PERCENT BUYING	**97.7%**	**92.4%**	**98.1%**	**99.0%**	**99.3%**	**99.8%**	**99.7%**	**99.7%**
Owned dwellings	**66.7**	**38.7**	**57.7**	**64.6**	**73.6**	**82.4**	**84.4**	**92.3**
Mortgage interest and charges	43.7	13.0	26.8	41.2	52.7	62.9	67.3	76.9
Mortgage interest	40.8	11.9	24.2	38.6	49.0	58.8	63.5	73.1
Interest paid, home equity loan	4.2	1.0	2.4	2.8	5.4	5.8	7.6	7.9
Interest paid, home equity line of credit	5.5	1.1	2.5	4.4	5.1	7.7	8.1	13.2
Property taxes	65.3	36.5	55.8	63.6	72.3	81.7	83.6	91.8
Maintenance, repairs, insurance, other expenses	35.3	17.6	28.6	33.7	39.2	45.0	46.6	53.3
Homeowner's insurance	23.6	10.3	18.2	23.5	27.4	32.2	33.6	35.4
Ground rent	1.6	2.2	2.8	2.2	0.9	0.8	0.8	0.2
Maintenance and repair services	12.0	5.9	9.0	10.8	11.9	14.9	15.0	21.1
Painting and papering	1.0	0.5	0.7	0.9	0.8	1.2	1.5	2.2
Plumbing and water heating	3.4	2.0	2.6	3.2	3.5	3.9	3.8	5.9
Heat, air conditioning, electrical work	4.2	1.8	3.3	4.0	3.8	6.3	5.7	7.4
Roofing and gutters	1.0	0.3	0.8	1.0	1.4	1.3	1.4	1.7
Other repair and maintenance services	4.0	2.0	2.9	3.4	3.7	4.7	4.9	7.6
Repair, replacement of hard-surface flooring	0.6	0.3	0.3	0.5	0.6	0.6	0.8	1.0
Repair of built-in appliances	0.3	0.1	0.2	0.2	0.4	0.4	0.5	0.5
Maintenance and repair materials	4.9	1.8	3.8	4.2	5.8	7.5	7.4	7.7
Paints, wallpaper, and supplies	1.9	0.6	1.3	1.3	2.4	2.8	3.1	3.1
Tools, equipment for painting, wallpapering	1.9	0.6	1.3	1.3	2.4	2.8	3.1	3.1
Plumbing supplies and equipment	0.7	0.3	0.6	0.9	0.9	1.0	1.2	0.8
Electrical supplies, heating and cooling equipment	0.3	0.2	0.3	0.1	0.4	0.4	0.4	0.5
Hard-surface flooring, repair and replacement	0.3	0.1	0.1	0.4	0.4	0.3	0.2	0.5
Roofing and gutters	0.2	0.1	0.2	0.3	0.2	0.6	0.5	0.2
Plaster, paneling, siding, windows, doors, screens, awnings	0.6	0.3	0.5	0.5	0.7	0.9	1.1	0.9
Patio, walk, fence, driveway, masonry, brick, and stucco materials	0.4	0.1	0.3	0.2	0.5	0.5	0.7	0.5
Miscellaneous supplies and equipment	1.5	0.4	1.1	1.3	1.5	2.5	2.1	2.7
Property management and security	5.3	2.8	3.9	5.3	4.9	6.3	6.5	9.7
Property management	5.0	2.7	3.7	5.1	4.7	5.5	6.3	9.1
Management and upkeep services for security	1.3	0.6	1.0	1.3	1.0	1.7	1.1	2.4
Parking	2.4	1.4	2.3	2.7	2.8	2.9	2.0	3.1
Rented dwellings	**32.0**	**53.6**	**41.1**	**35.6**	**26.8**	**19.0**	**16.9**	**9.5**
Rent	31.0	52.1	40.1	34.4	25.9	18.1	16.2	8.8
Rent as pay	1.4	4.0	1.2	0.8	0.9	0.3	0.2	0.1
Maintenance, insurance, and other expenses	3.9	3.7	4.3	5.1	4.5	4.3	3.6	2.6
Tenant's insurance	2.9	2.5	3.0	4.2	3.5	3.1	2.6	2.1
Maintenance and repair services	0.5	0.5	0.5	0.4	0.4	0.6	0.6	0.4
Maintenance and repair materials	0.8	0.9	1.0	0.8	1.1	0.9	0.4	0.3
Other lodging	**18.8**	**6.9**	**11.0**	**15.0**	**19.2**	**22.5**	**26.6**	**39.4**
Owned vacation homes	5.5	1.4	3.7	3.3	5.4	6.5	7.2	12.5
Mortgage interest and charges	1.7	0.4	0.9	0.7	1.5	1.4	1.8	4.7
Property taxes	5.2	1.3	3.5	3.2	4.9	5.9	6.7	12.0
Maintenance, insurance, and other expenses	2.0	0.3	1.3	0.9	2.0	2.4	2.6	4.9
Housing while attending school	0.9	0.5	0.2	0.5	0.5	0.9	0.7	2.9
Lodging on trips	14.2	5.2	7.9	11.9	14.2	17.5	21.4	29.6

	total households	under $20,000	$20,000–$39,999	$40,000–$49,999	$50,000–$69,999	$70,000–$79,999	$80,000–$99,999	$100,000 or more
UTILITIES, FUELS, AND PUBLIC SERVICES, PERCENT BUYING	**97.7%**	**91.8%**	**98.5%**	**99.4%**	**99.5%**	**99.8%**	**99.7%**	**99.6%**
Natural gas	**49.8**	**35.1**	**44.5**	**49.3**	**52.4**	**55.1**	**58.9**	**65.6**
Electricity	**91.6**	**79.0**	**91.7**	**95.2**	**95.0**	**96.6**	**97.2**	**97.2**
Fuel oil and other fuels	**8.4**	**4.7**	**7.7**	**8.4**	**8.0**	**11.5**	**11.7**	**11.3**
Fuel oil	3.4	1.8	3.0	3.1	2.9	4.4	6.0	4.9
Coal, wood, and other fuels	0.7	0.5	0.7	0.8	0.8	1.1	0.9	0.9
Bottled gas	4.7	2.7	4.3	4.8	4.8	6.4	5.7	6.3
Telephone services	**92.8**	**82.6**	**93.3**	**95.6**	**95.7**	**96.7**	**96.8**	**97.3**
Residential telephone and pay phones	72.4	61.2	68.4	71.0	73.1	75.6	79.2	86.3
Cellular phone service	59.6	37.0	54.9	64.1	68.0	72.5	72.1	72.2
Phone cards	4.7	4.8	5.9	5.6	4.7	3.3	3.6	3.4
Voice over IP	1.3	0.6	0.9	1.2	1.2	2.1	1.6	2.6
Water and other public services	**62.6**	**41.3**	**56.8**	**62.2**	**69.2**	**73.9**	**75.2**	**79.9**
Water and sewerage maintenance	56.9	37.6	50.8	58.0	63.0	67.0	68.4	72.4
Trash and garbage collection	37.7	23.9	33.7	36.5	40.9	44.3	47.2	50.1
Septic tank cleaning	0.4	0.2	0.2	0.3	0.3	0.6	0.6	0.6

Source: Bureau of Labor Statistics, unpublished data from the 2008 Consumer Expenditure Survey

Table 8.6 Amount Buyers Spent on Shelter and Utilities by Household Income, <u>Average Quarter</u>, 2008

(average amount spent by households buying shelter and utilities during the average quarter, by before-tax income of household, 2008)

	total households	under $20,000	$20,000–$39,999	$40,000–$49,999	$50,000–$69,999	$70,000–$79,999	$80,000–$99,999	$100,000 or more
SHELTER, AMOUNT SPENT	**$2,605.44**	**$1,439.82**	**$1,744.44**	**$2,168.80**	**$2,533.35**	**$2,915.08**	**$3,108.44**	**$4,881.39**
Owned dwellings*	**2,533.50**	**1,261.13**	**1,423.62**	**1,965.99**	**2,306.94**	**2,676.52**	**2,834.70**	**4,231.49**
Mortgage interest and charges	2,189.04	1,437.91	1,461.09	1,675.12	1,864.37	2,139.73	2,119.88	3,020.30
Mortgage interest	2,193.23	1,471.36	1,515.99	1,707.69	1,895.88	2,154.84	2,106.21	2,949.73
Interest paid, home equity loan	616.21	486.91	631.66	385.45	530.60	582.46	578.57	761.47
Interest paid, home equity line of credit	640.11	491.96	432.78	449.66	497.90	569.19	577.54	805.91
Property taxes	673.15	443.45	449.65	532.95	563.69	638.24	717.62	1,066.32
Maintenance, repairs, insurance, other expenses	833.11	711.11	626.65	714.08	782.64	754.36	783.98	1,137.23
Homeowner's insurance	374.60	352.93	342.28	328.86	344.76	350.58	365.99	448.58
Ground rent	794.22	708.77	795.88	752.15	967.29	977.47	762.66	960.00
Maintenance and repair services	1,316.72	989.02	807.42	1,081.46	1,382.54	1,198.69	1,167.89	1,818.66
Painting and papering	1,773.54	1,457.01	999.31	1,411.21	1,990.26	1,870.93	1,452.04	2,244.77
Plumbing and water heating	403.35	343.82	312.70	380.76	408.12	452.63	434.15	459.20
Heat, air conditioning, electrical work	711.70	624.77	654.76	656.33	698.29	524.37	674.65	855.94
Roofing and gutters	2,324.52	1,031.06	1,512.23	1,515.53	2,895.71	2,827.33	2,370.19	2,760.71
Other repair and maintenance services	1,546.99	1,253.92	707.18	1,255.01	1,630.42	1,324.36	1,082.73	2,327.40
Repair, replacement of hard-surface flooring	1,600.91	1,807.02	1,167.75	1,774.50	1,131.85	908.33	1,794.08	2,152.06
Repair of built-in appliances	188.33	184.68	259.87	183.33	198.13	169.32	118.75	200.00
Maintenance and repair materials	359.67	243.85	226.53	386.57	416.31	312.30	525.51	369.88
Paints, wallpaper, and supplies	152.65	116.12	135.07	150.19	157.58	117.27	186.46	158.04
Tools, equipment for painting, wallpapering	16.40	12.49	14.49	16.15	16.91	12.64	20.03	16.96
Plumbing supplies and equipment	182.39	120.27	113.01	203.02	177.94	150.51	195.26	258.64
Electrical supplies, heating and cooling equipment	185.61	81.74	116.69	821.43	130.49	106.88	190.63	250.49
Hard-surface flooring, repair and replacement	885.58	1,048.26	441.62	1,458.11	643.59	668.27	850.00	987.50
Roofing and gutters	977.17	292.72	792.48	593.00	1,136.36	572.58	2,223.04	477.63
Plaster, paneling, siding, windows, doors, screens, awnings	564.52	333.06	271.86	167.16	1,346.15	705.17	608.57	448.08
Patio, walk, fence, driveway, masonry, brick, and stucco materials	94.44	47.75	111.02	98.96	112.50	100.93	121.15	56.73
Miscellaneous supplies and equipment	290.31	140.32	184.40	235.63	233.56	240.16	451.18	355.06
Property management and security	284.88	339.38	256.59	235.56	249.64	222.62	311.94	309.72
Property management	249.01	294.01	213.67	198.97	225.11	203.07	288.51	267.35
Management and upkeep services for security	213.00	275.63	210.51	180.62	169.25	175.45	187.28	240.79
Parking	93.51	87.30	100.72	74.91	78.37	77.92	114.48	108.20
Rented dwellings	**2,125.82**	**1,533.53**	**1,993.44**	**2,238.05**	**2,570.27**	**2,890.06**	**3,086.10**	**4,323.60**
Rent	2,108.22	1,469.11	1,979.49	2,261.86	2,574.82	2,927.15	3,144.63	4,484.23
Rent as pay	1,352.02	1,275.06	1,312.20	1,278.80	1,594.48	1,991.67	2,429.17	2,468.75
Maintenance, insurance, and other expenses	228.70	164.61	218.44	151.63	202.13	323.60	191.55	437.74
Tenant's insurance	95.42	82.48	86.31	71.85	111.89	89.90	96.50	131.04
Maintenance and repair services	773.94	432.53	759.33	351.88	604.38	1,410.25	546.67	1,425.00
Maintenance and repair materials	325.63	185.63	342.44	432.33	244.55	291.57	255.92	837.12
Other lodging	**926.58**	**601.60**	**634.66**	**545.57**	**669.45**	**682.56**	**697.56**	**1,393.15**
Owned vacation homes	1,373.72	1,014.99	934.01	690.54	1,153.95	918.86	937.62	1,946.53
Mortgage interest and charges	2,060.03	1,620.11	1,582.50	1,005.71	1,402.78	1,840.43	1,118.99	2,678.93
Property taxes	482.87	436.92	404.89	394.63	438.41	316.50	424.03	583.88
Maintenance, insurance, and other expenses	805.33	356.50	496.87	365.28	1,002.81	632.17	731.49	968.23
Housing while attending school	1,880.22	1,565.95	1,409.07	2,557.45	981.86	1,658.87	1,442.61	2,121.75
Lodging on trips	577.09	369.49	406.90	393.23	427.52	452.58	506.32	823.54

	total households	under $20,000	$20,000– $39,999	$40,000– $49,999	$50,000– $69,999	$70,000– $79,999	$80,000– $99,999	$100,000 or more
UTILITIES, FUELS, AND PUBLIC SERVICES, AMOUNT SPENT	**$933.60**	**$612.84**	**$785.40**	**$876.96**	**$973.47**	**$1,066.82**	**$1,137.17**	**$1,315.34**
Natural gas	**266.79**	**222.01**	**246.50**	**256.95**	**255.87**	**270.85**	**282.78**	**315.19**
Electricity	**369.36**	**290.66**	**324.50**	**337.07**	**375.89**	**399.13**	**402.61**	**481.44**
Fuel oil and other fuels	**571.51**	**511.88**	**558.51**	**492.50**	**556.46**	**584.59**	**636.83**	**619.41**
Fuel oil	851.40	744.09	817.19	792.98	877.26	826.15	827.94	941.49
Coal, wood, and other fuels	414.86	282.34	395.39	356.41	415.26	872.69	416.85	368.24
Bottled gas	341.52	365.68	356.63	288.75	341.00	338.24	375.52	334.60
Telephone services	**303.44**	**203.80**	**249.77**	**292.24**	**327.30**	**343.68**	**370.59**	**407.95**
Residential telephone and pay phones	161.32	146.16	155.41	159.86	162.92	158.52	168.38	177.40
Cellular phone service	269.62	205.28	222.30	252.23	278.72	287.33	305.64	330.94
Phone cards	59.17	46.15	60.78	51.39	65.27	59.02	80.69	64.94
Voice over IP	116.17	133.83	118.84	119.40	121.82	112.44	123.39	107.41
Water and other public services	**178.03**	**155.13**	**158.83**	**166.47**	**173.65**	**175.94**	**189.89**	**212.03**
Water and sewerage maintenance	146.03	129.06	133.29	135.77	144.13	144.99	154.54	169.84
Trash and garbage collection	73.39	63.05	65.68	66.95	70.46	71.24	76.26	89.08
Septic tank cleaning	225.00	361.53	173.23	125.00	189.84	213.14	157.94	276.59

Amount does not include principal reduction, which is considered an asset.
Source: Calculations by New Strategist based on the Bureau of Labor Statistics' 2008 Consumer Expenditure Survey

Table 8.7 Percent Buying Utilities and Fuels by Household Income, <u>Average Week</u>, 2008

(percent of households buying utilities and fuels during the average week, by before-tax income of household, 2008)

	total households	under $20,000	$20,000– $39,999	$40,000– $49,999	$50,000– $69,999	$70,000– $79,999	$80,000– $99,999	$100,000 or more
UTILITIES AND FUELS, PERCENT BUYING	**34.9%**	**29.4%**	**32.6%**	**34.4%**	**36.1%**	**36.7%**	**40.1%**	**40.2%**
Electricity and natural gas	**21.7**	**17.6**	**20.2**	**22.4**	**22.2**	**23.1**	**24.0**	**25.3**
Electricity	17.6	14.5	16.7	18.7	18.2	19.0	19.5	19.3
Natural gas	9.9	7.0	8.6	9.4	9.7	9.7	12.2	14.7
Fuel oil and other fuels	**5.5**	**3.7**	**4.5**	**4.9**	**5.5**	**6.4**	**8.4**	**7.8**
Fuel oil	1.3	0.7	1.2	1.3	1.6	1.7	2.0	1.1
Bottled and tank gas	1.9	1.3	1.8	1.6	1.4	1.9	2.2	3.2
Coal	0.5	0.1	0.3	0.6	0.6	0.6	0.5	0.8
Miscellaneous fuels	2.7	1.8	1.8	2.3	3.0	3.4	4.5	4.1
Telephone services	**22.4**	**18.5**	**20.8**	**22.4**	**23.4**	**23.4**	**25.9**	**25.5**

Source: Bureau of Labor Statistics, unpublished data from the 2008 Consumer Expenditure Survey

Table 8.8 Amount Buyers Spent on Utilities and Fuels by Household Income, <u>Average Week</u>, 2008

(average amount spent by households buying utilities and fuels during the average week, by before-tax income of household, 2008)

	total households	under $20,000	$20,000– $39,999	$40,000– $49,999	$50,000– $69,999	$70,000– $79,999	$80,000– $99,999	$100,000 or more
UTILITIES AND FUELS, AMOUNT SPENT	**$184.62**	**$132.86**	**$176.74**	**$179.47**	**$174.31**	**$195.18**	**$210.46**	**$227.60**
Electricity and natural gas	**158.61**	**124.91**	**145.63**	**152.93**	**152.17**	**158.23**	**176.72**	**195.73**
Electricity	139.80	109.59	127.48	135.91	139.06	144.68	152.33	172.32
Natural gas	97.78	86.53	95.09	92.78	87.51	93.21	103.78	110.92
Fuel oil and other fuels	**125.87**	**81.82**	**204.82**	**119.18**	**71.38**	**140.65**	**138.62**	**108.75**
Fuel oil	303.97	127.50	481.75	216.92	129.03	368.86	375.12	290.83
Bottled and tank gas	112.30	118.35	120.07	116.13	84.06	103.21	120.91	118.81
Coal	60.87	28.50	32.77	40.35	57.89	58.18	168.09	55.00
Miscellaneous fuels	25.93	17.51	53.21	43.67	14.90	17.78	14.38	25.55
Telephone services	**103.61**	**76.66**	**92.09**	**97.01**	**107.91**	**111.40**	**117.14**	**130.71**

Source: Calculations by New Strategist based on the Bureau of Labor Statistics' 2008 Consumer Expenditure Survey

Table 8.9 Percent of High-Income Households Buying Shelter and Utilities, <u>Average Quarter</u>, 2008

(percent of high-income households buying shelter and utilities during the average quarter, by before-tax income of household, 2008)

	total households	$100,000 or more	$100,000– $119,999	$120,000– $149,999	$150,000 or more
SHELTER, PERCENT BUYING	**97.7%**	**99.7%**	**99.4%**	**99.8%**	**99.8%**
Owned dwellings	**66.7**	**92.3**	**90.4**	**93.4**	**93.2**
Mortgage interest and charges	43.7	76.9	76.2	77.6	77.0
Mortgage interest	40.8	73.1	72.4	73.7	73.3
Interest paid, home equity loan	4.2	7.9	7.9	9.1	7.1
Interest paid, home equity line of credit	5.5	13.2	11.6	12.2	15.1
Property taxes	65.3	91.8	89.6	93.2	92.8
Maintenance, repairs, insurance, other expenses	35.3	53.3	53.0	53.4	53.5
Homeowner's insurance	23.6	35.4	36.8	37.4	32.8
Ground rent	1.6	0.2	0.5	0.1	0.1
Maintenance and repair services	12.0	21.1	18.8	18.8	24.5
Painting and papering	1.0	2.2	1.5	1.7	2.9
Plumbing and water heating	3.4	5.9	5.4	5.3	6.7
Heat, air conditioning, electrical work	4.2	7.4	6.0	6.4	9.3
Roofing and gutters	1.0	1.7	1.5	1.5	1.9
Other repair and maintenance services	4.0	7.6	7.4	6.4	8.6
Repair, replacement of hard-surface flooring	0.6	1.0	0.8	0.8	1.2
Repair of built-in appliances	0.3	0.5	0.2	0.3	0.8
Maintenance and repair materials	4.9	7.7	8.0	8.0	7.4
Paints, wallpaper, and supplies	1.9	3.1	3.0	3.3	3.1
Tools, equipment for painting, wallpapering	1.9	3.1	3.0	3.3	3.1
Plumbing supplies and equipment	0.7	0.8	0.9	0.7	0.9
Electrical supplies, heating and cooling equipment	0.3	0.5	0.5	0.6	0.5
Hard-surface flooring, repair and replacement	0.3	0.5	0.3	0.9	0.3
Roofing and gutters	0.2	0.2	0.4	0.2	0.0
Plaster, paneling, siding, windows, doors, screens, awnings	0.6	0.9	1.1	0.9	0.8
Patio, walk, fence, driveway, masonry, brick, stucco materials	0.4	0.5	0.7	0.5	0.4
Miscellaneous supplies and equipment	1.5	2.7	3.0	2.3	2.8
Property management and security	5.3	9.7	9.2	9.9	9.9
Property management	5.0	9.1	8.8	9.3	9.2
Management and upkeep services for security	1.3	2.4	2.2	2.5	2.5
Parking	2.4	3.1	3.6	2.3	3.2
Rented dwellings	**32.0**	**9.5**	**11.3**	**8.2**	**8.8**
Rent	31.0	8.8	10.6	7.6	8.3
Rent as pay	1.4	0.1	0.1	0.1	0.1
Maintenance, insurance, and other expenses	3.9	2.6	2.8	2.1	2.9
Tenant's insurance	2.9	2.1	2.3	1.9	2.1
Maintenance and repair services	0.5	0.4	0.3	0.4	0.5
Maintenance and repair materials	0.8	0.3	0.3	–	0.6
Other lodging	**18.8**	**39.4**	**31.0**	**37.0**	**48.0**
Owned vacation homes	5.5	12.5	8.5	10.6	17.1
Mortgage interest and charges	1.7	4.7	2.4	4.5	6.7
Property taxes	5.2	12.0	8.1	9.6	16.8
Maintenance, insurance, and other expenses	2.0	4.9	2.5	5.0	6.9
Housing while attending school	0.9	2.9	2.1	1.4	4.6
Lodging on trips	14.2	29.6	23.1	28.8	35.4

	total households	$100,000 or more	$100,000– $119,999	$120,000– $149,999	$150,000 or more
UTILITIES, FUELS, AND PUBLIC SERVICES, PERCENT BUYING	**97.7%**	**99.6%**	**99.5%**	**99.8%**	**99.7%**
Natural gas	**49.8**	**65.6**	**59.7**	**66.0**	**70.0**
Electricity	**91.6**	**97.2**	**96.7**	**97.5**	**97.3**
Fuel oil and other fuels	**8.4**	**11.3**	**11.4**	**10.4**	**11.8**
Fuel oil	3.4	4.9	4.5	4.0	5.7
Coal, wood, and other fuels	0.7	0.9	1.0	1.1	0.6
Bottled gas	4.7	6.3	6.5	5.7	6.5
Telephone services	**92.8**	**97.3**	**97.0**	**97.3**	**97.5**
Residential telephone and pay phones	72.4	86.3	82.4	87.5	88.7
Cellular phone service	59.6	72.2	70.7	72.8	73.0
Phone cards	4.7	3.4	3.6	3.1	3.3
Voice over IP	1.3	2.6	3.1	2.7	2.2
Water and other public services	**62.6**	**79.9**	**78.0**	**80.8**	**80.8**
Water and sewerage maintenance	56.9	72.4	70.1	72.4	74.4
Trash and garbage collection	37.7	50.1	47.0	52.3	51.3
Septic tank cleaning	0.4	0.6	0.4	0.5	0.9

Note: "–" means sample is too small to make a reliable estimate.
Source: Bureau of Labor Statistics, unpublished data from the 2008 Consumer Expenditure Survey

Table 8.10 Amount High-Income Buyers Spent on Shelter and Utilities, <u>Average Quarter</u>, 2008

(average amount spent by high-income households buying shelter and utilities during the average quarter, by before-tax income of household, 2008)

	total households	$100,000 or more	$100,000–$119,999	$120,000–$149,999	$150,000 or more
SHELTER, AMOUNT SPENT	**$2,605.44**	**$4,881.39**	**$3,795.42**	**$4,197.36**	**$6,221.95**
Owned dwellings*	**2,533.50**	**4,231.49**	**3,366.86**	**3,691.77**	**5,278.04**
Mortgage interest and charges	2,189.04	3,020.30	2,511.80	2,741.22	3,619.20
Mortgage interest	2,193.23	2,949.73	2,485.21	2,666.03	3,515.50
Interest paid, home equity loan	616.21	761.47	737.45	705.32	830.74
Interest paid, home equity line of credit	640.11	805.91	494.89	802.23	1,003.85
Property taxes	673.15	1,066.32	773.82	891.27	1,414.80
Maintenance, repairs, insurance, other expenses	833.11	1,137.23	824.59	920.51	1,534.91
Homeowner's insurance	374.60	448.58	396.88	427.71	512.01
Ground rent	794.22	960.00	1,001.02	288.89	1,150.00
Maintenance and repair services	1,316.72	1,818.66	1,271.61	1,450.12	2,351.85
Painting and papering	1,773.54	2,244.77	1,597.53	1,312.50	2,884.52
Plumbing and water heating	403.35	459.20	266.45	419.09	606.02
Heat, air conditioning, electrical work	711.70	855.94	544.20	860.36	1,020.84
Roofing and gutters	2,324.52	2,760.71	2,204.14	4,016.28	2,455.05
Other repair and maintenance services	1,546.99	2,327.40	1,682.28	1,498.36	3,200.96
Repair, replacement of hard-surface flooring	1,600.91	2,152.06	1,254.75	1,842.26	2,764.26
Repair of built-in appliances	188.33	200.00	348.96	115.91	184.94
Maintenance and repair materials	359.67	369.88	306.16	369.19	426.33
Paints, wallpaper, and supplies	152.65	158.04	167.68	140.21	162.98
Tools, equipment for painting, wallpapering	16.40	16.96	18.01	15.06	17.47
Plumbing supplies and equipment	182.39	258.64	145.64	279.62	341.67
Electrical supplies, heating and cooling equipment	185.61	250.49	188.00	427.82	143.33
Hard-surface flooring, repair and replacement	885.58	987.50	390.83	1,147.04	1,166.41
Roofing and gutters	977.17	477.63	519.23	439.71	243.75
Plaster, paneling, siding, windows, doors, screens, awnings	564.52	448.08	378.33	192.02	727.56
Patio, walk, fence, driveway, masonry, brick, stucco materials	94.44	56.73	47.18	22.06	104.05
Miscellaneous supplies and equipment	290.31	355.06	304.32	281.33	440.34
Property management and security	284.88	309.72	213.33	262.60	414.26
Property management	249.01	267.35	171.77	210.64	380.33
Management and upkeep services for security	213.00	240.79	205.16	256.93	254.86
Parking	93.51	108.20	81.27	112.45	130.76
Rented dwellings	**2,125.82**	**4,323.60**	**3,501.48**	**4,246.66**	**5,238.20**
Rent	2,108.22	4,484.23	3,695.83	4,459.61	5,322.73
Rent as pay	1,352.02	2,468.75	4,145.83	2,666.67	925.00
Maintenance, insurance, and other expenses	228.70	437.74	155.96	436.84	664.07
Tenant's insurance	95.42	131.04	118.80	163.24	122.66
Maintenance and repair services	773.94	1,425.00	207.26	1,608.55	1,903.70
Maintenance and repair materials	325.63	837.12	296.09	–	1,087.05
Other lodging	**926.58**	**1,393.15**	**1,071.28**	**1,056.28**	**1,736.39**
Owned vacation homes	1,373.72	1,946.53	1,715.74	1,790.20	2,105.18
Mortgage interest and charges	2,060.03	2,678.93	3,307.08	2,332.43	2,649.22
Property taxes	482.87	583.88	516.82	429.18	668.82
Maintenance, insurance, and other expenses	805.33	968.23	1,006.55	872.80	1,001.46
Housing while attending school	1,880.22	2,121.75	2,876.56	1,302.74	2,007.31
Lodging on trips	577.09	823.54	545.69	633.46	1,074.65

	total households	$100,000 or more	$100,000–$119,999	$120,000–$149,999	$150,000 or more
UTILITIES, FUELS, AND PUBLIC SERVICES, AMOUNT SPENT	**$933.60**	**$1,315.34**	**$1,163.75**	**$1,273.62**	**$1,466.95**
Natural gas	**266.79**	**315.19**	**285.22**	**293.68**	**349.62**
Electricity	**369.36**	**481.44**	**423.25**	**466.07**	**539.06**
Fuel oil and other fuels	**571.51**	**619.41**	**670.47**	**539.68**	**625.68**
Fuel oil	851.40	941.49	958.19	872.33	965.06
Coal, wood, and other fuels	414.86	368.24	445.53	358.49	279.92
Bottled gas	341.52	334.60	439.76	298.59	269.23
Telephone services	**303.44**	**407.95**	**365.71**	**410.74**	**440.59**
Residential telephone and pay phones	161.32	177.40	163.79	172.89	190.72
Cellular phone service	269.62	330.94	302.72	334.89	350.70
Phone cards	59.17	64.94	59.16	61.86	72.30
Voice over IP	116.17	107.41	116.21	92.03	110.37
Water and other public services	**178.03**	**212.03**	**189.22**	**206.32**	**233.88**
Water and sewerage maintenance	146.03	169.84	154.95	165.43	184.16
Trash and garbage collection	73.39	89.08	80.32	87.84	96.49
Septic tank cleaning	225.00	276.59	293.90	216.67	292.98

* Amount does not include principal reduction, which is considered an asset.
Note: "–" means sample is too small to make a reliable estimate.
Source: Calculations by New Strategist based on the Bureau of Labor Statistics' 2008 Consumer Expenditure Survey

Table 8.11 Percent of High-Income Households Buying Utilities and Fuels, Average Week, 2008

(percent of high-income households buying utilities and fuels during the average week, by before-tax income of household, 2008)

	total households	$100,000 or more	$100,000– $119,999	$120,000– $149,999	$150,000 or more
UTILITIES AND FUELS, PERCENT BUYING	**34.9%**	**40.2%**	**40.7%**	**41.3%**	**38.7%**
Electricity and natural gas	**21.7**	**25.3**	**24.7**	**24.8**	**26.3**
Electricity	17.6	19.3	19.1	18.5	20.3
Natural gas	9.9	14.7	14.0	14.7	15.2
Fuel oil and other fuels	**5.5**	**7.8**	**7.4**	**8.2**	**7.9**
Fuel oil	1.3	1.1	1.3	1.3	0.7
Bottled and tank gas	1.9	3.2	2.9	3.3	3.4
Coal	0.5	0.8	0.9	0.6	0.9
Miscellaneous fuels	2.7	4.1	3.8	3.9	4.5
Telephone services	**22.4**	**25.5**	**26.1**	**26.8**	**24.0**

Source: Bureau of Labor Statistics, unpublished data from the 2008 Consumer Expenditure Survey

Table 8.12 Amount High-Income Buyers Spent on Utilities and Fuels, Average Week, 2008

(average amount spent by high-income households buying utilities and fuels during the average week, by before-tax income of household, 2008)

	total households	$100,000 or more	$100,000– $119,999	$120,000– $149,999	$150,000 or more
UTILITIES AND FUELS, AMOUNT SPENT	**$184.62**	**$227.60**	**$209.58**	**$227.41**	**$247.36**
Electricity and natural gas	**158.61**	**195.73**	**180.19**	**196.42**	**210.46**
Electricity	139.80	172.32	161.89	173.53	181.59
Natural gas	97.78	110.92	98.00	113.09	121.73
Fuel oil and other fuels	**125.87**	**108.75**	**78.37**	**157.96**	**97.58**
Fuel oil	303.97	290.83	202.34	425.76	258.33
Bottled and tank gas	112.30	118.81	56.06	166.37	138.58
Coal	60.87	55.00	51.16	69.49	52.22
Miscellaneous fuels	25.93	25.55	29.63	36.79	14.79
Telephone services	**103.61**	**130.71**	**134.07**	**120.02**	**136.32**

Source: Calculations by New Strategist based on the Bureau of Labor Statistics' 2008 Consumer Expenditure Survey

Table 8.13 Percent Buying Shelter and Utilities by Household Type, <u>Average Quarter</u>, 2008

(percent of households buying shelter and utilities during the average quarter, by type of household, 2008)

	total married couples	married couples, no children	married couples with children				single parent, at least one child <18	single person
			total	oldest child under 6	oldest child 6 to 17	oldest child 18 or older		
SHELTER, PERCENT BUYING	99.2%	99.3%	99.2%	98.5%	99.3%	99.4%	96.1%	95.2%
Owned dwellings	83.2	86.0	81.5	67.2	82.5	88.4	41.0	49.3
Mortgage interest and charges	58.4	48.4	67.6	61.7	71.5	64.4	33.3	24.8
Mortgage interest	54.5	42.9	65.1	61.2	70.0	58.9	32.4	22.9
Interest paid, home equity loan	5.9	4.9	6.7	4.6	7.1	7.4	1.8	2.2
Interest paid, home equity line of credit	8.0	8.0	8.1	6.5	8.1	9.2	3.1	2.7
Property taxes	82.0	84.7	80.5	66.1	81.7	86.9	39.9	47.4
Maintenance, repairs, insurance, other expenses	44.3	45.8	43.6	38.7	44.7	44.5	21.6	25.8
Homeowner's insurance	31.2	31.4	31.3	27.9	31.8	32.3	13.6	15.2
Ground rent	1.2	1.2	1.2	1.4	1.4	0.6	1.6	2.2
Maintenance and repair services	13.9	16.3	12.2	10.4	12.6	12.6	7.1	10.7
Painting and papering	1.3	1.5	1.1	1.1	1.1	1.2	0.6	0.9
Plumbing and water heating	3.7	4.6	3.0	2.9	3.1	3.0	2.1	3.5
Heat, air conditioning, electrical work	5.0	5.9	4.4	4.3	4.5	4.2	3.1	3.7
Roofing and gutters	1.3	1.6	1.0	1.0	0.9	1.4	0.5	0.7
Other repair and maintenance services	4.7	5.7	3.9	3.2	4.1	3.8	2.1	3.6
Repair, replacement of hard-surface flooring	0.7	0.8	0.6	0.3	0.5	0.9	0.3	0.4
Repair of built-in appliances	0.4	0.4	0.4	0.1	0.5	0.5	0.2	0.2
Maintenance and repair materials	6.7	6.7	6.9	7.7	6.6	6.9	3.0	2.5
Paints, wallpaper, and supplies	2.8	2.6	3.0	3.4	3.0	2.8	1.3	0.7
Tools, equipment for painting, wallpapering	2.8	2.6	3.0	3.4	3.0	2.8	1.3	0.7
Plumbing supplies and equipment	0.8	1.0	0.8	0.6	0.8	0.8	0.5	0.4
Electrical supplies, heating and cooling equipment	0.4	0.4	0.4	0.5	0.4	0.5	0.1	0.3
Hard-surface flooring, repair and replacement	0.4	0.4	0.3	0.4	0.3	0.2	0.2	0.1
Roofing and gutters	0.3	0.3	0.3	0.2	0.2	0.7	0.0	0.1
Plaster, paneling, siding, windows, doors, screens, awnings	0.9	1.0	0.8	1.0	0.8	0.7	0.2	0.3
Patio, walk, fence, driveway, masonry, brick, and stucco materials	0.6	0.7	0.5	0.8	0.5	0.5	0.1	0.1
Miscellaneous supplies and equipment	1.9	2.0	1.9	2.5	1.7	1.7	1.0	0.8
Property management and security	5.3	6.3	4.6	5.4	5.2	3.0	3.1	6.5
Property management	5.0	5.9	4.4	5.4	4.9	2.8	2.9	6.0
Management and upkeep services for security	1.1	1.6	0.7	0.5	1.0	0.3	0.5	1.8
Parking	2.0	2.7	1.5	3.2	1.3	0.8	1.4	3.5
Rented dwellings	17.1	14.4	18.9	32.9	18.0	12.1	55.8	47.0
Rent	16.3	13.4	18.2	32.0	17.3	11.4	54.7	45.5
Rent as pay	0.6	0.6	0.6	1.1	0.4	0.5	3.5	2.3
Maintenance, insurance, and other expenses	2.9	2.7	3.4	6.5	3.2	2.0	4.9	5.0
Tenant's insurance	2.2	2.0	2.6	5.3	2.4	1.4	3.7	3.8
Maintenance and repair services	0.4	0.4	0.5	0.7	0.5	0.4	0.6	0.6
Maintenance and repair materials	0.6	0.5	0.7	0.9	0.7	0.4	1.0	0.9
Other lodging	25.4	28.7	23.4	17.1	24.0	26.2	11.0	12.0
Owned vacation homes	8.1	10.7	6.0	2.1	6.2	7.9	1.5	2.7
Mortgage interest and charges	2.3	2.9	1.9	0.7	1.9	2.5	0.5	0.8
Property taxes	7.7	10.2	5.5	1.9	5.7	7.4	1.2	2.6
Maintenance, insurance, and other expenses	2.9	4.1	1.9	0.8	1.7	3.0	0.7	0.8
Housing while attending school	1.3	1.2	1.6	0.6	0.9	3.4	0.4	0.6
Lodging on trips	18.8	20.5	18.2	14.8	19.0	18.9	9.7	9.3

	total married couples	married couples, no children	married couples with children				single parent, at least one child <18	single person
			total	oldest child under 6	oldest child 6 to 17	oldest child 18 or older		
UTILITIES, FUELS, AND PUBLIC SERVICES, PERCENT BUYING	99.6%	99.5%	99.8%	99.6%	99.8%	99.9%	97.5%	93.8%
Natural gas	56.0	53.5	58.2	53.0	58.4	61.1	42.3	40.6
Electricity	96.6	96.7	96.6	94.2	97.1	97.0	89.0	82.8
Fuel oil and other fuels	10.9	12.7	9.5	9.6	10.0	8.6	5.4	5.4
Fuel oil	4.1	4.8	3.6	3.6	3.6	3.5	2.3	2.6
Coal, wood, and other fuels	1.0	1.2	0.8	0.6	0.6	1.2	0.4	0.4
Bottled gas	6.4	7.4	5.7	5.7	6.3	4.7	3.0	2.6
Telephone services	96.9	96.8	97.1	94.4	97.6	97.6	91.9	85.6
Residential telephone and pay phones	83.5	85.7	82.0	67.3	82.9	89.2	59.2	59.8
Cellular phone service	65.5	59.7	70.2	69.5	70.4	70.1	63.7	46.0
Phone cards	5.2	4.3	5.4	6.6	4.9	5.5	4.2	3.2
Voice over IP	1.6	1.3	1.9	2.8	1.8	1.7	1.6	0.9
Water and other public services	73.7	72.4	75.1	68.9	75.5	78.1	52.8	46.6
Water and sewerage maintenance	66.6	65.2	67.6	63.0	67.7	70.2	48.3	42.6
Trash and garbage collection	46.0	43.9	48.0	40.0	50.7	48.2	30.8	26.1
Septic tank cleaning	0.6	0.6	0.6	0.4	0.6	0.7	–	0.2

Note: "–" means sample is too small to make a reliable estimate.
Source: Bureau of Labor Statistics, unpublished data from the 2008 Consumer Expenditure Survey

Table 8.14 Amount Buyers Spent on Shelter and Utilities by Household Type, <u>Average Quarter</u>, 2008

(average amount spent by households buying shelter and utilities during the average quarter, by type of household, 2008)

	total married couples	married couples, no children	married couples with children — total	oldest child under 6	oldest child 6 to 17	oldest child 18 or older	single parent, at least one child <18	single person
SHELTER, AMOUNT SPENT	**$3,047.98**	**$2,640.99**	**$3,413.96**	**$3,527.44**	**$3,639.88**	**$2,958.42**	**$2,324.85**	**$1,972.93**
Owned dwellings*	**2,803.50**	**2,271.66**	**3,294.16**	**3,790.27**	**3,559.79**	**2,643.06**	**2,650.05**	**1,871.17**
Mortgage interest and charges	2,312.71	1,925.30	2,539.34	2,951.65	2,717.93	1,962.55	2,120.05	1,826.32
Mortgage interest	2,318.73	1,996.93	2,492.25	2,842.37	2,635.43	1,982.05	2,087.53	1,855.44
Interest paid, home equity loan	582.08	545.22	561.74	563.29	592.99	510.05	589.20	624.89
Interest paid, home equity line of credit	671.69	592.71	704.37	868.07	700.34	642.55	618.18	493.77
Property taxes	735.33	694.06	783.40	767.95	804.93	755.27	647.81	540.59
Maintenance, repairs, insurance, other expenses	854.56	946.44	778.59	563.37	751.93	936.20	566.13	824.76
Homeowner's insurance	388.23	432.79	348.61	291.40	345.55	383.29	284.00	352.98
Ground rent	801.72	950.00	703.91	677.97	675.18	851.82	691.35	760.92
Maintenance and repair services	1,481.55	1,464.90	1,512.70	913.38	1,412.55	1,982.13	752.47	1,063.71
Painting and papering	2,067.91	2,363.79	1,832.08	1,034.86	2,316.74	1,488.79	1,548.18	1,187.93
Plumbing and water heating	380.49	386.51	365.13	239.88	336.50	492.20	540.42	390.64
Heat, air conditioning, electrical work	805.70	932.90	686.24	517.12	533.87	1,066.17	373.77	620.23
Roofing and gutters	2,513.08	2,090.55	3,080.77	589.36	3,802.01	3,390.00	1,294.61	1,647.01
Other repair and maintenance services	1,719.26	1,500.13	1,981.33	1,426.95	1,750.66	2,698.75	488.78	1,416.90
Repair, replacement of hard-surface flooring	1,799.62	1,414.10	2,325.00	888.64	2,475.00	2,450.53	1,645.83	1,092.61
Repair of built-in appliances	219.23	252.56	194.89	40.00	203.24	185.29	113.10	87.50
Maintenance and repair materials	382.62	349.17	399.53	299.06	382.65	494.59	213.08	257.50
Paints, wallpaper, and supplies	161.23	168.68	145.65	148.24	165.08	108.63	128.13	97.92
Tools, equipment for painting, wallpapering	17.30	18.10	15.64	15.91	17.71	11.65	13.67	10.42
Plumbing supplies and equipment	216.07	174.74	232.57	132.14	145.31	437.01	61.76	101.74
Electrical supplies, heating and cooling equipment	193.45	228.95	153.98	173.04	182.69	103.13	155.00	215.18
Hard-surface flooring, repair and replacement	850.00	578.38	1,128.33	312.14	1,475.78	1,017.71	1,005.68	940.91
Roofing and gutters	1,098.39	300.00	1,666.13	78.13	1,355.88	2,015.00	137.50	700.00
Plaster, paneling, siding, windows, doors, screens, awnings	638.64	676.01	648.17	670.67	638.27	653.93	90.00	476.85
Patio, walk, fence, driveway, masonry, brick, and stucco materials	100.85	89.55	109.31	88.49	75.56	184.57	8.33	72.73
Miscellaneous supplies and equipment	288.99	273.63	314.30	269.57	314.88	351.89	182.32	182.59
Property management and security	277.08	333.77	199.73	144.85	242.49	129.49	383.31	288.76
Property management	245.91	297.15	177.11	135.25	211.71	120.42	395.52	240.31
Management and upkeep services for security	208.71	229.35	184.72	97.17	208.50	129.03	84.18	231.53
Parking	100.51	120.96	71.98	50.47	67.58	131.85	98.18	94.67
Rented dwellings	**2,557.25**	**2,467.17**	**2,584.98**	**2,484.96**	**2,612.37**	**2,680.89**	**1,920.24**	**1,850.88**
Rent	2,576.30	2,511.76	2,591.58	2,481.26	2,637.07	2,660.24	1,839.68	1,830.31
Rent as pay	1,484.82	1,409.43	1,437.95	1,282.37	1,275.68	1,858.80	1,582.83	1,222.33
Maintenance, insurance, and other expenses	298.47	348.05	257.87	160.42	255.90	454.06	189.78	189.46
Tenant's insurance	115.78	140.70	98.65	78.61	115.53	95.66	65.09	83.24
Maintenance and repair services	971.34	1,387.84	725.53	347.31	847.28	835.90	118.22	619.58
Maintenance and repair materials	400.00	291.33	441.15	458.52	220.27	1,231.43	622.98	284.34
Other lodging	**1,001.65**	**1,094.32**	**910.45**	**648.42**	**869.19**	**1,077.41**	**686.28**	**720.35**
Owned vacation homes	1,318.36	1,475.63	1,068.56	904.91	1,011.73	1,172.72	1,848.97	1,366.07
Mortgage interest and charges	2,139.01	2,546.68	1,690.19	1,336.49	1,706.28	1,725.31	2,105.21	1,911.39
Property taxes	467.29	506.21	411.75	344.92	412.72	420.31	742.07	499.22
Maintenance, insurance, and other expenses	744.67	825.98	510.13	368.90	376.20	662.16	1,176.52	1,077.56
Housing while attending school	1,994.40	1,878.21	2,065.99	4,709.52	2,087.50	1,758.51	408.55	1,441.53
Lodging on trips	637.67	653.26	638.07	417.28	665.95	692.40	481.80	445.57

	total married couples	married couples, no children	married couples with children				single parent, at least one child <18	single person
			total	oldest child under 6	oldest child 6 to 17	oldest child 18 or older		
UTILITIES, FUELS, AND PUBLIC SERVICES, AMOUNT SPENT	**$1,120.29**	**$1,011.35**	**$1,191.52**	**$971.31**	**$1,207.41**	**$1,294.70**	**$849.72**	**$603.42**
Natural gas	**293.25**	**279.49**	**302.55**	**262.07**	**307.36**	**315.57**	**249.12**	**208.85**
Electricity	**426.57**	**380.08**	**453.38**	**368.33**	**464.88**	**482.67**	**366.05**	**251.31**
Fuel oil and other fuels	**554.86**	**589.74**	**513.20**	**526.52**	**482.00**	**568.17**	**494.14**	**603.47**
Fuel oil	837.16	840.32	844.48	837.47	802.72	926.84	834.38	864.24
Coal, wood, and other fuels	489.84	549.78	431.67	333.77	568.97	341.52	221.15	185.63
Bottled gas	336.76	387.31	269.51	320.42	260.46	253.82	212.88	366.70
Telephone services	**348.49**	**295.94**	**386.24**	**329.78**	**379.30**	**430.76**	**305.21**	**205.10**
Residential telephone and pay phones	169.15	164.33	172.34	162.28	169.70	181.07	162.11	138.96
Cellular phone service	292.56	237.89	325.17	281.19	319.23	361.41	284.34	195.00
Phone cards	56.68	45.85	59.38	60.05	63.01	53.09	48.15	50.62
Voice over IP	115.78	112.11	117.91	101.51	99.17	170.15	95.55	125.59
Water and other public services	**192.64**	**177.30**	**200.93**	**173.52**	**205.28**	**208.08**	**170.56**	**139.37**
Water and sewerage maintenance	157.80	144.27	165.55	143.22	168.37	172.75	144.37	113.48
Trash and garbage collection	77.55	75.47	78.67	71.58	78.69	82.13	66.02	62.88
Septic tank cleaning	217.73	219.20	218.10	191.45	202.50	257.31	–	123.33

Amount does not include principal reduction, which is considered an asset.
Note: "–" means sample is too small to make a reliable estimate.
Source: Calculations by New Strategist based on the Bureau of Labor Statistics' 2008 Consumer Expenditure Survey

Table 8.15 Percent Buying Utilities and Fuels by Household Type, Average Week, 2008

(percent of households buying utilities and fuels during the average week, by type of household, 2008)

| | total married couples | married couples, no children | married couples with children | | | | single parent, at least one child <18 | single person |
			total	oldest child under 6	oldest child 6 to 17	oldest child 18 or older		
UTILITIES AND FUELS, PERCENT BUYING	**37.2%**	**35.9%**	**37.9%**	**38.5%**	**36.6%**	**39.9%**	**33.5%**	**30.9%**
Electricity and natural gas	**23.3**	**23.1**	**23.3**	**24.9**	**21.8**	**24.9**	**21.8**	**18.9**
Electricity	18.7	18.6	18.6	19.4	17.6	19.9	17.7	15.7
Natural gas	11.1	11.0	11.2	12.9	10.0	12.1	9.7	7.9
Fuel oil and other fuels	**6.6**	**6.3**	**7.0**	**5.3**	**7.2**	**7.8**	**3.6**	**3.9**
Fuel oil	1.5	1.4	1.5	0.5	1.5	2.2	0.8	1.0
Bottled and tank gas	2.3	2.3	2.5	2.9	2.6	2.1	1.1	1.4
Coal	0.5	0.6	0.5	0.6	0.5	0.3	0.5	0.4
Miscellaneous fuels	3.3	3.1	3.4	2.4	3.6	3.7	2.1	1.8
Telephone services	**23.9**	**22.4**	**24.9**	**24.3**	**24.3**	**26.4**	**21.8**	**19.8**

Source: Bureau of Labor Statistics, unpublished data from the 2008 Consumer Expenditure Survey

Table 8.16 Amount Buyers Spent on Utilities and Fuels by Household Type, Average Week, 2008

(average amount spent by households buying utilities and fuels during the average week, by type of household, 2008)

| | total married couples | married couples, no children | married couples with children | | | | single parent, at least one child <18 | single person |
			total	oldest child under 6	oldest child 6 to 17	oldest child 18 or older		
UTILITIES AND FUELS, AMOUNT SPENT	**$204.97**	**$181.05**	**$218.53**	**$194.31**	**$221.04**	**$229.36**	**$181.25**	**$141.16**
Electricity and natural gas	**173.86**	**154.20**	**184.27**	**169.79**	**191.32**	**182.44**	**157.93**	**118.73**
Electricity	154.82	133.42	168.28	152.86	177.66	163.06	143.71	100.70
Natural gas	104.78	98.91	104.21	97.37	104.80	108.08	91.35	82.93
Fuel oil and other fuels	**125.60**	**136.25**	**103.56**	**64.19**	**90.44**	**142.42**	**78.18**	**153.89**
Fuel oil	302.03	352.08	234.21	10.00	196.62	313.06	236.14	309.28
Bottled and tank gas	113.30	95.15	104.40	58.97	110.89	130.33	36.79	158.52
Coal	67.31	46.77	93.75	232.76	57.69	39.39	48.89	54.29
Miscellaneous fuels	27.08	34.09	19.58	10.97	13.13	34.25	12.08	34.08
Telephone services	**114.93**	**92.68**	**131.07**	**120.45**	**134.20**	**132.08**	**108.18**	**77.32**

Source: Calculations by New Strategist based on the Bureau of Labor Statistics' 2008 Consumer Expenditure Survey

Table 8.17 Percent Buying Shelter and Utilities by Race and Hispanic Origin, Average Quarter, 2008

(percent of households buying shelter and utilities during the average quarter, by race and Hispanic origin of householder, 2008)

	total households	Asian	black	Hispanic	non-Hispanic white and other
SHELTER, PERCENT BUYING	**97.7%**	**97.4%**	**97.0%**	**98.0%**	**97.8%**
Owned dwellings	**66.7**	**54.9**	**46.3**	**51.6**	**72.2**
Mortgage interest and charges	43.7	42.3	31.7	36.5	46.7
Mortgage interest	40.8	41.6	31.0	35.5	43.2
Interest paid, home equity loan	4.2	1.6	1.9	2.6	4.8
Interest paid, home equity line of credit	5.5	3.5	1.1	1.8	6.7
Property taxes	65.3	54.2	44.8	50.6	70.8
Maintenance, repairs, insurance, other expenses	35.3	27.2	21.5	23.0	39.3
Homeowner's insurance	23.6	15.8	14.7	13.8	26.5
Ground rent	1.6	0.3	0.9	2.0	1.7
Maintenance and repair services	12.0	12.8	6.8	5.8	13.7
Painting and papering	1.0	0.7	0.8	0.5	1.2
Plumbing and water heating	3.4	3.8	2.0	1.4	4.0
Heat, air conditioning, electrical work	4.2	5.3	2.1	2.1	4.9
Roofing and gutters	1.0	0.7	0.6	0.6	1.2
Other repair and maintenance services	4.0	3.8	1.8	1.9	4.7
Repair, replacement of hard-surface flooring	0.6	0.4	0.6	0.3	0.6
Repair of built-in appliances	0.3	0.2	0.3	0.1	0.3
Maintenance and repair materials	4.9	2.1	2.2	3.7	5.6
Paints, wallpaper, and supplies	1.9	0.8	0.8	1.5	2.1
Tools, equipment for painting, wallpapering	1.9	0.8	0.8	1.5	2.1
Plumbing supplies and equipment	0.7	0.2	0.4	0.4	0.8
Electrical supplies, heating and cooling equipment	0.3	0.1	0.2	0.3	0.4
Hard-surface flooring, repair and replacement	0.3	0.2	0.2	0.3	0.3
Roofing and gutters	0.2	–	0.1	0.1	0.3
Plaster, paneling, siding, windows, doors, screens, awnings	0.6	0.1	0.2	0.7	0.7
Patio, walk, fence, driveway, masonry, brick, stucco materials	0.4	–	0.1	0.3	0.4
Miscellaneous supplies and equipment	1.5	0.7	0.5	0.9	1.7
Property management and security	5.3	9.3	2.4	3.1	6.2
Property management	5.0	9.0	2.4	3.0	5.8
Management and upkeep services for security	1.3	2.1	0.3	0.6	1.5
Parking	2.4	5.4	0.8	2.0	2.7
Rented dwellings	**32.0**	**42.7**	**51.4**	**47.1**	**26.7**
Rent	31.0	42.5	50.5	45.6	25.7
Rent as pay	1.4	1.6	2.8	2.4	1.0
Maintenance, insurance, and other expenses	3.9	4.0	4.1	2.6	4.1
Tenant's insurance	2.9	3.6	2.9	1.3	3.1
Maintenance and repair services	0.5	–	0.7	0.6	0.4
Maintenance and repair materials	0.8	0.4	0.9	0.9	0.8
Other lodging	**18.8**	**16.8**	**8.6**	**9.8**	**21.8**
Owned vacation homes	5.5	2.6	2.1	2.5	6.5
Mortgage interest and charges	1.7	0.6	0.9	1.1	1.9
Property taxes	5.2	2.5	2.1	2.4	6.1
Maintenance, insurance, and other expenses	2.0	1.3	0.7	0.6	2.4
Housing while attending school	0.9	1.3	0.3	0.3	1.1
Lodging on trips	14.2	13.6	6.5	7.5	16.5

	total households	Asian	black	Hispanic	non-Hispanic white and other
UTILITIES, FUELS, AND PUBLIC SERVICES, PERCENT BUYING	**97.7%**	**98.5%**	**97.6%**	**98.0%**	**97.7%**
Natural gas	**49.8**	**57.4**	**43.7**	**51.5**	**50.5**
Electricity	**91.6**	**90.5**	**89.9**	**89.0**	**92.3**
Fuel oil and other fuels	**8.4**	**2.2**	**2.9**	**4.3**	**9.9**
Fuel oil	3.4	1.5	1.4	1.2	4.0
Coal, wood, and other fuels	0.7	0.1	0.5	0.3	0.8
Bottled gas	4.7	0.7	1.1	2.8	5.5
Telephone services	**92.8**	**93.9**	**91.3**	**93.9**	**92.9**
Residential telephone and pay phones	72.4	66.1	68.9	65.6	73.9
Cellular phone service	59.6	65.2	54.7	63.3	59.8
Phone cards	4.7	14.7	3.0	15.5	3.3
Voice over IP	1.3	3.2	1.0	1.1	1.4
Water and other public services	**62.6**	**55.7**	**55.4**	**56.6**	**64.7**
Water and sewerage maintenance	56.9	53.1	53.7	54.4	57.7
Trash and garbage collection	37.7	33.7	27.4	36.3	39.5
Septic tank cleaning	0.4	–	0.0	0.2	0.4

Note: "Asian" and "black" include Hispanics and non-Hispanics who identify themselves as being of the respective race alone. "Hispanic" includes people of any race who identify themselves as Hispanic. "Other" includes people who identify themselves as non-Hispanic and as Alaska Native, American Indian, Asian (who are also included in the Asian column), or Native Hawaiian or other Pacific Islander as well as non-Hispanics reporting more than one race. "–" means sample is too small to make a reliable estimate.
Source: Bureau of Labor Statistics, unpublished data from the 2008 Consumer Expenditure Survey

Table 8.18 Amount Buyers Spent on Shelter and Utilities by Race and Hispanic Origin, Average Quarter, 2008

(average amount spent by households buying shelter and utilities during the average quarter, by race and Hispanic origin of householder, 2008)

	total households	Asian	black	Hispanic	non-Hispanic white and other
SHELTER, AMOUNT SPENT	**$2,605.44**	**$3,516.92**	**$2,057.34**	**$2,472.49**	**$2,712.92**
Owned dwellings*	**2,533.50**	**3,861.00**	**2,126.30**	**2,583.38**	**2,571.14**
Mortgage interest and charges	2,189.04	3,239.69	1,944.45	2,412.62	2,190.14
Mortgage interest	2,193.23	3,115.92	1,936.71	2,401.17	2,198.21
Interest paid, home equity loan	616.21	3,098.13	518.36	655.20	619.19
Interest paid, home equity line of credit	640.11	712.25	565.13	667.08	641.07
Property taxes	673.15	999.66	500.05	600.96	698.71
Maintenance, repairs, insurance, other expenses	833.11	756.61	676.75	642.70	863.08
Homeowner's insurance	374.60	367.56	352.81	389.34	375.68
Ground rent	794.22	850.00	450.82	792.91	821.39
Maintenance and repair services	1,316.72	843.26	1,064.68	1,004.03	1,355.47
Painting and papering	1,773.54	2,502.90	1,581.71	1,905.32	1,780.87
Plumbing and water heating	403.35	351.31	455.56	324.65	403.15
Heat, air conditioning, electrical work	711.70	662.52	436.85	360.19	753.02
Roofing and gutters	2,324.52	2,592.75	1,606.25	1,204.69	2,486.21
Other repair and maintenance services	1,546.99	588.46	1,322.29	1,320.19	1,571.41
Repair, replacement of hard-surface flooring	1,600.91	479.49	1,158.90	1,357.81	1,685.34
Repair of built-in appliances	188.33	81.25	168.00	82.14	194.85
Maintenance and repair materials	359.67	324.28	440.77	375.41	352.56
Paints, wallpaper, and supplies	152.65	253.66	161.73	213.40	145.62
Tools, equipment for painting, wallpapering	16.40	27.13	17.28	22.88	15.64
Plumbing supplies and equipment	182.39	102.63	80.63	344.51	176.54
Electrical supplies, heating and cooling equipment	185.61	420.83	429.41	126.52	177.86
Hard-surface flooring, repair and replacement	885.58	1,261.25	470.00	813.79	908.93
Roofing and gutters	977.17	–	2,141.67	436.36	945.19
Plaster, paneling, siding, windows, doors, screens, awnings	564.52	128.57	750.00	358.33	589.55
Patio, walk, fence, driveway, masonry, brick, stucco materials	94.44	–	92.50	134.38	91.25
Miscellaneous supplies and equipment	290.31	179.05	454.72	296.47	280.09
Property management and security	284.88	286.30	286.67	169.07	292.90
Property management	249.01	254.48	256.85	145.95	255.96
Management and upkeep services for security	213.00	181.80	249.17	156.56	214.83
Parking	93.51	79.01	77.88	69.23	96.44
Rented dwellings	**2,125.82**	**2,742.79**	**1,829.09**	**2,157.85**	**2,208.72**
Rent	2,108.22	2,695.34	1,771.01	2,148.27	2,202.82
Rent as pay	1,352.02	1,240.54	1,367.42	1,252.07	1,378.79
Maintenance, insurance, and other expenses	228.70	117.15	184.25	259.86	233.27
Tenant's insurance	95.42	96.21	74.48	85.16	99.12
Maintenance and repair services	773.94	–	482.31	558.18	881.98
Maintenance and repair materials	325.63	307.89	244.68	273.90	349.33
Other lodging	**926.58**	**819.92**	**821.97**	**738.64**	**945.40**
Owned vacation homes	1,373.72	1,565.68	1,857.31	1,264.84	1,353.28
Mortgage interest and charges	2,060.03	3,388.39	3,354.08	1,801.83	1,984.89
Property taxes	482.87	522.79	305.24	317.50	501.60
Maintenance, insurance, and other expenses	805.33	685.45	327.54	664.66	833.72
Housing while attending school	1,880.22	1,644.85	1,574.14	2,112.96	1,874.77
Lodging on trips	577.09	552.61	410.23	470.64	594.39

	total households	Asian	black	Hispanic	non-Hispanic white and other
UTILITIES, FUELS, AND PUBLIC SERVICES, AMOUNT SPENT	**$933.60**	**$831.17**	**$921.85**	**$881.55**	**$942.92**
Natural gas	**266.79**	**233.33**	**304.90**	**205.94**	**271.04**
Electricity	**369.36**	**309.05**	**400.29**	**366.74**	**364.85**
Fuel oil and other fuels	**571.51**	**622.37**	**498.88**	**295.22**	**593.24**
Fuel oil	851.40	747.73	797.30	712.30	859.47
Coal, wood, and other fuels	414.86	711.36	149.47	126.47	458.63
Bottled gas	341.52	196.32	244.20	131.41	360.60
Telephone services	**303.44**	**297.65**	**319.71**	**327.74**	**297.06**
Residential telephone and pay phones	161.32	143.06	187.64	163.12	157.15
Cellular phone service	269.62	264.58	290.54	299.83	261.66
Phone cards	59.17	66.18	81.68	62.29	54.17
Voice over IP	116.17	84.61	147.47	113.74	113.38
Water and other public services	**178.03**	**200.70**	**180.57**	**197.08**	**175.09**
Water and sewerage maintenance	146.03	162.57	152.66	157.06	143.39
Trash and garbage collection	73.39	75.76	65.43	71.49	74.58
Septic tank cleaning	225.00	–	16.67	111.36	237.79

* Amount does not include principal reduction, which is considered an asset.
Note: "Asian" and "black" include Hispanics and non-Hispanics who identify themselves as being of the respective race alone. "Hispanic" includes people of any race who identify themselves as Hispanic. "Other" includes people who identify themselves as non-Hispanic and as Alaska Native, American Indian, Asian (who are also included in the Asian column), or Native Hawaiian or other Pacific Islander as well as non-Hispanics reporting more than one race. "–" means sample is too small to make a reliable estimate.
Source: Calculations by New Strategist based on the Bureau of Labor Statistics' 2008 Consumer Expenditure Survey

Table 8.19 Percent Buying Utilities and Fuels by Race and Hispanic Origin, Average Week, 2008

(percent of households buying utilities and fuels during the average week, by race and Hispanic origin of householder, 2008)

UTILITIES AND FUELS, PERCENT BUYING	total households	Asian	black	Hispanic	non-Hispanic white and other
	34.9%	31.4%	33.8%	36.4%	34.9%
Electricity and natural gas	**21.7**	**21.0**	**21.3**	**21.9**	**21.7**
Electricity	17.6	16.1	16.9	18.6	17.6
Natural gas	9.9	12.9	9.6	9.4	10.0
Fuel oil and other fuels	**5.5**	**3.6**	**3.4**	**3.9**	**6.0**
Fuel oil	1.3	0.4	1.0	0.5	1.4
Bottled and tank gas	1.9	0.7	1.2	1.0	2.1
Coal	0.5	0.8	0.9	0.2	0.5
Miscellaneous fuels	2.7	2.4	1.4	2.7	2.9
Telephone services	**22.4**	**19.9**	**22.4**	**26.0**	**21.9**

Note: "Asian" and "black" include Hispanics and non-Hispanics who identify themselves as being of the respective race alone. "Hispanic" includes people of any race who identify themselves as Hispanic. "Other" includes people who identify themselves as non-Hispanic and as Alaska Native, American Indian, Asian (who are also included in the Asian column), or Native Hawaiian or other Pacific Islander as well as non-Hispanics reporting more than one race.
Source: Bureau of Labor Statistics, unpublished data from the 2008 Consumer Expenditure Survey

Table 8.20 Amount Buyers Spent on Utilities and Fuels by Race and Hispanic Origin, Average Week, 2008

(average amount spent by households buying utilities and fuels during the average week, by race and Hispanic origin of householder, 2008)

UTILITIES AND FUELS, AMOUNT SPENT	total households	Asian	black	Hispanic	non-Hispanic white and other
	$184.62	$153.55	$194.00	$173.68	$185.02
Electricity and natural gas	**158.61**	**137.66**	**171.42**	**151.90**	**157.78**
Electricity	139.80	111.15	157.48	131.74	138.60
Natural gas	**97.78**	**86.06**	**102.29**	**92.37**	**97.90**
Fuel oil and other fuels	125.87	25.00	102.03	54.34	134.88
Fuel oil	303.97	13.89	221.78	123.53	321.28
Bottled and tank gas	112.30	42.03	52.07	109.38	118.10
Coal	60.87	40.00	51.76	70.59	62.22
Miscellaneous fuels	25.93	10.88	13.29	12.13	28.82
Telephone services	**103.61**	**91.96**	**114.53**	**106.93**	**101.46**

Note: "Asian" and "black" include Hispanics and non-Hispanics who identify themselves as being of the respective race alone. "Hispanic" includes people of any race who identify themselves as Hispanic. "Other" includes people who identify themselves as non-Hispanic and as Alaska Native, American Indian, Asian (who are also included in the Asian column), or Native Hawaiian or other Pacific Islander as well as non-Hispanics reporting more than one race.
Source: Calculations by New Strategist based on the Bureau of Labor Statistics' 2008 Consumer Expenditure Survey

Table 8.21 Percent Buying Shelter and Utilities by Region, Average Quarter, 2008

(percent of households buying shelter and utilities during the average quarter, by region of residence, 2008)

	total households	Northeast	Midwest	South	West
SHELTER, PERCENT BUYING	**97.7%**	**97.7%**	**97.1%**	**97.5%**	**98.7%**
Owned dwellings	**66.7**	**65.4**	**68.8**	**68.2**	**63.2**
Mortgage interest and charges	43.7	43.0	45.4	42.2	44.9
Mortgage interest	40.8	38.2	41.9	40.2	43.0
Interest paid, home equity loan	4.2	6.3	5.3	3.1	3.0
Interest paid, home equity line of credit	5.5	6.8	7.1	4.0	5.1
Property taxes	65.3	64.8	67.8	65.9	62.3
Maintenance, repairs, insurance, other expenses	35.3	32.5	36.6	35.2	36.2
Homeowner's insurance	23.6	21.3	26.3	24.1	22.0
Ground rent	1.6	0.8	1.4	1.8	2.2
Maintenance and repair services	12.0	12.6	12.5	11.1	12.3
Painting and papering	1.0	1.3	0.8	0.9	1.2
Plumbing and water heating	3.4	3.8	3.3	3.1	3.8
Heat, air conditioning, electrical work	4.2	4.4	4.6	4.1	3.9
Roofing and gutters	1.0	1.3	1.0	1.2	0.6
Other repair and maintenance services	4.0	4.2	4.2	3.5	4.5
Repair, replacement of hard-surface flooring	0.6	0.5	0.7	0.6	0.5
Repair of built-in appliances	0.3	0.2	0.3	0.3	0.4
Maintenance and repair materials	4.9	4.8	5.4	4.7	5.1
Paints, wallpaper, and supplies	1.9	1.9	2.4	1.7	1.8
Tools, equipment for painting, wallpapering	1.9	1.9	2.4	1.7	1.8
Plumbing supplies and equipment	0.7	0.7	0.6	0.8	0.8
Electrical supplies, heating and cooling equipment	0.3	0.3	0.3	0.4	0.3
Hard-surface flooring, repair and replacement	0.3	0.2	0.3	0.2	0.4
Roofing and gutters	0.2	0.2	0.2	0.2	0.3
Plaster, paneling, siding, windows, doors, screens, awnings	0.6	0.7	0.5	0.7	0.7
Patio, walk, fence, driveway, masonry, brick, stucco materials	0.4	0.3	0.2	0.4	0.5
Miscellaneous supplies and equipment	1.5	1.5	1.6	1.4	1.6
Property management and security	5.3	4.6	3.5	4.7	9.0
Property management	5.0	4.5	3.4	4.4	8.3
Management and upkeep services for security	1.3	0.9	0.4	1.2	2.5
Parking	2.4	2.2	1.6	2.3	3.6
Rented dwellings	**32.0**	**33.1**	**29.6**	**30.3**	**36.4**
Rent	31.0	32.3	28.1	29.4	35.6
Rent as pay	1.4	1.4	1.4	1.3	1.4
Maintenance, insurance, and other expenses	3.9	3.4	4.8	3.3	4.4
Tenant's insurance	2.9	2.3	3.8	2.3	3.4
Maintenance and repair services	0.5	0.4	0.5	0.5	0.5
Maintenance and repair materials	0.8	0.8	0.8	0.8	0.8
Other lodging	**18.8**	**18.9**	**20.7**	**16.3**	**21.0**
Owned vacation homes	5.5	7.1	5.4	5.0	5.0
Mortgage interest and charges	1.7	2.1	1.2	1.8	1.6
Property taxes	5.2	6.8	5.2	4.8	4.5
Maintenance, insurance, and other expenses	2.0	2.8	2.0	1.5	2.1
Housing while attending school	0.9	1.0	1.0	0.9	0.7
Lodging on trips	14.2	13.0	16.0	12.0	17.2

	total households	Northeast	Midwest	South	West
UTILITIES, FUELS, AND PUBLIC SERVICES, PERCENT BUYING	97.7%	97.4%	96.6%	98.3%	98.2%
Natural gas	49.8	50.1	64.2	33.4	61.3
Electricity	91.6	88.6	90.9	93.8	91.2
Fuel oil and other fuels	8.4	19.0	6.6	5.7	5.8
Fuel oil	3.4	14.2	1.1	1.2	0.5
Coal, wood, and other fuels	0.7	1.4	0.5	0.6	0.6
Bottled gas	4.7	5.2	5.1	4.1	4.9
Telephone services	92.8	94.1	90.7	93.4	93.1
Residential telephone and pay phones	72.4	77.0	69.8	72.7	70.7
Cellular phone service	59.6	56.7	59.5	59.4	62.3
Phone cards	4.7	5.4	3.4	3.8	6.8
Voice over IP	1.3	2.7	1.4	0.9	0.8
Water and other public services	62.6	49.0	61.0	68.5	66.1
Water and sewerage maintenance	56.9	41.7	53.2	65.1	59.8
Trash and garbage collection	37.7	22.0	38.8	37.3	50.3
Septic tank cleaning	0.4	0.6	0.5	0.3	0.2

Source: Bureau of Labor Statistics, unpublished data from the 2008 Consumer Expenditure Survey

Table 8.22 Amount Buyers Spent on Shelter and Utilities by Region, <u>Average Quarter</u>, 2008

(average amount spent by households buying shelter and utilities during the average quarter, by region of residence, 2008)

	total households	Northeast	Midwest	South	West
SHELTER, AMOUNT SPENT	**$2,605.44**	**$3,076.88**	**$2,297.36**	**$2,173.79**	**$3,223.09**
Owned dwellings*	**2,533.50**	**3,013.68**	**2,283.70**	**2,067.35**	**3,218.61**
Mortgage interest and charges	2,189.04	2,227.78	1,771.42	1,947.42	2,963.86
Mortgage interest	2,193.23	2,277.42	1,769.79	1,945.35	2,932.75
Interest paid, home equity loan	616.21	605.66	486.89	589.41	914.60
Interest paid, home equity line of credit	640.11	730.43	518.88	576.52	795.22
Property taxes	673.15	1,078.92	709.77	480.29	612.63
Maintenance, repairs, insurance, other expenses	833.11	967.45	777.88	771.39	888.22
Homeowner's insurance	374.60	383.97	327.74	394.61	389.75
Ground rent	794.22	875.00	848.93	632.06	947.57
Maintenance and repair services	1,316.72	1,412.46	1,225.74	1,240.20	1,442.82
Painting and papering	1,773.54	1,546.64	878.57	1,897.75	2,474.17
Plumbing and water heating	403.35	341.56	349.10	393.51	518.19
Heat, air conditioning, electrical work	711.70	935.63	632.86	755.63	520.08
Roofing and gutters	2,324.52	2,140.19	2,307.52	2,075.22	3,449.61
Other repair and maintenance services	1,546.99	1,571.32	1,699.46	1,271.97	1,721.85
Repair, replacement of hard-surface flooring	1,600.91	1,674.48	1,536.94	1,507.59	1,733.16
Repair of built-in appliances	188.33	248.86	173.28	150.00	215.91
Maintenance and repair materials	359.67	318.40	451.54	342.63	316.01
Paints, wallpaper, and supplies	152.65	125.00	133.79	171.21	173.20
Tools, equipment for painting, wallpapering	16.40	13.38	14.33	18.33	18.65
Plumbing supplies and equipment	182.39	204.41	235.59	172.76	137.67
Electrical supplies, heating and cooling equipment	185.61	172.41	296.30	190.54	107.35
Hard-surface flooring, repair and replacement	885.58	823.68	877.68	832.61	940.28
Roofing and gutters	977.17	942.71	1,623.61	1,205.00	409.68
Plaster, paneling, siding, windows, doors, screens, awnings	564.52	505.38	1,250.98	387.31	353.85
Patio, walk, fence, driveway, masonry, brick, stucco materials	94.44	110.00	106.82	94.51	82.61
Miscellaneous supplies and equipment	290.31	219.67	412.58	266.36	247.58
Property management and security	284.88	658.19	219.47	217.93	210.60
Property management	249.01	610.74	193.62	177.62	171.46
Management and upkeep services for security	213.00	311.47	252.44	198.78	189.82
Parking	93.51	122.58	87.82	89.14	85.93
Rented dwellings	**2,125.82**	**2,316.66**	**1,688.39**	**1,893.84**	**2,661.64**
Rent	2,108.22	2,276.97	1,685.70	1,868.89	2,645.57
Rent as pay	1,352.02	1,398.94	1,105.19	1,389.10	1,470.89
Maintenance, insurance, and other expenses	228.70	337.02	231.48	213.68	174.89
Tenant's insurance	95.42	94.59	81.97	111.17	94.30
Maintenance and repair services	773.94	1,726.88	961.32	433.33	422.55
Maintenance and repair materials	325.63	300.00	389.00	325.00	281.85
Other lodging	**926.58**	**1,414.31**	**774.01**	**826.83**	**844.95**
Owned vacation homes	1,373.72	2,123.18	1,157.06	1,008.98	1,327.27
Mortgage interest and charges	2,060.03	3,097.30	1,797.98	1,404.10	2,305.25
Property taxes	482.87	676.30	567.12	374.22	329.37
Maintenance, insurance, and other expenses	805.33	1,404.95	542.60	533.45	696.19
Housing while attending school	1,880.22	1,929.70	1,822.75	1,785.64	2,043.31
Lodging on trips	577.09	736.91	496.97	563.66	568.26

	total households	Northeast	Midwest	South	West
UTILITIES, FUELS, AND PUBLIC SERVICES, AMOUNT SPENT	**$933.60**	**$1,056.49**	**$912.73**	**$931.15**	**$857.35**
Natural gas	**266.79**	**363.05**	**314.39**	**222.52**	**189.22**
Electricity	**369.36**	**367.50**	**309.23**	**439.24**	**316.21**
Fuel oil and other fuels	**571.51**	**787.58**	**558.89**	**364.96**	**329.65**
Fuel oil	851.40	881.02	874.29	695.26	653.43
Coal, wood, and other fuels	414.86	631.34	404.17	285.71	235.78
Bottled gas	341.52	313.95	493.66	270.06	297.99
Telephone services	**303.44**	**301.42**	**293.86**	**311.91**	**300.96**
Residential telephone and pay phones	161.32	163.91	154.53	170.25	151.02
Cellular phone service	269.62	266.19	261.26	275.75	271.03
Phone cards	59.17	55.60	48.46	71.67	56.03
Voice over IP	116.17	126.87	105.66	119.09	101.54
Water and other public services	**178.03**	**181.10**	**156.60**	**170.29**	**209.56**
Water and sewerage maintenance	146.03	161.89	128.03	140.38	163.33
Trash and garbage collection	73.39	90.28	68.31	66.41	79.70
Septic tank cleaning	225.00	212.89	203.50	163.46	505.00

Amount does not include principal reduction, which is considered an asset.
Source: Calculations by New Strategist based on the Bureau of Labor Statistics' 2008 Consumer Expenditure Survey

Table 8.23 Percent Buying Utilities and Fuels by Region, Average Week, 2008

(percent of households buying utilities and fuels during the average week, by region of residence, 2008)

	total households	Northeast	Midwest	South	West
UTILITIES AND FUELS, PERCENT BUYING	**34.9%**	**34.8%**	**35.9%**	**34.9%**	**34.2%**
Electricity and natural gas	**21.7**	**20.5**	**22.2**	**22.3**	**20.9**
Electricity	17.6	17.4	17.1	19.0	16.2
Natural gas	9.9	9.5	13.1	7.2	11.4
Fuel oil and other fuels	**5.5**	**6.5**	**5.3**	**5.1**	**5.5**
Fuel oil	1.3	3.0	0.9	1.1	0.5
Bottled and tank gas	1.9	1.6	1.9	1.8	2.1
Coal	0.5	0.3	0.4	0.5	0.6
Miscellaneous fuels	2.7	2.1	3.0	2.5	3.2
Telephone services	**22.4**	**22.9**	**22.9**	**22.4**	**21.6**

Source: Bureau of Labor Statistics, unpublished data from the 2008 Consumer Expenditure Survey

Table 8.24 Amount Buyers Spent on Utilities and Fuels by Region, Average Week, 2008

(average amount spent by households buying utilities and fuels during the average week, by region of residence, 2008)

	total households	Northeast	Midwest	South	West
UTILITIES AND FUELS, AMOUNT SPENT	**$184.62**	**$225.88**	**$171.79**	**$185.75**	**$161.67**
Electricity and natural gas	**158.61**	**181.06**	**159.60**	**161.99**	**133.49**
Electricity	139.80	139.91	123.25	159.10	120.69
Natural gas	97.78	134.07	109.86	83.31	73.47
Fuel oil and other fuels	**125.87**	**291.02**	**98.87**	**64.72**	**83.73**
Fuel oil	303.97	509.93	190.91	94.44	208.33
Bottled and tank gas	112.30	116.46	152.43	84.78	114.15
Coal	60.87	135.29	51.35	54.90	40.35
Miscellaneous fuels	25.93	50.24	18.54	18.58	29.65
Telephone services	**103.61**	**98.43**	**91.43**	**113.05**	**105.09**

Source: Calculations by New Strategist based on the Bureau of Labor Statistics' 2008 Consumer Expenditure Survey

Table 8.25 Percent Buying Shelter and Utilities by Education, <u>Average Quarter</u>, 2008

(percent of households buying shelter and utilities during the average quarter, by highest level of education of householder, 2008)

	total households	less than high school graduate	high school graduate	some college	associate's degree	college graduate total	bachelor's degree	master's, professional, doctorate
SHELTER, PERCENT BUYING	**97.7%**	**97.0%**	**97.7%**	**95.8%**	**99.0%**	**99.1%**	**99.0%**	**99.4%**
Owned dwellings	**66.7**	**52.8**	**66.3**	**59.9**	**70.2**	**78.1**	**75.9**	**82.0**
Mortgage interest and charges	43.7	24.1	37.8	40.4	50.0	59.2	58.0	61.5
Mortgage interest	40.8	21.5	34.7	38.3	46.2	56.2	54.9	58.5
Interest paid, home equity loan	4.2	2.4	4.1	3.6	6.2	5.1	5.3	4.9
Interest paid, home equity line of credit	5.5	2.1	4.1	5.0	5.3	8.8	8.2	9.7
Property taxes	65.3	50.2	64.2	58.9	68.8	77.6	75.4	81.5
Maintenance, repairs, insurance, other expenses	35.3	23.5	33.0	33.0	39.1	43.7	41.8	47.1
Homeowner's insurance	23.6	14.8	22.7	22.4	28.6	28.3	28.0	28.8
Ground rent	1.6	3.4	2.5	1.2	1.1	0.4	0.5	0.1
Maintenance and repair services	12.0	5.2	9.5	11.0	11.0	18.5	16.2	22.7
Painting and papering	1.0	0.4	0.7	1.0	1.1	1.6	1.4	2.1
Plumbing and water heating	3.4	1.4	2.9	2.8	2.8	5.7	4.8	7.3
Heat, air conditioning, electrical work	4.2	1.6	3.3	3.9	3.8	6.8	5.8	8.5
Roofing and gutters	1.0	0.6	0.9	1.0	0.9	1.5	1.3	1.9
Other repair and maintenance services	4.0	1.5	2.9	3.9	4.1	6.3	5.4	7.8
Repair, replacement of hard-surface flooring	0.6	0.3	0.4	0.5	0.4	0.8	0.9	0.8
Repair of built-in appliances	0.3	0.1	0.1	0.4	0.2	0.5	0.4	0.7
Maintenance and repair materials	4.9	3.3	4.1	4.8	7.1	5.9	5.6	6.5
Paints, wallpaper, and supplies	1.9	1.1	1.5	1.8	2.7	2.4	2.2	2.8
Tools, equipment for painting, wallpapering	1.9	1.1	1.5	1.8	2.7	2.4	2.2	2.8
Plumbing supplies and equipment	0.7	0.5	0.8	0.7	0.9	0.7	0.6	0.8
Electrical supplies, heating and cooling equipment	0.3	0.3	0.3	0.3	0.4	0.3	0.3	0.4
Hard-surface flooring, repair and replacement	0.3	0.2	0.2	0.3	0.2	0.3	0.4	0.3
Roofing and gutters	0.2	0.3	0.2	0.2	0.4	0.2	0.2	0.1
Plaster, paneling, siding, windows, doors, screens, awnings	0.6	0.4	0.5	0.6	0.9	0.8	0.7	0.9
Patio, walk, fence, driveway, masonry, brick, and stucco materials	0.4	0.2	0.2	0.4	0.5	0.5	0.4	0.7
Miscellaneous supplies and equipment	1.5	0.7	1.0	1.3	2.1	2.2	2.2	2.1
Property management and security	5.3	1.6	3.8	4.9	4.7	9.2	8.2	10.8
Property management	5.0	1.6	3.5	4.7	4.5	8.6	7.8	10.1
Management and upkeep services for security	1.3	0.3	0.9	1.1	1.2	2.2	1.8	3.0
Parking	2.4	0.7	1.8	2.4	2.3	3.9	3.3	4.8
Rented dwellings	**32.0**	**44.7**	**32.2**	**36.8**	**29.9**	**22.6**	**24.4**	**19.3**
Rent	31.0	43.0	31.5	35.8	28.7	21.6	23.6	18.2
Rent as pay	1.4	3.0	1.5	1.5	0.7	0.6	0.6	0.5
Maintenance, insurance, and other expenses	3.9	2.8	3.1	4.9	5.4	4.0	4.5	3.2
Tenant's insurance	2.9	1.4	2.1	3.8	4.2	3.3	3.7	2.5
Maintenance and repair services	0.5	0.7	0.3	0.4	0.7	0.5	0.6	0.4
Maintenance and repair materials	0.8	1.0	0.9	1.0	0.8	0.5	0.6	0.4
Other lodging	**18.8**	**6.4**	**13.4**	**17.9**	**19.7**	**30.3**	**26.5**	**37.2**
Owned vacation homes	5.5	1.6	3.9	5.2	5.7	9.0	7.2	12.2
Mortgage interest and charges	1.7	0.4	0.8	1.7	1.8	3.0	2.3	4.1
Property taxes	5.2	1.6	3.7	5.0	4.9	8.5	6.7	11.8
Maintenance, insurance, and other expenses	2.0	0.3	1.4	1.6	1.6	3.7	2.9	5.1
Housing while attending school	0.9	0.1	0.4	1.1	0.8	1.7	1.5	2.0
Lodging on trips	14.2	4.9	10.1	13.1	15.0	23.3	20.5	28.3

	total households	less than high school graduate	high school graduate	some college	associate's degree	college graduate		
						total	bachelor's degree	master's, professional, doctorate
UTILITIES, FUELS, AND PUBLIC SERVICES, PERCENT BUYING	**97.7%**	**96.9%**	**98.6%**	**95.0%**	**99.1%**	**99.0%**	**98.9%**	**99.2%**
Natural gas	**49.8**	**41.6**	**45.8**	**47.8**	**47.9**	**59.5**	**58.9**	**60.5**
Electricity	**91.6**	**87.4**	**92.8**	**88.1**	**93.9**	**94.5**	**94.0**	**95.5**
Fuel oil and other fuels	**8.4**	**7.0**	**8.6**	**7.8**	**11.4**	**8.4**	**8.5**	**8.3**
Fuel oil	3.4	2.4	3.4	2.7	4.8	4.0	3.7	4.6
Coal, wood, and other fuels	0.7	0.7	0.9	0.7	0.8	0.7	0.7	0.6
Bottled gas	4.7	4.3	4.8	4.8	6.6	4.1	4.4	3.6
Telephone services	**92.8**	**90.5**	**94.0**	**88.6**	**95.3**	**95.4**	**94.8**	**96.5**
Residential telephone and pay phones	72.4	71.4	74.0	64.7	74.7	76.5	74.6	80.1
Cellular phone service	59.6	43.5	56.5	61.6	63.9	67.4	66.1	69.8
Phone cards	4.7	9.3	4.2	3.2	3.5	4.2	4.0	4.5
Voice over IP	1.3	0.2	1.0	1.1	1.7	2.2	2.0	2.6
Water and other public services	**62.6**	**51.3**	**60.9**	**60.8**	**68.2**	**69.5**	**68.6**	**71.2**
Water and sewerage maintenance	56.9	46.5	54.6	55.3	61.6	63.8	63.0	65.3
Trash and garbage collection	37.7	31.4	35.1	37.5	41.7	42.0	41.2	43.4
Septic tank cleaning	0.4	0.2	0.5	0.3	0.3	0.5	0.4	0.5

Source: Bureau of Labor Statistics, unpublished data from the 2008 Consumer Expenditure Survey

Table 8.26 Amount Buyers Spent on Shelter and Utilities by Education, <u>Average Quarter</u>, 2008

(average amount spent by households buying shelter and utilities during the average quarter, by highest level of education of householder, 2008)

	total households	less than high school graduate	high school graduate	some college	associate's degree	college graduate total	bachelor's degree	master's, professional, doctorate
SHELTER, AMOUNT SPENT	**$2,605.44**	**$1,579.05**	**$1,950.94**	**$2,442.28**	**$2,605.85**	**$3,798.88**	**$3,544.29**	**$4,255.09**
Owned dwellings*	**2,533.50**	**1,414.11**	**1,768.52**	**2,434.88**	**2,557.38**	**3,538.39**	**3,375.99**	**3,808.56**
Mortgage interest and charges	2,189.04	1,679.13	1,637.10	2,051.45	2,142.10	2,687.78	2,628.37	2,788.66
Mortgage interest	2,193.23	1,755.94	1,651.01	2,033.65	2,187.35	2,655.92	2,592.97	2,762.13
Interest paid, home equity loan	616.21	455.25	569.16	636.90	512.90	714.84	775.24	597.11
Interest paid, home equity line of credit	640.11	810.26	575.12	535.20	523.81	714.03	702.86	731.67
Property taxes	673.15	387.73	517.74	610.96	627.33	927.84	876.96	1,012.59
Maintenance, repairs, insurance, other expenses	833.11	628.45	669.49	816.35	750.35	1,030.68	901.01	1,237.34
Homeowner's insurance	374.60	343.58	340.65	362.74	365.16	417.18	395.05	455.48
Ground rent	794.22	773.97	768.57	844.21	960.81	745.14	730.61	823.08
Maintenance and repair services	1,316.72	1,041.46	1,049.40	1,312.44	1,334.94	1,476.32	1,310.28	1,688.38
Painting and papering	1,773.54	806.08	1,500.00	2,091.75	1,281.25	1,933.54	1,509.29	2,449.28
Plumbing and water heating	403.35	247.41	368.07	355.65	450.09	448.59	379.55	529.88
Heat, air conditioning, electrical work	711.70	648.30	720.63	592.18	842.15	743.00	753.43	730.41
Roofing and gutters	2,324.52	2,631.82	2,357.50	1,999.50	3,560.17	2,219.90	2,038.10	2,438.24
Other repair and maintenance services	1,546.99	1,340.30	903.76	1,551.09	1,240.16	1,891.25	1,641.42	2,206.22
Repair, replacement of hard-surface flooring	1,600.91	826.47	1,931.25	1,502.94	1,445.51	1,662.80	1,647.73	1,711.51
Repair of built-in appliances	188.33	100.00	167.31	198.75	228.95	195.50	169.38	222.79
Maintenance and repair materials	359.67	330.68	352.72	378.91	251.34	400.17	437.57	342.46
Paints, wallpaper, and supplies	152.65	178.98	129.93	138.93	141.17	171.03	179.63	158.33
Tools, equipment for painting, wallpapering	16.40	19.25	13.98	14.89	15.15	18.41	19.33	17.02
Plumbing supplies and equipment	182.39	128.92	187.20	160.00	177.66	212.50	281.56	119.69
Electrical supplies, heating and cooling equipment	185.61	122.22	235.34	179.41	131.98	209.56	246.09	144.38
Hard-surface flooring, repair and replacement	885.58	883.33	866.25	745.59	698.75	1,002.94	1,292.76	286.00
Roofing and gutters	977.17	1,061.72	1,512.50	439.58	603.85	1,320.31	1,426.14	462.50
Plaster, paneling, siding, windows, doors, screens, awnings	564.52	226.83	531.38	980.42	381.87	504.55	499.64	502.15
Patio, walk, fence, driveway, masonry, brick, and stucco materials	94.44	215.28	79.55	45.51	137.24	96.00	113.41	76.52
Miscellaneous supplies and equipment	290.31	228.47	288.22	305.68	165.88	331.28	268.06	444.51
Property management and security	284.88	287.74	213.33	287.35	238.00	317.08	276.15	372.69
Property management	249.01	269.52	187.57	252.37	205.30	275.17	248.46	311.27
Management and upkeep services for security	213.00	159.00	164.94	216.67	164.66	239.64	190.14	293.77
Parking	93.51	83.85	94.57	87.71	82.53	98.51	91.69	106.97
Rented dwellings	**2,125.82**	**1,682.40**	**1,971.84**	**2,022.54**	**2,171.83**	**2,868.03**	**2,684.61**	**3,287.21**
Rent	2,108.22	1,652.69	1,925.60	2,003.46	2,172.81	2,902.22	2,702.20	3,364.94
Rent as pay	1,352.02	1,123.14	1,577.38	1,154.67	1,628.52	1,672.84	1,518.65	2,071.88
Maintenance, insurance, and other expenses	228.70	288.30	208.28	181.19	259.31	252.99	228.82	314.02
Tenant's insurance	95.42	91.30	71.15	94.99	100.42	107.87	106.62	111.10
Maintenance and repair services	773.94	715.00	557.26	372.56	1,015.07	1,052.45	845.61	1,510.71
Maintenance and repair materials	325.63	223.72	365.70	395.53	352.11	250.50	243.97	265.97
Other lodging	**926.58**	**500.51**	**730.84**	**760.64**	**679.06**	**1,173.43**	**1,099.99**	**1,267.62**
Owned vacation homes	1,373.72	802.34	1,230.80	1,066.40	857.91	1,721.18	1,730.47	1,708.88
Mortgage interest and charges	2,060.03	1,474.42	1,941.96	1,602.05	1,431.25	2,447.81	2,359.44	2,542.82
Property taxes	482.87	292.72	451.40	390.76	337.12	579.94	616.48	543.01
Maintenance, insurance, and other expenses	805.33	550.74	1,070.59	547.09	444.03	867.05	960.45	771.25
Housing while attending school	1,880.22	565.38	1,277.38	1,505.90	1,105.19	2,353.59	2,191.11	2,550.00
Lodging on trips	577.09	380.33	447.94	489.45	509.12	697.81	657.22	750.58

	total households	less than high school graduate	high school graduate	some college	associate's degree	college graduate		
						total	bachelor's degree	master's, professional, doctorate
UTILITIES, FUELS, AND PUBLIC SERVICES, AMOUNT SPENT	**$933.60**	**$795.90**	**$896.72**	**$907.10**	**$972.19**	**$1,040.55**	**$1,013.87**	**$1,088.38**
Natural gas	**266.79**	**250.69**	**272.41**	**251.13**	**253.59**	**281.58**	**274.90**	**293.36**
Electricity	**369.36**	**356.49**	**366.24**	**362.66**	**367.52**	**383.41**	**376.48**	**395.67**
Fuel oil and other fuels	**571.51**	**517.63**	**558.94**	**482.92**	**651.36**	**633.56**	**602.78**	**689.33**
Fuel oil	851.40	760.68	815.36	775.47	910.89	918.28	907.33	936.10
Coal, wood, and other fuels	414.86	290.49	417.05	495.00	533.44	381.72	372.95	397.81
Bottled gas	341.52	373.36	345.04	284.74	407.69	338.42	331.71	353.85
Telephone services	**303.44**	**255.19**	**285.53**	**311.04**	**319.62**	**331.60**	**325.92**	**341.65**
Residential telephone and pay phones	161.32	160.29	158.13	158.42	161.93	166.19	163.78	170.21
Cellular phone service	269.62	252.38	261.84	275.76	280.23	273.59	275.70	269.97
Phone cards	59.17	68.55	57.51	54.35	51.79	54.93	59.09	48.37
Voice over IP	116.17	148.96	115.91	108.63	156.36	108.18	110.48	104.90
Water and other public services	**178.03**	**170.84**	**169.13**	**179.61**	**172.83**	**188.14**	**185.55**	**192.62**
Water and sewerage maintenance	146.03	141.90	141.66	146.34	141.53	152.01	150.53	154.52
Trash and garbage collection	73.39	68.32	69.95	73.57	72.16	78.09	76.70	80.45
Septic tank cleaning	225.00	111.11	239.44	218.33	237.50	231.67	225.00	246.57

* Amount does not include principal reduction, which is considered an asset.
Source: Calculations by New Strategist based on the Bureau of Labor Statistics' 2008 Consumer Expenditure Survey

Table 8.27 Percent Buying Utilities and Fuels by Education, <u>Average Week</u>, 2008

(percent of households buying utilities and fuels during the average week, by highest level of education of householder, 2008)

UTILITIES AND FUELS, PERCENT BUYING	total households	less than high school graduate	high school graduate	some college	associate's degree	college graduate total	bachelor's degree	master's, professional, doctorate
	34.9%	**34.7%**	**35.0%**	**33.1%**	**35.9%**	**36.1%**	**35.1%**	**37.9%**
Electricity and natural gas	**21.7**	**21.6**	**21.9**	**19.8**	**23.1**	**22.5**	**21.4**	**24.6**
Electricity	17.6	18.5	18.7	15.4	18.6	17.7	16.8	19.4
Natural gas	9.9	8.4	8.7	9.3	9.9	12.2	11.7	13.1
Fuel oil and other fuels	**5.5**	**3.6**	**5.2**	**6.0**	**6.6**	**5.9**	**5.9**	**5.9**
Fuel oil	1.3	0.9	1.7	1.1	1.9	1.0	0.9	1.2
Bottled and tank gas	1.9	1.3	1.4	2.6	1.9	2.0	2.1	1.8
Coal	0.5	0.1	0.5	0.6	0.4	0.5	0.3	0.8
Miscellaneous fuels	2.7	1.6	2.4	2.9	2.9	3.3	3.2	3.5
Telephone services	**22.4**	**23.4**	**22.3**	**20.6**	**23.0**	**23.3**	**22.4**	**25.0**

Source: Bureau of Labor Statistics, unpublished data from the 2008 Consumer Expenditure Survey

Table 8.28 Amount Buyers Spent on Utilities and Fuels by Education, <u>Average Week</u>, 2008

(average amount spent by households buying utilities and fuels during the average week, by highest level of education of householder, 2008)

UTILITIES AND FUELS, AMOUNT SPENT	total households	less than high school graduate	high school graduate	some college	associate's degree	college graduate total	bachelor's degree	master's, professional, doctorate
	$184.62	**$167.25**	**$183.28**	**$179.55**	**$205.26**	**$190.97**	**$183.84**	**$203.30**
Electricity and natural gas	**158.61**	**158.26**	**155.47**	**155.70**	**157.20**	**164.09**	**158.72**	**172.66**
Electricity	139.80	129.29	137.49	146.10	146.36	140.91	137.79	145.87
Natural gas	97.78	121.10	95.76	88.94	92.21	98.27	92.12	108.58
Fuel oil and other fuels	**125.87**	**96.09**	**149.14**	**107.12**	**190.08**	**108.15**	**95.40**	**131.98**
Fuel oil	303.97	151.69	311.31	219.44	410.36	360.61	328.41	410.17
Bottled and tank gas	112.30	99.25	105.11	123.37	148.92	100.50	98.10	104.49
Coal	60.87	58.33	40.38	44.83	180.95	63.27	46.88	75.95
Miscellaneous fuels	25.93	43.67	37.24	21.68	34.35	15.20	15.26	14.78
Telephone services	**103.61**	**87.84**	**99.73**	**107.27**	**109.01**	**110.13**	**111.88**	**107.08**

Source: Calculations by New Strategist based on the Bureau of Labor Statistics' 2008 Consumer Expenditure Survey

CHAPTER 9

Buyers of Personal Care, Reading Material, Education, and Tobacco, 2008

The personal care category includes everything from haircuts, facials, and manicures to cosmetics, shampoo, and tooth-paste. Average household spending on personal care products and services fell 13 percent between 2000 and 2008, after adjusting for inflation. Spending on reading material fell by an even larger 37 percent. Spending on education increased sharply between 2000 and 2008, with the average household boosting its spending on college tuition by 43 percent.

Quarterly spending

During the average quarter of 2008, 62 percent of households spent on personal care products or services, 42 percent bought reading material, 14 percent had education expenses, and 21 percent bought tobacco products. Twenty percent of households purchased newspaper and magazine subscriptions during the average quarter of 2008, spending an average of $57 on these items. Those most likely to pay for newspaper and magazine subscriptions are householders aged 65 or older. Five percent of households paid for college tuition during the average quarter of 2008. Among those who paid college tuition, average spending on the category during the quarter was $3,244.

Weekly spending

During the average week of 2008, 34 percent of households purchased personal care products and 9 percent spent on personal care services. Those spending on personal care products during the average week devoted $18 to the category. Those buying personal care services spent a larger $46, with average spending on services for females ($33) more than twice as much as spending on services for males ($15). Householders aged 75 or older are most likely to spend on personal care services for females.

Top Personal Care Categories

(personal care products and services bought by the largest percentage of households during an average week, 2008)

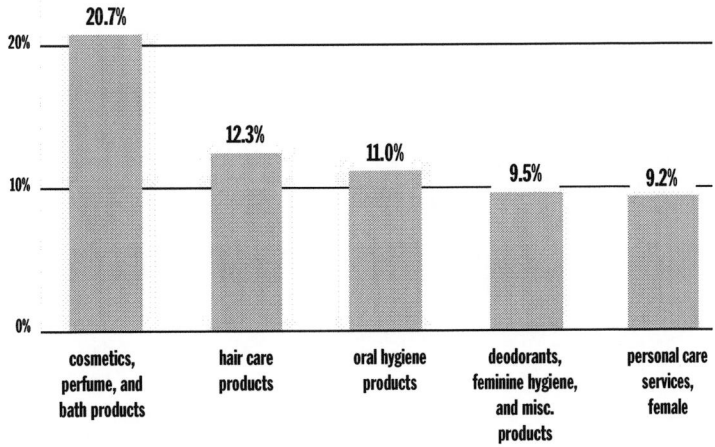

Table 9.1 Percent Buying Personal Care Products and Services, Reading Material, Education, and Tobacco by Age, <u>Average Quarter</u>, 2008

(percent of households buying personal care products and services, reading material, education, and tobacco during the average quarter, by age of householder, 2008)

	total households	under 25	25 to 34	35 to 44	45 to 54	55 to 64	65 to 74	75+
PERSONAL CARE, PERCENT BUYING	**62.2%**	**48.0%**	**57.7%**	**63.5%**	**65.4%**	**65.3%**	**64.8%**	**62.5%**
Wigs and hairpieces	0.8	1.5	1.1	1.1	0.7	0.6	0.3	0.1
Electric personal care appliances	3.4	4.3	4.1	3.6	3.8	3.4	2.2	1.8
Personal care services	61.3	46.0	56.3	62.5	64.5	64.7	64.2	62.1
READING, PERCENT BUYING	**41.6**	**25.9**	**34.3**	**38.4**	**43.9**	**47.8**	**50.4**	**46.6**
Newspaper and magazine subscriptions	20.1	4.2	9.9	14.4	20.8	26.5	32.1	35.0
Newspapers and magazines, nonsubscription	15.9	13.1	15.8	16.2	18.2	17.8	16.5	8.3
Books purchased through book clubs	1.5	0.1	1.0	1.3	1.5	2.0	1.9	2.1
Books not purchased through book clubs	19.6	14.3	18.8	20.4	21.3	22.9	20.3	13.2
EDUCATION, PERCENT BUYING	**14.0**	**22.0**	**15.5**	**19.5**	**20.2**	**8.7**	**3.1**	**1.8**
College tuition	5.0	11.1	5.5	3.3	8.4	4.5	1.2	0.9
Elementary and high school tuition	1.7	0.1	0.9	3.7	3.0	0.7	0.6	0.2
Vocational and technical schools tuition	0.3	0.3	0.3	0.4	0.6	0.1	0.2	0.0
Other school tuition	0.4	0.3	0.4	0.5	0.8	0.5	0.3	0.1
Other school expenses including rentals	3.5	2.9	3.6	6.4	5.0	2.0	0.5	0.5
Books, supplies for college	4.0	15.3	5.1	2.5	6.1	1.9	0.4	0.1
Books, supplies for elementary, high school	3.4	0.9	3.9	7.6	4.5	1.4	0.4	0.2
Books, supplies for vocational and technical schools	0.1	0.3	0.1	0.2	0.2	0.2	0.1	–
Books, supplies for day care, nursery school	0.1	0.1	0.4	0.3	0.1	0.0	0.0	–
Books, supplies for other schools	0.2	0.0	0.2	0.6	0.2	0.2	0.2	0.1
TOBACCO, PERCENT BUYING	**21.5**	**22.5**	**22.2**	**23.0**	**27.2**	**22.2**	**17.0**	**7.1**
Cigarettes	18.7	20.1	19.3	19.5	24.4	19.5	14.3	5.5
Other tobacco products	3.8	3.7	4.2	4.3	4.0	3.9	3.2	1.9

Note: "–" means sample is too small to make a reliable estimate.
Source: Bureau of Labor Statistics, unpublished data from the 2008 Consumer Expenditure Survey

Table 9.2 Amount Buyers Spent on Personal Care Products and Services, Reading Material, Education, and Tobacco by Age, Average Quarter, 2008

(average amount spent by households buying personal care products and services, reading material, education, and tobacco during the average quarter, by age of householder, 2008)

	total households	under 25	25 to 34	35 to 44	45 to 54	55 to 64	65 to 74	75+
PERSONAL CARE, AMOUNT SPENT	**$120.82**	**$85.81**	**$113.05**	**$130.28**	**$130.27**	**$125.26**	**$110.28**	**$115.52**
Wigs and hairpieces	76.92	82.07	88.30	72.94	64.58	45.54	162.04	141.07
Electric personal care appliances	51.97	43.53	60.91	52.59	51.70	50.45	43.50	47.28
Personal care services	118.81	82.65	109.70	128.17	128.16	123.55	109.17	114.53
READING, AMOUNT SPENT	**69.54**	**45.67**	**57.21**	**66.06**	**70.58**	**81.90**	**74.53**	**70.76**
Newspaper and magazine subscriptions	57.28	43.85	39.93	49.77	54.52	67.00	59.19	62.26
Newspapers and magazines, nonsubscription	22.71	15.18	20.08	20.92	23.19	24.24	26.17	31.58
Books purchased through book clubs	63.62	59.09	82.63	60.00	72.68	62.56	55.56	50.00
Books not purchased through book clubs	65.38	55.58	61.64	68.92	67.11	68.57	64.62	56.84
EDUCATION, AMOUNT SPENT	**1,782.60**	**1,887.45**	**1,162.93**	**1,127.27**	**2,401.26**	**2,396.62**	**2,543.73**	**2,400.55**
College tuition	3,243.68	3,089.12	2,524.68	2,273.78	3,806.03	3,813.68	3,058.67	3,079.07
Elementary and high school tuition	2,812.28	150.00	1,090.38	2,822.40	3,023.17	2,028.38	5,678.88	7,379.41
Vocational and technical schools tuition	1,467.24	258.33	576.56	1,015.54	2,533.64	337.50	1,059.38	58.33
Other school tuition	849.43	316.96	673.57	1,164.36	801.67	1,148.33	327.21	117.86
Other school expenses including rentals	297.36	181.59	230.99	208.63	417.97	354.48	485.56	647.50
Books, supplies for college	387.59	395.09	280.71	341.21	449.30	454.79	383.75	614.29
Books, supplies for elementary, high school	124.04	95.65	85.06	117.24	152.11	168.39	120.35	112.50
Books, supplies for vocational and technical schools	467.86	1,558.04	68.75	538.33	323.61	216.67	60.71	–
Books, supplies for day care, nursery school	94.64	12.50	83.78	95.69	235.00	37.50	50.00	–
Books, supplies for other schools	147.92	112.50	196.67	133.90	225.00	111.11	90.00	34.38
TOBACCO, AMOUNT SPENT	**364.88**	**272.84**	**333.75**	**378.76**	**398.36**	**393.58**	**332.17**	**302.81**
Cigarettes	380.10	278.75	349.75	398.76	409.90	405.42	357.28	320.38
Other tobacco products	193.60	144.05	161.13	216.86	203.42	217.68	166.15	203.39

Note: "–" means sample is too small to make a reliable estimate.
Source: Calculations by New Strategist based on the Bureau of Labor Statistics' 2008 Consumer Expenditure Survey

Table 9.3 Percent Buying Personal Care Products and Services, School Supplies, and Smoking Accessories by Age, <u>Average Week</u>, 2008

(percent of households buying personal care products and services, school supplies, and smoking accessories during the average week, by age of householder, 2008)

	total households	under 25	25 to 34	35 to 44	45 to 54	55 to 64	65 to 74	75+
PERSONAL CARE, PERCENT BUYING	38.6%	26.9%	37.6%	43.0%	41.1%	38.7%	38.3%	34.3%
Personal care products	34.0	24.2	33.6	38.4	37.6	33.7	32.8	26.2
Hair care products	12.3	9.0	12.6	15.4	14.9	11.0	10.0	6.3
Hair accessories	2.3	2.0	3.1	2.8	2.4	1.8	1.6	1.2
Oral hygiene products	11.0	6.2	9.5	12.4	11.8	11.7	12.7	8.8
Shaving products	3.9	2.8	3.6	5.5	4.9	3.2	2.7	2.1
Cosmetics, perfume, and bath products	20.7	15.8	20.6	23.4	23.4	20.6	18.5	15.6
Deodorants, feminine hygiene, misc. products	9.5	6.6	9.8	12.6	11.1	8.8	6.9	5.0
Electric personal care appliances	0.8	0.5	0.5	0.8	1.0	1.2	0.8	0.3
Personal care services	9.5	4.5	8.6	9.8	8.1	10.3	11.1	13.8
Personal care service for females	9.2	4.5	7.9	9.5	8.0	10.0	10.9	13.8
Personal care service for males	9.2	4.4	8.5	9.6	7.8	10.1	10.7	13.0
SCHOOL SUPPLIES, PERCENT BUYING	8.8	5.9	8.9	10.7	10.3	8.1	8.4	4.9
SMOKING ACCESSORIES, PERCENT BUYING	1.4	1.0	1.3	1.3	2.0	1.6	0.9	0.8

Source: Bureau of Labor Statistics, unpublished data from the 2008 Consumer Expenditure Survey

Table 9.4 Amount Buyers Spent on Personal Care Products and Services, School Supplies, and Smoking Accessories by Age, <u>Average Week</u>, 2008

(average amount spent by households buying personal care products and services, school supplies, and smoking accessories during the average week, by age of householder, 2008)

	total households	under 25	25 to 34	35 to 44	45 to 54	55 to 64	65 to 74	75+
PERSONAL CARE, AMOUNT SPENT	$27.40	$23.42	$27.00	$30.51	$29.20	$26.99	$24.95	$21.33
Personal care products	18.26	16.90	16.99	20.23	20.61	17.66	16.23	12.51
Hair care products	10.69	12.36	9.78	10.57	11.66	10.95	10.94	6.98
Hair accessories	5.26	5.10	5.11	5.34	5.00	5.06	4.32	4.31
Oral hygiene products	6.12	6.94	5.36	5.65	5.76	6.76	6.84	6.56
Shaving products	9.33	10.43	11.48	9.12	9.20	7.91	9.06	5.74
Cosmetics, perfume, and bath products	14.06	10.33	13.08	15.58	16.30	12.99	13.41	10.08
Deodorants, feminine hygiene, misc. products	6.55	7.45	5.53	7.22	6.50	6.58	4.95	7.94
Electric personal care appliances	28.95	10.87	33.33	32.00	24.74	30.00	30.67	33.33
Personal care services	46.19	49.33	51.45	54.87	52.47	43.54	38.04	29.19
Personal care service for females	32.54	33.71	37.63	38.61	37.05	30.18	26.67	20.48
Personal care service for males	15.08	15.68	17.28	17.68	16.65	14.34	12.34	9.42
SCHOOL SUPPLIES, AMOUNT SPENT	10.23	11.00	7.97	12.95	12.91	7.00	7.38	6.95
SMOKING ACCESSORIES, AMOUNT SPENT	4.35	9.62	2.40	7.14	4.02	4.38	4.30	3.66

Source: Calculations by New Strategist based on the Bureau of Labor Statistics' 2008 Consumer Expenditure Survey

Table 9.5 Percent Buying Personal Care Products and Services, Reading Material, Education, and Tobacco by Household Income, Average Quarter, 2008

(percent of households buying personal care products and services, reading material, education, and tobacco during the average quarter, by before-tax income of household, 2008)

	total households	under $20,000	$20,000–$39,999	$40,000–$49,999	$50,000–$69,999	$70,000–$79,999	$80,000–$99,999	$100,000 or more
PERSONAL CARE, PERCENT BUYING	**62.2%**	**41.9%**	**55.3%**	**61.2%**	**66.0%**	**71.5%**	**74.3%**	**83.2%**
Wigs and hairpieces	0.8	0.9	0.9	1.0	0.6	0.7	0.8	0.6
Electric personal care appliances	3.4	2.0	2.8	3.5	3.5	4.2	4.5	4.9
Personal care services	61.3	40.8	54.2	60.1	65.0	70.4	73.3	82.7
READING, PERCENT BUYING	**41.6**	**27.3**	**34.4**	**40.0**	**45.1**	**49.4**	**49.6**	**58.8**
Newspaper and magazine subscriptions	20.1	12.3	16.0	18.0	20.6	23.9	23.9	32.1
Newspapers and magazines, nonsubscription	15.9	10.1	13.7	17.1	19.0	19.5	17.2	20.4
Books purchased through book clubs	1.5	0.9	1.0	1.8	1.7	1.4	1.7	2.2
Books not purchased through book clubs	19.6	10.1	13.2	17.3	20.9	24.6	25.3	34.5
EDUCATION, PERCENT BUYING	**14.0**	**9.6**	**8.6**	**10.5**	**13.6**	**17.2**	**18.7**	**24.8**
College tuition	5.0	3.5	2.7	3.4	4.7	5.5	6.2	10.1
Elementary and high school tuition	1.7	0.3	0.7	0.8	1.5	1.9	2.8	4.6
Vocational and technical schools tuition	0.3	0.1	0.2	0.4	0.3	0.4	0.4	0.6
Other school tuition	0.4	0.2	0.3	0.4	0.4	0.3	0.7	1.0
Other school expenses including rentals	3.5	1.5	2.1	2.9	3.4	4.9	5.5	6.5
Books, supplies for college	4.0	5.0	2.4	2.1	3.3	4.1	4.5	6.3
Books, supplies for elementary, high school	3.4	1.8	2.6	3.0	3.3	5.0	4.7	5.4
Books, supplies for vocational and technical schools	0.1	0.1	0.1	0.2	0.2	0.2	0.2	0.2
Books, supplies for day care, nursery school	0.1	0.0	0.1	0.1	0.1	0.4	0.3	0.2
Books, supplies for other schools	0.2	0.1	0.2	0.1	0.2	0.3	0.2	0.5
TOBACCO, PERCENT BUYING	**21.5**	**21.3**	**22.2**	**23.7**	**24.0**	**24.4**	**21.5**	**16.5**
Cigarettes	18.7	18.9	20.1	21.0	20.8	20.9	18.8	13.0
Other tobacco products	3.8	3.0	2.8	3.5	4.7	5.1	3.9	4.8

Source: Bureau of Labor Statistics, unpublished data from the 2008 Consumer Expenditure Survey

Table 9.6 Amount Buyers Spent on Personal Care Products and Services, Reading Material, Education, and Tobacco by Household Income, <u>Average Quarter</u>, 2008

(average amount spent by households buying personal care products and services, reading material, education, and tobacco during the average quarter, by before-tax income of household, 2008)

	total households	under $20,000	$20,000–$39,999	$40,000–$49,999	$50,000–$69,999	$70,000–$79,999	$80,000–$99,999	$100,000 or more
PERSONAL CARE, AMOUNT SPENT	**$120.82**	**$78.43**	**$88.08**	**$98.97**	**$111.27**	**$114.22**	**$130.81**	**$185.23**
Wigs and hairpieces	76.92	59.18	87.68	111.32	55.47	157.35	46.73	61.89
Electric personal care appliances	51.97	35.24	42.73	49.71	52.10	38.36	57.87	68.88
Personal care services	118.81	77.39	86.17	96.19	109.59	112.16	128.47	181.78
READING, AMOUNT SPENT	**69.54**	**49.45**	**54.86**	**57.13**	**65.32**	**64.74**	**71.95**	**98.65**
Newspaper and magazine subscriptions	57.28	53.39	53.89	50.18	55.82	49.01	54.22	67.61
Newspapers and magazines, nonsubscription	22.71	19.75	20.42	19.21	22.71	22.67	23.67	27.54
Books purchased through book clubs	63.62	58.44	47.76	54.55	66.87	85.28	64.82	72.41
Books not purchased through book clubs	65.38	45.15	52.92	54.86	60.01	58.64	68.58	84.16
EDUCATION, AMOUNT SPENT	**1,782.60**	**1,451.11**	**957.99**	**1,103.64**	**1,043.96**	**1,109.43**	**1,470.85**	**3,020.47**
College tuition	3,243.68	2,984.03	2,105.08	2,492.93	2,094.88	2,344.09	2,629.98	4,554.57
Elementary and high school tuition	2,812.28	1,799.42	1,400.82	1,233.43	1,107.84	1,068.56	2,356.63	4,122.21
Vocational and technical schools tuition	1,467.24	193.27	385.99	487.86	565.44	868.42	620.71	3,092.67
Other school tuition	849.43	215.16	342.57	908.57	518.75	677.42	603.36	1,340.00
Other school expenses including rentals	297.36	207.33	186.82	197.21	184.75	270.34	263.49	465.67
Books, supplies for college	387.59	364.79	364.92	319.95	357.10	381.90	415.47	431.11
Books, supplies for elementary, high school	124.04	88.91	77.94	149.41	121.69	120.49	98.92	167.77
Books, supplies for vocational and technical schools	467.86	1,000.88	158.99	79.69	190.00	357.81	128.13	796.67
Books, supplies for day care, nursery school	94.64	78.31	32.56	37.50	130.36	73.72	77.00	128.26
Books, supplies for other schools	147.92	54.27	93.00	32.50	59.78	178.85	42.50	260.20
TOBACCO, AMOUNT SPENT	**364.88**	**310.00**	**352.95**	**359.79**	**406.20**	**391.99**	**406.51**	**381.52**
Cigarettes	380.10	319.15	365.82	382.66	429.62	406.08	433.71	391.77
Other tobacco products	193.60	187.19	181.38	148.48	176.59	217.91	158.42	248.91

Source: Calculations by New Strategist based on the Bureau of Labor Statistics' 2008 Consumer Expenditure Survey

Table 9.7 Percent Buying Personal Care Products and Services, School Supplies, and Smoking Accessories by Household Income, Average Week, 2008

(percent of households buying personal care products and services, school supplies, and smoking accessories during the average week, by before-tax income of household, 2008)

	total households	under $20,000	$20,000–$39,999	$40,000–$49,999	$50,000–$69,999	$70,000–$79,999	$80,000–$99,999	$100,000 or more
PERSONAL CARE, PERCENT BUYING	**38.6%**	**29.5%**	**33.5%**	**34.3%**	**39.8%**	**43.3%**	**46.6%**	**51.2%**
Personal care products	**34.0**	**26.2**	**29.5**	**31.4**	**35.5**	**37.7**	**40.4**	**44.2**
Hair care products	12.3	8.6	10.4	10.5	12.2	15.0	16.4	16.9
Hair accessories	2.3	1.7	1.7	1.6	2.1	2.7	3.5	3.5
Oral hygiene products	11.0	7.9	9.6	9.6	11.0	12.5	13.2	15.4
Shaving products	3.9	2.4	2.4	3.1	4.0	4.8	6.0	6.3
Cosmetics, perfume, and bath products	20.7	15.0	17.9	18.8	21.8	22.4	24.5	28.4
Deodorants, feminine hygiene, misc. products	9.5	6.6	7.3	8.4	8.7	12.7	12.3	14.3
Electric personal care appliances	0.8	0.5	0.5	0.8	0.8	0.4	1.1	1.3
Personal care services	**9.5**	**5.7**	**7.6**	**5.5**	**8.9**	**12.0**	**12.4**	**16.6**
Personal care service for females	9.2	5.5	7.5	5.2	8.6	11.3	11.9	16.4
Personal care service for males	9.2	5.4	7.4	5.5	8.8	11.3	12.1	16.1
SCHOOL SUPPLIES, PERCENT BUYING	**8.8**	**4.3**	**6.6**	**7.5**	**9.1**	**9.5**	**11.3**	**15.8**
SMOKING ACCESSORIES, PERCENT BUYING	**1.4**	**1.1**	**1.4**	**1.3**	**0.9**	**1.4**	**1.8**	**1.9**

Source: Bureau of Labor Statistics, unpublished data from the 2008 Consumer Expenditure Survey

Table 9.8 Amount Buyers Spent on Personal Care Products and Services, School Supplies, and Smoking Accessories by Household Income, Average Week, 2008

(average amount spent by households buying personal care products and services, school supplies, and smoking accessories during the average week, by before-tax income of household, 2008)

	total households	under $20,000	$20,000–$39,999	$40,000–$49,999	$50,000–$69,999	$70,000–$79,999	$80,000–$99,999	$100,000 or more
PERSONAL CARE, AMOUNT SPENT	**$27.40**	**$26.49**	**$19.02**	**$21.21**	**$20.34**	**$28.04**	**$29.28**	**$43.87**
Personal care products	**18.26**	**19.96**	**13.10**	**15.55**	**16.36**	**19.35**	**19.54**	**25.93**
Hair care products	10.69	12.08	8.94	9.42	9.54	11.40	9.40	14.11
Hair accessories	5.26	4.65	5.87	5.61	3.73	3.28	6.30	5.37
Oral hygiene products	6.12	9.62	4.64	5.19	6.60	6.27	5.82	6.84
Shaving products	9.33	11.77	8.92	8.80	10.83	10.56	9.60	10.40
Cosmetics, perfume, and bath products	14.06	14.77	8.62	11.09	13.17	14.85	15.57	20.09
Deodorants, feminine hygiene, misc. products	6.55	9.17	6.13	7.12	5.24	6.46	5.43	7.61
Electric personal care appliances	28.95	37.72	42.28	32.93	25.00	19.51	25.93	28.57
Personal care services	**46.19**	**46.93**	**32.68**	**36.27**	**33.46**	**40.38**	**46.30**	**66.19**
Personal care service for females	32.54	33.45	22.68	24.88	23.69	29.62	33.42	46.00
Personal care service for males	15.08	15.02	10.61	11.98	11.15	13.25	14.88	21.58
SCHOOL SUPPLIES, AMOUNT SPENT	**10.23**	**13.89**	**6.53**	**6.74**	**7.87**	**9.38**	**13.78**	**11.86**
SMOKING ACCESSORIES, AMOUNT SPENT	**4.35**	**4.05**	**2.56**	**2.56**	**8.27**	**2.78**	**3.85**	**7.53**

Source: Calculations by New Strategist based on the Bureau of Labor Statistics' 2008 Consumer Expenditure Survey

Table 9.9 Percent of High-Income Households Buying Personal Care Products and Services, Reading Material, Education, and Tobacco, Average Quarter, 2008

(percent of high-income households buying personal care products and services, reading material, education, and tobacco during the average quarter, by before-tax income of household, 2008)

	total households	$100,000 or more	$100,000–$119,999	$120,000–$149,999	$150,000 or more
PERSONAL CARE, PERCENT BUYING	**62.2%**	**83.2%**	**80.0%**	**82.9%**	**85.9%**
Wigs and hairpieces	0.8	0.6	1.0	0.7	0.2
Electric personal care appliances	3.4	4.9	5.4	5.3	4.4
Personal care services	61.3	82.7	79.4	82.3	85.6
READING, PERCENT BUYING	**41.6**	**58.8**	**55.5**	**56.5**	**63.1**
Newspaper and magazine subscriptions	20.1	32.1	28.4	29.9	36.6
Newspapers and magazines, nonsubscription	15.9	20.4	20.6	19.8	20.8
Books purchased through book clubs	1.5	2.2	2.7	1.8	2.1
Books not purchased through book clubs	19.6	34.5	29.8	33.4	39.2
EDUCATION, PERCENT BUYING	**14.0**	**24.8**	**22.1**	**23.8**	**27.7**
College tuition	5.0	10.1	8.3	10.0	11.7
Elementary and high school tuition	1.7	4.6	3.3	3.8	6.2
Vocational and technical schools tuition	0.3	0.6	0.3	0.8	0.7
Other school tuition	0.4	1.0	0.7	1.2	1.1
Other school expenses including rentals	3.5	6.5	7.4	5.5	6.5
Books, supplies for college	4.0	6.3	5.8	6.7	6.5
Books, supplies for elementary, high school	3.4	5.4	5.3	5.6	5.4
Books, supplies for vocational and technical schools	0.1	0.2	0.1	0.3	0.2
Books, supplies for day care, nursery school	0.1	0.2	0.3	0.2	0.2
Books, supplies for other schools	0.2	0.5	0.5	0.3	0.6
TOBACCO, PERCENT BUYING	**21.5**	**16.5**	**20.9**	**17.1**	**12.4**
Cigarettes	18.7	13.0	17.6	13.3	8.9
Other tobacco products	3.8	4.8	5.7	4.7	4.2

Source: Bureau of Labor Statistics, unpublished data from the 2008 Consumer Expenditure Survey

Table 9.10 Amount High-Income Buyers Spent on Personal Care Products and Services, Reading Material, Education, and Tobacco, _Average Quarter_, 2008

(average amount spent by high-income households buying personal care products and services, reading material, education, and tobacco during the average quarter, by before-tax income of household, 2008)

	total households	$100,000 or more	$100,000–$119,999	$120,000–$149,999	$150,000 or more
PERSONAL CARE, AMOUNT SPENT	**$120.82**	**$185.23**	**$153.38**	**$172.12**	**$217.94**
Wigs and hairpieces	76.92	61.89	52.50	66.30	85.42
Electric personal care appliances	51.97	68.88	67.43	65.52	72.83
Personal care services	118.81	181.78	149.31	168.72	214.77
READING, AMOUNT SPENT	**69.54**	**98.65**	**88.45**	**91.90**	**110.03**
Newspaper and magazine subscriptions	57.28	67.61	65.19	63.26	71.53
Newspapers and magazines, nonsubscription	22.71	27.54	26.14	26.24	29.52
Books purchased through book clubs	63.62	72.41	68.07	71.33	77.75
Books not purchased through book clubs	65.38	84.16	78.10	79.53	90.58
EDUCATION, AMOUNT SPENT	**1,782.60**	**3,020.47**	**1,789.02**	**1,911.87**	**4,458.16**
College tuition	3,243.68	4,554.57	2,738.47	2,778.06	6,618.94
Elementary and high school tuition	2,812.28	4,122.21	3,016.38	2,405.52	5,299.15
Vocational and technical schools tuition	1,467.24	3,092.67	517.65	2,829.61	4,436.15
Other school tuition	849.43	1,340.00	1,966.32	836.78	1,384.26
Other school expenses including rentals	297.36	465.67	357.19	324.68	646.50
Books, supplies for college	387.59	431.11	370.77	360.71	523.49
Books, supplies for elementary, high school	124.04	167.77	125.57	165.13	203.78
Books, supplies for vocational and technical schools	467.86	796.67	370.83	429.81	1,361.67
Books, supplies for day care, nursery school	94.64	128.26	105.17	291.18	72.62
Books, supplies for other schools	147.92	260.20	140.69	313.64	325.43
TOBACCO, AMOUNT SPENT	**364.88**	**381.52**	**381.52**	**351.44**	**409.11**
Cigarettes	380.10	391.77	380.31	368.67	433.30
Other tobacco products	193.60	248.91	220.84	234.44	291.14

Source: Calculations by New Strategist based on the Bureau of Labor Statistics' 2008 Consumer Expenditure Survey

Table 9.11 Percent of High-Income Households Buying Personal Care Products and Services, School Supplies, and Smoking Accessories, Average Week, 2008

(percent of high-income households buying personal care products and services, school supplies, and smoking accessories during the average week, by before-tax income of household, 2008)

	total households	$100,000 or more	$100,000– $119,999	$120,000– $149,999	$150,000 or more
PERSONAL CARE, PERCENT BUYING	**38.6%**	**51.2%**	**51.2%**	**51.1%**	**51.3%**
Personal care products	**34.0**	**44.2**	**45.9**	**45.0**	**41.8**
Hair care products	12.3	16.9	18.6	16.4	15.6
Hair accessories	2.3	3.5	3.2	3.7	3.7
Oral hygiene products	11.0	15.4	15.6	15.7	14.8
Shaving products	3.9	6.3	6.5	6.3	6.0
Cosmetics, perfume, and bath products	20.7	28.4	27.8	29.9	27.8
Deodorants, feminine hygiene, misc. products	9.5	14.3	17.1	14.5	11.4
Electric personal care appliances	0.8	1.3	1.0	0.8	2.1
Personal care services	**9.5**	**16.6**	**14.0**	**15.9**	**19.8**
Personal care service for females	9.2	16.4	13.9	15.7	19.5
Personal care service for males	9.2	16.1	13.7	15.4	19.1
SCHOOL SUPPLIES, PERCENT BUYING	**8.8**	**15.8**	**13.9**	**16.9**	**16.8**
SMOKING ACCESSORIES, PERCENT BUYING	**1.4**	**1.9**	**1.6**	**1.4**	**2.5**

Source: Bureau of Labor Statistics, unpublished data from the 2008 Consumer Expenditure Survey

Table 9.12 Amount High-Income Buyers Spent on Personal Care Products and Services, School Supplies, and Smoking Accessories, Average Week, 2008

(average amount spent by high-income households buying personal care products and services, school supplies, and smoking accessories during the average week, by before-tax income of household, 2008)

	total households	$100,000 or more	$100,000– $119,999	$120,000– $149,999	$150,000 or more
PERSONAL CARE, AMOUNT SPENT	**$27.40**	**$43.87**	**$33.22**	**$39.01**	**$58.61**
Personal care products	**18.26**	**25.93**	**19.74**	**24.85**	**33.88**
Hair care products	10.69	14.11	10.42	12.72	19.73
Hair accessories	5.26	5.37	5.92	4.83	5.61
Oral hygiene products	6.12	6.84	6.53	6.12	7.77
Shaving products	9.33	10.40	7.87	10.21	13.38
Cosmetics, perfume, and bath products	14.06	20.09	14.22	19.73	26.50
Deodorants, feminine hygiene, misc. products	6.55	7.61	6.32	8.56	8.63
Electric personal care appliances	28.95	28.57	35.71	20.73	27.27
Personal care services	**46.19**	**66.19**	**56.70**	**54.97**	**80.19**
Personal care service for females	32.54	46.00	39.42	38.12	55.80
Personal care service for males	15.08	21.58	18.10	18.00	26.33
SCHOOL SUPPLIES, AMOUNT SPENT	**10.23**	**11.86**	**10.78**	**13.06**	**11.81**
SMOKING ACCESSORIES, AMOUNT SPENT	**4.35**	**7.53**	**3.68**	**5.71**	**11.02**

Source: Calculations by New Strategist based on the Bureau of Labor Statistics' 2008 Consumer Expenditure Survey

Table 9.13 Percent Buying Personal Care Products and Services, Reading Material, Education, and Tobacco by Household Type, Average Quarter, 2008

(percent of households buying personal care products and services, reading material, education, and tobacco during the average quarter, by type of household, 2008)

	total married couples	married couples, no children	married couples with children				single parent, at least one child <18	single person
			total	oldest child under 6	oldest child 6 to 17	oldest child 18 or older		
PERSONAL CARE, PERCENT BUYING	**69.7%**	**71.9%**	**69.1%**	**65.9%**	**69.9%**	**69.6%**	**53.2%**	**53.9%**
Wigs and hairpieces	0.7	0.3	0.8	0.3	0.9	1.1	3.2	0.3
Electric personal care appliances	4.3	3.9	4.5	4.1	4.6	4.7	3.1	2.2
Personal care services	68.9	71.2	68.2	65.0	68.8	69.0	51.4	53.2
READING, PERCENT BUYING	**47.9**	**52.6**	**45.0**	**39.6**	**45.0**	**48.3**	**27.1**	**36.5**
Newspaper and magazine subscriptions	25.7	31.8	21.3	18.2	19.5	26.4	7.6	15.7
Newspapers and magazines, nonsubscription	17.4	17.8	17.2	14.5	17.7	17.9	13.2	13.8
Books purchased through book clubs	1.9	1.9	1.8	1.7	1.8	2.0	0.9	1.0
Books not purchased through book clubs	23.4	23.6	24.1	22.9	25.2	23.0	14.2	16.0
EDUCATION, PERCENT BUYING	**17.8**	**7.5**	**27.3**	**13.2**	**31.1**	**29.3**	**20.3**	**7.1**
College tuition	6.1	4.5	7.7	4.3	4.0	15.9	2.9	3.5
Elementary and high school tuition	2.8	0.3	5.0	1.4	7.4	3.0	2.6	0.2
Vocational and technical schools tuition	0.4	0.3	0.4	0.4	0.4	0.5	0.0	0.1
Other school tuition	0.6	0.5	0.8	0.6	1.1	0.6	0.2	0.2
Other school expenses including rentals	4.8	1.5	8.0	3.4	10.1	6.9	6.8	1.1
Books, supplies for college	4.1	2.6	5.4	3.4	2.8	11.1	2.7	4.1
Books, supplies for elementary, high school	4.8	0.4	8.7	1.5	13.8	4.1	9.5	0.2
Books, supplies for vocational and technical schools	0.1	0.1	0.1	0.1	0.2	0.2	0.1	0.1
Books, supplies for day care, nursery school	0.2	–	0.5	1.6	0.3	–	0.3	–
Books, supplies for other schools	0.4	0.1	0.6	0.4	0.9	0.3	–	0.2
TOBACCO, PERCENT BUYING	**20.7**	**19.1**	**21.0**	**16.7**	**20.8**	**23.7**	**19.5**	**17.4**
Cigarettes	17.3	15.7	17.3	13.0	16.6	21.0	18.6	15.1
Other tobacco products	4.7	4.6	4.9	4.6	5.0	4.7	1.0	2.9

Note: "–" means sample is too small to make a reliable estimate.
Source: Bureau of Labor Statistics, unpublished data from the 2008 Consumer Expenditure Survey

Table 9.14 Amount Buyers Spent on Personal Care Products and Services, Reading Material, Education, and Tobacco by Household Type, Average Quarter, 2008

(average amount spent by households buying personal care products and services, reading material, education, and tobacco during the average quarter, by type of household, 2008)

	total married couples	married couples, no children	married couples with children				single parent, at least one child <18	single person
			total	oldest child under 6	oldest child 6 to 17	oldest child 18 or older		
PERSONAL CARE, AMOUNT SPENT	**$135.55**	**$131.23**	**$140.52**	**$116.81**	**$143.51**	**$148.71**	**$122.38**	**$90.73**
Wigs and hairpieces	51.89	100.76	39.76	43.75	32.35	47.99	100.24	78.45
Electric personal care appliances	55.65	53.38	58.20	62.81	56.45	58.92	40.19	44.04
Personal care services	133.30	129.15	137.96	114.29	141.48	145.17	118.10	89.76
READING, AMOUNT SPENT	**76.42**	**78.73**	**74.37**	**61.51**	**74.52**	**80.39**	**52.80**	**59.68**
Newspaper and magazine subscriptions	59.06	62.46	53.97	45.05	53.03	58.84	44.94	55.59
Newspapers and magazines, nonsubscription	24.32	25.53	23.37	20.73	21.71	27.49	22.18	20.65
Books purchased through book clubs	64.52	59.16	60.19	76.95	63.19	47.50	52.91	58.59
Books not purchased through book clubs	68.14	66.94	69.43	50.81	72.25	75.17	52.92	59.76
EDUCATION, AMOUNT SPENT	**1,878.01**	**2,678.68**	**1,711.63**	**775.06**	**1,334.61**	**2,651.57**	**743.99**	**2,046.06**
College tuition	3,344.88	3,591.96	3,157.53	1,451.16	2,818.22	3,582.64	2,051.87	3,415.55
Elementary and high school tuition	2,954.34	4,874.14	3,043.99	1,267.83	3,066.68	3,417.38	2,263.92	3,201.67
Vocational and technical schools tuition	842.26	1,044.17	839.53	454.38	642.11	1,286.54	312.50	1,305.00
Other school tuition	976.19	701.06	1,065.36	344.26	1,183.96	1,133.77	397.37	282.61
Other school expenses including rentals	321.15	451.90	308.92	182.09	278.38	422.66	223.97	345.23
Books, supplies for college	414.22	427.87	419.62	278.97	399.82	454.04	247.43	362.32
Books, supplies for elementary, high school	128.00	121.62	131.36	57.12	127.41	170.11	105.21	97.92
Books, supplies for vocational and technical schools	316.07	189.58	475.00	96.43	200.00	919.44	41.67	188.64
Books, supplies for day care, nursery school	84.78	–	86.11	95.99	67.74	–	89.81	–
Books, supplies for other schools	167.57	197.73	166.13	46.25	212.50	49.24	–	80.00
TOBACCO, AMOUNT SPENT	**390.17**	**386.62**	**376.55**	**340.97**	**358.03**	**419.62**	**311.59**	**305.93**
Cigarettes	411.97	410.81	399.87	365.89	393.14	421.84	317.24	321.89
Other tobacco products	209.46	202.77	198.51	202.44	181.80	226.53	176.46	161.33

Note: "–" means sample is too small to make a reliable estimate.
Source: Calculations by New Strategist based on the Bureau of Labor Statistics' 2008 Consumer Expenditure Survey

Table 9.15 Percent Buying Personal Care Products and Services, School Supplies, and Smoking Accessories by Household Type, Average Week, 2008

(percent of households buying personal care products and services, school supplies, and smoking accessories during the average week, by type of household, 2008)

| | total married couples | married couples, no children | married couples with children | | | | single parent, at least one child <18 | single person |
			total	oldest child under 6	oldest child 6 to 17	oldest child 18 or older		
PERSONAL CARE, PERCENT BUYING	**45.6%**	**40.7%**	**49.2%**	**44.1%**	**49.5%**	**51.8%**	**38.2%**	**27.8%**
Personal care products	**40.5**	**35.0**	**44.5**	**38.4**	**44.8**	**47.8**	**36.2**	**23.1**
Hair care products	15.1	11.2	18.0	14.0	18.0	20.7	16.2	6.8
Hair accessories	2.9	1.5	3.9	3.7	4.4	3.3	3.3	1.2
Oral hygiene products	13.7	11.6	15.1	11.8	14.9	17.6	9.9	7.2
Shaving products	5.0	3.8	5.9	5.1	6.2	5.9	4.2	2.1
Cosmetics, perfume, and bath products	24.9	21.0	27.9	23.1	27.4	32.1	21.4	13.2
Deodorants, feminine hygiene, misc. products	12.0	8.5	14.8	13.1	14.2	16.7	10.4	5.3
Electric personal care appliances	1.0	1.1	1.0	0.6	0.8	1.7	0.7	0.4
Personal care services	**11.9**	**12.2**	**11.8**	**12.9**	**11.9**	**11.2**	**6.2**	**7.3**
Personal care service for females	11.5	11.8	11.4	11.7	11.6	10.9	6.0	7.3
Personal care service for males	11.6	11.8	11.5	12.7	11.6	10.4	6.1	7.1
SCHOOL SUPPLIES, PERCENT BUYING	**11.4**	**8.3**	**14.1**	**12.5**	**15.1**	**13.4**	**7.9**	**5.1**
SMOKING ACCESSORIES, PERCENT BUYING	**1.4**	**1.2**	**1.6**	**1.3**	**1.3**	**2.4**	**1.6**	**1.0**

Source: Bureau of Labor Statistics, unpublished data from the 2008 Consumer Expenditure Survey

Table 9.16 Amount Buyers Spent on Personal Care Products and Services, School Supplies, and Smoking Accessories by Household Type, Average Week, 2008

(average amount spent by households buying personal care products and services, school supplies, and smoking accessories during the average week, by type of household, 2008)

| | total married couples | married couples, no children | married couples with children | | | | single parent, at least one child <18 | single person |
			total	oldest child under 6	oldest child 6 to 17	oldest child 18 or older		
PERSONAL CARE, AMOUNT SPENT	**$30.16**	**$29.59**	**$31.56**	**$34.00**	**$30.98**	**$31.22**	**$20.48**	**$24.76**
Personal care products	**19.81**	**18.72**	**21.20**	**19.70**	**20.01**	**23.93**	**14.71**	**16.33**
Hair care products	10.97	11.72	10.75	11.50	9.99	11.62	7.72	12.46
Hair accessories	4.91	4.73	5.10	3.54	5.28	5.74	5.41	6.09
Oral hygiene products	6.36	7.05	5.89	4.42	5.91	6.42	4.44	5.84
Shaving products	9.18	9.69	9.18	11.79	8.62	8.97	7.19	10.80
Cosmetics, perfume, and bath products	15.43	14.76	16.54	16.12	15.97	17.62	11.03	12.85
Deodorants, feminine hygiene, misc. products	6.50	6.48	6.71	6.32	6.47	7.35	5.39	6.42
Electric personal care appliances	27.72	29.91	24.51	29.82	28.05	19.39	36.23	38.64
Personal care services	**48.07**	**45.00**	**51.44**	**57.70**	**53.79**	**42.42**	**40.65**	**42.51**
Personal care service for females	34.03	31.64	36.55	41.94	37.67	30.60	28.15	29.67
Personal care service for males	15.76	14.82	16.77	19.58	17.39	13.52	13.22	13.62
SCHOOL SUPPLIES, AMOUNT SPENT	**10.59**	**8.12**	**11.76**	**4.96**	**12.75**	**13.70**	**12.87**	**7.92**
SMOKING ACCESSORIES, AMOUNT SPENT	**4.96**	**8.47**	**3.05**	**3.13**	**3.73**	**2.93**	**1.83**	**3.85**

Source: Calculations by New Strategist based on the Bureau of Labor Statistics' 2008 Consumer Expenditure Survey

Table 9.17 Percent Buying Personal Care Products and Services, Reading Material, Education, and Tobacco by Race and Hispanic Origin, Average Quarter, 2008

(percent of households buying personal care products and services, reading material, education, and tobacco during the average quarter, by race and Hispanic origin of householder, 2008)

	total households	Asian	black	Hispanic	non-Hispanic white and other
PERSONAL CARE, PERCENT BUYING	**62.2%**	**61.4%**	**48.5%**	**54.0%**	**65.6%**
Wigs and hairpieces	0.8	0.2	3.9	0.4	0.3
Electric personal care appliances	3.4	2.6	2.5	2.9	3.7
Personal care services	61.3	60.8	46.3	53.1	64.9
READING, PERCENT BUYING	**41.6**	**30.8**	**25.7**	**18.7**	**47.6**
Newspaper and magazine subscriptions	20.1	12.6	8.4	6.5	24.0
Newspapers and magazines, nonsubscription	15.9	9.7	14.4	8.2	17.3
Books purchased through book clubs	1.5	0.4	0.6	0.8	1.7
Books not purchased through book clubs	19.6	16.2	9.0	7.6	23.1
EDUCATION, PERCENT BUYING	**14.0**	**17.5**	**9.9**	**12.9**	**14.8**
College tuition	5.0	7.5	2.8	3.2	5.6
Elementary and high school tuition	1.7	2.2	0.9	1.6	1.8
Vocational and technical schools tuition	0.3	0.2	0.3	0.4	0.3
Other school tuition	0.4	0.7	0.3	0.3	0.5
Other school expenses including rentals	3.5	3.7	1.9	2.9	3.8
Books, supplies for college	4.0	5.9	2.8	2.9	4.4
Books, supplies for elementary, high school	3.4	2.6	3.1	4.7	3.3
Books, supplies for vocational and technical schools	0.1	0.2	0.1	0.3	0.1
Books, supplies for day care, nursery school	0.1	0.3	0.1	0.3	0.1
Books, supplies for other schools	0.2	0.7	0.0	0.2	0.3
TOBACCO, PERCENT BUYING	**21.5**	**12.3**	**19.9**	**12.1**	**23.1**
Cigarettes	18.7	12.1	18.4	11.4	19.8
Other tobacco products	3.8	0.4	2.0	0.9	4.5

Note: "Asian" and "black" include Hispanics and non-Hispanics who identify themselves as being of the respective race alone. "Hispanic" includes people of any race who identify themselves as Hispanic. "Other" includes people who identify themselves as non-Hispanic and as Alaska Native, American Indian, Asian (who are also included in the Asian column), or Native Hawaiian or other Pacific Islander as well as non-Hispanics reporting more than one race.
Source: Bureau of Labor Statistics, unpublished data from the 2008 Consumer Expenditure Survey

Table 9.18 Amount Buyers Spent on Personal Care Products and Services, Reading Material, Education, and Tobacco by Race and Hispanic Origin, <u>Average Quarter,</u> 2008

(average amount spent by households buying personal care products and services, reading material, education, and tobacco during the average quarter, by race and Hispanic origin of householder, 2008)

	total households	Asian	black	Hispanic	non-Hispanic white and other
PERSONAL CARE, AMOUNT SPENT	**$120.82**	**$96.59**	**$155.17**	**$97.30**	**$119.67**
Wigs and hairpieces	76.92	12.50	87.40	24.40	68.18
Electric personal care appliances	51.97	91.76	41.53	53.73	52.95
Personal care services	118.81	93.52	152.87	95.80	117.75
READING, AMOUNT SPENT	**69.54**	**72.89**	**46.24**	**50.68**	**72.66**
Newspaper and magazine subscriptions	57.28	59.49	41.29	46.69	58.60
Newspapers and magazines, nonsubscription	22.71	21.51	20.22	20.30	23.22
Books purchased through book clubs	63.62	119.51	75.00	64.38	63.10
Books not purchased through book clubs	65.38	76.67	55.41	55.77	66.45
EDUCATION, AMOUNT SPENT	**1,782.60**	**2,329.41**	**1,221.81**	**1,243.48**	**1,911.19**
College tuition	3,243.68	3,886.72	2,989.17	2,576.42	3,318.93
Elementary and high school tuition	2,812.28	3,144.38	1,261.83	2,881.75	2,926.65
Vocational and technical schools tuition	1,467.24	1,262.50	771.00	1,320.00	1,573.28
Other school tuition	849.43	521.01	735.34	874.04	858.67
Other school expenses including rentals	297.36	361.97	301.84	233.59	304.30
Books, supplies for college	387.59	394.50	403.88	339.55	389.89
Books, supplies for elementary, high school	124.04	116.38	83.81	130.30	128.54
Books, supplies for vocational and technical schools	467.86	111.46	181.82	434.62	503.85
Books, supplies for day care, nursery school	94.64	54.55	254.17	101.79	80.77
Books, supplies for other schools	147.92	127.31	31.25	122.06	153.57
TOBACCO, AMOUNT SPENT	**364.88**	**330.82**	**278.84**	**293.24**	**382.18**
Cigarettes	380.10	326.06	283.98	295.17	401.56
Other tobacco products	193.60	285.00	161.40	206.94	195.34

Note: "Asian" and "black" include Hispanics and non-Hispanics who identify themselves as being of the respective race alone. "Hispanic" includes people of any race who identify themselves as Hispanic. "Other" includes people who identify themselves as non-Hispanic and as Alaska Native, American Indian, Asian (who are also included in the Asian column), or Native Hawaiian or other Pacific Islander as well as non-Hispanics reporting more than one race.
Source: Calculations by New Strategist based on the Bureau of Labor Statistics' 2008 Consumer Expenditure Survey

Table 9.19 Percent Buying Personal Care Products and Services, School Supplies, and Smoking Accessories by Race and Hispanic Origin, Average Week, 2008

(percent of households buying personal care products and services, school supplies, and smoking accessories during the average week, by race and Hispanic origin of householder, 2008)

	total households	Asian	black	Hispanic	non-Hispanic white and other
PERSONAL CARE, PERCENT BUYING	38.6%	33.5%	34.9%	41.9%	38.7%
Personal care products	34.0	28.6	31.4	39.3	33.6
Hair care products	12.3	9.0	9.4	16.7	12.1
Hair accessories	2.3	1.8	2.8	2.9	2.1
Oral hygiene products	11.0	8.7	9.8	12.1	11.0
Shaving products	3.9	2.2	2.5	4.6	3.9
Cosmetics, perfume, and bath products	20.7	19.2	21.1	24.9	20.1
Deodorants, feminine hygiene, misc. products	9.5	6.6	8.5	11.2	9.4
Electric personal care appliances	0.8	0.2	0.5	0.6	0.8
Personal care services	9.5	6.9	6.2	6.2	10.4
Personal care service for females	9.2	6.6	6.1	5.9	10.1
Personal care service for males	9.2	6.7	6.1	6.0	10.1
SCHOOL SUPPLIES, PERCENT BUYING	8.8	8.8	3.8	6.5	9.9
SMOKING ACCESSORIES, PERCENT BUYING	1.4	0.6	0.7	1.1	1.5

Note: "Asian" and "black" include Hispanics and non-Hispanics who identify themselves as being of the respective race alone. "Hispanic" includes people of any race who identify themselves as Hispanic. "Other" includes people who identify themselves as non-Hispanic and as Alaska Native, American Indian, Asian (who are also included in the Asian column), or Native Hawaiian or other Pacific Islander as well as non-Hispanics reporting more than one race.
Source: Bureau of Labor Statistics, unpublished data from the 2008 Consumer Expenditure Survey

Table 9.20 Amount Buyers Spent on Personal Care Products and Services, School Supplies, and Smoking Accessories by Race and Hispanic Origin, Average Week, 2008

(average amount spent by households buying personal care products and services, school supplies, and smoking accessories during the average week, by race and Hispanic origin of householder, 2008)

	total households	Asian	black	Hispanic	non-Hispanic white and other
PERSONAL CARE, AMOUNT SPENT	$27.40	$33.35	$20.48	$20.58	$29.48
Personal care products	18.26	23.96	14.15	16.71	19.15
Hair care products	10.69	10.69	8.01	8.25	11.54
Hair accessories	5.26	2.81	3.55	4.08	5.69
Oral hygiene products	6.12	6.64	5.44	5.03	6.29
Shaving products	9.33	12.05	7.11	8.70	9.64
Cosmetics, perfume, and bath products	14.06	23.19	10.89	12.66	14.89
Deodorants, feminine hygiene, misc. products	6.55	7.70	5.75	6.46	6.60
Electric personal care appliances	28.95	8.33	17.31	26.56	30.49
Personal care services	46.19	62.59	43.48	33.55	47.56
Personal care service for females	32.54	44.38	30.36	23.43	33.53
Personal care service for males	15.08	20.47	14.21	11.42	15.48
SCHOOL SUPPLIES, AMOUNT SPENT	10.23	10.41	12.76	8.29	10.23
SMOKING ACCESSORIES, AMOUNT SPENT	4.35	14.04	2.86	2.86	5.23

Note: "Asian" and "black" include Hispanics and non-Hispanics who identify themselves as being of the respective race alone. "Hispanic" includes people of any race who identify themselves as Hispanic. "Other" includes people who identify themselves as non-Hispanic and as Alaska Native, American Indian, Asian (who are also included in the Asian column), or Native Hawaiian or other Pacific Islander as well as non-Hispanics reporting more than one race.
Source: Calculations by New Strategist based on the Bureau of Labor Statistics' 2008 Consumer Expenditure Survey

Table 9.21 Percent Buying Personal Care Products and Services, Reading Material, Education, and Tobacco by Region, <u>Average Quarter</u>, 2008

(percent of households buying personal care products and services, reading material, education, and tobacco during the average quarter, by region of residence, 2008)

	total households	Northeast	Midwest	South	West
PERSONAL CARE, PERCENT BUYING	**62.2%**	**65.8%**	**61.2%**	**60.8%**	**62.6%**
Wigs and hairpieces	0.8	0.9	0.7	1.0	0.4
Electric personal care appliances	3.4	2.6	3.8	3.5	3.6
Personal care services	61.3	65.0	60.2	59.8	61.7
READING, PERCENT BUYING	**41.6**	**46.2**	**44.4**	**35.8**	**44.4**
Newspaper and magazine subscriptions	20.1	22.3	23.0	16.6	20.9
Newspapers and magazines, nonsubscription	15.9	19.8	16.0	14.3	15.2
Books purchased through book clubs	1.5	1.5	1.6	1.2	1.7
Books not purchased through book clubs	19.6	21.0	19.9	15.4	25.1
EDUCATION, PERCENT BUYING	**14.0**	**12.8**	**16.3**	**12.7**	**14.8**
College tuition	5.0	5.1	6.0	4.3	5.1
Elementary and high school tuition	1.7	1.5	2.3	1.5	1.7
Vocational and technical schools tuition	0.3	0.1	0.3	0.2	0.5
Other school tuition	0.4	0.4	0.3	0.4	0.6
Other school expenses including rentals	3.5	2.9	4.6	2.9	3.8
Books, supplies for college	4.0	4.0	5.0	3.3	4.3
Books, supplies for elementary, high school	3.4	2.4	3.3	4.0	3.3
Books, supplies for vocational and technical schools	0.1	0.1	0.2	0.1	0.2
Books, supplies for day care, nursery school	0.1	0.2	0.2	0.1	0.1
Books, supplies for other schools	0.2	0.3	0.3	0.2	0.2
TOBACCO, PERCENT BUYING	**21.5**	**21.0**	**23.3**	**23.1**	**17.4**
Cigarettes	18.7	18.1	20.4	19.7	15.6
Other tobacco products	3.8	3.5	4.2	4.3	2.8

Source: Bureau of Labor Statistics, unpublished data from the 2008 Consumer Expenditure Survey

Table 9.22 Amount Buyers Spent on Personal Care Products and Services, Reading Material, Education, and Tobacco by Region, <u>Average Quarter</u>, 2008

(average amount spent by households buying personal care products and services, reading material, education, and tobacco during the average quarter, by region of residence, 2008)

	total households	Northeast	Midwest	South	West
PERSONAL CARE, AMOUNT SPENT	**$120.82**	**$122.23**	**$109.22**	**$123.74**	**$126.70**
Wigs and hairpieces	76.92	70.28	80.99	87.63	46.51
Electric personal care appliances	51.97	53.53	47.72	47.36	63.27
Personal care services	118.81	120.63	106.98	121.69	124.59
READING, AMOUNT SPENT	**69.54**	**76.44**	**65.97**	**60.81**	**78.68**
Newspaper and magazine subscriptions	57.28	67.67	54.95	51.68	57.92
Newspapers and magazines, nonsubscription	22.71	27.21	22.99	19.63	22.28
Books purchased through book clubs	63.62	72.28	54.40	60.59	70.61
Books not purchased through book clubs	65.38	65.55	60.45	62.34	72.27
EDUCATION, AMOUNT SPENT	**1,782.60**	**3,005.41**	**1,515.02**	**1,478.58**	**1,630.93**
College tuition	3,243.68	5,415.57	2,861.27	2,778.60	2,543.63
Elementary and high school tuition	2,812.28	4,976.87	1,601.78	2,537.84	3,319.58
Vocational and technical schools tuition	1,467.24	1,192.86	573.48	655.95	2,548.58
Other school tuition	849.43	797.37	1,047.79	701.22	921.88
Other school expenses including rentals	297.36	400.17	210.08	274.91	368.95
Books, supplies for college	387.59	453.53	364.75	419.55	322.81
Books, supplies for elementary, high school	124.04	93.72	144.47	115.29	138.85
Books, supplies for vocational and technical schools	467.86	187.50	151.32	181.25	951.04
Books, supplies for day care, nursery school	94.64	68.06	71.05	145.83	65.00
Books, supplies for other schools	147.92	73.00	134.68	216.25	146.43
TOBACCO, AMOUNT SPENT	**364.88**	**383.75**	**379.98**	**348.47**	**361.10**
Cigarettes	380.10	405.91	396.31	364.67	365.36
Other tobacco products	193.60	194.87	173.52	202.00	203.83

Source: Calculations by New Strategist based on the Bureau of Labor Statistics' 2008 Consumer Expenditure Survey

Table 9.23 Percent Buying Personal Care Products and Services, School Supplies, and Smoking Accessories by Region, <u>Average Week</u>, 2008

(percent of households buying personal care products and services, school supplies, and smoking accessories during the average week, by region of residence, 2008)

	total households	Northeast	Midwest	South	West
PERSONAL CARE, PERCENT BUYING	**38.6%**	**38.3%**	**35.9%**	**39.2%**	**40.4%**
Personal care products	**34.0**	**33.1**	**30.7**	**35.1**	**36.1**
Hair care products	12.3	11.6	11.4	12.3	13.7
Hair accessories	2.3	1.8	2.0	2.5	2.7
Oral hygiene products	11.0	11.4	9.8	11.4	11.1
Shaving products	3.9	3.4	3.7	4.1	4.0
Cosmetics, perfume, and bath products	20.7	19.8	18.5	21.7	22.1
Deodorants, feminine hygiene, misc. products	9.5	8.7	8.5	10.0	10.2
Electric personal care appliances	0.8	0.9	0.9	0.5	0.9
Personal care services	**9.5**	**10.7**	**9.8**	**8.7**	**9.4**
Personal care service for females	9.2	10.5	9.6	8.4	9.0
Personal care service for males	9.2	10.3	9.3	8.5	9.1
SCHOOL SUPPLIES, PERCENT BUYING	**8.8**	**8.6**	**8.0**	**7.9**	**11.2**
SMOKING ACCESSORIES, PERCENT BUYING	**1.4**	**1.2**	**1.4**	**1.4**	**1.5**

Source: Bureau of Labor Statistics, unpublished data from the 2008 Consumer Expenditure Survey

Table 9.24 Amount Buyers Spent on Personal Care Products and Services, School Supplies, and Smoking Accessories by Region, <u>Average Week</u>, 2008

(average amount spent by households buying personal care products and services, school supplies, and smoking accessories during the average week, by region of residence, 2008)

	total households	Northeast	Midwest	South	West
PERSONAL CARE, AMOUNT SPENT	**$27.40**	**$28.68**	**$27.41**	**$24.87**	**$30.36**
Personal care products	**18.26**	**18.76**	**18.21**	**15.62**	**22.02**
Hair care products	10.69	11.94	11.57	8.56	12.30
Hair accessories	5.26	4.40	5.05	4.45	6.42
Oral hygiene products	6.12	6.07	5.63	5.79	6.95
Shaving products	9.33	10.79	9.38	8.60	9.52
Cosmetics, perfume, and bath products	14.06	14.05	13.58	11.84	17.94
Deodorants, feminine hygiene, misc. products	6.55	7.22	6.26	6.18	6.77
Electric personal care appliances	28.95	31.76	26.09	24.07	32.97
Personal care services	**46.19**	**44.63**	**43.46**	**49.19**	**46.16**
Personal care service for females	32.54	31.02	30.83	34.61	32.85
Personal care service for males	15.08	14.73	14.06	15.94	15.14
SCHOOL SUPPLIES, AMOUNT SPENT	**10.23**	**9.26**	**10.74**	**10.86**	**9.69**
SMOKING ACCESSORIES, AMOUNT SPENT	**4.35**	**3.23**	**4.23**	**2.96**	**8.05**

Source: Calculations by New Strategist based on the Bureau of Labor Statistics' 2008 Consumer Expenditure Survey

Table 9.25 Percent Buying Personal Care Products and Services, Reading Material, Education, and Tobacco by Education, <u>Average Quarter</u>, 2008

(percent of households buying personal care products and services, reading material, education, and tobacco during the average quarter, by highest level of education of householder, 2008)

	total households	less than high school graduate	high school graduate	some college	associate's degree	college graduate		
						total	bachelor's degree	master's, professional, doctorate
PERSONAL CARE, PERCENT BUYING	**62.2%**	**44.4%**	**57.5%**	**61.2%**	**66.3%**	**74.8%**	**72.3%**	**79.3%**
Wigs and hairpieces	0.8	1.4	0.8	0.8	0.5	0.6	0.6	0.6
Electric personal care appliances	3.4	1.9	2.7	4.0	4.1	4.1	4.2	4.0
Personal care services	61.3	43.2	56.7	60.1	65.3	74.1	71.4	78.9
READING, PERCENT BUYING	**41.6**	**23.1**	**36.1**	**41.2**	**45.7**	**54.8**	**51.6**	**60.5**
Newspaper and magazine subscriptions	20.1	11.6	17.3	18.5	20.2	28.0	26.3	31.2
Newspapers and magazines, nonsubscription	15.9	9.8	14.7	16.9	17.8	18.7	18.3	19.5
Books purchased through book clubs	1.5	1.0	1.2	1.3	2.1	1.8	1.6	2.0
Books not purchased through book clubs	19.6	5.6	12.1	19.6	22.3	32.5	29.4	38.1
EDUCATION, PERCENT BUYING	**14.0**	**6.2**	**9.8**	**17.1**	**14.9**	**19.0**	**19.1**	**19.0**
College tuition	5.0	1.1	2.8	6.9	5.0	7.6	7.5	7.7
Elementary and high school tuition	1.7	0.7	1.0	1.5	1.3	3.0	2.9	3.3
Vocational and technical schools tuition	0.3	0.1	0.4	0.4	0.2	0.3	0.3	0.3
Other school tuition	0.4	0.2	0.2	0.4	0.6	0.8	0.7	0.9
Other school expenses including rentals	3.5	1.3	2.7	3.8	3.9	4.9	5.0	4.7
Books, supplies for college	4.0	0.7	2.2	7.1	3.8	5.1	5.3	4.9
Books, supplies for elementary, high school	3.4	2.7	3.0	3.0	4.0	4.2	4.4	3.8
Books, supplies for vocational and technical schools	0.1	0.2	0.1	0.1	0.2	0.2	0.2	0.1
Books, supplies for day care, nursery school	0.1	0.1	0.1	0.1	0.2	0.2	0.3	0.1
Books, supplies for other schools	0.2	0.1	0.2	0.2	0.2	0.4	0.3	0.6
TOBACCO, PERCENT BUYING	**21.5**	**25.4**	**28.4**	**22.4**	**22.6**	**12.3**	**14.1**	**9.0**
Cigarettes	18.7	23.1	24.8	19.8	19.7	9.9	11.5	6.9
Other tobacco products	3.8	3.3	5.0	3.7	3.7	3.1	3.4	2.5

Source: Bureau of Labor Statistics, unpublished data from the 2008 Consumer Expenditure Survey

Table 9.26 Amount Buyers Spent on Personal Care Products and Services, Reading Material, Education, and Tobacco by Education, Average Quarter, 2008

(average amount spent by households buying personal care products and services, reading material, education, and tobacco during the average quarter, by highest level of education of householder, 2008)

	total households	less than high school graduate	high school graduate	some college	associate's degree	college graduate total	bachelor's degree	master's, professional, doctorate
PERSONAL CARE, AMOUNT SPENT	**$120.82**	**$82.98**	**$99.83**	**$116.66**	**$118.06**	**$149.68**	**$139.86**	**$165.77**
Wigs and hairpieces	76.92	52.22	103.67	97.50	68.75	57.76	65.52	43.53
Electric personal care appliances	51.97	36.77	41.76	54.84	58.01	57.60	56.07	60.30
Personal care services	118.81	82.12	97.90	113.88	115.55	147.61	137.91	163.35
READING, AMOUNT SPENT	**69.54**	**46.56**	**52.26**	**60.78**	**63.54**	**91.02**	**81.29**	**105.91**
Newspaper and magazine subscriptions	57.28	49.76	51.30	50.57	55.70	65.78	59.64	75.08
Newspapers and magazines, nonsubscription	22.71	19.36	22.43	22.01	21.70	24.57	23.00	27.23
Books purchased through book clubs	63.62	48.47	60.95	57.01	75.12	68.82	59.97	82.11
Books not purchased through book clubs	65.38	47.35	48.93	56.93	54.67	78.46	71.73	87.79
EDUCATION, AMOUNT SPENT	**1,782.60**	**518.33**	**991.96**	**1,407.12**	**1,330.73**	**2,717.15**	**2,399.55**	**3,290.14**
College tuition	3,243.68	1,578.83	1,859.31	2,468.73	2,503.31	4,508.87	4,026.60	5,353.75
Elementary and high school tuition	2,812.28	507.19	1,740.91	1,636.35	2,902.80	3,833.50	3,495.73	4,354.14
Vocational and technical schools tuition	1,467.24	601.79	2,703.57	903.47	670.24	1,017.50	605.65	1,780.17
Other school tuition	849.43	290.00	689.13	995.95	389.91	1,005.52	1,084.42	902.20
Other school expenses including rentals	297.36	144.74	187.55	242.51	293.72	405.46	367.96	478.23
Books, supplies for college	387.59	374.65	370.93	367.60	379.77	416.54	377.59	491.12
Books, supplies for elementary, high school	124.04	94.46	94.68	107.05	103.47	167.68	150.39	204.72
Books, supplies for vocational and technical schools	467.86	961.36	340.00	139.58	218.33	418.75	214.06	900.00
Books, supplies for day care, nursery school	94.64	227.78	143.75	59.62	26.47	81.82	82.76	68.18
Books, supplies for other schools	147.92	250.00	86.25	104.76	61.90	201.25	263.39	146.83
TOBACCO, AMOUNT SPENT	**364.88**	**375.94**	**372.97**	**363.51**	**383.35**	**328.48**	**322.08**	**346.67**
Cigarettes	380.10	383.36	391.65	377.85	401.37	341.13	336.54	354.70
Other tobacco products	193.60	217.41	174.36	181.76	195.03	218.59	200.52	262.01

Source: Calculations by New Strategist based on the Bureau of Labor Statistics' 2008 Consumer Expenditure Survey

Table 9.27 Percent Buying Personal Care Products and Services, School Supplies, and Smoking Accessories by Education, <u>Average Week</u>, 2008

(percent of households buying personal care products and services, school supplies, and smoking accessories during the average week, by highest level of education of householder, 2008)

	total households	less than high school graduate	high school graduate	some college	associate's degree	college graduate		
						total	bachelor's degree	master's, professional, doctorate
PERSONAL CARE, PERCENT BUYING	**38.6%**	**32.9%**	**35.6%**	**38.1%**	**41.7%**	**43.3%**	**43.4%**	**43.1%**
Personal care products	**34.0**	**29.9**	**31.9**	**33.7**	**36.9**	**37.1**	**37.6**	**36.1**
Hair care products	12.3	10.8	11.1	13.0	14.4	12.8	13.2	12.0
Hair accessories	2.3	2.2	1.8	2.3	2.0	2.8	3.1	2.3
Oral hygiene products	11.0	9.7	10.6	9.8	11.8	12.6	12.1	13.4
Shaving products	3.9	2.5	3.4	3.6	4.5	5.0	5.6	3.8
Cosmetics, perfume, and bath products	20.7	18.3	18.9	21.0	23.2	22.5	22.7	22.2
Deodorants, feminine hygiene, misc. products	9.5	7.6	8.8	9.5	11.8	10.3	10.7	9.4
Electric personal care appliances	0.8	0.4	0.7	0.7	0.9	1.0	0.8	1.4
Personal care services	**9.5**	**4.8**	**8.3**	**8.7**	**9.8**	**13.1**	**12.1**	**15.0**
Personal care service for females	9.2	4.7	8.1	8.5	9.5	12.7	11.6	14.8
Personal care service for males	9.2	4.7	8.1	8.4	9.4	12.7	11.7	14.4
SCHOOL SUPPLIES, PERCENT BUYING	**8.8**	**4.1**	**6.6**	**9.1**	**9.6**	**12.5**	**11.2**	**15.1**
SMOKING ACCESSORIES, PERCENT BUYING	**1.4**	**1.4**	**1.2**	**1.7**	**1.5**	**1.2**	**1.1**	**1.5**

Source: Bureau of Labor Statistics, unpublished data from the 2008 Consumer Expenditure Survey

Table 9.28 Amount Buyers Spent on Personal Care Products and Services, School Supplies, and Smoking Accessories by Education, <u>Average Week</u>, 2008

(average amount spent by households buying personal care products and services, school supplies, and smoking accessories during the average week, by highest level of education of householder, 2008)

	total households	less than high school graduate	high school graduate	some college	associate's degree	college graduate		
						total	bachelor's degree	master's, professional, doctorate
PERSONAL CARE, AMOUNT SPENT	**$27.40**	**$14.93**	**$22.20**	**$25.83**	**$27.94**	**$36.65**	**$35.00**	**$39.73**
Personal care products	**18.26**	**11.89**	**15.28**	**17.62**	**18.81**	**23.23**	**23.75**	**22.25**
Hair care products	10.69	7.43	9.80	10.50	10.79	12.81	12.33	13.97
Hair accessories	5.26	3.15	4.00	4.31	6.03	6.69	7.37	4.35
Oral hygiene products	6.12	4.87	5.78	5.82	5.94	6.92	7.41	6.13
Shaving products	9.33	6.00	8.61	8.68	7.87	11.27	11.25	11.02
Cosmetics, perfume, and bath products	14.06	7.85	11.41	13.35	12.82	19.31	20.04	17.98
Deodorants, feminine hygiene, misc. products	6.55	7.22	5.69	5.80	8.88	6.54	6.72	6.40
Electric personal care appliances	28.95	16.28	23.53	35.82	20.88	32.35	33.33	30.88
Personal care services	**46.19**	**28.33**	**36.21**	**45.06**	**48.31**	**55.22**	**51.69**	**60.44**
Personal care service for females	32.54	20.13	25.43	31.49	33.89	39.16	36.97	42.31
Personal care service for males	15.08	8.72	11.96	14.74	15.96	17.97	16.95	19.53
SCHOOL SUPPLIES, AMOUNT SPENT	**10.23**	**8.13**	**8.77**	**11.00**	**12.23**	**10.29**	**9.83**	**10.88**
SMOKING ACCESSORIES, AMOUNT SPENT	**4.35**	**2.96**	**4.10**	**6.94**	**6.85**	**3.23**	**3.64**	**3.33**

Source: Calculations by New Strategist based on the Bureau of Labor Statistics' 2008 Consumer Expenditure Survey

CHAPTER 10

Transportation Buyers, 2008

Transportation is the second biggest expense of American households, behind only spending on shelter. In 2008, the average household spent 7 percent less on transportation than in 2000, after adjusting for inflation. Gasoline is by far the biggest transportation expense.

Quarterly spending

During the average quarter of 2008, 90 percent of households bought gasoline. The buyers spent $697 fueling their vehicles. More than half of households spent money to repair their vehicles during the average quarter, and slightly more than half paid for vehicle insurance. A smaller one-third of households paid vehicle finance charges. Only 1.3 percent of households purchased a new car or truck during the average quarter of 2008. Those who bought new cars spent an average of $23,500, while those who bought new trucks spent $28,212.

Weekly spending

During the average week of 2008, 68 percent of households purchased gasoline, spending an average of $68 on the category. The percentage of households that spent on gasoline during the average week peaks at 74 percent among householders aged 35 to 54. Gas buyers in those age groups spent an average of $75 to $77 on the product.

Transportation Buyers' Top 10

(transportation categories bought by the largest percentage of households during an average quarter, 2008)

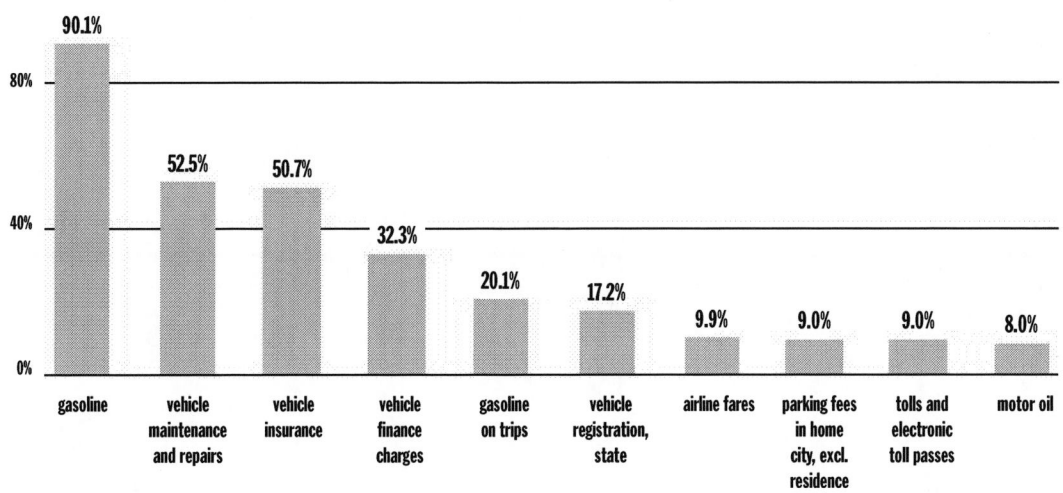

Table 10.1 Percent Buying Transportation by Age, <u>Average Quarter</u>, 2008

(percent of households buying transportation during the average quarter, by age of householder, 2008)

TRANSPORTATION, PERCENT BUYING	total households	under 25	25 to 34	35 to 44	45 to 54	55 to 64	65 to 74	75+
	94.8%	90.0%	96.0%	96.8%	96.9%	96.8%	94.4%	84.3%
Vehicle purchases	**4.7**	**5.5**	**5.6**	**5.4**	**5.7**	**4.3**	**2.9**	**1.7**
Cars and trucks, new	1.3	0.8	1.3	1.4	1.6	1.5	1.0	0.7
New cars	0.8	0.6	0.7	0.7	1.0	1.0	0.7	0.4
New trucks	0.5	0.1	0.6	0.6	0.5	0.6	0.3	0.3
Cars and trucks, used	3.2	4.0	4.0	3.7	4.0	2.5	1.9	0.9
Used cars	1.8	2.6	1.8	2.0	2.3	1.5	1.0	0.5
Used trucks	1.5	1.4	2.2	1.7	1.7	1.0	0.9	0.4
Other vehicles	0.4	0.9	0.4	0.4	0.3	0.4	0.2	0.1
Gasoline and motor oil	**90.7**	**83.0**	**91.1**	**94.2**	**93.1**	**93.2**	**90.5**	**79.2**
Gasoline	90.1	82.1	90.3	93.5	92.4	92.6	90.0	78.9
Diesel fuel	1.8	0.7	1.5	2.2	2.2	2.4	1.9	0.7
Gasoline on trips	20.1	15.7	19.2	21.3	22.9	23.7	19.2	10.9
Motor oil	8.0	7.3	8.0	9.4	9.5	8.3	6.7	3.3
Motor oil on trips	20.1	15.7	19.2	21.3	22.9	23.7	19.2	10.9
Other vehicle expenses	**80.8**	**65.2**	**82.5**	**86.3**	**85.7**	**85.2**	**78.0**	**63.0**
Vehicle finance charges	32.3	25.2	42.2	40.1	37.5	32.3	19.1	7.1
Automobile finance charges	17.1	16.0	22.7	17.3	20.7	17.5	10.9	5.1
Truck finance charges	17.5	10.1	23.6	25.4	19.8	16.7	9.2	2.0
Motorcycle and plane finance charges	1.4	1.3	2.0	2.4	1.5	0.8	0.2	0.0
Other vehicle finance charges	1.4	1.2	1.4	1.9	1.6	1.7	1.3	0.3
Maintenance and repairs	52.5	39.9	52.0	56.0	58.4	56.7	50.1	38.1
Coolant, additives, brake and transmission fluids	5.0	4.4	5.1	5.6	6.4	5.1	3.6	2.3
Tires—purchased, replaced, installed	7.8	6.2	7.1	9.2	10.0	8.1	6.2	3.9
Vehicle products and cleaning services	3.6	2.0	3.9	3.4	4.1	3.9	3.9	3.0
Parts, equipment, and accessories	8.7	8.7	8.2	9.7	10.3	9.4	6.8	4.2
Vehicle audio equipment, excluding labor	0.2	0.3	0.3	0.2	0.2	0.2	0.2	–
Vehicle video equipment	0.3	0.1	0.4	0.3	0.4	0.2	0.3	0.1
Body work and painting	1.2	0.5	0.9	1.2	1.5	1.7	1.0	1.2
Clutch and transmission repair	1.2	0.9	1.1	1.1	1.5	1.3	1.1	1.0
Drive shaft and rear-end repair	0.3	0.1	0.2	0.3	0.3	0.4	0.2	0.2
Brake work	4.8	3.0	3.6	5.6	6.5	5.2	4.2	2.3
Repair to steering or front-end	1.2	0.6	1.1	1.1	1.5	1.6	0.9	0.8
Repair to engine cooling system	1.7	1.2	1.4	1.5	2.4	2.0	1.6	1.3
Motor tune-up	4.4	2.3	4.0	5.0	5.1	5.5	3.8	2.9
Lube, oil change, and oil filters	33.8	24.3	33.7	35.7	37.2	36.1	33.7	25.0
Front-end alignment, wheel balance, rotation	2.5	1.0	2.0	3.0	2.9	3.2	2.4	1.8
Shock absorber replacement	0.3	0.2	0.1	0.4	0.4	0.5	0.4	0.1
Tire repair and other repair work	5.9	3.6	4.9	5.8	6.9	6.8	6.4	4.6
Exhaust system repair	0.9	0.6	0.9	0.8	1.1	1.1	0.9	0.4
Electrical system repair	2.2	1.2	1.6	2.4	2.5	2.7	2.1	1.7
Motor repair, replacement	2.6	1.6	2.2	2.8	3.2	3.0	2.1	1.9
Auto repair service policy	0.5	0.4	0.3	0.4	0.7	0.8	0.5	0.3
Vehicle accessories including labor	0.5	0.2	0.3	0.3	0.7	0.6	0.5	0.3
Vehicle air conditioning repair	0.9	0.4	0.5	0.7	1.3	1.4	0.7	0.8

	total consumer units	under 25	25 to 34	35 to 44	45 to 54	55 to 64	65 to 74	75+
Vehicle insurance	50.7%	33.2%	54.3%	57.4%	55.1%	52.7%	45.6%	35.9%
Vehicle rental, leases, licenses, other charges	43.3	30.6	41.9	46.5	48.7	48.1	40.6	30.9
Leased and rented vehicles	6.5	2.5	7.8	7.4	7.5	7.6	4.7	2.7
Rented vehicles	2.8	1.3	3.1	2.7	3.6	4.0	1.9	0.9
Auto rental	0.5	0.5	0.6	0.5	0.5	0.6	0.3	0.4
Auto rental on trips	2.0	0.7	1.9	1.7	2.7	3.1	1.5	0.5
Truck rental	0.2	0.2	0.5	0.4	0.2	0.1	0.1	–
Truck rental on trips	0.1	0.0	0.1	0.1	0.3	0.2	0.1	0.0
Leased vehicles	3.8	1.2	4.9	4.9	4.2	3.9	2.9	1.8
Car lease payments	2.3	0.9	2.8	2.4	2.6	2.1	2.0	1.6
Truck lease payments	1.8	0.4	2.4	2.8	2.0	2.0	1.0	0.2
Vehicle registration, state	17.2	10.1	16.2	18.5	20.6	18.5	16.4	12.6
Vehicle registration, local	2.1	0.8	1.6	2.3	2.6	2.4	2.7	1.4
Driver's license	5.2	4.4	5.3	5.8	5.5	5.5	4.6	3.8
Vehicle inspection	6.4	3.8	5.7	6.7	7.4	7.0	6.5	5.1
Parking fees	11.4	11.1	12.3	12.1	13.5	13.0	8.4	4.4
Parking fees in home city, excluding residence	9.0	9.8	10.1	9.5	10.4	10.2	6.5	3.5
Parking fees on trips	3.1	1.9	3.0	3.5	4.1	3.8	2.3	0.9
Tolls and electronic toll passes	9.0	4.8	8.6	10.9	10.9	10.6	7.5	3.4
Tolls on trips	6.2	3.9	5.7	6.8	7.1	7.5	5.9	3.5
Towing charges	0.9	1.7	1.0	1.2	1.1	0.7	0.6	0.5
Global positioning services	0.5	0.3	0.4	0.4	0.6	0.5	0.7	0.4
Automobile service clubs	5.0	1.2	2.4	3.9	6.2	7.0	7.0	6.8
Public transportation	**18.2**	**17.8**	**19.4**	**17.6**	**20.5**	**20.0**	**15.4**	**12.3**
Airline fares	9.9	6.7	8.9	9.9	11.6	12.4	9.5	6.3
Intercity bus fares	4.0	3.6	3.5	3.9	4.4	4.5	4.2	3.1
Intracity mass transit fares	7.0	8.5	8.8	6.9	7.5	7.2	5.1	4.1
Local transportation on trips	4.8	3.6	4.4	4.9	5.5	5.6	5.1	3.1
Taxi fares and limousine service on trips	4.8	3.6	4.4	4.9	5.5	5.6	5.1	3.1
Taxi fares and limousine service	3.0	4.7	4.5	2.6	3.0	2.5	1.8	2.5
Intercity train fares	3.9	3.2	3.5	3.7	4.5	4.6	3.8	2.9
Ship fares	2.2	1.0	1.5	2.2	2.9	2.9	2.4	1.7
School bus	0.0	–	0.0	0.1	0.1	0.0	–	–

Note: "–" means sample is too small to make a reliable estimate.
Source: Bureau of Labor Statistics, unpublished data from the 2008 Consumer Expenditure Survey

Table 10.2 Amount Buyers Spent on Transportation by Age, <u>Average Quarter,</u> 2008

(average amount spent by households buying transportation during the average quarter, by age of householder, 2008)

	total households	under 25	25 to 34	35 to 44	45 to 54	55 to 64	65 to 74	75+
TRANSPORTATION, AMOUNT SPENT	**$2,200.87**	**$1,543.13**	**$2,259.72**	**$2,492.67**	**$2,645.59**	**$2,342.72**	**$1,673.10**	**$1,145.39**
Vehicle purchases	**14,560.25**	**8,985.94**	**13,981.44**	**14,400.09**	**14,593.86**	**17,602.00**	**16,436.90**	**15,002.44**
Cars and trucks, new	25,487.50	19,970.45	26,088.28	25,904.01	25,443.91	25,853.62	27,594.80	22,637.14
New cars	23,500.00	19,872.18	25,906.94	23,969.52	23,477.16	22,151.25	26,447.01	20,815.34
New trucks	28,212.24	21,833.93	26,321.88	28,110.55	28,823.11	31,175.00	29,856.62	25,720.19
Cars and trucks, used	10,374.53	6,961.63	10,520.68	10,475.47	10,287.53	12,531.50	10,198.39	9,680.49
Used cars	9,508.71	6,759.98	8,349.86	9,579.95	9,658.51	12,271.03	9,293.81	10,173.61
Used trucks	11,204.83	7,348.72	12,193.55	11,278.90	10,780.12	12,673.02	10,819.57	8,960.81
Other vehicles	9,596.43	7,610.00	8,158.54	9,725.66	11,552.68	12,105.56	6,798.53	12,075.00
Gasoline and motor oil	**748.22**	**594.59**	**755.43**	**888.84**	**885.62**	**755.50**	**565.12**	**370.28**
Gasoline	697.37	568.81	708.16	834.30	829.92	692.97	512.75	342.35
Diesel fuel	633.33	698.57	763.31	687.33	601.48	608.19	445.83	651.89
Gasoline on trips	179.96	123.79	179.14	181.69	176.33	191.24	203.86	162.78
Motor oil	31.28	27.93	30.37	28.47	37.16	31.92	25.04	29.80
Motor oil on trips	1.82	1.26	1.81	1.83	1.78	1.93	2.06	1.63
Other vehicle expenses	**731.51**	**524.66**	**713.81**	**768.27**	**866.05**	**770.19**	**591.96**	**516.55**
Vehicle finance charges	241.79	230.34	247.78	247.11	243.90	238.44	229.29	184.61
Automobile finance charges	196.13	212.16	191.65	213.05	201.33	184.85	171.64	159.78
Truck finance charges	222.02	220.55	236.72	218.19	217.12	224.05	200.95	198.98
Motorcycle and plane finance charges	126.85	80.26	113.50	109.14	162.34	167.21	122.83	158.33
Other vehicle finance charges	279.86	67.65	229.23	225.65	266.51	356.76	506.20	334.00
Maintenance and repairs	329.52	241.79	272.22	315.58	408.69	359.75	281.93	293.76
Coolant, additives, brake and transmission fluids	18.34	13.62	18.93	16.40	17.73	23.39	13.87	23.57
Tires—purchased, replaced, installed	398.24	341.57	372.81	387.47	425.20	419.81	371.16	410.91
Vehicle products and cleaning services	42.22	25.90	42.86	42.39	43.43	48.53	40.77	32.28
Parts, equipment, and accessories	126.53	143.20	105.50	107.60	154.19	126.17	111.82	139.10
Vehicle audio equipment, excluding labor	251.19	406.45	213.33	120.24	335.71	297.83	121.05	–
Vehicle video equipment	301.72	387.50	341.07	235.58	304.55	337.50	264.39	378.13
Body work and painting	640.57	630.10	577.53	645.47	733.28	611.13	480.77	681.93
Clutch and transmission repair	756.20	374.72	756.86	661.06	928.25	670.34	722.30	907.93
Drive shaft and rear-end repair	397.00	506.25	239.71	336.21	515.38	357.89	514.13	490.00
Brake work	313.32	263.90	260.10	289.60	345.26	332.17	341.35	290.33
Repair to steering or front-end	447.50	385.25	400.22	425.22	522.88	464.42	467.20	273.42
Repair to engine cooling system	322.53	230.49	355.07	277.07	376.99	333.99	228.11	293.37
Motor tune-up	257.86	211.20	249.49	240.51	247.81	281.34	275.47	297.77
Lube, oil change, and oil filters	52.14	44.78	49.86	54.30	55.82	54.88	48.41	43.13
Front-end alignment, wheel balance, rotation	135.08	168.32	119.49	133.67	139.97	144.41	111.46	142.72
Shock absorber replacement	357.26	755.00	263.64	358.55	410.42	324.50	255.92	351.92
Tire repair and other repair work	224.10	185.63	243.97	217.25	233.55	202.44	216.52	258.59
Exhaust system repair	270.00	224.15	261.08	235.42	270.39	290.42	330.56	266.28
Electrical system repair	318.26	262.50	287.26	332.20	316.47	356.92	292.64	301.67
Motor repair, replacement	668.65	427.97	681.71	671.36	742.56	681.52	556.43	618.78
Auto repair service policy	901.42	745.63	1,380.17	1,161.36	754.17	925.32	673.61	662.88
Vehicle accessories including labor	661.11	95.00	191.13	244.12	1,647.01	240.32	138.54	189.17
Vehicle air conditioning repair	300.55	135.23	277.36	396.96	303.74	284.55	271.38	287.83

	total consumer units	under 25	25 to 34	35 to 44	45 to 54	55 to 64	65 to 74	75+
Vehicle insurance	$438.54	$414.76	$396.43	$426.95	$496.44	$453.49	$404.20	$415.10
Vehicle rental, leases, licenses, other charges	271.81	161.55	304.90	304.81	283.96	282.12	226.16	167.27
Leased and rented vehicles	1,038.43	655.00	1,067.89	1,146.67	1,006.27	1,028.68	1,016.61	821.00
Rented vehicles	322.71	237.97	259.12	326.01	333.59	385.66	300.92	257.98
Auto rental	292.79	222.45	331.05	289.81	299.06	362.89	153.70	149.29
Auto rental on trips	307.91	155.60	239.43	285.44	311.06	371.67	300.52	348.47
Truck rental	328.26	64.58	211.50	414.29	606.25	201.79	392.50	–
Truck rental on trips	460.71	150.00	181.82	572.50	404.17	661.76	585.00	25.00
Leased vehicles	1,520.08	1,119.70	1,533.49	1,556.92	1,525.96	1,631.62	1,446.86	1,123.43
Car lease payments	1,244.69	822.80	1,130.37	1,240.53	1,253.23	1,543.48	1,306.28	1,013.78
Truck lease payments	1,371.58	1,069.74	1,359.57	1,328.63	1,375.49	1,473.10	1,471.21	1,046.05
Vehicle registration, state	128.06	128.94	127.94	136.55	130.45	126.50	127.79	98.51
Vehicle registration, local	108.69	94.30	98.02	116.59	115.83	101.95	108.86	104.08
Driver's license	35.98	33.05	37.86	37.70	37.86	35.36	30.87	30.60
Vehicle inspection	42.24	40.00	37.57	45.66	45.46	42.00	37.00	40.88
Parking fees	81.65	88.94	71.61	83.59	88.72	82.99	60.08	97.53
Parking fees in home city, excluding residence	86.17	94.74	75.22	90.62	95.71	85.76	56.82	98.01
Parking fees on trips	48.71	30.08	41.42	42.77	48.28	55.07	60.61	86.44
Tolls and electronic toll passes	57.43	37.09	57.35	62.26	61.64	59.92	43.99	36.12
Tolls on trips	17.46	14.17	15.60	16.94	19.59	18.47	16.87	15.35
Towing charges	122.61	153.18	118.68	138.24	111.19	104.85	115.95	99.02
Global positioning services	105.50	252.78	71.59	123.65	106.75	116.98	85.62	88.46
Automobile service clubs	88.42	73.16	80.96	83.83	89.89	95.96	89.22	82.43
Public transportation	**698.61**	**317.60**	**534.96**	**753.34**	**772.27**	**790.23**	**815.82**	**697.95**
Airline fares	867.80	443.12	728.58	961.21	947.72	906.29	852.18	809.28
Intercity bus fares	69.71	43.78	61.35	59.40	67.10	71.19	97.08	98.17
Intracity mass transit fares	215.06	185.93	233.15	232.92	237.52	219.51	148.73	113.73
Local transportation on trips	63.72	32.25	44.06	56.93	61.93	78.83	54.99	134.39
Taxi fares and limousine service on trips	37.42	18.92	25.85	33.42	36.39	46.31	32.29	78.90
Taxi fares and limousine service	109.16	79.49	105.02	138.33	124.00	104.17	97.24	81.50
Intercity train fares	144.82	81.70	136.64	132.54	149.44	127.47	151.11	262.54
Ship fares	424.10	148.76	255.39	269.17	397.02	404.09	880.21	667.96
School bus	437.50	–	362.50	269.44	525.00	200.00	–	–

Note: "–" means sample is too small to make a reliable estimate.
Source: Calculations by New Strategist based on the Bureau of Labor Statistics' 2008 Consumer Expenditure Survey

Table 10.3 Percent Buying Transportation by Age, <u>Average Week</u>, 2008

(percent of households buying transportation during the average week, by age of householder, 2008)

	total households	under 25	25 to 34	35 to 44	45 to 54	55 to 64	65 to 74	75+
TRANSPORTATION, PERCENT BUYING	70.7%	62.9%	73.0%	76.2%	76.1%	72.1%	66.7%	50.0%
Gasoline	67.9	60.2	70.3	73.9	73.7	69.0	63.6	46.0
Diesel fuel	0.8	0.1	0.6	1.1	0.9	0.9	0.4	0.6
Motor oil	1.6	2.0	1.1	1.9	1.8	1.8	1.3	1.1
Coolant, additives, brake and transmission fluids	1.4	1.7	1.3	1.6	1.5	1.5	1.6	0.6
Other vehicle expenses	15.9	9.8	15.4	16.8	19.1	17.2	15.8	10.2
Maintenance and repairs	6.1	4.2	5.4	5.9	7.3	7.3	6.6	4.0
Vehicle audio equipment, excluding labor	0.1	0.2	–	0.1	0.1	0.0	–	–
Vehicle products and cleaning services	1.3	1.3	1.1	1.3	1.6	1.6	1.1	0.4
Miscellaneous auto repair, servicing	5.2	3.2	4.5	5.0	6.0	6.2	5.7	3.8
Vehicle insurance	9.2	4.7	9.7	10.3	11.3	9.5	8.0	5.6
Vehicle rental, leases, licenses, and other charges	2.5	1.4	2.2	2.7	2.5	3.1	3.1	1.2
Tolls and electronic toll passes	2.5	1.4	2.2	2.7	2.5	3.1	3.1	1.2
Taxi fares and limousine service	1.0	1.7	1.3	0.8	0.9	1.0	0.4	1.2

Note: "–" means sample is too small to make a reliable estimate.
Source: Bureau of Labor Statistics, unpublished data from the 2008 Consumer Expenditure Survey

Table 10.4 Amount Buyers Spent on Transportation by Age, <u>Average Week</u>, 2008

(average amount spent by households buying transportation during the average week, by age of householder, 2008)

	total households	under 25	25 to 34	35 to 44	45 to 54	55 to 64	65 to 74	75+
TRANSPORTATION, AMOUNT SPENT	$99.00	$70.61	$90.05	$106.30	$115.51	$101.04	$85.91	$84.34
Gasoline	67.63	57.47	66.92	77.22	75.10	67.69	53.16	42.66
Diesel fuel	82.89	76.92	82.81	82.08	94.68	73.33	84.62	78.95
Motor oil	9.43	6.97	10.62	12.37	10.50	7.91	6.40	6.19
Coolant, additives, brake and transmission fluids	8.45	10.24	6.72	8.13	7.28	9.66	10.90	7.27
Other vehicle expenses	143.37	92.55	114.29	133.19	163.33	145.05	143.46	207.68
Maintenance and repairs	18.30	15.13	16.02	16.24	23.83	14.76	15.61	26.50
Vehicle audio equipment, excluding labor	150.00	65.00	–	111.11	260.00	100.00	–	–
Vehicle products and cleaning services	12.60	6.40	6.25	9.85	16.46	7.74	6.36	107.69
Miscellaneous auto repair, servicing	16.67	13.40	17.78	13.97	19.80	14.70	16.96	16.49
Vehicle insurance	232.21	173.94	169.79	205.04	258.53	247.32	264.88	354.90
Vehicle rental, leases, licenses, and other charges	11.43	16.06	12.50	10.07	13.55	10.42	10.22	11.38
Tolls and electronic toll passes	11.43	16.06	12.50	10.07	13.55	10.42	10.22	11.38
Taxi fares and limousine service	34.69	20.96	30.16	37.33	18.28	30.30	89.19	72.73

Note: "–" means sample is too small to make a reliable estimate.
Source: Calculations by New Strategist based on the Bureau of Labor Statistics' 2008 Consumer Expenditure Survey

Table 10.5 Percent Buying Transportation by Household Income, Average Quarter, 2008

(percent of households buying transportation during the average quarter, by before-tax income of household, 2008)

	total households	under $20,000	$20,000–$39,999	$40,000–$49,999	$50,000–$69,999	$70,000–$79,999	$80,000–$99,999	$100,000 or more
TRANSPORTATION, PERCENT BUYING	**94.8%**	**82.3%**	**95.6%**	**98.1%**	**98.7%**	**99.4%**	**99.5%**	**99.5%**
Vehicle purchases	**4.7**	**2.9**	**4.0**	**4.2**	**5.5**	**4.9**	**6.4**	**6.6**
Cars and trucks, new	1.3	0.3	0.7	1.0	1.3	1.5	2.2	2.8
New cars	0.8	0.2	0.5	0.5	0.7	1.2	1.5	1.7
New trucks	0.5	0.1	0.3	0.5	0.6	0.3	0.7	1.1
Cars and trucks, used	3.2	2.3	3.1	3.2	3.9	3.3	3.9	3.3
Used cars	1.8	1.4	1.7	1.4	2.1	1.7	2.4	1.8
Used trucks	1.5	0.9	1.4	1.9	1.8	1.7	1.6	1.5
Other vehicles	0.4	0.3	0.2	0.0	0.4	0.2	0.4	0.6
Gasoline and motor oil	**90.7**	**72.7**	**91.1**	**95.3**	**96.3**	**98.0**	**98.3**	**98.2**
Gasoline	90.1	72.0	90.6	94.7	95.6	97.5	97.8	97.3
Diesel fuel	1.8	0.7	1.1	2.2	2.2	2.4	3.0	2.8
Gasoline on trips	20.1	9.4	13.7	18.2	22.2	25.5	28.4	34.0
Motor oil	8.0	5.8	8.5	9.3	9.4	10.7	8.9	6.8
Motor oil on trips	20.1	9.4	13.7	18.2	22.2	25.5	28.4	34.0
Other vehicle expenses	**80.8**	**54.6**	**78.5**	**85.8**	**90.1**	**91.9**	**93.8**	**94.3**
Vehicle finance charges	32.3	10.0	25.5	36.3	41.6	44.1	47.8	45.7
Automobile finance charges	17.1	5.6	13.5	19.6	21.5	21.9	22.7	25.6
Truck finance charges	17.5	4.2	12.6	17.5	23.1	25.6	29.6	26.2
Motorcycle and plane finance charges	1.4	0.2	0.8	1.1	2.1	3.1	2.2	1.8
Other vehicle finance charges	1.4	0.3	0.8	1.7	1.5	1.4	2.4	3.0
Maintenance and repairs	52.5	31.8	48.9	54.3	59.7	62.6	63.6	65.9
Coolant, additives, brake and transmission fluids	5.0	3.9	5.7	5.7	5.7	6.0	5.3	3.9
Tires—purchased, replaced, installed	7.8	4.2	6.7	6.9	8.6	9.9	9.8	11.6
Vehicle products and cleaning services	3.6	1.5	2.7	3.2	3.8	4.7	5.3	6.2
Parts, equipment, and accessories	8.7	5.5	8.1	9.0	10.2	13.4	10.1	9.2
Vehicle audio equipment, excluding labor	0.2	0.2	0.3	0.1	0.1	0.2	0.4	0.3
Vehicle video equipment	0.3	0.0	0.2	0.2	0.4	0.4	0.2	0.6
Body work and painting	1.2	0.5	0.9	1.0	1.3	1.4	1.7	2.3
Clutch and transmission repair	1.2	0.8	1.1	0.8	1.3	1.0	1.6	1.8
Drive shaft and rear-end repair	0.3	0.1	0.2	0.2	0.4	0.4	0.4	0.4
Brake work	4.8	2.3	3.9	4.1	5.3	6.2	6.0	7.5
Repair to steering or front-end	1.2	0.5	0.9	1.4	1.4	1.7	1.5	1.7
Repair to engine cooling system	1.7	1.0	1.6	1.3	1.6	2.1	2.4	2.6
Motor tune-up	4.4	2.1	3.5	4.0	4.3	5.7	5.3	7.7
Lube, oil change, and oil filters	33.8	18.9	29.6	35.2	39.1	40.0	41.8	45.3
Front-end alignment, wheel balance, rotation	2.5	0.9	2.0	2.1	2.8	3.2	4.1	4.2
Shock absorber replacement	0.3	0.2	0.3	0.2	0.4	0.2	0.4	0.4
Tire repair and other repair work	5.9	3.0	4.9	5.6	6.1	6.5	7.2	9.5
Exhaust system repair	0.9	0.5	0.8	0.3	1.2	1.5	1.0	1.2
Electrical system repair	2.2	1.4	2.1	1.8	2.1	3.1	2.2	3.0
Motor repair, replacement	2.6	1.4	2.2	1.7	2.8	3.6	3.5	3.9
Auto repair service policy	0.5	0.2	0.4	0.5	0.6	0.7	0.6	0.8
Vehicle accessories including labor	0.5	0.1	0.3	0.5	0.4	0.7	0.8	0.8
Vehicle air conditioning repair	0.9	0.4	0.6	0.8	0.9	1.1	1.2	1.7

	total households	under $20,000	$20,000–$39,999	$40,000–$49,999	$50,000–$69,999	$70,000–$79,999	$80,000–$99,999	$100,000 or more
Vehicle insurance	50.7%	31.0%	48.7%	56.1%	57.9%	59.4%	62.2%	59.1%
Vehicle rental, leases, licenses, other charges	43.3	23.6	35.1	40.6	47.5	53.5	55.4	65.3
Leased and rented vehicles	6.5	1.9	3.7	4.9	6.3	7.6	8.9	14.8
Rented vehicles	2.8	0.9	1.5	2.2	2.9	2.7	3.4	6.8
Auto rental	0.5	0.3	0.5	0.4	0.6	0.8	0.5	0.8
Auto rental on trips	2.0	0.6	0.9	1.3	2.0	1.5	2.5	5.1
Truck rental	0.2	0.1	0.2	0.3	0.2	0.3	0.1	0.5
Truck rental on trips	0.1	0.0	0.0	0.2	0.1	0.1	0.3	0.5
Leased vehicles	3.8	1.0	2.2	2.8	3.4	5.4	5.8	8.6
Car lease payments	2.3	0.7	1.6	1.8	1.9	2.5	3.5	4.7
Truck lease payments	1.8	0.3	0.6	1.1	1.7	3.4	2.7	4.8
Vehicle registration, state	17.2	9.6	15.2	16.5	20.6	21.4	21.1	23.0
Vehicle registration, local	2.1	1.3	1.8	1.9	2.5	3.1	2.6	2.8
Driver's license	5.2	3.2	4.7	5.0	5.9	5.5	5.9	7.1
Vehicle inspection	6.4	3.6	5.4	6.0	7.2	9.5	8.2	8.5
Parking fees	11.4	5.2	6.7	8.8	11.3	13.6	16.4	22.8
Parking fees in home city, excluding residence	9.0	4.5	5.6	7.2	9.1	10.6	12.5	17.5
Parking fees on trips	3.1	0.8	1.4	2.0	2.9	3.7	4.8	7.7
Tolls and electronic toll passes	9.0	2.9	4.5	7.4	9.2	11.2	13.4	19.5
Tolls on trips	6.2	2.0	3.7	5.6	7.0	7.4	8.5	12.2
Towing charges	0.9	0.8	0.9	1.0	0.9	1.1	1.1	1.0
Global positioning services	0.5	0.1	0.3	0.3	0.3	0.7	0.8	1.2
Automobile service clubs	5.0	2.5	3.9	3.9	4.9	7.2	7.6	8.2
Public transportation	**18.2**	**15.8**	**13.4**	**14.7**	**16.1**	**17.0**	**20.5**	**30.0**
Airline fares	9.9	4.4	5.4	7.5	9.8	10.3	13.0	21.7
Intercity bus fares	4.0	2.6	2.4	3.4	3.6	3.9	5.5	7.5
Intracity mass transit fares	7.0	9.3	6.3	6.3	5.1	5.7	5.7	8.6
Local transportation on trips	4.8	2.0	2.4	4.2	4.8	5.4	6.6	10.5
Taxi fares and limousine service on trips	4.8	2.0	2.4	4.2	4.8	5.4	6.6	10.5
Taxi fares and limousine service	3.0	3.2	2.8	2.5	2.2	2.6	2.9	4.2
Intercity train fares	3.9	1.9	2.0	3.1	3.6	4.6	5.4	8.1
Ship fares	2.2	0.5	1.1	1.9	1.8	2.3	3.1	5.8
School bus	0.0	–	0.0	0.0	0.0	–	–	0.1

Note: "–" means sample is too small to make a reliable estimate.
Source: Bureau of Labor Statistics, unpublished data from the 2008 Consumer Expenditure Survey

Table 10.6 Amount Buyers Spent on Transportation by Household Income, <u>Average Quarter</u>, 2008

(average amount spent by households buying transportation during the average quarter, by before-tax income of household, 2008)

	total households	under $20,000	$20,000–$39,999	$40,000–$49,999	$50,000–$69,999	$70,000–$79,999	$80,000–$99,999	$100,000 or more
TRANSPORTATION, AMOUNT SPENT	**$2,200.87**	**$960.16**	**$1,534.35**	**$1,781.85**	**$2,290.47**	**$2,549.61**	**$2,910.12**	**$3,884.45**
Vehicle purchases	**14,560.25**	**6,946.17**	**11,802.84**	**12,577.70**	**14,082.51**	**15,852.95**	**15,393.28**	**20,770.39**
Cars and trucks, new	25,487.50	17,951.93	22,125.63	23,660.68	24,174.02	21,061.13	24,554.22	29,126.27
New cars	23,500.00	15,514.99	21,283.55	19,366.50	22,796.96	20,573.26	22,774.32	26,979.07
New trucks	28,212.24	21,656.24	23,644.20	28,957.78	24,698.66	22,870.97	28,264.44	31,788.84
Cars and trucks, used	10,374.53	5,105.66	9,400.74	9,136.44	10,896.63	13,067.94	10,508.69	14,876.52
Used cars	9,508.71	5,165.64	8,020.08	8,828.62	10,497.05	12,150.45	9,888.87	13,362.50
Used trucks	11,204.83	5,022.09	10,691.95	9,168.51	11,254.12	13,907.19	11,454.33	16,385.76
Other vehicles	9,596.43	6,430.79	10,462.41	14,737.50	11,377.50	15,532.61	7,360.14	11,047.27
Gasoline and motor oil	**748.22**	**431.16**	**575.06**	**687.43**	**787.47**	**899.92**	**959.18**	**1,070.75**
Gasoline	697.37	409.99	542.25	645.93	732.11	831.99	881.24	991.36
Diesel fuel	633.33	508.52	523.77	498.87	794.15	653.94	725.99	609.89
Gasoline on trips	179.96	139.70	172.96	159.98	169.61	201.53	192.45	196.71
Motor oil	31.28	26.12	26.66	32.36	32.65	29.81	36.88	38.86
Motor oil on trips	1.82	1.41	1.74	1.62	1.71	2.03	1.95	1.99
Other vehicle expenses	**731.51**	**405.54**	**520.55**	**588.33**	**702.47**	**809.81**	**876.22**	**1,165.88**
Vehicle finance charges	241.79	190.01	201.73	212.87	231.55	251.93	268.89	285.50
Automobile finance charges	196.13	181.07	182.15	183.86	190.36	208.52	210.80	209.35
Truck finance charges	222.02	188.29	195.39	201.84	217.89	221.29	235.75	246.21
Motorcycle and plane finance charges	126.85	93.61	74.69	105.37	89.37	125.65	175.45	179.78
Other vehicle finance charges	279.86	157.20	191.21	288.91	227.03	348.94	295.95	307.03
Maintenance and repairs	329.52	228.88	253.09	238.92	301.86	342.64	359.81	498.35
Coolant, additives, brake and transmission fluids	18.34	18.03	19.82	17.12	20.26	17.50	20.08	15.04
Tires—purchased, replaced, installed	398.24	295.00	321.60	354.20	392.13	371.78	423.75	512.06
Vehicle products and cleaning services	42.22	21.84	31.77	39.84	36.33	35.28	54.92	54.25
Parts, equipment, and accessories	126.53	105.85	105.31	97.42	122.06	97.64	141.10	188.36
Vehicle audio equipment, excluding labor	251.19	142.40	214.68	288.46	254.17	305.00	163.51	342.42
Vehicle video equipment	301.72	178.48	366.49	182.14	248.30	184.62	389.47	333.33
Body work and painting	640.57	628.27	592.08	354.64	667.19	1,044.64	614.39	626.96
Clutch and transmission repair	756.20	800.10	544.87	535.76	691.79	744.75	770.58	1,039.43
Drive shaft and rear-end repair	397.00	548.87	349.11	426.47	447.14	402.86	381.10	403.57
Brake work	313.32	241.81	252.01	278.68	341.32	271.92	326.68	380.80
Repair to steering or front-end	447.50	352.21	372.00	323.23	419.23	429.61	571.60	568.25
Repair to engine cooling system	322.53	253.89	256.74	295.00	386.79	279.57	226.16	424.05
Motor tune-up	257.86	195.59	212.85	183.27	229.69	282.05	303.28	313.95
Lube, oil change, and oil filters	52.14	41.58	43.49	47.53	49.84	52.00	58.07	65.16
Front-end alignment, wheel balance, rotation	135.08	111.22	106.84	182.98	113.64	116.56	150.36	154.88
Shock absorber replacement	357.26	516.56	327.67	228.33	314.19	270.83	288.07	484.88
Tire repair and other repair work	224.10	159.87	207.33	193.33	230.96	201.42	204.00	276.67
Exhaust system repair	270.00	200.13	243.27	281.82	270.36	290.00	282.03	311.07
Electrical system repair	318.26	270.59	296.03	260.42	360.98	291.42	288.31	376.52
Motor repair, replacement	668.65	495.99	589.63	845.48	545.45	717.51	816.76	730.61
Auto repair service policy	901.42	514.63	901.12	866.67	529.69	1,231.85	667.97	1,167.47
Vehicle accessories including labor	661.11	110.26	127.61	171.28	278.21	416.67	224.09	1,578.35
Vehicle air conditioning repair	300.55	134.92	336.93	266.88	254.12	228.10	312.91	392.34

	total households	under $20,000	$20,000–$39,999	$40,000–$49,999	$50,000–$69,999	$70,000–$79,999	$80,000–$99,999	$100,000 or more
Vehicle insurance	$438.54	$303.21	$355.55	$381.75	$436.18	$450.67	$496.19	$601.21
Vehicle rental, leases, licenses, other charges	271.81	154.52	172.03	205.27	219.26	281.96	280.39	436.75
Leased and rented vehicles	1,038.43	841.48	749.62	890.55	836.36	1,216.79	1,000.50	1,239.02
Rented vehicles	322.71	314.83	260.18	272.91	270.34	295.28	286.72	379.24
Auto rental	292.79	288.25	169.00	150.61	381.78	280.26	306.52	344.88
Auto rental on trips	307.91	229.01	307.93	233.97	246.18	321.27	276.71	353.52
Truck rental	328.26	419.23	151.19	403.13	145.65	103.79	288.64	509.04
Truck rental on trips	460.71	11.43	576.67	497.22	420.83	187.50	363.39	483.15
Leased vehicles	1,520.08	1311.41	1065.69	1,353.88	1,299.20	1,588.43	1,376.86	1,829.81
Car lease payments	1,244.69	1186.58	1008.96	1,247.73	1,049.09	1,188.62	1,075.42	1,501.32
Truck lease payments	1,371.58	1314.77	1071.74	1,008.63	1,337.42	1,285.45	1,476.98	1,470.58
Vehicle registration, state	128.06	98.33	113.26	117.59	124.72	118.64	136.54	161.27
Vehicle registration, local	108.69	97.93	90.91	95.34	113.52	98.14	119.24	131.59
Driver's license	35.98	33.20	34.39	41.35	36.05	37.16	37.20	35.83
Vehicle inspection	42.24	39.78	36.76	42.24	42.42	41.41	41.43	48.73
Parking fees	81.65	64.73	55.19	65.08	59.92	67.26	70.32	114.62
Parking fees in home city, excluding residence	86.17	67.15	54.67	69.32	63.05	69.50	74.56	124.73
Parking fees on trips	48.71	38.08	45.94	37.63	36.77	48.24	46.44	56.51
Tolls and electronic toll passes	57.43	32.92	31.55	39.31	52.73	47.08	55.88	76.80
Tolls on trips	17.46	12.15	18.69	12.30	17.54	16.53	18.50	18.96
Towing charges	122.61	151.01	146.55	99.47	107.97	102.27	110.59	123.76
Global positioning services	105.50	40.77	72.75	165.15	73.15	76.39	71.95	136.25
Automobile service clubs	88.42	76.79	79.84	84.03	87.93	83.92	82.79	103.19
Public transportation	**698.61**	**310.28**	**435.69**	**431.84**	**603.14**	**768.46**	**747.89**	**1,165.20**
Airline fares	867.80	582.48	646.62	540.25	691.65	836.58	808.90	1,158.01
Intercity bus fares	69.71	56.58	88.24	53.33	57.92	54.69	52.45	85.24
Intracity mass transit fares	215.06	121.65	183.42	181.12	225.89	242.01	282.25	344.67
Local transportation on trips	63.72	28.74	44.60	35.84	45.97	61.97	73.45	87.88
Taxi fares and limousine service on trips	37.42	16.85	26.15	21.03	26.99	36.36	43.13	51.62
Taxi fares and limousine service	109.16	69.26	99.28	114.40	100.79	115.13	110.34	154.78
Intercity train fares	144.82	65.88	100.41	81.61	114.53	209.29	162.15	185.78
Ship fares	424.10	1569.98	361.67	95.68	309.02	468.06	309.49	451.17
School bus	437.50	–	442.06	318.75	225.00	–	–	475.00

Note: "–" means sample is too small to make a reliable estimate.
Source: Calculations by New Strategist based on the Bureau of Labor Statistics' 2008 Consumer Expenditure Survey

Table 10.7 Percent Buying Transportation by Household Income, <u>Average Week</u>, 2008

(percent of households buying transportation during the average week, by before-tax income of household, 2008)

	total households	under $20,000	$20,000– $39,999	$40,000– $49,999	$50,000– $69,999	$70,000– $79,999	$80,000– $99,999	$100,000 or more
TRANSPORTATION, PERCENT BUYING	70.7%	50.6%	64.4%	73.0%	77.7%	82.4%	81.6%	84.1%
Gasoline	67.9	47.9	61.9	70.8	74.8	79.1	79.2	80.5
Diesel fuel	0.8	0.0	0.5	0.8	0.9	0.8	1.5	1.4
Motor oil	1.6	1.0	1.3	1.8	1.8	1.9	2.1	1.9
Coolant, additives, brake and transmission fluids	1.4	1.0	1.2	1.7	1.5	1.7	2.5	1.4
Other vehicle expenses	15.9	8.7	12.8	13.5	18.4	20.6	22.1	22.5
Maintenance and repairs	6.1	3.2	4.3	4.2	6.9	7.8	8.8	10.4
Vehicle audio equipment, excluding labor	0.1	–	–	–	0.0	–	0.1	0.2
Vehicle products and cleaning services	1.3	0.7	1.0	0.9	1.6	1.8	1.4	1.9
Miscellaneous auto repair, servicing	5.2	2.6	3.4	3.6	5.7	6.2	7.9	9.0
Vehicle insurance	9.2	5.7	7.9	8.6	11.2	11.4	12.9	10.8
Vehicle rental, leases, licenses, and other charges	2.5	1.0	1.4	2.0	2.6	3.5	3.5	4.7
Tolls and electronic toll passes	2.5	1.0	1.4	2.0	2.6	3.5	3.5	4.7
Taxi fares and limousine service	1.0	1.0	0.8	1.0	0.9	0.2	0.5	1.8

Note: "–" means sample is too small to make a reliable estimate.
Source: Bureau of Labor Statistics, unpublished data from the 2008 Consumer Expenditure Survey

Table 10.8 Amount Buyers Spent on Transportation by Household Income, <u>Average Week</u>, 2008

(average amount spent by households buying transportation during the average week, by before-tax income of household, 2008)

	total households	under $20,000	$20,000– $39,999	$40,000– $49,999	$50,000– $69,999	$70,000– $79,999	$80,000– $99,999	$100,000 or more
TRANSPORTATION, AMOUNT SPENT	$99.00	$68.79	$78.02	$92.26	$98.89	$105.09	$126.49	$128.68
Gasoline	67.63	46.74	54.88	63.55	66.39	73.57	81.25	89.02
Diesel fuel	82.89	10.09	74.75	65.79	72.53	67.53	76.03	107.80
Motor oil	9.43	3.71	11.01	5.65	8.89	8.95	8.57	15.46
Coolant, additives, brake and transmission fluids	8.45	6.56	5.67	9.36	10.67	9.70	8.00	9.42
Other vehicle expenses	143.37	133.00	121.66	158.01	140.66	133.92	168.07	150.71
Maintenance and repairs	18.30	12.05	15.08	12.68	20.96	12.76	17.20	23.85
Vehicle audio equipment, excluding labor	150.00	–	–	–	–	–	188.89	169.57
Vehicle products and cleaning services	12.60	5.27	6.76	5.56	22.22	7.22	13.33	16.23
Miscellaneous auto repair, servicing	16.67	11.99	16.34	13.33	18.21	13.96	14.20	19.71
Vehicle insurance	232.21	195.36	185.90	238.98	215.86	228.06	274.05	286.41
Vehicle rental, leases, licenses, and other charges	11.43	8.30	12.58	9.05	14.73	12.43	10.80	10.66
Tolls and electronic toll passes	11.43	8.30	12.58	9.05	14.73	12.43	10.80	10.66
Taxi fares and limousine service	34.69	47.67	17.87	33.33	30.11	14.29	32.61	35.43

Note: "–" means sample is too small to make a reliable estimate.
Source: Calculations by New Strategist based on the Bureau of Labor Statistics' 2008 Consumer Expenditure Survey

Table 10.9 Percent of High-Income Households Buying Transportation, <u>Average Quarter</u>, 2008

(percent of high-income households buying transportation during the average quarter, by before-tax income of household, 2008)

	total households	$100,000 or more	$100,000–$119,999	$120,000–$149,999	$150,000 or more
TRANSPORTATION, PERCENT BUYING	**94.8%**	**99.5%**	**99.6%**	**99.2%**	**99.5%**
Vehicle purchases	**4.7**	**6.6**	**6.2**	**7.9**	**6.0**
Cars and trucks, new	1.3	2.8	2.4	2.9	3.0
New cars	0.8	1.7	1.7	1.4	1.8
New trucks	0.5	1.1	0.8	1.5	1.2
Cars and trucks, used	3.2	3.3	3.4	3.8	2.9
Used cars	1.8	1.8	1.4	2.3	1.8
Used trucks	1.5	1.5	2.0	1.6	1.1
Other vehicles	0.4	0.6	0.5	1.2	0.4
Gasoline and motor oil	**90.7**	**98.2**	**98.6**	**98.3**	**97.9**
Gasoline	90.1	97.3	97.9	97.4	96.8
Diesel fuel	1.8	2.8	2.9	2.5	2.9
Gasoline on trips	20.1	34.0	29.5	33.1	38.3
Motor oil	8.0	6.8	7.3	7.4	6.0
Motor oil on trips	20.1	34.0	29.5	33.1	38.3
Other vehicle expenses	**80.8**	**94.3**	**94.5**	**95.4**	**93.4**
Vehicle finance charges	32.3	45.7	46.1	51.7	41.3
Automobile finance charges	17.1	25.6	24.2	28.7	24.6
Truck finance charges	17.5	26.2	26.6	30.1	23.4
Motorcycle and plane finance charges	1.4	1.8	2.4	2.1	1.2
Other vehicle finance charges	1.4	3.0	2.5	2.9	3.4
Maintenance and repairs	52.5	65.9	65.5	67.9	64.9
Coolant, additives, brake and transmission fluids	5.0	3.9	4.1	4.3	3.5
Tires—purchased, replaced, installed	7.8	11.6	11.1	10.9	12.4
Vehicle products and cleaning services	3.6	6.2	5.7	4.8	7.5
Parts, equipment, and accessories	8.7	9.2	9.8	9.5	8.6
Vehicle audio equipment, excluding labor	0.2	0.3	0.3	0.1	0.5
Vehicle video equipment	0.3	0.6	0.2	0.8	0.9
Body work and painting	1.2	2.3	1.6	2.3	2.9
Clutch and transmission repair	1.2	1.8	1.8	1.6	1.9
Drive shaft and rear-end repair	0.3	0.4	0.3	0.7	0.2
Brake work	4.8	7.5	7.3	7.7	7.6
Repair to steering or front-end	1.2	1.7	1.6	1.5	2.0
Repair to engine cooling system	1.7	2.6	2.6	2.9	2.5
Motor tune-up	4.4	7.7	6.2	7.5	9.0
Lube, oil change, and oil filters	33.8	45.3	45.7	45.6	44.7
Front-end alignment, wheel balance, rotation	2.5	4.2	4.7	4.2	3.7
Shock absorber replacement	0.3	0.4	0.4	0.3	0.6
Tire repair and other repair work	5.9	9.5	9.0	9.1	10.0
Exhaust system repair	0.9	1.2	1.2	1.3	1.3
Electrical system repair	2.2	3.0	2.7	2.6	3.4
Motor repair, replacement	2.6	3.9	3.6	4.2	3.9
Auto repair service policy	0.5	0.8	0.6	0.8	1.0
Vehicle accessories including labor	0.5	0.8	0.6	0.9	1.0
Vehicle air conditioning repair	0.9	1.7	1.5	2.3	1.6

	total households	$100,000 or more	$100,000– $119,999	$120,000– $149,999	$150,000 or more
Vehicle insurance	50.7%	59.1%	60.8%	61.4%	56.2%
Vehicle rental, leases, licenses, other charges	43.3	65.3	60.3	63.7	70.4
Leased and rented vehicles	6.5	14.8	12.3	12.2	18.5
Rented vehicles	2.8	6.8	4.7	5.7	9.3
Auto rental	0.5	0.8	0.8	0.7	1.0
Auto rental on trips	2.0	5.1	3.2	4.0	7.4
Truck rental	0.2	0.5	0.4	0.3	0.7
Truck rental on trips	0.1	0.5	0.3	0.6	0.6
Leased vehicles	3.8	8.6	8.1	7.0	10.0
Car lease payments	2.3	4.7	5.0	3.7	5.3
Truck lease payments	1.8	4.8	3.8	4.0	6.2
Vehicle registration, state	17.2	23.0	22.2	24.2	23.0
Vehicle registration, local	2.1	2.8	3.8	2.3	2.2
Driver's license	5.2	7.1	7.3	7.5	6.7
Vehicle inspection	6.4	8.5	7.6	9.1	8.8
Parking fees	11.4	22.8	18.6	20.2	28.1
Parking fees in home city, excluding residence	9.0	17.5	13.9	15.9	21.6
Parking fees on trips	3.1	7.7	6.1	6.3	10.0
Tolls and electronic toll passes	9.0	19.5	14.4	18.3	24.4
Tolls on trips	6.2	12.2	9.7	10.4	15.5
Towing charges	0.9	1.0	1.0	0.8	1.2
Global positioning services	0.5	1.2	0.8	1.3	1.4
Automobile service clubs	5.0	8.2	7.2	9.2	8.5
Public transportation	**18.2**	**30.0**	**24.0**	**26.3**	**37.3**
Airline fares	9.9	21.7	16.7	18.9	27.5
Intercity bus fares	4.0	7.5	6.7	6.0	9.3
Intracity mass transit fares	7.0	8.6	6.7	6.7	11.4
Local transportation on trips	4.8	10.5	8.9	9.1	12.8
Taxi fares and limousine service on trips	4.8	10.5	8.9	9.1	12.8
Taxi fares and limousine service	3.0	4.2	3.4	3.3	5.6
Intercity train fares	3.9	8.1	6.8	6.5	10.2
Ship fares	2.2	5.8	5.3	5.1	6.6
School bus	0.0	0.1	0.2	0.1	0.1

Source: Bureau of Labor Statistics, unpublished data from the 2008 Consumer Expenditure Survey

Table 10.10 Amount High-Income Buyers Spent on Transportation, <u>Average Quarter</u>, 2008

(average amount spent by high-income households buying transportation during the average quarter, by before-tax income of household, 2008)

	total households	$100,000 or more	$100,000– $119,999	$120,000– $149,999	$150,000 or more
TRANSPORTATION, AMOUNT SPENT	**$2,200.87**	**$3,884.45**	**$3,270.70**	**$3,855.44**	**$4,408.11**
Vehicle purchases	**14,560.25**	**20,770.39**	**18,418.80**	**18,309.72**	**24,889.81**
Cars and trucks, new	25,487.50	29,126.27	25,490.91	27,571.28	32,607.88
New cars	23,500.00	26,979.07	24,937.57	20,445.28	31,867.96
New trucks	28,212.24	31,788.84	26,723.00	34,083.95	32,093.54
Cars and trucks, used	10,374.53	14,876.52	14,152.99	13,364.58	16,930.79
Used cars	9,508.71	13,362.50	14,882.99	10,076.53	15,169.63
Used trucks	11,204.83	16,385.76	12,925.75	18,222.42	19,817.13
Other vehicles	9,596.43	11,047.27	9,087.50	10,561.69	13,896.62
Gasoline and motor oil	**748.22**	**1,070.75**	**1,002.20**	**1,077.54**	**1,122.93**
Gasoline	697.37	991.36	935.65	994.90	1,035.34
Diesel fuel	633.33	609.89	495.37	792.57	597.85
Gasoline on trips	179.96	196.71	184.63	204.44	199.88
Motor oil	31.28	38.86	41.35	28.37	45.04
Motor oil on trips	1.82	1.99	1.87	2.06	2.02
Other vehicle expenses	**731.51**	**1,165.88**	**981.94**	**1,087.60**	**1,371.36**
Vehicle finance charges	241.79	285.50	247.40	295.92	311.70
Automobile finance charges	196.13	209.35	187.01	214.42	223.38
Truck finance charges	222.02	246.21	222.28	256.95	259.48
Motorcycle and plane finance charges	126.85	179.78	120.80	188.33	272.39
Other vehicle finance charges	279.86	307.03	277.54	352.39	298.88
Maintenance and repairs	329.52	498.35	414.67	454.85	598.04
Coolant, additives, brake and transmission fluids	18.34	15.04	13.14	12.21	19.02
Tires—purchased, replaced, installed	398.24	512.06	482.61	448.46	570.83
Vehicle products and cleaning services	42.22	54.25	41.90	51.57	63.04
Parts, equipment, and accessories	126.53	188.36	125.61	194.76	242.15
Vehicle audio equipment, excluding labor	251.19	342.42	138.89	110.71	488.78
Vehicle video equipment	301.72	333.33	211.36	341.23	350.85
Body work and painting	640.57	626.96	442.75	530.57	764.60
Clutch and transmission repair	756.20	1,039.43	1,016.29	1,202.72	965.16
Drive shaft and rear-end repair	397.00	403.57	326.67	436.40	408.33
Brake work	313.32	380.80	332.92	403.97	402.15
Repair to steering or front-end	447.50	568.25	450.31	718.03	576.63
Repair to engine cooling system	322.53	424.05	385.69	473.36	419.78
Motor tune-up	257.86	313.95	258.17	332.90	334.26
Lube, oil change, and oil filters	52.14	65.16	59.96	64.28	70.12
Front-end alignment, wheel balance, rotation	135.08	154.88	148.88	154.35	161.96
Shock absorber replacement	357.26	484.88	577.98	492.59	411.16
Tire repair and other repair work	224.10	276.67	238.03	247.02	323.18
Exhaust system repair	270.00	311.07	275.86	255.95	372.80
Electrical system repair	318.26	376.52	341.73	377.48	396.99
Motor repair, replacement	668.65	730.61	872.73	686.46	654.08
Auto repair service policy	901.42	1,167.47	1,392.34	1,061.90	1,107.00
Vehicle accessories including labor	661.11	1,578.35	353.97	221.18	2,996.91
Vehicle air conditioning repair	300.55	392.34	394.31	382.24	401.57

	total households	$100,000 or more	$100,000–$119,999	$120,000–$149,999	$150,000 or more
Vehicle insurance	$438.54	$601.21	$519.04	$580.58	$689.17
Vehicle rental, leases, licenses, other charges	271.81	436.75	375.56	343.84	535.35
Leased and rented vehicles	1,038.43	1,239.02	1,198.17	1,017.76	1,357.59
Rented vehicles	322.71	379.24	320.06	311.28	431.41
Auto rental	292.79	344.88	408.73	212.31	355.47
Auto rental on trips	307.91	353.52	275.78	296.62	401.28
Truck rental	328.26	509.04	589.86	375.78	516.15
Truck rental on trips	460.71	483.15	234.62	364.66	657.27
Leased vehicles	1,520.08	1,829.81	1,628.89	1,531.68	2,099.13
Car lease payments	1,244.69	1,501.32	1,446.93	1,308.81	1,632.03
Truck lease payments	1,371.58	1,470.58	1,412.87	1,315.34	1,565.78
Vehicle registration, state	128.06	161.27	151.87	170.15	162.41
Vehicle registration, local	108.69	131.59	106.82	127.16	168.95
Driver's license	35.98	35.83	34.62	32.97	38.99
Vehicle inspection	42.24	48.73	46.13	46.09	52.31
Parking fees	81.65	114.62	75.88	90.36	147.16
Parking fees in home city, excluding residence	86.17	124.73	84.52	94.52	160.68
Parking fees on trips	48.71	56.51	39.01	50.24	67.80
Tolls and electronic toll passes	57.43	76.80	76.17	62.27	84.34
Tolls on trips	17.46	18.96	17.08	18.02	20.36
Towing charges	122.61	123.76	118.75	88.33	142.23
Global positioning services	105.50	136.25	65.12	139.31	167.71
Automobile service clubs	88.42	103.19	99.51	106.39	103.52
Public transportation	**698.61**	**1,165.20**	**855.16**	**1,087.03**	**1,365.53**
Airline fares	867.80	1,158.01	855.14	1,111.11	1,330.65
Intercity bus fares	69.71	85.24	53.75	82.69	104.85
Intracity mass transit fares	215.06	344.67	307.80	294.20	381.94
Local transportation on trips	63.72	87.88	55.21	76.70	111.90
Taxi fares and limousine service on trips	37.42	51.62	32.42	45.03	65.72
Taxi fares and limousine service	109.16	154.78	103.20	149.92	181.94
Intercity train fares	144.82	185.78	99.48	163.42	242.66
Ship fares	424.10	451.17	376.33	476.86	487.42
School bus	437.50	475.00	227.94	239.29	787.50

Source: Calculations by New Strategist based on the Bureau of Labor Statistics' 2008 Consumer Expenditure Survey

Table 10.11 Percent of High-Income Households Buying Transportation, Average Week, 2008

(percent of high-income households buying transportation during the average week, by before-tax income of household, 2008)

	total households	$100,000 or more	$100,000– $119,999	$120,000– $149,999	$150,000 or more
TRANSPORTATION, PERCENT BUYING	**70.7%**	**84.1%**	**83.1%**	**85.4%**	**84.1%**
Gasoline	67.9	80.5	80.7	82.0	79.2
Diesel fuel	0.8	1.4	0.4	1.4	2.4
Motor oil	1.6	1.9	2.7	1.9	1.3
Coolant, additives, brake and transmission fluids	1.4	1.4	1.7	1.3	1.1
Other vehicle expenses	15.9	22.5	20.9	23.6	23.4
Maintenance and repairs	6.1	10.4	8.5	10.3	12.4
Vehicle audio equipment, excluding labor	0.1	0.2	0.1	0.2	0.4
Vehicle products and cleaning services	1.3	1.9	2.0	1.8	1.9
Miscellaneous auto repair, servicing	5.2	9.0	7.3	9.0	10.8
Vehicle insurance	9.2	10.8	12.3	11.4	8.9
Vehicle rental, leases, licenses, and other charges	2.5	4.7	3.0	5.4	5.9
Tolls and electronic toll passes	2.5	4.7	3.0	5.4	5.9
Taxi fares and limousine service	**1.0**	**1.8**	**0.9**	**1.4**	**2.9**

Source: Bureau of Labor Statistics, unpublished data from the 2008 Consumer Expenditure Survey

Table 10.12 Amount High-Income Buyers Spent on Transportation, Average Week, 2008

(average amount spent by high-income households buying transportation during the average week, by before-tax income of household, 2008)

	total households	$100,000 or more	$100,000– $119,999	$120,000– $149,999	$150,000 or more
TRANSPORTATION, AMOUNT SPENT	**$99.00**	**$128.68**	**$123.36**	**$135.68**	**$128.54**
Gasoline	67.63	89.02	84.36	93.96	89.89
Diesel fuel	82.89	107.80	111.63	86.62	117.08
Motor oil	9.43	15.46	15.04	16.58	15.08
Coolant, additives, brake and transmission fluids	8.45	9.42	14.55	6.06	7.02
Other vehicle expenses	143.37	150.71	158.39	155.62	139.80
Maintenance and repairs	18.30	23.85	20.84	18.88	29.18
Vehicle audio equipment, excluding labor	150.00	169.57	537.50	105.88	123.81
Vehicle products and cleaning services	12.60	16.23	4.00	5.59	36.65
Miscellaneous auto repair, servicing	16.67	19.71	17.63	18.47	22.07
Vehicle insurance	232.21	286.41	252.97	299.47	321.42
Vehicle rental, leases, licenses, and other charges	11.43	10.66	9.97	12.10	9.81
Tolls and electronic toll passes	11.43	10.66	9.97	12.10	9.81
Taxi fares and limousine service	**34.69**	**35.43**	**22.99**	**37.23**	**38.78**

Source: Calculations by New Strategist based on the Bureau of Labor Statistics' 2008 Consumer Expenditure Survey

Table 10.13 Percent Buying Transportation by Household Type, Average Quarter, 2008

(percent of households buying transportation during the average quarter, by type of household, 2008)

	total married couples	married couples, no children	married couples with children				single parent, at least one child <18	single person
			total	oldest child under 6	oldest child 6 to 17	oldest child 18 or older		
TRANSPORTATION, PERCENT BUYING	**99.0%**	**98.7%**	**99.3%**	**98.9%**	**99.4%**	**99.4%**	**90.8%**	**87.6%**
Vehicle purchases	**5.9**	**4.7**	**6.9**	**6.4**	**6.7**	**7.5**	**3.7**	**2.7**
Cars and trucks, new	1.8	1.7	1.7	1.8	1.7	1.7	0.5	0.6
New cars	1.0	1.0	1.0	0.6	1.0	1.1	0.4	0.5
New trucks	0.8	0.7	0.8	1.2	0.7	0.6	0.2	0.2
Cars and trucks, used	3.7	2.7	4.7	4.2	4.4	5.5	3.0	1.9
Used cars	2.0	1.5	2.4	1.8	2.0	3.3	1.8	1.2
Used trucks	1.8	1.2	2.4	2.4	2.4	2.3	1.4	0.7
Other vehicles	0.5	0.3	0.5	0.4	0.7	0.3	0.1	0.2
Gasoline and motor oil	**97.3**	**97.1**	**97.5**	**96.4**	**98.1**	**97.0**	**84.8**	**80.4**
Gasoline	96.8	96.5	97.0	96.1	97.6	96.6	84.2	79.5
Diesel fuel	2.7	3.2	2.4	1.9	2.4	2.5	0.6	0.7
Gasoline on trips	25.7	26.8	25.8	24.5	27.2	24.2	13.6	13.9
Motor oil	9.5	9.3	9.4	6.8	9.7	10.4	5.6	5.2
Motor oil on trips	25.7	26.8	25.8	24.5	27.2	24.2	13.6	13.9
Other vehicle expenses	**90.0**	**88.5**	**91.7**	**90.8**	**92.1**	**91.4**	**73.3**	**66.2**
Vehicle finance charges	41.1	33.0	47.8	50.3	47.7	46.7	29.2	16.2
Automobile finance charges	20.0	17.0	22.5	20.6	19.7	28.5	16.9	9.4
Truck finance charges	25.1	18.2	30.7	35.0	33.2	23.8	12.7	6.5
Motorcycle and plane finance charges	1.8	1.4	2.0	2.2	2.1	1.8	0.6	0.7
Other vehicle finance charges	2.3	2.4	2.3	1.6	2.5	2.3	0.2	0.3
Maintenance and repairs	61.3	60.4	62.4	59.6	62.4	64.2	45.4	39.6
Coolant, additives, brake and transmission fluids	5.8	5.1	6.5	5.5	6.7	6.6	3.7	3.4
Tires—purchased, replaced, installed	9.5	8.3	10.5	10.1	9.7	12.2	6.9	4.7
Vehicle products and cleaning services	4.4	4.7	4.3	3.9	4.8	3.8	3.0	2.9
Parts, equipment, and accessories	10.6	10.0	10.9	9.3	11.6	10.6	6.1	5.3
Vehicle audio equipment, excluding labor	0.2	0.2	0.3	0.4	0.2	0.3	0.1	0.2
Vehicle video equipment	0.4	0.3	0.4	0.1	0.5	0.5	0.3	0.1
Body work and painting	1.5	1.6	1.5	0.6	1.4	2.3	0.7	0.8
Clutch and transmission repair	1.4	1.5	1.4	1.1	1.4	1.5	0.8	0.8
Drive shaft and rear-end repair	0.3	0.3	0.3	0.2	0.4	0.3	0.2	0.2
Brake work	5.9	5.1	6.7	4.0	6.4	8.6	4.6	2.7
Repair to steering or front-end	1.4	1.4	1.5	1.1	1.5	1.6	1.1	0.7
Repair to engine cooling system	2.1	1.7	2.3	1.9	1.9	3.3	0.9	1.2
Motor tune-up	5.4	5.4	5.3	5.2	5.2	5.5	3.9	2.8
Lube, oil change, and oil filters	39.5	39.0	40.3	37.8	40.1	42.2	30.3	25.7
Front-end alignment, wheel balance, rotation	3.1	3.0	3.2	2.8	3.1	3.6	2.2	1.7
Shock absorber replacement	0.4	0.5	0.3	0.2	0.3	0.5	0.3	0.3
Tire repair and other repair work	7.1	7.3	7.2	6.7	6.6	8.6	4.5	4.3
Exhaust system repair	1.1	0.8	1.3	1.1	1.2	1.7	0.4	0.8
Electrical system repair	2.4	2.4	2.4	1.6	2.4	3.0	2.3	1.6
Motor repair, replacement	3.2	2.8	3.3	2.3	2.9	4.4	1.9	1.7
Auto repair service policy	0.6	0.7	0.5	0.4	0.5	0.6	0.6	0.4
Vehicle accessories including labor	0.6	0.5	0.7	0.5	0.6	0.9	0.4	0.3
Vehicle air conditioning repair	1.2	1.2	1.2	1.2	1.0	1.8	0.3	0.7

	total married couples	married couples, no children	married couples with children				single parent, at least one child <18	single person
			total	oldest child under 6	oldest child 6 to 17	oldest child 18 or older		
Vehicle insurance	57.6%	53.2%	61.0%	60.3%	62.1%	59.6%	46.9%	37.5%
Vehicle rental, leases, licenses, other charges	51.7	51.9	52.5	50.1	53.0	53.1	32.1	33.1
Leased and rented vehicles	8.1	8.0	8.8	8.9	8.8	8.7	4.7	4.5
Rented vehicles	3.4	3.9	3.3	3.0	2.9	4.0	2.1	2.2
Auto rental	0.5	0.5	0.5	0.4	0.5	0.5	0.9	0.5
Auto rental on trips	2.5	2.9	2.3	2.0	2.0	2.9	0.9	1.5
Truck rental	0.2	0.3	0.2	0.4	0.2	0.2	0.3	0.2
Truck rental on trips	0.2	0.2	0.3	0.3	0.2	0.4	0.1	0.0
Leased vehicles	5.0	4.4	5.8	5.9	6.1	5.1	2.8	2.4
Car lease payments	2.8	2.8	3.1	2.3	3.1	3.4	1.5	1.8
Truck lease payments	2.7	2.0	3.4	4.0	3.7	2.3	1.4	0.6
Vehicle registration, state	21.4	21.2	22.1	18.9	21.5	25.1	12.6	11.8
Vehicle registration, local	2.8	2.8	2.8	2.8	2.7	2.8	1.3	1.4
Driver's license	6.3	5.9	6.7	5.8	6.5	7.4	4.7	3.4
Vehicle inspection	7.8	7.3	8.2	6.7	7.9	9.8	5.1	4.2
Parking fees	13.8	13.8	14.2	15.0	14.8	12.5	7.6	9.2
Parking fees in home city, excluding residence	10.4	10.1	11.0	12.1	11.1	10.0	5.9	8.0
Parking fees on trips	4.5	4.8	4.4	3.8	5.0	3.8	2.0	1.6
Tolls and electronic toll passes	11.3	11.1	11.7	11.0	12.4	11.1	5.9	6.0
Tolls on trips	7.9	8.4	7.6	6.4	7.7	8.2	3.9	4.2
Towing charges	0.9	0.7	1.1	1.4	1.0	1.2	0.8	0.8
Global positioning services	0.6	0.7	0.6	0.3	0.8	0.5	0.2	0.4
Automobile service clubs	5.9	7.6	4.7	2.7	4.6	6.0	2.7	4.4
Public transportation	**17.8**	**18.2**	**17.7**	**18.1**	**16.5**	**19.6**	**16.2**	**18.9**
Airline fares	11.7	13.4	10.6	8.8	10.7	11.5	6.3	8.6
Intercity bus fares	4.4	5.4	3.5	2.9	3.5	4.0	2.7	4.0
Intracity mass transit fares	5.4	4.1	6.3	8.1	5.0	7.4	8.6	8.2
Local transportation on trips	5.6	6.4	5.1	4.2	4.8	6.1	3.3	4.5
Taxi fares and limousine service on trips	5.6	6.4	5.1	4.2	4.8	6.1	3.3	4.5
Taxi fares and limousine service	2.0	1.9	2.0	3.0	1.8	2.0	2.2	4.5
Intercity train fares	4.5	5.2	4.0	3.0	3.8	4.9	3.1	3.5
Ship fares	3.0	3.7	2.4	1.4	2.3	3.3	1.4	1.3
School bus	0.1	–	0.1	–	0.1	0.2	0.1	–

Note: "–" means sample is too small to make a reliable estimate.
Source: Bureau of Labor Statistics, unpublished data from the 2008 Consumer Expenditure Survey

Table 10.14 Amount Buyers Spent on Transportation by Household Type, Average Quarter, 2008

(average amount spent by households buying transportation during the average quarter, by type of household, 2008)

	total married couples	married couples, no children	married couples with children				single parent, at least one child <18	single person
			total	oldest child under 6	oldest child 6 to 17	oldest child 18 or older		
TRANSPORTATION, AMOUNT SPENT	$2,792.74	$2,467.72	$3,037.63	$2,580.94	$2,999.09	$3,374.57	$1,647.75	$1,198.28
Vehicle purchases	15,803.52	17,479.59	14,737.61	14,277.93	14,818.70	14,841.17	12,789.20	11,395.32
Cars and trucks, new	26,407.86	25,662.72	26,874.13	27,983.52	27,090.59	26,073.41	29,787.50	21,957.94
New cars	23,964.46	24,025.49	24,183.93	24,800.40	24,891.91	22,648.89	24,547.92	20,994.02
New trucks	28,644.74	28,142.65	29,220.19	29,712.28	28,307.19	30,490.63	40,265.28	24,566.18
Cars and trucks, used	11,279.14	12,928.10	10,518.66	9,092.39	10,363.87	11,355.91	9,927.14	8,040.29
Used cars	10,256.44	12,097.80	9,444.28	5,041.48	8,953.61	11,317.77	8,344.60	8,136.64
Used trucks	12,153.47	13,736.67	11,508.09	12,139.08	11,415.42	11,260.78	11,475.56	7,777.05
Other vehicles	10,411.67	11,039.06	10,509.91	7,666.48	10,127.74	14,941.00	8,005.00	7,029.76
Gasoline and motor oil	915.27	773.80	1,021.90	855.17	1,017.84	1,127.68	614.63	430.45
Gasoline	845.66	699.19	954.55	799.07	944.26	1,064.34	587.38	403.56
Diesel fuel	633.61	596.95	677.86	751.82	721.90	568.58	657.46	598.65
Gasoline on trips	198.07	200.47	194.60	165.72	204.35	193.08	155.74	138.20
Motor oil	33.56	35.61	32.05	25.00	30.36	37.56	30.03	27.70
Motor oil on trips	2.00	2.02	1.97	1.67	2.06	1.95	1.57	1.40
Other vehicle expenses	858.01	769.80	920.27	768.13	907.24	1,032.85	588.80	490.36
Vehicle finance charges	261.92	251.30	264.61	244.95	271.10	265.77	204.17	187.04
Automobile finance charges	203.13	189.34	208.41	198.20	211.66	208.96	203.92	165.98
Truck finance charges	230.04	220.78	234.47	223.32	235.37	242.13	191.04	203.67
Motorcycle and plane finance charges	142.92	216.54	99.26	84.17	113.74	80.68	101.64	67.80
Other vehicle finance charges	289.38	320.85	255.53	152.64	287.96	240.04	179.17	310.29
Maintenance and repairs	363.82	342.47	376.40	278.89	379.95	424.23	262.81	265.52
Coolant, additives, brake and transmission fluids	19.06	19.57	18.33	17.60	18.69	18.19	17.53	13.63
Tires—purchased, replaced, installed	423.24	460.91	398.96	383.32	424.51	371.53	288.01	367.78
Vehicle products and cleaning services	49.43	48.93	48.90	36.93	45.30	64.32	26.99	30.57
Parts, equipment, and accessories	131.91	115.78	137.88	98.82	131.51	170.34	99.18	123.11
Vehicle audio equipment, excluding labor	239.29	275.00	225.00	139.20	164.06	330.15	106.82	173.75
Vehicle video equipment	301.32	306.82	301.70	112.50	340.87	265.63	231.03	412.50
Body work and painting	688.80	632.21	729.28	571.88	932.45	531.22	540.07	574.69
Clutch and transmission repair	797.70	721.03	848.39	484.03	962.85	821.52	978.44	701.54
Drive shaft and rear-end repair	338.39	392.24	296.77	420.45	240.71	350.00	697.73	416.67
Brake work	341.39	348.39	338.85	269.40	341.23	354.75	217.96	295.85
Repair to steering or front-end	488.29	511.21	458.22	448.89	418.21	525.00	343.81	398.65
Repair to engine cooling system	321.60	298.55	329.46	150.39	294.49	427.37	258.43	376.26
Motor tune-up	279.90	312.73	246.98	253.24	257.22	226.59	203.06	246.02
Lube, oil change, and oil filters	57.19	53.46	61.00	58.71	59.83	64.12	43.01	43.34
Front-end alignment, wheel balance, rotation	148.54	149.33	151.58	196.48	141.72	145.87	95.72	103.18
Shock absorber replacement	336.11	365.56	293.18	148.96	345.00	295.59	305.77	398.39
Tire repair and other repair work	248.34	235.37	255.39	262.74	260.24	245.03	183.86	187.85
Exhaust system repair	262.85	289.29	249.43	283.73	260.87	224.42	274.31	302.24
Electrical system repair	321.37	320.80	314.26	260.67	314.06	329.28	352.33	317.26
Motor repair, replacement	667.51	704.68	632.49	650.32	613.10	650.46	529.32	664.09
Auto repair service policy	826.23	772.50	989.80	571.71	1,049.47	1,067.80	1,616.80	801.28
Vehicle accessories including labor	904.17	254.33	1,481.06	165.74	2,841.81	393.54	82.39	176.92
Vehicle air conditioning repair	324.38	322.17	330.44	221.61	413.16	299.86	256.25	220.90

	total married couples	married couples, no children	married couples with children				single parent, at least one child <18	single person
			total	oldest child under 6	oldest child 6 to 17	oldest child 18 or older		
Vehicle insurance	$488.55	$462.67	$495.05	$396.41	$448.96	$636.88	$341.06	$333.06
Vehicle rental, leases, licenses, other charges	310.22	280.37	342.58	337.98	359.25	316.43	288.49	194.70
Leased and rented vehicles	1,163.27	1,029.99	1,267.52	1,216.86	1,391.05	1,085.78	1,226.22	734.15
Rented vehicles	353.39	332.43	377.68	348.92	398.72	361.88	506.16	246.93
Auto rental	293.09	251.56	344.27	554.76	343.09	258.82	541.57	233.17
Auto rental on trips	337.86	323.80	358.59	301.61	378.06	356.74	277.27	253.36
Truck rental	444.79	366.35	451.04	292.36	616.25	384.09	704.55	64.71
Truck rental on trips	448.96	533.75	412.93	301.52	426.14	451.92	384.38	441.67
Leased vehicles	1,654.20	1,576.82	1,719.88	1,642.31	1,818.19	1,576.03	1,653.26	1,168.40
Car lease payments	1,319.15	1,257.79	1,385.46	1,313.20	1,488.26	1,252.42	1,076.87	1,144.10
Truck lease payments	1,442.69	1,365.44	1,483.48	1,452.19	1,490.51	1,492.38	1,328.68	1,092.67
Vehicle registration, state	139.12	135.53	139.98	126.52	149.77	131.53	118.83	105.58
Vehicle registration, local	115.18	104.18	125.45	117.53	132.87	117.95	121.92	92.22
Driver's license	35.96	34.74	37.20	45.59	36.29	34.63	39.30	33.14
Vehicle inspection	43.14	42.36	42.59	36.96	44.55	42.23	36.39	38.16
Parking fees	81.89	77.07	85.41	93.25	75.02	100.92	94.01	77.24
Parking fees in home city, excluding residence	86.68	78.85	91.92	101.16	79.74	108.82	105.68	80.58
Parking fees on trips	50.50	56.62	45.75	46.06	45.03	46.92	49.02	41.83
Tolls and electronic toll passes	61.81	51.80	68.21	83.18	63.65	68.11	55.94	44.25
Tolls on trips	18.14	17.61	18.81	23.67	16.30	20.57	17.67	16.81
Towing charges	114.89	104.41	118.20	111.17	127.25	109.76	182.91	135.54
Global positioning services	121.25	127.24	108.75	223.28	98.03	98.50	54.41	74.40
Automobile service clubs	96.40	95.33	97.39	89.51	88.31	111.68	68.25	73.07
Public transportation	**963.96**	**1,009.76**	**926.88**	**640.73**	**969.62**	**1,022.86**	**451.17**	**395.38**
Airline fares	1,040.18	953.88	1,125.57	874.46	1,168.66	1,172.47	702.16	549.27
Intercity bus fares	78.97	91.23	67.19	41.44	75.00	66.77	54.37	60.05
Intracity mass transit fares	271.26	211.25	296.86	322.28	234.46	353.10	174.88	133.96
Local transportation on trips	70.19	76.92	65.12	40.06	60.33	81.72	41.64	47.88
Taxi fares and limousine service on trips	41.22	45.17	38.24	23.51	35.44	47.98	24.47	28.13
Taxi fares and limousine service	133.46	105.59	146.32	97.57	155.23	175.64	168.69	77.90
Intercity train fares	169.00	170.49	175.50	130.96	175.78	191.18	123.79	109.93
Ship fares	505.13	667.21	331.20	158.93	261.17	457.50	192.01	274.22
School bus	392.86	–	447.92	–	562.50	268.75	210.71	–

Note: "–" means sample is too small to make a reliable estimate.
Source: Calculations by New Strategist based on the Bureau of Labor Statistics' 2008 Consumer Expenditure Survey

Table 10.15 Percent Buying Transportation by Household Type, _Average Week_, 2008

(percent of households buying transportation during the average week, by type of household, 2008)

	total married couples	married couples, no children	married couples with children				single parent, at least one child <18	single person
			total	oldest child under 6	oldest child 6 to 17	oldest child 18 or older		
TRANSPORTATION, PERCENT BUYING	**78.7%**	**73.9%**	**82.7%**	**82.0%**	**81.9%**	**84.6%**	**68.7%**	**55.7%**
Gasoline	**76.1**	**70.8**	**80.2**	**79.5**	**79.6**	**81.9**	**67.0**	**52.2**
Diesel fuel	**1.0**	**0.9**	**1.2**	**1.0**	**1.4**	**0.9**	**0.2**	**0.4**
Motor oil	**2.0**	**1.7**	**2.4**	**2.0**	**2.2**	**2.9**	**0.9**	**0.9**
Coolant, additives, brake and transmission fluids	**1.7**	**1.4**	**2.0**	**0.9**	**1.8**	**2.9**	**0.9**	**0.9**
Other vehicle expenses	**19.3**	**17.9**	**20.3**	**19.1**	**19.0**	**23.5**	**11.6**	**11.2**
Maintenance and repairs	7.9	8.4	7.8	6.8	7.0	9.7	4.0	3.8
Vehicle audio equipment, excluding labor	0.1	0.0	0.2	0.3	0.1	0.2	–	0.0
Vehicle products and cleaning services	1.6	1.8	1.6	1.6	1.4	2.1	1.0	0.7
Miscellaneous auto repair, servicing	6.8	7.1	6.6	6.0	5.9	8.0	3.3	3.3
Vehicle insurance	10.9	9.6	11.9	11.0	11.1	13.9	7.9	6.6
Vehicle rental, leases, licenses, and other charges	2.9	2.4	3.2	3.4	3.1	3.2	1.2	1.7
Tolls and electronic toll passes	2.9	2.4	3.2	3.4	3.1	3.2	1.2	1.7
Taxi fares and limousine service	**0.8**	**0.8**	**0.9**	**1.0**	**0.6**	**1.4**	**0.6**	**1.3**

Note: "–" means sample is too small to make a reliable estimate.
Source: Bureau of Labor Statistics, unpublished data from the 2008 Consumer Expenditure Survey

Table 10.16 Amount Buyers Spent on Transportation by Household Type, _Average Week_, 2008

(average amount spent by households buying transportation during the average week, by type of household, 2008)

	total married couples	married couples, no children	married couples with children				single parent, at least one child <18	single person
			total	oldest child under 6	oldest child 6 to 17	oldest child 18 or older		
TRANSPORTATION, AMOUNT SPENT	**$114.04**	**$102.29**	**$122.51**	**$107.15**	**$112.33**	**$149.56**	**$72.84**	**$72.35**
Gasoline	**76.48**	**64.85**	**84.42**	**77.53**	**80.72**	**95.09**	**57.27**	**47.94**
Diesel fuel	**78.85**	**64.84**	**88.03**	**71.00**	**94.16**	**84.78**	**35.29**	**88.57**
Motor oil	**10.34**	**9.04**	**11.34**	**14.78**	**13.24**	**7.82**	**7.06**	**5.75**
Coolant, additives, brake and transmission fluids	**8.98**	**7.97**	**9.74**	**8.24**	**8.29**	**11.38**	**6.45**	**6.82**
Other vehicle expenses	**156.83**	**159.59**	**156.57**	**130.08**	**135.72**	**200.34**	**98.62**	**126.87**
Maintenance and repairs	18.69	18.38	18.71	19.26	17.24	20.29	16.96	14.58
Vehicle audio equipment, excluding labor	177.78	0.00	194.12	90.00	320.00	168.18	–	100.00
Vehicle products and cleaning services	11.73	16.29	7.32	5.73	7.86	8.06	4.17	7.58
Miscellaneous auto repair, servicing	16.59	17.58	15.09	15.83	12.79	17.73	16.56	14.89
Vehicle insurance	260.94	279.33	252.36	208.79	219.06	321.86	135.96	202.71
Vehicle rental, leases, licenses, and other charges	10.88	10.37	11.91	11.95	9.71	15.22	6.03	14.20
Tolls and electronic toll passes	10.88	10.37	11.91	11.95	9.71	15.22	6.03	14.20
Taxi fares and limousine service	**32.10**	**32.00**	**32.22**	**37.00**	**41.38**	**22.38**	**14.29**	**44.09**

Note: "–" means sample is too small to make a reliable estimate.
Source: Calculations by New Strategist based on the Bureau of Labor Statistics' 2008 Consumer Expenditure Survey

Table 10.17 Percent Buying Transportation by Race and Hispanic Origin, Average Quarter, 2008

(percent of households buying transportation during the average quarter, by race and Hispanic origin of householder, 2008)

TRANSPORTATION, PERCENT BUYING	total households	Asian	black	Hispanic	non-Hispanic white and other
	94.8%	94.5%	88.7%	94.0%	95.8%
Vehicle purchases	**4.7**	**3.0**	**3.6**	**5.0**	**4.9**
Cars and trucks, new	1.3	1.4	0.6	0.9	1.4
New cars	0.8	1.1	0.4	0.4	0.9
New trucks	0.5	0.3	0.3	0.5	0.5
Cars and trucks, used	3.2	1.6	2.8	3.9	3.1
Used cars	1.8	0.9	1.9	2.2	1.7
Used trucks	1.5	0.6	1.0	1.7	1.5
Other vehicles	0.4	0.1	0.2	0.2	0.4
Gasoline and motor oil	**90.7**	**87.5**	**80.2**	**87.4**	**92.9**
Gasoline	90.1	87.0	79.9	87.0	92.2
Diesel fuel	1.8	0.1	0.5	0.9	2.2
Gasoline on trips	20.1	17.5	9.3	13.5	22.8
Motor oil	8.0	3.9	5.9	8.0	8.3
Motor oil on trips	20.1	17.5	9.3	13.5	22.8
Other vehicle expenses	**80.8**	**76.1**	**68.8**	**75.3**	**83.6**
Vehicle finance charges	32.3	24.4	29.1	31.4	32.9
Automobile finance charges	17.1	16.1	18.7	15.7	17.0
Truck finance charges	17.5	9.7	13.2	18.3	18.1
Motorcycle and plane finance charges	1.4	1.2	0.1	0.9	1.6
Other vehicle finance charges	1.4	0.1	0.1	0.5	1.8
Maintenance and repairs	52.5	49.4	42.0	47.5	55.0
Coolant, additives, brake and transmission fluids	5.0	3.3	4.7	6.1	4.9
Tires—purchased, replaced, installed	7.8	6.4	6.6	6.5	8.2
Vehicle products and cleaning services	3.6	3.3	2.8	2.6	3.9
Parts, equipment, and accessories	8.7	4.6	4.8	8.1	9.3
Vehicle audio equipment, excluding labor	0.2	0.1	0.2	0.3	0.2
Vehicle video equipment	0.3	0.5	0.1	0.2	0.4
Body work and painting	1.2	0.9	0.6	0.9	1.4
Clutch and transmission repair	1.2	0.3	0.9	1.1	1.3
Drive shaft and rear-end repair	0.3	0.2	0.1	0.1	0.3
Brake work	4.8	5.1	4.2	3.9	5.0
Repair to steering or front-end	1.2	0.8	1.0	0.8	1.3
Repair to engine cooling system	1.7	1.2	1.2	1.3	1.9
Motor tune-up	4.4	6.7	3.1	5.5	4.5
Lube, oil change, and oil filters	33.8	33.9	27.2	29.4	35.4
Front-end alignment, wheel balance, rotation	2.5	1.7	2.1	1.9	2.7
Shock absorber replacement	0.3	–	0.3	0.3	0.3
Tire repair and other repair work	5.9	5.3	4.3	4.4	6.3
Exhaust system repair	0.9	0.6	0.6	0.4	1.0
Electrical system repair	2.2	1.6	1.5	1.7	2.3
Motor repair, replacement	2.6	2.2	1.9	3.0	2.6
Auto repair service policy	0.5	0.5	0.6	0.2	0.6
Vehicle accessories including labor	0.5	0.4	0.3	0.2	0.5
Vehicle air conditioning repair	0.9	0.5	0.4	0.7	1.0

	total households	Asian	black	Hispanic	non-Hispanic white and other
Vehicle insurance	50.7%	42.2%	44.7%	49.2%	51.9%
Vehicle rental, leases, licenses, other charges	43.3	44.3	28.5	36.1	46.8
Leased and rented vehicles	6.5	8.5	3.6	4.9	7.2
Rented vehicles	2.8	5.1	1.9	1.8	3.2
Auto rental	0.5	0.9	0.6	0.2	0.5
Auto rental on trips	2.0	3.6	1.0	1.4	2.2
Truck rental	0.2	0.6	0.2	0.2	0.3
Truck rental on trips	0.1	0.3	0.1	0.0	0.2
Leased vehicles	3.8	3.9	1.8	3.1	4.2
Car lease payments	2.3	2.7	1.2	1.8	2.5
Truck lease payments	1.8	1.3	0.7	1.5	2.1
Vehicle registration, state	17.2	13.0	10.8	15.2	18.6
Vehicle registration, local	2.1	1.1	1.6	1.6	2.3
Driver's license	5.2	4.4	4.0	3.3	5.6
Vehicle inspection	6.4	4.9	4.8	5.9	6.7
Parking fees	11.4	16.6	6.7	7.8	12.7
Parking fees in home city, excluding residence	9.0	13.8	5.7	6.5	9.9
Parking fees on trips	3.1	4.4	1.4	1.5	3.6
Tolls and electronic toll passes	9.0	12.3	5.4	8.7	9.6
Tolls on trips	6.2	7.3	2.7	4.2	7.1
Towing charges	0.9	1.0	0.9	1.0	0.9
Global positioning services	0.5	0.2	0.2	0.1	0.6
Automobile service clubs	5.0	5.8	3.0	2.0	5.8
Public transportation	**18.2**	**35.2**	**18.5**	**18.3**	**18.1**
Airline fares	9.9	16.7	5.0	6.2	11.2
Intercity bus fares	4.0	6.8	2.6	2.8	4.4
Intracity mass transit fares	7.0	17.7	12.6	10.9	5.6
Local transportation on trips	4.8	7.2	2.5	2.6	5.5
Taxi fares and limousine service on trips	4.8	7.2	2.5	2.6	5.5
Taxi fares and limousine service	3.0	4.0	2.9	3.2	3.0
Intercity train fares	3.9	5.8	2.0	2.2	4.4
Ship fares	2.2	2.8	1.1	1.3	2.6
School bus	0.0	0.1	0.0	0.2	0.0

Note: "Asian" and "black" include Hispanics and non-Hispanics who identify themselves as being of the respective race alone. "Hispanic" includes people of any race who identify themselves as Hispanic. "Other" includes people who identify themselves as non-Hispanic and as Alaska Native, American Indian, Asian (who are also included in the Asian column), or Native Hawaiian or other Pacific Islander as well as non-Hispanics reporting more than one race. "–" means sample is too small to make a reliable estimate.
Source: Bureau of Labor Statistics, unpublished data from the 2008 Consumer Expenditure Survey

Table 10.18 Amount Buyers Spent on Transportation by Race and Hispanic Origin, <u>Average Quarter</u>, 2008

(average amount spent by households buying transportation during the average quarter, by race and Hispanic origin of householder, 2008)

	total households	Asian	black	Hispanic	non-Hispanic white and other
TRANSPORTATION, AMOUNT SPENT	**$2,200.87**	**$2,254.95**	**$1,753.15**	**$2,053.28**	**$2,288.65**
Vehicle purchases	**14,560.25**	**20,391.72**	**13,559.78**	**12,899.60**	**14,911.83**
Cars and trucks, new	25,487.50	26,611.69	31,581.05	22,021.15	25,375.17
New cars	23,500.00	22,989.45	27,826.25	21,897.09	23,265.76
New trucks	28,212.24	39,773.33	32,498.08	22,132.29	28,558.02
Cars and trucks, used	10,374.53	14,592.58	9,614.13	10,815.98	10,384.11
Used cars	9,508.71	8,571.47	9,031.38	10,219.93	9,423.80
Used trucks	11,204.83	23,384.92	10,332.32	11,273.54	11,251.34
Other vehicles	9,596.43	12,512.50	11,590.48	10,265.28	9,557.05
Gasoline and motor oil	**748.22**	**725.79**	**703.79**	**776.70**	**750.06**
Gasoline	697.37	694.87	684.69	740.03	692.87
Diesel fuel	633.33	906.25	580.85	772.58	623.40
Gasoline on trips	179.96	160.13	143.39	188.18	181.33
Motor oil	31.28	30.55	21.80	29.49	32.60
Motor oil on trips	1.82	1.62	1.46	1.90	1.83
Other vehicle expenses	**731.51**	**754.41**	**632.75**	**686.10**	**750.69**
Vehicle finance charges	241.79	256.12	245.01	251.38	239.94
Automobile finance charges	196.13	213.42	220.51	221.20	188.57
Truck finance charges	222.02	270.49	227.08	230.66	219.96
Motorcycle and plane finance charges	126.85	143.85	75.00	87.09	130.75
Other vehicle finance charges	279.86	333.33	245.00	292.00	278.18
Maintenance and repairs	329.52	304.96	267.48	279.90	343.42
Coolant, additives, brake and transmission fluids	18.34	17.40	19.22	20.22	17.83
Tires—purchased, replaced, installed	398.24	422.95	304.73	357.11	415.82
Vehicle products and cleaning services	42.22	42.22	50.18	58.40	39.90
Parts, equipment, and accessories	126.53	98.38	84.48	117.72	131.16
Vehicle audio equipment, excluding labor	251.19	151.92	280.00	189.81	260.71
Vehicle video equipment	301.72	301.42	258.33	348.33	297.86
Body work and painting	640.57	590.86	484.77	721.43	642.83
Clutch and transmission repair	756.20	962.10	523.88	789.72	777.54
Drive shaft and rear-end repair	397.00	375.00	340.63	687.50	390.52
Brake work	313.32	296.39	263.49	272.17	324.75
Repair to steering or front-end	447.50	403.09	409.22	458.93	450.98
Repair to engine cooling system	322.53	355.43	270.90	237.69	337.63
Motor tune-up	257.86	292.46	217.53	168.42	278.29
Lube, oil change, and oil filters	52.14	52.87	47.67	51.13	52.82
Front-end alignment, wheel balance, rotation	135.08	158.93	125.82	137.04	135.59
Shock absorber replacement	357.26	–	286.36	292.86	379.03
Tire repair and other repair work	224.10	245.42	218.22	165.74	230.46
Exhaust system repair	270.00	331.64	217.24	253.13	277.21
Electrical system repair	318.26	347.17	304.11	366.42	316.81
Motor repair, replacement	668.65	624.67	698.95	569.34	681.73
Auto repair service policy	901.42	1,409.24	838.84	844.57	913.60
Vehicle accessories including labor	661.11	144.38	251.92	139.47	722.12
Vehicle air conditioning repair	300.55	301.85	360.71	201.07	309.41

	total households	Asian	black	Hispanic	non-Hispanic white and other
Vehicle insurance	$438.54	$511.38	$429.38	$424.63	$441.84
Vehicle rental, leases, licenses, other charges	271.81	327.52	208.82	265.47	278.61
Leased and rented vehicles	1,038.43	992.78	783.50	1,078.43	1,053.39
Rented vehicles	322.71	239.53	288.64	293.99	328.65
Auto rental	292.79	262.09	299.61	390.63	286.11
Auto rental on trips	307.91	209.21	256.89	252.76	316.29
Truck rental	328.26	188.10	266.18	436.25	314.00
Truck rental on trips	460.71	321.77	382.69	62.50	478.13
Leased vehicles	1,520.08	1,840.32	1,241.94	1,511.94	1,541.94
Car lease payments	1,244.69	1,362.83	1,057.99	1,200.14	1,266.06
Truck lease payments	1,371.58	1,166.60	1,239.77	1,538.10	1,361.11
Vehicle registration, state	128.06	136.91	121.20	136.07	127.60
Vehicle registration, local	108.69	141.20	130.78	100.00	107.42
Driver's license	35.98	47.83	38.15	32.76	35.99
Vehicle inspection	42.24	53.89	38.66	47.98	41.88
Parking fees	81.65	121.39	75.60	81.74	82.06
Parking fees in home city, excluding residence	86.17	132.46	78.32	89.34	86.58
Parking fees on trips	48.71	43.56	41.49	33.72	49.93
Tolls and electronic toll passes	57.43	78.22	62.69	70.97	55.98
Tolls on trips	17.46	17.31	16.14	26.84	16.70
Towing charges	122.61	86.32	149.72	147.66	114.89
Global positioning services	105.50	191.67	79.69	183.33	105.74
Automobile service clubs	88.42	83.82	81.00	82.78	89.26
Public transportation	**698.61**	**903.67**	**346.55**	**520.69**	**782.18**
Airline fares	867.80	1,381.75	606.82	907.17	882.55
Intercity bus fares	69.71	85.36	61.26	87.00	69.15
Intracity mass transit fares	215.06	272.69	190.18	211.63	224.37
Local transportation on trips	63.72	56.04	40.08	106.18	62.32
Taxi fares and limousine service on trips	37.42	32.91	23.58	62.36	36.60
Taxi fares and limousine service	109.16	125.31	102.81	108.23	110.22
Intercity train fares	144.82	119.88	89.74	141.02	148.64
Ship fares	424.10	506.52	196.67	194.32	456.05
School bus	437.50	2,375.00	237.50	306.67	483.33

Note: "Asian" and "black" include Hispanics and non-Hispanics who identify themselves as being of the respective race alone. "Hispanic" includes people of any race who identify themselves as Hispanic. "Other" includes people who identify themselves as non-Hispanic and as Alaska Native, American Indian, Asian (who are also included in the Asian column), or Native Hawaiian or other Pacific Islander as well as non-Hispanics reporting more than one race. "–" means sample is too small to make a reliable estimate.
Source: Calculations by New Strategist based on the Bureau of Labor Statistics' 2008 Consumer Expenditure Survey

Table 10.19 Percent Buying Transportation by Race and Hispanic Origin, <u>Average Week</u>, 2008

(percent of households buying transportation during the average week, by race and Hispanic origin of householder, 2008)

	total households	Asian	black	Hispanic	non-Hispanic white and other
TRANSPORTATION, PERCENT BUYING	**70.7%**	**66.4%**	**65.4%**	**71.0%**	**71.4%**
Gasoline	**67.9**	**65.1**	**63.5**	**68.3**	**68.5**
Diesel fuel	**0.8**	**–**	**0.4**	**0.3**	**0.9**
Motor oil	**1.6**	**0.9**	**1.6**	**1.8**	**1.6**
Coolant, additives, brake and transmission fluids	**1.4**	**1.1**	**1.4**	**1.4**	**1.4**
Other vehicle expenses	**15.9**	**11.7**	**13.7**	**15.8**	**16.3**
Maintenance and repairs	6.1	5.0	5.2	5.2	6.4
Vehicle audio equipment, excluding labor	0.1	–	0.1	–	0.1
Vehicle products and cleaning services	1.3	0.8	1.6	1.4	1.2
Miscellaneous auto repair, servicing	5.2	4.5	3.9	4.3	5.5
Vehicle insurance	9.2	5.7	8.8	9.7	9.2
Vehicle rental, leases, licenses, and other charges	2.5	3.1	1.9	2.8	2.5
Tolls and electronic toll passes	2.5	3.1	1.9	2.8	2.5
Taxi fares and limousine service	**1.0**	**1.1**	**0.6**	**1.4**	**1.0**

Note: "Asian" and "black" include Hispanics and non-Hispanics who identify themselves as being of the respective race alone. "Hispanic" includes people of any race who identify themselves as Hispanic. "Other" includes people who identify themselves as non-Hispanic and as Alaska Native, American Indian, Asian (who are also included in the Asian column), or Native Hawaiian or other Pacific Islander as well as non-Hispanics reporting more than one race. "–" means sample is too small to make a reliable estimate.
Source: Bureau of Labor Statistics, unpublished data from the 2008 Consumer Expenditure Survey

Table 10.20 Amount Buyers Spent on Transportation by Race and Hispanic Origin, <u>Average Week</u>, 2008

(average amount spent by households buying transportation during the average week, by race and Hispanic origin of householder, 2008)

	total households	Asian	black	Hispanic	non-Hispanic white and other
TRANSPORTATION, AMOUNT SPENT	**$99.00**	**$104.68**	**$95.18**	**$97.34**	**$99.71**
Gasoline	**67.63**	**63.42**	**63.81**	**67.86**	**68.10**
Diesel fuel	**82.89**	**–**	**72.09**	**136.67**	**81.61**
Motor oil	**9.43**	**16.67**	**7.64**	**10.56**	**9.62**
Coolant, additives, brake and transmission fluids	**8.45**	**4.55**	**6.67**	**7.19**	**9.09**
Other vehicle expenses	**143.37**	**234.07**	**152.89**	**138.31**	**142.69**
Maintenance and repairs	18.30	13.12	13.60	15.06	19.22
Vehicle audio equipment, excluding labor	150.00	–	100.00	–	157.14
Vehicle products and cleaning services	12.60	9.76	4.88	5.88	14.75
Miscellaneous auto repair, servicing	16.67	13.03	14.62	16.24	16.76
Vehicle insurance	232.21	469.31	226.88	214.05	235.32
Vehicle rental, leases, licenses, and other charges	11.43	6.84	12.77	13.12	11.29
Tolls and electronic toll passes	11.43	6.84	12.77	13.12	11.29
Taxi fares and limousine service	**34.69**	**49.11**	**56.14**	**16.67**	**37.11**

Note: "Asian" and "black" include Hispanics and non-Hispanics who identify themselves as being of the respective race alone. "Hispanic" includes people of any race who identify themselves as Hispanic. "Other" includes people who identify themselves as non-Hispanic and as Alaska Native, American Indian, Asian (who are also included in the Asian column), or Native Hawaiian or other Pacific Islander as well as non-Hispanics reporting more than one race. "–" means sample is too small to make a reliable estimate.
Source: Calculations by New Strategist based on the Bureau of Labor Statistics' 2008 Consumer Expenditure Survey

Table 10.21 Percent Buying Transportation by Region, <u>Average Quarter</u>, 2008

(percent of households buying transportation during the average quarter, by region of residence, 2008)

	total households	Northeast	Midwest	South	West
TRANSPORTATION, PERCENT BUYING	**94.8%**	**91.9%**	**94.9%**	**95.1%**	**96.5%**
Vehicle purchases	**4.7**	**4.3**	**5.4**	**4.5**	**4.8**
Cars and trucks, new	1.3	1.4	1.2	1.3	1.2
New cars	0.8	1.0	0.7	0.8	0.8
New trucks	0.5	0.4	0.6	0.5	0.4
Cars and trucks, used	3.2	2.9	3.8	3.0	3.1
Used cars	1.8	1.6	2.2	1.6	1.7
Used trucks	1.5	1.3	1.6	1.4	1.5
Other vehicles	0.4	0.2	0.4	0.3	0.5
Gasoline and motor oil	**90.7**	**82.0**	**91.4**	**93.0**	**93.5**
Gasoline	90.1	81.4	90.8	92.5	92.7
Diesel fuel	1.8	0.7	1.5	2.4	2.2
Gasoline on trips	20.1	17.3	21.8	18.2	23.7
Motor oil	8.0	6.1	8.7	8.5	8.0
Motor oil on trips	20.1	17.3	21.8	18.2	23.7
Other vehicle expenses	**80.8**	**74.2**	**81.8**	**81.9**	**83.5**
Vehicle finance charges	32.3	25.7	32.4	36.3	31.2
Automobile finance charges	17.1	14.4	17.1	18.8	16.4
Truck finance charges	17.5	13.1	17.8	20.2	16.5
Motorcycle and plane finance charges	1.4	1.0	1.5	1.4	1.5
Other vehicle finance charges	1.4	0.7	1.8	1.5	1.6
Maintenance and repairs	52.5	47.5	54.9	53.3	53.0
Coolant, additives, brake and transmission fluids	5.0	5.4	5.2	5.1	4.2
Tires—purchased, replaced, installed	7.8	7.8	7.2	8.0	8.3
Vehicle products and cleaning services	3.6	2.6	3.8	3.2	4.9
Parts, equipment, and accessories	8.7	7.1	8.6	9.2	9.1
Vehicle audio equipment, excluding labor	0.2	0.2	0.2	0.2	0.3
Vehicle video equipment	0.3	0.4	0.3	0.2	0.3
Body work and painting	1.2	1.2	1.0	1.2	1.5
Clutch and transmission repair	1.2	1.0	1.5	1.1	1.3
Drive shaft and rear-end repair	0.3	0.4	0.3	0.2	0.3
Brake work	4.8	6.8	5.4	3.5	4.5
Repair to steering or front-end	1.2	1.8	1.4	0.9	1.0
Repair to engine cooling system	1.7	1.6	1.6	1.6	2.1
Motor tune-up	4.4	4.6	3.1	4.1	6.2
Lube, oil change, and oil filters	33.8	29.9	36.3	35.1	32.2
Front-end alignment, wheel balance, rotation	2.5	2.4	2.6	2.7	2.3
Shock absorber replacement	0.3	0.3	0.3	0.2	0.5
Tire repair and other repair work	5.9	6.7	6.4	5.1	5.8
Exhaust system repair	0.9	1.4	1.0	0.6	0.8
Electrical system repair	2.2	2.1	2.0	1.9	2.8
Motor repair, replacement	2.6	2.2	2.6	2.4	3.1
Auto repair service policy	0.5	0.6	0.6	0.5	0.5
Vehicle accessories including labor	0.5	0.7	0.5	0.4	0.3
Vehicle air conditioning repair	0.9	0.9	0.7	0.9	1.1

	total households	Northeast	Midwest	South	West
Vehicle insurance	50.7%	45.3%	49.9%	52.3%	53.5%
Vehicle rental, leases, licenses, other charges	43.3	51.0	43.4	38.9	44.0
Leased and rented vehicles	6.5	8.4	8.0	4.1	7.2
Rented vehicles	2.8	2.8	2.7	2.1	4.2
Auto rental	0.5	0.6	0.5	0.4	0.7
Auto rental on trips	2.0	1.7	2.0	1.4	3.2
Truck rental	0.2	0.3	0.2	0.2	0.3
Truck rental on trips	0.1	0.2	0.1	0.1	0.1
Leased vehicles	3.8	5.8	5.5	2.0	3.3
Car lease payments	2.3	3.7	3.0	1.3	1.8
Truck lease payments	1.8	2.9	2.9	0.8	1.6
Vehicle registration, state	17.2	14.3	20.2	15.3	19.8
Vehicle registration, local	2.1	1.1	2.3	3.3	0.9
Driver's license	5.2	5.2	5.3	5.2	5.0
Vehicle inspection	6.4	11.0	1.2	8.1	5.0
Parking fees	11.4	14.0	12.8	8.4	12.7
Parking fees in home city, excluding residence	9.0	11.1	10.5	6.3	10.3
Parking fees on trips	3.1	3.8	3.1	2.7	3.3
Tolls and electronic toll passes	9.0	20.3	5.7	7.3	5.7
Tolls on trips	6.2	11.2	6.2	4.6	4.5
Towing charges	0.9	0.9	1.2	1.0	0.6
Global positioning services	0.5	0.6	0.5	0.4	0.6
Automobile service clubs	5.0	7.9	4.1	3.1	6.7
Public transportation	**18.2**	**27.4**	**16.4**	**11.7**	**23.0**
Airline fares	9.9	10.0	9.2	7.4	14.6
Intercity bus fares	4.0	4.1	3.9	3.0	5.6
Intracity mass transit fares	7.0	16.5	5.0	3.3	7.4
Local transportation on trips	4.8	5.3	4.9	3.3	7.0
Taxi fares and limousine service on trips	4.8	5.3	4.9	3.3	7.0
Taxi fares and limousine service	3.0	5.9	3.5	1.2	3.2
Intercity train fares	3.9	3.9	4.0	2.8	5.5
Ship fares	2.2	2.3	2.1	1.8	3.0
School bus	0.0	0.1	0.0	0.0	0.1

Source: Bureau of Labor Statistics, unpublished data from the 2008 Consumer Expenditure Survey

Table 10.22 Amount Buyers Spent on Transportation by Region, Average Quarter, 2008

(average amount spent by households buying transportation during the average quarter, by region of residence, 2008)

	total households	Northeast	Midwest	South	West
TRANSPORTATION, AMOUNT SPENT	$2,200.87	$2,279.00	$2,148.83	$2,158.60	$2,259.45
Vehicle purchases	14,560.25	15,659.32	13,394.78	15,042.27	14,407.79
Cars and trucks, new	25,487.50	25,156.20	25,688.91	26,252.13	24,692.77
New cars	23,500.00	23,984.65	22,300.72	24,342.95	22,455.77
New trucks	28,212.24	26,255.13	29,404.91	28,071.23	28,097.16
Cars and trucks, used	10,374.53	10,511.89	9,559.19	10,671.20	10,825.00
Used cars	9,508.71	8,899.84	8,380.47	10,160.99	10,470.56
Used trucks	11,204.83	11,941.98	11,129.17	11,009.86	11,010.14
Other vehicles	9,596.43	15,591.18	10,291.89	8,404.69	9,136.50
Gasoline and motor oil	748.22	727.18	728.55	789.85	716.18
Gasoline	697.37	692.17	673.93	738.61	658.22
Diesel fuel	633.33	691.22	579.50	659.02	604.19
Gasoline on trips	179.96	152.62	195.14	177.92	184.76
Motor oil	31.28	26.75	32.14	32.84	30.57
Motor oil on trips	1.82	1.54	1.97	1.80	1.87
Other vehicle expenses	731.51	863.71	673.80	677.51	778.42
Vehicle finance charges	241.79	226.00	223.35	251.05	254.71
Automobile finance charges	196.13	182.53	173.54	209.14	206.28
Truck finance charges	222.02	217.01	206.39	227.64	231.30
Motorcycle and plane finance charges	126.85	156.12	149.66	97.43	130.50
Other vehicle finance charges	279.86	276.43	203.95	280.36	367.31
Maintenance and repairs	329.52	385.13	297.00	295.48	378.45
Coolant, additives, brake and transmission fluids	18.34	17.69	15.67	19.98	19.18
Tires—purchased, replaced, installed	398.24	414.01	391.01	361.82	449.21
Vehicle products and cleaning services	42.22	41.25	39.00	44.55	42.96
Parts, equipment, and accessories	126.53	150.32	120.00	109.48	145.67
Vehicle audio equipment, excluding labor	251.19	169.74	184.21	409.72	180.00
Vehicle video equipment	301.72	262.50	216.67	298.81	484.00
Body work and painting	640.57	584.88	715.10	530.21	770.72
Clutch and transmission repair	756.20	1,033.42	664.73	737.50	721.37
Drive shaft and rear-end repair	397.00	293.24	479.46	331.25	524.00
Brake work	313.32	335.32	321.42	267.74	332.92
Repair to steering or front-end	447.50	472.93	439.49	391.94	510.20
Repair to engine cooling system	322.53	309.10	269.63	282.25	423.31
Motor tune-up	257.86	291.97	215.79	233.62	284.46
Lube, oil change, and oil filters	52.14	52.54	49.26	51.96	55.52
Front-end alignment, wheel balance, rotation	135.08	159.23	159.54	111.16	130.78
Shock absorber replacement	357.26	370.45	444.83	296.05	335.29
Tire repair and other repair work	224.10	245.03	178.54	259.79	204.85
Exhaust system repair	270.00	297.74	262.26	269.67	241.23
Electrical system repair	318.26	262.32	315.39	318.48	356.82
Motor repair, replacement	668.65	576.58	619.64	678.59	758.04
Auto repair service policy	901.42	679.55	1,005.80	988.24	867.00
Vehicle accessories including labor	661.11	244.40	189.90	1,617.76	317.74
Vehicle air conditioning repair	300.55	377.06	281.25	322.80	241.23

	total households	Northeast	Midwest	South	West
Vehicle insurance	$438.54	$506.38	$375.29	$444.18	$442.94
Vehicle rental, leases, licenses, other charges	271.81	335.13	296.44	191.15	301.28
Leased and rented vehicles	1,038.43	1,279.47	991.01	905.00	979.99
Rented vehicles	322.71	344.77	286.62	330.37	329.09
Auto rental	292.79	281.05	220.00	370.63	283.85
Auto rental on trips	307.91	328.14	294.64	276.09	328.24
Truck rental	328.26	367.86	110.94	443.75	247.00
Truck rental on trips	460.71	417.71	484.62	498.21	282.50
Leased vehicles	1,520.08	1,677.49	1,296.64	1,471.77	1,726.29
Car lease payments	1,244.69	1,262.43	1,067.93	1,256.44	1,509.86
Truck lease payments	1,371.58	1,434.62	1,211.93	1,507.28	1,474.37
Vehicle registration, state	128.06	91.05	134.76	99.82	178.73
Vehicle registration, local	108.69	151.82	89.65	98.56	173.40
Driver's license	35.98	44.48	36.46	29.65	38.60
Vehicle inspection	42.24	55.00	47.73	31.04	46.77
Parking fees	81.65	117.42	75.70	67.13	70.74
Parking fees in home city, excluding residence	86.17	130.27	79.18	68.78	71.21
Parking fees on trips	48.71	51.80	43.43	48.31	51.22
Tolls and electronic toll passes	57.43	64.14	38.07	54.38	63.74
Tolls on trips	17.46	19.92	15.54	18.34	13.68
Towing charges	122.61	123.91	108.61	123.28	149.56
Global positioning services	105.50	120.97	109.69	112.80	80.00
Automobile service clubs	88.42	88.67	80.57	93.05	89.46
Public transportation	**698.61**	**673.68**	**637.80**	**697.13**	**768.95**
Airline fares	867.80	1,051.58	760.74	787.74	899.61
Intercity bus fares	69.71	94.74	61.82	70.45	59.73
Intracity mass transit fares	215.06	273.00	176.39	177.46	161.42
Local transportation on trips	63.72	71.63	48.76	73.70	61.71
Taxi fares and limousine service on trips	37.42	42.06	28.66	43.29	36.25
Taxi fares and limousine service	109.16	131.44	121.05	85.45	75.79
Intercity train fares	144.82	180.10	145.38	140.50	127.06
Ship fares	424.10	418.07	452.43	362.99	469.64
School bus	437.50	810.00	266.67	331.25	310.00

Source: Calculations by New Strategist based on the Bureau of Labor Statistics' 2008 Consumer Expenditure Survey

Table 10.23 Percent Buying Transportation by Region, <u>Average Week</u>, 2008

(percent of households buying transportation during the average week, by region of residence, 2008)

	total households	Northeast	Midwest	South	West
TRANSPORTATION, PERCENT BUYING	**70.7%**	**66.9%**	**70.9%**	**73.3%**	**69.3%**
Gasoline	**67.9**	**62.7**	**68.4**	**70.9**	**66.6**
Diesel fuel	**0.8**	**0.2**	**0.5**	**0.9**	**1.2**
Motor oil	**1.6**	**1.4**	**1.2**	**2.2**	**1.2**
Coolant, additives, brake and transmission fluids	**1.4**	**1.0**	**1.6**	**1.8**	**1.0**
Other vehicle expenses	**15.9**	**18.9**	**14.2**	**16.0**	**15.0**
Maintenance and repairs	6.1	6.4	6.0	6.0	6.2
Vehicle audio equipment, excluding labor	0.1	–	0.1	0.1	0.1
Vehicle products and cleaning services	1.3	1.3	1.2	1.4	1.1
Miscellaneous auto repair, servicing	5.2	5.4	5.1	4.9	5.5
Vehicle insurance	9.2	9.5	8.3	10.2	8.3
Vehicle rental, leases, licenses, and other charges	2.5	5.5	1.2	2.2	1.7
Tolls and electronic toll passes	2.5	5.5	1.2	2.2	1.7
Taxi fares and limousine service	**1.0**	**2.5**	**0.6**	**0.6**	**0.6**

Note: "–" means sample is too small to make a reliable estimate.
Source: Bureau of Labor Statistics, unpublished data from the 2008 Consumer Expenditure Survey

Table 10.24 Amount Buyers Spent on Transportation by Region, <u>Average Week</u>, 2008

(average amount spent by households buying transportation during the average week, by region of residence, 2008)

	total households	Northeast	Midwest	South	West
TRANSPORTATION, AMOUNT SPENT	**$99.00**	**$108.57**	**$91.50**	**$101.35**	**$95.05**
Gasoline	**67.63**	**68.06**	**64.81**	**69.14**	**67.61**
Diesel fuel	**82.89**	**100.00**	**57.69**	**81.52**	**95.00**
Motor oil	**9.43**	**13.67**	**6.67**	**7.44**	**14.52**
Coolant, additives, brake and transmission fluids	**8.45**	**7.84**	**7.45**	**8.99**	**8.16**
Other vehicle expenses	**143.37**	**150.19**	**140.04**	**149.44**	**128.66**
Maintenance and repairs	18.30	22.17	16.11	17.03	18.91
Vehicle audio equipment, excluding labor	150.00	–	200.00	133.33	140.00
Vehicle products and cleaning services	12.60	22.14	6.56	7.30	20.72
Miscellaneous auto repair, servicing	16.67	20.63	14.65	16.87	14.84
Vehicle insurance	232.21	276.87	226.17	222.21	216.04
Vehicle rental, leases, licenses, and other charges	11.43	13.55	7.44	11.11	10.18
Tolls and electronic toll passes	11.43	13.55	7.44	11.11	10.18
Taxi fares and limousine service	**34.69**	**43.87**	**23.44**	**29.03**	**26.23**

Note: "–" means sample is too small to make a reliable estimate.
Source: Calculations by New Strategist based on the Bureau of Labor Statistics' 2008 Consumer Expenditure Survey

Table 10.25 Percent Buying Transportation by Education, <u>Average Quarter</u>, 2008

(percent of households buying transportation during the average quarter, by highest level of education of householder, 2008)

						college graduate		
TRANSPORTATION, PERCENT BUYING	total households	less than high school graduate	high school graduate	some college	associate's degree	total	bachelor's degree	master's, professional, doctorate
	94.8%	**86.6%**	**94.4%**	**95.3%**	**97.4%**	**98.0%**	**97.5%**	**99.0%**
Vehicle purchases	**4.7**	**4.0**	**5.1**	**4.9**	**5.3**	**4.4**	**4.5**	**4.4**
Cars and trucks, new	1.3	0.5	1.0	1.2	1.5	1.9	1.7	2.2
New cars	0.8	0.3	0.7	0.7	0.8	1.2	0.9	1.7
New trucks	0.5	0.2	0.3	0.4	0.7	0.7	0.9	0.5
Cars and trucks, used	3.2	3.3	3.8	3.4	3.3	2.4	2.6	2.2
Used cars	1.8	1.5	2.0	2.1	1.7	.1.4	1.6	1.1
Used trucks	1.5	1.8	1.8	1.3	1.7	1.0	1.0	1.1
Other vehicles	0.4	0.3	0.4	0.4	0.5	0.2	0.3	0.2
Gasoline and motor oil	**90.7**	**79.1**	**90.2**	**91.1**	**95.0**	**95.4**	**95.0**	**96.0**
Gasoline	90.1	78.4	89.7	90.4	94.5	94.6	94.2	95.3
Diesel fuel	1.8	1.4	1.7	2.0	2.7	1.8	2.0	1.4
Gasoline on trips	20.1	8.8	14.5	20.5	22.3	29.6	27.0	34.2
Motor oil	8.0	9.2	9.1	7.8	9.6	6.1	6.4	5.5
Motor oil on trips	20.1	8.8	14.5	20.5	22.3	29.6	27.0	34.2
Other vehicle expenses	**80.8**	**63.3**	**79.6**	**81.0**	**86.8**	**88.7**	**87.9**	**89.9**
Vehicle finance charges	32.3	20.4	33.3	34.2	40.7	33.3	34.8	30.6
Automobile finance charges	17.1	10.0	16.2	18.8	21.4	18.7	18.8	18.6
Truck finance charges	17.5	11.3	18.3	18.2	22.2	17.9	19.5	15.1
Motorcycle and plane finance charges	1.4	0.5	2.2	1.3	2.7	0.7	0.8	0.6
Other vehicle finance charges	1.4	0.3	2.2	1.6	2.1	1.0	1.2	0.7
Maintenance and repairs	52.5	39.3	49.5	52.3	57.2	60.6	59.9	61.8
Coolant, additives, brake and transmission fluids	5.0	5.5	5.4	5.4	5.9	3.8	4.2	3.1
Tires—purchased, replaced, installed	7.8	5.6	7.2	8.0	9.0	8.9	8.9	8.8
Vehicle products and cleaning services	3.6	1.4	2.9	3.3	4.5	5.3	5.1	5.8
Parts, equipment, and accessories	8.7	8.2	9.3	9.1	10.7	7.3	7.1	7.8
Vehicle audio equipment, excluding labor	0.2	0.2	0.1	0.3	0.1	0.3	0.3	0.3
Vehicle video equipment	0.3	0.1	0.2	0.2	0.7	0.5	0.4	0.6
Body work and painting	1.2	0.5	0.9	1.4	1.5	1.7	1.7	1.8
Clutch and transmission repair	1.2	1.0	1.1	1.3	1.2	1.4	1.3	1.6
Drive shaft and rear-end repair	0.3	0.2	0.2	0.2	0.1	0.4	0.3	0.5
Brake work	4.8	3.4	4.1	4.4	5.4	6.1	6.0	6.2
Repair to steering or front-end	1.2	0.6	1.1	1.3	1.4	1.4	1.4	1.3
Repair to engine cooling system	1.7	1.4	1.6	1.5	2.0	2.1	2.0	2.3
Motor tune-up	4.4	3.0	3.3	4.0	5.1	6.2	5.7	6.9
Lube, oil change, and oil filters	33.8	21.2	30.2	33.8	37.7	42.0	41.1	43.7
Front-end alignment, wheel balance, rotation	2.5	1.2	2.0	2.2	3.4	3.6	3.2	4.4
Shock absorber replacement	0.3	0.3	0.2	0.3	0.6	0.3	0.2	0.5
Tire repair and other repair work	5.9	3.7	5.1	5.6	5.8	7.9	7.1	9.2
Exhaust system repair	0.9	0.7	1.0	0.8	1.2	0.9	0.9	0.8
Electrical system repair	2.2	1.8	1.8	2.0	2.2	2.8	2.8	2.8
Motor repair, replacement	2.6	1.9	2.4	2.7	2.0	3.0	3.0	3.1
Auto repair service policy	0.5	0.4	0.5	0.5	0.8	0.6	0.5	0.6
Vehicle accessories including labor	0.5	0.1	0.4	0.5	0.4	0.7	0.7	0.7
Vehicle air conditioning repair	0.9	0.5	0.8	0.8	0.8	1.3	1.2	1.4

	total households	less than high school graduate	high school graduate	some college	associate's degree	college graduate total	bachelor's degree	master's, professional, doctorate
Vehicle insurance	50.7%	39.9%	51.5%	50.5%	56.2%	53.8%	54.9%	52.0%
Vehicle rental, leases, licenses, other charges	43.3	25.4	37.6	43.0	46.0	56.7	54.4	60.9
Leased and rented vehicles	6.5	1.6	4.6	5.8	6.9	10.9	9.4	13.8
Rented vehicles	2.8	0.6	1.6	2.4	2.8	5.5	4.5	7.1
Auto rental	0.5	0.0	0.5	0.6	0.5	0.8	0.7	0.9
Auto rental on trips	2.0	0.3	1.0	1.4	1.9	4.1	3.3	5.5
Truck rental	0.2	0.1	0.1	0.3	0.2	0.4	0.4	0.4
Truck rental on trips	0.1	0.1	0.1	0.1	0.2	0.3	0.2	0.4
Leased vehicles	3.8	1.1	3.1	3.5	4.3	5.9	5.2	7.1
Car lease payments	2.3	0.7	2.1	2.0	2.3	3.4	2.8	4.4
Truck lease payments	1.8	0.4	1.4	1.6	2.2	3.0	2.9	3.3
Vehicle registration, state	17.2	11.3	16.7	17.7	19.4	19.6	19.6	19.7
Vehicle registration, local	2.1	2.0	2.1	1.9	2.0	2.4	2.4	2.3
Driver's license	5.2	3.3	4.9	5.9	5.6	5.8	5.9	5.5
Vehicle inspection	6.4	4.6	5.9	6.4	6.7	7.6	7.5	7.6
Parking fees	11.4	3.4	6.2	11.6	11.3	19.9	17.4	24.5
Parking fees in home city, excluding residence	9.0	2.7	4.5	9.3	9.3	16.0	14.0	19.4
Parking fees on trips	3.1	0.7	1.8	2.9	2.6	5.7	4.7	7.7
Tolls and electronic toll passes	9.0	2.9	6.1	8.2	8.4	15.3	14.4	17.0
Tolls on trips	6.2	2.0	4.1	6.0	6.4	10.2	8.9	12.6
Towing charges	0.9	0.7	0.8	1.2	1.1	0.9	0.9	0.9
Global positioning services	0.5	0.1	0.5	0.5	0.6	0.7	0.7	0.7
Automobile service clubs	5.0	2.2	4.0	4.4	5.7	7.6	7.2	8.5
Public transportation	**18.2**	**13.4**	**12.1**	**16.9**	**15.4**	**27.8**	**24.6**	**33.6**
Airline fares	9.9	2.6	5.6	9.0	9.7	18.1	15.6	22.6
Intercity bus fares	4.0	1.4	2.7	4.3	3.7	6.2	5.5	7.5
Intracity mass transit fares	7.0	8.5	5.0	6.3	4.7	9.5	8.0	12.1
Local transportation on trips	4.8	1.2	2.8	4.4	4.7	8.8	7.9	10.5
Taxi fares and limousine service on trips	4.8	1.2	2.8	4.4	4.7	8.8	7.9	10.5
Taxi fares and limousine service	3.0	2.8	2.1	2.6	2.4	4.5	3.7	5.8
Intercity train fares	3.9	1.0	2.4	3.8	3.6	6.8	5.8	8.4
Ship fares	2.2	0.7	1.4	2.0	2.7	3.8	3.5	4.4
School bus	0.0	0.0	0.0	0.1	–	0.1	0.1	0.0

Note: "–" means sample is too small to make a reliable estimate.
Source: Bureau of Labor Statistics, unpublished data from the 2008 Consumer Expenditure Survey

Table 10.26 Amount Buyers Spent on Transportation by Education, <u>Average Quarter</u>, 2008

(average amount spent by households buying transportation during the average quarter, by highest level of education of householder, 2008)

	total households	less than high school graduate	high school graduate	some college	associate's degree	college graduate total	college graduate bachelor's degree	college graduate master's, professional, doctorate
TRANSPORTATION, AMOUNT SPENT	$2,200.87	$1,458.49	$1,983.03	$2,105.62	$2,469.97	$2,701.32	$2,598.84	$2,882.47
Vehicle purchases	14,560.25	9,601.18	12,063.09	13,490.43	15,913.90	19,744.36	19,057.89	20,999.20
Cars and trucks, new	25,487.50	19,661.32	21,468.63	25,788.26	25,375.65	28,323.68	27,983.14	28,608.03
New cars	23,500.00	17,693.33	19,431.79	23,737.50	22,346.52	26,750.21	24,841.03	28,370.41
New trucks	28,212.24	23,239.77	25,925.00	28,557.95	28,609.12	29,725.00	29,737.94	29,956.37
Cars and trucks, used	10,374.53	7,830.79	9,586.67	9,493.81	12,661.98	13,024.49	13,482.78	12,103.00
Used cars	9,508.71	6,020.45	8,417.41	9,506.85	11,265.29	12,016.13	11,486.46	13,379.24
Used trucks	11,204.83	9,068.23	10,691.57	9,325.58	13,856.44	14,278.64	16,291.42	10,741.67
Other vehicles	9,596.43	9,965.00	8,960.37	10,857.39	7,291.04	10,885.71	9,627.00	13,795.00
Gasoline and motor oil	748.22	638.58	726.22	741.65	815.71	795.80	793.15	800.40
Gasoline	697.37	611.22	682.80	690.70	757.25	731.41	730.63	732.74
Diesel fuel	633.33	630.00	709.88	633.46	547.26	606.25	682.79	399.45
Gasoline on trips	179.96	166.62	186.69	175.38	182.11	181.02	180.99	181.12
Motor oil	31.28	27.71	30.99	32.21	37.53	30.35	30.53	29.98
Motor oil on trips	1.82	1.67	1.88	1.78	1.84	1.83	1.83	1.83
Other vehicle expenses	731.51	517.73	678.49	713.14	776.82	848.96	822.49	895.62
Vehicle finance charges	241.79	211.28	248.06	246.98	245.54	240.20	239.39	241.89
Automobile finance charges	196.13	176.00	203.17	201.29	182.10	197.46	198.31	195.86
Truck finance charges	222.02	213.31	227.62	225.18	229.48	214.23	206.22	232.74
Motorcycle and plane finance charges	126.85	130.32	102.42	116.21	141.45	187.68	231.33	97.62
Other vehicle finance charges	279.86	281.90	259.01	256.01	291.94	337.87	359.03	275.37
Maintenance and repairs	329.52	241.23	300.77	321.75	336.96	381.79	376.89	390.47
Coolant, additives, brake and transmission fluids	18.34	19.74	16.87	17.35	19.60	19.47	17.28	24.84
Tires—purchased, replaced, installed	398.24	306.65	397.51	381.20	400.67	438.44	422.34	468.69
Vehicle products and cleaning services	42.22	33.52	50.34	40.72	39.10	40.96	41.88	39.53
Parts, equipment, and accessories	126.53	95.71	129.49	131.88	141.22	128.99	110.49	159.13
Vehicle audio equipment, excluding labor	251.19	166.67	348.21	283.00	152.27	226.72	135.19	347.79
Vehicle video equipment	301.72	359.09	276.39	476.47	247.31	280.56	221.62	343.33
Body work and painting	640.57	870.65	617.22	585.79	413.10	713.61	783.94	592.66
Clutch and transmission repair	756.20	498.27	797.62	679.80	975.86	824.65	822.54	822.36
Drive shaft and rear-end repair	397.00	291.18	340.48	456.25	535.42	426.92	387.10	490.69
Brake work	313.32	244.70	313.79	285.24	340.17	340.54	324.42	369.07
Repair to steering or front-end	447.50	352.05	393.75	401.31	520.36	519.96	518.49	521.08
Repair to engine cooling system	322.53	299.29	294.39	357.41	292.66	339.32	339.58	337.61
Motor tune-up	257.86	157.48	202.69	259.20	305.53	295.93	290.42	303.96
Lube, oil change, and oil filters	52.14	46.67	50.13	51.59	50.16	55.71	54.63	57.54
Front-end alignment, wheel balance, rotation	135.08	134.45	165.58	125.67	111.06	131.89	129.44	135.22
Shock absorber replacement	357.26	325.81	331.25	382.69	373.18	368.18	350.00	380.66
Tire repair and other repair work	224.10	154.28	210.95	249.46	216.96	235.45	229.27	244.09
Exhaust system repair	270.00	168.94	257.45	287.05	245.04	320.11	382.78	200.00
Electrical system repair	318.26	352.86	307.16	301.50	293.81	330.14	331.14	328.43
Motor repair, replacement	668.65	464.38	616.77	730.84	705.15	724.59	767.65	651.04
Auto repair service policy	901.42	688.16	953.24	852.78	958.33	947.73	1,128.92	694.67
Vehicle accessories including labor	661.11	225.00	132.89	239.58	387.20	1,231.62	1,825.00	164.49
Vehicle air conditioning repair	300.55	308.33	347.26	250.00	237.66	311.90	296.58	335.21

	total households	less than high school graduate	high school graduate	some college	associate's degree	college graduate		
						total	bachelor's degree	master's, professional, doctorate
Vehicle insurance	$438.54	$370.45	$425.76	$433.85	$450.91	$474.07	$452.15	$515.48
Vehicle rental, leases, licenses, other charges	271.81	166.07	237.58	247.45	278.46	327.78	304.68	364.92
Leased and rented vehicles	1,038.43	1,110.65	1,074.24	991.97	1,117.54	1,020.95	1,036.93	1,002.60
Rented vehicles	322.71	262.05	321.52	312.50	321.92	330.14	313.17	350.04
Auto rental	292.79	1,050.00	202.78	422.95	239.90	268.18	278.87	251.70
Auto rental on trips	307.91	293.18	318.88	250.00	309.05	320.60	303.88	337.59
Truck rental	328.26	76.92	412.50	387.04	339.06	305.26	295.39	306.88
Truck rental on trips	460.71	300.00	528.57	305.56	273.75	537.04	341.25	690.24
Leased vehicles	1,520.08	1,558.96	1,430.16	1,414.59	1,593.66	1,591.79	1,596.53	1,587.41
Car lease payments	1,244.69	1,185.14	1,083.57	1,212.62	1,550.98	1,290.77	1,304.23	1,275.68
Truck lease payments	1,371.58	1,271.34	1,472.24	1,331.72	1,384.20	1,354.07	1,281.05	1,470.44
Vehicle registration, state	128.06	111.13	120.98	125.45	132.22	138.75	138.47	139.10
Vehicle registration, local	108.69	95.15	104.79	105.96	119.54	116.88	111.98	125.76
Driver's license	35.98	35.51	38.48	36.20	35.28	34.26	33.97	34.80
Vehicle inspection	42.24	41.81	42.04	43.89	33.41	43.91	43.20	45.12
Parking fees	81.65	45.40	61.54	73.22	62.68	97.34	89.87	106.85
Parking fees in home city, excluding residence	86.17	45.80	66.43	78.31	63.24	102.19	94.65	112.04
Parking fees on trips	48.71	40.54	42.53	42.94	44.49	53.66	50.54	57.16
Tolls and electronic toll passes	57.43	62.16	59.32	54.59	45.73	59.52	60.17	58.50
Tolls on trips	17.46	23.12	15.56	15.65	17.15	18.47	17.37	19.83
Towing charges	122.61	101.69	129.11	148.55	106.98	107.14	97.07	123.30
Global positioning services	105.50	79.17	115.56	85.78	108.06	112.32	90.67	151.76
Automobile service clubs	88.42	87.78	88.63	79.50	92.80	91.07	89.44	93.74
Public transportation	**698.61**	**333.27**	**502.25**	**535.37**	**688.12**	**939.27**	**828.45**	**1,085.18**
Airline fares	867.80	778.64	651.03	672.84	725.93	1,030.61	918.63	1,169.68
Intercity bus fares	69.71	73.06	69.70	63.86	66.85	73.14	65.56	83.03
Intracity mass transit fares	215.06	179.48	199.60	179.43	201.88	258.08	245.53	272.67
Local transportation on trips	63.72	41.73	50.54	44.06	86.18	72.45	58.73	90.92
Taxi fares and limousine service on trips	37.42	24.40	29.73	25.91	50.64	42.54	34.49	53.39
Taxi fares and limousine service	109.16	158.71	89.95	82.39	108.99	112.92	108.92	117.57
Intercity train fares	144.82	74.25	134.60	106.64	122.42	173.15	148.37	203.78
Ship fares	424.10	262.68	401.48	322.46	383.21	496.34	488.60	506.44
School bus	437.50	287.50	150.00	329.17	–	484.38	284.09	2,625.00

Note: "–" means sample is too small to make a reliable estimate.
Source: Calculations by New Strategist based on the Bureau of Labor Statistics' 2008 Consumer Expenditure Survey

Table 10.27 Percent Buying Transportation by Education, Average Week, 2008

(percent of households buying transportation during the average week, by highest level of education of householder, 2008)

	total households	less than high school graduate	high school graduate	some college	associate's degree	college graduate total	bachelor's degree	master's, professional, doctorate
TRANSPORTATION, PERCENT BUYING	70.7%	61.3%	70.0%	71.2%	74.8%	73.9%	75.1%	71.6%
Gasoline	67.9	58.3	67.7	68.4	72.8	70.6	71.6	68.7
Diesel fuel	0.8	0.7	0.7	0.7	1.6	0.7	0.8	0.4
Motor oil	1.6	1.8	2.1	1.5	1.6	1.2	1.1	1.2
Coolant, additives, brake and transmission fluids	1.4	1.4	1.5	1.5	2.1	1.1	1.1	1.1
Other vehicle expenses	15.9	10.8	14.8	15.9	17.0	18.9	18.7	19.4
Maintenance and repairs	6.1	3.8	5.1	5.4	7.0	8.4	8.1	8.9
Vehicle audio equipment, excluding labor	0.1	0.0	0.0	0.1	–	0.1	0.1	–
Vehicle products and cleaning services	1.3	0.9	1.1	1.3	1.8	1.4	1.6	1.1
Miscellaneous auto repair, servicing	5.2	3.0	4.3	4.4	5.7	7.3	7.0	7.9
Vehicle insurance	9.2	6.9	9.4	9.9	10.4	9.3	9.4	9.0
Vehicle rental, leases, licenses, and other charges	2.5	1.3	1.8	2.2	2.2	3.9	3.5	4.6
Tolls and electronic toll passes	2.5	1.3	1.8	2.2	2.2	3.9	3.5	4.6
Taxi fares and limousine service	1.0	1.2	0.5	1.1	0.5	1.4	1.3	1.7

Note: "–" means sample is too small to make a reliable estimate.
Source: Calculations by New Strategist based on the Bureau of Labor Statistics' 2008 Consumer Expenditure Survey

Table 10.28 Amount Buyers Spent on Transportation by Education, Average Week, 2008

(average amount spent by households buying transportation during the average week, by highest level of education of householder, 2008)

	total households	less than high school graduate	high school graduate	some college	associate's degree	college graduate total	bachelor's degree	master's, professional, doctorate
TRANSPORTATION, AMOUNT SPENT	$99.00	$85.00	$97.96	$98.08	$110.86	$102.29	$100.20	$106.38
Gasoline	67.63	59.72	67.13	66.60	74.80	69.62	70.54	67.83
Diesel fuel	82.89	81.43	87.88	55.71	93.55	95.59	96.39	90.00
Motor oil	9.43	7.91	8.13	8.22	9.26	14.78	12.39	18.64
Coolant, additives, brake and transmission fluids	8.45	8.82	8.84	7.95	7.58	9.01	9.01	8.04
Other vehicle expenses	143.37	148.80	148.21	146.96	156.37	132.38	124.97	145.70
Maintenance and repairs	18.30	21.96	14.98	27.22	13.78	16.11	17.53	13.48
Vehicle audio equipment, excluding labor	150.00	500.00	100.00	145.45	–	87.50	84.62	–
Vehicle products and cleaning services	12.60	7.53	7.02	28.80	8.47	8.51	9.03	7.02
Miscellaneous auto repair, servicing	16.67	18.54	15.28	20.86	14.29	15.42	16.52	13.76
Vehicle insurance	232.21	219.94	223.49	219.19	243.75	251.35	229.10	294.78
Vehicle rental, leases, licenses, and other charges	11.43	10.24	10.44	10.96	14.22	12.21	11.78	12.75
Tolls and electronic toll passes	11.43	10.24	10.44	10.96	14.22	12.21	11.78	12.75
Taxi fares and limousine service	34.69	37.29	66.67	23.81	18.75	31.94	29.77	36.09

Note: "–" means sample is too small to make a reliable estimate.
Source: Bureau of Labor Statistics, unpublished data from the 2008 Consumer Expenditure Survey

Appendix A: Average Household Spending Trends: 2000 to 2008

Household spending is down because of the Great Recession. In 2008, the average household spent $50,486—6 percent more than in 2000, after adjusting for inflation. According to data collected annually by the Bureau of Labor Statistics' Consumer Expenditure Survey, household spending reached an all-time high in 2006 of $51,688 not only because of the easy money of the housing bubble, but also because the cost of necessities was climbing. Then the recession took hold. Between 2006 and 2008, spending by the average household fell 2 percent—down $1,202—as the hard times hit.

Although overall household spending was rising between 2000 and 2006, an examination of spending trends during those years reveals two opposing forces at work. On the one hand, the numbers show that some households were awash in the easy money that resulted from surging housing prices and the abuse of home equity loans. On the other hand, the cost of necessities was rising, forcing many households to trim their spending on discretionary items well before the official start of the recession.

Average household spending on housing increased by 13 percent between 2000 and 2006, after adjusting inflation. That figure includes a 24 percent rise in property taxes as well as a 21 percent rise in spending on mortgage interest as the rate of homeownership reached a record high and some families bought larger homes than they could afford. Spending on audio and visual equipment and services grew 24 percent as some spent their home equity on big-screen TVs and other electronic toys. Average household spending on household services also grew substantially during those years.

Ominously, however, the cost of necessities was climbing sharply. The average household spent 47 percent more on gasoline in 2006 than in 2000, after adjusting for inflation. Spending on utilities and heating fuels rose 17 percent during those years. Health insurance spending climbed 27 percent, and education spending increased 20 percent. The middle class was being squeezed, and consumers were cutting back. Spending on used vehicles plummeted 24 percent between 2000 and 2006, while spending on new vehicles fell 4 percent. Spending on women's clothes declined 11 percent, and spending on footwear was down 24 percent. Despite the record high homeownership rate, spending on household furnishings and equipment fell 6 percent between 2000 and 2006.

Those who track the government's Consumer Expenditure Survey could not have been surprised by these declines or the even deeper cuts that followed. For years, spending trends have suggested that American households were struggling. Between 2006 and 2008, spending on mortgage interest fell nearly 5 percent. Cash contributions were down 13 percent. Spending on clothing and vehicles continued to plummet. Households also cut their spending on alcoholic beverages, food away from home, and furniture. American consumers are proving to be cautious spenders, with enormous consequences for our economy.

Households spent more, then cut back, on many items

(percent change in spending by the average household on selected products and services, 2000–06 and 2006–08; in 2008 dollars)

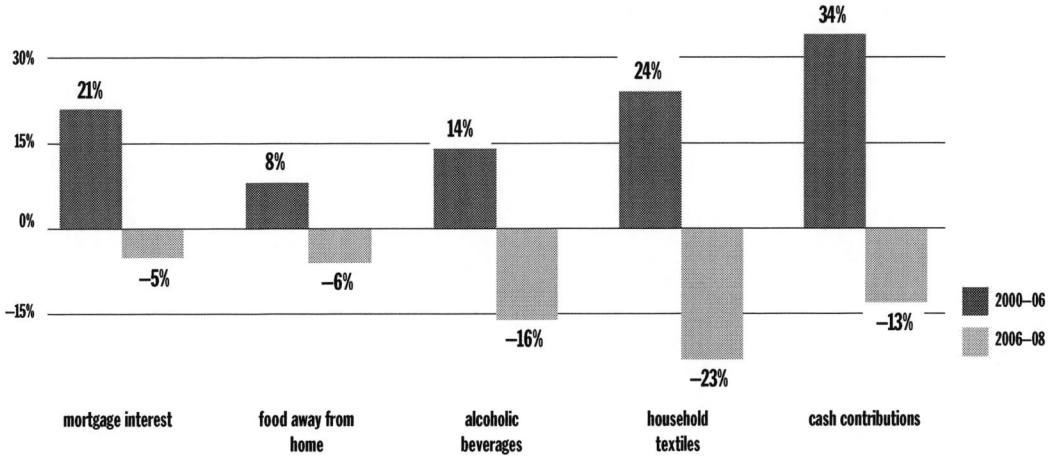

Average Household Spending Trends, 2000 to 2008

(average annual spending of total households, 2000 to 2008; percent change, 2000–06, 2006–08, and 2000–08; in 2008 dollars)

	2008	2006	2000	percent change 2000–06	percent change 2006–08	percent change 2000–08
Number of households (in 000s)	120,770	118,843	109,367	8.7%	1.6%	10.4%
Average annual spending of consumer units	$50,486	$51,688	$47,568	8.7	-2.3	6.1
FOOD	**6,443**	**6,526**	**6,449**	**1.2**	**−1.3**	**−0.1**
Food at home	**3,744**	**3,649**	**3,777**	**−3.4**	**2.6**	**−0.9**
Cereals and bakery products	507	476	566	−15.9	6.4	−10.5
Cereals and cereal products	170	153	195	−21.7	11.3	−12.8
Bakery products	337	325	371	−12.6	3.8	−9.2
Meats, poultry, fish, and eggs	846	851	994	−14.4	−0.6	−14.9
Beef	239	252	298	−15.3	−5.2	−19.7
Pork	163	168	209	−19.7	−2.8	−21.9
Other meats	106	112	126	−11.2	−5.5	−16.1
Poultry	159	151	181	−16.9	5.6	−12.3
Fish and seafood	128	130	138	−5.3	−1.8	−6.9
Eggs	51	40	43	−7.0	29.1	20.0
Dairy products	430	393	406	−3.3	9.4	5.8
Fresh milk and cream	168	150	164	−8.7	12.4	2.6
Other dairy products	261	243	241	0.9	7.2	8.2
Fruits and vegetables	657	632	651	−2.9	3.9	0.9
Fresh fruits	222	208	204	2.2	6.6	8.9
Fresh vegetables	212	206	199	3.7	2.9	6.6
Processed fruits	116	116	144	−19.0	−0.4	−19.3
Processed vegetables	107	101	105	−3.4	5.5	1.9
Other food at home	1,305	1,294	1,159	11.7	0.8	12.6
Sugar and other sweets	129	133	146	−8.7	−3.4	−11.8
Fats and oils	104	92	104	−11.5	13.2	0.2
Miscellaneous foods	680	670	546	22.6	1.6	24.5
Nonalcoholic beverages	342	355	313	13.4	−3.5	9.4
Food prepared by consumer unit on trips	49	46	50	−8.2	6.7	−2.0
Food away from home	**2,698**	**2,877**	**2,672**	**7.7**	**−6.2**	**1.0**
ALCOHOLIC BEVERAGES	**444**	**531**	**465**	**14.1**	**−16.3**	**−4.5**
HOUSING	**17,109**	**17,478**	**15,403**	**13.5**	**−2.1**	**11.1**
Shelter	**10,183**	**10,330**	**8,895**	**16.1**	**−1.4**	**14.5**
Owned dwellings	6,760	6,959	5,754	20.9	−2.9	17.5
Mortgage interest and charges	3,826	4,008	3,300	21.5	−4.5	16.0
Property taxes	1,758	1,761	1,424	23.7	−0.2	23.4
Maintenance, repair, insurance, other expenses	1,176	1,191	1,032	15.4	−1.2	14.0
Rented dwellings	2,724	2,766	2,543	8.8	−1.5	7.1
Other lodging	698	606	598	1.3	15.3	16.8
Utilities, fuels, and public services	**3,649**	**3,628**	**3,112**	**16.6**	**0.6**	**17.3**
Natural gas	531	544	384	41.6	−2.3	38.3
Electricity	1,353	1,352	1,139	18.7	0.1	18.8
Fuel oil and other fuels	192	147	121	21.5	30.3	58.3
Telephone services	1,127	1,161	1,097	5.9	−2.9	2.8
Water and other public services	446	424	370	14.6	5.2	20.5
Household services	**998**	**1,012**	**855**	**18.4**	**−1.4**	**16.7**
Personal services	383	420	408	3.0	−8.7	−6.0
Other household services	614	593	448	32.4	3.6	37.2
Housekeeping supplies	**654**	**684**	**603**	**13.4**	**−4.3**	**8.5**
Laundry and cleaning supplies	148	161	164	−1.5	−8.2	−9.6
Other household products	350	352	283	24.7	−0.7	23.9
Postage and stationery	156	170	158	7.8	−8.1	−1.0
Household furnishings and equipment	**1,624**	**1,824**	**1,937**	**−5.8**	**−11.0**	**−16.1**
Household textiles	126	164	133	24.1	−23.4	−4.9
Furniture	388	494	489	1.1	−21.5	−20.6
Floor coverings	45	51	55	−6.8	−12.2	−18.2

	2008	2006	2000	percent change 2000–06	percent change 2006–08	percent change 2000–08
Major appliances	$204	$257	$236	8.9%	−20.7%	−13.7%
Small appliances and miscellaneous housewares	113	116	109	7.0	−2.9	3.9
Miscellaneous household equipment	749	740	914	−19.0	1.2	−18.1
APPAREL AND RELATED SERVICES	**1,801**	**2,001**	**2,321**	**−13.8**	**−10.0**	**−22.4**
Men and boys	**427**	**474**	**550**	**−13.8**	**−9.9**	**−22.4**
Men, aged 16 or older	344	377	430	−12.3	−8.8	−20.0
Boys, aged 2 to 15	83	97	120	−19.0	−14.6	−30.9
Women and girls	**718**	**802**	**906**	**−11.5**	**−10.5**	**−20.8**
Women, aged 16 or older	597	672	759	−11.5	−11.1	−21.3
Girls, aged 2 to 15	121	130	148	−11.7	−7.1	−18.0
Children under age 2	**93**	**103**	**103**	**0.0**	**−9.3**	**−9.3**
Footwear	**314**	**325**	**429**	**−24.3**	**−3.3**	**−26.8**
Other apparel products and services	**248**	**299**	**333**	**−10.1**	**−17.1**	**−25.4**
TRANSPORTATION	**8,604**	**9,086**	**9,274**	**−2.0**	**−5.3**	**−7.2**
Vehicle purchases	**2,755**	**3,654**	**4,274**	**−14.5**	**−24.6**	**−35.5**
Cars and trucks, new	1,305	1,920	2,007	−4.3	−32.0	−35.0
Cars and trucks, used	1,315	1,675	2,213	−24.3	−21.5	−40.6
Other vehicles	134	58	54	7.3	132.4	149.2
Gasoline and motor oil	**2,715**	**2,378**	**1,614**	**47.3**	**14.2**	**68.2**
Other vehicle expenses	**2,621**	**2,515**	**2,852**	**−11.8**	**4.2**	**−8.1**
Vehicle finance charges	312	318	410	−22.4	−2.0	−23.9
Maintenance and repairs	731	735	780	−5.8	−0.5	−6.3
Vehicle insurance	1,113	946	973	−2.7	17.6	14.4
Vehicle rentals, leases, licenses, other charges	465	515	689	−25.3	−9.7	−32.5
Public transportation	**513**	**539**	**534**	**1.0**	**−4.9**	**−3.9**
HEALTH CARE	**2,976**	**2,954**	**2,583**	**14.4**	**0.7**	**15.2**
Health insurance	1,653	1,565	1,229	27.3	5.7	34.5
Medical services	727	716	710	0.8	1.6	2.4
Drugs	482	549	520	5.5	−12.2	−7.3
Medical supplies	114	125	124	0.9	−8.8	−7.9
ENTERTAINMENT	**2,835**	**2,537**	**2,329**	**8.9**	**11.7**	**21.7**
Fees and admissions	616	647	644	0.5	−4.8	−4.3
Audio and visual equipment and services	1,036	968	778	24.4	7.1	33.2
Pets, toys, and playground equipment	704	440	418	5.4	60.0	68.6
Other entertainment products and services	479	482	491	−2.0	−0.6	−2.5
PERSONAL CARE PRODUCTS AND SERVICES	**616**	**625**	**705**	**−11.4**	**−1.4**	**−12.6**
READING	**116**	**125**	**183**	**−31.5**	**−7.2**	**−36.5**
EDUCATION	**1,046**	**948**	**790**	**20.0**	**10.3**	**32.4**
TOBACCO PRODUCTS AND SMOKING SUPPLIES	**317**	**349**	**399**	**−12.4**	**−9.2**	**−20.5**
MISCELLANEOUS	**840**	**904**	**970**	**−6.9**	**−7.0**	**−13.4**
CASH CONTRIBUTIONS	**1,737**	**1,996**	**1,490**	**33.9**	**−13.0**	**16.5**
PERSONAL INSURANCE AND PENSIONS	**5,605**	**5,628**	**4,207**	**33.8**	**−0.4**	**33.2**
Life and other personal insurance	317	344	499	−31.1	−7.8	−36.5
Pensions and Social Security	5,288	5,284	–	–	–	–
PERSONAL TAXES	**1,789**	**2,597**	**3,897**	**−33.4**	**−31.1**	**−54.1**
Federal income taxes	1,817	1,827	3,012	−39.3	−0.6	−39.7
2008 tax stimulus	−784	–	–	–	–	–
State and local income taxes	542	554	703	−21.1	−2.2	−22.9
Other taxes	213	216	183	18.2	−1.3	16.7
GIFTS FOR PEOPLE IN OTHER HOUSEHOLDS	**1,209**	**1,232**	**1,354**	**−9.0**	**−1.9**	**−10.7**

Note: Spending by category does not add to total spending because gift spending is also included in the preceding product and service categories and personal taxes are not included in the total. "–" means data are unavailable.
Source: Bureau of Labor Statistics, 2000 and 2008 Consumer Expenditure Surveys, Internet site http://www.bls.gov/cex/; calculations by New Strategist

Appendix B: About the Consumer Expenditure Survey

History

The Consumer Expenditure Survey is an ongoing study of the day-to-day spending of American households. In taking the survey, government interviewers collect spending data on products and services as well as the amount and sources of household income, changes in saving and debt, and demographic and economic characteristics of household members. The Bureau of the Census collects data for the Consumer Expenditure Survey under contract with the Bureau of Labor Statistics, which is responsible for analysis and release of the survey data.

Since the late 19th century, the federal government has conducted expenditure surveys about every 10 years. Although the results have been used for a variety of purposes, their primary application is to track consumer prices. Beginning in 1980, the Consumer Expenditure Survey became a continuous survey with annual release of data (with a lag time of about two years between data collection and release). The survey is used to update prices for the market basket of products and services used in calculating the Consumer Price Index.

Description of the Consumer Expenditure Survey

The Consumer Expenditure Survey consists of two separate surveys: an interview survey and a diary survey. In the interview portion of the survey, respondents are asked each quarter for five consecutive quarters to report their expenditures for the previous three months. The interview survey records purchases of big-ticket items such as houses, cars, and major appliances as well as recurring expenses such as insurance premiums, utility payments, and rent. It covers about 95 percent of all expenditures.

Expenditures on small, frequently purchased items are recorded during a two-week period by the diary survey. These detailed records include expenses for food and beverages purchased in grocery stores and at restaurants as well as other items such as tobacco, housekeeping supplies, nonprescription drugs, and personal care products and services. The diary survey is intended to capture expenditures respondents are likely to forget or recall incorrectly over longer periods of time.

Data collection and processing

Two separate, nationally representative samples are used for the interview and diary surveys. For the interview survey, about 7,000 consumer units are interviewed on a rotating panel basis each quarter for five consecutive quarters. Another 7,000 consumer units keep weekly diaries of spending for two consecutive weeks. Data collection is carried out in 91 areas of the country.

The Bureau of Labor Statistics reviews, audits, and cleanses the data, then weights them to reflect the number and characteristics of all U.S. consumer units. Like any sample survey, the Consumer Expenditure Survey is subject to two major types of error. Nonsampling error occurs when respondents misinterpret questions or interviewers are inconsistent in the way they ask questions or record answers. Respondents may forget items, recall expenses incorrectly, or deliberately give wrong answers. A respondent may remember how much he or she spent at the grocery store but forget the items picked up at a local convenience store. Most surveys of alcohol consumption or spending on alcohol, for example, suffer from underreporting. Nonsampling error can also be caused by mistakes during the various stages of data processing and refinement.

Sampling error occurs when a sample does not accurately represent the population it is supposed to represent. This kind of error is present in every sample-based survey and is minimized by using a proper sampling procedure. Standard error tables documenting the extent of sampling error in the Consumer Expenditure Survey are available from the Bureau of Labor Statistics at http://www.bls.gov/cex/csxstnderror.htm.

Although the Consumer Expenditure Survey is the best source of information about the spending behavior of American households, it should be treated with caution because of the above problems. Comparisons with consumption data from other sources show that Consumer Expenditure Survey data tend to underestimate expenditures except for rent, fuel, telephone service, furniture, transportation, and personal care services. Despite these problems, the data reveal important spending patterns by demographic segment that can be used to better understand consumer behavior.

Definition of consumer unit

The Consumer Expenditure Survey uses the consumer unit as the sampling unit rather than the household, which is the sampling unit used by the Census Bureau. The term "household" is used interchangeably with the term "consumer unit" in this book for convenience, although they are not exactly the same. Some households contain more than one consumer unit.

The Bureau of Labor Statistics defines consumer unit as (1) members of a household who are related by blood, marriage, adoption, or other legal arrangements; (2) a person living alone or sharing a household with others or living as a roomer in a private home or lodging house or in permanent living quarters in a hotel or motel, but who is financially independent; or (3) two or more persons living together who pool their income to make joint expenditure decisions. The bureau defines financial independence in terms of "the three major expenses categories: housing, food, and other living expenses. To be considered financially independent, at least two of the three major expense categories have to be provided by the respondent."

The Census Bureau uses the household as its sampling unit in the decennial census and in the monthly Current Population Survey. The Census Bureau's household "consists of all persons who occupy a housing unit. A house, an apartment or other group of rooms, or a single room is regarded as a housing unit when it is occupied or intended for occupancy as separate living quarters; that is, when the occupants do not live and eat with any other persons in the structure and there is direct access from the outside or through a common hall."

The definition goes on to specify that "a household includes the related family members and all the unrelated persons, if any, such as lodgers, foster children, wards, or employees who share the housing unit. A person living alone in a housing unit or a group of unrelated persons sharing a housing unit as partners is also counted as a household. The count of households excludes group quarters."

Because there can be more than one consumer unit in a household, consumer units outnumber households by several million. Young adults under age 25 head most of the additional consumer units.

For more information

If you want to know more about the Consumer Expenditure Survey, contact the specialists at the Bureau of Labor Statistics at (202) 691-6900, or visit the Consumer Expenditure Survey home page at http://www.bls.gov/cex/. The web site includes news releases, technical documentation, and current and historical summary-level data.

Glossary

age The age of the reference person.

alcoholic beverages Includes beer and ale, wine, whiskey, gin, vodka, rum, and other alcoholic beverages.

annual spending Shown in Appendix A, the Bureau of Labor Statistics calculates the annual average for all households in a segment, not just for those that purchased an item. The averages are calculated by integrating the results of the diary (weekly) and interview (quarterly) portions of the Consumer Expenditure Survey. For items purchased by most households—such as bread—average annual spending figures are a fairly accurate account of actual spending. For products and services purchased by few households during a year's time—such as cars—the average annual amount spent is much less than what purchasers spend.

apparel, accessories, and related services Includes the following:

• *men's and boys' apparel* Includes coats, jackets, sweaters, vests, sport coats, tailored jackets, slacks, shorts and short sets, sportswear, shirts, underwear, nightwear, hosiery, uniforms, and other accessories.

• *women's and girls' apparel* Includes coats, jackets, furs, sport coats, tailored jackets, sweaters, vests, blouses, shirts, dresses, dungarees, culottes, slacks, shorts, sportswear, underwear, nightwear, uniforms, hosiery, and other accessories.

• *infants' apparel* Includes coats, jackets, snowsuits, underwear, diapers, dresses, crawlers, sleeping garments, hosiery, footwear, and other accessories for children.

• *footwear* Includes articles such as shoes, slippers, boots, and other similar items. It excludes footwear for babies and footwear used for sports such as bowling or golf shoes.

• *other apparel products and services* Includes material for making clothes, shoe repair, alterations and sewing patterns and notions, clothing rental, clothing storage, dry cleaning, sent-out laundry, watches, jewelry, and repairs to watches and jewelry.

baby boom Americans born between 1946 and 1964.

cash contributions Includes cash contributed to persons or organizations outside the consumer unit including court-ordered alimony, child support payments, and support for college students, and contributions to religious, educational, charitable, or political organizations.

consumer unit (1) All members of a household who are related by blood, marriage, adoption, or other legal arrangements; (2) a person living alone or sharing a household with others or living as a roomer in a private home or lodging house or in permanent living quarters in a hotel or motel, but who is financially independent; or (3) two or more persons living together who pool their income to make joint expenditure decisions. Financial independence is determined by the three major expense categories: housing, food, and other living expenses. To be considered financially independent, at least two of the three major expense categories have to be provided by the respondent. For convenience, called household in the text of this report.

consumer unit, composition of The classification of interview households by type according to (1) relationship of other household members to the reference person; (2) age of the children of the reference person; and (3) combination of relationship to the reference person and age of the children. Stepchildren and adopted children are included with the reference person's own children.

education Includes tuition, fees, books, supplies, and equipment for public and private nursery schools, elementary and high schools, colleges and universities, and other schools.

entertainment Includes the following:

• *fees and admissions* Includes fees for participant sports; admissions to sporting events, movies, concerts, plays; health, swimming, tennis, and country club memberships, and other social recreational and fraternal organizations; recreational lessons or instructions; and recreational expenses on trips.

• *audio and visual equipment and services* Includes television sets; radios; cable TV; tape recorders and players; video cassettes, tapes, and discs; video cassette recorders and video disc players; video game hardware and software; personal digital audio players; streaming and downloading audio and video; sound components; CDs, records, and tapes; musical instruments; and rental and repair of TV and sound equipment.

• *pets, toys, hobbies, and playground equipment* Includes pet food, pet services, veterinary expenses, toys, games, hobbies, and playground equipment.

• *other entertainment equipment and services* Includes indoor exercise equipment, athletic shoes, bicycles, trailers, campers, camping equipment, rental of cameras and trailers, hunting and fishing equipment, sports equipment, winter sports equipment, water sports equipment, boats, boat motors and boat trailers, rental of boats, landing and docking fees, rental and repair of sports equipment, photographic equipment, film, photo processing, photographer fees, repair and rental of photo equipment, fireworks, pinball and electronic video games.

expenditure The transaction cost including excise and sales taxes of goods and services acquired during the survey period. The full cost of each purchase is recorded even though full payment may not have been made at the date of purchase. Expenditure estimates include gifts. Excluded from expenditures are purchases or portions of purchases directly assignable to business purposes and periodic credit or installment payments on goods and services already acquired.

federal income tax Includes federal income tax withheld in the survey year to pay for income earned in survey year plus additional tax paid in survey year to cover any underpayment or underwithholding of tax in the year prior to the survey.

financial products and services Includes accounting fees, legal fees, union dues, professional dues and fees, other occupational expenses, funerals, cemetery lots, dating services, shopping club memberships, and unclassified fees and personal services.

food Includes the following:

• *food at home* Refers to the total expenditures for food at grocery stores or other food stores during the interview period. It is calculated by multiplying the number of visits to a grocery or other food store by the average amount spent per visit. It excludes the purchase of nonfood items.

• *food away from home* Includes all meals (breakfast, lunch, brunch, and dinner) at restaurants, carry-outs, and vending machines, including tips, plus meals as pay, special catered affairs such as weddings, bar mitzvahs, and confirmations, and meals away from home on trips.

Generation X Americans born between 1965 and 1976, also known as the baby-bust generation.

gifts for people in other households Includes gift expenditures for people living in other consumer units. The amount spent on gifts is also included in individual product and service categories.

health care Includes the following:

• *health insurance* Includes health maintenance plans (HMOs), Blue Cross/Blue Shield, commercial health insurance, Medicare, Medicare supplemental insurance, long-term care insurance, and other health insurance.

• *medical services* Includes hospital room and services, physicians' services, services of a practitioner other than a physician, eye and dental care, lab tests, X-rays, nursing, therapy services, care in convalescent or nursing home, and other medical care.

• *drugs* Includes prescription and nonprescription drugs, internal and respiratory over-the-counter drugs.

• *medical supplies* Includes eyeglasses and contact lenses, topicals and dressings, antiseptics, bandages, cotton, first aid kits, contraceptives; medical equipment for general use such as syringes, ice bags, thermometers, vaporizers, heating pads; supportive or convalescent medical equipment such as hearing aids, braces, canes, crutches, and walkers.

Hispanic origin The self-identified Hispanic origin of the consumer unit reference person. All consumer units are included in one of two Hispanic origin groups based on the reference person's Hispanic origin: Hispanic or non-Hispanic. Hispanics may be of any race.

household According to the Census Bureau, all the people who occupy a household. A group of unrelated people who share a housing unit as roommates or unmarried partners is also counted as a household. Households do not include group quarters such as college dormitories, prisons, or nursing homes. A household may contain more than one consumer unit. The terms "household" and "consumer unit" are used interchangeably in this report.

household furnishings and equipment Includes the following:

• *household textiles* Includes bathroom, kitchen, dining room, and other linens, curtains and drapes, slipcovers and decorative pillows, and sewing materials.

• *furniture* Includes living room, dining room, kitchen, bedroom, nursery, porch, lawn, and other outdoor furniture.

• *carpet, rugs, and other floor coverings* Includes installation and replacement of wall-to-wall carpets, room-size rugs, and other soft floor coverings.

• *major appliances* Includes refrigerators, freezers, dishwashers, stoves, ovens, garbage disposals, vacuum cleaners, microwave ovens, air-conditioners, sewing machines, washing machines, clothes dryers, and floor-cleaning equipment.

• *small appliances and miscellaneous housewares* Includes small electrical kitchen appliances, portable heating and cooling equipment, china and other dinnerware, flatware, glassware, silver and other serving pieces, nonelectric cookware, and plastic dinnerware. Excludes personal care appliances.

• *miscellaneous household equipment* Includes computer hardware and software, luggage, lamps and other lighting fixtures, window coverings, clocks, lawn mowers and gardening equipment, hand and power tools, telephone answering devices, personal digital assistants, Internet services away from home, office equipment for home use, fresh flowers and house plants, rental of furniture, closet and storage items, household decorative items, infants' equipment, outdoor equipment, smoke alarms, other household appliances, and small miscellaneous furnishing.

household services Includes the following:

• *personal services* Includes baby sitting, day care, and care of elderly and handicapped persons.

• *other household services* Includes computer information services; housekeeping services; gardening and lawn care services; coin-operated laundry and dry-cleaning of household textiles; termite and pest control products; moving, storage, and freight expenses; repair of household appliances and other household equipment; reupholstering and furniture repair; rental and repair of lawn and gardening tools; and rental of other household equipment.

housekeeping supplies Includes soaps, detergents, other laundry cleaning products, cleansing and toilet tissue, paper towels, napkins, and miscellaneous household products; lawn and garden supplies, postage, stationery, stationery supplies, and gift wrap.

life and other personal insurance Includes premiums from whole life and term insurance; endowments; income and other life insurance; mortgage guarantee insurance; mortgage life insurance; premiums for personal life liability, accident and disability; and other non–health insurance other than homes and vehicles.

Millennial generation Americans born between 1977 and 1994.

occupation The occupation in which the reference person received the most earnings during the survey period. The occupational categories follow those of the Census of Population. Categories shown in the tables include the following:

• *self-employed* Includes all occupational categories; the reference person is self-employed in own business, professional practice, or farm.

• *wage and salary earners, managers and professionals* Includes executives, administrators, managers, and professional specialties such as architects, engineers, natural and social scientists, lawyers, teachers, writers, health diagnosis and treatment workers, entertainers, and athletes.

• *wage and salary earners, technical, sales, and clerical workers* Includes technicians and related support workers; sales representatives, sales workers, cashiers, and sales-related occupations; and administrative support, including clerical.

• *retired* People who did not work either full- or part-time during the survey period.

pensions and Social Security Includes all Social Security contributions paid by employees; employees' contributions to railroad retirement, government retirement and private pensions programs; retirement programs for self-employed.

personal care Includes products for the hair, oral hygiene products, shaving needs, cosmetics, bath products, suntan lotions, hand creams, electric personal care appliances, incontinence products, other personal care products, personal care services such as hair care services (haircuts, bleaching, tinting, coloring, conditioning treatments, permanents, press, and curls), styling and other services for wigs and hairpieces, body massages or slenderizing treatments, facials, manicures, pedicures, shaves, electrolysis.

quarterly spending Quarterly spending data are collected in the interview portion of the Consumer Expenditure Survey. The quarterly spending tables show the percentage of households that purchased an item during an average quarter, and the amount spent during the quarter on the item(s) by purchasers. Not all items are included in the interview portion of the Consumer Expenditure Survey.

reading Includes subscriptions for newspapers, magazines, and books through book clubs; purchase of single-copy newspapers and magazines, books, and encyclopedias and other reference books.

reference person The first member mentioned by the respondent when asked to "Start with the name of the person or one of the persons who owns or rents the home." It is with respect to this person that the relationship of other consumer unit members is determined. Also called the householder or head of household.

region Consumer units are classified according to their address at the time of their participation in the survey. The four major census regions of the United States are the following state groupings:

• *Northeast* Connecticut, Maine, Massachusetts, New Hampshire, New Jersey, New York, Pennsylvania, Rhode Island, and Vermont.

• *Midwest* Illinois, Indiana, Iowa, Kansas, Michigan, Minnesota, Mississippi, Nebraska, North Dakota, Ohio, South Dakota, and Wisconsin.

• *South* Alabama, Arkansas, Delaware, District of Columbia, Florida, Georgia, Kentucky, Louisiana, Maryland, Mississippi, North Carolina, Oklahoma, South Carolina, Tennessee, Texas, Virginia, and West Virginia.

• *West* Alaska, Arizona, California, Colorado, Hawaii, Idaho, Minnesota, Nevada, New Mexico, Oregon, Utah, Washington, and Wyoming.

shelter Includes the following:

• *owned dwellings* Includes interest on mortgages, property taxes and insurance, refinancing and prepayment charges, ground rent, expenses for property management and security, homeowner's insurance, fire insurance and extended coverage, landscaping expenses for repairs and maintenance contracted out (including periodic maintenance and service contracts), and expenses of materials for owner-performed repairs and maintenance for dwellings used or maintained by the consumer unit, but not dwellings maintained for business or rent.

• *rented dwellings* Includes rent paid for dwellings, rent received as pay, parking fees, maintenance, and other expenses.

• *other lodging* Includes all expenses for vacation homes, school, college, hotels, motels, cottages, trailer camps, and other lodging while out of town.

• *utilities, fuels, and public services* Includes natural gas, electricity, fuel oil, coal, bottled gas, wood, other fuels; residential telephone service, cell phone service, phone cards; water, garbage, trash collection; sewerage maintenance, septic tank cleaning; and other public services.

state and local income taxes Includes state and local income taxes withheld in the survey year to pay for income earned in survey year plus additional taxes paid in the survey year to cover any underpayment or underwithholding of taxes in the year prior to the survey.

tobacco and smoking supplies Includes cigarettes, cigars, snuff, loose smoking tobacco, chewing tobacco, and smoking accessories such as cigarette or cigar holders, pipes, flints, lighters, pipe cleaners, and other smoking products and accessories.

transportation Includes the following:

• *vehicle purchases (net outlay)* Includes the net outlay (purchase price minus trade-in value) on new and used domestic and imported cars and trucks and other vehicles, including motorcycles and private planes.

• *gasoline and motor oil* Includes gasoline, diesel fuel, and motor oil.

• *other vehicle expenses* Includes vehicle finance charges, maintenance and repairs, vehicle insurance, and vehicle rental licenses and other charges.

• *vehicle finance charges* Includes the dollar amount of interest paid for a loan contracted for the purchase of vehicles described above.

• *maintenance and repairs* Includes tires, batteries, tubes, lubrication, filters, coolant, additives, brake and transmission fluids, oil change, brake adjustment and repair, front-end alignment, wheel balancing, steering repair, shock absorber replacement, clutch and transmission repair, electrical system repair, repair to cooling system, drive train repair, drive shaft and rear-end repair, tire repair, vehicle video equipment, other maintenance and services, and auto repair policies.

• *vehicle insurance* Includes the premium paid for insuring cars, trucks, and other vehicles.

• *vehicle rental, licenses, and other charges* Includes leased and rented cars, trucks, motorcycles, and aircraft, inspection fees, state and local registration, drivers' license fees, parking fees, towing charges, tolls on trips, and global positioning services.

• *public transportation* Includes fares for mass transit, buses, trains, airlines, taxis, private school buses, and fares paid on trips for trains, boats, taxis, buses, and trains.

weekly spending Weekly spending data are collected in the diary portion of the Consumer Expenditure Survey. The data show the percentage of households that purchased an item during the average week, and the amount spent per week on the item(s) by purchasers. Not all items are included in the diary portion of the Consumer Expenditure Survey.

Index

cold cuts, 115–178
college
    books and supplies, 311–332
    support for students, 93–114
    tuition, 311–332
compact discs, 49–91
computer
    hardware for nonbusiness use, 231–273
    information services, 231–273
    installation, 231–273
    repair of systems for nonbusiness use, 231–273
    software for nonbusiness use, 231–273
condiments, 115–178
contact lenses. *See* Eyeglasses and contact lenses.
contributions, cash, 93–114
    to charities, 93–114
    to educational organizations, 93–114
    to non-household members, 93–114
    to political organizations, 93–114
    to religious organizations, 93–114
cookies, 115–178
cooking stoves, 231–273
cookware, nonelectric, 231–273
cornmeal, 115–178
cosmetics, 311–332
costumes, 5–47
crackers, 115–178
cream
    fresh, 115–178
    nondairy, 115–178
credit card memberships, 93–114
cupcakes, 115–178
curtains, 231–273

dairy products, 115–178
dating services, 93–114
day care, adult, 231–273
day care centers, nursery schools, and preschools, 231–273
    books and supplies for, 311–332
decorative items for the home, 231–273
delivery services, 231–273
dental, services, 209–230
deodorants, 311–332
desserts, prepared, 115–178
detergents, 231–273
diesel fuel, 333–368
dining room
    furniture, 231–273
    linens, 231–273
dinner, at restaurants, 115–178
dinnerware, 231–273
docking and landing fees, 49–91
doctor's services. *See* Physician's services.
donations. *See* Contributions.
doughnuts, 115–178
draperies, 231–273
dresses, 5–47
drinks
    alcoholic, 115–178
    fruit juice, canned and bottled, 115–178
    fruit juice, fresh, 115–178
    fruit juice, frozen, 115–178
    fruit-flavored, non-carbonated, 115–178
    nonalcoholic, 115–178
driver's license, 333–368
drugs
    nonprescription, 209–230
    prescription, 209–230

dry cleaning. *See* Laundry and dry cleaning.
dryers. *See* Clothes dryers.

education, 311–332. *See also* College; Day care centers,
        nursery schools, and preschools; Elementary school;
        High school; and School.
    contributions to, 93–114
    gifts of, 179–207
eggs, 115–178
electrical work, 275–310
electricity, 275–310
elementary school
    books and supplies, 311–332
    tuition, 311–332
entertainment, 49–91
    gifts of, 179–207
equipment
    exercise, 49–91
    fishing, 49–91
    hunting, 49–91
    infants', 231–273
    medical, 209–230
    recreational, 49–91
    sound, 49–91
    sports, 49–91
    water sports, 49–91
    winter sports, 49–91
eye care services, 209–230
eyeglasses and contact lenses, 209–230

fats and oils, 115–178
fees
    accounting, 93–114
    and admissions to entertainment events, 49–91
    docking and landing, 49–91
    for recreational lessons, 49–91
    legal, 93–114
    parking, 333–368
    union and professional, 93–114
feminine hygiene products, 311–332
film, 49–91
finance charges
    except mortgage and vehicle, 93–114
    mortgage, 275–310
    vehicle, 333–368
fireworks, 49–91
fish and seafood
    canned, 115–178
    fresh, 115–178
    frozen, 115–178
fishing equipment, 49–91
flatware, 231–273
floor. *See also* Carpeting; and Rugs, nonpermanent.
    cleaning equipment, electric, 231–273
    coverings, 231–273
flour, 115–178
flowers. *See* Plants and fresh flowers.
food. *See also* Restaurants.
    at home, 115–178
    away from home, 115–178
    gifts of, 179–207
    prepared by consumer unit on trips, 115–178
footwear. *See* Shoes.
frankfurters, 115–178
freezers. *See* Refrigerators and freezers.
freight express, household, 231–273